D0893296

Mental Illness:
Changes and Trends

Mental Illness: Changes and Trends

Edited by

Philip Bean
University of Nottingham

JOHN WILEY & SONS
Chichester · New York · Brisbane · Toronto · Singapore

RC 458
M46
1983

Library of Congress Cataloging in Publication Data
Main entry under title:

Mental illness. Changes and trends

  Includes index.
  1. Mental illness—Addresses, essays, lectures.
2. Psychotherapy—Addresses, essays, lectures.
3. Mental health services—Addresses, essays, lectures.
I. Bean, Philip. [DNLM: 1. Mental disorders. WM 100
M5494]RC458.M46   1983   362.2   82–8603
                               AACR2

ISBN 0 471 10240 7

British Library Cataloguing in Publication Data:

Mental Illness.
  1. Mental illness
  I. Bean, Philip
  616.89   RA790

ISBN 0 471 10240 7

Photosetting by Thomson Press (India) Ltd., New Delhi

Printed in Great Britain by
Page Bros (Norwich) Ltd

The Contributors

Ron Baker

At the time of writing Ron Baker was a Professor of Social Work at the University of New South Wales, Sydney, Australia. He holds qualifications in social work, psychiatric social work, and mental and general nursing. He is currently a freelance social work educator and part time consultant to the Ockenden Venture.

For eight years Ron Baker was a full time social work practitioner in Australia and the UK working primarily in the mental health field. For the past twelve years he has been a social work educator as Lecturer, Senior Lecturer and Professor at the Universities of Bradford (1970–74), Monash, Melbourne, Australia (1974–77), and New South Wales (1977–81). He has several areas of interest and current research which include the development of social work practice theory and skills, curriculum design, human rights with specific reference to refugees, interpersonal helping, the relationship between ideologies, and social work intervention and mental health/illness.

Over the past ten years he has published regularly in Australian, British, and international professional social work journals and contributed five chapters to books on social welfare and social work practice. He is the author of *The Interpersonal Process in Generic Social Work: An Introduction* (2nd Ed., 1978) and is currently preparing another book (with C. Pritchard) entitled *Policy Priorities for Social Work Practice: Challenges and Opportunities in the 1980s*, published in 1982.

Philip Bean

Philip Bean is a Lecturer in the Department of Social Administration and Social Work, University of Nottingham. Prior to that he was a research officer for the Medical Research Council and before that a probation officer in the Inner London Probation and After-Care Service. In 1979 he was Visiting Professor at the University of Manitoba, Canada, this award being granted by the Canadian Federal Government on an open competitive basis. Philip Bean's main interests are in the fields of criminology, mental health, and social philosophy where he has published widely. Included in the list of publications are *The Social Control of Drugs* (Martin Robertson, 1974); *Rehabilitation and Deviance* (Routledge and

Kegan Paul, 1976); *Compulsory Admissions to Mental Hospitals* (John Wiley, 1980) and *Punishment: a Philosophical and Criminological Inquiry* (Martin Robertson, 1981).

Anthony Clare

Anthony Clare graduated in medicine at University College, Dublin in 1966. He worked first in the United States and Ireland before coming to the Maudsley Hospital in 1970 and moved to the Institute of Psychiatry in 1975. He is the author of *Psychiatry in Dissent* (Tavistock, 1976; 1980) and *Let's Talk About Me* (BBC, 1981), and co-author with Paul Williams of *Psychological Disorders in General Practice* (Academic Press, 1979) plus numerous papers on psychiatry in general practice, ethics, education, alcoholism, and controversial issues in psychiatry. Currently Medical Adviser to MIND and a Consultant Adviser to the WHO.

Antony Flew

Professor of Philosophy, University of Reading since 1973. Formerly in the same position in the University of Keele from 1954. He has had many temporary visiting appointments in the USA, Canada, Malawi, and Australia; as well as short British Council tours in Brazil, Thailand, and the Argentine. He is Vice-President of the Rationalist Press Association, founder member of the Council of the Freedom Association, and sometime Chairman of the Executive of the Voluntary Euthanasia Society (Exit). The most relevant publications are: *Crime or Disease?* (London: Macmillan, 1973); 'Delinquency and Mental Disease', in M. Goldinger (Ed.) *Punishment and Human Rights* (Morristown, NJ: General Learning Press, 1974); and *A Rational Animal* (Oxford: Clarendon, 1978). But among the other books are: *God and Philosophy* (London: Hutchinson, 1966); *Evolutionary Ethics* (London: Macmillan, 1967); *An Introduction to Western Philosophy* (London, and Indianapolis: Thames and Hudson, and Bobbs-Merrill, 1971); *Thinking about Thinking* (London: Collins/Fontana, 1975); *Sociology, Equality and Education* (London: Macmillan, 1976); and *The Politics of Procrustes* (London: Temple Smith, 1981).

Hugh Freeman

Hugh Freeman is a Senior Consultant Psychiatrist to the Salford Health Authority (Teaching) and Honorary Lecturer at the Universities of Manchester and Salford. He is the author of numerous publications on social psychiatry, epidemiology, and psychopharmacology, and has edited a number of books on these subjects, as well as being concerned in the editing of several international journals. He is a Consultant to the World Health Organization and has acted as adviser on mental health services to the governments of four countries. His current research includes the epidemiology and long-term care of schizophrenia, investigation of new psychotropic drugs, and evaluation of the WHO European mental health programme.

Larry Gostin

Larry O. Gostin is Legal Director of MIND (The National Association for Mental Health) and is the Western European and United Kingdom editor of the *International Journal of Law and Psychiatry*. He has written extensively and is the author of the definitive work on the Mental Health Act of England and Wales (*A Human Condition*, 2 vols.). He represents mentally ill and mentally handicapped patients in a wide variety of courts and tribunals in the United Kingdom and Europe. He has brought several landmark cases before the European Court and European Commission of Human Rights.

Martin Herbert

Martin Herbert was educated at Durban High School and Natal University, South Africa. He did his professional clinical psychology training at the Institute of Psychiatry, Maudsley Hospital, London, in 1958 and was later awarded a Ph.D in Clinical Psychology. In 1966 he went to the University of Leicester, first in the Psychology department, later in the School of Social Work where he became Director and Professor.

Martin Herbert has practised as an Honorary Consultant in the National Health Service for many years and in particular directed his own child treatment research unit working in the natural environment of children and adolescents with psychological problems. He has published widely including papers on childhood problems and therapeutics and his books include *Conduct Disorders of Childhood and Adolescence* (John Wiley & Sons, 1978); *Behavioural Treatment of Problem Children* (Academic Press, 1981); and *Psychology for Social Workers* (Macmillan, 1981).

Derek Jehu

Derek Jehu is a Professor in the Psychological Service Centre, University of Manitoba, where his responsibilities include the Directorship of the Sexual Dysfunction Clinic. Before emigrating to Canada in 1976 he lectured at the University of Liverpool and held a Chair at the University of Leicester. He is a practising clinical psychologist, a Fellow of the British Psychological Society, and a Clinical Fellow of the Behaviour Therapy and Research Society. Among his previous publications are *Learning Theory and Social Work* (Routledge, and Kegan Paul, 1967); *Behaviour Modification in Social Work* (John Wiley, 1972); and *Sexual Dysfunction: A Behavioural Approach to Causation, Assessment and Treatment* (John Wiley, 1979).

Rachel Jenkins

Rachel Jenkins is a Clinical Lecturer in the General Practice Research Unit, Institute of Psychiatry, University of London and Honorary Senior Registrar in the Bethlem Royal and Maudsley Hospitals. Her research interests include the outcome of neurotic illness in general practice, sex differences in minor psychiatric morbidity, the contribution of minor psychiatric morbidity to sickness absence, and the association of unemployment with minor psychiatric morbidity. Her publications include seven scientific papers.

Stewart MacPherson

Stewart MacPherson is a Lecturer in Social Administration at the University of Nottingham. He has a BA in Sociology and Politics from the University of Keele, an M. Phil in Social Administration from the University of York, and a Ph. D from the University of Nottingham. During 1972/73 he taught social policy and administration at Makerere University, Uganda, and was Visiting Lecturer in Social Administration at the University of Dar-es-Salaam, Tanzania, in 1974. From 1977 to 1979 he was Lecturer in Social Policy at the University of Papua New Guinea. He contributed to *Introducing Social Policy* (RKP, 1979) and is author of *Social Policy in the Third World* (Harvester, 1982) and *Primary Health Care and Development* (forthcoming). One of his main interests is social policy and underdevelopment.

Philip McLean

Philip McLean qualified in medicine at the University of Edinburgh. He trained in psychiatry at the Royal Edinburgh Hospital and at the University Hospital of the West Indies in Jamaica. He is Consultant Psychiatrist at Mapperley Hospital, Nottingham. He is the Director of the Trent Regional Addiction Unit and is on the teaching staff of the University of Nottingham.

    Philip McLean's main interest is in the development of treatment services for those with alcohol and drug dependency problems, with the emphasis on integrated local community resources for the alcoholic and on the development and application of pharmacological techniques in the treatment of drug addiction.

Richard Mindham

Richard Mindham qualified from Guy's Hospital Medical School in 1959. He then worked in various hospitals in general medicine, paediatrics, obstetrics and gynaecology, and neurology before starting training in psychiatry at the York Clinic, Guy's Hospital in 1964. He moved to the Bethlem Royal and Maudsley Hospitals in 1965 and completed the diploma in psychological medicine with the University of London in 1968. He then entered the Institute of Psychiatry, first as a research worker and later as a Lecturer in psychiatry, where he did research in psychopharmacology and neuropsychiatry. In 1972 he moved to Nottingham as a Senior Lecturer in psychiatry in the new Medical School and in 1977 was appointed to his present post of Nuffield Professor of Psychiatry at the University of Leeds. His research interests are in psychopharmacology, the psychiatric aspects of physical illness, neuropsychiatry and particularly in Parkinson's disease.

Alfred Minto

Alfred Minto graduated in medicine at Aberdeen University in 1951. He has worked in mental hospitals in the United Kingdom being particularly associated with Duncan MacMillan at Mapperley Hospital, Nottingham in developing the open door policy, day care, and industrial therapy. He was for nine years on the National Advisory Council for the Employment of Disabled People advising the Secretary of State as well as being a member of the council of the National Association of Mental Health and chairman of its Clinical Services Committee, 1970–1973. He was until 1981 Consultant Psychiatrist, Mapperley Hospital, but is now Medical Director, Rampton Hospital, one of the four special hospitals in England and Wales, providing treatment in conditions of maximum security for mentally disordered patients with dangerous propensities.

Norval Morris

Norval Morris is Julius Kreeger Professor of Law and Criminology at the University of Chicago. He was born in Auckland, New Zealand and studied first at Melbourne University and later at London University where he was awarded his Ph.D. and the Hutchinson Silver Medal for the outstanding thesis over a period of four years in the fields of law, political science, international relations, and political history. He is a barrister and solicitor of the Victorian Supreme Court, the South Australian Supreme Court, and the High Court of Australia. He has held a number of visiting professorships and was between 1975 and 1978 Dean of the University of Chicago Law School. He has been an Australian delegate to a number of United Nations Congresses, and since becoming an American citizen in 1973 has been actively involved in a number of commissions in Illinois. He has published widely in the fields of criminology and law.

Felix Post

Felix Post was born in 1913 in Berlin. In 1933 he moved to London to continue his medical studies at St Bartholomew's Hospital. What was intended as a temporary stay turned into emigration, and he qualified in 1939. In the course of several general hospital appointments he came under the influence of the leading psychiatrist Dr. A. J. (later Professor Sir Aubrey) Lewis, and commenced psychiatric training at first in one of the war-time branches of the Maudsley Hospital and later at the Edinburgh department. He served as a specialist in the RAMC, but since 1947 until retirement in 1978 was consultant psychiatrist at the joint Bethlem Royal and Maudsley Hospitals. Again under Aubrey Lewis' influence, he originated the first geriatric department in a psychiatric teaching hospital, and his publications have mainly been on late life psychiatry. He has been president of the psychiatric section of the Royal Society of Medicine, secretary of the geriatric section of the World Psychiatric Association, and chairman of the Group for Old Age, which later became the old age section of the Royal College of Psychiatrists, which recently made him an Honorary Fellow.

Herschel Prins

Herschel Prins is Director, School of Social Work, University of Leicester. He has worked as a probation officer and psychiatric social worker and also as an inspector in the Probation and After-Care Department of the Home Office. For five years he was a lecturer in the Department of Psychiatry, Faculty of Medicine, University of Leeds, before moving to Leicester as a senior lecturer in 1972. His main interests are in the fields of mental health and criminology. He is the author of over seventy articles in the learned and professional journals and of four books, the latest of these—*Offenders, Deviants or Patients*—was published in 1980. He was a member of the Parole Board for England and Wales 1978–1981 and is a member of the Mental Health Review Tribunal for the Trent Regional Health Authority Area. The views expressed in his chapter, however, are his own, and should not be taken to represent these bodies.

Andrew Scull

Andrew Scull is currently an Associate Professor of Sociology at the University of California, San Diego. He previously held faculty positions at Princeton University and the University of Pennsylvania. He is the author of *Decarceration: Community Treatment and the Deviant* (Prentice-Hall, 1977); *Museums of Madness: the Social Organization of Insanity in Nineteenth Century England* (London: Allen Lane/Penguin Books; New York: St Martin's); editor of *Madhouses, Mad-doctors, and Madmen: The Social History of Psychiatry in the Victorian Era* (London: Athlone/Philadelphia: University of Pennsylvania

Press, 1981); and has written numerous journal articles. He was educated at Balliol College, Oxford, and at Princeton University. During 1976–1977, he held an American Council of Learned Societies' Fellowship at the University of London; and for 1981–1982, he was awarded a Guggenheim Fellowship.

Michael Shepherd

Michael Shepherd is Professor of Epidemiological Psychiatry, Institute of Psychiatry, University of London (1968–) and Honorary Physician to the Bethlem Royal and Maudsley Hospitals and King's College Hospitals. Honorary Director, General Practice Research Unit. Founder editor of *Psychological Medicine*. His publications include twelve books, and approximately 200 scientific papers.

Thomas Szasz

Thomas Szasz is a Professor of Psychiatry at the State University of New York in Syracuse. Born in Budapest, Hungary in 1920, he emigrated to the United States in 1938 and received his medical degree from the University of Cincinnati in 1944. He began his professional career as a privately practicing psychoanalyst and a staff member at the Chicago Institute for Psycho-analysis. After a period of service in the United States Navy, he accepted a Professorship at the State University of New York in Syracuse in 1956, where he has completed more than 25 years of teaching, research, and writing. He is a Life Fellow of the American Psychiatric Association and a Life Member of the American Psychoanalytic Association. Thomas Szasz is the author of more than 400 articles and book reviews and of 17 books, among them *The Myth of Mental Illness, The Manufacture of Madness*, and most recently, *Sex: Facts, Frauds, and Follies*.

Peter Tyrer

Peter Tyrer has been a Consultant Psychiatrist at Mapperley Hospital since 1979. Before this he worked as a Senior Lecturer in Psychiatry at the University of Southampton. He received his psychiatry training at St Thomas' Hospital, St John's Hospital, Buckinghamshire, and the Maudsley Hospital, London.

His main interests are the treatment of neurosis and the expansion of psychiatric services in general practice. He has carried out a number of clinical trials of both drug and non-pharmacological treatments in psychotic disorder.

CONTENTS

xiii

Introduction

Traditionally, books on mental illness have tended to be written around one or perhaps two specialisms. Here, a number of different specialisms have been included where each is seen as making an important but unique contribution to the subject matter. There are chapters by philosophers, lawyers, psychologists, sociologists, and social workers, as well as by psychiatrists and even then from psychiatrists offering different approaches to their discipline. The book is not, therefore, a textbook written in the traditional textbook style, rather it is an attempt to bring together a group of authors, many of whom are acknowledged experts in their field and with international reputations, to produce new knowledge and fresh thinking on the subject. Where overlap occurs, or where there is sharp disagreement between the authors, an editorial note has been inserted directing the reader to the alternative place in the text.

All the contributions are original, that is they have not been published before, and whilst the aim throughout has been to produce a book within one field (i.e. mental illness as opposed to mental handicap or psychopathy) each chapter should also be seen as standing in its own right. Any conclusions, such as there are, ought not give the impression that the matter ends there, for the debate about mental illness is a continuing one. In some of the chapters the authors have been concerned to show the boundaries of their approach to the subject, in others future trends are predicted, and in others there are criticisms of existing practices. It has been neither possible nor desirable to produce a standardized format for the chapters so that where the book could be seen as lacking a measure of homogeneity it more than makes up for it in originality.

One of the many difficulties involved in using a multi-disciplinary approach is that there may be little or no agreement about basic terms. Indeed, 'mental illness' itself is regarded by some of the authors as a myth and by others as open to question. Probably none of the authors are entirely satisfied with the term but may continue to use it, however hesitatingly, because no other is able to convey a similar meaning or is more acceptable. But for all its disadvantages 'mental illness' at least implies a recognized field of study with conventionally accepted boundaries. Its use throughout should not imply that the debate about 'mental illness' is regarded as closed, quite the reverse, merely that it is the most convenient in the circumstances and especially so in the absence of alternatives. 'Mental disorder', for example, is no better, nor is 'psychiatric illness', nor are any which imply that the 'mind' can be ill or diseased for all are open to objections.

Similar difficulties arise with other terms like 'psychotic', 'neurotic', or even 'insanity'. These difficulties merely reflect the ambiguous nature of the subject matter and have to be accepted as such. No attempt has been made to produce a conformity for to do so would be spurious, and whilst some authors are critical of current psychiatric terminology and others are not, these differences have to be seen for what they are—inherent in the nature of the subject. It is to be hoped that this book has helped to clarify some of the issues, for that is as much as can be expected.

A further difficulty surrounds the topics covered. This is primarily an editorial problem and one which always leads to the accusation of editorial bias in some form or another. Yet inevitably there will be omissions and there may appear to be duplications, or rather an excess of contributions in one area and a shortage in others. The editor must bear responsibility and of course to some extent bias exists. It cannot be otherwise, and whilst attempts have been made to cover as wide a range of topics as possible, different editors would doubtless have made different choices. Again, all that can be hoped is that the range, and indeed the quality, is sufficient to offset the defects.

Finally, something needs to be said about the chapters themselves. Sometimes in contributed volumes there is an editorial introduction summarizing the main points of the chapters, and sometimes the chapters are subdivided into sections. Here there is no editorial introduction nor are there subdivisions. There are many reasons for presenting the book in this way, not the least being that it would be almost impossible to summarize the main points of each chapter, and furthermore, it seemed that to do so would reduce the chapter to a level which is inappropriate. For, to repeat the point, each chapter stands in its own right, and as such needs no introduction or summary. As for subdivisions, this was more difficult. Originally the intention had been to arrange the contributions into sections, for example, mental illness and the law, mental illness and the community, and clinical aspects of mental illness, etc. This approach was soon abandoned for the sections themselves provided distinctions which were artificial and served no useful purpose. Accordingly the chapters have been arranged on the basis of their content where a chapter is more likely to be connected to the previous one than any other. Basic difficulties remain; where to start and where to finish. Those chapters relating to the legal system appeared to be the most likely from which to begin—or rather others appeared less likely. However, I do not wish to convey any sense of priority in the ordering of the chapters, and to end the book with a chapter on 'Mental Illness in the Third World' is, I hope, a way of stating that the end of this book is the point from which others may begin.

It is my pleasant duty to thank all who have made this book possible, and particularly to the authors themselves.

Department of Social Administration and Social Work   Philip Bean
University of Nottingham
December 1981

Mental Illness: Changes and Trends
Edited by Philip Bean
© 1983 John Wiley & Sons Ltd.

CHAPTER 1

Mental illness and the criminal law

NORVAL MORRIS
Julius Kreeger Professor of Law and Criminology,
The University of Chicago, USA

The layman often asks: 'What is the legal definition of insanity?' There is, of course, no such definition. Mental illness and mental retardation intersect with legal issues in complex and changing relationships, with sharply varying tests for the consequences of these intersections, so that, for example, the tests of mental illness are very different in relation to making a contract, making a will, standing trial for a crime, being held responsible for a crime, being compulsorily committed to a mental hospital, and many other civil and criminal issues. On reflection it is clear that the tests of legally operative insanity vary from one such legal situation to another, and that they should so vary—they are purposive, linked to very different legal consequences, and no single definition can possibly suffice.

This chapter concentrates on three such relationships between mental illness and the criminal law: the competency of a mentally ill accused person to be tried for a criminal offence; his (it mostly is a 'him' and the masculine pronoun will be used throughout without hint of sexism) responsibility for conduct that absent his mental illness would be found to be criminal; and the task of sentencing mentally ill criminals.

These three intersections between mental illness and the criminal law—'triability, responsibility, punishability'—by no means exhaust the list. The police frequently face the choice between invoking the powers of the State under the criminal law or under mental health legislation; so do other citizens who are victims of crime or involved with criminals. But these three are the focal points of much public anxiety and professional consideration and form the general frame of reference for the difficult balance between individual autonomy and State authority in relation to criminal behaviour by the mentally ill.

The United States rejoices in more luxuriant crime rates than those in the United Kingdom, with the result that there is more frequent litigation and legislative consideration of these issues in the United States. Though American practice in this field draws heavily on its English origins, there have been recent developments in all three of our topics where American law and practice has

1

moved away from its English base. To foreshadow discussions of these developments: in 'triability,' there have been recommendations in the United States for the abolition of the plea of 'unfitness to stand trial' and there has been legislative experimentation with the 'innocent only' trial; in 'responsibility', a new verdict of 'guilty but mentally ill', with novel consequences, has been introduced in three states and is likely to be emulated in many more; in 'punishability', there is steady legislative acceptance of increased punishment for those whose likelihood of criminality is seen as very high with some mentally ill criminals falling within this category. As yet, there is no single text in the United States recounting these various legislative developments and committee recommendations; for England and Wales the best single source is the 'Report of the Committee on Mentally Abnormal Offenders' (HMSO, 1975).

Mention must be made of two developments in the United States which have had substantial impact on the three relationships between mental illness and the criminal law considered in this chapter: a shift of population from mental hospitals to gaols and prisons, and a hardening of public attitudes towards the punishment of crime. Both form a necessary backdrop to understanding legislative and judicial change in this field; they can be briefly stated but their practical significance is great.

Over the past fifteen years, due to developments in psychiatry, in particular in the psychotropic drugs, and a change of professional and community attitudes toward the mentally ill, the back-wards of the state mental hospitals, where previously many mentally ill patients spent many years of their lives, have now been largely emptied. Mental hospitals have become institutions for relatively short-term treatment by comparison with earlier decades. As a result, more of the mentally ill and retarded are in the community, more get into trouble with the criminal law, and more thus find themselves in police lock-ups, gaols, and prisons. Public anxiety about mentally ill criminals is consequently increased. I am, of course, not recommending any reversal of this direction, the long-term back-wards had little indeed to recommend them; but the fact of this shift of population must be noted if developments, particularly in the United States, are to be understood.

Secondly, in recent years in the United States, with a substantial increase in the level of criminal violence, there has been an intensification of punitive attitudes towards criminals generally and an increasing disinclination to ameliorate or mitigate punishment because of any excuses for criminal behaviour. Prison terms have increased markedly. Mentally ill criminals have been caught up in these processes so that their terms of detention, whether in prisons or mental hospitals, have also increased and new powers to keep them out of the community have been developed.

The sequence of consideration of the three topics discussed in this chapter follows the sequence of a trial: first fitness for trial, then responsibility for crime, then sentencing.

Triability

On this topic there is a difference of terminology between England and the United States. The English term for incompetency to play the role at trial of an accused person is 'unfit to plead'; Americans, with their usual preference for brevity, favour 'unfit to stand trial'. But the pleas in both countries are closely similar, the words of the Supreme Court of the United States in *Dusky* v. *United States* (1960) capturing the essence of both by asking whether the accused 'has sufficient present ability to consult with his lawyer with a reasonable degree of rational understanding—and whether he has a rational as well as factual understanding of the proceedings against him'.

Unfitness to stand trial is a frequent plea as compared to the insanity plea, very many more accused persons being found unfit to stand trial, unfit to plead, in America and England, than are found not guilty by reason of insanity, yet it has received scant scholarly attention compared to the prodigious academic wrestling with the criminal responsibility of the mentally ill.

It is an old rule that persons who cannot meet the unfitness test should not be tried; they are not really present at trial; they may not be able properly to play the role of the accused person, to recall relevant events, to produce evidence and witnesses, to testify effectively on their own behalf, to help to confront hostile witnesses, and to project to the trier of facts a sense of their innocence. These notions are supported by both the conventional wisdom and much current practice. Nevertheless, there have been recommendations in the United States and in England that the plea of incompetence to stand trial should be abolished. Instead, a motion for trial continuance by reason of disability should be allowed up to a maximum of six months for the accused to maximize his fitness for trial. Psychiatric and psychological (or other) treatment, where appropriate, should be made available to him to this end during this period, in the least restrictive setting properly determined by the court. Thereafter, at the election of the prosecution, either the trial should proceed under rules of court designed so far as practicable to redress the trial disadvantages under which the accused labours or a *nolle prosequi* should be entered. In making this election there would be no impropriety in the State first pursuing civil commitment processes against the accused, it being understood that the prosecution will proceed to trial only if the accused is not civilly committed.

Initially, to advocate the abolition of the plea of unfitness for trial, and hence to favour the trial of some mentally ill, retarded, or otherwise gravely disadvantaged accused persons, seems heartless, useless, and, to Americans, possibly unconstitutional. Paradoxically, it is one situation of overlap between the mental health power of the State and the criminal law power where the case for reform in the general direction of these recommendations is compelling—and is being pursued.

Widespread legislative reforms move in the direction of this suggested reform, though uneasy compromise is all that has, as yet, been legislatively achieved. The American Bar Association Commission on the Mentally Disabled (American Bar Association, 1978) expressly accepted the proposal Robert Burt and I had earlier advanced (Burt and Norris, 1972), as did the report of the Butler Committee, referred to above, though varying the form of verdict for the 'convicted' incompetent.

It is no small suggestion that the long established incompetency plea should be changed into a mere motion for a continuance, but practice, principle, and Occam's Razor all cut in that direction. Perhaps the toughest issue that must be confronted is what to do about those who protractedly or permanently suffer serious psychological or physical (deaf-mutism) disadvantages as defendants in a criminal trial. But before analysing the various legislative experiments and recommendations of commentators concerning the unrestorable incompetent, the case of Theon Jackson must be examined.

At age twenty-seven, Theon Jackson was arrested in Indiana for a purse-snatching involving property of $4 value and a robbery of $5 in cash. The record is unclear whether any actual violence accompanied these crimes—whoever committed them. Jackson was a deaf-mute, with very little capacity to communicate, being unable to read, to write, or to use sign language. He was found unfit to plead, and committed to the custody of the Indiana Department of Mental Health to be held secure, as the law then provided, until he was fit for trial. Psychiatric testimony to the court hearing the plea of incompetency had been firm and uncontradicted that Jackson was most unlikely ever to become competent to stand trial; in effect, that he would forever be unfit for trial. He thus faced detention for the term of his natural life.

Prior to the charge of purse-snatching Jackson was free, civil commitment not having been pursued against (or for) him for 27 years; after the charge and the incompetency plea, he was indeterminately incarcerated, the safeguards of freedoms in both the criminal law and the law of mental health having been abrogated in his case. The manifest injustice of this result led the United States Supreme Court (*Jackson* v. *Indiana* (1971)) unanimously to prohibit his indeterminate detention, the narrow conclusion being that 'Indiana cannot constitutionally commit the petitioner for an indefinite period simply on account of his incompetency to stand trial on the charges filed against him,' the more ample holding being that:

a person charged by a State with a criminal offense who is committed solely on account of his incapacity to proceed to trial cannot be held more than the reasonable period of time necessary to determine whether there is a substantial probability that he will attain that capacity in the foreseeable future. If it is determined that this is not the case, then the State must either institute the customary civil commitment proceeding that would be required to commit indefinitely any other citizen, or release the defendant. Furthermore, even if it is determined that the defendant probably soon will be able to stand trial, his continued commitment must be justified by progress toward that goal.

The Court reached this conclusion on grounds of the denial to Theon Jackson both of equal protection and of due process, equal protection since he lacked the protections accorded civilly committed patients, due process since the 'nature and duration' of his confinement bore no 'reasonable relation to the purpose for which' he was committed, that is, to make him competent to stand trial. Given the evidence of Jackson's unrestorable incompetency, no period of commitment at all could be justified by the supposed purpose of helping him to become fit for trial, though, of course, under the mental health law a temporary detention pending a hearing on his civil commitment could be justified—but not the three years between Jackson's arrest and the decision of the Supreme Court.

One case mentioned by the Supreme Court in *Jackson* has had an extraordinary and troubling sequel—*People ex rel. Meyers* v. *Briggs* (1970). Donald Lang, an illiterate deaf-mute, was arrested for the murder of a lady of mercenary virtue and found unfit to stand trial. Six years later, the Illinois Supreme Court ordered that Lang should be tried or released. Since the State's chief witness had died by this time, Lang was not indicted. Five months after his release Lang was again arrested for another murder of a lady in circumstances similar to the first killing. The trial court, guided by the opinion in *Meyers* v. *Briggs*, proceeded to trial, trying to compensate for Lang's inability to communicate, and Lang was convicted. The appellate court reversed, holding that no trial procedures could sufficiently compensate for Lang's inability to communicate. At the time of this writing, Lang remains in custody of the Illinois Department of Mental Health.

All states, the District of Columbia, and the federal system prohibit the trial of the incompetent and have broadly similar criteria of incompetency. All these systems were as a result of the *Jackson* decision compelled to confront the problem of the unrestorable incompetent. There has been much legislative experimentation. Most states have provided for the hearing of pre-trial motions though the accused be unfit for trial if, for example, in the words of the Illinois statute, 'the defendant's presence is not essential to a fair determination of the issues,' but such motion leave the central problem of the unrestorable incompetent unresolved.

There are three paths that may be followed. The details of the legislative experiments and the recommendations of the commentators vary greatly, but they can be fairly grouped as follows:

Civil commitment (the rule in *Jackson*);
'Innocent only' trial;
Trial of the unrestorable incompetent (the Burt–Morris recommendation).

Let us consider the advantages and disadvantages of each.

The ruling in *Jackson* v. *Indiana* was plain. The only warrant for holding the accused who is unfit for trial is to make him fit for trial. Lacking movement in that direction, he must be released unless, of course, quite apart from the charge, he can be civilly committed. For most cases, such a direct, clear, and simple principle suffices; it certainly would have sufficed in Jackson's case. But it is less satisfactory in cases where, if the 'accused-patient' did the act with which he is charged, the grounds for his civil commitment as dangerous to others are strong, both in theory and practice, and if he did not they are not. It needs no extensive commentary to make the point that the base expectancy rate for Donald Lang's dangerousness to others increases drastically if he killed the first lady as distinct from if he was not with her when she died.

Thus, the *Jackson* ruling—civil commitment or release—solves all but a few cases of unrestorable incompetents who may be serious dangers to others if they did indeed do the acts with which they are charged. It is a fair but perhaps insufficient response, placing too heavy a burden on the fact finding processes in the civil commitment hearing.

A second solution offered to the problem of the unrestorable incompetent is the 'innocent only' trial. A modest form of 'innocent only' trial was recommended as their third and least preferred alternative by the American Bar Association's Commission on the Mentally Disabled. Their reasons for offering this alternative were to 'avoid both the uncertain constitutionality of proceeding to trial and distortion of the civil commitment process'. It is a *faute de mieux* solution, an unsatisfactory compromise; but it is finding acceptance in several states and must be considered even though it suffers the fatal taint of intermingling the criminal law and mental health law powers of the State.

Here, in summary, is the procedure proposed: trial postponement up to 180 days to achieve competency; then, or earlier if competency is unlikely to be restored, the state must either dismiss with prejudice the charges against the defendant or file 'a petition for evaluation'. This petition can be filed only if the defendant was charged with a crime involving serious bodily harm to another. Pursuant to the petition for evaluation a special commitment hearing will be held at which it must be established beyond reasonable doubt, in the American Bar Association version of the 'innocent only' trial, that:

(a) the person sought to be committed committed the criminal act or acts specified (no mental disorder at the time of such act or acts is relevant to this finding); and

(b) that he 'presents a substantial risk of serious bodily harm to others, such risk being defined as a substantial probability that in the foreseeable future he will inflict serious unjustified bodily harm on others as evidenced by conduct attempting, threatening, or inflicting such harm'.

This is, of course, a manifest blending of the two powers, dodging the safeguards of each. The American Bar Association's proposal is cautious in that it limits the special commitment to a period of 90 days, with subsequent renewals for 180 days each, the total period of commitment not to exceed three years nor to extend beyond the date the defendant would have become eligible for parole had he been convicted and given the maximum sentence. Similar 'innocent only' trials in some states are less cautiously confined.

The 'innocent only' trial leading to detention related to the term imposable pursuant to the original charge against the unrestorable incompetent may thus succeed in avoiding the constitutional obstacle on which Indiana foundered in *Jackson,* but it skirts the spirit of that decision and is an unprincipled blending of two great powers of the State leading to the protracted incarceration of one who has not been found guilty of a crime nor found to be mentally ill at a level to justify civil commitment.

Because of these problems with the 'innocent only' trial and because of the gap in the *Jackson* ruling regarding the unrestorable incompetent, there is substantial pressure for the abolition of the incompetency plea so that the unrestorable incompetent, thought to be a danger to others, may be taken to trial under special rules of court designed so far as practicable to compensate for his physical or psychological adversities. Those favouring this reform urge that the incompetency plea has nothing to offer that cannot better be otherwise achieved, that it is perjorative and injurious without influencing the balance of authority and autonomy between the State and the citizen. The accused citizen has a right to be tried at his maximum level of competence, to play the role of an accused person, provided he does not unduly delay trial. The State has a right to the best available fact finding at criminal trials and to as competent an accused as possible for this purpose, subject to the accused's rights to bail and to a speedy trial. And both bail and speedy trial will have to bend to a degree to the need sometimes to treat in custody the psychologically or physically lesser competent accused to help him reach his maximum competence. All this can be conveniently and sensibly incorporated into rules of court dealing with continuances. And a six month continuance should define the normal outer limits for such a delay. Thereafter, civil commitment or trial would ensue, with the State having the right to a deferred election on this question; so that if the 'accused-patient' is civilly committed, a *nolle prosequi* follows as of right, and if he is not civilly committed, the State may proceed with the prosecution if it thinks this course socially desirable.

Is this argument for the trial of the mentally ill meant to suggest that the accused's mental illness or retardation is irrelevant to the efficiency and fairness of a trial? Not at all. It goes no further than to urge that trial should be deferred to allow the mentally ill or retarded accused to be as fit mentally for trial as treatment in or out of a mental hospital (on bail or not) can make him, and that it may then be socially desirable to take him to trial with special rules of discovery, corroboration, jury warnings, and new trials designed to minimize his personal physical or mental disadvantages. If, after the continuance for treatment, he remains gravely impaired, civil commitment will normally adequately meet all society's needs for protection and the accused's treatment needs; but in exceptional cases they will not, and then a criminal trial should follow with a conviction, if it ensues, leading to sentencing cognizant of the special problems of sentencing the mentally ill.

Hence, just as in exceptional cases we take the amnesiac to criminal trial, and those whose memory fails them because of the long time between the events at issue and the trial (in the charming conceit of an English judge, 'he is the man who has lost his diary or doesn't have one'), just as we take to trial one whose disruptive behaviour precludes his physical presence (or run the trial with him in restraint), or as we pursue a criminal trial though important witnesses are dead or unavailable, so in exceptional circumstances and by carefully adapted means we should take some unrestorable incompetents to trial.

Before abandoning this preferred solution to the problem of the unrestorable incompetent, the Report of the English Committee on Mentally Abnormal Offenders, the Butler Committee Report, merits consideration. That committee took the same view of the problem as did the American Bar Association Committee on the Mentally Disabled, following the recommendation of the Burt–Morris article (1972). They recommended a maximum deferment of trial of the incompetent for six months (actually, two periods of three months, an interstitial further hearing on incompetence to justify further deferment of trial being required after three months) and if the incompetence remains and the prosecution wishes to proceed a trial should follow "to the fullest extent possible having regard to the medical condition of the defendant."

The Butler Committee addressed one common objection to such a trial:

It may be asked how the prosecution can establish their case if the defendant is unable to make a proper defence and in particular how they can prove intention in these circumstances. The answer is that intention is proved as it almost always is in court: by inference from the evidence of what the defendant did.

If an acquittal followed such a trial the only possibility for detaining the defendant would be by civil commitment. What should follow a conviction? In the view of the American Bar Association Commission, ordinary sentencing powers, not including capital punishment, should apply, sensitized, one would hope, to the particular problems of sentencing the mentally ill. The Butler Committee took a different view and followed a path which as yet is, unfortunately, not available in the United States.

In England and Wales when a criminal is convicted and there is evidence that he is mentally ill or retarded the sentencing court may make an order for his in-patient or out-patient treatment in a mental hospital 'with or without a restriction order'. The 'restriction order' gives power to the Home Secretary to control trial and final release of the convicted person. The Butler Committee adapted these processes to convictions following trials of unrestorable incompetents, and recommended that the court be given power to make any of the following social or medical orders: (a) an order for in-patient treatment in a hospital with or without a restriction order; (b) an order for hospital out-patient treatment; (c) an order for forfeiture of any firearm, motor vehicle, etc., used in crime; (d) a guardianship order; (e) any disqualification (e.g., from driving) normally open to the court to make on conviction; (f) discharge without any order.

The differences between English and American practice in sentencing the mentally ill become apparent. The trial recommended by the Butler Committee is the same as that recommended by the American Bar Association as the best solution to the problem of the unrestorable incompetent in the United States; but the English committee varies its sentencing recommendations because: '[W]e cannot envisage any circumstances in which an overtly penal disposal—prison, borstal, or fine—would be suitable for such a defendant' (at p. 157). This difference in the recommendations of the two main committees in the United States and in England which have considered the problem of the unrestorable incompetent is of interest: they agree in principle to the necessity for criminal trials in some such cases, diverging in sentencing powers which reflect more sophisticated powers in the English judge in sentencing mentally ill criminals.

So much for the competency of the mentally ill to be tried or held in custody if not tried; let us turn now to their responsibility for criminal conduct.

Responsibility

It is no easy task to cut through the accumulated cases, commentaries, and confusions concerning the responsibility of the mentally ill for conduct otherwise criminal to the underlying issues of principle; but an attempt to do so must be made. Those issues are *au fond* legal, moral, and political, not medical or psychological, though, of course, the developing insights of psychiatry and psychology are of close relevance.

A structural point is a necessary preliminary. Evidence of mental illness is always admissible on the question of the accused's intent to commit the criminally prohibited harm. There is no need for a 'special defence of insanity' to that end. Nevertheless, such a special defence gradually evolved in English Common Law and found acceptance throughout the Common Law world. It flourished in the nineteenth century, its launching pad being the 'rules' enunciated by the House of Lords in relation to Daniel McNaughtan's killing of Sir Edward Drummond in 1843.

The dramatic events of major criminal trials, particularly in the latter three quarters of the nineteenth century, became important battlegrounds for psychiatry and psychiatrists, public dramatic ceremonials in which professional standing was proclaimed and tested. Inexorably, conflict developed between the disciplines of law and psychiatry with their distinct supporting epistemologies—the language and concepts of the law, free will, moral choice, guilt and innocence, confronting those of psychiatry, determinism, degrees of cognitive and volitional control, classification of diseases and definition of treatments. Complicating these inherent confrontations were the different consequences of the application of the two competing systems: the binary system of the law, guilt or innocence, and, if the former, punishment to close the equation; the continuum of psychiatry, degrees of illness and opportunities for 'cure' to be determined in the last resort only by the fact of non-destructive life in the community.

The attempt clearly to articulate a special defence based on insanity was made in 1843. Daniel McNaughtan was found 'not guilty on the ground of insanity' of the murder of Sir Edward Drummond, secretary to the then Prime Minister, Robert Peel. The verdict caused public concern. The judges of the Queen's Bench were invited to attend the House of Lords to advise their Lordships on the proper rules relating to the defence of insanity to a criminal charge. They did so, though one, Mr Justice Maule, expressed his dissatisfaction with this role. The judges' response to the Lords' questions form the McNaughtan Rules, which remain the basis of this defence throughout the Common Law world. The heart of these rules is that, to establish a defence on the ground of insanity, 'it must be clearly proved that at the time of the committing of the act, the party accused was labouring under such a defect of reason, from disease of the mind, as not to know the nature and quality of the act he was doing; or if he did know it, that he did not know he was doing what was wrong'.

A recent book by Richard Moran (Moran, 1981), is a careful analysis of the events of the killing of Drummond and the trial of McNaughtan in which the argument is made that McNaughtan was not seriously mentally ill, may have been a hired killer, and did not himself fall within 'the McNaughtan Rules'. The book also settles—for all time it is hoped—the proper spelling of the accused's name, McNaughtan. Be these facts as they may, the *McNaughtan Rule*, or the right-wrong test as it became known in the United States, remained the dominant statement of the defence of insanity for over a century. Under the *McNaughtan Rule* as adopted in the United States, the psychiatrist was asked whether the defendant could tell right from wrong at the time of the unlawful act. Many psychiatrists criticized this approach because it did not take into account scientific knowledge pertaining to mental illness. Some pointed out that few if any persons could be said fully to lack the capacity to distinguish right from wrong.

In 1954, the Court of Appeals for the District of Columbia rejected the *McNaughtan Rule* and formulated a new test of criminal responsibility in *Durham* v. *United States* (1954). Writing for the court, judge David Bazelon stated that an accused must be exculpated from criminal responsibility if his unlawful act was the product of mental disease or mental defect. The court explicitly stated that a jury would have to find an accused not guilty by reason of insanity unless they believed beyond a reasonable doubt that he was *not* suffering from a diseased or defective mental condition at the time of the crime, or that his criminal act was *not* the product of such abnormality. The court hoped that this new test would enable juries to make better use of psychiatric testimony pertaining to the accused's mental health.

Durham immediately evoked a great deal of controversy. Critics contended that by failing to state what mental characteristics were an essential ingredient of the concepts of mental disease or defect, the court had forfeited its control over the legal determination of insanity to medical experts who assigned medical meanings to these terms. The weekend flip-flop case, *In re Rosenfield* (1957), is often pointed to as proof of this abnegation of authority. In that case a psychiatrist testified on a Friday afternoon that a person with a 'sociopathic personality' did not suffer from a mental disease. The following Monday morning, the psychiatrist's hospital announced a new policy which defined a 'psychopathic or sociopathic personality' as a mental disease. Although the defendant's condition had clearly remained unchanged, the likelihood of his insanity defence being successful was dramatically altered by the proffered change in medical terminology.

In response to the problems that it perceived to be inherent in the *Durham* Rule—the difficulty of medical terminology and the problem of the causal link between the illness and the crime—the American Law Institute's Model Penal Code formulated yet other tests of irresponsibility for crime on the ground of insanity. Section 4–01(1) of the Code states that 'a person is not responsible for criminal conduct if at the time of such conduct as a result of mental disease or defect he lacks substantial capacity either to appreciate the criminality [wrongfulness] of his conduct or to conform his conduct to the requirements of the law'. This rule was adopted by the Court of Appeals for the District of Columbia in *United States* v. *Brawner* (1972). The Court acknowledged the leading defects in its own earlier applied *Durham* Rule and in particular, rather unfairly bewailed the excessive influence that rule gave psychiatrists allowing them, it suggested, to testify beyond the scope of their medical and psychological knowledge. The court cited 'undue dominance by the experts giving testimony' as a principal reason for its decision to depart from the *Durham* rule.

The *Brawner* court agreed that the objective of *Durham*, 'to put before the jury information that is within the expert's domain to aid the jury in making a broad and comprehensive judgment' remained sound, but they advanced several reasons for adopting the American Law Institute's test of criminal responsibility. This rule retained the core requirement of causality between the mental illness and the incident charged. A defendant would be able successfully to assert the defence of insanity only if, as a result of his mental illness, he lacked the substantial capacity required for criminal responsibility. The court went on to define 'mental disease or defect' as 'any abnormal condition of the mind which substantially affects mental or emotional processes and substantially impairs behaviour controls'. According to the *Brawner* court, this definition had been successful in enabling medical experts to testify on the subject of mental illness, while preventing them from relying too heavily on medical labels in their testimony. Finally, the court expressed the view that justice dictates that persons without substantial capacity to know or control their actions should not be held criminally responsible.

Both the *Brawner* court and the majority of those who were responsible for the American Law Institute's Model Penal Code rejected an alternative test of responsibility for crime first advanced by the English Royal Commission on Capital Punishment in 1953 by which the accused should be found not guilty by reason of insanity if, in the view of the jury, he was so mentally ill at the time of crime that he 'ought not be convicted'. (HMSO, 1953). This type of formulation, leaving the moral issue naked to the jury, though probably reflecting the operational reality of this defence, was rejected by the majority of those responsible for the American Law Institute's Model Penal Code and the majority of the court in *Brawner* on the ground that it gave insufficient guidance to the jury.

The ALI–*Brawner* test has been accepted in many state criminal codes. It is clearly the dominant articulation of the insanity defence in the United States. However, several states have created their own distinctive law pertaining to the criminal responsibility of an accused.

In a series of recent cases, *Wells–Gorshen–Conley–White*, the California Supreme Court has corrupted and confounded the mental illness–*mens rea* relationship. The sound principle, that mental illness may be relevant to disproving the presence of a state of mind necessary to first degree murder or necessary to the 'malice aforethought', which is the distinguishing characteristic of murder in California, has been pushed to an unacceptable complexity and confusion in the law of homicide in that state. It is not necessary here to trace those developments; the largest part of the difficulty these cases present is to be found in the central role still accorded 'malice aforethought' in the California doctrine of 'diminished capacity' and in the elusive emphases given in *Gorshen* and *Conley* to the accused's capacity to identify to some degree with the suffering of his victim as a precondition to the full possession of a prohibited mental state. Structures of talmudic complexity have been built around the relationship between mental illness and 'malice aforethought'.

A more recent development, this time legislative rather than judicial, promises to be of great practical importance. Indiana and Illinois have followed Michigan's lead in enacting legislation designed to draw the weak old fangs of the special defence of insanity, to preserve its facade but drastically to change the realities behind it. Many states are moving to follow their lead. Pursuant to a 1975 amendment to the Michigan Code of Criminal Procedure, those found 'guilty but mentally ill' may be sentenced as if they had been convicted of the offence charged and may be held either in the Department of Corrections or transferred to the custody of the Department of Mental Health. Wherever held, the duration of confinement cannot exceed what could be imposed pursuant to a conviction without the mental illness rider unless, of course, they qualify for civil commitment at the expiration of the sentence.

Hence, if an accused person in Michigan, Indiana, or Illinois pleads not guilty by reason of insanity, the result may be any one of the following: (a) not guilty, or (b) not guilty by reason of insanity, or (c) guilty but mentally ill, or (d) guilty.

The Michigan special defence of insanity ((b) above) is the American Law Institute–*Brawner* test providing that a person is 'legally insane' if at the time of the alleged crime 'as a result of mental illness...that person lacks substantial capacity either to appreciate the wrongfulness of his conduct or to conform his conduct to the requirements of the law'.

By contrast—or is it contrast—'mental illness' for purposes of the new alternative verdict of guilty but mentally ill ((c) above) is defined as 'a substantial disorder of thought or mood which significantly impairs judgment, behaviour, capacity to recognize reality, or ability to cope with the ordinary demands of life'.

'Significant impairment' must as a matter of logic occur at an earlier threshold of psychopathology than 'substantial capacity' for a verdict of guilty but mentally ill ever to be reached. And juries are so instructed. It cannot be unequivocally obvious to them, even if it is to lawyers and legislators. But in practice they probably find the alternative helpful. 'Guilty but mentally ill' appears to a degree in early experience with this defence to supplant 'not guilty by reason of insanity'. Juries must find *beyond reasonable doubt* that the accused had substantial capacity to appreciate the wrongfulness of his conduct and to conform to the law's demands (to avoid (b) above) and yet that he was suffering a substantial disorder of thought or mood which significantly impaired his judgment, behaviour, capacity to recognize reality, or ability to cope with the ordinary demands of life (to fall within (c) above). Forgive the repetition, but these are not easy distinctions—it is like trying to think of a very large grey animal with a trunk without thinking of an elephant. But, as I say, juries can do it—probably because they are informed as to the consequences of each verdict.

The maximum consequences in Michigan pursuant to each verdict are: not guilty, discharge; not guilty by reason of insanity, civil standards for commitment and release; guilty but mentally ill, a sentence by the trial judge to the maximum for the crime charged, which will be served in prison or in a mental hospital; guilty, commitment to prison up to maximum period for the crime charged.

Since, in Michigan, Indiana, and Illinois any mentally ill prisoner may, with appropriate consent, be transferred to a mental hospital, the distinctions between 'guilty' and 'guilty but mentally ill' are not of translucent clarity. Both groups may be given psychiatric treatment in both types of institutions and for the same maximum periods. The punishment, setting aside capital punishment, may be the same; it is a matter for discussion whether the stigma of guilty but mentally ill is or is not any less than guilty *simpliciter*.

The argument grows burdensome. The Michigan statute has survived constitutional challenge before the Supreme Court of Michigan. Can it survive the challenge of analytic principle? I think not. It seems to me on its face and in its operation a means of drawing such acquitting and destigmatizing teeth as were left in the special defence of insanity—and they were not many—while pretending to preserve the moral values embedded in the ideas underlying the special defence. No one is deceived; certainly not the prisoner.

One advantage to the accused survives the new verdict if the Michigan pattern is followed in states returning to the atavism of capital punishment; both those found not guilty by reason of insanity and those found guilty but mentally ill side-step the executioner.

A final nicety about the Michigan, Indiana, and Illinois statutes. They are triggered by the accused pleading not guilty by reason of insanity. They are not triggered and cannot be the verdict if the accused argues that his mental illness at the time of the crime precluded his conviction on *mens rea* grounds but does not plead not guilty by reason of insanity.

What then has happened in Michigan pursuant to this new initiative? During the seven years prior to the advent of the 'guilty but mentally ill' verdict, 279 persons had been found not guilty by reason of insanity. During 1975, the year the new verdict was enacted, 33 persons were found not guilty by reason of insanity. The following year, 32 persons successfully asserted this defence. Between 1977 and 1980, approximately 57 persons were acquitted by reason of insanity each year. The 'guilty but mentally ill' verdict was successfully asserted by approximately 80 persons a year in Michigan between 1979 and 1981. Of these 80 persons, half were found to be mentally ill at the time of their admission to prison. Only half of this group presently need any special mental health programme.

It is my view that injustice and inefficiency invariably flow from any blending of the criminal law and mental health law powers of the state; each is sufficient unto itself to achieve a just balance between freedom and authority, each has its own interested constituency—mixed together only the likelihood of injustice is added. In accordance with this thesis, I favour, as do several other commentators, the abolition of the special defence of insanity. A fall-back alternative position, in no way conflicting with the separation thesis, is for the abolition of the special defence and for legislative substitution of a qualified defence of diminished responsibility to a charge of murder having the effect, if successful, of a conviction of manslaughter with the usual sentencing discretion attached to that crime.

How would the law operate under the proposed abolition? The sick mind of the accused would be relevant to his guilt since he may, for that reason, have lacked the prohibited state of mind required for conviction of the offence with which he has been charged or of any other offence of which he may be convicted on such a charge (in the language of the trade, 'lesser included offence')' If guilty of such a crime, his sick mind is relevant to fair sentencing. If innocent, that is all the criminal law has to do with the matter though, of course, like any other citizen he may be civilly committed if he is mentally ill and is a danger to himself or others or is incapable of caring for himself. On many of these issues the psychiatrist has useful insights; on none should psychiatry frame the operative rule, define the cut-line between guilt and innocence, between detention and freedom. Whenever this happens, the law is perverted in practice and psychiatry is brought into disrepute. The English and American judges went wrong in the nineteenth century; it is time we returned to older and truer principles.

No state has yet abolished the defence of insanity. However, two commissions of enquiry—one in England and one in New York—have moved far towards this view. The Butler Commission in 1975 recommended the substantial reduction of the reach of the special defence, placing their main reliance on diminished responsibility to solve the problems with which that defence was meant to grapple. To closely similar effect, but going further in the direction of complete abolition of the special defence than the Butler Committee, a report entitled 'The Insanity Defense in New York' made in 1978 by a distinguished committee prepared under the direction of William A. Carnahan, Deputy Commissioner and Counsel to the New York Department of Mental Hygiene (hereinafter the Carnahan Report) recommended the abolition of the special defense of insanity and the adoption of a rule of 'diminished capacity under which evidence of abnormal mental condition would be admissible to affect the degree of crime for which an accused could be convicted'.

The Butler Committee recommended the retention of a special defence of insanity in a few very rare cases of 'severe mental illness' and 'severe subnormality'. They recommended 'a specific exemption from conviction of any defendant who, at the time of the act or omission charged, was suffering from severe mental illness or severe subnormality . . . notwithstanding technical proof of *mens rea*'. The Butler Committee definitions of 'severe mental illness' and 'severe subnormality' are extensive and difficult. They certainly narrowly confine the defence. And part of the reason for the Butler Committee's compromise here is the statistical reality of what has happened in England and Wales to the special defence of insanity pursuant to the legislative introduction of diminished responsibility in the Homicide Act of 1957. That Act provided in section 2(1):

Where a person kills or is party to the killing of another, he shall not be convicted of murder if he was suffering from such abnormality of mind . . . as substantially impaired his mental responsibility for his acts and omissions in doing or being a party to the killing.

Prior to 1957, of all persons committed for trial for murder in England about 20 per cent were found unfit to stand trial and diverted from criminal process and about 20 per cent were found not guilty by reason of insanity (the terminology is adapted from English to American usage). As that Act has had its impact, by the late 1970s, about two per cent are unfit and diverted, less than one per cent are found not guilty by reason of insanity, and about 37 per cent fall under the diminished responsibility provisions.

The same thing would happen in the United States. The Butler Committee's recommendation of a restricted retention of a special defence of insanity is thus almost a *de minimis* inconsequential recognition of an extremely severely mentally ill or retarded group who need not be brought within criminal processes.

There are three points to be made in favour of a legislatively introduced rule of 'diminished responsibility' in the United States of the type now well tested by English juries.

First, for some exceptional murder charges *mens rea* principles may not suffice to reduce murder to manslaughter in cases where such a reduction is desirable. I hypothesize an accused clearly psychotic and paranoic believing he is commanded by God to kill. He has heard voices to that effect and is in no doubt of his moral duty. He probably does not fall within any *mens rea* provisions reductive of his crime from murder to manslaughter (unless one sets out on the unacceptable path of California case law). Yet such cases are, it is submitted, better treated and sentenced as manslaughter than as murder. A legislative provision modelled on the English Homicide Act of 1957 would achieve that result.

Secondly, where states impose mandatory sentences on those convicted of murder, some escape mechanisms for the mentally ill from those sentences (other than by their frustration by charge bargaining) is desirable. The evil to be remedied here lies in the mandatory sentence not in the criminal law relating to mentally ill criminals; but the only politically acceptable remedy may be legislative enunciation of a doctrine of diminished responsibility.

Thirdly, diminished responsibility is, on close analysis, apart from the two special problems in the two previous paragraphs, a shift of sentencing discretion to a degree from judge to jury, the jury under diminished responsibility lowering the maximum (and sometimes the minimum) sentencing range within which the judge will impose sentence. In some states there may be advantages in such a limitation of judicial discretion.

Sentencing the mentally ill

Whatever rules apply to trying the mentally ill and to holding them responsible or not responsible for their crimes, an appreciable flow of psychologically disturbed and intellectually retarded persons pass to conviction and sentencing through the criminal courts. The filtering mechanisms of unfitness to plead and the special defence of insanity are insufficient to insulate many mentally ill from being convicted of crime.

In England and the United States those offenders thought to be mentally ill are frequently remanded for psychiatric assessment as part of a pre-sentence report;

but there is scant scholarship on what use should be made, when the sentence comes to be determined, of advice in such reports that the criminal is mentally ill. Nor has it proved easy, from observing practice and drinking with judges, to perceive any general principles guiding the exercise of sentencing discretion in such cases. Sometimes the mentally ill are seen as morally less culpable and therefore will be less severely punished; in other cases, somewhat randomly, they are seen as likely to be more dangerous and therefore to require separation or longer separation from the community than would have been ordered had they not been mentally ill. Despite these apparently contradictory tendencies, there is general agreement on one proposition: the mental illness of the convicted offender is relevant to just and efficient sentencing. Relevant, but how? To what purposes? By what measures? Does it mitigate punishment? Does it aggravate punishment? Both? How?

English law and practice in this area is in advance of that obtaining in the United States. In particular, the power given to English criminal courts to make treatment orders and hospital orders for the psychiatric out-patient and in-patient treatment for mentally ill offenders is in advance of equivalent powers in the United States which are to be found either in conditions of probation orders or in placement in psychiatric sections of prisons or, very rarely, in transfers between prisons and mental hospitals.

In this chapter it is impracticable to seek to survey the extraordinary diversity of treatment modalities, out-patient and in institutions, for mentally ill offenders in England and the United States. Generally it is no exaggeration to suggest that they do not attract the best available facilities. The focus in this chapter is rather on questions of sentencing powers, on which, particularly in the United States, there has been considerable controversy.

An excellent summary of treatment practices in England and Wales of mentally abnormal offenders is to be found in the Butler Committee Report referred to above.

One recent development in England does merit attention. As noted earlier, English law and practice permits the judge sentencing a mentally ill person convicted of a crime to make an order for his hospital treatment 'with a restriction order'. The European Commission of Human Rights has recently considered several cases challenging the use of such restriction orders, finding them to be an offence against human rights.

Section 60(1) of the Mental Health Act of 1959 empowers criminal courts to direct that, where appropriate, a convicted person shall be dealt with by way of medical treatment rather than by way of punishment, if necessary in a special mental hospital for the criminally insane. Section 65(1) provides that, having considered the nature of the offence, the antecedents of the offender and the risk of his committing further offences if set free, and where also necessary for the protection of the public, the court may direct that the hospital order be subject to special restrictions regarding discharge, with or without a time limit. Such restrictions have been imposed primarily for the protection of the public and overriding responsibility for the patient's control—though not his treatment—is vested in the Home Secretary (*X* v. *United Kingdom, Application No. 6998/75*).

The Home Secretary, under Section 66, has special powers in connection with the discharge of restricted patients. If he is satisfied that the restriction order is no longer required for the protection of the public, he may direct that the restrictions be lifted. While a restriction order is in effect the Home Secretary may, if he thinks fit, discharge a patient either absolutely or conditionally. If the discharge is conditional, the Home Secretary may, at any time while the restriction order is in force, recall the patient by warrant to the hospital.

This restriction order was recently considered in *X* v. *United Kingdom*. The applicant was convicted of grievous bodily harm in November, 1968, and compulsorily committed to Broadmoor hospital for an indefinite period, in accordance with Sections 60 and 65 of the Act. The Home Secretary conditionally discharged the applicant in May, 1971. But in April, 1974, after several complaints by his wife, the applicant was recalled to Broadmoor, where he was further detained until his death in 1979 (the Commission retained the application after his death in view of the wishes of next of kin, and because of the issues of general interest it raised).

The Commission of Human Rights held that the applicant's recall and subsequent detention pursuant to the Home Secretary's power under Section 66 violated Article 5, Section 4 of the Convention for the Protection of Human Rights and Fundamental Freedoms. Article 5, Section 4 provides: 'Everyone who is deprived of his liberty by arrest or detention shall be entitled to take proceedings by which the lawfulness of his detention shall be decided speedily by a court and his release ordered if the detention is not lawful.' The Commission, following its decision in *Winterwerp* v. *The Netherlands* (1979), stated that it would be contrary to the object and purposes of Article 5 to immunize this category of confinement from subsequent review of lawfulness merely because the initial decision to commit issued from a court since 'the reasons initially warranting confinement of this kind may cease to exist'. The Commission concluded that persons of unsound mind have the right to a periodic judicial review of the lawfulness of their detention, and that such review must encompass the substantive justification for the deprivation of liberty. It found that the 1968 criminal court decision committing the applicant was an insufficient basis for his further detention nearly six years later and that *habeas corpus* proceedings do not provide a sufficient review for patients subject to a restriction order.

As a consequence of these decisions, new powers to introject judicial control into release pursuant to hospital restriction orders will have to be developed.

Let us now return to more general issues concerning sentencing the mentally ill for their crimes. There is both in England and in the United States an apparent paradox in the impact of mental illness on sentencing in that it is both ameliorative or reductive of punishment, on grounds of lesser moral fault, and at the same time aggravating or increasing punishment, on grounds of the offender's greater dangerousness. This ambivalence of attitude, these divergent pressures on punishment in practice, pervade the problem of sentencing the mentally ill. What is offered here are examples of statutory increments of punishment by reason of mental illness in the United States, followed by a theoretical discussion of how these contrary pressures, both to reduce and to increase punishment by reason of the accused's mental illness, may be brought into better focus and reconciled.

Statutes on 'sexual psychopaths' or 'sexually dangerous persons' spread like a rash of injustice across the United States from 1938 onwards, covering twenty-five states and the District of Columbia. All aim better to protect the public 'from persons with criminal propensities to the commission of sex offences'. In their orgin they claimed to be civil in form, not punitive, committing the mentally ill criminal with a propensity to sexual offences to indeterminate treatment until 'cured'. The earlier statutes sought to intercept the 'sexual psychopath' even before he was convicted of a crime, any crime, sexual or otherwise; but these unqualified preemptive strikes seemed so clearly unjust that later statutes have tended to require a conviction of some crime, usually a sexual crime (with great difficulties of definition), as a condition precedent to their invocation. The cloak of civil commitment, thin to begin with, became transparent with the decision of the United States Supreme Court in *Baxstrom* v. *Herold* (1966), and statutes passed subsequent to that case have tended to confine the duration of detention (and treatment, if any) to that which could have been ordered pursuant to a criminal conviction.

The cloak of civil commitment being removed, what remains? The mentally ill sexual offender must be seen as less morally guilty than the same offender guilty of an offence of identical severity and with an identical criminal record; hence the justification for an extension of state power over the mentally ill offender must rest on a belief in his increased dangerousness.

Sexual psychopathy is an insufficiently precise diagnosis to sustain such far-reaching legislative intervention; psychiatrists disagree profoundly on its definition and all modern nosologies reject it as a diagnostic entity.

There is little of principle that can be said in defence of these statutes. Most were immediate legislative reactions to sensational sexual crimes and illustrate a legislative capacity to conceal excessive punitiveness behind a veil of psychiatric treatment, independently of knowledge of the efficacy of, or provision for, such treatment. At base lies the false assumption of a unity between sexual offences and mental illness, certainly mental illness subject to effective treatment within the constraints of human rights.

Sexual psychopath statutes are also based on yet further false premises, in particular, that sexual offenders start with minor sexual offences and move on to more serious ones—that exhibitionism or voyeurism proceeds to rape—and that serious sexual offenders have higher rates of recidivism than other criminals—which they do not.

The literature on these statutes in extensive and need not be canvassed here. Let curt conclusions from that literature suffice: the best one can say in favour of these statutes is that they have been rarely and sporadically applied, except in California, Indiana, and Wisconsin, where mistaken enthusiasm outran both good sense and a sense of justice. These three states apart, the judiciary elsewhere in the United States remains uneasy in applying sexual psychopath statutes.

Where applied they have tended to sweep into their net minor sexual offenders, the inadequate repetitive voyeurs and exhibitionists, rather than those who commit serious crimes of sexual violence. They are exercises in retributive justice masquerading as 'treatment'; they are one paradigm of injustice flowing from an unprincipled blending of powers under the criminal law and the mental health law.

These vituperations are, of course, not meant to deny that some sexual offenders are mentally ill, in need of treatment, and that the community is in need of protection from them. The indictment is different. It is, *au fond*, that sexual criminality is a mistaken classification for these purposes, for the invocation of special powers. A sexual offender may be mentally ill and properly civilly committed; a sexual offender may be likely to repeat his crime and properly punished for it; but no blending of sexual crime and mental illness can justify varying ordinary rules of civil commitment or of the criminal law. For these purposes, armed robbers and serious sexual offenders are jurisprudentially identical, though the former are more likely to repeat their crimes.

The vigour and cogency of the scholarly attack on sexual psychopath laws led to their rejection by the three main commissions in the United States which have contributed nationally in the past quarter century to reform of the criminal law: the American Law Institute's Model Panel Code; the Model Sentencing Act of the Advisory Council of Judges of the National Council on Crime and Delinquency; and the National Commission on Reform of Federal Criminal Laws, (the Brown Commission.) All three reject 'sexual psychopathy,' 'psychopathy', and the more recent 'sociopathy' as acceptable referents for legislation; but all three, in rejecting that path of increasing punishment because of the mental illness of the accused, set out on another path we must now follow.

Criminal law, as a system of deterrent threats, aims to assist the potential offender resist criminality by means of the threat of punishment if he does not. Sexual psychopath laws are based on the premise that such threats are insufficient for certain psychologically disturbed sexual offenders. In their best case they rest on a view of such offenders as psychologically incapable, or less capable, of controlling their sexual instincts under the going rate of deterrent threat and therefore properly requiring added deterrence, more protracted detention and special treatment to assist their responsiveness to normal controls for the sake of the community and, in a sense, for their own sake. The category of legislation to which we now turn—Dangerous Offender Laws—preserves the element of predicting future criminality despite normal criminal law deterrent threats, which is involved in the Sexual Psychopath Laws, but applies this concept to wider groups of offenders. Again, provision is made for large threats and longer incapacitation, the former to maximize deterrence, the latter because while the criminal is in prison he can commit crimes only against others in prison (prisoners and guards) and because both the passage of an extended term of years and the ageing process will reduce the duration of the offender's life of crime in the community. Dangerous Offender Laws share with Sexual Psychopath Laws a belief in the predictability of criminal conduct.

Three categories of serious offenders are normally included in the Dangerous Offender Laws: habitual criminals, professional criminals, and psychologically disturbed criminals. Each category merits close consideration and raises jurisprudential problems distinct from the other two, but in this chapter discussion will be confined to the third category, psychologically disturbed offenders, where again a link is forged between mental illness and crime leading to an increment of punishment.

The products of the three influential commissions referred to above—the Model Penal Code, the Model Sentencing Act, and the Final Report of the Brown Commission—all recommended enactment of special and increased punishment for psychologically disturbed dangerous offenders. These recommendations have been accepted expressly or implicitly in at least ten states which have special sentencing provisions permitting increased punishment of mentally disturbed offenders thought likely to commit further crimes.

The paradigm of these proposals for sentencing reform and of this legislative flurry is Section 7.03(3) of the Model Penal Code which authorized a court, when sentencing a person convicted of felony, to extend the term of imprisonment beyond the maximum provided for that category of felon when 'the defendant is a dangerous, mentally abnormal person whose commitment for an extended period of time is necessary for protection of the public'. A precondition of such a sentence is a psychiatric examination 'resulting in the conclusions that his mental condition had been characterized by a pattern of repetitive or compulsive behaviour or by persistent aggressive behaviour with heedless indifference to consequences; and that such condition makes him a serious danger to others'.

I have it on the best authority that the dangerous mentally abnormal offender provisions of the Model Penal Code were the bargaining counter for the exclusion of any sexual psychopath provisions from the Code.

The Model Sentencing Act followed suit. Section 5 defines 'dangerous offenders' as those who have committed or attempted certain violent crimes and who are found by the court to be 'suffering from a severe mental or emotional disorder indicating a propensity toward continuing dangerous criminal activity'.

One marvels at the confidence reposed in the diagnostic and predictive capacities of psychiatrists by these provisions despite the caution in the accompanying commentary. The commentary to Section 5 recognizes that the concept of dangerousness is 'difficult to accept', that 'the behavioural sciences do not now have sufficient expertise to carry out this assignment adequately', but nevertheless claims to have provided 'a legally and socially precise delineation of dangerous persons and a legally and clinically careful procedure for identifying them'.

To complete this trilogy of 'model' legislation, the National Commission on Reform of Federal Criminal Laws, recommended that extended terms of imprisonment be provided for 'dangerous special offenders' and included an offender whose 'mental condition is abnormal and makes him a serious danger to the safety of others' and who committed the felony for which he is being sentenced 'as an instance of aggressive behaviour with heedless indifference to the consequences of such behaviour'. As usual with such recommendations, a comprehensive psychiatric examination and report are required as a precondition to the imposition of such an extended term.

In a variety of ways ten states have followed these recommendations. Other states, of course, can and do reach similar results, without express legislative direction, extending the duration of imprisonment of the mentally ill beyond the term that would have been imposed had they not been so diagnosed. That result may be achieved, as a matter of judicial discretion, whenever likely future criminality is authorized expressly or implicitly as a ground for aggravation of sentence and reliance is placed in the mental illness of the convicted person as indicative of likely future criminality. Of course, when extended terms are legislatively provided, the stakes are higher.

One can thus draw the conclusion that in the prevailing jurisprudence of the past twenty years in the United States, in legislation, theory and practice, in the legislative commissions, legislatures and courts, the mental illness of the convicted criminal when it leads to predictions of his increased 'dangerousness' is a ground for increasing the severity or the duration of his sentence. His mental illness may led to his imprisonment, when he would not have been imprisoned for what he did had he not been mentally ill, or to the extension of the term of his imprisonment.

There is, of course, a pervasive theme running at 180 degrees to the punitive direction we have been considering. Mental illness is widely seen and frequently legislatively prescribed as a ground for ameliorating punishment, for avoiding imprisonment, or for reducing its term. We turn now to legislative provisions for such mitigation of sentences imposed on the mentally ill.

So pervasive is this theme of lesser punishment being appropriate because of the lesser degree of moral guilt of the mentally ill that a few examples should suffice to lay the factual basis for its later analysis.

A convenient opening example is the American Law Institute's Model Penal Code, which provides that in determining whether it is necessary to imprison a convicted offender, the fact that 'there were substantial grounds tending to excuse or justify the defendant's criminal conduct, though failing to establish a defense', should be 'accorded weight in favor of withholding sentence of imprisonment'. This is often the situation in relation to a failed defence of insanity or to a situation where the crime committed is not of sufficient gravity to attract such a defence though the offender is mentally ill—one does not plead this defence to minor charges.

Moving forward twenty years to more recently recommended sentencing reforms, House Bill 6915 in the declining days of the 96th Congress provided that the first purpose of sentencing is to 'assure that the severity of the sentence is proportionate and directly related to the culpability of the defendant and the harm done'. In this Bill and in the related Senate Bill 1722, sentencing courts are directed 'in determining the particular sentence to be imposed' to consider 'the history and characteristics of the defendant'. In addition, Senate Bill 1722 directs the Sentencing Commission, in producing sentencing guidelines, to consider the relevance of a defendant's 'mental and emotional condition to the extent that such condition mitigates the defendant's culpability or to the extent that such condition is otherwise plainly relevant'.

The Model Sentencing and Corrections Act is also express on the matter of mental illness as a mitigating factor: '[M]itigating factors may include... the defendant was suffering from a mental or physical condition that significantly reduced his culpability for the offense'. This provision directs the Sentencing Commission to include this factor in guidelines for the sentencing judges and those judges to include this element in their assessment of the sentence to be imposed in an individual case.

But it is labouring the obvious. Pre-sentence psychiatric and psychological assessments are often drafted and applied to give the court understanding of the psychopathology of the convicted offender. The express and latent effects of such pre-sentence reports are frequently to lessen the offender's moral culpability in the eyes of the sentencing judge and hence, in practice, to mitigate the sentence.

How may one resolve the conflict between the mitigating and aggravating effects of mental illness on punishment? Let me offer, without elaborating the argument, a view on how this apparent paradox should be resolved.

Within retributive limitations on punishment, the finer-tuning of moral fault allows for mercy, clemency, and parsimony in punishment of the mentally ill. It is not a sentimental but rather a judicious use of the heavy weapon of punishment to lighten its impact on the less morally guilty to the extent that decent community sentiment allows. Psychological and social adversities may both properly have this influence on punishment, and we risk little by recognizing their sometimes undue criminogenic pressure and mitigating punishment accordingly. Since parsimony in the use of punishment is desirable in itself, mitigation of punishment on grounds of mental illness is both justified and socially desirable unless it increases the risk to the community beyond that which it bears from the ordinary limitations on the operation of the criminal justice system generally.

This may flow from reduced general deterrence from the sentence known to be imposed or increased social risk from the criminal so sentenced.

As to general deterrence and the punishment of the mentally ill: those who contemplate crime rather than those who find themselves caught to their horror in it do not calculate cost in punishment contingencies sufficiently precisely or make such assessments sufficiently frequently to lead to the rejection of the impulse to clemency in punishment of the mentally ill.

As to the increased risk to the community flowing from the likely dangerousness of the criminal, itself a product of mental illness: the present submission is that though in jurisprudential analysis aggravation of punishment up to a deserved maximum may properly supplant any argument for mitigation on grounds of lesser moral fault, the empirical preconditions of such aggravation are restrictive and will in practice rarely be encountered.

The key is this: the mentally ill convicted criminal's base expectancy rate must be shown by reliable evidence to be substantially higher than the base expectancy rate of another criminal with an identical record and convicted of a closely similar crime of violence but who is not mentally ill. The likely recidivism of the mentally ill offender must substantially exceed the likely recidivism of the sane offender. If that cannot be shown, then he should be sentenced on the low side of the deserved range if his criminality is related to his mental illness.

It is my submission that this principle governs both main sentence fine-tuning decisions: the in–out decision and, if imprisonment is ordered, the duration decision.

It is important to insist on clear and compelling evidence of a higher base expectancy rate attributable to mental illness before it can, in justice, increase punishment. This is not the occasion to reaffirm scepticism in psychiatric clinical predictions generally; the literature on this is compelling. And even when sociological predictors are added, and sophisticated statistical techniques and research methodologies are applied, there will be very few cases indeed where the principle enunciated in the previous paragraphs will justify an increase in punishment. But that does not invalidate the principle; to the contrary, it tends to affirm its importance and to stress the need for more reliable data than we now have as a precondition to any increase of punishment of the mentally ill relying on the mediating concept of their unestablished heightened dangerousness.

Hence the conclusion: the range of deserved punishment being otherwise determined, the judge should sentence the mentally ill offender toward the bottom of the deserved range to the extent that his mental illness was causally related to his crime (or to his earlier crimes), unless reliable evidence is adduced that because of his mental illness this offender is substantially more likely than others in that range to be involved in similar or more serious crimes in the future.

This conclusion should not be seen as support for the current tendency to misuse 'dangerousness' to increase punishment. I very much oppose that tendency, seeing it as based on uncritical acceptance of specious predictions claiming reliability grossly in excess of truth. But if and when base expectancy predictions of future criminality meet the criteria I have suggested, they should properly infuse a just sentencing system.

References

American Bar Association (1978). Commission on the mentally disabled (2 Mentally Disabled Law Reporter 617).
Burt, R., and Morris N. (1972). A proposal for the abolition of the incompetency plea. *University of Chicago Law Review*, Vol. 66.
HMSO (1953). Royal Commission on Capital Punishment Cmnd. 8932 (The Gowers Commission).
HMSO (1975). Report of the committee on mentally abnormal offenders Cmnd. 6244 (The Butler Committee Report).
Moran, R. (1981). *Knowing Right from Wrong: The Insanity Defense of Daniel McNaughtan*, Free Press.
New York (1978). The insanity defense in New York (Carnahan Report).

Cases Cited

Baxtrom v. *Herold* (383 U.S. 107 (1966))
People v. *Conley*, 64 cal. 2d 310, 411 P.2d 911, 49 Cal. Rptr. 815 (1966).
Durham v. *United States* (214 F. 2d. 862 (1954)).
Dusky v. *United States* (362 U.S. 402 (1960)).
People v. *Gorshen*, 51 Cal. 2d. 761, 336 P. 2d. 442 (1949).
Jackson v. *Indiana* (406 U.S. 715 (1971)).
People ex rel. Meyers v. *Briggs* (46 Ill. 2d. 281 263 NE 2d. 109 (1970)).
Inre Rosenfield (157 F. Supp. 18 D.D.C. (1957)).
United States v. *Brawner* (471 F. 2d. 969 D.C.C. (1972)).
People v. *Wells*, 33 Cal. 2d. 330, 202 P. 2d. 53 (1949), *cert.* denied, 383 U.S. 863 (1949).
People v. *White*, 117 Cal. App. 2d. 270, 172 Cal. Reptr. 612 (Cal Ct App. 1981).
Winterwerp v. *The Netherlands, Application No. 6301/73*, Judgment of the European Commission of Human Rights (October 24, 1979).
X v. *United Kingdom, Application No. 6998/75* Judgment of European Commission of Human Rights (5 Nov. 1981) Para 11.

Mental Illness: Changes and Trends
Edited by Philip Bean
© 1983 John Wiley & Sons Ltd.

CHAPTER 2

The ideology of entitlement: the application of contemporary legal approaches to psychiatry

LARRY O. GOSTIN
Legal director, mind

One of the principal controversies at the interface of psychiatry and law is whether the 'rights' of people designated as mentally ill, should be a major focus in seeking to improve their status and quality of life. This 'ideology of entitlement', at face value, appears to be an ill-conceived philosophy upon which to promote the interests of any socially impoverished group of people. There is a traditional affinity of law and lawyers to people with wealth and property. The law is perceived as a profession which is aligned with the defence of power and established interests. There can be few underprivileged people who feel comfortable with the law and who are aware of its use to promote their interests and to meet their social needs. The law is associated more with the removal of liberty and privileges than with the protection of morally justified values.

The influence of law in mental health was firmly established by the Lunacy Laws which enabled the legal profession comprehensively to review the decisions of other professions such as medicine and social work. The new 'ideology of entitlement' supported in this paper is not equivalent to the comprehensive legalism established under the Lunacy Laws which has been discredited in a number of quarters (Jones, 1972, 1980; Clare, 1980; Sedgwick, 1982). Nor would it be proper to defend entirely the 'new legalism' so evident in the United States which is emerging in Great Britain. What I will seek to do is to set out the three broad strategies of the legal approach: to obtain a right to adequate health and social services; to set limits on psychiatric activities based, in part, upon the principle of consent; and to prevent discrimination solely on the basis of a psychiatric classification. I will first seek to place the legal approach in perspective by suggesting significant limitations on its utility and by emphasizing that it is only one strategy for securing a comprehensive mental health service.

I   The ideology of entitlement: searching for parameters

The legal approach to mental health is considered inappropriate on a number of grounds. There is the perception that the legal profession is seeking to substitute its discretion for that of the medical and social work professions. It should be observed that there is little in the traditions, training or experience of judges or members of the legal profession to commend them in preference to professionals traditionally associated with humanism. Professor Kathleen Jones—whose historical assessment of British mental health legislation effectively discredited the 'legal formalism' of the Lunacy Laws (Jones, 1972)—suggests that legal intervention can only be remedial and not creative or inspiring: 'The need is not for increased legal formalism, but for human commpassion and professional skill...Legal enactments have been tried repeatedly and contributed little to genuine psychiatric progress' (Jones, 1980).

Professor Jones' argument is directed against a legal formalism that few would support. Contemporary legal philosophy goes behond the technical formalism associated with the Lunacy Laws. It does not seek to erect a cumbersome legal framework or to introduce technical legal procedures. Thus, the argument that the 'new legalism' is treading an historically discredited path does not take account of contemporary legal thought, although it is fair to react cautiously to any proposal which relies entirely upon legal or judicial decision-making. It is also improper to suggest that law and humanism are mutually exclusive—that there exists a sterile choice between 'legal enactments and restrictions' or 'genuine psychiatric advance', but not both. This language serves only to caricature the problem but not to assess it.

Traditional legalism is founded upon the application of a body of law to individual cases so that relatively consistent and fixed results accrue from reasonably equivalent factual circumstances. Such attempts to promote consistency and reasonable objectivity in psychiatric decision-making are, in principle, sound. However, those who oppose legal intervention argue that a formalistic or mechanistic approach is not suited to a field of human endeavour which is, by its nature, individualistic and unpredictable; while 'remedial law' can lay down relatively fixed and simplistic rules to penalize illegal activity, it cannot formulate a logical regulatory framework for complex issues relating to human behaviour. It is true that the law has not succeeded in trying to prescribe in detail the circumstances in which compulsory psychiatric intervention is justified; there is perhaps no other body of law which has undergone as many fundamental changes in approach and philosophy as mental health law. Nevertheless, where decisions involve the removal of a person's liberty or some other right of self-determination, it is no answer to say that the law should not control this activity because, by its nature there are no reliable and consistent factors which could govern such decisions. If this were the case, the remedy would not be to leave medical discretion unfettered; rather, it would suggest that discretion should not be exercised at all, and certainly not under the authority of law.

The most compelling argument against the traditional legal approach to psychiatry is that it is essentially negative and reactive; the law reacts to events and attempts to control them once they have occurred, but it cannot shape or influence them in a positive way. The law can examine narrow issues such as the occasional misuse of medical authority or the technical unlawfulness of admission. It can even regulate in some detail the provision of mental health services by setting boundaries and monitoring professional practice. However, it cannot effectively examine and resolve the more fundamental mental health issues.

Whatever one's views of the aetiology or indeed the existence of mental illness, there can be little doubt that emotional distress is one of the most important social problems of the day. Much of this suffering could be reduced by effective community health and social services, including ordinary and group accommodation, employment and specialized occupational training, crisis intervention, and medical, nursing, and social support systems. One of the principal objectives, then, of any strategy to improve the mental health services is to develop effective community-based alternatives to traditional institutional care. However, policy analysis and creative ideas relating to the provision of services to people suffering from mental distress seldom emanate from the legal profession or from the law. Moreover, the law appears incapable of contributing to the development of effective services as this requires long-term planning, budgeting, building, and management. Clearly these aspects of effective service provision are not within the competency of the courts or the law. Nor do members of the legal profession have the experience or expertise in areas of health and social services to enable them to identify needs and to propose workable solutions.

In sum, the legal approach to psychiatry has traditionally and perhaps necessarily been narrow and predictable. It has become an almost routinized and highly reactive counterbalance to medical and other professional authority. It has therefore virtually lost any identity of its own, save as being regulatory and critical of established psychiatric interests in a most predictable way (Sedgwick, 1982).

My argument is that a new role has been developing in law which can and should be used as a strategy in the provision of services. It would be quite wrong for the reasons given above to consider the law as the exclusive or the most important element in the provision of medical and social services. Yet a distinctive role can be identified. I will further argue that there is an important place for the law in setting limits on established psychiatric measures relating, for example, to compulsory admission and treatment and even to particularly hazardous measures taken with the consent of the patient. The final role of law is to ensure the civil status of those who are the consumers of psychiatric services.

One must accept the fact that pernicious legal and social consequences sometimes are secondary features of the receipt of psychiatric services. Here the law can make a distinctive contribution to uphold a person's personal status and dignity. This approach does not pretend to offer a solution to the more collective problems relating to deficiency in services, but the more individualistic approach of the law, nevertheless, has its own legitimacy in upholding the integrity of people who have felt dehumanized by institutions, by the opprobrium of society and by the discriminatory character of current legislation.

II   The ideology of entitlement: the contribution of law to the provision of adequate health and social services

The premise of the ideology of entitlement is that access to health and social services should not be based upon charitable or professional discretion, but upon enforceable rights. The rules of equity and fairness are deeply entrenched principles of law. From a broad legal perspective, a parliament is not obliged to pass ligislation to provide health and social services. However, once it chooses to provide services it cannot arbitrarily deprive or exclude certain individuals or client groups. If there is an unreasonable denial of a service, the remedy is, or should be, provided by the law.

The right to a service, of course, does not emanate from intangible, jurisprudential or moral philosophy, but from statute and, in some jurisdictions, from a written constitution. Great Britain, for example, provides a reasonably comprehensive health and social service. There is a wide ranging body of legislation which provides a general entitlement to treatment, care, housing, and social services (Finch, 1981; Gostin and Rassaby, 1980; Jacob, 1978). Thus, the provision of services is, from its origin, integrally associated with law. Improvements in the nature or quality of that service lie, at least in part, on enforcement of the law or in its reform. It should be observed that this approach relies upon 'open-textured' or 'enabling' legislation which must be supported by adequate financing, efficient management, and good practice. However, the law can, and sometimes does, place specific statutory duties on central or local government authorities which can be enforced through the courts or by administrative remedies. The objective of the ideology of entitlement is to establish the right to a service which can be enforced at the behest of a client group or an individual. This draws the attention of the relevant authorities to their legal and social obligations to particularly underprivileged client groups and draws public attention to under-provision and under-resourcing in areas of concern.

It would be wrong to suggest that the law has entirely solved the problems relating, for example, to traditional under-financing of mental handicap, psychogeriatric or community medical, nursing, and social services. However, the law can and does have a positive and substantial impact. It should also be observed that other more direct means of securing a fair proportion of resources in mental health have been unsuccessful. Traditionally, underprivileged people in mental distress have had very little impact on the political process. Consumers of psychiatric services are not organized, their interests have not been articulated forcefully by mental health professionals, and they have been denied the right to the franchise and other rights associated with the exercise of political choice and influence. It is perhaps unsurprising that 35 per cent of NHS beds are in mental illness or mental handicap hospitals and yet only 18 per cent of NHS resources are allocated to these areas (DHSS, 1978a).* Given the traditional impoverishment and rightlessness of consumers of psychiatric services it is reasonable to look beyond the established philosophies based upon professional and the charitable discretion and to examine the alternative strategy of the ideology of entitlement.

It may be helpful to examine some of the specific legal strategies utilized in Great Britain and in the United States in order to assess their impact. Before doing so I would emphasize that it is not possible at present to measure the success of the legal strategy in terms of its cumulative effect on the provision of services. In particular, one could not be certain whether legal intervention, on balance, has improved the mental health services. Is the quality of life for patients who require hospital care improved? Are more people who do not require in-patient care able to leave the hospital? Are there more adequate support facilities in the community? Are humane professionals rejecting mental health because of the restraints and complexities introduced by the law? These questions are unanswerable but lie at the core of the debate concerning the efficacy of the legal approach.

Illustrations of the contemporary legal approach in Great Britain

The Secretary of State for Health and Social Services has overall responsibility for the promotion of comprehensive health and social services, to secure improvement in the physical and mental health of people in England and Wales, and in the prevention, diagnosis, and treatment of illness. He has a duty to provide, to the extent he considers necessary, and to meet all reasonable requirements, hospital and other accommodation, services, and facilities for the prevention, diagnosis, treatment, and after-care of persons who are or have been suffering from illness including mental disorder. The Secretary of State may delegate any of his functions to Regional, District, or Special Health Authorities. The law in England and Wales, then, provides a comprehensive statutory entitlement to health services (National Health Service Act, 1977, sections 1–5). National health and other social legislation places equivalent duties on social service authorities to provide services for the prevention, care and after-care of persons designated as mentally ill (DHSS, 1974).

* See also Chapter 16.

The objective of the legal approach is to identify judicial or administrative remedies in cases where authorities do not comply with their legal responsibilities toward those suffering from mental illness. It may be argued that this is a usurpation of legislative functions (Wald and Friedman, 1978) and that it is for Parliament and local government to determine how scarce resources should be allocated. While this may be true, it is a simplistic notion as to how resources are dispersed. There are a number of factors which determine spending priorities and it appears valid to seek the intervention of the courts where resources are withdrawn or provided at a disproportionately low level to certain individuals or client groups.

Parliament specially provided a remedy for such instances in the hands of the Secretary of State for Health and Social Services. Where the Secretary of State is of the opinion, on complaint or otherwise, that a health authority has failed to carry out any functions conferred on it under National Health Service legislation, he may, after such enquiry as he thinks fit, make an order declaring it in default. The effect of such an order is that members of the authority forth-with vacate their office and new members are appointed who will comply with their statutory obligations (National Health Service Act, 1977, section 85). Similar powers are given to the Secretary of State under mental health legislation should be find a local authority social services department to be in default (Mental Health Act, 1959, section 142). The default powers are, in theory, an important remedy for the person who is unable to obtain effective health or social services which reasonably should have been provided under existing legislation. A patient is entitled to ask the Secretary of State to examine whether there has been a failure to comply with relevant legislation and to consider a default finding. In practice, successive Secretaries of State have been extremely reluctant to exercise their default powers, largely because of the political consequences of using compulsion on local government officials. Accordingly, legal reform should be directed toward obtaining new and more effective remedies where statutory responsibilities have not been fulfilled. It should be observed, however, that even with the limitations on current remedies, formal requests to the Secretary of State to exercise his default powers have drawn attention to inadequate provision of services and have produced some significant alterations in the pattern of services. Potentially, there is the right to judicial review of the Secretary of State's decision, although this strategy has been called into question as a result of a recent decision by the Court of Appeal (_R_ v. _Secretary of State for Social Services ex parte, HINCKS_, 1980). There are also accompanying strategies through constituency Members of Parliament and all-party mental health and disablement groups. A combination of these strategies have resulted in improvement in services for elderly people with mental distress, including an undertaking to provide government financing for private care for individuals where no NHS beds are available; default powers have also resulted in the provision of hostel accommodation for a special hospital patient, and in the provision of a hospital bed for a person with Huntington's chorea (MIND, in press). Similar default powers in the Education Act 1944 have resulted in greater rights to education for mentally handicapped children (Gostin, 1979c; Advisory Centre for Education/MIND, 1981).

Sometimes members society themselves use the law to try to prevent former patients from living normally in the community. General planning and licensing laws have been used to try to prevent the building of supported accommodation in the community. The legal approach has at times allied itself with mental health professionals and judicial approval has been successfully gained for community housing services which otherwise would not have existed (*In re Brent and Harrow AHA and Praetorial Housing Association*, 1978).

The search for effective remedies in the British context has gone beyond judicial or administrative remedies under health and social service legislation. The European Convention of Human Rights is available to member states and individual applicants from contracting parties within the Council of Europe. The organs of the Convention (The European Commission and Court) have recently been concerned with mental health cases, particularly emanating from Great Britain. The European Commission of Human Rights held admissible a complaint that the conditions and treatment provided in Broadmoor Hospital constituted a violation of Article 3 of the European Convention in that they were inhuman and degrading (*Smith* v. The United Kingdom, 1981); shortly after the commission's admissibility decision, they sent an international fact finding delegation to Broadmoor. Thereafter it was reported that £120 million had been allocated to improve hospital conditions. In a further case, the European Commission of Human Rights found admissible a complaint from a special hospital patient under Article 3 concerning the use of seclusion. The commission endorsed a settlement between the parties which included minimal guidelines in the use of seclusion and an *ex gratia* payment (*A* v. *United Kingdom*, 1980).

Social benefits have also been secured using a legal approach: mobility allowance was granted to Down's syndrome patients (MIND, in press); a local hospital bed was found for a special hospital patient who remained detained in a high security hospital because of a union dispute (*Ashingdane* v. *Secretary of State for Social Services and Others*, 1980); employment was secured for a former patient (*Chandler* v. *Surrey County Council*, 1977); and accommodation was secured for patients in hospital because of their homelessness (Gostin and Rassaby, 1980).

Concepts of individual liberty and the need for personal health and social services in the community are, or should be, interrelated. A legal approach which has as its sole objective the closure of psychiatric hospitals and the discharge of patients is misconceived. There is little advantage for people suffering from human distress to discharge them into the community without a home, employment or occupation, or medical, nursing, or social support. A writ of *habeas corpus*, for example, as a legal tool can only free a person from confinement in hospital; however, it cannot ensure that he or she will receive help in the community. *Habeas corpus* has been a time-honoured remedy against unlawful confinement offered by the law in the Anglo-Saxon jurisdictions. It has been sought in mental health cases since the eighteenth century (*R* v. *Turlington*, 1761. See also *R* v. *Board of Control and others ex parte Rutty*, 1956) and continues to be used to the present day (Gostin, 1977; MIND, In press). While *habeas corpus* cannot itself affect service provision, it does at least free the individual to pursue his own life and does compel local government to discontinue its traditional reliance on hospitals as a place for 'treatment' of those designated as mentally ill. In several recent *habeas corpus* applications the individuals did not want any support or supervision in the community. Rather, they wanted to be free from any outside interference in their lives; achieving such objectives is a traditional function of the law.In other cases patients could not be discharged from secure hospitals unless provision could first be found in local NHS hospitals or residential accommodation (*R* v. *Secretary of State ex parte Medway*, 1976; *R* v. *Secretary of State ex parte Powell*, 1978; *Kynaston* v. *Secretary of State for the Home Department and Secretary of State for the Department of Health and Social Security* 1982). In each of these cases the responsible authorities provided the accommodation and/or released the patient once the legal action was filed and, in one case, on the day that the case was being heard in the House of Lords. Indeed, a repeated feature of the contemporary legal approach in Great Britain is that cases involving service delivery or individual liberty are seldom resolved in the courts because government has agreed to provide the service or release the patient as a consequence of the threat or initiation of legal action.

The United States

The legal profession in the United States has had a profound affect on the mental health system in that country. Indeed, so prolific and diverse have been its activities that it is difficult to determine any overriding objective or strategy. Any attempt at charting the course of legal activity in the United States would result in oversimplification; more complete descriptions of the legal activities in America are contained elsewhere (Wald and Friedman, 1978; Gostin, 1979a; Mental Health Law Project, 1981) and there are several textbooks and journals devoted entirely to mental health law in America (Brooks, 1974 and 1980; *Mental Disability Law Reporter*).

A notable characteristic of American federalism is that domestic policy has been substantially determined by the courts; the judiciary has introduced its own social morality to try to ensure reasonable access to services for those designated as mentally ill. The judicial landmarks are not difficult to draw. A series of cases from the late 1960s onwards criticized the very existence of psychiatric institutions. The constitutional parameters of these cases were complex and diverse, but broadly relied upon the fact that patients were involuntarily detained. If the government was to deprive individuals of their liberty, the argument went, it was bound to provide (and here the judicial prescriptions varied) some minimal treatment or habilitation (*Donaldson* v. *O'Connor*, 1975).

Two conceptual obstacles have impeded a major shift in resources from institutions to the community. First, as stated above, the basis of the constitutional claims rested largely upon the legal status of patients; voluntary patients or people in the community were, therefore, not entitled to equivalent constitutional protection. Subsequent cases have sought to circumvent this obstacle by, for example, proclaiming a constitutional right to protection from harm (*New York State Association for Retarded Children* v. *Carey*, 1975); however, this constitutional path has never firmly established itself. The second conceptual obstacle was to be the pivotal factor; the success of this strategy was to be an important measure of the success of the legal approach itself. It involved the power and willingness of the judiciary to compel government to provide community-based alternatives to institutional care. The concept of affirmative action found its most complete expression in a Federal District Court case emanating from the state of Texas: 'Constitutional rights are hollow if there are in fact no alternatives to institutionalization. The State may not circumvent the Constitution simply by refusing to create any alternatives to incarceration; it must act affirmatively to foster such alternatives' (*Morales* v. *Tutman*, 1974).

One should be reminded of the radical nature of such judicial pronouncements. The United States has never sought to enshrine in its law any comprehensive right to health or social services, although federal legislation has been enacted providing an incentive to states to develop community-based psychiatric and social services. The United States Supreme Court recently refused to uphold any constitutional or statutory right to care in the community (*Pennhurst State School and Hospital* v. *Halderman*, 1981). Although the Supreme Court has not conclusively decided that there is not constitutional right, it will now be difficult for the legal profession to pursue such a course in the courts.

It would be improper to be over-critical of judicial intervention in the United States, particularly since it has come in the wake of chronic legislative and executive neglect of the needs of people suffering from mental distress. Nonetheless, it is regrettable that important policy decisions have been taken within the narrow context of litigation. The disadvantages of this judicial approach are that the courts are limited by the particular facts and issues raised in the immediate case and they are able only to set *minimal* standards based upon non-specific constitutional principles; they are unfamiliar with the range and appropriateness of treatment approaches and facilities; and they are ill-equipped to assure long-term compliance with, and implementation of, their judgments.

Conspicuously absent from American policy is a comprehensive legislative and political assessment of the needs of people suffering from mental distress and long-term programmes designed to meet those needs. (Compare the fragmented approach of the United States illustrated by judicial intervention on a case-by-case basis, with the integrated approach in national health and social service legislation and in the White Papers on service provision in Great Britain (DHSS, 1971 and 1975).) One must pause and reflect about the policy of institutional closure in many developed countries including the United States and Great Britain. In Britain, there are some 120,000 people receiving care in institutions, while in the United States there are approximately 200,000. It would be a grave mistake to close all psychiatric hospitals without considering the effect it would have on people whose only home and means of support are in the institutions. Is it going to be possible to fundamentally improve the lives of so many individuals, each with different and unique needs, without additional expenditure? The economics are complex and have been explore elsewhere (MIND, 1977). However, in common sense terms much of the money presently spent on hospital services goes into maintenance, heating, and staffing of large institutions; inevitably much of this expenditure will continue until the institutions are entirely closed and the hospital property is sold. Before institutions can be closed it will not be possible to adequately maintain two parallel systems of care at no additional cost. It is difficult to see how the quality of life for those who are left behind in the institution will improve, and how people with mental distress in the community will be provided with the homes, jobs, medical, and social support they need. Clearly, legal intervention as an exclusive strategy is not capable of ensuring that the needs of these people are met, and other political, social, and educational methods are necessary. In Britain the government has argued that no additional expenditure will required (DHSS, 1981a). In America the process they call 'deincarceration' or, more to the point, 'dumping'* was based, in part, upon principles of economic retrenchment. Indeed, one of the first experiments in substantially reducing the hospital population was undertaken in California by the then Governor Reagan. This was based upon a policy of budget reduction. Several years later one of Mr Reagan's first decisions as President was to drastically curtail programmes previously passed by Congress to provide community services and advocacy for people with mental illness.

It is curious that similar policies of deinstitutionalization were advocated by civil libertarians opposed in principle to involuntary confinement. In many cases strategies of institutional closure have resulted in new forms of regimentation, impoverishment and deprivation in the community. In many instances the same clinical approaches were transferred from hospitals to nursing homes and hostels (Barnett, 1978). More importantly, when institutions were closed, there was nowhere for patients to go because of the absence of any coherent strategy. They ended up in prison, or exploited by private landlords, readmitted to other institutions, or just homeless, neglected and alone.

To avoid similar patterns in Great Britain and elsewhere sufficient provision will have to be made to achieve effective and humane integration of those

* See also Chapter 15.

designated as mentally ill into ordinary homes, schools, and industries. Government will have to build and to adapt community resources in sufficient numbers, educate the wider community to be more tolerant of those considered deviant, and reduce the community's false reliance on total institutional care and the 'medicalization' of deviance.

III Limitations on the practice of psychiatry

Psychiatry is a profession with a traditional affinity to humanism; its *raison d'etre* is to care for people with deep emotional and human distress. It is, moreover, a specialism of medicine which has well established traditions of healing the sick and which is guided by scrupulous ethical principles (Bloch and Chedoff, 1981). When one examines the caring traditions and benevolent principles underlying the profession, it is curious that it has been so closely associated with power and its abuse.

Psychiatrists remain confident that they exist only to tend the ill and that their activities do not have any social or political implications. They, like other members of the medical profession, purport to care only for the interests of the patient. They assert that psychiatry relies upon objective assessment and scientific principles which are not governed by social or personal values.

The tools of psychiatry (for example, involving psychotherapeutic techniques and social support) are to a great extent less intrusive than those used in most other specialisms of medicine. Why then should psychiatrists be so maligned and criticized? The now influential school of critical psychiatry would say that the reason is the absence of any objective evidence for the existence of the very subject of psychiatric inquiry, that is, mental illness. (See e.g. Laing, 1965; Scheff, 1966; Goffman, 1968; Szasz, 1972. More recent critiques include Ingleby, 1981; Baruch and Treacher, 1978; Bean, 1980; Adlam and Rose, in press.) Classical psychiatry, it is argued, is based upon whole systems of prejudice about the nature of human behaviour and how it can be explained. Psychiatry seeks to encapsulate a complex and diverse human character into the language of scientific medicine—e.g. diagnosis, symptomatology, and behaviour prediction. The entire foundation of psychiatry is erected upon observed behaviour which is considered to be deviant, according to the unstated norms and values of the observer. From the behaviour, the psychiatrist infers a physical disorder which is relevant to a medical state wider than, and apart from, the specific behaviour. The symptoms are grouped and classified (diagnosis) and the disease is then expected to take a certain course (prognosis).

Whatever one's views about the existence of mental illness or its aetiology, it must be acknowledged that there exists a deep intuitive recognition of the existence of insanity, at least in its extreme forms. There is a common sense acceptance that madness is not a myth invented by medicine. Moreover, one is aware that 'crazy behaviour' or extreme feelings of emotion can cause grave suffering to individuals and their families which sometimes can be alleviated by medical, nursing, or social support. It may be, as some argue, that this is a placebo effect, and occurs only because sufferers *believe* in the effectiveness of treatment (Ingleby, 1981). In response one need only observe that few of its critics have offered any clear alternative to psychiatrists and other traditional mental health professionals; their continuing involvement in tending the mentally distressed has never effectively been placed into question.

The principal concern of those who advocate a legal approach is that psychiatrists have gone much further than simply caring for people who are thought by themselves and others to suffering from mental distress. Psychiatrists have established themselves as 'experts' in deviance and have claimed exclusive abilities to identify insanity when it would not be possible for the lay person to do so. The diagnosis is not based upon observable behaviour and there are no other openly stated and objective criteria. Law and society, moreover, have simply relinquished any responsibility for designation and treatment of mental illness. British mental health legislation defines mental disorder as mental illness, mental impairment, psychopathic disorder and 'any other disorder or disability of mind'. Mental illness is left undefined. This legislative framework appears to encompass a wide variety of people whose character, attitudes, or intelligence are considered abnormal. It is when psychiatry enters the grey areas of personality disorder or neurosis, or when it claims an ability to identify an 'illness' which is not apparent to the rest of us that it is most vulnerable as a profession.

The legal approach, then, is not part of the fabric of anti-psychiatry. Its aim is to ensure, particularly where compulsion is involved, that the expert, minimally, can explain and justify his or her decision to the lay person and that there exists some objective behavioural criteria. Psychiatric decisions have been based upon 'expert' opinion and, predictably, doctors have insisted upon their expertise. In this way they have avoided a wider review of their decisions. The 'experts', according to the legal approach, should be required to state the grounds for their decisions in terms which are open to examination by others. The confrontation should then be on the question of the adequacy of the grounds advanced and not on the basis of presumed expertise. This is the area of disagreement at the interface of law and psychiatry. The legal approach does not accept unsupported claims of knowledge in areas of diagnosis, behaviour prediction, or treatment. In each context the law requires some observable evidence to support professional judgments.

There is a sense of contradiction in the way that contemporary psychiatry presents itself. Psychiatry purports to be a specialism of medicine; it strives toward objectivity and has an affinity with the natural sciences. The psychiatric journals bristle with research to establish the empirical efficacy of somatic treatments. At the same time, psychiatry asks not to be held to account for its views in an objective and scientific way. It asks, rather, to operate under the ambiguous parameters of 'clinical judgment', which relies not upon an empiricist view, but upon unspoken areas of personal intuition and subjective judgments. Psychiatrists are often loath to explain and to justify their opinions, except perhaps to fellow professionals. Medical thought concerning the propriety of allowing those designated as mentally ill to exercise judgment in respect of admission or treatment decisions appears to be this: Mental patients are considered to be detained in hospital because they are considered a danger to themselves or others and/or that they are unable to make reasonably informed judgments concerning the need for treatment. Members of the medical profession are delegated the task of determining those who are dangerous or lacking competence, and then to substitute their judgment for that of the person concerned. It is the benefit that is said to accrue to the patient which is thought to justify the deprivation of his or her ordinary right to self-determination. It follows that society operates on the assumption that psychiatrists can reliably and validly diagnose particular forms of mental disorder, that psychiatrists have an ability to predict future behaviour in cases where the lay person could not, that psychiatric treatments with reasonably established efficacy exist, and that psychiatrists can make reasonably consistent and objective judgments concerning the need for a treatment response to a particular medical condition. The evidence to support each of these assumptions is highly equivocal.

Diagnoses

One of the most researched areas in psychiatry and social science is the ability of practitioners to make reliable and valid diagnoses of mental illness. Reliability is a term used to describe the frequency of agreement when two or more independent observers answer the same question; that is the ability of psychiatrists to agree upon a diagnosis when viewing the same person or an identical set of symptoms. Research has repeatedly demonstrated that psychiatrists cannot make reliable diagnoses under normal clinical conditions (Morse, 1978; Gostin, 1975). There are observers such as Clare (1980) who argue that more recent findings show higher levels of reliability. However, even these minimal levels of reliability were obtained only when researchers artificially imposed common standards for psychiatric participants in such areas as interview techniques, nosological nomenclature and training. Unfortunately such methods of refinement of diagnostic skills are not part of the actual practice of psychiatry on hospital wards and out-patient clinics. There remains very little evidence that psychiatric diagnoses are more reliable than judgments about human behaviour made by other professionals or indeed by laymen. The core of Clare's argument in defence of psychiatry (see also, Wing, 1978) is that the subjectivity of psychiatric perceptions of 'illness' and diagnosis and the resulting unreliability is hardly different from that which pertains in other specialisms of medicine.

However, it is difficult to accept that psychiatric judgments are qualitatively equivalent to those make in other specialisms of medicine (Adlam and Rose, in press; Iingleby, 1981), although there is some overlap. In psychiatry the 'illness' does not manifest itself in any verifiable or observable fashion; diagnosis is always referable back to the person's behaviour and how that behaviour is to be interpreted. Further, the diagnosis cannot be confirmed by other independent evidence—for example, there is no cognizable aetiology or measurable physiological process or overt symptomatology. The justification for the existence of the illness originates and remains wholly within the character or psyche of the 'patient'.

Even if the psychiatric profession could obtain high diagnostic reliability, serious problems would remain with their system of classification. Psychiatric diagnoses often do not convey specific and accurate information about how a patient is currently behaving, why he is behaving in that way or how he is likely to behave in the future. Diagnoses do not appear to be reasonably precise; the same behaviour or affect may be indicative of different diagnoses, while a single diagnosis may incorporate a large range of behaviour and affect. The value of diagnoses, therefore, for the purpose of determining, in a reasonably precise way, legally relevant issues such as compulsory admission, competency, and forcible treatment is problematic.

The most important characteristic of psychiatry, which distinguishes it from other specialisms of medicine, is that it is empowered to substitute, by compulsion if necessary, the psychiatrist's judgment concerning the need for admission and treatment for that of the patient. Psychiatry is the only branch of medicine which relies on compulsion admission to hospital and can corpel major forms of physical treatment on patients without their consent. The guiding principle of the legal approach is that, if the law is to delegate authority to the doctor to impose admission and treatment, it must also place reasonable fetters and boundaries on the exercise of that authority.

Admission

It has bever been difficult to show the importance of the law in relation to compulsory admission because of the traditional function of the law as a guardian of personal liberty. The right to an independent review of the need for detention in hospital is now well established in an international context (Curran and Harding, 1978; United Nations, 1981; *Winterwerp* v. *The Netherlands*, 1979; *X* v. *The United Kingdom*, 1981). A new legal formalism has particularly established itself in certain American jurisdictions where elaborate 'criminal due process' procedures have been introduced (*Lessard* v. *Schmidt*, 1972). These procedures involve notice of hearing, preliminary and full judicial hearings, the right to a state appointed lawyer, trial by jury, standard of proof (clear and convincing evidence), privilege against self-incrimination and transcripts taken at the hearing for the purposes of a possible appeal. The elaborateness of legal intervention in the United States probably carries with it unacceptably high social costs, in terms of diversion of scarce resources and the opprobrium placed upon the subject of the proceedings (Gostin, 1979a). However, the general value of an independent review is beyond question if only because such a right is afforded to every other individual in society faced either with loss of liberty or deprivation of a valued personal or property right.

The strategy of legal intervention in the United Kingdom has been, firstly, to establish a right of judicial review and, secondly, to make that review more effective in broad social terms. Both elements of this legal approach have had a large measure of success. The government was recently found to be in violation of Article 5(4) of the European Convention of Human Rights due to its failure to provide an independent review for certain categories of cases (*X* v. *United Kingdom* 1981 Gostin, in press) and related 'second generation' cases have already been filed with the Commission (MIND, in press). These relate to the inordinate time sometimes needed to arrange a hearing; the right to legal aid for paid representation and the right to natural justice at the hearing.

The second aspect of legal strategy has been to improve the quality of tribunal hearings. It has been observed that strict procedural guarantees afforded to prospective patients in civil commitment hearings in the United States did not appear to improve the accuracy of the decision-making process or even provide significant protection against unnecessary loss of liberty. Studies in the United States suggest that the performance of lawyers in civil commitment hearings have been perfunctory and highly mechanistic (Hiday, 1977; Cohen, 1966). Reports from several states have described counsel doing 'virtually nothing except stand passively at the hearing and add a falsely reassuring patina of respectability to the hearings' (Andalman and Chambers, 1974). (For related studies in Great Britain see Peay, 1981; Greenland, 1970; Gostin and Rassaby, 1980.)

The American experience demonstrates that the erection of a cumbersome legal edifice, without any thought as to the effect it will have on the decision-making process, is ill-judged. The prospective patient will benefit from a hearing and representation only if the decisions taken by the tribunal are based upon more complete information about the medical/social/after care aspects of the case. MIND operates a comprehensive tribunal representation service in England and Wales which informs all patients of their right to a tribunal and provides a legal or lay representative for any patient who requires one. Potential representatives in this scheme undergo an intensive training course with the purpose of apprising them of the broad medico/social/legal aspects of tribunal representation. The representative is trained to utilise appropriate legal procedures; to constructively examine medical opinion to ensure that it is based upon empirical evidence; to secure independent medical and/or social reports; to explore the availability of housing, employment, care or treatment in the community; and, where necessary, to compel local government to provide services if such provision could avoid the need for hospital care (Gostin and Rassaby, 1980).

Those who advocate the principles of anti-psychiatry may argue that this full participation in the civil commitment process simply legitimizes institutional care and confinement. While this may be so, it is the responsibility of the law to ensure that, where hospitals and institutional structures exist, they are used properly. The individual, minimally, must be afforded the dignity of having his point of view considered and the assistance of a representative for the purpose of avoiding unnecessary confinement. This may not be a radical or visionary solution to the conceptual problems of psychiatry, but it is of pragmatic and meaningful assistance to individuals whose own life choices are to be disregarded by society.

Treatment

Legal concern for the welfare and rights of the psychiatric patient has traditionally ceased at the hospital door on the assumption that, while the law could reasonably set procedural and substantive standards in respect of compulsory admission, it could not interfere in the clinical relationship which must be established following admission. This traditional legal view resulted in the failure of mental health legislation to establish general principles protecting the position of detained psychiatric patients to decide what treatment they should receive (Gostin, 1979b, 1981). The authority provided by law to administer treatment against the express wishes of detained patients has, in many countries, no apparent boundary based upon the nature of the treatment, its proven efficacy, its irreversible or adverse effects, or its risks (United Nations, 1981). This sets psychiatry apart from other specialisms of medicine where the law provides, at least in principle, a right to self determination. In law, a physically ill patient is free to make a decision which may be against his medical interests so long as he is able to understand the implication of that decision; the common law places no legal obstacle to a patient's decision to live in great pain or even to risk his or even to risk his or her life rather than to accept unwanted medical treatment.

The fundamental issue facing psychiatry and law regarding the therapeutic relationship are, firstly, competency and consent and, secondly, the efficacy and risks of the treatment proposed. In order to establish the relevance of law in the treatment decision one must either question the wisdom of the doctor or point to some specific criteria which are neither medical nor quasi-medical but are ultimately non-medical which makes the doctor the *wrong* person to apply them. A person's competency to consent to medical treatment is not a medical concept, but essentially lay and legal. The question to be put is not whether the patient is able to make a more informed and expert medical decision than the doctor, but whether he is able to understand the nature, purpose and risks of the treatment and to express his will rationally. A doctor may well be able to tell us the benefits of a particular treatment, but the decision about whether it is proper to impose it upon an unwilling patient, thus undermining his dignity and physical integrity, is ultimately a social and lay judgment and should not rest on medical grounds alone.

The second, and more controversial, role of law in regulating the therapeutic relationship relates to the nature of the treatments themselves. If it can be demonstrated that particular treatments used by any branch of medicine are irreversible, unusually hazardous or not fully established, their use should be subjected to rigorous examination and control. Put another way, psychiatry cannot logically assert an unqualified right to practice medicine unless it is prepared to demonstrate to others outside of the profession that the treatments it administers are, minimally, safe and effective.

There is no conclusive evidence in psychiatry concerning the aetiology of most forms of psychiatric illness, nor is there a clear understanding of why many treatments are thought to have a beneficial effect. Nevertheless, there is some evidence that each of the three major somatic treatments—electroconvulsive therapy, psychosurgery, and medication—are empirically effective in the treatment of particular psychiatric conditions.

It has to be observed that the therapeutic effect of each treatment is narrowly limited to particular clinical conditions and depends for its effectiveness on the way it is used. Moreover, use of certain treatments intensively or over long periods of time can result in adverse effects which far outweigh any potential benefit. The principal difficulty in respect of these treatments and the area of disagreement at the interface of medicine and law is as follows. Psychiatrists properly observe that the major somatic treatments can be beneficial and can have acceptable levels of risk. Accordingly, the medical view is that safeguards are not warranted and that decisions about treatment should be left exclusively to the medical profession. The difficulty with this position is the fact that in psychiatry, as in most professions, there is a wide range of competence and expertise as well as limited time and resources with which to take decisions. The consistent findings of the major hospital enquiries (e.g. S. E. Thames Regional Health Authority, 1976) and courts (e.g. *Mills* v. *Rogers*, 1982) in the last decade have shown that treatments are not necessarily limited to interventions with established efficacy and safety, and that the major somatic treatments are sometimes used far too extensively and can result in severe adverse effects for the patient. It should also be observed that psychiatrists have been shown to exhibit a singular style of treatment response and to categorize patients medically in a relatively fixed way which is independent of the symptoms observed. There appears to be an overall predisposition to diagnose psychopathology and a propensity in individual clinicians to diagnose and administer treatment according to their different experience and clinical orientation (Morse, 1978).

The justification for legal interference in the therapeutic relationship depends upon the context in which particular treatments are used. Brief illustrations of this principle, using the three major somatic treatments in psychiatry, may be useful. More complete discussions of these treatments and the principles involved are contained elsewhere (Palmer, 1981; Clare, 1978; Bridges and Bartlett, 1977; Gostin, 1980; Brooks, 1980).

Electroconvulsive therapy. Electroconvulsive therapy has been shown to be empirically effective in the treatment of severe endogenous depression (Freeman, *et al.*, 1978), although there is some evidence that the electrically induced convulsion is not the critical factor (Johnstone, *et al.*, 1980). More importantly, there is no clinical consensus as to its benefit in the treatment of other psychiatric conditions such as schizophrenia and there is no recognized professional body of opinion upholding its use as a method of behaviour control (Royal college of Psychiatrists, 1977). Electroconvulsive therapy, therefore, may be regarded as reasonably established in some clinical contexts but not in others. Electroconvulsive therapy is not normally considered hazardous, except to the extent that any treatment has certain hazards associated with it. It is not unusually hazardous when account is taken of the prospect of benefit to be expected from the treatment in appropriate cases. However, the anaesthetic which precedes ECT may be unusually hazardous to a patient who has just eaten a large meal or who suffers from a heart condition. Electroconvulsive therapy can be hazardous when administered in an unmodified form (i.e. without muscle relaxant and anaesthetic), where there are significant risks of bodily injury (Hansard, 1981; Bebbington, *et al.*, 1980), or when it is used intensively or over a long term where there is a risk of memory deficit and other adverse effects.

Psychotropic medication. In the general euphoria that followed the discovery of anti-psychotic medications, relatively little attention has been paid to their human costs. However, there is increasing evidence in the medical literature about the excessive use of psychotropic drugs and the adverse effects of their long-term administration (Michel and Kolakowska, 1981; Brooks, 1980). Prescribing by general practitioners and psychiatrists is criticized for the concurrent administration of more than one psychotropic drug—known as polypharmacy—prolonged use of drugs, and incorrect dosage.

There is no question that major tranquillizers have led to a revolution in psychiatric treatment, which has resulted in greater possibilities for patients to leave hospital and to live in the community. Nevertheless, the adverse effects of psychotropic medication are widespread, severe, and sometimes irreversible. It must be observed that the adverse effects of medication occur even where it is responsibly and competently administered. The side effects include dryness of the mouth, lethargy, and Parkinsonian symptoms including gross involuntary movements of the mouth and limbs; damage to the nervous system, in certain circumstances, can be irreversible—for example, with tardive diskinesia (American Psychiatric association, 1980).

Psychosurgery. There is now a considerable body of literature concerning the therapeutic and ethical aspects of psychosurgery (Bridges and Bartlett, 1977; Valenstein, 1977, 1980; Gostin, 1980), and certain conclusions can be reached on the practice of psychosurgery—both past and present. There is some contemporary evidence that psychosurgery is an empirically effective treatment for affective disorders such as depression and anxiety states. However, psychosurgery was observed from its earliest use not to be effective in the treatment of schizophrenia. Nevertheless, it is estimated that some two-thirds of the 10 000 operations conducted between 1942 and 1954 in Britain were on patients diagnosed as schizophrenic. Contemporary psychosurgery is also used in the treatment of schizophrenia despite the fact that rarely is there any marked clinical improvement. There is also inconclusive evidence as to the effectiveness of psychosurgery in a number of highly diverse medical and social conditions—for example, psychosurgery has been performed in the cases of anorexia nervosa, sexual deviation, hyper-responsiveness, aggressiveness and anti-social behaviour. Between 1974–76 there were 16 different types of lesions made in a minimum of 14 cerebral sites (Barraclough and Mitchell–Heggs, 1978). Despite the multiplicity of existing surgical interventions, together with their use on almost the entire range of psychiatric and social conditions, the use of psychosurgery is not the subject of specific legal or administrative regulation.*

This assessment of the major somatic treatments and the role of law in setting parameters to psychiatric practice may be viewed by radical observers to be misguided. Sedgwick (1982) has argued that, if the law uses the language of 'abuse', it must acknowledge that there is a proper 'use' for such psychiatric activities. Ingleby (1981), in turn, argues that even if there were empirical evidence for the somatic treatments it may be no more than a placebo effect and, in any case, it does not prove there is any organic origin to the problem. My view is that one must respond to psychiatry on its own terms and in relation to its acceptance in society. It purports to be a specialism of medicine which is concerned with the alleviation of human suffering. If a patient defines his problem as medical and consents to a treatment with demonstrated empirical effectiveness, there can be no rational ground for society or the law to intervene. The language of 'use' or 'misuse' can only have relevance if it is applied within the context of ordinary medical conventions relating to the efficacy of treatments. This requires that the efficacy and risks of the treatment must be tested according to accepted scientific principles used in all forms of medicine. There are many physical treatments in medicine which have alleviated suffering although the extant evidence as to efficacy is exclusively empirical. Evidence for the major

---

* The Mental Health (Amendment Act) 1982 places special safeguards over the use of psychosurgery on detained patients.

somatic treatments in psychiatry, therefore, is not qualitatively different from that used in other branches of medicine.

It has been the burden of this part of the paper to show that there is no orthodoxy in psychiatric thought concerning the three major somatic treatments. The objective of the legal approach is to provide safeguards for the patient in either of two situations. First, the patient who refuses to consent to a treatment should be entitled to protection under the law. This places the psychiatric patient in a similar position to physically ill patients who object to receiving certain treatments. Second, a treatment should not be administered unless the doctor can demonstrate that it is reasonably efficacious (even if the proof is only empirical) and that it acts without disproportionate risks or adverse effects.

IV   Maintaining the civil and social status of those designated mentally ill

The final legal approach to contemporary mental health problems is to undo much of the false legalism inherited from legislation devised in the Victorian era. The contemporary legal principle is that legislation should not place extra jurisprudential, social or political burdens on those designated as mentally ill unless these are justified by substantial and reasonable societal objectives such as public safety. Put another way, the legal approach seeks to avoid discrimination which is based upon inaccurate professional and/or social beliefs about the behaviour and capabilities of those who suffer from mental distress. Such attitudes have resulted in mental health legislation which, when examined carefully, is almost entirely devoted, not to provision of services and help, but to the systematic withdrawal of liberties and civil rights or status which are afforded to other members of society. Basic societal rights or privileges such as enfranchisement, jury service, access to the courts, control of one's own possessions and finance, licences to drive or engage in a profession, immigration, unimpeded communication or association, are withdrawn without ever asking the question—is the individual capable of exercising the right or privilege at issue?

This approach has both a substantive and procedural element. Substantively, legislators should require particular and substantial evidence in each individual case to show that the person will do significant damage to himself or others if he or she is permitted to exercise the right. This would place the person designated as mentally ill in an equivalent position to other members of society. It is possible to justify the withdrawal of any right or privilege to any person if such a case could be made. The right to vote, drive a car or have access to the courts, for example, can be withdrawn if, *on any grounds*, the person is shown not to be capable. Why, then, should these rights or privileges be withdrawn systematically in the psychiatric context simply on the basis of a medical or social label and without the need for evidence in the individual case? Procedurally, the legal approach would require that people who are to have a right or privilege removed must first have an idependent review where they can put their point of view and present their own evidence. Such a procedural entitlement is considered fundamental in every other non-psychiatric context, even where the issue involves only small sums of money or property where, what is at stake, is much less important to individual dignity. This procedural entitlement would also place those designated as mentally ill in a similar position to other members of society. There follows a brief examination of two highly selected areas of concern where people are rather arbitrarily deprived of basic rights or privileges based upon unfounded paternalistic attitudes toward 'illness' and deviance. The right of access to the courts and enfranchisement have been chosen as illustrations because of their importance in establishing the civil and social status of any vulnerable group in society.

Access to the Courts

Section 141 of the Mental Health Act, 1959 places a significant impediment on any person seeking to bring civil or criminal proceedings against any person carrying out functions in pursuance of the Act. In many important cases, such as wrongful imprisonment, the Mental Health Act does not simply impede, but effectively prevents a psychiatric patient from obtaining legal redress. In Kynaston's case (1981), for example, a psychiatric patient was placed in the invidious position of not being permitted even to present a claim to the domestic courts that he was a sane person detained in a maximum security hospital without lawful justification.

The Kynaston case (and the related case of *Ashingdane*, 1980) are currently being considered by the European Commission of Human Rights. The grounds for the application are under Article 5(1) (e) as there was no objective evidence of mental illness to justify detention; Article 5(5) as he was prevented from enforcing a right to compensation through the courts; Article 6(1) as he was unable to have a court hearing before having a fundamental civil right (i.e. access to the courts) withdrawn; Article 13 as he was denied an effective remedy before a national authority; and Article 14 since there was discrimination in that psychiatric patients are singled out in English law for restriction on their rights of access to the courts.

Given a law which, on its face, appears to deprive a vulnerable class of people of a formidable number of basic human rights, it is interesting to examine the historical context and purpose of this provision. The Dillwyn Committee on Lunacy Law expressed the concern that 'some years ago there was an action brought against a medical man for illegally signing an order for detention for a patient.... It appears to me there should be some relief to medical men'. Similarly, the Royal Commission on Lunacy and Mental Disorder (1926) spoke of a 'certification strike' by medical practitioners because of their alleged vulnerability to legal actions by patients. Thus, the historical origin of the withdrawal of a basic right to those designated as mentally ill arose, not because of any evidence that they were incapable of reasonably exercising the right, but because of the perceived need to protect the medical profession (Gostin, 1975).

The earliest precursor to section 141 of the Mental health Act, 1959 was section 12 of the Lunacy Amendment Act, 1889. The terms of section 12 were re-enacted in section 33 of the Lunacy Act, 1890 and section 62 of the Mental Deficiency Act, 1913. A similar impediment to judicial process was carried over into the Mental Treatment Act, 1930. However, throughout this period the terms of the provision changed, almost imperceptively, until now it has resulted in a rigid judicial attitude toward people suffering from mental distress. In *Pountney's* case (1975) an actual conviction of a nurse for assaulting a patient was overturned on the basis that the patient had no unqualified right to sue. Lord Simon stated that psychiatric patients are 'inherently likely to harass those concerned with them by groundless charges and litigation'.

The concept that all, or even a substantial majority, of patients in psychiatric hospitals would be likely to bring unwarranted litigation unless barred by section 141, contains an antiquated and unsupported notion of how patients are likely to behave. Clearly the range of behaviour of people designated as mentally ill is just as diverse as for any section of the population. The vast majority of people (some, for example, with depressed emotions or retarded cognitive development) are admitted to hospital under a set of circumstances which do not justify infringement of their rights. Mere entry into hospital does not justify the conclusion that the patient would be more likely than the population at large to bring vexatious or unnecessary litigation. Indeed an examination of the number of actions brought by psychiatric patient indicates the opposite conclusion—i.e. that the majority of patients are too withdrawn, isolated and unsure to pursue even their genuine legal interests (Gostin, 1975). The Mental Health (Amendment) Act proposes substantial reform of Section 141.

Enfranchisement

In order to vote in the United Kingdom the person's name must appear on the register of electors as a resident of a particular locality. Any place where the elector legitimately resides may be used as an address which qualifies the person for entry onto the register. The single exception is found in section 4(3) of the Representation of the People Act, 1949, as amended by the Mental Health Act, 1959. Section 4(3) prevents any 'patient' who resides in a psychiatric hospital from using that address for electoral purposes. Prior to recent court decisions, this effectively disenfranchised some 120 000 people.

The fundamental objection to section 4(3) is that it deprives a citizen of the right to vote, not on the basis of individual fitness, but solely on a residential criterion. An informal patient who has a home address can be registered and can either visit a polling station or be treated as an absentee voter. Equally capable patients from the same hospital will be deprived of the vote simply because they have no alternative address. Closer scrutiny of section 4(3) reveals further anomalies. Homeless patients in general or geriatric hospitals are entitled to use the hospital as their place of residence for voting purposes. Accordingly, a patient in a psychiatric unit of a district general hospital is entitled to vote whereas a resident in a psychiatric hospital, possibly with the same psychiatric classification, is not. In effect, the system disenfranchises people who are homeless and confined to psychiatric hospitals simply because community services are inadequate.

A brief examination of the contemporary history relating to the enfranchisement of psychiatric patients illustrates the value of the legal approach. The 1973/74 Speakers' Conference on Electoral Reform recommended that patients in mental illness and mental handicap hospitals should be placed on the same footing as those in general hospitals; implementation of this recommendation would result in the repeal of section 4(3), a rather simple matter requiring very little Parliamentary time. Both major political parties while in government agreed in principle to the Speakers' recommendation but neither would devote Parliamentary time to the issue. (It may be interesting to observe, however, that Parliamentary time was made available to amend the 1949 Act to prevent prisoners from standing for elected office following the election of Robert Sands to Parliament.)

The fact that successive governments deliberately decided not to delegate Parliamentary time to the enfranchisement of such a large social minority presents an insight into legislative perceptions of those designated as mentally ill. It is difficult to conceive of any other social minority which would remain so insular and non-vocal after being denied the franchise despite the rare unanimity of responsible opinion that the law was unjust and discriminatory. The issue is not necessarily that a significant number of patients would choose to vote, but that they should be regarded by elected officials as constituents to whom they are accountable.

It is where political and social strategies fail that the legal approach is sometimes needed. Two recent test cases—for those designated mentally ill (*Wild and Others* v. *Electoral Registration Officer for Warrington*, 1976) and mentally handicapped (*Smith and Others* v. *Jackson*, 1981)—established the right to vote for the great majority of those formerly disenfranchised (Gostin, 1976). The grounds argued in the two cases show how legal analysis is used to construe ordinary language to achieve a just result. Both courts accepted the view that the majority of people in psychiatric hospitals could not legally be regarded as 'patients' because they resided in hospital predominately for social, as opposed to medical, purposes. Following the *Wild* and *Smith* decisions circulars were issued to hospital and electoral registration officers on a national basis asking them to comply with the judgments. The Mental Health (Amendment) Act 1982 proposes to amend section 4(3) in order to enfranchise informal patients.

Similar legal approaches have been followed in a number of related areas in England (MIND, in press) and North America (Mental Health Law Project, 1981; National Legal Resources Service, 1981). The fact that contemporary legal approaches have been used so extensively to undo earlier legislation based upon inappropriate social perceptions of 'mental illness' is itself an indictment of the law. The legal profession has never felt comfortable with social issues and it is only recently that it has concerned itself with examining the social and legal situation of those designated as mentally ill. Yet, broad jurisprudential principles of treating similarly situated groups with reasonable equality has meant a greater measure of success in this particular area of legal endeavour.

Conclusion

Legal intervention in the activities of psychiatrists has resulted in deeply felt criticism. Psychiatric opinion continues to adhere to the sentiments contained in such familiar expressions as 'doctor knows best' or 'leave it to me'. This is a message very firmly directed toward the legal profession. Psychiatry has remained adament that it is therapeutically harmful to interpose legal standards or procedures into the doctor/patient relationship; it has resisted any attempt from outside the profession to examine and regulate its activities. Yet, mental health legislation in Great Britain to come into force in 1983 (see DHSS, 1976, 1978b) and elsewhere (United Nations, 1981) shows that the new legalism will influence events in psychiatry for the foreseeable future.

It is important to remain vigilant to any attempt by the legal profession to erect a superstructure of technical procedures or cumbersome legal regulations; nor should the law be permitted to substitute the discretion of lawyers and courts for that of mental health professionals on matters of treatment. However, the new legal approach to psychiatry does not usurp the function of the caring professions. It seeks only to alter public perceptions of the mental health services, which should place an emphasis on the person distressed and not on the concerns of society or the profession. Once this principle is accepted it follows that services should be provided, as of right, according to the needs of the person and not at the discretion of the professional; a person's consent should be the operative factor and not what *others* feel would be in the individual's best interests; and the receipt of services should be for the benefit of the person and not to provide an automatic rationale for society to diminish the civil and social status of the individual. These are the fundamental principles of the new legal approach to psychiatry. The legal profession is not opposed to psychiatry in principle but seeks only to ensure that, if psychiatry is to retain its affinity to medicine and humanism, it must serve principally those who suffer from mental distress and not societal or professional self-interests.

References

Adlam, D., and Rose, N. (In press). The politics of psychiatry, *Power and Politics*.
Advisory Centre for Education/MIND (1981). *Education to Nineteen: The Right of All Mentally Handicapped People*, ACE/MIND, London.

American Psychiatric Association (1980). Task force on late neurological effects of antipsychotic drugs, report, *Am. J. Psychiat.*, **135**, 1163 (1980).

Andalman and Chambers (1974). Effective counsel for persons facing commitment: a survey, a polemic and a proposal, *Mississippi L. J.*, **45**, 43–91.

Barnett, C. (1978). Treatment rights of the mentally ill nursing home residents, *U. Pa. L. Rev.*, **126**, 578.

Barraclough, B. M., and Mitchell-Heggs, N. A. (1978). Use of neurosurgery for psychological disorder in British Isles, *Brit. Med. J.*, **12**, 1591–93.

Baruch, G., and Treacher, A. (1978). *Psychiatry Observed*, Routledge and Kegan Paul, London.

Bean, P. T. (1980). *Compulsory Admissions to Mental Hospitals*, John Wiley & Sons, London.

Bebbington *et al.* (1980). Letter, *Lancet*, **i**, March 15.

Bloch, S., and Chedoff, P., eds. (1981). *Psychiatric Ethics*, OUP, Oxford.

Bridges, P. K., and Bartlett, J. R. (1977). Psychosurgery: yesterday and today, *Brit. J. Psychiat.*, **131**, 249–60.

Brooks, A. D. (1974 with 1980 Supp.). *Law, Psychiatry and the Mental Health System*, Little Brown and Co., Boston.

Brooks, A. (1980). The constitutional right to refuse antipsychotic medications, *Bull. Am. Acad. of Psychiat. & Law*, **8**, 179–221.

Clare, A. (1980). *Psychiatry in Dissent: Controversial Issues in Thought and Practice*, 2nd ed., Tavistock, London.

Clare, A. (1978). Therapeutic and ethical aspects of electro-convulsive therapy: a British perspective, *Int. J. Law & Psychiat.*, **1**, 237–53.

Cohen, F. (1966). The function of the attorney and the commitment of the mentally ill, *Tex. L. Rev.*, **44**, 427–31.

Curran, W. J., and Harding, T. W. (1978). *The Law and Mental Health: Harmonizing Objectives*. World Health Organization, Geneva.

Department of Health and Social Security (1971). *Better Services for the Mentally Handicapped*, Cmnd. 4683, HMSO, London.

Department of Health and Social Security (1974). Circular 19/74.

Department of Health and Social Security (1975). *Better Services for the Mentally Ill*, Cmnd. 6233, HMSO, London.

Department of Health and Social Security (1976). *A Review of the Mental Health Act 1959*, HMSO, London.

Department of Health and Social Security (1978a). *Health and Personal Social Services for 1976/77*, HMSO, London.

Department of Health and Social Security (1978b). *Review of the Mental health Act 1959*, Cmnd. 7320, HMSO, London.

Department of Health and Social Security (1981). *Care in the Community: A consultative Document of Moving Resources for Care in England*, HMSO, London. Accompanied by Health Circular HC(81)9 and Local Authority Circular LAC (81)5.

Department of Health and Social Security (1981b). *Reform of mental health legislation* Cmnd. 8405 HMSO, London.

Finch, J. D. (1981). *Health Services Law*, Sweet and Maxwell, London.

Freeman, C. P. L., Basson, J. V., and Crighton, A. (1978). Double-blind trial of electro-convulsive therapy (ECT) and simulated ECT in depressive illness', *Lancet*, **1**, 738–40.

Goffman, E. (1968). *Asylums*, Penguin, New York.

Gostin, L. (1975). *A Human Condition: The Mental Health Act 1959 to 1975: Observations, Analysis and Proposals for Reform*, Vol. 1, MIND, London.

Gostin, L. (1976). A mental patient's right to vote, *Poly L. Rev.*, **2**, 17–21.

Gostin, L. (1977). *A Human Condition: The Law Relating to Mentally Abnormal Offenders*, vol. 2, MIND, London.

Gostin, L. (1979a). Current legal concepts in mental retardation in the United States: emerging constitutional issues, in *Tredgold's Mental Retardation* (Craft, M., ed.) 294-312.

Gostin, L. (1979b). 'The merger of incompetency and certification: the illustration of unauthorised medical contact in the psychiatric context', *Int. J. Law & Psychiat.*, **2**, 126-67.

Gostin, L. (1979c). The right of a mentally handicapped child to receive education, *Disability Rights Handbook*, 45-47.

Gostin, L. (1980). Ethical considerations of psychosurgery: the unhappy legacy of the prefrontal lobotomy, *J. Med. Ethics*, **6**, 149-54.

Gostin, L. (1981). Observations on consent to treatment and review of clinical judgment in psychiatry: a discussion paper, *J. Roy. Soc. Med.*, **74**, 742-52.

Gostin, (in press). Human rights, judicial review and the mentally disordered offender, *Criminal Law Review*.

Gostin, L. and Rassaby, E. (1980). *Representing the Mentally Ill and Handicapped: A Guide to Mental Health Review Tribunals*. Quartermaine House, Surrey.

Greenland, C. (1970). *Mental Illness and Civil Liberty*, G. Bell and Sons, London.

Hansard (1981). Adjournment Debate on Electro-Convulsive Therapy (Broadmoor Hospital), 26 January, 742-50.

Hiday, V. A. (1977). The role of counsel in civil commitment: changes, effects and determinants, *J. Psychiat. & Law*, Winter 1977, 551-69.

Ingleby, D. (1981). Understanding mental illness, in *Critical Psychiatry: The Politics of Mental Health* (Ingleby, ed.), Penguin, Middlesex.

Jacob, J. (1978). *Speller's Law Relating to Hospitals and Kindred Institutions*, H. K. Lewis Ltd., London.

Johnstone, E. C., Deakin, J. F. W., Lawler, P., Frith, C. D., Stevens, M., McPherson, K., and Crow, T. J. (1980). The Northwick Park electro-convulsive therapy trial, *Lancet*, **ii**, 1317-20.

Jones, K. (1972). *A History of the Mental Health Services*, Routledge and Kegan Paul, London.

Jones, K. (1980). The limitations of the legal approach to mental health, *Int. J. Law and Psychiat.*, **3**, 1-16.

Laing, R. D. (1965). *The Divided Self*, Penguin, London.

Mental Disability Law Reporter. ABA Commission on the Mentally Disabled, Washington.

Mental Health Law Project (1981). *Summary of Activities*, MHLP, Washington.

Michel, K., and Kolakowska, T. (1981). A survey of prescribing psychotropic drugs in two psychiatric hospitals, *Brit. J. Psychiat.*, **138**, 217-21.

MIND (1977). *Evidence to the Royal Commission on the NHS with Regard to Services for Mentally Ill People*, MIND, London.

MIND (in press). *Mental Health Case Docket*, London, MIND.

Morse, S. (1978). Crazy behavior, morals, and science: an analysis of mental health law, *S. Cal. L. Rev.*, **51**, 527-654.

National Legal Resources Service (1981). *Annual Report*. National Institute for Mental Retardation, Toronto.

Palmer, R. (ed.) (1981). *Electroconvulsive Therapy: An Appraisal*, OUP, Oxford.

Peay, J. (1981). Mental health review tribunals: just or efficacious sateguards? *Law and Human Behaviour*, **5**, 161-186.

Royal College of Psychiatrists (1977). Memorandum on the use of electro-convulsive therapy, *Brit. J. Psychiat.*, **131**, 261-72.

Sedgwick, P. (1982). *Psycho Politics*, Pluto Press, London.
S. E. Thames Regional Health Authority (1976). *Committee of Enquiry into St Augustine's* Hospital. *Report*, HMSO, London.
Scheff, T. (1966). *Being Mentally Ill*, Chicago, Aldine.
Szasz, T. (1972. *The Myth of Mental Illness*, Paladin, N. Y.
United Nations (1981). *The Protection of Persons Suffering from Mental Disorder*, Association Internationale De Droit Penal, Siracusa, Sicily.
Valenstein, E. S. (1977). The Practice of Neurosurgery: A Survey of the Literature 1971–1976. *Report to the National Commission for the Protection of Human Subjects of Biomedical and Behavioural Research*. Appendix: Psychosurgery. Department of Health and Education and Welfare, Washington.
Valenstine, E. S. (ed.) (1980). *The Psychosurgery Debate: Scientific, Legal and Ethical Perspectives*, W. H. Freeman and Co., San Francisco.
Wald, P. M., and Friedman, P. R. (1978). The politics of mental health advocacy in the United States, *Int. J. Law & Psychiat.*, **1**, 137–52.
Wing, J. (1978). *Reasoning about Madness*, OUP, Oxford.

Cases Cited

A. v. The United Kingdom. Application No. 6840/74. Report of the European Commission of Human Rights, 16 July 1980.
Ashingdane v. *Secretary of State for Social Services and Others*. Court of Appeal, 18 February 1980, unreported. Transcript available from MIND.
Chandler v. *Surrey County Council*. Industrial Tribunal. Case no. 22760/77. See also *O'Brien* v. *Prudential Assurance Co. Ltd.*, EAT, 13 December 1978; *Nobody Wants You: 40 Cases of Discrimination at Work* (1978), MIND, London. (Case transcripts available from MIND.)
Donaldson v. *O'Connor* (1975) 422 U.S. 563.
In re Brent and Harrow AHA and Praetorian Housing Association, 1978. Unreported. Decision available from MIND, application no. 0/532/78.
Kynaston v. *Secretary of State for the Home Department and Secretary of State for the Department of Health and Social Security*, 1982 J.S.W.L. 104, C. A.
Morales v. *Turman* 383 F Supp. 53 125 (E. D. Tex. 1974).
Lessard v. *Schmidt* (1972). 349 F. Supp. 1078 (E. D. Wisc. 1972), *vacated and remanded on other grounds*, 414 U.S. 473 (1974).
Mills v. *Rogers*. U.S. Supreme Court decided 18 June 1982.
New York State Association for Retarded Children v. *Carey*, 393 F. Supp. (E.D.N.Y. 1975).
Pennhurst State School and Hospital v. *Halderman* 67 L. Ed. 2d.694 (1981).
R. v. *Board of Control and Others ex parte Rutty* (1956) I All ER 769.
R. v. *Bracknell Justices ex parte Griffiths* (1975) 3 W.L.R. 140 (*Pountney's* case).
R. v. *Secretary of State ex parte Medway* (1976) 62 Cr. App. R. 85.
R. v. Secretary of State for the Home Department, ex parte Powell, Q.B.D., 21 December 1978. Reported in Gostin, L., and Rassaby, E. (1980). *Representing the Mentally Ill and Handicapped*, Quartermaine House, Surrey.
R. v. *Secretary of State for Social Services ex parte HINCKS* (1980) J.S.W.L. 113, H. C.
R. v. *Turlington* (1761) 2 Burr.1115.
Smith v. *The United Kingdom* (1981). Application no. 6870/75. Report on admissibility, 12 and 14 May 1977, Report as to the merits, 7 May 1981.
Smith and Others v. *Jackson* (1981). County Court for Blackburn, Unreported. Transcript available from MIND.

Wild and Others v. *Electoral Registration Officer for Warrington* (1976). County Court, Unreported. Transcripts available from MIND.
Winterwerp v. *The Netherlands* (1979). Application no. 6301/73, Commission Report 15 December 1977. Judgment of the European Court of Human Rights, 24 October 1979.
X. v. *The United Kingdom* (1981). *Application no. 6998/75.* Report of the European Commission of Human Rights, 16 July 1980. Report of the European Court of Human Rights, Judgment given 5 Nov. 1981.

Mental Illness: Changes and Trends
Edited by Philip Bean
© 1983 John Wiley & Sons Ltd.

CHAPTER 3

Dangerous behaviour: some implications for mental health professionals

HERSCHEL PRINS
Director, School of Social Work, University of Leicester

> *Between the acting of a dreadful thing*
> *And the first motion, all the interim is*
> *Like a phantasma or a hideous dream.*
>
> Julius Caesar II(i)

Introduction

This chapter is addressed primarily to those mental health professionals (i.e. psychiatrists, psychologists, nurses, and social workers) who are likely to encounter the so-called dangerous offender or dangerous patient. However, it is hoped that the remarks that follow will be of interest to a wider circle of readers, whose involvement though more peripheral, may none the less be productive of anxiety and stress. Such readers are likely to include police officers, general medical practitioners, lawyers, and sentencers (e.g. magistrates and judges in both lower and superior courts). Since this chapter appears in a major text devoted primarily to questions concerning mental illness it is necessary to remind readers that, as Tennent (1975) states, not all mentally disordered offenders are dangerous and not all dangerous offenders are necessarily mentally disordered. Tennent suggests that three types of relationships may be discerned between 'aberrant or dangerous behaviour and mental disorder'. First, dangerous behaviour can occur as a result of mental illness (though the incidence is low (Prins, 1980)). Second, some aberrant and dangerous behaviour may occur in those offenders with mental illness, but for whom treatment of the mental illness will not necessarily affect this behaviour. Third, dangerous behaviour may be found in individuals without any evidence of mental disorder. Dangerous and potentially dangerous behaviour is likely to come to the attention of the psychiatric, penal, and allied professions either at the stage at which institutional care has to be considered or at a time when release is being countenanced. It may also be a vital question when recall to an institution is being considered because the individual's behaviour is considered to be dangerous or potentially dangerous. The material in this chapter is presented under the following headings: Historical and Legal Context; Ethical Aspects; Definitions of Dangerousness; Prediction and Prognostication; Assessment and Management; Conclusions. As already suggested, dangerous behaviour may not be specifically connected with mental illness; it therefore seems appropriate to deal with the notions of dangerous behaviour generally rather than divide it into 'normal' on the one hand and 'abnormal' on the other for in most cases the same issues of management arise.

Historical and legal context

In mediaeval times and even earlier, the term 'dangerous' seems to have been applied in a general way to those persons or groups of persons who were felt to menace the survival of the State. Rennie (1978), reminds us of the extent to which the poor and the disadvantaged were frequently referred to as the 'dangerous classes'. Indeed, the assumption is implicit in the Poor Law legislation of England from the time of Elizabeth I onwards, that the poor were not only 'idle' but also dangerous. 'For nearly four hundred years, from the thirteenth through the sixteenth centuries, the English criminal law was obsessed with vagrants and beggars, who were viewed as a great danger to society' (Rennie, 1978). It was only from the eighteenth century onwards that the 'psychiatrization of delinquency' occurred (Foucault, 1978). Foucault suggests that psychiatry in the nineteenth century was used to delineate those individuals who were 'dangerous' and to denote the stigmata that accompanied this delineation, for example, moral and instinctive insanity and degeneration. (See also Prins, 1980.) In order to deal with incomprehensible behaviour—whether it took the form of some bizarre killing or some minor peculation—Foucault suggests that new legal-psychiatric categories were introduced. He cites as examples the introduction of the terms necrophilia (1840), kleptomania (around 1860), and exhibitionism (around 1876). Foucault reminds us in his illuminating socio-legal commentary that the developing relationship between psychiatry and the law was not only complex but bound up inextricably with developments in the behavioural sciences, philosophy, and politics. During the twentieth century, mental health professionals (notably but not exclusively, psychiatrists) have become increasingly involved in offering their views about a wide range of social behaviour that goes far beyond that of formal mental illness. In addition, their views are frequently sought about an individual's potential for harm or for further harm, as for example, in recent years when psychiatrists have been brought in increasingly to advise the police and militia on the handling of terrorists (Danto, 1980). Not all psychiatrists have readily accepted such responsibilities. The views of one psychiatrist are worth quoting here and could well be taken to represent the opinions of other mental health professionals. 'In deviation from the normal, particularly where behaviour is concerned, there may not necessarily be a medical contribution at all. The treatment may be purely legal or social action. The aim is to bring the behaviour into conformity... The psychiatrist comes into the study of some human problems only by invitation, and this invitation may not be wholehearted. *It is as if the psychiatrist is expected to claim authority in every problem of living, only to have that claim challenged even while his help is being sought...*' (Kahn, 1971) (present writer's italics).

Society then is clearly ambivalent as to the interventions of these mental health professionals, or secular priests, as North (1972) calls them, in dealing with deviant or criminal conduct. Indeed, as we shall see later, such professionals are often placed in a 'no win' situation, for if they collectively recommend not to release a potentially dangerous offender/patient they may well be criticized for being over-cautious, but if they do recommend release they will be accused of not having sufficient regard for the protection of the community. Thus, such mental health and allied professionals must always expect to suffer some degree of alienation from society (Prins, 1974).

In the United Kingdom, unlike some other jurisdictions, dangerous individuals are not specifically designated by statute (Levine, 1975). It is true, however, that the law recognizes such offences as dangerous driving, endangering the lives of passengers, having vehicles in a dangerous condition, or being in possession of dangerous drugs. Dangerous behaviour may of course be implied in prosecutions for negligence. Offenders who persist in crime, but not always in dangerous physical assaultive crime, may be liable to be sentenced to Extended Imprisonment (formerly called Preventive Detention) if the court is satisfied on the basis of previous criminal record and present offence that they are eligible for such a sentence. However, the criteria for the imposition of such a penalty are quite strict. It is true, however, that the dangerous proclivities of some offenders or offender/patients are recognized in the relevant mental health statutes. Thus we find in those sections of the Mental Health Act, 1959 dealing with compulsory admission the term 'in the interest of his own health or safety *or with a view to the protection of other persons*' (author's italics). More specifically, the dangerous proclivities of some offender/patients are recognized in the relevant statutes establishing and maintaining our Special Hospitals (e.g. Broadmoor, Rampton, and Moss Side) in that they exist, *inter alia*, for those offender/patients who exhibit 'dangerous, violent or criminal propensities' (Mental Health Act, 1959; restated in the National Health Service Act, 1977). In discussing the legal and administrative provisions required for those offenders considered to be dangerous, the Butler Committee on Mentally Abnormal Offenders (Home Office and DHSS, 1975) made a number of important recommendations. First, that a *new form of sentence* should be introduced from which release would be dependent *entirely on the issue of dangerousness*. Such a sentence would be for offenders who are dangerous and who present a history of mental disorder which could *not* be dealt with under the Mental Health Act, and for whom the life sentence was not thought to be appropriate. The sentence would be reviewable at two-yearly intervals. Upon discharge, the offender would be under compulsory supervision and subject to statutory review. Second, the imposition of such a sentence would be restricted to those convicted for offences which caused or might have caused grave harm to others. The Committee (in Appendix 4 of the Report) provided two schedules indicating what would constitute such offences. Amongst others, they included murder, manslaughter, rape, arson and criminal damage endangering life, firearms and explosives offences, hi-jacking, infliction of grievous bodily harm with intent, sexual offences, robbery, aggravated burglary, ill-treatment of children, and carrying an offensive weapon in a public place. Third, the Home Secretary would have the power to transfer a prisoner serving a reviewable sentence from prison to hospital under section 72 of the Mental Health Act, 1959. In such circumstances, a restriction order (Sec. 65) would be placed upon the discharge of the prisoner from hospital. Fourth, the two-yearly review would be carried out by the Parole Board and release would be on licence of unlimited duration; however, the *conditions* of the licence would be subject to a two-yearly review with the possibility of their eventual removal. It is apparent from the labours of the committee that they were anxious to give legal and administrative recognition to classes of persons who can be considered to be dangerous. Such recognition has introduced the notion of a new legal category and it raises a number of ethical issues. Some of these will now be considered.

Ethical aspects: who is to be detained, for how long and under what conditions?

For those involved in decision making concerning the detention or release of the person exhibiting dangerous or potentially dangerous behaviour, a number of ethical issues present themselves for examination. It is of course very easy to be 'wise after the event' (Webb, 1976) and the present writer has described elsewhere a number of instances in which prompt action *might* have averted a tragedy (Prins, 1975, 1980, 1981). Few dilemmas present to mental health professionals more starkly than those that involve them in balancing the need to act as agents of control and custody in the interests of society on the one hand, and the interests of the offender or patient on the other. Walker (1978), in an important paper, has discussed some of these problems very lucidly. He is concerned that we should limit as far as possible the infliction of measures that would deprive the potential dangerous offender of his liberty for very long periods of time. He suggests, as others have done, that such measures of detention should be used only to 'prevent serious and lasting hardship to other individuals, of a kind, which, once caused, cannot be remedied'. He propounds a set of five useful rules that might go some way towards resolving some of the ethical dilemmas involved. First, he suggests that we might exclude property offences from our consideration since most loss or damage to property can be remedied by compensation. He would also exclude from consideration of grave harm, cases of temporary alarm (for example, threats with imitation or unloaded weapons), and minor threats to decency, for example, indecent exposure. This last exclusion seems somewhat questionable since the amount of psychological harm caused may well depend upon the circumstances in which the offence took place; some children, and not a few adults find the confrontation involved in an act of indecent exposure very frightening. However, he *includes* the offences of rape, blackmail, kidnapping, and by implication, all serious assaults. Walker does not state that the harm must *actually have been done*. If the offender *intended* the harm or must have appreciated that harm was a highly likely result of what he did or attempted he would come within Walker's first rule. However, it seems likely that this question of intent would be a difficult matter to establish in this context. Secondly, he suggests a further safeguard against unjustified detention, namely that the actions or behaviour to which his first rule would apply should not be isolated, out of character episodes. Previous similar conduct would help to establish whether or not a pattern existed, as would, for example, declared intentions of future vengeance. Thirdly, Walker suggests that a further rule would operate in the offender's favour if the incentives for his initial offending has ceased to exist, or, through incapacity, he was considered to be unlikely to repeat his behaviour. The former criterion might be less easy to substantiate than the latter since it has not been unknown for those who have murdered to find surrogate victims (Terence Iliffe, who murdered his fourth wife, being a good case in point). Fourthly, Walker argues that if there is any possibility of the use of measures other than detention, they should be used. He also suggests a greater use of supervision and control in the community. Although one has much sympathy with this point of view, it must be acknowledged, however, that some professionals in this field, for example, local authority social workers and probation officers, have declared their disquiet about acquiring any greater powers of control over potentially dangerous offenders than they have available at present. One would suggest they may have failed to recognize that unless they are prepared to move increasingly into the social control arena, many so-called dangerous and potentially dangerous offenders may be detained in prisons and hospitals for longer than is necessary. Walker also makes the further suggestion that it should be possible to disqualify people from undertaking certain jobs, for example, responsibility for the care of children. As he rightly points out, we are not normally reluctant to disqualify those adjudged to be dangerous motorists from holding driving licences. Fifthly, he suggests that if we do have to impose measures of preventive detention, then the conditions of that detention should be as humane and tolerable as possible.

Recent allegations about malpractice in some of our mental hospitals and penal establishments would encourage the belief that the humanity suggested by Walker may sometimes be more honoured in the breach than the observance (see DHSS, 1980). The reluctance of mental health professionals to initiate more active interventions with dangerous or potentially dangerous clients or patients might to some extent be diminished by the implementation of the kind of safeguards and limitations suggested by Walker. Within such a clearly defined framework those mental health professionals who have to deal with dangerous or potentially dangerous individuals might feel a little less self-conscious about imposing their authority and power to impose sanctions. Some of this reluctance to intervene will be discussed later in this chapter.

Definitions of dangerousness

Dangerousness can, of course, mean different things to different people. As Tennent (1975) suggests, there are 'many forms of danger, both of people and of objects, concrete or abstract. We speak of social danger, political danger, moral danger as well as physical danger'. The present author has raised the question elsewhere as to who should be regarded as the more dangerous, the murderer, the rapist, the arsonist, the bank-robber, the drunken driver, the embezzler, the spy, the revolutionary, or the zealot? (Prins, 1975). It is easy to agree with Walker (1978) when he suggests that our main concern is with 'dangerous people'. As he points out, 'dangerousness is not an objective quality, but an ascribed quality like trustworthiness. We feel justified in talking about a person as dangerous if he has indicated by word or deed that he is more likely than most people to do serious harm, or act in way that is likely to result in serious harm. . . .' Walker also suggests that most people would interpret harm in this context to means such acts as homicide, rape, mutilation, or the promotion of destitution. This propensity to cause serious personal harm featured in the deliberations of the Butler Committee in their discussion of the question of dangerousness. 'We have come to equate dangerousness with a tendency to cause serious physical injury or lasting psychological harm. Physical violence is, we think, what the public are most worried about, but the psychological damage which may be suffered by some victims of other crime is not to be underrated' (Home Office and DHSS, 1975). The present writer had equated elsewhere dangerousness with impulsive, uncensored, personal violence towards others and sometimes towards self (Prins, 1975). Scott (1977), in his seminal paper on this subject, reminds us that in considering dangerousness, the social context is vitally important; it is 'easier to say what dangerousness is not than what it is. It is not simply that which is noxious or evil, and it is not necessarily a violent or explosive trait in an individual'. As Scott suggests, the man who smokes on an oil tanker is potentially dangerous by reason of the explosive material around him; if he refuses repeatedly to 'douse that glim', it is likely to be assumed that he has dangerous intentions rather than that he is merely careless or feckless. As will be seen when matters concerning assessment and management are considered, the social context of the offender or patient adjudged to be dangerous is of paramount importance. At this point comment is necessary concerning the relationship between violence, described by Scott (1977) as aggression concentrated into brief time and dangerousness. In general, the nature of the behaviour which society is likely to describe as dangerous is that which is also violent. But, as Sarbin (1967) has wisely pointed out, the concepts of danger and the concepts of violence are not necessarily coterminous. As he says 'violence denotes action; danger denotes a relationship'. In the same paper, Sarbin also makes an interesting observation concerning the etymology of the word danger. Contrary to popular belief, it is in fact derived from the Latin *dominiarium*—meaning Lordship or Sovereignty and not ascribable to physicalist conceptions. Sarbin goes on to suggest that this derivation has an important meaning in terms of the position held by individuals in the social structure based on relative power and esteem. He also argues that this meaning has important implications in relation to a man's concept of his social identity and to the actions that he or others may take as a social animal to confirm or deny it. We may conclude this section by agreeing with a quotation from Scott (1977). 'Dangerousness then is an unpredictable and untreatable tendency to inflict or risk irreversible injury or destruction, or to induce others to do so.'

Prediction and prognostication

It is a sad truism that there are no statistical or actuarial measures available that offer the prediction of dangerousness with any degree of certainty, although useful beginnings have been made in this area by Nicol *et al.* (1972), Payne *et al.* (1974), Megargee (1976), Greenland (1978), Soothill *et al.* (1980), and Monahan (1981). Despite the fact that much research has been carried out into the prediction of antisocial behaviour generally (see for example, Simon, 1971), this research merely seems to suggest that although actuarial techniques can discriminate between high-risk and low-risk groups, there will always be a residual majority in the middle-risk groups whose re-offending rates are too near 'fifty-fifty' to be of much use prognostically. Kozol and his colleagues (Kozol *et al.*, 1972) obtained follow-up information on a sample of offender/patients who had been discharged despite the fact that the mental health professionals responsible for their care had classified them as being dangerous. *Only about a third of the group actually became involved in violence on discharge.* It is now a well established fact that mental health professionals tend to err on the side of caution when asked to make predictions about future behaviour. In what has now become a classic study, Steadman and Cocozza (1974) examined a group of allegedly dangerous mentally abnormal offenders who had been freed from detention as a result of what is now regarded as a famous American Supreme Court decision (in the case of Baxstrom). In this case it had been held that Baxstrom (an offender/patient) had been detained unconstitutionally. One effect of the Baxstrom decision, was that a large number of other offender/patients had to be discharged into the community. Steadman and Cocozza were provided therefore with a unique opportunity to test out the validity or otherwise of prolonged detention for so-called criminally insane and dangerous offenders. As a result of their large scale and careful survey the authors concluded that mental health professionals were over cautious in their predictions and that prolonged incarceration was not required for the majority of such offender/patients. However, it should be noted that a large number of these offender/patients were over fifty years of age when released. Had the research involved a younger and potentially more aggressive age group, their findings might have been different. However, there has now been more recent confirmation of the Steadman and Cocozza findings in the work of Thornberry and Jacoby (1979): they followed up a not dissimilar group of patients who had also been released as a result of a court decision (in the Dixon case in 1971). At many points the results obtained by Thornberry and Jacoby are very similar to those obtained by Steadman and Cocozza. In summary we may conclude that these two major studies confirm the view that there is a strong tendency to over-predict the likelihood of further harm being caused by allegedly dangerous offender/patients following their release into the community. However, as indicated earlier in this chapter, there have also been a number of disturbing instances in which one might conclude with hindsight that further harmful behaviour might have been prevented if earlier action had been taken. With this uncomfortable anecdotal evidence in mind we may now turn to questions of assessment and management.

Assessment and management

In the absence of any foolproof actuarial devices and the tendency for those concerned to come up with what statisticians choose to describe as false positives, are we left with *any* indicators of the *probability* of future dangerous behaviour? It has been suggested, no doubt somewhat cynically, that nothing predicts behaviour like behaviour. For example, exhibitionists (indecent exposers) tend to repeat their offences, but only seldom do they go on to indulge in more serious sexual criminality. (However, it is worth noting here (from a prognostic point of view), that where acts of indecent exposure are also associated with even minor assaultive behaviour, the likelihood of engagement in later serious sexual criminality is quite strong.) Thus the detailed circumstances of offences should be studied carefully since they will frequently offer useful prognostic clues. This matter will be returned to later. Men with several convictions for violence are considerably more likely than their fellows to be convicted of violence in the future. The Butler Committee, in recognizing the limitations of objective assessment, wondered whether it was better to rely upon a 'continuing process of treatment and subjective assessment in which checks on adjustment are constantly made in the light of the developing pattern evinced by the individual concerned'. (Home Office and DHSS, 1975). Such assessment presupposes good team-work amongst the mental health and other professionals concerned and also presupposes agreed and open lines of communication. That this team-work may sometimes be lacking and communication often be faulty is well attested to in a thoughtful and disturbing paper by Pfohl (1979).

Good working relationships with colleagues are essential in dealing with the dangerous or potentially dangerous offender/patient whose problems are not only multifaceted but whose alienation from society may seem to have a contagious quality. As already mentioned, those who work with these individuals must share some of this alienation, for, in the eyes of society, they can never win whatever decision they may make, either corporately or alone. These questions cannot be developed in detail here, but one or two points can be made briefly. First, we must acknowledge the irrational elements in some of these team relationships; for example the reluctance to give up and to share, with their accompanying elements of anxiety, anger, doubt, and frustration. Some of these aspects have been well identified by Graham and Sher (1976). Secondly, in order for working relationships with others to be successful, it is essential to be clear about objectives and to demonstrate a capacity for sharing knowledge and skills. Thirdly, a degree of flexibility in the assignment and acceptance of tasks is essential as is the ability to give up notions of 'going it alone'. Finally, there must be a consequential development of openness, trust and respect for each other's contributions. One important factor that may militate against all these desirable outcomes is the manner in which mental health professionals receive quite separate education and training. They are also subject, very largely, to differing terms and conditions of employment with resultant differences in perceived status and prestige. At the present author's university efforts are being made to remedy this situation, at least as far as it concerns medical undergraduates. In Leicester's new medical school, 20 per cent of the total teaching in the first two years is allocated to the behavioural sciences ('Man in Society' as it is called). The students are exposed to contributions from psychologists, psychiatrists, social workers, and sociologists. In addition, they are attached to families and visit a very wide range of health care, social and penal institutions. In 1980, the first cohort of what may prove to be a group of more socially-conscious and socially-orientated doctors graduated, it is hoped with a greater understanding of patients as people, but with no loss to their other essential medical expertise.

Opportunity can also be taken for other methods of inter-disciplinary education and discussion, particularly at the post-graduate level. The present author has been running experimental short courses on the problems presented by the mentally abnormal offender. A wide range of multi-disciplinary workers have been present and these courses have met with quite a degree of success. (For an account, see Prins (1979).) There is of course no magic to bring to the task of assessment (as some would perhaps like to think). As Scott (1977) said, 'it is patience, thoroughness and persistence in ... (this) ... process, rather than any diagnostic or interviewing brilliance that produces results. In this sense the telephone, the written request for past records and the checking of information against other informants are the important diagnostic devices ... ' Reference has already been made to the need to examine in detail the full circumstances of offences involving serious personal harm. The bare details of the offence itself or its legal classification give no real indication of the possible degree of harm involved. The three following examples will hopefully make this point clear.

Case (I)

This concerns the case of a man convicted of rape. His victim had been subjected to more than one sexual assault, both per vaginam and per anum, in the course of the offence. She had also been tied up whilst the assaults took place. In addition, the attacker had used a leather belt to induce unconsciousness, only releasing this 'garrotte' in order to bring his victim round sufficiently for a further assault to take place. The formal charge of rape afforded no indication as to the disturbing nature of the man's behaviour and this was only revealed when the full police reports and statements were made available.

Case (II)

This concerns a man serving a two-year prison sentence for indecent assault on a boy of 15. Examination of the detailed police account of the case revealed that the youth's attacker used both considerable force and fear to hold down the youth during the assault. Thus, the legal and judicial classification of the offence in this case gave no real clue as to its seriousness or possible ominous prognostications as to future behaviour.

Case (III)

This concerned the case of a man convicted of raping a small girl. During the attack, the child had struggled and screamed. Her assailant had held his hand over her mouth to stifle her screams and had he not been interrupted by the fortunate arrival of a passer-by he might well have found himself on a murder or at least a manslaughter charge.

Of all the mental health professionals, social workers are often in a pre-eminent position to become involved in the social backgrounds of dangerous or potentially dangerous offender/patients and are thereby able to observe and monitor subtle changes in behaviour. Sometimes these changes will be caused by physical (organic) factors and non medically qualified mental health professionals need to have a basic working knowledge of these if danger signs are not to be missed. (See for example the work of Mark and Ervin, 1970 and Monroe, 1978.) In days gone by social workers were taught the value of taking a detailed social history from patient or relations. They were also encouraged to see how this history taking could add to the picture of the person derived from other professionals. In this way, a full assessment could be made of the person's situation, the social and familial stresses within it, and, in the light of this, his or her potential for recovery. Unfortunately, the reorganization of local authority social services departments in the United Kingdom, of local government areas and of the National Health Service, has brought about rapid movements of staff, some consequential dilution of specialist skills, and a lack of continuity of staffing. The author's experience as a teacher of social workers leads him to believe that there is still a considerable degree of reluctance on the part of social work students and the newly qualified to deal with the mentally ill, particularly the potentially violent and the more severely disturbed.*

Numerous writers on social, psychiatric, and forensic matters have confirmed the need for a full investigation of the social history and current situation in cases where dangerous behaviour has occurred or was considered to be likely. Such a need is well attested to by Blair (1971) in his discussion of the case of *Richard Holmes*. Holmes, aged twenty-two, was sentenced to life imprisonment for wounding with intent to murder. Shortly after sentence, he committed suicide. In Blair's sensitive and detailed account of this sad case, he draws attention to the fact that the prison medical officer did not feel it necessary to interview Holmes's parents, nor, apparently, were reports called for from 'any psychiatric social worker or probation officer'. He suggests that had full and detailed information been available, not only would a much clearer understanding of this young man's history and mental state have been possible, but a tragedy might also have been averted.

Occasionally, social workers have been stridently over critical of psychiatrists, not infrequently on the basis of very flimsy experience and knowledge. Lest social workers in the mental health team consider that they are the only people concerned about possible abuses of patients' rights, the comments of Dr McGrath formerly Medical Superintendent of Broadmoor should be noted. 'It is enormously important for the hospital to keep in touch with the after-care agencies who often feel out of their depth in caring for homicides in the community, and who have to be supported to cope with the repugnance at their own feeling that they may be instruments in the readmission of a patient who has not yet offended again. This potential guilt is not the sole prerogative of the . . . caseworker, but is shared by doctors, who do not delight in incarcerating the legally defenceless . . . ' (McGrath, 1968).

The need for a careful review of the total social situation of the dangerous or potentially dangerous offender/patient has already been stressed. Sometimes mental health professionals seem reluctant to ask questions that might give important prognostic clues, often on the grounds of concern over the invasion of the offender/patient's privacy. Some other aspects of this reluctance are now considered. One important and additional reason for such reluctance may be the tendency for mental health professionals in this field, be they social workers,

*See also Chapter 18.

psychiatrists, psychologists, or other staff, to *over-identify* with the dangerous offender/patient. Because of this, they may not take into account important aspects of the individual's less desirable behaviour as reported by family members and others. Johnston (1967), has stated that 'many psychiatrists identify too closely with the patient and become too sympathetic with his problem, and as a result, come up with a judgement which is not based on the stark reality of the situation'.

Usdin (1967), states that we may often miss the clues given us by our offender/patients or clients. He suggests that we do not like to hear some of the things that these people are saying; as he puts it, 'we might get alarmed or insulted....' He goes on to suggest that the mechanism of denial is not one reserved solely for patients,... 'quite often our antennae did not pick up what they were saying and that they were relating important material.... As numerous studies have reported, the suicidal patient nearly always gives warnings that he is contemplating suicide. There is no reason to believe that the homicidal patient does not do likewise...' Confirmation of this is demonstrated in some recent studies of violence which have shown a high incidence of mental illness *coupled with premonitory signs*. For example, Faulk (1974), in a study of 25 men remanded in prison on charges of seriously assaulting their wives or co-habitees, found in almost 70 per cent of cases that there were premonitory signs of violence. Seven of the wives had received a warning but had not acted upon this. Cuthbert (1970), has also drawn attention to this phenomenon in homicide cases.

As MacDonald (1967) has suggested, this reluctance to intervene may be due also to the fact that the 'non-directive psychiatric interview facilitates avoidance of violence when this is the wish of the patient, his relatives and the physician'. Many professionals are likely to be uncertain in their reactions to threats of violence, particularly if these are homicidal. These threats may be met too easily with a bland reassurance such as 'You wouldn't do anything like that would you?' When a person with a background of violent behaviour threatens extreme violence, for example, towards a spouse, the traditional professional psychothe-rapeutic response might be to say something like 'This must upset you a lot, would you like to tell me a bit more about your marriage...?' As MacDonald has suggested, it might be better to ask, 'what plans have you made...?'

In trying to assess the offender's potential for dangerous behaviour a number of areas of examination need to be borne in mind. These are now enumerated and commented upon.

First, what seem to have been the nature of any past precipitating stress factors in the offender's social environment? Have these been removed? If not, to what extent can they perhaps be moderated if the offender is allowed to go free in the community? Reference has already been made to Walker's rule on this. Sadly, as suggested earlier, an offender who has caused serious harm to a relative or other close social contact may still need to destroy a surrogate. To what extent was the original offence behaviour caused by provocation, conscious or unconscious? In this context, MacDonald (1967) quotes the example of the 'female hysterical character who continues to wear dresses that are several inches too short and to behave in a flirtatious manner despite the angry response of a jealous husband...' He quotes the further example of the youth who had been hospitalized for threatening to kill his father. The boy rang his father to ask him if he would take him home for the day. The father indicated that he would be down 'right away'. The boy asked how long that would be. The father, who only lived twenty minutes away, said 'two hours'. One needs to be on the alert constantly for the victim precipitated encounter in which the probable victim is continually provoking the potentially dangerous person. These people may of course be drawn into such encounters to satisfy pseudo-sado-masochistic or similar needs. At a more practical level mental health professionals should be on the alert for ways in which they might prevent the means of destruction being available too readily. One should remember here the ease with which *Graham Young* appeared to have secured a form of employment which gave him easy access to the means of destroying others (Holden, 1974). A more recent example was the case of the sixteen-year-old American girl, quoted in The Guardian of 31 January 1979. She is alleged to have killed two men, wounded eight children aged between six and fourteen and a policemen in a sniping attack, before finally surrendering to the police. She was said to like television violence and setting fire to cats by pouring petrol on their tails. More ominous perhaps, is the statement made by a school classmate. 'Her father bought her a rifle for Christmas and she was always boasting about the guns her father had.' The suggestion made by Walker (1978) and referred to earlier, that certain individuals might well be disqualified from placing themselves in situations in which they may be especially vulnerable is highly relevant here. A quotation from Shakespeare's *King John* is also very apt: 'How oft the sight of means to do ill deeds makes ill deeds done.' (Cited by MacDonald).

Second, what is the offender's capacity for sympathetic identification with others? In what way may the previous history given by both the offender/patient and those near to him confirm or refute this? Has he still some capacity left for learning by experience?

Third, does he seem to derive satisfaction from the infliction of pain or suffering on others? Can it be ascertained whether his violence is directed against a particular individual for specific reasons or is it directed against the world in general? Is he the sort of person who continually feels threatened and/or persecuted? The need for all mental health professionals to understand fully paranoid states and morbid jealousy is of paramount importance in this work. Not all this learning should come from clinical sources; the world's great literature can be used to enhance understanding and empathy. Who has provided a better description of morbid jealousy than Shakespeare?

But jealous souls will not be answered so;
They are not ever jealous for the cause,
But jealous for they are jealous; tis a monster
Begot upon itself, born on itself.
Othello. III.iii

Fourth, in addition to personal behaviour and expressions of attitude, are there other indicators that might be of use? Sometimes, the eliciting of violent or sadistic phantasies or preoccupations may provide useful clues. However, too much importance should not be attached to this, because the extent to which such preoccupations are indulged in by those who never actually behave dangerously is not known. Having said this, *some* clues do seem to have ominous prognostications, especially when phantasies are *also* acted upon. Brittain (1970), in his paper on the sadistic murderer, has provided a detailed account of the manner in which some people develop, *but at the same time attempt to conceal*, their sadistic and murderous phantasies. (Present author's italics.) One may wonder whether the course of events might have been different if those responsible for Graham Young's supervision in the community had gained access to his room and noted the significance of the ominous array of articles it contained.

Fifth, can any clues be gained from choice of previous employments or occupations? Scott (1977) suggests that very occasionally these may provide us with useful hints. Butchering and work in abattoirs is *sometimes* found in the employment records of those convicted of particularly sadistic offences; sadistic children sometimes show a preference for work as veterinary surgeons, showing an unusual interest in sick and damaged animals. Scott noted how quickly these died in their care, as did their own pets.

Finally, can anything be learned from the way in which the offender talks about his offence and his behaviour? Occasionally, it is difficult to distinguish between a near hysterical threat of murderous intent and one that is made quietly, calmly, but with absolute conviction. It is frequently an ominous sign if the offence is discussed in a dispassionate guilt free manner. However, it should be remembered that after the perpetration of a particularly serious offence, such as homicide, many protective mechanisms come into play. These may present as a callous indifference. Much time is needed for these mechanisms to be dissipated and the underlying attitudes revealed. It is the author's experience that some offenders serving life sentences for murder seem very reluctant to acknowledge their guilt and this makes consideration for parole a highly problematic issue.

So far, comment has been made rather generally about techniques of investigation and assessment and less has been said about the more personal attributes the mental health professional should bring to his or her dealings with dangerous or potentially dangerous individuals. It is probably no accident that this most important aspect has been left so late for consideration; most workers are reluctant to admit freely that such persons may frighten them. Sometimes it is very difficult to put this fear into words. Some may say that they have a 'hunch', or, others will say, 'it is something in his eyes'. This may sound absurd; indeed the present author has been criticized by one colleague (Webb, 1976), for explaining dangerous behaviour *post hoc* and for suggesting that hunches should be relied upon. But sometimes professionals *may* have to act upon informed hunches rather that upon proven facts and then try to apply what they have learned from one case to the next the hard way. Professionals may well ask themselves, 'what is it we are afraid of?' All of us can certainly be afraid of physical violence. Lion (1972) has drawn attention to this aspect, including the fact that some dangerous persons may not only wish to be controlled, but in fact are afraid of their own dangerous or violent urges. Cox (1974), in a paper on the psychotherapist's anxiety in dealing with offender/patients, provides a useful reminder of the importance of the professionals' anxieties in this area. He also suggests that some offender/patients may be frightened to talk about their feelings and phantasies because they feel the therapist is himself too frightened to want to listen to them. As indicated earlier, denial is not the sole prerogative of offender/patients. As professionals, of what are we afraid, if it is not the threat of immediate violence? Is it the fear that we may *unwittingly provoke* a violent assault, or are we more afraid that our own egos may be overwhelmed by that of the dangerous offender/patient? Is it the fear that somehow we may be engulfed and destroyed by his violent phantasy system? As already indicated, it is only after an intensive study of the individual, his past history and his life style that clues may be afforded as to the likelihood of violent and possible unpredictable outbursts. A useful illustration of this would be an assault committed in circumstances that amounted to homosexual panic. The so-called normal person who violently attacks another because of an alleged homosexual overture, may well need to have his own actions understood more in terms of his own possible repressed homosexuality than solely as the reactions of an outraged male responding to an unwelcome overture. As a general rule, one would suggest that the greater degree of violence shown, the more precarious the so called normal person's defences may be. These phenomena have been discussed very sensitively by Woods (1975).

In order for mental health professionals to operate effectively and humanely in work with dangerous and potentially dangerous clients, it is necessary for them to have tried to come to terms with their *own* potential for violent or dangerous behaviour. It is therefore helpful to try to learn to behave calmly when explosive behaviour threatens. If the 'scream' can be kept out of the voice this may help. In certain circumstances, an attempt may have to be made to remove quietly and firmly a dangerous weapon from a person intent on using it. A quiet voice and calm movements will probably help; with some potentially violent offender/patients it is probably best to avoid eye-ball to eye-ball confrontation by looking at them obliquely. As Jordan and Packman (1978) have pointed out, there is no particularly good reason why social workers, or other mental health professionals for that matter, should be naturally adept at dealing with violent situations. They suggest that the kind of person who, for example, wishes to be a social worker may frequently be of a personality type not suited to engagement in violent confrontations. They are unlike policemen in the main, who Jordan and Packman suggest, might reasonably be expected to be 'rather extroverted, confident, physically large and physically brave'; there are no good reasons for suggesting that mental health professionals should be any of these things. In fact, the opposite may be nearer the truth, for by and large they are quite likely to be recruited from the ranks of the more introverted and possibly less physically robust. It may be that such workers and others are sometimes particularly effective in these explosive situations, because, unlike officers of the law, they are not usually in a position to enforce or carry through any kind of physical submission. They have only themselves and their personal skills to rely upon. They may, therefore, be the best people to open up lines of communication. In this connection one can return to the work of Sarbin. He suggests elsewhere in the paper already referred to that danger is not to be construed solely as the expression of a personality trait, but rather as a relationship of relative power in a role-system. If this is so, then a counsellor or other mental health professional may find communication easier in a danger laden situation than may a police officer or other easily identified law enforcement officer. As he says 'The experience of potential danger alters the perceptual accuracy of guards, policemen and others in reciprocal positions to... those... defined as non-persons. Misperceptions may lead to premature power displays which in turn exacerbate the degradation process...' (Sarbin, 1967).

Summary

We can now summarize some of the essential attributes needed by those who have to work with dangerous offender/patients or in situations where danger may threaten.

First, to be honest with oneself and to acknowledge our own potential for violence. This can only come about through effective support and supervision by more experienced colleagues. These colleagues can alert us to our blind-spots and to the dangers of over-identification and denial already referred to.

Second, the need to remember that a panic reaction in a moment of particular stress may prevent the registration of significant words or messages from the dangerous client. It may also mean that the importance of certain things left unsaid is overlooked.

Third, the development of a capacity to take a *total* view of the person adjudged to be dangerous or potentially dangerous. This will include all the points made earlier about the need for a careful in-depth examination of the person's social situation and the forces operating for stress—both past and present.

Fourth, the need to present oneself as a still centre in dangerous or potentially dangerous situations. This may often itself convey calm to the person in a state of tension and turmoil.

Fifth, after careful consideration of the situation the worker may have to take his or her courage in both hands and intervene quite directly; for example, by removing a weapon or dangerous implement from someone who is threatening to use it. This is always a finely poised matter; there may be little time for reflection, and the situation can only be judged as it appears at a particular point in time. As previously suggested, a calm voice, an averted gaze, and slow calm movements augur for a better response than a panic-stricken grab or strident command. In general, it is better to sit than to stand. To stand in a confronting position in relation to a potentially dangerous offender may make him feel even more anxious, overwhelmed or panic stricken. A position taken at the *rear* of such an individual may be particularly threatening.

Sixth, the need to be prepared to respond speedily to rapidly developing crisis situations. The telephone is perhaps an under-used device in this type of work. From time to time, offender/patients feel that things are beginning to 'blow up'. The opportunity for temporary readmission, compulsorily, or (preferably) otherwise, should not be missed. George Stürup, who was for many years medical superintendent of Denmark's famous institution for psychopaths at Herstedvester, relates how a former inmate appeared at their gates and asked how many offences he had to commit before he could be readmitted! Fortunately, Stürup and his colleagues acted upon such a *cri de coeur* and arranged for the man's readmission. (Stürup, 1968). McGrath (1958) has described a somewhat similar provision at Broadmoor. It could well be that some of the disasters that have occurred might have been avoided if our social, penal, and psychiatric services had been geared to provide more temporary asylums or, as is now happening in some areas, if crisis intervention services staffed by mental health professionals had been readily available. Support for the introduction of such schemes may be found in a paper by Craft (1974). He suggests that staff knew offenders so well 'that they could swiftly locate and treat the dangerous mood that almost always prefaced mayhem, danger, and absconsion.'

Seventh, by attempting to mobilize the offender/parent's 'cognitive resources to discuss what he fears may happen' (Ball, 1977). Such work may include asking questions about intent (as already discussed). It will also include discussion of the use of alcohol and other drugs which, as is well established, may precipitate or facilitate violent and unpredictable behaviour. Sometimes, it may be possible to talk through a potentially dangerous episode. In addition, one can attempt to point out the likely consequences of further dangerous behaviour in some cases. This is unlikely to be successful with severely paranoid or delusionally jealous clients; with others who are more in touch with reality, it may well appeal to the rational part of their being, to their ego and to their self respect.

Finally, as already stated, some dangerous offenders try to give premonition of the harm they feel they may do and yet others seem to respond positively to attempts to contain them.

Conclusions

The purpose of this chapter has been to demonstrate the multi-disciplinary nature of the task of dealing with dangerous or potentially dangerous offender/patients. The distinction between those who are mentally ill and those who are 'normal' has, for the purposes of brevity and clarity, deliberately been blurred. It is essential for all professionals who work with these individuals not only to have a keen regard for their social situations and the stresses within them, but for the professionals concerned to try to become more aware of their own anxieties and blind-spots. Unless we are to detain all potentially dangerous offender/patients indefinitely, we shall from time to time have to take risks, even though hindsight may teach us that our judgment may have been at fault. The problem was well summed up by the Aarvold Committee in its enquiry into offender/patients subject to restriction orders. 'The making of recommendations and decisions about the discharge and continuing care of. . . (dangerous). . . mentally disordered offenders entails, fundamentally, the assessment and prediction, by one group of human beings, of the probable future behaviour of another. Prescribed procedures can offer real safeguards against the chance of human error going undetected, but we do not believe that in this situation there can be an absolute guarantee of infallibility. Indeed, there might be a risk that the adoption of over-elaborate proceedings could reduce the quality of judgments made, by *weakening the sense of personal responsibility* which those who care for these unfortunate individuals bring to their tasks . . .' (Home Office, 1973) (present author's italics). It behoves all those mental health professionals working in this field to aspire to the standards of professional competence envisaged by Judge Aarvold and his colleagues.

References

Ball, M. (1977). Issues of violence in family casework, *Social Case Work*, **58**, 3–12.
Blair, D. (1971). Life sentence then suicide. The sad case of Richard Holmes, *Med. Sci. Law*, **11**, 162–179.
Brittain, R. P. (1970). The sadistic murderer, *Med. Sci. Law*, **10**, 198–208.
Cox, M. (1974). The psychotherapist's anxiety: liability or asset? (With special reference to offender-patients), *Brit. J. Criminol.*, **14**, 1–17.
Craft, M. (1974). A description of a new community forensic psychiatric service, *Med. Sci. Law*, **14**, 268–272.
Cuthbert, T. M. (1970). A portfolio of murderers, *Brit. J. Psychiat.*, **116**, 1–10.
Danto, B. L. (1980). The boomerang bullet: suicide among snipers and assassins, *Int. J. Off. Ther. and Comp. Criminol.*, **24**, 41–57.
DHSS (1980). *Report of the review of Rampton Hospital* (Bonton Report) Cmnd. 8073 HMSO, London.

Faulk, M. (1974). Men who assault their wives, *Med. Sci. Law*, **14**, 180–183.
Foucault, M. (1978). About the concept of the 'dangerous individual' in 19th-century legal psychiatry, *Int. J. Law and Psychiat.*, **1**, 1–18.
Graham, H., and Sher, M. (1976). Social work and general medical practice. Personal accounts of a three year attachment, *Brit. J. Soc. Wk.*, **6**, 233–249.
Greenland, C. (1978). The prediction and management of dangerous behaviour: social policy issues, *Int. J. Law and Psychiat.*, **I**, 205–222.
Holden, A. (1974). *The St. Albans Poisoner. The Life and Crime of Graham Young*, Hodder and Stoughton, London.
Home Office (1973). *Report on the Review of Procedures for the Discharge and Supervision of Psychiatric Patients subject to Special Restrictions (Aarvold Committee)*, Cmnd. 5191, HMSO, London.
Home Office, and DHSS (1975). *Report of the Committee on Mentally Abnormal Offenders (Butler Committee)*, Cmnd. 6244, HMSO, London.
Johnston, W. C. (1967).Releasing the dangerous offender, in *The Clinical Evaluation of the Dangerousness of the Mentally Ill*, (Ed. J. R. Rappeport), pp. 29–34, Charles C. Thomas, Illinois.
Jordan, B., and Packman, J. (1978). *Training for social work with violent families*, in *Violence and the Family*, (Ed. J. P. Martin), pp. 325–343, John Wiley, London.
Kahn, J. H. (1971). Uses and abuses of child psychiatry: problems of diagnosis and treatment of psychiatric disorder, *Brit. J. Med. Psychol.*, **44**, 229–238.
Kozol, H. L., Boucher, A. M., and Garofalo, R. F. (1972). The diagnosis and treatment of dangerousness, *Crime and Delinquency*, **18**, 371–392.
Levine, D. (1975). *The Concept of Dangerousness: Criticism and Compromise* (Paper presented to National Criminology Conference, Cambridge University, 9–11 July, 1975), Institute of Criminology (Mimeo) Cambridge.
Lion, J. R. (1972). *Evaluation and Management of the Violent Patient*, Charles C. Thomas, Illinois.
MacDonald, J. M. (1967). Discussant in *The Clinical Evaluation of the Dangerousness of the Mentally Ill* (Ed. J. R. Rappeport), pp. 58–61, Charles C. Thomas, Illinois.
McGrath, P. G. (1958). The treatment of the psychotic offender, *Howard J.*, **X**, 38–44.
McGrath, P. G. (1968). *Custody and release of dangerous offenders*, in *The Mentally Abnormal Offender* (Eds. A. V. S. de Rueck and R. Porter), pp. 121–126, J. and A. Churchill, London.
Mark, V. H., and Ervin, F. R. (1970). *Violence and the Brain*, Harper and Row, Maryland.
Megargee, E. I. (1976). The Prediction of dangerous behaviour, *Criminal Justice and Behaviour*, **3**, 3–22.
Monahan J. (1981). *Predicting Violent Behaviour. An Assesment of Clinical Techniques*. Sage Publications, London.
Monroe, R. R. (1978). *Brain Dysfunction in Aggressive Criminals*, Lexington Books, Toronto.
Nicol, A. R., Gunn J. G., Foggitt, R. H., and Gristwood, J. (1972). The quantitative assessment of violence in adult and young offenders, *Med. Sci. Law*, **12**, 275–282.
North, M. (1972). *The Secular Priests*, Allen and Unwin, London.
Payne, C., McCabe, S., and Walker, N. (1974). Predicting offender-patients' reconvictions. *Brit. J. Psychiat.*, **125**, 60–64.
Pfohl, S. (1979). From whom will we be protected? Comparative approaches to the assessment of dangerousness, *Int. J. Law and Psychiat.*, **2**, 55–78.
Prins, H. (1974). Motivation in social work, *Social Work Today*, **5**, 40–43.
Prins, H. (1975). A danger to themselves and to others. (Social workers and potentially dangerous clients.), *Brit. J. Soc. WK.*, **5**, 297–309.

Prins, H. (1979). Socio-forensic studies: a promising field for future development, *Med. Sci. Law*, **19**, 108–110.

Prins, H. (1980). *Offenders Deviants or Patients*, Tavistock Publications, London.

Prins, H. (1981). Dangerous people or dangerous situations: some implications for assessment and management. *Medicine science and the law*, **21**, 125–133.

Rennie, Y. (1978). *The Search for Criminal Man*, Lexington Books, Toronto. (pp. 3–5).

Sarbin, T. R. (1967). The dangerous individual: an outline of social identity transformations, *Brit. J. Criminol.*, **7**, 285–295.

Scott, P. D. (1977). Assessing dangerousness in criminals, *Brit. J. Psychiat.*, **131**, 127–142.

Simon, F. H. (1971). *Prediction Methods in Criminology, Home Office Research Studies No. 7*. HMSO, London.

Soothill, K. L., Way, C. K., and Gibbens, T. C. N. (1980). Subsequent Dangerousness Among Compulsory Hospital Patients', *Brit. J. Criminol.*, **20**, 289–295.

Steadman, H. J. and Cocozza, J. J. (1974). *Careers of the Criminally Insane*, Lexington Books, Toronto.

Stürup, G. (1968). *Treating the Untreatable: Chronic Criminals at Herstedvester*, Johns Hopkins, Baltimore.

Tennent, T. G. (1975). The dangerous offender, in *Contemporary Psychiatry* (Eds. T. Silverstone, and B. Barraclough), pp. 308–315, Headley Brothers, Ashford, Kent.

Thornberry, T. P. and Jacoby, J. E. (1979). *The Criminally Insane*, University of Chicago Press, Chicago.

Usdin, G. L. (1967). *Broader Aspects of Dangerousness*, in *The Clinical Evaluation of the Dangerousness of the Mentally Ill* (Ed. J. R. Rappeport), pp. 43–47, Charles C. Thomas, Illinois.

Walker, N. (1978). Dangerous people, *Int. J. Law and Psychiat.*, **1**, 37–50.

Webb, D. (1976). Wise after the event: some comments on 'a danger to themselves and to others', *Brit. J. Soc. Wk.*, **6**, 91–96.

Woods, S. (1975). Violence, psychotherapy of pseudohomosexual panic, in *Violence and Victims*, (Ed. S. A. Pasternack), pp. 61–70, Spectrum Publications, New York.

Mental Illness: Changes and Trends
Edited by Philip Bean
© 1983 John Wiley & Sons Ltd.

CHAPTER 4

The nature of psychiatric theory

PHILIP BEAN
Lecturer, Department of Social Administration,
University of Nottingham

When a psychiatrist is asked how he decides that a patient is mentally ill he would I think reply according to his medical training and in terms of the medical paradigm. That is, the patient (or someone with knowledge of the patient) complains of symptoms and the doctor perceives signs; on this basis a diagnosis is made. The symptoms and signs are said to be explained by the disease condition; i.e. a constellation of related symptoms and signs with a characteristic prognosis. So, if symptoms X and signs Y exist then disease Z exists; this being the obvious case where X and Y are both necessary and sufficient conditions of Z. Of course matters are rarely so clear cut. In physical medicine for example symptoms and signs can be sufficient but not necessary conditions, or necessary but not sufficient conditions as with body temperatures. Moreover the medical paradigm has no adequate definition of disease contained within it, for some diseases like tuberculosis are defined by their cause, others like ulcerative colitis by their pathology and others like migraine by their symptoms (Kendell, 1975, p. 19).

Paradigms are, by definition, a loose collection of ideas surrounding a central theme, in this instance the explanation of disease as an ideal type. The examples given above show that the medical paradigm is no exception. Lacking a single theory of disease, the paradigm consists of a set of propositions built up over time on a variable conceptual basis. A great deal of uninformed criticism has been directed at psychiatry contrasting it unfavourably with general medicine and suggesting often by implication that general medicine has a firm methodology and psychiatry a more fragile one. But this is not necessarily so. General medicine has acquired new ways of thinking over time, and has come to resemble what Kendell describes as a mansion which has been refurnished without clearing out the old furniture. Among the furnishings are antiques which may not be of the highest quality (ibid. p. 20). The search for a sound methodology in general medicine has to continue for there remains disagreement about the nature of disease, and about how it is transmitted—and hence about signs and symptoms.

Indeed in some respects psychiatry is more favourably placed. Modern general medicine has evolved slowly although there have been occasional sudden breakthroughs when discoveries were made which have revolutionized thinking. These have produced new paradigms; for example by the use of new technologies like the microscope which have led to the discovery of bacteria. However, new methods have been grafted on to earlier ways of thinking without earlier ways being abandoned—hence Kendell's comparison with furnishings. Psychiatry in contrast uses the same clinical descriptive model introduced by Sydenham in the seventeenth century, i.e. disease is diagnosed by a cluster of signs and symptoms and has a characteristic time course (ibid. p. 21) Kendell may regard it as lamentable that no new models have been devised but he recognizes that there are advantages in the existing system, one of which is that psychiatry avoids many of the problems in general medicine, with its multiplicity of models and concepts.

On the other hand there are many areas where psychiatry appears to be more severely disadvantaged; not the least being the divergence of modern psychiatry into different 'schools', sometimes based on the mental or social conditions of the patients, and sometimes on the methods of treatment. So the psychoanalyst may have little in common with the organically orientated psychiatrist, and may even be antagonistic, although both may operate within the same view of themselves i.e. as doctors offering treatment. Between these extremes are a number of other 'schools' where the approaches may differ according to the work setting, i.e. psychiatrists working in the mental hospital find themselves having little in common with those working in child guidance clinics. However, these differences are more superficial than real, for real differences exist only at the extremes of the disciplines and remain in the minority. Modern psychiatry is dominated by 'general psychiatrists', by which I mean those who do not have a firm theoretical stance, are more eclectic in their approach and perhaps more pragmatic, using a variety of methods and accepting the strengths and defects of each theory. 'General psychiatry' is well recognized in Britain as standing for a middle-of-the-road view. It is perhaps less well known elsewhere, where theoretical positions are maintained more strenuously but it is to this group that I wish to direct attention for they also pose the most interesting questions.

Psychiatric theory is therefore dominated by the medical view. Whether it should be or not are in part ethical and in part sociological questions which for the purposes of this chapter I wish to ignore—not because I believe they are unimportant, but because I wish to look at another neglected area of psychiatry; the nature of the theory itself. In doing so I wish to raise questions about the psychiatrist's methodology which is inevitably tied to the theory.

Decisions about specific illnesses

When a psychiatrist assesses a patient he makes a diagnosis. He cannot avoid this unless he also avoids all forms of classification and offers the same treatment to everyone. Diagnosis is a form of classification where patients suffering from like conditions are categorized together. In psychiatry, as in medicine generally, classifications are based on the so-called disease condition. Recently psychiatrists have become preoccupied with achieving greater levels of reliability in their diagnosis. They have argued, and rightly so, that the accuracy of the prognostic and therapeutic inferences derived from a diagnosis can never be higher than the accuracy with which, in any given situation, that diagnosis can be made (ibid. p. 27). The means by which greater reliability can be achieved has taken various forms including a demand for greater concordance in training, and for more sophisticated classificatory systems. (Shepherd, *et al.*, 1968).

I do not wish to deprecate these attempts to increase diagnostic reliability, for there is overwhelming evidence to suggest that improvement is long overdue. But again psychiatrists do a disservice to themselves if they create the impression that diagnostic unreliability is uniquely theirs. Reliability is a problem in all areas where personal judgments are involved,—and this includes other branches of medicine as well as psychology and social work. Diagnostic reliability may be more of a problem in psychiatry than elsewhere in medicine but is not unique to it, for the old idea that all diagnosis is an art not a science is another way of recognizing the same thing. The dangers come from pursuing reliability and forgetting the assumptions upon which it is based; the assumptions being that mental illnesses are illnesses like all others, that they exist in a value free world of science, and that we can be clear about the correct methods of assessments. And of course mental illnesses are not like other illnesses. Since mental illnesses are defined and diagnosed only at the clinical descriptive level psychiatrists make their diagnosis without knowledge of the underlying disease condition and have to proceed as if one existed. They leave themselves open to the accusation that mental illnesses are of a qualitatively different order, or at the extreme that no illness exists at all.

There is another sense in which mental illnesses differ and that is in boundaries of the condition. Consider the definition of illness given by Sir Aubrey Lewis.

In order for mental illness to be inferred disorder of function must be detectable at a discreet and differential level, that is hardly conceivable when mental activity as a whole is taken as an irreducible datum. If non-conformity can be detected only in total behaviour, while all the particular psychological functions seem unimpaired health will be presumed not illness (Lewis, 1953, p. 118).

Lewis' distinction between mental illness and non-conformity is hardly satisfactory for non-conformity can also be discreet and differential. (The burglar living an otherwise impeccable life is not unknown.) A more important distinction stems from Lewis' view that disease can only be established by an examination of individual objects and events. But this view weakens the scientific context of the subject matter for the study of disease is thereby reduced to a study of the individual manifestations and the natural history within individual patients. Lewis does not say that psychiatrists should search only for individual objects and events but he wishes to emphasize their importance, which means the importance of the patient's background and previous mental state. And by pushing psychiatry in this direction he also leaves it open to the charge of being imprecise.

For the problem is this: in order for sciences to advance, reality must be viewed as unchanging or universal so that disease A will have the same reality whether it be in patients X, Y, or Z. A disease like depression is assumed to have a common nature like all other depressions. If depression means anything it means something which is not this or that depression, but some kind of universal depressiveness. In examining the unchanging reality of phenomena, terms can be used as abstract concepts susceptible to empirical investigation, or to scientific investigation. Cats or dogs have a universal 'cattiness' or 'dogginess' which means something more to zoologists that 'this cat' or 'that dog', and, by the same argument, 'depression' or 'schizophrenia' must mean something more than 'this depressed person' or 'this schizophrenic person'. This theory of universals which is derived from Plato has enabled all classificatory systems to develop and all sciences to distinguish between phenomena common to it and that which is not.

Plato's theory of universals is not without its difficulties. What, for example are we to make of 'man' or other animals in an evolutionary process? At what point do they stop being 'something else' and start being 'man' or whatever? Even so, science could not proceed without regard to Plato's methods of classification, and medicine in general and psychiatry in particular is no exception. Yet it is also obvious that cats can differ, in physique, and some would say in their 'personality'—so presumably can depressed patients or schzophrenic patients and other psychotics. When Lewis was demanding that psychiatrists look at the individual features of patients he was not being unreasonable in that sense. Moreover he was operating within the traditions of all scientific advances, for individual differences require consideration at two stages; at the beginning of scientific endeavour where classificatory systems are in their infancy, and at a later stage where classifications exist but refinements are added based on observation of minutae. The orthopaedic surgeon mends broken legs but has to recognize that broken legs differ in structure and function. I want to insist, however, that the difference is one of emphasis. The methodology of the surgeon is not one based first and foremost on the individuality of patients yet Lewis' definition surely is. (It may seem unfair to single out Sir Aubrey Lewis for criticism but as so few psychiatrists have spelt out their methodology those who have done so tend unfortunately to attract the criticism.)

Examining the individual aspects of the patient is not a method unique to psychiatry for all sciences require it in varying form. The uniqueness, and the corresponding weakness, is to pursue an individualized approach where diagnosis becomes a generalist and particularistic stance with the latter assuming prominence. For this is what Lewis is urging psychiatrists to do. The diagnostic method is then in two parts; first in Plato's terms there is a search for the unchanging reality of the disease and this is then set against the Aristotelian version of the objects and events of the individual patient—a method described by one writer as a 'psychic shuffle'. Yet it is not the 'psychic shuffle' which is the problem, for that is inevitable, it is the attraction towards the patients' life style that demonstrates the fragile nature of psychiatric methodology.

This debate may seem connected remotely to the modern psychiatrists task. Many modern psychiatrists would I think say that no patients are alike and individual features must be important. So take for example a middle aged man otherwise hale and hearty not given to reflective ruminations. Modern psychiatrists may say he would appear to be of a different order, psychiatrically speaking, to the unhappy man whose morbid worldly-view has persisted throughout his life. But to accept this argument is to display a bias towards the Aristotelian view, or the 'substance' as Aristotle called it, where little can be understood about the disease and a great deal about the patient. I do not, however, wish to be unsympathetic to the psychiatrists' task for where attempts have been made to search far for that 'unchanging reality' the results have often been disappointing. Kendell reminds us that the study of depression has produced no agreement about the nature of endogenous or reactive depressions, whether they are one and the same, or extremes of a continuum. Historically, similar attempts to extricate psychiatry from these and similar methodological difficulties have led to no great advance (Kendell, 1976).

One method has been to posit the existence of some other unchanging reality, possibly innate which would be discovered eventually by empirical methods. This type of approach was advanced by Kraepelin, who it will be remembered maintained that mental diseases could be classified according to patients reactions. In 1854 he published his now famous description of depression calling it *La Folie Circulaire*, and with rare insight proposed the name manic-depressive insanity, to distinguish it from dementia praecox. By 1913 he had extended his definition to include the whole domain of periodic and circular insanity, simple mania, and melancholia, all of which he saw as part of a single morbid process. He suggested that a series of subordinate forms may be described at some later point, or that small groups be entirely separated.

Kraepelin was of course convinced that manic depressive insanity was based on an aetiology of a morbid anatomy which would subsequently be discovered. Like other psychiatrists of that period he found he had to be content to describe clinical features, yet believed that the conditions he was describing were somehow fixed entities in the body, whose discovery and classification would be a matter of time. Manic-depressive insanity was to Kraepelin a product of nature not of the environment. In a similar vein Henry Maudsley, a contemporary of Kraepelin spoke of 'the organization', or of a character which was fixed by birth. Maudsley thought that no one could escape the tyranny of the organization that was innate in him. Maudsley would have agreed with Kraepelin who considered that manic-depressive insanity often follows serious disappointments such as family deaths or hardships, but these were 'sparks' which ignited the organization. The organization defined the origin of the malady which according to Maudsley and Kraepelin was possibly innate.

Kraepelin and other psychiatrists of this tradition reflected the philosophical stance of Hobbes who wrote of a relatively unfixed character against which the person must be forever watchful. These speculative notions about the nature of man were translated by Kraepelin into statements of intent about the future course of psychiatry even though he lacked the anatomical correlated that he was convinced existed and was forced to rely, as psychiatrists still are, on clinical data and on the symptomatology and the course of the illness (Kendell, 1976). Whilst one may admire Kraepelin's attempt to classify a condition as wide as manic depressive insanity, he opened the way to a number of areas of confusion which still remain. First, what is the nature of that organization and included in this how to distinguish between the 'organization' and those 'reactive sparks' which set off manic depressive insanity? Second, how to define the boundaries of the condition? and third, how to determine the nature of the condition distinguishing between the severe and less severe forms?

But before coming to the specific features of Kraepelin's argument we can attack it first at the level of social theory. For to assume, as Kraepelin and Maudsley did, that there exists an 'organization' is to see the patient as a person having certain wants, needs, or even instincts which are assumed to arise independently of a social context. In modern social theory Kraepelin's model of man is that of the abstract individual (Lukes, 1973). In this sense Kraepelin's position was not dissimilar to that described by Hobbes', 'where men spring out of the earth, and suddenly like mushrooms came to maturity without any kinds of engagements to each other' (quoted in ibid. p. 77). To Kraepelin depressed patients were bearers of certain psychobiological features and the social world interacted with that invariant condition. In its modern form abstract individualism shows itself in the work of Eysenck, who wants to explain attitudes by reference to antecedent conditions, in particular the modifications of the individual's central nervous system. These explanations operate in abstraction from the historical, economic, sociological and perhaps even anthropological context (ibid. p. 120). Similarly Freud's view of man is of an abstract individual born with a sort of 'treasure chest' of instinctual desires located in the id. (Hobbes used the terms 'appetites' and 'aversions' but the model is the same). In Freudian terms those desires generate a type of activity which may or may not be channelled into acceptable social directions.

Abstract individualism is open to more specific criticisms. It has been attacked as a narrow and superficial dogma by Marx who saw it as axiomatic that man was not an abstract human being squatting outside the world. Man was the human world, man was the state, the society and the institutions of that society (Lukes,

1973). To Marx, Kraepelin's views would appear as based on the invalid assumption that man was a product of nature, not of history, nor of human society. Many non-Marxists have taken up the point. Bradley for instance had little sympathy with the view of man as an abstraction. Man for Bradley, was a social being who was only real because he was social, he was not in Kraepelin's terms (or in Freudian terms) real because he was born with innate instinctual desires (Lukes, 1973).

We need not extend this criticism of Kraepelin, for we can return to the more specific criticisms cited earlier. First, what is the nature of that organization? And here we find that Kraepelin's and Maudsley's version of an organization is similar to Aristotle's 'essence'; that is what you are by your nature and which cannot be changed without losing that intrinsic quality of being 'you' or your basic personality. But 'essence' or 'organization' is merely as Bertrand Russell says, 'a convenient way of collecting attributes into bundles.' It is a way of providing a linguistic convenience and giving a collective name for a number of attributes. Or if it is not then it denotes something altogether different and unknowable and therefore vague within this context, (Russell, 1946).

Second, what are the boundaries of the condition particularly where disease conditions are said to interact between instinctual desires and the environment? Or to put the question another way, which environmental factors are revelvant? Are not some more relevant that others and if so on what basis are weights attributed to the respective environmental factors? An examination of the Maudsley Hospital Institute of Psychiatry Item Sheet will illustrate my point. Items include family history, children's development, education, work history, war history, friendships, delinquency, sexual history (including examples of infidelity), as well as the number and types of children born to the subject—which may include illegitimate children. So a sort of 'shopping list' is produced where internal and external factors hitherto undefined determine the extent of the list. The factors appear to have been collected on the basis of some clinical or statistical variables although I would suggest that there exists another assumption which we can call the 'evil-begets-evil assumption' which also dominates. Here the psychiatrist is confronted with an unpleasantness, i.e. mental illness, and searches around in the patient's environment to link it with another evil, say, defective family relationships or some such similar event.

Thirdly, there is the problem of how to distinguish between the severe and less severe forms. And here we find that the only basis by which distinctions can be made are through professional or clinical judgments—indeed there is little in Kraepelin's theory which would suggest otherwise. To use Maudsley's terminology there is the 'organization' and the 'reactive sparks' where presumably the 'organization' is the major factor and is by definition vague. Now these 'reactive sparks' can be evaluated—at least on a commonsense basis where say the death of a close relative could be seen as more serious than the loss of a job. But of course that commonsense view may not always accord with empirical observation. And if it did not how could the psychiatrist account for differences? He could only do so by showing that the close relative was perhaps not as close as originally believed, or perhaps by reference to the 'organization' And if he does he ought not to be suprised if he is accused of supporting a theory which lacks precision.

Mental illness as a disease of the mind

To say, as do most psychiatric textbooks that mental illnesses are diseases or disorders of mind places psychiatry in a difficult if not impossible position. A mind whether disordered or not is in the Cartesian sense not witnessable by other observers, its career is private and unlike the body the mind is not in space nor subject to mechanical laws. How then can it be treated, or rather how can it ever be diseased? It may be fashionable to dismiss Cartesian dualism but whatever one's metaphysical disposition dualism helps provide a distinction between life and death and between the animate and inanimate (Teichman, 1974, p. 106). Furthermore it allows us to comprehend the mind other than in behaviourist or materialist concerns and as such offers a model of explanation not reduced to scientific laws of behaviour or to studies of the human brain. It also offers an elementary distinction between a mind and a soul and between a mind and a brain which other theories do not.

But Cartesian dualism hardly helps the psychiatrist. If a mind is not subject to mechanical laws and is not in space or time the empirical base of psychiatry is suspect. And if there is no 'ghost in the machine' as Gilbert Ryle says then the psychiatrist must resort to behaviourism or materialism; the former concerned with analysing behaviour and the states of the human nervous system which underlies such behaviour, and the latter concerned with contingent identities, i.e. identifying mental events with brain events. I suppose that of the two materialism would be more favoured by the modern psychiatrist but I know of few psychiatrists who would see themselves as materialists and fewer who were out and out behaviourists. Most would grudgingly accept that dualism had some value and in so doing place themselves in a position where they need give a satisfactory account of the relationship between what Descartes called the spiritual and the corporeal, and the mind and other minds. Once they accept dualism they accept the Cartesian view that the mind is indivisible and non-extended, it is complete and united with the body; hardly a view which lends itself to empirical enquiry. Yet to accept behaviourism is to accept a restricted view of human beings and to accept materialism is to accept the doubtful logic of the materialist argument (Teichman 1974).

But it is not easy to be rid of dualistic views. It may not be necessary to accept the whole Cartesian argument particularly that part where Descartes asserted the mind was deterministic, and governed by the laws of physics as was the body, yet the doctrine as advanced by Plato draws heavily on the mind as a means of understanding. In the *Phaedo* Plato talks of the way the soul uses the body as an instrument of perception and 'is not dragged by the body into the region of the changeable nor wanders or is confused' rather the soul (or mind) returns into herself and reflects and ceases from erring ways. 'And this state of the soul is called wisdom.'

The notion of 'reflection' in Plato, or 'judgment' in Descartes, provides one of the strongest arguments in support of dualism. When Descartes in the Second Meditation says that judgment is essential to perception he is saying that we do more than 'see' things, we comprehend and evaluate and assess. And when Plato speaks of reflecting he is also speaking of judgments in the Cartesian sense. Psychiatrists themselves speak freely of judgments and reflections when they talk of introspection in patients. As and when they do, they are implying a rather sophisticated form of dualism where the mind reflects on the mind and evaluates its feelings and thoughts or its mental state. Or in Gilbert Ryle's terms insight is 'a non-optical species of perception where the person regards a mental state or process of his own' (Ryle, 1973, p. 157).

To talk of 'introspection' is to talk of something over and above a metaphysical conception of the world; introspections are held by many psychiatrists to be the factor which distinguishes the psychotic from the normal. A disease of the mind is said to exist when introspection is absent. Introspection, in the Freudian sense, allows the ego to be enlarged and enables human beings to be rational, to forecast future events and deal with them more rationally. When psychiatrists say of a patient that he does not introspect they are saying more than he is unreflective, they are saying he has little or no control over his feelings or emotions. Introspection becomes a means of producing order, for without introspection in Plato's terms the 'world spins round, and the person is like a drunkard when he touches change.'

Introspection becomes a rather special 'ghost in the machine', and for psychiatrists who use the term—and from my experience almost all of them do—they are pushed towards a Cartesian view of the world. Now there is nothing intrinsically wrong with that, at least in the philosophical sense for Cartesian dualism has much to commend it. The difficulty is that in terms of this discussion it does little to help the psychiatrist defend his specialism as an empirical science to be compared favourably with medicine. At a philosophical level there may be advantages but at the empirical there are none. Plato calls the mind the 'unseen' and the body the 'seen', and introspection, to use Ryle's term, is defined as 'a non-sensuous inner perception' (Ryle, 1973, p. 148). Moreover, Ryle subjects the term to a form of criticism which I fear is largely unanswerable by modern psychiatrists intent on retaining it as an indication of success or failure in treatment.

There are some states of mind which cannot be coolly scrutinized, since the fact that we are in those states involves that we are not cool or the fact that we are cool involves that we are not in those states. No one could introspectively scrutinize the state of panic or fury since the dispassionateness exercised in scientific observation is by the definition of panic and fury not the state of mind of the victim of those turbulences. Similarly since a convulsion of merriment is not the state of mind of the sober experimentalist the enjoyment of a joke is also not an introspective happening... Yet nothing disastrous follows from this restriction. We are not shorter of information about panic or amusement than other states of mind.

Whilst the term introspection has been used throughout, 'insight' is I think the term more favoured by psychiatrists. Yet 'insight' is more evaluative than introspection, and as such makes the psychiatrists' position less tenable. The schizophrenic could be introspective—using the term in its widest sense since he may regard, in a non-optical way, a mental state or process of his own but would not be insightful. Insight means more than looking at the mental processes, it means evaluating them and coming to acceptable conclusions—acceptable that is to the psychiatrist—and which if those conclusions do not lead to wisdom immediately, it is to be hoped they will in the future when the patient has learned to adjust his behaviour. Insight, therefore, becomes a special type of normative term, so that were psychiatric definitions of health or disease to hinge on the use of insight, psychiatric theory would become nothing more than a normative theory. And by a normative theory I mean a theory that converts facts and laws into required means and ends, where the objectives themselves are desired by the formulator or by those in whose service the theorist stands. Normative theories are about ideal ways of behaving or acting, or as far as institutions are concerned, of operating. Normative theories state the ends to be achieved in advance and produce arguments and convert data to satisfy those ends. They are theories about morality, where the morality is contained within the theories themselves and/or in the required ends. Both features are necessary; normative theories which do not contain normative statements within the theory would not convert facts but merely state them, and those which had no normative ends could not satisfy the requirements of the ideal ways of behaving.

In spite of the many difficulties imposed on psychiatric theory by Cartesian dualism psychiatrists seem unable to dispense with that mode of thinking. The problem is not of course confined to psychiatrists for sociologists and other social scientists have to contend with accusations that their theories are also normative. Yet in psychiatry the normative component seems more acute, perhaps because psychiatrists are concerned with the patient's own normative assessments. Consider the diagnosis of depression for this gives the most immediate impact to the argument. Most psychiatric textbooks define depression as a disorder of mood (Cohen, 1967; Lewis, 1967). The *Psychiatric Dictionary* defines it in terms of a lowering of mood tone (feelings of painful dejection), difficulty in thinking and psychomotor retardation (1970). The *International Journal of Psychoanalysis* has a more elaborate definition. 'A pathological state of conscious psychic suffering and guilt accompanied by a marked reduction in the sense of personal values and a diminution of mental psycho-motor and even organic activity unrelated to actual deficiency' (Nacht, and Racamier, 1960).

Included in both definitions are some normative statements and some not, the latter for these purposes we can call happenings. Because human actions involve physical movements we tend to assume that explanations of the movements are explanations of the actions. Alisdair MacIntyre cites the example where he nods his head and is asked why he did it. If he answers by reference to a nervous tic he is referring to something that happens to him. If on the other hand he explains the nod by saying that he has been asked a question and was answering it by a 'Yes' he is explaining the nod by an action. He is pointing to the purpose it serves (MacIntyre, 1972, p. 57). Or to give a slightly different example, an arm raising relative to a body is not the same thing as a man raising his arm. The difference is that one involves the movement of an object, i.e. a happening, and the other involves a purpose in that movement, i.e. an action. The man whose arm was raised relative to the body can explain the motion by stating what is happening to him; if the man was raising his arm the explanation would be in terms of a purpose or an action, perhaps as giving a signal or pointing to some object.

Translating this distinction to the field of mental illnesses we can see that where psychiatrists are concerned with the physical symptoms of the patient they concentrate on happenings—or what philosophers call passions. So for example to say that a person has a certain expression or has a disturbance of sleep is a description about what is happening to him. It does not explain the patient's behaviour nor does it explain why the patient behaves in a particular way. Similarly, assume for a moment that the patient took a large quantity of sleeping tablets and was admitted to a hospital where as a result of the activities of the medical staff the patient recovered. In this example we have described what happened to the patient. However, if we were to say this patient attempted suicide we begin to ascribe a purpose to the patient's activities and as such move toward an explanation of his actions.

The distinction between happenings and actions defined above tends to oversimplify the point but used in this way we can see that Freud's discoveries were largely about what happened to his patients, they did not provide explanations of the patient's actions. For my main point is that actions unlike happenings are normative statements, that is they relate to certain social rules, and evaluations about behaviour are in terms of those rules. Human actions cannot be analysed in causal terms but only in terms of rules which are social and can be broken—and there are different ways in which that can be done and in different social contexts. Only in the light of rules and by the standards they provide can we intelligibly evaluate behaviour. Remembering is not just a mental state it is to be sure that we were correct about something that occurred in the past. Similarly to learn something is to improve at something or to get something right (Benn and Peters, 1975). By the same argument we cannot explain the actions of motor-car drivers who stop at traffic lights without explaining their behaviour in terms of the rules governing behaviour at traffic lights. If the car driver fails to stop we cannot explain his behaviour in terms of the colour of the lights for a red light does not cause people to stop (or not stop) in the way that heat causes iron to expand. In this sense, Kant's suggestion that there are two different types of causation because men live in physiological and normative worlds is a metaphysical way of bringing out the logical distinctions of the two sorts of explanation.

To see how psychiatrists confuse happenings and actions we need only look again at the Item Sheet of the Professorial Unit of the Maudsley Hospital, London. Here 300 items of information are gathered covering the patient's family history, past personal history, premorbid personality together with the aetiology, symptomatology, treatment, and outcome of the illness. Irrespective of the reliability of such a document we find the whole range of features from 'tics and other dyskenic phenomena' to being 'suspicious irritable and perplexed' being enclosed. Whereas the former group may be happenings the latter are not. And whilst I have used depression as the example schizophrenia could have been used too, for thought disorder implies a level of inappropriateness of response and reply, which is another way of saying that patients are adjudged in the light of social rules and according to whether they have got things right.

Notice that I am not saying that mental illnesses such as depression or schizophrenia are 'social conditions' for that is a truism; I am saying that the psychiatric methods of explanation of the disease are a mixture of actions (normative) and happenings (non-normative). And it would follow that treatment too becomes a mixture of normative and non-normative methods, where the patient reassesses his feelings in normative terms and where success or failure in treatment is adjudged by that assessment. Psychiatrists sometimes claim to by-pass the normative elements by suggesting that the method of treatment can be non-normative as say when antidepressant drugs or tranquillizers are given to patients. But it will not do to argue that the normative components can so readily be by-passed by reference to some underlying disease condition which is 'cured' by the actions of tranquillizers. For as Jeff Coulter has pointed out we cannot say that the disease is what tranquillizers tranquillize since there are no logical grounds for arguing from the status of the treatment medium to the status of the precipitating medium (Coulter, 1973, p. 27).

So it is not simply a question of adjusting a definition to make problems vanish. Furthermore, the psychiatrist who defines depression in terms of happenings only, is still faced with a multiplicity of normative questions presented by the patient. Unlike the patient with a heart condition who points to a pain near his heart the depressed patient cannot indicate that he is in pain (unless that is he is prepared to accept psychic pain as pain which is doubtful) but can and will say he feels sad, unworthy, ashamed etc. And because these normative symptoms are the mainstay of the psychiatrist's diagnosis they must also be included in the definition.

Specific disease conditions

Up to this point I have argued that the use of the word mind with its dualistic overtones provides a poor empirical base for the science of psychiatry. However in practice, or rather in diagnostic terms, psychiatrists rarely talk in such global terms, rather they classify conditions into disorders of mood or feeling (depression), disorders of thought (schizophrenia), etc., so that 'the mind' becomes a catch-all generic term used for convenience to delineate the boundaries of the discipline. It is only the layman, or the psychiatrist talking as layman who would speak of 'the balance of the mind being disturbed' or 'being out of one's mind'. Even so psychiatrists would still assert that disorders of mood or thought are sub-categories used to break down the components into more manageable points—at least that is what some psychiatric textbooks convey.

But are they? Well if they are then they lack a certain elementary precision for to see the mind as comprising feelings, thoughts, and the will, (to use the three major categories of illnesses) is to take an unwarranted conceptual leap. Nor is it clear from such a typology how, if at all, overlap occurs, nor when overlap occurs which category is likely to dominate. Are disorders of thoughts to be more dominant than disorders of feeling, and in what way if at all are the two connected? And it is because these questions cannot be answered that psychiatrists are led into those endless diagnostic debates about whether the patient had an underlying depressive condition in an overlying schizophrenia, or an underlying schizophrenia in an overlying depressive condition when patients show symptoms of both.

The usual response from psychiatrists when faced with such questions about categories of mind is to reply in terms of their limited existing knowledge base and hope that as research develops more certainty will be acquired. Psychiatry, it is said is a young science exhibiting all the defects appropriate to its development. This of course may well be true except that, if the previous analysis is correct, few advances are likely to occur whilst it retains strong normative components. But the point I want to make is not directed wholly at the classificatory system as much as at the language used by psychiatrists operating that system. Consider 'disorders of mood'. A disorder of mood is not necessarily a disorder of feeling although it is often used by psychiatrists as if it were. But moods monopolize, according to Ryle (p. 96), whereas feelings are partial and non-predictive. By this I mean that to say 'I am in a lazy or industrious mood is to describe why I am not in any other mood and why when confronted with new work I shall put it on one side. To say 'I am in a lazy mood' is to describe more than my feelings about work but to predict my attitude to future work. Moods may be short-lived or not but they are total and describe more than one's feelings. To say 'I am in a lazy mood' is different from saying 'I feel lazy'.

Feelings may exist within moods but are more transient. In Ryle's terms 'feelings are things that come and go or wax and wane in a few seconds' (p. 97). To say I feel happy or depressed is to say that I feel happy or depressed now, but nothing in that statement suggests that I am likely to continue to feel happy or depressed tomorrow. Nor can anyone predict how that happiness will be affected by changes in circumstances, say a partial rebuff or another piece of good news. Feelings are with us all the time, moods are not. We do not say yesterday I was in the following moods, and list them as if they changed regularly, but we might easily say 'yesterday I felt happy until I heard so and so, then felt sad for a little time until ...' and we frequently describe our feelings as 'mixed'.

The confusion between a mood and a feeling underlines this part of the debate. Perhaps it is as Ryle suggests that theorists have felt constrained to operate within three permitted pigeon-holes, Thought, Will, and Feeling, and as moods do not fit the first two they must be made to fit the third (p. 97). And the discussion on disorders of thought is no less clear. How many thoughts are correct and how many incorrect before a diagnosis of schizophrenia is made? And can thoughts be somehow separated from feelings as if there were emotional processes and cognitive ones? The answer to this question is I think no; I do not have two mental processes operating when I think and only one when I feel, even though many diagnostic categories suggest otherwise.

I am arguing that psychiatry is characterized by an over abundance of terms which lack precision, and which of themselves help reduce the quality of psychiatric theory. Were attention given to these matters even at a straightforward linguistic level then some improvement could certainly be made. For this loose way of thinking extends to many areas of psychiatric practice including that within the legal system (except that is in the area related to the insanity defences. See Chapter 1). A close examination of legislation such as the 1959 Mental Health Act, tells us a great deal about the status of psychiatry but little about the content of its theory. (For it is part of the modern paradox that the legal status of psychiatry has outpaced its theoretical development.) Under the 1959 Act psychiatric theory is represented by a series of unproven assertions, particularly that where the Act says 'mental illness is an illness like any other illness'. In this Act itself, mental illness itself is not defined; and nor is psychopathy or mental subnormality yet they remain categories under which psychiatrists may recommend a patient be detained.

One may well ask how and under what circumstances has such legal sloppiness occurred? And the answer must be in sociological rather than jurisprudential terms where psychiatry has been cast into an elevated role irrespective of the quality of its theory. I do not believe that psychiatrists intentionally promoted themselves but having been accorded that position were, until recently, reluctant to renounce it. They accepted it with little criticism from themselves and with few self-doubts.

It is none the less clear that the theoretical basis upon which psychiatrists operate—that is within certain parts of the legal system—is faulty. Consider the assertion that 'mental illness is an illness like any other'; a position derived originally from a Royal Commission which preceded modern mental health legislation in Britain (see Bean, 1980, ch. 4). Now even if the assertion is true, which is doubtful, it is obvious that mental illness is different in a number of important respects. First, as the Commission recognized, mental illness makes many patients incapable of protecting themselves or their interests so that if they are neglected or exploited it may be necessary to have authority to insist on providing them with proper care. Secondly, in many cases mental illness affects the patients judgment so that he does not realize that he is ill, and the illness can only be treated against the patient's wishes at the time. Finally, in many cases mental illness affects the patient's behaviour in such a way that it is necessary in the interests of other people or of society in general to insist on removing the patient for treatment even if he is unwilling. We find therefore that the assertion is more a statement of intent where the intention is political, aimed at placing psychiatry within the framework of medicine in order to achieve certain political ends. Other aims are social such as reducing the stigma of the patient diagnosed as mentally ill, whilst others a mixture of the social and political where the intentions are to increase the status of psychiatry, up-grade the mental hospitals, and encourage highly trained medical personnel to work in the psychiatric field. These aims may be laudable in themselves, but cannot be derived from the level of psychiatric theory and practice which existed at the time, and the Commission was dishonest to try.

This example illustrates the importance and difficulty of extracting the political and social components of psychiatric theory from the theory itself. Unlike many other applied sciences the theory becomes less neutral and is more tied to social changes or political ends. Perhaps this is what is so circular about the whole discussion; the theory is regarded as weak and so political and social ends intrude and they do so because the theory is regarded as weak. But it is difficult to break the circularity.

One approach is to abandon all pretence of making psychiatry a non-normative discipline and move towards the position where older terms like moral treatment become resurrected and provided with new meaning. Psychiatry would then become a form of moral education. Such a view has been advanced before and has a certain persuasive ring about it. Given that psychiatrists may find it impossible to deal in non-normative concepts the strength of the argument remains clear. Alternatively one could accept Karl Menninger's view that classifying psychiatric patients is both unscientific and unnecessary since all forms of mental illness are the same and differ only in degree and form (Menninger, *et al.*, 1963). Both positions seem to be councils of despair, the latter being worse since it supports the notion that mental illness exists but no attempt is made to understand the nature of that phenomenon, nor to try to explain it.

Neither does it meet the points about methodology which are central to this chapter.

Conclusion

Enough has been said, I think, to show that psychiatric theory needs attention at various points. It is a sad reflection of modern psychiatry to note how little attention has been given to these matters—with one or two notable exceptions that is. There has, I think, been a consistent theme running through modern psychiatry that it must be promoted as a facsimile of medicine—an obvious outcome of the psychiatrists' medical training. Of course psychiatry has close theoretical associations with medicine generally, but it may diverge sharply at certain points, and the fact that psychiatrists are trained as doctors is a historical rather than a logical reason for continuing the connection. Whether that connection is valid or not has to be demonstrated.

A philosophical contribution to the study of psychiatry need not be a one way movement of ideas, for psychiatry has much to teach philosophy. Even so, philosophers cannot abdicate responsibility from the basic task; that is to examine the nature of psychiatric theory and the logic of theory construction. They can and should avoid many of the pitfalls into which some others have fallen, notably in the social sciences where, for example, a sociology of medicine has too often been changed imperceptibly to a sociology *in* medicine and where the social scientist has lost independence and credibility, having become immersed in psychiatric thinking. Edmund Pelligrino is right when he says the philosopher will be helpful to medicine and advance his own discipline only if he remains a *bona fide* philosopher (Pelligrino, 1976, p. 25). But to move into psychiatric areas, and particularly those which concern mental illness is a daunting task for most philosophers. In this paper I have tried to do no more than point the way where hopefully others may follow, and in so doing have taken a broad rather than narrow view of psychiatric methodology.

In taking a broad view it has become difficult to see psychiatry as a facsimile of medicine—indeed in many respects psychiatric methodology divides at certain crucial points. In saying this I do not want to convey that medicine *qua* medicine is a science and psychiatry not, for medicine as a practice is more opaque than we normally take it to be (Gorovitz, and MacIntyre, 1976) and psychiatry less so. Nor is it a question of seeing medicine and psychiatry at different points on a scientific continuum where psychiatry is rated lower on a scientific scale. It may be that this is the way psychiatrists see themselves and hope for improvement with greater reliability of diagnosis, etc. If so, I remain unconvinced that their position on the continuum will be changed—at least in the near future. We may find eventually that we are talking about quite different disciplines, which may resemble each other in personnel, aims, and objectives but operate from different theoretical suppositions, and where to state it baldly one is concerned with happenings the other with individual actions.

References

Bean, P. T. (1980). *Compulsory Admissions to Mental Hospitals*. John Wiley and Sons.
Benn, S. I., and Peters, R. S. (1975). *Social Principles and the Democratic State*. George Allen and Unwin.
Cohen, R. A. (1967). Manic-depressive reactions. In Freedman, A. M. *et al.* (Eds.) *Comprehensive Textbook in Psychiatry*. Williams and Wilkins.
Coulter, J. (1973). *Approaches to Insanity*. Martin Robertson.
Gorovitz, S., and MacIntyre, A. (1976). Towards a theory of medical fallibility. *Journal of Medicine and Philosophy*. **1**, No. 1. 51–71.
Kendell, R. E. (1975). *The Role of Diagnosis in Psychiatry*. Basil Blackwell.
Kendell, R. E. (1976). *The Classification of Depressive Illness*. Oxford University Press.
Lewis, Sir A. (1953). Health as a social concept. *British Journal of Sociology*. **4**, 109–124.
Lewis, Sir A. (1967). Melancholia: a historical review. In Lewis, Sir A. *The State of Psychiatry*. Routledge and Kegan Paul.
Lukes, S. (1973). *Individualism*. Basil Blackwell.
MacIntyre, A. (1972). A mistake about causality. In Laslett, R., and Runciman, W. G. (Eds.) *Philosophy Politics and Society*. Basil Blackwell. (2nd Series).
Menninger, K. *et al.* (1963). *The Vital Balance*. Viking Press.
Nacht, S., and Racamier, P. C. (1960). Symposium on depressive illness, *International Journal of Psychoanalysis* **41**, 481–496.
Pelligrino, E. (1976). Philosophy of medicine: problematic and potential. *Journal of Medicine and Philosophy*, **1**, No. 1, 5–31.
Russell, B. (1946). *A history of Western Philosophy*. George Allen and Unwin.
Ryle, G. (1973). *The Concept of Mind*. Penguin.
Shepherd, M. *et al.* (1968). An experimental approach to psychiatric diagnosis. *Acta Psychiatrica Scandinavica*.
Teichman, J. (1974). *The Mind and the Soul*. Routledge and Kegan Paul.

Mental Illness: Changes and Trends
Edited by Philip Bean
© 1983 John Wiley & Sons Ltd.

CHAPTER 5

Mental illness as strategy

THOMAS SZASZ
*Professor of Psychiatry, State University of New York,
Syracuse, USA*

> *What a thing means is simply what habits it involves.... there is no
> distinction of meaning so fine as to consist in anything but a possible
> difference of practice.*
>
> Charles Saunders Peirce (1878)

Introduction

Every person of average intelligence and a measure of general education knows, or could be helped to understand, that language may be used in two quite different ways—namely, to assert or describe, and to advocate or prescribe. For example, we can say 'The door is closed', or 'Please close the door'. Although the difference between these two modes of communication is obvious, misunderstanding or denying it lies at the heart of much of the confusion and controversy concerning psychiatric matters.

A good deal of this confusion derives from the fact that the term 'mental illness' appears to refer to a disease, but actually refers to a decision. I point here to a simple, but strictly forbidden, truth about psychiatry—namely, that its practitioners usually first decide what to do about a person, and then 'discover' the appropriate diagnostic label with which to justify their decision. For example, if psychiatrists want to commit a person, they 'discover' that he is dangerously psychotic; if they want to get him acquitted of a criminal charge by reason of insanity, they 'discover' that he was, at the precise moment of his criminal act, suffering from a mental illness that deprived him of criminal responsibility; if they want to provide an abortion for a woman in a country where the only legal abortions are those deemed to be therapeutic, then they 'discover' that she suffers from a mental illness for which the 'indicated treatment' is abortion. In short, psychiatrists use mental illness terms as if they were descriptions (of psychopathological conditions from which persons suffer), whereas in practice these terms usually function as prescriptions (about how persons allegedly suffering from such conditions should be treated by others) (Szasz, 1961, 1970).

To be sure, many mental illness terms possess a certain descriptive content. For example, terms such as "depression" or "paranoia" identify certain configurations or patterns of behaviour in much the same way as do terms like 'neatness' or 'unreliability'. However, like the use of all terms descriptive of human behaviour, the use of mental illness terms is also fraught with much arbitrariness, partly because of their imprecision and partly because of the covert value judgments they carry that make their meaning vary not only with the behaviour of the person described but also with the character of the person doing the describing.

The differences between the descriptive and the prescriptive dimensions of diseases—or, to put it differently, between the conceptual and the strategic uses of disease terms—can be easily illustrated with the case of leprosy. Fifty years ago, leprosy meant Hansen's disease, an infectious disease characterized by certain clinical manifestations; and it also meant social segregation. The former meaning was the descriptive or conceptual content of the term 'leprosy', whereas the latter meaning was the practical or strategic consequence of attaching the term to a person. Today, the medical concept of leprosy is the same as it was fifty years ago, but its social consequences are vastly different.

As it is intellectually possible to sever the medical concept of leprosy from its social consequences, so it is possible to sever the psychiatric concept of mental illness from its social consequences, and to consider the latter while ignoring the former. This is precisely my plan in this essay. Accordingly, I shall present an empirically consequential, and an inferentially strategic, analysis of the term 'mental illness'. The time-honoured principle that if we want to know the motives for an act we should look to its consequences lies rightly at the heart of a great deal of law-making, because it recognizes the inescapable truth that in real life, predictable consequences quickly become personal motives.

The debate in psychiatry about mental illness has long ago bogged down, it seems to me, partly because the debaters do not specify or do not agree on what the criteria ought to be for counting something as a disease, or as a mental disease; and, partly because doubt over whether the term 'mental illness' refers to a positively identified disease or to a putative disease or to a non-disease overshadows the argument and the evidence the debaters present. All of this, I hope, can be prevented by clearly identifying the social consequences of using mental illness terms, consequences that will remain the same whatever the true nature of mental illness turns out to be. Unless, of course, we change those consequences. Perhaps only in this way will we be able to come to grips in psychiatry with the crucial differences between the biological consequences of diseases and the social consequences of diagnoses—and with the complex interplay between the two.

Diagnoses: Medical, Pathological, and Psychiatric

In contrast to psychiatric diagnostic terms, medical diagnostic terms are condensed and precise descriptions of some aspect of the patient's body: for example, fracture of the fibula means that one of the bones in the patient's leg is broken; lobar pneumonia that he has an infection in one or several lobes of his lung; and so forth. Although such descriptions often imply a strategy or tactic concerning treatment (that is, what the doctor should do to alleviate the abnormality), nevertheless, correctly used, medical diagnoses are not simply made to justify treatment. The validity of this statement is supported by an important part of modern medical practice—namely, the expectation that antemortem clinical diagnoses should correspond to, and when possible should be corroborated by, post-mortem pathological diagnoses.

Although it is usually assumed (especially by non-physicians) that medical diagnoses are made about living persons, this is a very incomplete view of the facts of medical life. The most accurate diagnoses are actually those made post-mortem—that is, after the patient dies and the pathologist examines his body. In modern hospitals, post-mortem diagnoses are widely used as a check on the accuracy of the so-called clinical diagnoses made on living patients and on the propriety of the treatments to which they have been subjected. Moreover, in legal or forensic medicine, where coroners are called upon to decide the cause of death in persons who have died violently or without being attended by a physician, the post-mortem diagnosis serves both to establish certain facts (about the dead body and what it reveals about how it became such) and to guide the behaviour of the authorities toward certain survivors (for example, whether to charge a suspect with murder or whether to accord survivors certain special death benefits).

The post-mortem diagnosis is thus both a description of a condition and a potential prescription for action; nevertheless, it is not simply or predominantly a strategic device. For example, when the body of a person who apparently had committed suicide by drowning is examined by a pathologist, the purpose of the examination is to determine what caused the person's death. Should the pathologist discover that not only is there no water in the cadaver's lungs, but that its trachea had been fractured, he will conclude that the dead person did not commit suicide but was killed by strangling. Although this diagnosis may lead to the indictment of a suspect for murder, the diagnosis itself—that is, the fractured trachea—is a descriptive finding. Although psychiatric diagnoses, too, may possess both a descriptive and a prescriptive aspect, the former element is often imaginary or fictitious, concealing the fact that the diagnosis has a purely prescriptive function. (The post-mortem psychiatric diagnosis of lunacy, to be discussed presently, constitutes a dramatic example of this fundamental role of psychiatric diagnosis.)

A perusal of psychiatric textbooks would give the reader the impression that mental illness terms or psychiatric diagnoses posses descriptive content much as bodily illness terms or medical diagnoses do. But this is not true. Admittedly, in so far as mental illness terms—for example, depression or paranoia—are used as the names of certain recurring patterns of personal behaviours, they belong, as I have already noted, in the same class as do terms describing recurring patterns of 'non-psychiatric' personal behaviours—such as sloppiness or punctuality. However, although I accept the validity of these terms in the sense mentioned above, I reject the contention that they are the names of diseases, similar to diabetes or cancer. Moreover—and it is important to keep this in mind in reading this essay—regardless of the value of the proper descriptive uses of mental illness terms, it is a subject with which I shall not be concerned here. Instead, I shall focus on the prescriptive or strategic uses of such terms.

I believe that dispensing (for the time being, at least) with the descriptive meanings of mental illness terms will help us to see some of the traditional confusions and controversies concerning psychiatry more clearly than we have previously been able. To begin with, this approach frees us from considering whether statements using mental illness terms are true or false. For example, the sentence 'Close the door!' cannot be said to be true or false. It is a command or injunction that expresses a desire and prescribes an action of which we may approve or disapprove, one which we may obey or disobey. Thus, when asked to close the door, we may say such things in reply as, 'Yes sir, right away'; or 'I understand you want the door closed, but I prefer that it stay open'; or 'If you want the door closed, you close it'; and so forth. Let me illustrate how these considerations help us to cut through some confusions concerning the use of mental illness terms.

Suppose someone says: 'Jones suffers from paranoid schizophrenia'. As a descriptive statement, we would either have to agree or disagree, and hence say something like, 'Yes, you are right, he does,' or 'No, you have made a mistake, he does not'. Both answers imply that paranoid schizophrenia exists, that Jones may or may not have it, and that although Jones may not have it, some other people do. What I shall try to do in this essay is shown that while the sentence 'Jones suffers from paranoid schizophrenia' is grammatically descriptive, rhetorically (actually or practically) it is prescriptive and means something like: 'Jones should be confined in a mental hospital; should be acquitted as insane of the crimes he has committed; should not be taken seriously for the views he holds', and so forth. Once the translation of 'mental illness' from description to prescription is accomplished, we are free of the obligation to accept or reject the assertion about what I regard to be a non-existent or metaphorical illness; at the same time, we are free to respond to the injunction, previously implicit but now rendered explicit, with a clear assertion of our own concerning the problem or situation at hand.

So we must come back to our starting point—to the fact that the central epistemological muddle of psychiatry derives from the semantic structure and syntactic use of the term 'mental illness' that make it appear as if this term referred to an abnormality, disorder, or illness similar to bodily disease such as cancer and heart disease. However, this is not so. The term 'mental illness' does not denote an objectively identifiable condition or phenomenon. So the question remains: What is it?

One answer is that 'mental illness' is an abstract noun designating a supposed mental condition or state. Thus, asking what mental illness is like asking what emotions, motives, and thoughts are. Every one of these terms refers to a construct we create to describe and explain how or why persons act or fail to act the way they do. This much is, indeed, obvious and usually uncontested. The next step I propose to take is less so.

Long before people used philosophical, psychological, and psychiatric constructs to explain human conduct, they used religious constructs. In particular, deities, both good and evil, were regarded as agents that not only acted *qua* themselves but that also caused human beings to act. Thus, there is an important similarity between terms such as 'God' and 'devil' on the one hand, and terms such as 'mental illness' and 'insanity' on the other: both sets of terms point to mental constructs with no identifiable, objective referents in the real world. More importantly still, both sets of terms are used not only to explain human acts but also to justify them.

In keeping with the principle that the meaning of a word, especially of an abstract noun, is best determined by inferring it from its actual use, I shall identify, by illustrative examples, the principal uses/meanings of mental illness. I have divided these uses/meanings into three categories: (1) mental illness as accusation or incrimination; (2) mental illness as excuse or exoneration; and (3) mental illness as denial of moral conflict and evasion of personal responsibility.

Mental illness as strategy

Why are dead people sometimes declared insane? What does it mean to make such a diagnosis? Is it similar to making a post-mortem medical diagnosis? If not, what does such a diagnosis accomplish?

Imitating doctors, traditional psychiatrists insist that posthumous psychiatric diagnoses are just as valid as posthumous medical diagnoses. The adepts at this arcane art even speak about 'psychiatric autopsies'. But producing metaphors proves nothing: calling one's beloved an angel falls short of proving that she is a divine creature.

The empirical rationale behind an autopsy is the fact that every dead person leaves behind a dead body (except where the body is destroyed in the process of death, as, for example, in a major explosion or fire). The dead body, called the cadaver, can be examined and tested by sophisticated methods, as a result of which it is usually possible to establish what diseases, if any, the person suffered from before he died and why he died. But what does a dead person leave behind on which a psychiatric autopsy could be based? If the person has committed suicide, he or she may leave behind a suicide note. Dead people also leave behind their work (including writings or other artistic productions, if they are artists) and the remarks of others about them. Obviously, these 'remains' have nothing in common with bodily remains. Moreover, the psychiatrist possesses no special methods (such as tissue staining, microscopy, chemical analysis, etc.) with which to examine these 'materials'. In short, the psychiatric autopsy is only a pretentious imitation of a real autopsy.

But if this is so, what purpose does it serve to make a psychiatric diagnosis of a dead person? The answer is that it serves strategic functions for those who make it and for those whom it affects, in ways I shall demonstrate in a moment. However, before presenting the prototype of this sort of use of mental illness terms, I want to remark briefly on the historical model for this practice—namely, the posthumous theological 'diagnosis' of a person as a saint. To the non-conformist observer, such a *posthumous elevation* of dead individuals does not prove that they were saints or that there exists a condition called 'sanctity' or 'sainthood' (except as an abstract noun or moral judgment in the mind of the diagnostician).[1] However, since now nearly everyone is a devout 'psychiatric conformist', nearly everyone accepts the practice of the *posthumous execration* of persons as insane and the validity of the proposition that there exists a condition called insanity (above and beyond its existence as an abstract noun or moral judgment in the mind of the diagnostician).

Although the debate about the sanctity of this or that dead person cannot help or harm that person, it can, and indeed does, help the Church and the faithful: the process of deliberating about the sainthood of a person and the act of declaring him or her a saint 'prove' that sainthood exists and that theological experts know how to recognize it. After the Church declares a person a saint, the theological 'diagnosis' serves to organize the behaviour of the faithful toward the image of that person as well as toward the ruling hierarchy of the priesthood. In short, the whole process serves to enhance the prestige and power of the institution enjoying ideological dominance—in this case, the Church.

We can now observe the same process unfolding in psychiatry. Although diagnosing dead people as insane cannot help or harm them, it can, and indeed does, help psychiatry, psychiatrists, and the true believers in this modern faith: the process of deliberating about the 'mental condition' of a dead person and the act of declaring him or her mentally ill "prove" to the psychiatrically enlightened that mental illness exists and that the psychiatric experts know how to recognize it. And after psychiatry declares a person insane, the psychiatric diagnosis serves to organize the behaviour of the members of society toward the image of that person, as well as toward the ruling hierarchy of the psychiatric priesthood. Finally, the whole process again serves to enhance the prestige and power of the institution enjoying ideological dominance—in this case, psychiatry. Here, briefly, is how the posthumous diagnosis of lunacy developed to serve this function.

From the fifteenth century onward, suicide was a felony in English law. It was punished as self-murder, by burying the deceased at the crossroads instead of in consecrated ground, and by confiscating his worldly goods and bestowing them on the sovereign. These punishments symbolized the gravity of the offence—a crime against God and Church (hence the religious penalty) as well as against king and country (hence the secular penalty). From the thirteenth century, English law also recognized the concept of lunacy as an excuse to crime, but this excuse was applied very infrequently to suicides (Fedden, 1938). For reasons that need not concern us here, in the early eighteenth century death from suicide became more common in London than it had been until then; at the same time, coroner's juries began to bring in more and more verdicts of lunacy. S. E. Sprott (1961), a student of suicide in England, describes this development as follows:

In the eighteenth century juries increasingly brought in findings of insanity *in order* to save the family from the consequences of a verdict of felony; the number of deaths recorded as "lunatic" grew startlingly in relation to the number recorded as self-murder, whereas in the previous century, according to a modern legal authority, ninety per cent of self-killers sat on by coroners' juries had been returned as having made away with themselves. *Devices* were employed to save or bestow the goods of the deceased, and by the 1760s confiscation of goods seems to have become rare. (Emphasis added.) (p. 112.)

Fifty years later English sentiment overwhelmingly favoured the view that 'Every human being must wish to soften the rigour of our law respecting suicide' (p. 158). But the law about suicide that was now disturbing the living was made by human beings and could have been modified or repealed by human beings. For example, suicide could have been declared a human right, an idea that is still a decidedly minority view. In fact, the law declaring the suicide's burial at the crossroads was repealed only in 1823, and that decreeing the confiscation of his property was repealed only in 1870. That these laws were not repealed earlier was due in large part to the fact that there was no need to do so since they could be readily circumvented by 'finding' that the persons who killed themselves did so while they were temporarily insane. Such a finding was, of course, purely strategic. To pretend otherwise, to believe that such a diagnosis of 'lunacy' tells us something about what the dead person in question was like when he was alive, would be like believing that a one way street sign tells us something about what the condition of the road-bed of the street is like. In actuality, what each of these signs does is to instruct us about how we ought to conduct ourselves—concerning burying the dead person in the one case, concerning traversing the road in the other. To put it differently, posthumous diagnoses of lunacy constituted a new set of rules, in effect repealing the old rules (the prevailing laws) concerning suicide; however, since this fact had to be concealed, the purely rule-making character of the diagnosis itself was also concealed. Of course, all this was quite obvious, as William Blackstone's (1755–65) following remarks illustrate:

The law of England wisely and religiously considers that no man has the power to destroy life, but by commission from God, the author of it; and as the suicide is guilty of a double offence, one spiritual, in evading the prerogative of the Almighty, and rushing into His immediate presence uncalled for, the other temporal, against the sovereign, who has an interest in the preservation of all his subjects, the law has therefore ranked this among the highest crimes, making it a peculiar species of felony committed on one's self (pp. 211–12).

Nevertheless, the fact is that while Blackstone was composing his immortal *Commentaries on the Laws of England*, those laws were already in the process of being subverted by the new science of psychiatry (or mad-doctoring, as it was then called). Noting that for any offence against the law to count as a crime, it is necessary that the person who commits it be 'in his senses', Blackstone added this prescient warning against the use of the concept of insanity as an excuse for crime:

But this excuse (of lunacy) ought not to be strained to the length to which our coroner's juries are apt to carry it, viz., that every act of suicide is an evidence of insanity; as if every man who acts contrary to reason had no reason at all; for the same argument would prove every other criminal *non compos*, as well as the self-murderer (p. 212).

While Blackstone here foresaw and forewarned against the infinitely elastic strategic use of the concept of insanity as an excuse for crime, it was precisely this function of insanity that has made the concept so useful to those bent on destroying the rule of law. Moreover, what Blackstone failed to foresee was that the concept of insanity could be used equally elastically and effectively to incriminate innocent individuals as 'sick' and to deprive them of dignity and liberty through psychiatric stigmatization and incarceration. To these uses of the concept of mental illness I shall now turn.

Mental illness as accusation of incrimination

Albert Schweitzer's doctoral dissertation, titled *A Psychiatric Study of Jesus* was actually nothing but a pretentious refutation of the diagnostic denigration of Jesus by contemporary psychiatrists. One of the experts Schweitzer cites declared that 'Everything that we know about him (Jesus) conforms so perfectly to the clinical picture of paranoia that it is hardly conceivable that people can even question the accuracy of the diagnosis' (p. 40). Another psychiatrist offered this diagnosis of the Christian man-God:

A hybrid, tainted from birth by heredity, who even in his early youth as a born degenerate attracted attention by an extremely exaggerated self-consciousness combined with high intelligence and a very slightly developed sense of family and sex. His self-consciousness slowly unfolded until it rose to a fixed delusional system, the peculiarities of which were determined by the intensive religious tendencies of the time and by his one-sided preoccupation with the writings of the Old Testament (p. 37).

In view of the fact that hundreds of millions of people regard Jesus as a divinity, the defamatory meaning and use of mental illness terms in these 'diagnoses' could hardly be more obvious.

Sigmund Freud, the founder of psychoanalysis and supposedly one of the great masters of the science of psychopathology, was exceedingly fond of this sort of use of psychiatric terms (Szasz, 1970). For example, he called Leonardo da Vinci a homosexual (Freud, 1909), and Woodrow Wilson a borderline psychotic (Freud, and Bullitt, 1967). Adler and Jung, first his colleagues and later his competitors, he called 'paranoid' and 'crazy' (Clark, 1980). Earnest Jones, Freud's official biographer, diagnosed two other pioneer psychoanalysts as mad: Otto Rank was 'psychotic' and Sandor Ferenczi had 'latent psychotic trends' (Jones, 1957).

The accusatory and incriminatory use/meaning of mental illness is equally obvious when the term is deployed in a military setting. In 1971, Jack Anderson reported the case of a young Navy officer whose complaint of chest pain was interpreted as malingering to avoid duty in Vietnam. At the famed Bethesda Naval Hospital, a psychiatrist diagnosed the officer as 'a sociopath, a condition often identified with criminal tendencies, and consigned him to a restrictive psychiatric ward'. Facing a dishonorable discharge, the officer retained a civilian lawyer who successfully fought the order while a civilian doctor diagnosed the patient as suffering from a duodenal ulcer.

Psychopathological labels are often used to demean individuals who hold religious or political views different from those of the diagnostician. The diagnosis also serves to disqualify the labelled person's beliefs from deserving respect. For example, in 1980, Egyptian President Anwar Sadat was quoted as asserting that the Lybian leader, Muammad Gadaffi, 'suffers from schizophrenia'. Said Sadat: 'It was while speaking with Gadaffi that I noticed that he had a split personality. He found it very difficult to hide his second personality'.

In nineteenth-century Germany, when many Jews regarded assimilation through conversion to Christianity not only possible but desirable, a Jewish leader asserted that 'a Jew who preferred a non-existent state and nation (Israel) to Germany ought to be put under police protection not because his views were dangerous but because he was obviously insane' (Clemons, 1972). But as times change, so do psychopathological fashions. In 1972, a group of Jewish-American psychiatrists writing in the *American Journal of Psychiatry* expressed the opposite view, declaring that 'Formal religious conversion out of the Jewish community into another religious community occurs relatively infrequently nowadays in the absence of gross psychopathology' (Ostow, *et al.*, 1972).

As the climate of opinion changes and as people want to praise or blame different sorts of conduct, psychopathological labels get attached to a wide variety of behaviours—and get detached from others, for example, homosexuality. Thus, certain patterns of human behaviour that, until recently, were considered to be socially acceptable, are now considered to be the manifestations of mental diseases. For example, in 1975, at the 52nd annual meeting of the American Orthopsychiatric Association, a leading black psychiatrist declared that: 'Until we see racism as a mental illness, we will continue to treat the victims rather than the carriers'. At the same meeting, the Committee on Minority Group Children told a press conference that 'Racism is the number one public health problem' and that 'Racism is probably the only contagious mental disease' (Herndon, 1975).

Another new mental illness is homophobia. Its discovery can be traced directly to the American Psychiatric Association's decision, in 1973, to delete homosexuality from its official roster of mental diseases. In 1978, in a letter to the editor of *The New York Times*, the co-executive directors of the National Gay Task Force reminded readers of the *Times* of the APA's action and added: 'Mental health professionals, however, have identified a condition known as homophobia, which is defined as irrational fear and hatred of homosexuals and homosexuality' (O'Leary and Voeller, 1978). According to the author of a recent, much-praised book on how to raise children, 'homophobia, not homosexuality, is the disease of our times' (Pogrebin, 1981).

In the mid-1970s, we witnessed a similar reversal of the traditional diagnostic judgment concerning smoking. Long a favourite activity of psychiatrists, smoking was now added to the list of mental diseases. A report articulating this view, appearing in *The New York Times* in 1975, informed the reader that 'A psychiatrist who is a leading expert on drug addiction has suggested that heavy cigarette smokers have all the behavioral traits of drug abusers and has urged that people who smoke a pack a day or more should be described as suffering from a "compulsive smoking disorder"' (Brody, 1975).

Here too, the strategic nature of the use of mental illness labels is perfectly clear. The psychiatrist quoted in this article was Jerome Jaffe, the chief drug abuse bureaucrat in the Nixon Administration. Jaffe supported his proposal to call smokers mentally ill with this revealing argument: 'After all, you don't see television performers or other celebrities publicly boozing it up or shooting heroin'. That is certainly true. But would it not be more honest for Jaffe and like-minded psychiatrists to say that they disapprove of smoking, or that smoking causes (bodily) diseases, instead of asserting that they are describing a (new, mental) disease? Although it was evident that Jaffe was here using the mental illness label as a strategic device and not as the name of a disease, the illusion that mental diseases so generated are nevertheless real 'entities' is steadily gaining ground. Indeed, official psychiatry does not merely deny that calling smoking an illness is a *lie*, it actually affirms it as a *truth*: One of the mental diseases listed in the American Psychiatric Association's (1980) new roster of such diseases is 'tobacco dependence'.

But these are only some of the more trivial instances of the accusatory use of the term 'mental illness'. The most important such use of mental illness terms occurs in the context of commitment, the diagnosis being regarded as a justification for depriving the sick person of his liberty. Descriptions of the psychoses in psychiatric textbooks abound with examples, as the following cases, from *Noyes' Modern Clinical Psychiatry*, illustrate (Kolb, 1968).

The first story begins with this sentence: 'P. G. was committed to a hospital for mental disease because of his peculiar religious ideas and rites, one of them being the practice of going about nude' (p. 407). Looked at non-psychiatrically, this sentence makes hardly any sense at all. In the first place, every religious idea is peculiar to those who do not believe it and who do not believe in the broader religious mythology from which it issues. Furthermore, in so-called free societies, holding 'peculiar religious ideas' is considered to be an essential aspect of individual and political freedom. Lastly, the meaning of 'going about nude' depends on the context: in one's own home, it is a right; in a public place, it is a crime. Thus, from the very first sentence of this case history, we are confronted with a psychiatric account that purports to describe an illness that a so-called patient has (psychosis), while it actually covertly justifies an act in which a psychiatrist engages (commitment).

The rest of the story is an account of what psychiatrists regard as the typical case history of paranoia. I shall cite only the more relevant parts of it:

Prior to his marriage at age 26 he had paid little attention to persons of the opposite sex. At that age he married his landlady, a woman of 66, "as a humane act"; this was his characterization of the match when he entered the hospital. When questioned concerning his sex life, he stated that men had aroused him sexually more than women, for whom he had no sexual desire (p. 407).

In accordance with the standard psychiatric scenario, the author here established a putative linkage between (repressed) homosexuality and paranoia, as if that proved that paranoia was a disease with a known aetiology. Revealingly, nothing in this long case history is said about the patient's occupation or work record. Instead much is made of the patient's 'peculiar' religious ideas. We also get a glimpse at the collusion between the patient and his psychiatrists concerning the commitment:

About this time (when he was 40 years old) he began to go to isolated spots and to walk about nude, explaining that he was taking "sun baths". Gradually he made fewer attempts to retire from sight when taking his "sun bath" ... Finally after having been warned on repeated occasions by the local constable that he must not continue his exhibitionistic practices, the patient was committed to a hospital for mental disorders (p. 408).

The method in this madness is obvious enough: the patient wanted free room and board and went about obtaining those goods and services in the manner prescribed for doing so in his society. To show that this pattern is typical rather than isolated, I shall cite two more case histories from this textbook, illustrating the same sort of collusion between psychotic and psychiatrist culminating in commitment.

The patient, 'A. R.'—diagnosed as suffering from simple schizophrenia—was a poor student and then a poor worker. At age 19 he gave up his job as a machine operator in a factory and showed no further interest in securing employment. When asked if he worked, he replied, 'What do I want to work for? I have a father and sister working and they are enough'. He appeared quite self-satisfied and felt that he should have a position of importance (p. 376).

At this point in his life, A. R. was arrested for peeping into women's bedrooms. 'Through the influence of his father . . . the charge was dropped . . . A year later he was again arrested but again was released on the intercession of his father' (p. 376). Since these strategies failed to achieve what seemed to be their intended effect, the patient escalated his symptoms:

He came to say little unless addressed and grew antagonistic toward his father and sister. He would remain out until midnight and then come home, eat a large meal, read until 2 a.m. and sleep until noon. Finally, after his third arrest for peeping, he was committed to a hospital for mental disorders (p. 376).

Lawrence C. Kolb, the author of the text, comments: 'Such a case illustrates how an individual is unable to complete the transition from adolescence to maturity with its adult heterosexual and social adjustments' (p. 376). That may or may not be true. Kolb does not know (nor do I) whether this man was unable or unwilling to make this transition. In any case, why regard him as suffering from an illness and why commit him to a mental hospital? I maintain that the imagery of illness-and-helplessness attached to such an individual, and the imagery of hospital-and-treatment attached to the institution in which he is confined, function as justifications for this particular (psychiatric) method of handling 'the problem'. To be sure, in this sort of case, the 'patient' himself incriminates himself as a mental patient. After he does so long enough and persistently enough, his self-incrimination is given official sanction: he is diagnosed as suffering from schizophrenia and is committed.

The case history Kolb offers as typical of catatonic schizophrenia exhibits the same pattern. This patient, 'A. C.', married when he was twenty and stopped working when he was 24. We are not told who supported him after that. What we are told is this:

Two months before commitment the patient began to talk about how he had failed, had "spoiled" his whole life, that it was now "too late".·One night his wife was awakened by his talking. He told her of having several visions but refused to describe them. He stated that someone was after him and trying to blame him for the death of a certain man. He had been poisoned, he said. . . . He had periods of laughing and shouting and became so noisy and unmanageable that it was necessary to commit him (pp. 379–380).

Again, the pattern seems clear enough. The patient produces 'symptoms' which have the effect of coercing those about him to take care of him.[2] Sooner or later, psychiatrists are called upon to produce a 'diagnosis' of 'mental illness' which has the effect of counter-coercing the patient into commitment.

In the context of civil commitment mental illness terms are used to justify depriving persons of their liberty. In the context of certain criminal trials they are used to justify depriving persons of their lives. According to Texas law, persons convicted of capital crimes may be sentenced either to life imprisonment or to death, depending on the juries' opinion about 'the guilty man's inclinations to commit crimes in the future'. Since 1967, a Texas psychiatrist named James Grigson testified in no less than 70 such proceedings. In every one of them he testified under oath that in his professional opinion the defendant was a 'sociopath' who was and will remain dangerous to society. In every case but one the jury unanimously voted for the death penalty. In 1981, this use of psychiatric testimony came under the scrutiny of the Supreme Court of the United States. Its decision concerning this practice highlights once more the strategic use of mental illness terms, illustrating at the same time the persistent denial of this fact (Barbash, 1981).

A Texan named Ernest Smith was convicted of taking part in robbing a grocery store during which his accomplice killed a clerk. A judge asked Grigson to see Smith in jail to determine if he was competent to stand trial. The psychiatrist said he was. After a jury found Smith guilty, but before he was sentenced, Grigson testified in court, as required by law in capital cases, and told the jury that Smith was a 'severe sociopath' who showed no remorse for his crime and would always be a threat to society. The jury sentenced him to death. The death sentence was overturned by the Supreme Court. Chief Justice Warren Burger (1981) found the procedure unconstitutional because 'no one warned the defendant that whatever he told Grigson (the psychiatrist) during their 90-minute talk could be used to sentence him to death', and because he was not allowed to consult a lawyer beforehand. Said Burger, 'Just as the Fifth Amendment prevents a criminal defendant from being made the "deluded instrument of his own conviction", it protects him as well from being the "deluded instrument of his own execution"'.

The Supreme Court here rejected the practice of using psychiatric self-incrimination to justify a death sentence. However, the procedure used to bring about civil commitment is exactly the same, the two practices differing only in their aims and consequences. Without psychiatric testimony Texas courts could not send felons to the death chamber. *Mutatis mutandis*, without such testimony courts throughout the country could not send 'patients' to mental hospitals. As I pointed out some time ago (Szasz, 1963), if suspected mental patients were given the same protections against self-incrimination that convicted criminals are, the practice of civil commitment—the very pivot of psychiatry—would come to a grinding halt. It is ironic, indeed, that the Supreme Court protects a convicted murderer from being the 'deluded instrument of his own execution', but does not protect an innocent citizen from being the 'deluded instrument of his own commitment'.

Mental illness as excuse or exoneration

For obvious reasons, mental illness terms are used to excuse or exculpate only in situations where a person has committed an illegal act or is accused of having committed such an act. People do not plead insanity for engaging in legal acts or meritorious deeds.

Before it was fashionable to plead insanity, it was customary to plead demonic possession. Indeed, the psychiatric practices I shall be surveying in this section rest squarely on the graves in which the practices based on appeals to demonic possession are buried. From time to time, some of the remains buried there are exhumed and enjoy a brief reincarnation, as the following stories illustrate.

In 1974, a 47-year-old Phoenix (Arizona) man 'rammed his car into the front door of St Francis Xavier Catholic Church, then ran up the aisle and began destroying altar pieces'. It took eight parishioners to restrain him. The police took him to the local psychiatric hospital where 'he told the officers: "I was possessed by the devil and he made me do it"' ('The devil...', 1974).

The same claim was made recently by a young man in Connecticut charged with murder. His claim was supported not only by his relatives and friends but by his attorney as well. On February 16, 1981, Arne Cheyenne Johnson got into an argument with Alan Bono and stabbed him to death. The case, according to the *New York Times*, involved 'a family that seems utterly convinced of the Devil's presence in their house and a defense attorney who intends to force evidence of that influence onto the court (Clendinen, 1981). 'The courts have dealt with the existence of God", says Martin Minella, the attorney. "Now they're going to have to deal with the existence of the Devil"'. Johnson's girlfriend, Deborah Glatzel, has told the lawyer and the reporters that her brother had been possessed by the Devil and that he had said that 'he had seen the beast (devil) go into Cheyenne's body and it was the beast who had committed the crime'. The reporter for the *Times* notes that this case arises at a time when there is a growing belief in the country in religion and the paranormal and cites a 'national Gallup Poll taken 15 months ago for the journal *Christianity Today* (which) showed that 34 per cent of adults believe that 'the Devil is a personal being who directs evil forces and influences people to do wrong"'.

Of course, the more sophisticated about us no longer believe that the Devil makes people do wrong things; they know that it is mental illness that does it. In 1980, Michael Tindall, who had served as a helicopter pilot in Vietnam, was charged with taking part in smuggling hashish from Morocco to Gloucester (Mass.). He insisted that he did it 'because of a need to relive the excitement he experienced in combat', and that this need was a symptom of his illness, the

'Vietnam Syndrome' ('Vietnam syndrome...', 1980). In September, 1980, a Federal Court jury in Boston acquitted Tindall of the charges against him. 'It was', reported a combined AP-UPI dispatch about the verdict, 'the first time the Vietnam Syndrome—an emotional malady recognized by the American Psychiatric Association and the Veterans' Administration as post-traumatic stress—had been used successfully as a defense in connection with a pre-meditated crime'.

In 1973, Abbie Hoffman, who became famous as the leader of the so-called Yippies in the 1960s, was arrested in New York City for selling three pounds of cocaine to undercover agents. He skipped bail and went underground. In 1980, he surfaced, and after plea bargaining, pleaded guilty to a charge of third-degree criminal sale of a dangerous narcotic. Without plea bargaining, Hoffman would have faced charges that could have brought him a prison term of 15 years to life. With a new face (he had undergone plastic surgery) and a new girlfriend (he had divorced his wife), Hoffman seemed ready to cash in on his fame and to enjoy life as a celebrity. 'When he emerged from six and half years of hiding last September', commented *Time* magazine (April 20, 1981, p. 106), Hoffman expected that no-one would seriously want to lock him up for selling $36 000 worth of cocaine and then jumping bail. In court last week he admitted the sale but called it 'an act of insanity'. In short, Hoffman did not admit that he broke the law, but attributed his violation of the drug laws to a presumably isolated act of insanity. I say presumably isolated, because he did not attribute his other acts—such as his work 'for the environment', of which he was inordinately proud—to insanity. Surprised at being sentenced to jail, Hoffman continued to try to con the public, and perhaps himself, with new psychiatric tricks. Although he had never been in the armed services, he announced that he 'suffers from 'post-Vietnam syndrome'—a manic-depressive condition he said was induced by his antiwar activities'.... Hoffman, who is taking a tranquillizer daily, said, I fought the war just as hard as any of those veterans' (Hoffman, 1981).

Many diagnoses of mental illness are just as ludicrous as those Abbie Hoffman has offered on his own behalf, but with this difference: they are put forward and are supported by respected psychiatrists. The psychiatric testimony offered in the trial of Dan White is a case in point (Szasz, 1981).

In November, 1978, Dan White, a former San Francisco policeman, killed San Francisco Mayor George Moscone with four shots, and City Supervisor Harvey Milk with five shots. He fired two shots into the heads of each of his victims at point-blank range, execution-style. Charged with two counts of first degree murder, he pleaded 'diminished responsibility' to both counts. Several psychiatrists testified in support of the contention that White was mentally ill and hence 'had diminished responsibility'. One of the experts for the defence, Dr Martin Blinder, diagnosed White's condition as 'a manic-depressive syndrome dating back to adolescence', the symptoms of which 'were escalated by an exclusive diet of junk food—Twinkies, cupcakes, and Cokes...' (Blinder, 1979). The jury bought what the press called the 'Twinkie defence', and found White guilty only of manslaughter. When White entered the California prison system, the psychiatrists and psychologists who examined him declared that White 'has no apparent symptoms of mental disorder' and did not need psychiatric care (Workman, 1979).

Actually, every case in which a law-breaker is declared to be not guilty by reason of insanity and is then treated as a mental patient illustrates the mechanism of using the idea of mental illness as an excuse. There is a continuous stream of such cases reported in the press.

In July, 1980, Anthony Baekland—whose great-grandfather had developed one of the first plastics and patented it under the name 'Bakelite'—returned to New York from England, after having spent seven years in a British mental hospital for stabbing his mother to death. Six days later he was charged with trying to stab to death his 87-year-old grandmother. 'A police spokesman said Mr Baekland had "readily admitted" the stabbing. . . . 'Again, Mr Baekland was 'remanded for psychiatric examination' ('Ex-patient. . .', 1980).

In October, 1980, an Oakland (Michigan) Circuit Judge found a 70-year-old woman innocent by reason of insanity in the shooting death of a fellow churchgoer. The bare facts in this case were that on July 29, 1979, Mrs Verdia Lee Billings arrived late for church services in the New Hope Missionary Baptist Church in Pontiac, Michigan. On arriving, Mrs Billings took a pew in front of Mrs Roger Mae Wiley, whereupon 'Mrs Wiley stood up, pulled a revolver from her purse, and fired twice into the woman's back'. Mrs Billings fell dead. Mrs Wiley was examined by psychiatrists who told the judge that she suffered from a 'psychosis' manifested by the 'delusion that younger members of the church's nursing unit were seeking to replace elder members' (McClear, 1980).

Enough said. As in every case where the issue is commitment, mental illness terms are used to incriminate or inculpate, so in every case where the issue is the insanity defence, mental illness terms are used to excuse or exonerate. Moreover, not only are these two patterns of use reciprocal and symmetrical, they are also, in a sense, identical: for in every case where a person is committed, his psychiatric inculpation excuses him of certain basic, albeit marginal social rule-violations, and in every case where a person is excused by reason of insanity, his psychiatric exculpation incriminates him as mentally ill.

Mental illness as denial of moral conflict and evasion of personal responsibility

The acts of accusing and excusing, inculpating and exculpating involve, as a rule, clear-cut issues and situations in which individuals are blamed or forgiven. But in certain situations involving moral conflicts and questions of personal responsibility, the lines between good and evil, right and wrong, legal and illegal are not so neatly drawn. In these situations, too, mental illness terms may be used strategically—to obscure guilt, to resolve ambivalence, to bring about a result ustified by compassion, and so forth. Long before the days of modern psychiatry, Shakespeare had laid bare this tactical use of the idea of madness.

Aided and abetted by his wife, Macbeth murders his way to the pinnacle of political power. His victory is spoiled, however: Lady Macbeth starts to hallucinate blood on her hands, is tormented by anguish, cannot rest or sleep. Her husband concludes that she is sick and sends for a doctor. But the doctor wants none of it. He tells Macbeth that his wife is 'Not so sick, my lord / As she is troubled with thick-coming fancies, / That keep her from her rest'.

Macbeth is not satisfied. He presses the doctor with these immortal lines: 'Cure her of that: / Canst thou not minister to a mind disease'd, / Pluck from the memory a rooted sorrow, / Raze out the written troubles of the brain, / and with some sweet oblivious antidote / Cleanse the stuff'd bosom of that perilous stuff / Which weights upon her heart?' The doctor, however, recognizes that what ails his 'patient' is not a disease and cannot be cured by pills. His famous answer is: Therein the patient/Must minister to himself' (Act V, Scene 3). Lady Macbeth is not sick. She is guilty of the wrongs she has done. Her husband knows this but does not want to know it, does not want to admit it. The modern psychiatrist and the modern popular mind accept and legitimize precisely that intellectual and moral evasion which the doctor in *Macbeth* repudiates.

One of the crassest examples of the use of mental illness terms to obscure moral conflicts and avoid political decision-making occurs in the relationship between psychiatrists and pregnant women. Since time immemorial, some pregnant women (and their husbands or lovers) have sought abortions. Until recently, performing abortions was medically unsafe as well as legally prohibited. In the post-Second World War years, it became fashionable, in the United States as well as elsewhere, to allow pregnant women to have therapeutic abortions based not only on objectively verifiable medical criteria, such as severe renal disease with hypertension, but also on subjective and unverifiable psychiatric criteria, that is, the existence of mental illness. For example, in 1968 a new abortion law was enacted in California permitting therapeutic abortions on mental health grounds. During the first six months of that year, almost 2000 women were found to require therapeutic abortions 'to safeguard their mental health', while only 55 abortions were done to safeguard the women's physical health. By the time the first nine months of 1968 elapsed, 5000 therapeutic abortions were done in California, virtually all of them for psychiatric reasons. In the 1970s, when abortion was legalized, the psychiatric disabilities so common to pregnant women disappeared just as suddenly as they had appeared two decades earlier (Szasz, 1970).

Thus, whenever and wherever abortion on demand is illegal but psychiatric therapeutic abortion is legal, the psychiatrist becomes a bootlegger of abortion. In this respect, the psychiatrist who 'prescribes' abortions follows in the footsteps of the physician who, during Prohibition, 'prescribed' liquor.) In

Switzerland, for example, abortion on demand is still prohibited, while abortion justified on psychiatric grounds is popular.

Another area in which mental illness terms are used to obscure moral conflict and evade personal responsibility is the area of so-called drug abuse. The use of illegal psychoactive substances is now widespread, in the United States as well as in the rest of the Western world. Although it is obvious that no-one is compelled to take these substances and that, therefore, in the final analysis, people take drugs because they want to take them; and although it is also obvious that beyond this simple fact, there are countless complex cultural, religious, and legal reasons for the so-called drug problem—it is now fashionable to attribute the problem to the 'drug-abusing' persons' mental illnesses. In addition to thus blaming the problem on mental illness, it is also fashionable to blame the drug itself and those who make it available—both the 'dope' and the 'pusher' being viewed as 'seducers' who 'infect' the innocent individuals who then succumb to the 'mental illness' called 'addiction' (Szasz, 1974).

The evasions implicit in this imagery were dramatized in late 1980, when New York State Governor Hugh Carey attributed an epidemic of gold-chain snatching in New York City to a 'Russian design to wreck America by flooding the nation with deadly heroin'. Explained Carey (1980): 'In the streets, you know what's going on. Women are afraid to walk with a chain around their neck. Why? Somebody's grabbing that chain to get enough money for a fix.... If the Russians were using nerve gas on us we'd certainly call out the troops. This is more insidious than nerve gas. Nerve gas passes off. This doesn't. It kills. I'm not overstating the case'.

As these examples illustrate, and as all history teaches us, there is no foolishness too great for people to advance, and to accept, so long as it serves their interests. Among these foolishnesses, the idea of mental illness now ranks near the top.

Summary

I have advanced the thesis that it is senseless to debate what 'mental illness' is or means without identifying and recognizing the precise situation in which the term is used. Although mental illness terms seem to refer to conditions or phenomena, on the model of medical diseases, like injuries of infections—in the main, they refer to strategies or tactics, on the model of moral or legal claims, like accusations or excuses. In actual practice, mental illness terms are used to harm as well as to help people, to inculpate them and to exculpate them, to make them feel guilty and to protect them from feeling guilty. Psychiatric concepts and terms have come into being and remain viable not because they are true but because they are useful. In this essay I have tried to show how they are useful.

I realize, of course, that although what I have presented may be quite persuasive, it may suffer from a fatal flaw: it is too obvious. The strategic meaning/function of mental illness terms is, indeed, so obvious that it is perhaps of no use to demonstrate it: everyone knows it already, as the following pathetic story—condensed and quoted from a judicial decision rendered in the Criminal Court of New York City on January 27, 1981—illustrates.

On New Year's Eve, 1980, Anthony Spagna, an 80-year-old man living in a cold-water tenement on the Lower East Side, was arrested by the police. At the time of his arrest, the first in his life, Mr Spagna lived totally alone and forgotten, his last remaining relatives and friends having died five years ago. The arrest came about when, with the temperature having plunged to record lows, unable to obtain any heat, and having nowhere to turn, Mr Spagna lit a small fire on the bare floor of his room. He was huddled in bed shivering when taken into custody. Unable to find other shelter for him, the police took him to Bellevue Hospital. But the hospital did no want him. It was at this point that the court fell back on the strategic use of psychiatric illness terms and on the procedures they justify. What is particularly interesting about this case is, of course, not that a court employed this device, which courts frequently employ, but that it did so with a good deal of pride and self-righteousness. In its opinion, rendered by Judge Stanley Gartenstein, the court declared:

Because of the intransigence of a system which must bend the individual to its peculiarities on the one hand, and its inadequacy of facilities on the other hand, the only *instrumentality whereby Mr. Spagna could be somewhat assured of a safe place to stay temporarily was an order*... remanding him for mental examination to determine competency... Cognizant that the State of New York has not seen fit to acknowledge the existence of this human being on the one hand, or, on the other to guarantee his safety, we, prosecutor, defense counsel and the court, have fully shared in the complicity of creating this *device* to save his life. We have done so openly and with pride... (emphasis added; *People* v. *Spagna*, 1981).

Judge Gartenstein did not order—and would not have dreamed of ordering—Mr Spagna to have a barium enema, in order to house him on a medical ward; or a cystoscopy, in order to house him on a urology ward; or a brain scan, in order to house him on a neurological ward. Had the judge dreamed of such a thing and tried to realize it, it is he, not Mr Spagna, who would have ended up in the mental hospital. But Judge Gartenstein did order Mr Spagna to have a 'mental examination', in order to house him on a psychiatric ward.

Notes

1. This is true, however, only for the non-conformist observer. Persons who believe in saints are convinced that the abstract noun 'sanctity' refers to a demonstrable condition, just as they are convinced of the truth of other religious propositions. For example, the coffin of Bernadette Soubirou, the saint of Lourdes (who died in 1893), was opened three times to examine the body for signs of putrefaction, its absence being regarded by the

church as an indication of sanctity. For true believers in Roman Catholicism, the demonstration of a miracle thus constitutes proof of the existence of sanctity, obscuring the fact that calling a person a saint is a figure of speech. Similarly, for true believers in psychiatry, the demonstration of the miraculous cures of mental patients with chemicals now constitute proofs of the existence of mental illnesses, obscuring the fact that calling a person mentally ill is also a figure of speech (Szasz, 1961, 1977).

2. Psychiatrists are fond of debating whether persons—especially so-called mental patients—do what they do consciously or unconsciously. They have even convinced many contemporary philosophers and legal scholars that consciousness and unconsciousness are objectively discoverable attributes of motives much as, say, cancerousness and non-cancerousness are attributes of cells. That idea is also false. Indeed, it too derives its strength from successfully concealing practical strategic consequences behind putative descriptive conditions. Unless the boundaries and implications of distinguishing between conscious or unconscious motives are carefully drawn and strictly limited, I consider the debate to be ill-conceived and prefer not to be drawn into it.

References

American Psychiatric Association (1980). *Diagnostic and Statistical Manual of Mental Disorders (DSM-III)*, Third Ed., American Psychiatric Association, Washington, D. C., pp. 176–178.

Anderson, J. (1971). Disliked officer labeled 'sociopath'. *Syracuse Post-Standard*, January 5, 1971, p. 4.

Barbash, F. (1981). Court rules defendant may bar psychiatric exam in capital case, *The Washington Post*, May 19, 1981 p. A–9.

Blackstone, W. (1755–65). *Commentaries on the Laws of England: Of Public Wrongs*, Beacon Press (1962), Boston.

Blinder, M. (1979). Quoted in Jennigs, D., Jury told of turmoil within White, *San Francisco Chronicle*, May 7, 1979, p. 1.

Brody, J. (1975). Heavy smoking called a disorder, *The New York Times*, June 5, 1975, p. 38.

Burger, W. (1981). Quoted in Miranda: Out of the doghouse, *Time*, June 1, 1981, p. 64.

Carey, H. (1980). Quoted in Greenspan, A., Gold-chain grabbers? Carey blames Soviet heroin-war strategy, *New York Post*, September 26, 1980, p. 10.

Clark, R. W. (1980). *Freud, The Man and the Cause*, Cape and Weidenfeld and Nicolson, London.

Clemons, W. (1972). Quoted in The Promise and the Land, Review of *A History of Zionism*, by Walter Lacqueur, *Newsweek*, October 16, 1972, p. 64.

Clendinen, D. (1981). Defendant in a murder trial puts the devil on trial, *The New York Times*, March 23, 1981, pp. B-1 and B-6.

Ex-patient is held in 2d stabbing, *The New York Times*, July 29, 1980, p. B-4.

Fedden, H. R. (1938). *Suicide: A Social and Historical Study*, Peter Davies, London.

Freud, S. (1909). Leonardo da Vinci and a memory of his childhood. In *The Standard Edition of the Complete Psychological Works of Sigmund Freud*, vol. XI, pp. 57–137. Hogarth Press, London, (1957).

Freud, S., and Bullitt, W. C. (1967). *Thomas Woodrow Wilson: A Psychological Study*. Houghton Mifflin, Cambridge, Mass.

Herndon, A. (1975). Racism said to be America's chief mental health problem, *Psychiatric News*, April 16, 1975, p. 25.

Hoffman, A. (1981). Quoted in Hoffman to ask Carey for pardon, *Syracuse Post-Standard*, April 9, 1981, p. A-5.

Jones, E. (1957). *The Life and Work of Sigmund Freud*, Basic Books, New York, Vol. III, pp. 45–46, 73–74, 174.

Kolb, L. C. (1968). *Noyes' Modern Clinical Psychiatry*, Seventh Edition, Saunders, Philadelphia.

Marnham, P. (1981). *Lourdes: A Modern Pilgrimage*, Coward, McCann & Geoghegan, New York.

McClear, J. (1980). Insanity led to killing in church, judge rules, *Detroit News*, October 16, 1980, p. 4.

O'Leary, J., and Voeller, B. (1978). 'Homophobes.' (Letter to the Editor), *The New York Times*, November 29, 1978, p. 14.

Ostow, M., Blumental, M. J., Arlow, J. A., and Neubauer, P. B. (1972). The Jewishness of Jewish young people, *American Journal of Psychiatry*, **129**, 553–561, p. 555

Peirce, C. S. (1878). *Values in a Universe of Chance: Selected Writings of Charles Saunders Peirce, 1839–1914*, ed. by P. P. Weimer, P. 123. Doubleday Anchor, Garden City, N. Y.

People v. *Spagna* (1981). 108 Misc. 2d 1 (Courts of the State of New York), January 27, 1981.

Pogrebin, L. C. (1981). *Growing Up Free*, McGraw-Hill, New York, p. 288.

Sadat, A. (1980). Quoted in Gadaffi 'schizophrenic', *The Press* (Christchurch, New Zealand), June 10, 1980, p. 4.

Sprott, S. E. (1961). *The English Debate on Suicide: From Donne to Hume*, Open Court, LaSalle, Illinois.

Szasz, T. S. (1961). *The Myth of Mental Illness*, Harper and Row, New York.

Szasz, T. S. (1963). *Law, Liberty, and Psychiatry*. Macmillan, New York.

Szasz, T. S. (1970). *Ideology and Insanity*, Doubleday, Garden City, New York.

Szasz, T. S. (1974). *Ceremonial Chemistry*, Doubleday, Garden City, New York.

Szasz, T. S. (1977). *The Theology of Medicine*, Harper and Row, New York.

Szasz, T. S. (1981). The political use of psychiatry in the United States: The case of Dan White, *American Journal of Forensic Psychiatry*, **2**, pp. 1–11.

'The devil made him do it', *Syracuse Herald Journal*, April 29, 1974, p. 1.

'Vietnam syndrome frees vet', *Detroit News*, September 21, 1980, pp. 1-A and 3-A.

Workman, B. (1979). Dan White isn't getting mental treatment in jail, *San Francisco Chronicle*, May 24, 1979, p. 4.

Mental Illness: Changes and Trends
Edited by Philip Bean
© 1983 John Wiley & Sons Ltd.

CHAPTER 6

Mental health, mental disease, mental illness: 'the medical model'

ANTONY FLEW
Professor of Philosophy,
University of Reading

> *The mentally ill, far from being guilty persons who merit punishment,*
> *are sick people whose miserable state deserves all the consideration*
> *due to suffering humanity.*
>
> Philippe Pinel (1745–1826)

I An engagement with a Reith lecturer

1   In the version printed by *The Listener* on 6 November 1980 Ian Kennedy begins the first of his 1980 Reith Lectures with a satisfactorily arresting paragraph: 'Six years ago the American Psychiatric Association took a vote and decided homosexuality was not an illness. So, since 1974, it hasn't been an illness. How extraordinary, you may think, to decide what an illness is, by taking a vote. What exactly is going on here?' (p. 600).

It is a good question, and equally good whether the 'here' is construed as referring to these Reith Lectures or to those proceedings of the American Psychiatric Association (APA). In the former understanding Kennedy's answer is immediate and explicit: 'I've set as my task the unmasking of medicine.' And, although his nerve then weakens a little with the disclaimer that 'It isn't that I think there's something sinister behind the mask', the second paragraph still concludes: 'The first step on the way to understanding modern medicine, looking behind the mask, is to unravel the rhetoric of medicine' (p. 600).

In the latter understanding Kennedy's answer is implicit first in his second sentence: 'So, since 1974, it hasn't been an illness.' For this comment shows that he is taking that conference resolution as a piece of pure legislation, an authoritative decision laying down what the law is to be. Certainly this must have been at least part of the story. For, just as the general American Medical Association (AMA) publishes its *Standard Nomenclature of Diseases and Operations*, so the APA too maintains a more particular *Diagnostic and Statistical Manual of Mental Disorder*. One intended consequence, therefore, of

115

the conference resolution must have been corresponding deletions from future editions of that handbook. Nevertheless another and larger part of the story has to have been belated public recognition that homosexuality as such is not, and never was, a kind of illness; an illness, that is, on all fours with pneumonia, yellow fever, or leprosy. In this aspect the APA decision becomes like that of a Debates Union resolving 'That there is no God'; rather than like that of a legislature passing a law criminalizing, or decriminalizing, some class of actions. And, of course, it is this recognition resolution which is needed to provide, and which does in fact provide, the rationale required for the operational decision to revise the *Diagnostic Manual*; and the practice based thereon.

2   Kennedy now sets himself 'to unravel the rhetoric of medicine'. It is, as soon appears, a task for which his defective conceptual equipment is quite insufficient. He starts by assuming that those plain persons his listeners will insist that '"Illness" . . . is a technical term, a term of scientific exactitude. Whether someone has an illness, is ill, is a matter of objective fact' (p. 600). Certainly, whether someone feels ill, is suffering some pain, or has been in any way incapacitated, is indeed 'a matter of objective fact'. But, equally certainly none of the words employed in the previous sentence, nor the terms 'illness' and even 'disease', are in their primary and original usages technical. I need no expert to tell me that I feel terrible, that I have a splitting headache, and that when I try to get up and walk I collapse into a helpless heap on the floor. By contrast, I do need a doctor: first, to diagnose to which of all the various syndromes distinguished and labelled by medical researchers my condition of ill-ness is to be attributed; and, second, to prescribe a treatment enabling me to escape disease and to get back to health.

3   Accepting his own false suggestion that all the key words here are technical, Kennedy next considers what he characterizes as 'the strangely disquieting insight that illness involves not merely the existence of certain facts; it involves a judgement on those facts'. In his usage, which happens to be flat contrary to that of an earlier generation of philosophers, judging is a matter of deciding, not what the facts are, but what is to be done. Thus he continues: 'And it is doctors who do the judging. A choice exists whether to categorize particular circumstances as amounting to an illness. Power is vested in the doctor, and the power is not insignificant . . . medical practice is, above all, a political enterprise, one in which judgments about people are made.

   It becomes important, then, to discover whether there are boundaries to this word, this concept "illness". Can it be applied willy-nilly on the say-so of the doctor, or are there limits to his power? (p. 600). To determine this Kennedy begins by citing some conditions about which there is unanimous agreement—leprosy, cancer, appendicitis: 'We all agree that these are illnesses, because we accept two propositions. The first is that there is a normal state in which the appendix is not inflamed, and breathing is easy while resting. Secondly, it is appropriate to judge someone who deviates from this norm as ill.'

We have to examine the two explicit assumptions in turn: 'Take the first...
This seems simple enough. It isn't of course. For a start, it's *only* our convention
to call such deviations illness. Others in other cultures may view such conditions
entirely differently' (p. 600: italics supplied). It is one mark of the defective
conceptual equipment aforementioned that Kennedy—along with, I fear, two or
three other recent Reith Lecturers—never thinks to question two further,
unstated assumptions. He does not, that is, doubt: either, first, that we may
validly deduce the absence of objective knowledge from the subsistence of
disagreement and from nothing else besides; or, second, that, from premises
asserting only that something is in some group a matter of accepted convention, a
similarly compulsive argument goes straight through to the conclusion that that
is *only*, that that is *merely*, that that is *nothing but*, the (arbitrary) convention of
that group. (Compare and contrast, for instance, Flew, 1976, Chapters 2–3, and
Flew, 1975, *passim*.)

However, 'in our society', Kennedy continues, 'we cleave to science and the
scientific principle of a demonstrable state of normality and a causative agent
which brings about an abnormality... What is the state we should regard as
normal?' Here he does indicate what is, I shall be contending, the correct answer:
'We think in terms of a machine which has a design, which is the norm, and which
malfunctions when it does not perform according to the design'. Indeed we do.
For, although most of us have come to believe that no organism ever was in fact
designed, that all—like Topsy—'just growed'; still every biologist since the
Founding Father Aristotle has had to insist that organisms, and perhaps still
more the parts of organisms, must be thought of in a teleological way. The
challenge facing evolutionists has always been to explain how such overwhelming observed appearances of design could possibly have come about if not
through the actual operation of intention and intelligence. (For an account of
Darwin's contribution, and its true originality, see Flew, 1978, Chapter 1.)

There are, as Kennedy sees it, two shortcomings in any such biological ideal of
the normal: 'One weakness is that it is crude. We like to think of ourselves as
more than machines. We have emotions, moods, and feelings which affect our
physical states. A further weakness is that we may not all agree on the design, the
blueprint, against which to measure our performance or our state' (p. 600).
Under the first head it has at once to be admitted that those various psychological
attributes and potentialities which distinguish rational animals from the brutes
may give rise to special, possibly even insuperable, difficulties. We might, that is
to say, find that an account of (physical) health developed on these lines could not
be satisfactorily transposed to cover its supposed analogue, mental health.

Under the second head it must first be said again that the (alleged)
impossibility of achieving unanimous assent constitutes no kind of refutation.
Fresh interest and instruction are to be found in Kennedy's illustration: 'For
example, women have the capacity to bear children. In the old days, it was
considered part of the design for women that they bore children. A woman who

did not bear children departed from this design . . . you'll recall that Julius Caesar urged his wife to touch Antony so as to be cured of her barrenness' (p. 600). The crucial distinction, here characteristically and ruinously collapsed, is, in Aristotelian terms, that between potentiality and actuality. Applied particularly it is the distinction between simply being capable of bearing children and actually bearing them: the Caesar of history would not have attributed either a disease or any other sort of physical disorder to a Vestal Virgin who had in fact remained, as she was most imperatively bound to remain, a virgin and childless; while Calpurnia's trouble was that—her own longings and all her husband's no doubt strenuously faithful services notwithstanding—she had succeeded neither in conceiving nor in bringing forth. It is the physical condition resulting in this abnormal incapacity which, both today and 'In the old days', has to be scored either as a disease or an illness or as some other defection from perfect health and fitness. (Incidentally, I trust that no one would push forward to remedy that particular condition, if this is its only consequence, unless requested so to do by the patient herself.)

The final adversative clause in the last sentence of the previous paragraph should suggest, what will be argued more fully later, that, if we are going to define both health and the various kinds of defection from it along the lines suggested by Kennedy, then we shall have to dig a deep divide. It will run: between, on the one hand, terms of this present semi-technical and properly value-neutral sort; and, on the other hand, various everyday words in their ordinary usages. These everyday words carry the implication that the conditions to which they are applied are at least presumptively bad for and/or unwelcome to their patients—hence anyone relieving those conditions will typically be both serving the interests and observing the wishes of these patients.

The best programme so far proposed for making and maintaining such a chasm is to be found in an article 'On the Distinction between Disease and Illness' (Boorse, 1975). 'It is disease, the theoretical concept' Boorse writes, 'that applies indifferently to organisms of all species . . . it is to be analyzed in biological rather than ethical terms. The point is that illnesses are merely a subclass of diseases, namely those diseases that have certain normative features . . . An illness must be, first, a reasonably *serious* disease with incapacitating effects that make it undesirable . . . Secondly, to call a disease an illness is to view its owner as deserving special treatment and diminished moral accountability' (p. 56: italics original).

Boorse writes as if he were doing no more than explicate a distinction already embodied in established usage. In the title of the present paper, for instance, we have: not 'a Distinction'; but 'the Distinction'. Certainly, it requires no praeternaturally sensitive ear to insist that the syndromes distinguished and labelled by medical researchers should be rated diseases rather than illnesses, and to refuse to tolerate the describing of so very tolerable an affliction as athlete's foot as an illness. No doubt Boorse is also right in his claim that medical extbooks count every kind of physiological disorder as a disease; that they nclude among the diseased both the victims of gunshot wounds and persons orn blind as well as the syphilitc. But that, as he himself appreciates, is not lay isage. More seriously, even the professionals appear inclined to construe the erms 'health', 'disease' and 'disorder' as all essentially prescriptive. Again, 3oorse himself notes and protests this fact: 'With few exceptions, clinicians and ihilosophers are agreed that health is an essentially evaluative notion. According o this consensus view, a value-free science of health is impossible' (Boorse, 1975,). 50).

I therefore suggest that he is being rather too modest, that the truth is that he is ecommending a highly desirable measure of conceptual reform; and, further-nore, that this is a measure possessing the great practical political merit of going vith rather than against the grain of our linguistic habits.

4 In the paragraph following next after the one which ended with the misinterpreted reference to *Julius Caesar*, Kennedy draws his moral: 'The point s clear. What is the normal state against which to measure abnormality is a product of social and cultural values and expectations. It is not some static objectively identifiable fact . . . So, if illness has as its first criterion some deviation from the norm, some abnormality, it too will vary and change in its meaning' (p. 600).

Certainly, if the criteria for the application of some term are changed, then its meaning must alter correspondingly. But the crucial and crucially disputations contention here, surely, reformulated in Boorse's clearer and more incisive words, is that health and disease are essentially evaluative notions, 'that a value-free science of health is impossible'. It is important to realize that this contention is false, that there can be and are non-prescriptive theoretical ideals. Consider, for example, the status of the First Law of Motion in classical mechanics or of the Principle of Population in the theoretical scheme of Thomas Robert Malthus (Flew, 1978, Chapter 2). Both lay down ideal norms, all deviations from which have to be explained: explained by reference to 'impressed forces' in the former case; and in the latter by the operation of various 'positive and preventive checks'. But no one (one hopes) is rooting: either for the removal of all impressing forces; or for the liquidation of all checks on population growth.

It is in the same way possible to develop a completely detached, objective, non-prescriptive ideal norm of health; an ideal norm defined in terms of the fulfilling of the functions which organs and organisms appear to have, yet have not, been designed to fulfil. And, whatever may be the truth about even professional usage in a human context, these in fact are the concepts already applied to the brutes. No one is so free from the taint of speciesism that they would either intend or interpret the 'Diseased' label under a specimen of *drosophila melanogaster* to imply an imperative need for treatment and cure.

As examples of diagnoses supposedly varying with variations in the socially accepted ideal norm of health Kennedy cites 'some of those accused of witchcraft by Cotton Mather in 17th-century Massachussetts'. Forgetting—as so many do—how the evidence against these unfortunates was fabricated, Kennedy takes it for granted that they must all have had something in common; in addition, that is, to their defining collective characteristic of having been successfully charged with the (surely impossible) offence of witchcraft. Indeed he takes it for granted that there must actually have been something wrong with the lot of them. They would, he goes on, 'probably now be described as epileptics, or as suffering from Huntington's chorea, and seen as ill and certainly not as evil' (p. 600).

Running through these and other examples Kennedy detects 'the theme of responsibility'. He continues: 'As our views of each person's power to exercise dominion over his life changes, so will our concept of the borders between illness and evil. For evil is seen as a product of someone's choice, and thus something he may be held responsible for. Illness, by contrast, is something which overtakes him; and, once ill, he is absolved from the ordinary responsibilities of everyday life' (p. 600).

In welcoming the second two of these three propositions as both basic and substantially true we may be distracted to overlook the falsity of the first. (By the way: the third requires some amendment; to allow for the fact that illness absolves and excuses only and precisely to the extent that it incapacitates or handicaps. It is not the case that just any illness properly provides total absolution. This is something which people are perhaps more apt to forget in talking of mental than of physical illness.)

The reason why the first of these three propositions is false is that Kennedy is collapsing the distinction between connotation and denotation. What may change with changing beliefs about the extent of our capacities is the accepted denotation rather than the connotation of the key words. The fact that some people are discovered to have been incapacitated, in some dimension in which it was previously believed that they were not, is a reason, though not by itself a sufficient reason, for conceding that they were patients of some illness. But that same fact is no reason at all, not even an insufficient reason, for introducing some fresh sense or fresh criteria for the terms 'health' and 'illness'. So we shall, or we should, shift the frontier between the populations labelled 'the ill' and 'the healthy' in step with our discoveries about peoples' capacities and incapacities. Yet in doing this we shall not, most emphatically, be changing the membership qualifications for these two expanding and contracting clubs.

5   From all this Kennedy infers: that 'illness, a central concept of medicine, . . . is a matter of social and political judgment' (pp. 600–1); or, in what he appears to read as an alternative and equivalent formulation, 'that illness is an indeterminate concept, the product of social political and moral values which, as we have seen, fluctuate' (p. 601). The implications of this, we are assured, will strike us immediately: 'If "illness" is a judgment, the practice of medicine can be

understood in terms of power. He who makes the judgment wields the power' (p. 601).

That final statement just quoted might be unexceptionable, if only Kennedy were not so inclined to assume that the truth of such—shall we say?—sociological remarks must exclude that of all other kinds. In this he keeps bad company with all those fashionable 'sociologists of knowledge' who mistake it that their deliberately misnamed discipline is always and necessarily discrediting. The surely inescapable consequence would be that no belief falling within their compass can truly constitute an item of knowledge. Hence, since the compass now claimed is universal, it becomes a presupposition of the 'sociology of knowledge' that there neither are nor could be any beliefs truly deserving the diploma title 'knowledge'—with the implicit and radically inconsistent sole exception of those which are the outcome of the 'negotiated understandings' of the sociologists themselves (Flew, 1976, Chapter 2). But, of course, the expression of a medical judgment can perfectly well be, at one and the same time: both an assertion of some objective scientific truth; and part of an exercise of a life or death therapeutic power. Take, for example, the utterance, in some context which would guarantee their truth, of the arresting words: 'If we do not operate at once, the patient will be dead before dusk!'

The same failure to appreciate that two not necessarily exclusive descriptions may both be applicable simultaneously is found again in Kennedy's treatment of Smith's alleged malingering: 'Or the doctor may say, "There's nothing the matter with you, Smith." His notes may read: "Another malingerer!" It involves a judgment that Smith ought to be working and that the doctor is not going to aid him in avoiding this responsibility. Another doctor could just as well decide otherwise' (p. 601).

At this point we have a use for the distinction between the different locutionary and illocutionary forces of one and the same utterance, or speech-act (Austin, 1962). Roughly speaking: the former is what is said; while the latter is what is done by saying it. It was this distinction—or rather, this was one of the distinctions—which John Rex collapsed into a screaming chaos of confusion when, with reference to an Aunt Sally psychometrician, he wrote: 'What he does when he rates individuals or groups of individuals on a scale of measured intelligence is to say and to predict that one group of individuals rather than another should have privileges. It is of little use, therefore, that a writer like Eysenck should protest that there is a total disjunction between his scientific observations and his moral views. Scientific observations have political implications...' (Richardson and Spears, 1972, pp. 168–9).

Suppose someone says: 'This person has an IQ of 140 on the Binet scale'. Then, what and all that they are maintaining, the entire locutionary force of their words, is the proposition thus conventionally expressed. By itself, as Eysenck was so right to say, this carries no prescriptive implications. However, when that same proposition is uttered in some suitable context, the actual uttering of it may have the illocutionary force of recommending the allocation of a privilege; or, for that matter, of a handicap (Flew, 1976, pp. 67–70). For us the moral of this is that Kennedy has no business to infer: from the premise that a doctor's uttering, in such and such a context, the proposition 'Smith is malingering', has this or that illocutionary force; to the conclusion that that, and that alone, is also the locutionary force of that uttering.

Not only is this inference invalid. Its conclusion is also false. 'What sort of term is "malingering"?', Kennedy asks. His reply is: 'It involves a judgment that Smith ought to be working... Another doctor could just as well decide otherwise.' More than enough has been said to demonstrate that Kennedy interprets this as implying that the proposition 'Smith is malingering' is what he would call a judgment; and nothing else whatsoever but. This bold thesis is, nevertheless, quite grotesquely wrong. For to malinger precisely is to try to escape uncongenial tasks by pretending to be, in some relevant way, incapacitated. So, whatever else a doctor may be either saying or suggesting or doing when he says that someone is malingering, he most certainly is saying, whether honestly or dishonestly, whether truly or falsely, whether with or without warrant, that that person is not in fact, as she or he pretends to be, incapacitated. And that is a plain, or sometimes a not so plain, matter of neutrally descriptive fact.

6 Having satisfied himself that assertions of the presence or absence of illness are nothing but value judgments, and that they do not even in part characterize the condition of the patient, Kennedy seeks a fresh stamping ground: 'So far I have concentrated on the term illness. Let me now consider the concept of health. "Health", if it is to have any useful meaning, must refer to more than the mere absence of illness. It must have a positive quality. It must refer to all those factors which combine to represent man's aspirations and expectations... This is captured in the World Health Organization's definition of health as "not the mere absence of disease, but total physical, mental and social well-being"' (p. 602).

Kennedy's proposal is burdened by two fundamental faults. In the first place, there is no justification for the initial assumption that any useful and important notion must be essentially positive; notwithstanding that this seductive assumption was once harboured by Immanuel Kant. 'The above definition of freedom is *negative*,' Kant wrote of one disfavoured candidate, 'and consequently unfruitful as a way of grasping its essence...' (Paton, 1948, p. 114: italics original). The truth is—and both freedom and health provide illuminating illustrative instances—that often it is the ostensibly negative notion which 'wears the trousers'; that 'commonly enough the "negative" (looking) word marks the (positive) abnormality, while the "positive" word, *if* it exists, merely serves to rule out the suggestion of that abnormality' (Austin, 1961, p. 140: italics original; and compare Flew, 1973, pp. 45–51).

In the second place, it is preposterous to follow the World Health Organization in so redefining 'health' that the word becomes synonymous with the expression 'the supreme good for man'. Since health has been traditionally and, surely, correctly acknowledged to be one, albeit only one, main element in that supreme good, this silly manoeuvre must leave all its executants looking for some raw new verbal recruit to undertake the job performed previously, to everyone's complete satisfaction, by the old-time hooray word 'health'.

Neither of these two objections occurs to Kennedy. Instead he notices that many doctors are among those who join in ridiculing such over-ambitious and all-embracing definitions. They object on the grounds that the scope of their own qualifications is limited: 'We can't do anything about these things. We've got enough on our hands dealing with the illnesses about us.' (p. 602).

In view of all that Kennedy has already had to say about the alleged irrelevance of what we might uninstructedly have dignified with the title 'medical science', it is scarcely surprising that this modest professional objection leaves him unmoved. However—after concluding that, as just now redefined, 'health is far too important to be left entirely to doctors'—he proceeds to distinguish disease from illness on lines similar to those indicated in our Section 3, above.

Of course Kennedy does not really believe: either that there is no such thing as medical science; or that, whether or not there is, it is irrelevant to the diagnosis of disease and the treatment of illness. Or, at any rate, he does not believe either of these nonsenses consistently and all the time. His trouble, and ours, is that, having grasped or half-grasped a few sociological and philosophical insights, he has succumbed to the very usual temptation to apply newly acquired notions where there is no purchase for this application. Confusion is then worse confounded by his seeming inability to entertain the possibility that something might be either both this and that, or else in part this and in part that: that a single speech-act, for instance, might be both an exercise of power and an assertion of scientific fact; or that the meaning of a statement might be both in part neutrally descriptive and in part engaged prescriptive. The upshot is that Kennedy becomes committed to making and defending claims which he too finds, in his rather infrequent cooler moments, altogether unbelievable.

II Mental illness and the medical model

1 In the whole length of Part I there has been precious little direct mention of anything mental, as opposed to physical. Yet nothing said there is irrelevant to the announced subject of the present paper. It is significant that the example from which Kennedy began, as well as others cited later, are instances of disputatious conditions which, if they are to be described in a medical vocabulary, will have to be characterized as defections from *mental* health; *mental* diseases, that is, or *mental* illnesses, or, most generally, *mental* disorders. Indeed there is much internal evidence suggesting that Kennedy has swallowed the thesis of *The Myth*

of Mental Illness whole, and then generalized it to include the physical also (Szasz, 1961).

Much more important is the fact that my entire paper is intended as a defence of what has come to be called, usually with a slight sniff, the medical model. The nub of this matter, happily epitomized in my masthead motto from Philippe Pinel, is that our paradigms are and must be (physical) health, (physical) disease, and (physical) illness. It is and can be only and precisely in so far as there are some crucial similarities between conditions typically so described and other conditions, that those other conditions may properly and ingenuously be labelled either mental health or mental disease. An examination of the physical paradigms, and some sorting out of the commonest confusions surrounding them, is not, therefore, irrelevant. On the contrary, it is essential to the main business in hand.

I said that I propose to defend the medical model, so interpreted. But there will be nothing defensive about this defence. Quite the reverse. For it is, and should upon all hands be seen to be, a scandal that there are nowadays many persons enjoying the high status and high salaries normally and rightly accorded to qualified and practising doctors who, sometimes somewhat superciliously at that, repudiate the very idea that there actually are mental illnesses; which it is their professional duty to treat and, hopefully, to cure. Maybe there are not; and the great Pinel and all his successors were, or are, mistaken. Certainly these despisers of the medical model are among those who are in the best position to know whether or not that is so. But if it is, and there are indeed no mental illnesses, then the true moral is that both the APA and its several sister societies must go forthwith into an honourable, voluntary liquidation. It will not do, notwithstanding that it is—they tell me—rather widely done, to continue to luxuriate in the high status and high salaries aforementioned while in return practising what is thus brazenly confessed to be a kind of not-medicine directed at not-illnesses. Such persons need to be reminded that, in earlier and in this respect better days, it used to be customary for those who lost their faith to relinquish Holy Orders.

I have spoken carefully if strongly of 'the medical model, so interpreted'. The point is that several of those writing about, and against, what they have called the medical model have in fact directed their attacks at something else; though frequently believing that those attacks also disposed of the pretended priority of the physical paradigm. One patient defender lists five such attacking theses, all entirely different from and independent of one another, and none constituting a head-on challenge to the fundamental here propounded (Boorse, 1976, p. 62n; and compare Macklin, 1973, *passim*).

Another remarkable source and instance of confusion is to specify what is to be defended as 'the medical model' in a vocabulary far removed from traditionally Hippocratic concerns. It has, for example, been said to involve three things: first, 'that there is an underlying *cause* and consequently maladaptive behaviours cannot be treated directly because they are products of these causes. Second, changed behaviour is not really important unless the "real" trouble has been dealt with . . . Third, the distinction between what the subject does, his behaviour, and what the clinician expects, or knows to be there, is blurred, and failure to find the expected cause merely confirms the severity of the problem' (Ullman and Krasner, 1965, p. 5: italics original). In a later volume of *Case Studies in Behaviour Modification* the same authors define 'maladaptive behaviour'. It is 'behaviour that is considered inappropriate by those key people in a person's life who control reinforcers' (Ullman and Krasner, 1966, p. 20). But if this is what these Erewhonian 'straighteners' are proposing to 'cure' then it is not illness, which is primarily a problem for the sick person. They are instead proposing to 'cure' deviant conduct; which is a problem, where it is a problem at all, only for those shadowy and slightly sinister key figures 'who control reinforcers' (Flew, 1973; and compare Flew, 1978 Chapter 7).

It is, indeed, radically misguided to introduce the term 'behaviour' into the present context. For this introduction overrides and obscures two distinctions which are fundamental, respectively, to medicine in general and to psychological medicine in particular; that between what is or is not conduct, subject to the will; and that between those 'behaviours' which are and those which are not conventionally meaningful speech-acts.

Fortunately there is no call now to push any further in explorations of such fully realized possibilities of confusion and cross-purposes. Sufficient to reiterate the fundamental principle: that it is and can be only and precisely in so far as there are crucial similarities between central and typical cases of (physical) health, (physical) disease, or (physical) illness, on the one hand, and, on the other, certain other conditions, that we shall be able ingenuously and straightforwardly to describe those other conditions as *mental* health, *mental* disease, or *mental* illness. 'For the philosopher', the Marquis de Vauvenargues once remarked, 'clarity is a matter of good faith.' He might have added to that excellent maxim, 'and for everyone else as well'.

2 Developing suggestions put earlier, I propose now to distinguish two interpretations of the word 'health'; interpretations corresponding to the distinction between disease and illness (I3, above). One is (to be) neutral and detached, and negatively defined in terms of the absence of diseases; and also—in so far as these are distinguished from diseases—of wounds, congenital defects, and other similar disorders. The other is the everyday sense, again defined negatively; but this time in terms of the absence of illness, and of other such disorderly conditions understood as presumptively bad for the patients themselves. (By the way: the adverb 'presumptively' is inserted, as it was once before, in order to take care of awkward cases of persons whose illnesses are welcome to

them because they provide a let out. We do not want to have to say that severe asthma, for instance, whenever it ensures exemption for unpatriotic draftees, is not an illness.)

The main thing to emphasize about this proposal is that it opens up possibilities of incongruity: defections from health in the first and scientifically neutral understanding will not always and necessarily be congruous with defections from health in a lay understanding; nor yet the other way about. We have already offered illustrations of trivial diseases which do not make their patients ill. It is also at least conceptually possible that someone could feel very ill indeed, and be in some drastic way incapacitated, without there being any independently detectable physiological disorder to which this illness could be attributed. The first important practical consequence of this possibility of incongruity is that we shall need to be on guard against moves to treat and to 'cure' conditions which are unhealthy in the first sense, but not in the second, the layperson's; and, of course, the other way about.

Next we have to notice that in both senses of 'healthy' the healthy may be statistically quite abnormal. This truth is, when we are thinking about illness, sufficiently obvious. But it is perhaps not quite so obvious that it is possible to construct a conception of an ideal specimen on the basis of a study of actual specimens all of which may be in fact quite lamentably imperfect. A good proof-example, albeit of an artefact rather than an organism, is provided by the Norden bombsight. Apparently German technical intelligence in World War Two, working with nothing but shattered specimens extracted from crashed American bombers, succeeded in reconstructing the design, complete down to the last detail.

One might well be too embarrassed to insist upon points so simple and so luminous as those made in this Section 2 were it not for the fact that they are, even by people who ought to know better, especially in the context of the mental, constantly neglected. For example: this neglect is systematic in an otherwise most painstaking, conscientious study of a subject which surely above all others demands the hammering reiteration of such distinctions. Nowhere in *Russia's Political Hospitals* is there any sustained attempt to spell out the criteria for either mental disease or mental illness; and nowhere is there any explicit statement of the difference between statistical normality, which is indeed socially relative, and the other sort, which is not (Block and Reddaway, 1978; the most relevant passages are on pp. 23–7, 62, 67, 160, 165–6, and 248–55).

3   Again developing suggestions put earlier (I3 and 4, above), I propose that we should in its purely scientific understanding construe the term 'health' by reference to the functions which the organism or its organs look as if they had been designed to fulfil. This is no arbitrary proposal. For the Compact Edition of the *Oxford English Dictionary* gives the definition: 'Soundness of body; that condition in which its functions are duly and efficiently discharged.' Disease in

the relevant sense is, correspondingly, 'A condition of the body, or of some part or organ of the body, in which its functions are disturbed or deranged; a morbid physical condition; a departure from the state of health especially when caused by a structural change.' (Let us, instead of being petulant about the circularity introduced with the word 'morbid', simply notice, without further comment, that this dictionary definition embraces wounds and those other disorders which laypersons would not ordinarily call diseases.)

The key concept is that of function, and what we have to attend to is not actuality but potentiality. The tongue of a Trappist is not diseased merely because during a penitential fast it is employed neither in tasting nor talking. My rose bushes are not diseased simply because they are not taking in water which is not there. It will be time to begin asking questions about disease if when the Trappist eventually tries to exercise his tongue he finds that he cannot, and if when the bushes are inundated by a cloudburst still no water enters the system.

Another far more important point comes out when those two examples are compared further. In so far as both show that what matters here is potentiality rather than actuality, they are the same. But in other respects they are crucially different. Suppose that water is supplied to my rose bushes, and that none is then absorbed. That will constitute a sufficient reason for inferring that there must be something organically wrong, although what is organically wrong will not necessarily be a disease. Contrast with this the case of the fasting Trappist. He is a person and not a plant. So the fact that he does not eat when food is provided is no more sufficient to show that there is something organically wrong than is the fact that he refrains from making passes at pretty girls. In his case, but not in the case of the plants, there is room for questions about what he can do if he wants and what he could do if he tried. Indeed it is essential to the description of this particular example that there actually is a gap between what he is doing and what he could be doing if he chose. For anyone who suggests that a dumb eunuch is fitted for a Trappist vocation is altogether failing to grasp what monasticism is about.

The fundamental reality giving purchase to such questions is universally familiar and altogether inescapable. Yet it is a reality which professing social and psychological scientists are often in the last degree reluctant to admit. The truth is that we all are as rational animals creatures which can, and cannot but, make choices (Flew, 1978). The theoretical and practical implications of this ineluctable reality are not only of enormous human interest but also, and in consequence, intensely controversial. So I will try first simply to point to the facts without employing any theoretically loaded terms. The facts are: that in the happy bloom of health our bodies are partly, although always only partly, subject to our wills; and that there is a categorical difference between the claim that I moved my arm (without recourse to any extra-bodily apparatus) and the claim that my arm moved (without my moving it). Let us, in order to save words later, and in prudence following the grain of long-established verbal habits, distinguish movements of the former kind as movings, while reserving the word 'motions' for movements of the second kind. Non-movings and non-motions will, of course, in both kinds constitute the limiting or special case: remaining stock still is, for present purposes, just as much a form of action as leaping to your feet.

Once this difference between movings and motions has been pointed out, with every care to eschew premature theoretical commitment, then it becomes altogether obvious and undeniable that we are all most immediately acquainted with innumerable specimens of both kinds. It is just not on to attempt to conceal the subsistence of a difference: between, on the one hand, the case of—say—my liver, which however hard I try I cannot move at all except by shifting my whole torso; and, on the other hand, my hands, which I can move about whenever and however the fancy takes me. Nor is it possible to pretend that we are not forever, throughout all our waking hours, confronted with alternative possibilities of moving: when we are moving ourselves or any part of ourselves in one way, then we always could have moved ourselves or that part of ourselves in some other way; when we are contemplating any such moving, then there always is and has to be at least one alternative—if not another moving then simply not moving.

If the unreality of choice, as thus ostensibly defined and most directly and certainly known, really were a presupposition of the possibility of any psychological or sociological science, then the implication emerges totally clear: there could and can be no scientific psychology, no scientific sociology. No wonder that so many psychopersons and sociopersons, convinced that this presupposition does indeed obtain, will say or do almost anything in order to hush-up or to divert attention from the most central peculiarity of the nature of man! (I offer the shamefully trendy coinages 'psychoperson' and 'socioperson' to satisfy two long felt wants: a single word embracing practitioners of all the would be scientific psychological disciplines—psychology, psychoanalysis, psychiatry, and so on; and another similar single word embracing practitioners of all the aspiring social sciences—sociology, social anthropology, demography, and so on.)

I shall find occasion later to pay brief attention to one or two of the commonest misconceptions encouraging the belief that psychological and sociological enquiry shows this most manifest fact of our nature not to be a fact at all. But it has to be said at once that the fundamental distinctions just now drawn are not to be disposed of by objecting that there are marginal cases, which do not fit easily into either of two mutually exclusive categories; or that the differences pointed are to be discounted as mere differences of degree. Such objections can be, indeed are, made against almost every distinction of human concern. They should be dismissed. No doubt there are marginal cases. But, so long as the decisive majority is not marginal, we can and must insist on the difference between those which are centrally and paradigmatically of one kind and those which are, equally centrally and paradigmatically, of the other kind. Nor is it right to sneer at all differences of degree as *mere* differences of degree. The difference between this and that is, for present purposes, a difference of degree if and only if there is a spectrum of actual or possible cases shading by almost imperceptible steps from this to that. Are we therefore to disrespect as *merely* matters of degree the differences between sanity and insanity, age and youth, or riches and poverty (Flew, 1975, Sections 7.13ff)?

Suppose then that we take it as given that there is such a thing as being able to move or not to move at will; and that, in a most fundamental sense just now ostensibly explained, every agent could have done other than they did or did not do. How does this bear upon issues of the nature of health, construed as a theoretical ideal? In this way: to say that disease in a person is 'A condition of the body, or of some part or organ of the body, in which its functions are disturbed or deranged' is to provoke the question whether these functions do or do not include, besides mere motions, some movings or abstentions from movings.

The response to this gets us to the heart of the matter. For the concept of capability, of what we can or cannot do if we try, is central to the notion of (physical) health—at least in its primary application to human beings. For a man to be fit is not for him to do, but only to be able to do, whatever it is which he is fit to do. Certainly, to be fit to do what a sick or otherwise unfit man cannot do, does in fact always require the actual or potential proper functioning of organs which never are subject to the will. Nevertheless the criterion of the fit man's fitness is: not the propriety of these actual or hypothetical motions; but rather his capacities for not necessarily proper movings and not movings. So, if a definition of 'disease' in terms of the disturbance or derangement of functions is to be retained, we shall have to take it that the function of whatever is normally subject to our wills precisely is to be in this normal way thus subject; while at least the prime function of those organs not subject to our wills must be, correspondingly, to ensure the continuing efficiency and due subordination of those organs which are normally so subordinate. Death, as the end of all fitness for anything, is the ultimate limiting case of total malfunctioning.

In this perspective it becomes obvious that and why we cannot go on to apply the same idea to the whole organism; insisting, with Aristotle, that we too, like the organs of which we are composed, must have a function (*Nicomachean Ethics*, I(vii) 11–16: 1097 b29–1098 a20). More to the present point is the curious and piquant corollary that it must be egregiously grotesque for any doctors to allow themselves to be seduced by suggestions that there are no such things as choices or real alternatives. For, if that were so, then there could be no such things as either (human) health or (human) disease: 'Othello's occupation's gone'.

4   The question now arises how health, disease, and disorder—in these theoretical and purely scientific understandings—relate to health, illness, and other conditions construed as being of necessity either presumptively good or

presumptively bad for the persons so endowed or so afflicted. When and why do defections from health, in that first understanding, constitute suitable cases for treatment?

In an introduction to the *Principles of Morals and Legislation* Jeremy Bentham wrote: 'Health is the absence of disease, and consequently of all those kinds of pain which are among the symptoms of disease. A man may be said to be in a state of health when he is not conscious of any uneasy sensations, the primary seat of which can be anywhere in his body' (VI7). It was characteristic of Bentham, yet it is wrong, to present 'uneasy sensations' as the heart of the matter. For it is entirely possible to suffer an illness, even a fatal illness, without feeling (seriously) ill. Happily, this seems to have been the case with David Hume's terminal condition—'a wasting disease of the bowels'. One hopes that, with the help of modern techniques of anaesthesia and sedation, the same is becoming true of more and more actual illnesses. Certainly it is usual for patients of an illness to feel ill, especially if that illness is allowed to take its course; and certainly that is presumptively bad for them. Nevertheless the crux remains, surely, not pain but incapacitation?

The reason why medical treatment is desirable is at the same time the reason why it is necessary. For, although patients might have been able to avoid getting into their present conditions, those conditions themselves are conditions of incapacitation; and, as such, are precisely not of a kind which their patients are able to escape immediately, unaided, of their own volition. This again—though the point seems to elude many psychiatrists called to give expert testimony (Fingarette, 1972, pp. 97–120)—is the reason why so many jurisdictions now rule that no one is to be held criminally responsible for any behaviour, or for any failure to act, which is the inevitable result of some disease.

5   Much of what has been, and is, put down as some sort of defection from mental health does not satisfy this essential condition (Flew, 1973). But it is perverse to take this as a proof that there is no viable concept of mental health. Yet exactly that is done in a much reprinted and much respected work on *Social Science and Social Pathology*: 'For . . . the psychopath makes nonsense of every attempt to distinguish the sick from the healthy delinquent by the presence or absence of a psychiatric syndrome, or by symptoms of mental disorder which are independent of his objectionable behaviour. In his case no such symptoms can be diagnosed because it is just the absence of them which causes him to be classed as psychopathic. He is in fact, *par excellence*, and without shame or qualification, the model of the circular process by which mental abnormality is inferred from anti-social behaviour while anti-social behaviour is explained by mental abnormality' (Wootton, 1967, p. 250).

Yes, indeed: the astringent conclusions of the second two sentences are as sound as they are characteristic of their authoress. Yet they constitute no warrant whatsoever for the first statement. Certainly, where there neither is nor is going to be any incapacitation there can be no ill-health, whether physical or mental. So what really follows is that the correct next question for her, accepting that such psychopaths are not in fact sick, becomes this: whether they should, after all, be punished as mainline criminals; or whether they should be treated as if they were patients of some illness dangerous to others; or whether they should be handled in some new third way yet to be constructed. For us it is whether there is room anywhere for a kind of sickness to be distinguished as mental.

There have been, I suggest, various legitimate concepts here, at least two of which can find proper application. Their differences are determined by differences in the interpretation of the distinguishing adjective. Plato, who was the first major figure to develop a notion of psychological health, construed the key Greek word *psyche* as referring to a sort of incorporeal substance; taking all the behaviour which distinguishes men as rational agents as the manifesting work of these themselves unobservable entities—which are, he thought, what men ultimately and essentially are. This provided, at any rate in theory, a satisfyingly clear-cut principle for separating the sphere of psychological from that of physical medicine (Flew, 1973, I8). However, though much loose talk about the putative activities and interactions of the Unconscious and the Preconscious and the Conscious, of the Ego and the Id and the Superego, does encourage interpretation along such Platonic lines, it is at least doubtful whether any contemporary psychiatrists—with the possible exceptions of some Roman Catholics and Catholicizing Jungians—really intend their theoretical notions to be read in so substantial a way.

Turning quickly from Plato to the modern period, we find mental disorder generally understood as an affliction of the intellect. Thus Philippe Pinel, who did so much to have the demented cared for as the victims of a kind of sickness, once wrote: 'The storms of the revolution stirred up corresponding tempests in the passions of men, and overwhelmed not a few in a total ruin of their distinguished birthright of reason.' He proceeded to provide a memorable illustration: the unfortunate patient believing that he had been first guillotined and then afterwards reconstituted—if that is the appropriate word—with someone else's head (Pinel, 1962, pp. 9 and 69).

A different yet possibly complementary conception is to be found in its sharpest form in the early Freud's handling of hysteria. The disease gave rise to symptomatic tics and paralyses. The warrant for speaking of a disease or an illness was that these constitute incapacitations: the inability to prevent certain motions in the one case; and the inability in the other to effectuate any movings. The warrant for introducing the epithet 'mental' was that, absent any presently discernible organic lesions, there were supposed to be psychological causes; in particular unconscious motives, unconscious purposes, and unconscious intentions.

III   An engagement with Thomas Szasz

1   It is now twenty-two years since *The Myth of Mental Illness* was first published, and the bombardment then begun has to my own certain knowledge included eleven additional explosive books. The author, Dr Thomas Szasz, has done thereby a vast power of good. This good has been to show how much which has been put down as mental illness, and often even compulsorily treated as such, is falsely so described. I am myself second to none in my admiration for and commitment to this work. Nevertheless I shall now, not for the first time, argue that he is mistaken in his contention that there can be no application for any conception of mental illness.

He begins well by picking Freud's handling of hysteria as his paradigm; and suggesting, if not in this way outright saying, that most of what the layperson would think of as more or less gross insanity results from neurological disorder. In Chapter 1, 'Charcot's Contribution to the Problem of Hysteria', it looks as if Szasz is going to adopt a bold, uncompromisingly radical stance: patients classified by Charcot and his successors as mentally sick were and are, with whatever justification, in fact malingering. Szasz quotes Freud: '*First of all Charcot's work restored dignity to the subject*; gradually the sneering attitude, which the hysteric could reckon on meeting when she told her story, was given up, *she was no longer a malingerer, since Charcot had thrown the whole weight of his authority on the side of the reality and objectivity of hysterical phenomena*' (p. 25).

But later, taking a hint from the passages which he himself italicized in this quotation, Szasz allows the properly crucial issue of fact to drop out of view. The development begins in Chapter 2, 'The Logic of Classification and the Problem of Malingering'. At first it is tacitly recognized that the patients are not, after all, malingerers: 'The new rules are: "Persons *disabled* by phenomena which only look like illnesses of the body (i.e. hysteria) should be classified as ill"' (p. 41; italics supplied). But then we read, a few pages further on: 'With Freud and psychoanalysis . . . Hysteria was . . . viewed as unconscious malingering' (p. 46). Before this second chapter is out we have met an American psychoanalyst arguing 'that malingering is always the sign of a disease often more severe than neurotic disorder'. He adds the studiously preposterous comment: 'It is a disease which to diagnose requires particularly keen diagnostic acumen' (p. 48).

By the end of Chapter 7, 'Hysteria and Language', the development is complete. There is now no longer any question asked as to whether patients are or are not in fact incapacitated: 'From the standpoint of our present analysis, the entire change in renaming certain illness-like forms of behaviour from "malingering" to "hysteria" (and "mental illness") can be understood as nothing but a linguistic change... for the purpose of achieving a new type of action-orientedness... The verbal change, as first advocated by Charcot, served to command those dealing with "hysterics" to abandon their moral-condemnatory attitude toward them and to adopt instead a solicitous and benevolent attitude, such as befitted the physician vis-à-vis his patient' (p. 133). Consistent with this stage, which must surely have provided the main inspiration for the corresponding item in the Kennedy manifesto, is the apparent failure to notice, in discussing a quoted description of the notorious Ganser syndrome, categorical claims that the patients were in fact in the appropriate dimensions authentically incapacitated (pp. 250–1).

In so far as the issue here is indeed whether we are or are not dealing with conscious and deliberate malingerers, the philosopher in a professional capacity can at best hope to contribute only a few clarificatory observations before handing the investigation over to the medically qualified; suggesting perhaps that they might get many invaluable tips for testing out of the memoirs of doctors who have served their time in the armed forces of the crown. But if Szasz is after all prepared to live with the admissions of genuine disability made in Chapter 2, then it has to be emphasized that there is no mileage to be made here out of the constantly reiterated assertion that such supposed mental sickness cannot be referred to any discernible neurological disorder. For sickness, like illness, can be identified without appeal to sophisticated medical science; while the point of adding the qualification 'mental' simply is to indicate an aetiology psychological rather than physiological.

2   It remains only to list one or two of the confusions which may have misled Szasz, and which surely mislead others, to deny, neglect, or minimize fundamental distinctions of the kind adumbrated in Part II, 3, above. The first involves the first Freudian conception of the unconscious. We need to notice, what scarcely ever has been noticed, that in introducing talk of unconscious motives, unconscious purposes, and unconscious what have you, Freud made not one but two new conceptual moves. The obvious change was to permit the attribution of motives, purposes, and what have you to persons unaware—or who even vehemently and honestly deny—that they are so endowed. The much less obvious yet at least equally important change was to permit us to say that these unconscious motives or whatever give rise to bits of behaviour which are, in my terms, motions rather than movings (Flew, 1978, Chapter 8—a piece the first version of which was first published fully twenty-five years ago). In so far as this is correct, only the most perverse of Freudians could speak of unconscious malingering. For it is a necessary truth about your genuine malingerers that they wilfully pretend to be incapacitated in ways in which actually they are not; whereas an unconscious malingerer would, presumably, be genuinely incapacitated without (consciously) intending so to be—that is to say, no sort of malingerer at all.

Second, all the human sciences—psychological, sociological, and historical—labour to show that and how, in the light of all the perceived circumstances and of their own background and past development, people would not have been expected to do other than they did. It is all too easy and too common to infer from whatever successes may be achieved through the investigations of these sciences that, in reality, no one ever has any choice. Though perennially and powerfully tempting this inference is, nevertheless, altogether fallacious. Put as a pithy paradox the truth is that ordinarily we can only say that someone had no (real) choice, that they could not have done other than they did, when we are sure that, in the more fundamental senses ostensively defined in Part II, 3, above, they had and they did.

Consider, if I may license myself to redeploy two favourite illustrations: first, Luther before the Diet of Worms; and, second, the unfortunate businessman receiving from *The Godfather* an offer which he could not refuse. Certainly those acquainted with Luther might have known that he would in fact stand there; and that it would appear to him, in the everyday interpretation of those words, that 'I can no other. So help me God'. Yet none of this constitutes reason for drawing the abusive conclusion that Luther remained there erect and stationary because, and only because, he had fallen victim to a sudden paralysis.

The situation is the same with the man challenged by the Mafia gunman: 'I shall within thirty seconds have either your signature or your brains on this paper.' When we say that such a man had no choice what we mean is, not that he had no choice, but that he had no tolerable choice. An agent who acts under compulsion, however severe that compulsion, remains nonetheless an agent. He could, as some would, defy that compulsion. It is entirely different with the errant Mafioso, instantly gunned down from behind. He does not act under compulsion, since in the moment of death he ceases forever both to be and to act.

Any client of that second misconception—the first one about the presuppositions of the human sciences—is bound to be reluctant to acknowledge the realities of choice. A third misconception, which is similarly sure to sustain a similar reluctance, consists in the conviction that full determination by causes is incompatible with choice. Although this may well be true in the sense of 'cause' in which the effects caused are not human actions, it is certainly false in the sense of 'cause' in which we speak of the causes of that very different and peculiar type of effect (Flew, 1978, Chapters 2–3).

Most of us are not all the time inquiring into the causes of our own conduct. 'But that is no reason', we are told, 'for thinking that if you did preoccupy yourself with these causes you would not find them at work. You may remember that Sir Francis Galton was so much impressed with this possibility that for some time he kept account in a notebook of the occasions on which he made important choices with a full measure of this feeling of freedom; then shortly after each choice he turned his eye backward in search of constraints that might have been acting on him stealthily. He found it so easy to bring such constraining factors to light that he surrendered to the determinist view' (Blanshard, 1958, p. 6). The same necessitarian determinism is epitomized in the seemingly compelling argument of perhaps the sanest and least ideologically infatuated of contemporary criminologists: '... if causal theories explain why a criminal acts as he does, they also explain why he *must* act as he does' (Wilson, 1977, p. 58: italics original).

Oddly enough Szasz did once hold the secret of this knot in his hands, yet still did nothing to disentangle it. Thus he remarks: 'It should be kept in mind ... that my desire to see a play is the "cause" of my going to the theater in a sense very different from that in which we speak of "causal laws" in physics' (p. 88). So it should, and so it is. The unexploited secret is, in a nutshell, that whereas physical causes necessitate, the other sort of causes—call them personal causes—do not: personal causes, we may say in a phrase borrowed from Leibniz, incline but do not necessitate.

Given the sufficient (physical) causes of—say—an explosion or an eclipse, then of course it follows necessarily from the statement that these are their sufficient causes that these effects will in fact occur. Furthermore, it is also the case that these cause events must contingently (as opposed to logically) necessitate those effect events; that these must make the occurrence of those as a matter of fact inevitable, and their non-occurrence correspondingly impossible. With personal causes the case is altogether different. When, for instance, you give me or I give you cause to celebrate we may each thereby make it likely or predictable or intelligible that the other will in fact celebrate. Yet there is no question whatsoever of either contingent necessity or contingent impossibility. Neither you nor I become, by the presentation of sufficient causes of this second and personal kind, ineluctably destined willy-nilly to make whoopee. We can, and cannot but, choose; each and everyone choosing for themselves alone.

A final, Parthian shot. If, as I have suggested, there can be no sufficient physical causes of any item of behaviour which is at the same time an action, then we are all of us always as agents (physically) uncaused causes. Those who have a yen for the putative profundities of classical German philosophy will relish to add this as the most portentous of those distinctively human characteristics which religion is supposed to alienate from man on to its allegedly non-existent God (Feuerbach, 1957). For is not that God to every traditional theologian the Uncaused Cause of all things?

References

Aristotle (1926). *Nicomachean Ethics*, tr. H. Rackham. Heinemann and Putnam, London, and New York.
Austin, J. L. (1961). *Philosophical Papers* (Eds. J. O. Urmson and G. J. Warnock). Clarendon, Oxford.
Austin, J. L. (1962). *How to Do Things with Words* (Ed. J. O. Urmton), Clarendon, Oxford.
Bentham, J. (1948). *A Fragment on Government*, with *An Introduction to the Principles of Morals and Legislation* (Ed. W. Harrison). Blackwell, Oxford.

Blanshard, B. (1958). The case for determinism, in *Determinism and Freedom in the Age of Modern Science* (Ed. S. Hook). New York University Press, New York.

Block, S., and Reddaway, P. (1978). *Russia's Political Hospitals.*Futura, London.

Boorse, C. (1975). On the distinction between disease and illness, *Philosophy and Public Affairs*, **5**, 49–68.

Boorse, C. (1976). What a theory of mental health should be, *J. Theory Soc. Behaviour*, **6**, 1, 61–84.

Feuerbach, L. (1957). *The Essence of Christianity*, tr. G. Eliot. Harper, New York.

Fingarette, H. (1972). *The Meaning of Criminal Insanity*. University of California Press, Berkeley, Los Angeles and London.

Flew, A. G. N. (1973). *Crime or Disease?*. Macmillan, London.

Flew, A. G. N. (1975). *Thinking about Thinking*. Collins/Fontana, London. (Also as *Thinking Straight*. Prometheus, Buffalo, N. Y.)

Flew, A. G. N. (1976). *Sociology, Equality and Education*. Macmillan, London.

Flew, A. G. N. (1978). *A Rational Animal*. Clarendon, Oxford.

Macklin, R. (1972). Mental health and mental illness: some problems of definition and comcept formation, *Philosophy of Science*, **39**, 3, 341–65.

Macklin, R. (1973). The medical model in psychoanalysis and psychotherapy, *Comprehensive Psychiatry*, **14**, 1, 1–21.

Paton, H. J. (1948). *The Moral Law*. Hutchinson, London.

Pinel, P. (1962). *A Treatise on Insanity*. Hafner, New York. (A facsimile of the first English edition of 1806.)

Richardson, K., and Spears, D. (1972). (Eds.) *Race, Culture and Intelligence*. Penguin, Harmondsworth.

Szasz, T. (1961). *The Myth of Mental Illness*. Dell, New York.

Ullman, L. P., and Krasner, L. (1965). *Studies in Behavior Modification*. Holt, Rinehart and Winston, New York.

Ullman, L. P., and Krasner, L. (1966). *Case Studies in Behaviour Modification*. Holt, Rinehart and Winston, New York.

Wilson, J. Q. (1977). *Thinking about Crime*. Vintage, New York.

Wootton, B. (1967). *Social Science and Social Pathology* (4th Impression). Allen and Unwin, London.

Mental Illness: Changes and Trends
Edited by Philip Bean
© John Wiley & Sons Ltd.

CHAPTER 7

Treatment and cure in mental illness

ANTHONY W. CLARE
Senior Lecturer, Deputy Director of the
General Practice Research Unit, Institute
of Psychiatry; Honorary Consultant Psychiatrist,
Bethlem Royal and Maudsley Hospitals

Introduction

At the present time, the consensus of informed opinion appears to be that the efficacy of the various treatments of mental disorders is of a distressingly low level of magnitude. Cure—that is to say the permanent removal of distressing symptoms together with their cause—is a relatively infrequent occurrence. For the most part, the intrinsic complexity of the subject appears to bear the brunt of the blame for this state of affairs. In the words of one critic, 'if all the Nobel prize-winners of this century had worked in psychiatry the subject would have advanced only a little less slowly and none of them would have received the prize' (McKeown, 1976). It is certainly true that the rate of advance has been slow. The natural history of most common mental disorders has still to be established (Shepherd, 1981), the majority of treatments currently in use are empirical (Clare, 1980) and, in so far as treatments as varied as ECT and psychotherapy do appear to bring about remission, there is still much discussion as to the relative importance of placebo effect, spontaneous remission, and chance in effecting such change. (Hogan, 1979)* At the same time, when psychiatrists find themselves in possession of an apparently effective treatment, be it ECT or chlorpromazine, they tend to use it indiscriminately, like Leonceno's bad cobbler 'who tries to fit everybody with the same shoe' (Sudhoff, 1925).

Yet, some two decades ago psychiatry appeared poised on the threshold of revolutionary breakthroughs in treatment. However, the changes in psychiatry do not meet the criteria of what constitutes a revolution; there has been no overthrow of established systems of thought and no significant break with the major therapeutic schools of the past 100 years. The enthusiasm of those who talked of a therapeutic revolution now looks from the vantage-point of history singularly misplaced. The fact that different developments in therapy, from

* See also Chapter 2.

psychotherapy to psychotropics, from social psychiatry to behavioural approaches, have all in their time been dubbed 'revolutionary' only further illustrates the tendency of psychiatrists, in common with other active practitioners, to believe that they live 'in an age of rapid and impressive advance' (Lewis, 1979).

However, dashed hopes can produce a reaction in favour of therapeutic nihilism and, indeed, there is some evidence that this may have occurred. Nonpsychiatric medical practitioners do appear to see psychiatry as a speciality particularly preoccupied with intractable problems (Hutt *et al.*, 1979) although whether chronicity is any more a feature of psychiatric problems than of the conditions presenting in, for example, internal medicine or neurology, is open to question. However, when recovery does occur, the different members of the therapeutic team are often far from unanimous in predicting ultimate success—the revolving door of the 1960s and 1970s, through which scores of discharged 'recovered' patients returned in relapse, has exercised a sobering influence on even the most therapeutically sanguine of minds.

Perhaps it is not surprising if some psychiatrists despair of the whole notion of 'cure' and its applicability to psychiatric treatments. Antipsychiatrists too have questioned its relevance. 'Curing is so ambiguous a term' observed David Cooper (1967) 'one may cure bacon, hides, rubber, or patients. Curing usually implies the chemical treatment of raw materials so that they may taste better, be more useful or last longer. Curing is essentially a mechanistic perversion of medical ideals that is quite opposite to the authentic tradition of healing'. However, as Medawar (1972) pointed out in a pugnacious rebuttal of such a viewpoint, the notion of recovery is the one independent criterion by which the acceptability of psychoanalytic (and other psychiatric) notions can be judged. In the final analysis, in psychiatry as in medicine, the acid test of any treatment is that it should be shown to be effective. Its effectiveness too should be significantly superior to that obtained by chance. It is sobering to realize how few of psychiatry's treatments meet this fundamental test.

While the major issue concerning most psychiatric treatments is whether they work, it is by no means the only issue. There is much controversy over treatments which are commonly accepted as being effective. Such controversies are, for the most part, ethical and concern such issues as the morality and legality of compulsory treatment (Gostin, 1975; Roth, 1980; McGarry and Chodoff, 1981), the acceptability of bringing about behavioural changes desired by society but unwanted by the individual (Halleck, 1974; Karasu, 1981), and the justification of treatment approaches which appear to violate social mores (Jacobs *et al.*, 1975; Redlick, 1977). Overshadowing all of these is the vexed problems of what constitutes recovery.

The problem of outcome

Precise assessments of the therapeutic effects of various psychiatric treatments are jeopardized by the paucity of information available concerning the natural history of untreated mental illness. Spontaneous remission, even in the case of the most severe mental disorders, is not unknown. While such remissions are more likely to occur among a group of afflicted individuals who may be traditionally regarded as having a good prognosis (a first illness with an acute onset in response to massive and understandable stress in an individual with a well-established personality, social competence, and supportive social networks), it is nothing like as easy to identify the bulk of such patients with any degree of accuracy.

Such is the situation with regard to the most severe of all psychiatric disorders, namely schizophrenia. Despite the fact that a substantial number of drug studies have confirmed the powerful therapeutic effects of the neuroleptic drugs in ameliorating and, in many cases, eliminating psychotic symptoms in schizophrenic illnesses, there is remarkably little evidence to suggest that the 'cure' rate for the disorder has changed very much in the 90 years since Emil Kraepelin first described the condition. Indeed, one study, involving 20 years of regular observation of 200 patients has led one authoritative commentator to observe that the proportion of benign psychoses with complete life-long recovery has not been altered by modern physical treatment (Bleuler, 1974).

So how does one identify those patients who may respond particularly well to the drug while at the same time allowing those patients who do not need medication and who will make a spontaneous recovery to emerge? One study, of the efficacy of flupenthixol in the treatment of acute schizophrenia (Johnstone *et al.*, 1978), did show that an advantage of active medication over placebo emerges in the third week of treatment. Hirsch (1980) has suggested that a period of at least one week's observation without antipsychotic medication would identify those patients who begin to remit spontaneously and would spare them the disadvantages and the side-effects of unnecessary medication.

Given such findings, it is an understandable criticism of drug therapy in the treatment of schizophrenia that it merely dampens down or tranquillizes the afflicted patient (sometimes at a heavy price in terms of toxic sequelae and side-effects) while leaving the underlying disease process relatively untouched. Recent research suggests that such a view may be too simplistic. The commonly used drugs possess antipsychotic as well as sedative effects. The specific antipsychotic ability of neuroleptic medication to eliminate or diminish such symptoms as hallucinations, delusions, bizarre behaviour, and paranoid ideas appears to be pharmacologically related to the ability of such drugs to block dopamine transmission, particularly at post-synaptic receptor sites within the mesolimbic system (Creese *et al.*, 1978). Another specific effect of such drugs is their ability to reduce psychotic anxiety, excitement, and aggression with relatively little hypnotic effect compared with that resulting from traditional sedative drugs. Again, it is believed that this specific antipsychotic sedative action is related to the affinity of the neuroleptics for alpha-adrenergic receptors centrally. It can be distinguished from the non-specific sedative action of neuroleptics which diminish hyperarousal in anyone and is reflected in the strong hypnotic effects seen when neuroleptics are given to normal non-psychotic individuals.

A major advance in the pharmacotherapy of schizophrenia has been the recognition of the prophylactic effect of neuroleptic medication in preventing recurrence of schizophrenic symptoms. A systematic review of 24 methodologically sound double-blind controlled studies of maintenance therapy covering chronic in-patients and out-patients showed that 698 patients out of 1068 who received inert placebo (65 per cent) relapsed in contrast to 639 of 2127 patients on antipsychotics (30 per cent) (Davis, 1975). The value of long-acting depot injections for out-patient maintenance in schizophrenia has been emphasized in a number of double-blind, placebo-controlled trials (Hirsch et al., 1973; Hogarty et al., 1974; Falloon et al., 1978) but there is much controversy over who should receive item. It would seem important to identify those who do, for long-term neuroleptic medication is not without its attendant problems, carrying the risk of unwanted side-effects which include extrapyramidal symptoms (Johnson, 1978), tardive dyskinesia (Gibson, 1978), weight gain (Johnson and Breen, 1979), malignant neuroleptic syndrome of hypertonicity and hyperthermia (Vedrine, 1967), the sudden-death syndrome (Richardson, 1966), and skin-eye syndromes (Rubin and Slonicki, 1967). A number of studies of maintenance treatment have shown that about 20 per cent of patients withdrawn from treatment or switched to placebo do not relapse during the first one or two years (Leff and Wing, 1971; Hogarty et al., 1974). However, using a life table method of assessing the continued risk of relapse at any point in time, Hogarty and Ulrich (1977) calculated that at three years following discharge the rate of relapse was still 3 per cent per month or $2\frac{1}{2}$ to 3 times greater than for patients on maintenance therapy. Cheung (1981) reported a higher relapse rate in a randomized controlled trial of schizophrenics switched to benzodiazepines from neuroleptics after having been on the neuroleptics for 3–5 years, illustrating the risk involved in stopping maintenance therapy even after lengthy periods of treatment. It has been suggested (Leff and Vaughn, 1981) that one possible key to the problem may lie in an interaction between environmental stress, life events, and the disease process. In a two-year follow-up the chances of relapse were reduced for patients with schizophrenia living in families expressing low levels of emotion maintained on medication. Schizophrenics living in more favourable family situations may not require maintenance therapy to any comparable extent.

Somewhat similar issues confront therapists using drugs in the treatment and prophylaxis of bipolar affective illness. In general, attempts to predict treatment response in these disorders have been more successful than in the case of schizophrenia. Such heterogeneous indicators as upper socio-economic class, insidious onset, anorexia, weight loss, middle and late insomnia, and psychomotor disturbance are classically associated with a good prognosis (Petursson, 1979) whereas neurotic, hypochondriacal and hysterical traits, multiple prior episodes, and delusions are associated with a poor response. (Bielski and Friedel, 1976). In general, however, the relapse rate in affective illness is high. A recent

Medical Research Council trial reported that less than one in every three patients with a history of severe recurrent depression was relapse-free after three years despite active maintenance therapy involving lithium or amitriptyline (Glen *et al.*, 1981). The same study reported a relapse-free rate of 58 per cent in mild recurrently depressed patients maintained on active medication compared to 11 per cent maintained on placebo.

While such figures, sobering as they are, nonetheless point to a very definite therapeutic role for drugs in the treatment of psychotic illnesses, the relative failure of pharmacological treatments to bring about a cure in the majority of patients is seized upon by those who for various reasons remain sceptical of the power of physical agents to alter psychological events (Laing, 1967; Szasz, 1971). Claims are made on behalf of psychotherapy's efficacy in rooting out the underlying cause of such illnesses (compared with merely battening them down as drugs appear to do) despite the fact that there is little persuasive evidence to contest Freud's belief in 'the radical inaccessibility of the psychoses to analytic treatment' (Freud, 1932). If anything, the few systematic assessments of the efficacy of psychoanalysis and of analytically derived psychotherapies that have been undertaken point in quite the opposite direction. Such therapies, complex, time-consuming, and expensive as they may be, exercise such modest effects as they do in conditions which are relatively mild to begin with.

One of the most quoted studies, the Menninger Foundation's Psychotherapy Project (Kernberg *et al.*, 1972), which was designed 'to explore changes brought about by psychoanalytically-oriented psychotherapies and psychoanalysis' established that psychoanalysis only appeared suitable as a therapy for patients with high ego strength, good motivation, a high tolerance for anxiety, and relatively stable interpersonal relationships. A clear implication of the study's findings was that the therapy, because of its rigorous stripping away of defences and its exposure of the real problems at the heart of a patient's difficulties, could only be tolerated by individuals with relatively stable constitutions and personal and social circumstances. Such an attitude may appear at first glance defensible. After all, surgery is not offered to patients whose physical state would not enable them to survive the anaesthetic. However, such an analogy raises uncomfortable questions; it is only fair to point out, for example, that surgery is not offered to patients for whom less invasive treatments may be equally or more effective.

This conviction that psychotherapy brings about long-standing, deep and significant changes of personality, which is held and promulgated by psychotherapists, raises additional issues regarding treatment and cure which are well illustrated by reference to the work of David Malan and his colleagues at the Tavistock Clinic in London. This group has undertaken a number of studies of time-limited, psychoanalytically-based therapy and have made use of a distinction between so-called 'symptomatic' and 'dynamic' improvement. The subjectivity inherent in making such a distinction can be judged by examining the relatively detailed case histories provided by this group (Malan *et al.*, 1968) and assessing their ratings of improvement. Straightaway there are difficulties. The information provided is selective and tends generally to relate to those areas of functioning judged by the therapists to be important in the light of their preconceived theoretical system. Some important outcome criteria are not 'dynamic' in any psychological sense but are social while some judgments are in no way objective but are more in the manner of being clinical 'hunches'. A good example is Case No. 12, that of a man whose recovery from sexual difficulties is considered dynamically doubtful because on occasions he is unable to urinate in a public lavatory when other men are present and because he tends to lose an erection if his wife makes uncomplimentary remarks about his sexual technique.

Doubts about Malan's notions of 'dynamic' and 'symptomatic' recovery are far from academic. The study referred to, for instance, was of 45 patients who had been seen at the Tavistock Clinic for consideration of psychotherapy, who never received treatment and who were followed-up for between 2 and 6 years. Thirteen patients were judged by the researchers to be 'symptomatically' improved but still 'dynamically' doubtful (including Case 12 referred to above) while 11 patients were judged to be 'dynamically' as well as 'symptomatically' improved. The proportion of patients significantly benefited by no more than time will vary from 29 per cent to 53 per cent depending on the extent to which Malan's distinction concerning symptomatic and dynamic response is regarded as acceptable.

How 'dynamic' or deep does the response have to be to satisfy psychotherapists? An example given is that of homosexuality. For treatment to be dynamically successful, the homosexuality should not merely disappear (for this could clearly happen if the individual homosexual patient merely avoided opportunities for engaging in homosexual activities altogether) but should be replaced by heterosexual impulses, feelings, and activities. The authors agree with critics who regard such outcome criteria as somewhat exacting but point out that their therapeutic goal is 'normal emotional functioning'. An analogy is drawn with the physical treatment of breathlessness—if treatment is deeply as distinct from symptomatically effective, the patient should not only be able to breathe easily at rest but should be able to run normally and not just with excessive effort. So if the treatment of emotional symptoms is truly effective, the patient must be able to face loss, setback, challenge, and stress without developing the same or other symptoms.

Disagreement over the definition of recovery is by no means the only explanation of why there is still so little verified and dependable information on whether any of the many and varied forms of currently available psychotherapy work. The paucity of objective measures of agreed criteria of improvement, the flexible and ill-defined aims of treatment, the heterogeneous nature of the disorders selected for treatment, the dropping-out of patients on financial or psychological grounds, the lack of uniformity regarding the treatment techniques involved, the variable effects of the therapist's personality, and the disparity between therapists with regard to treatment skills all contribute to the problems involved.

However, disagreement over what constitutes recovery and cure is not confined to the psychotherapies. The same disagreement for example can be identified in current discussions concerning the efficacy of the treatment of alcohol dependence.* How to gauge the relative importance of spontaneous recovery, the use of antabuse, the role of Alcoholics Anonymous, the impact of specially designed treatment packages and the efficacy of psychotherapy is complicated by the fact that at the present time there is disagreement over what constitutes an appropriate therapeutic response. The most freqnently used indicators of positive response to treatment include abstinence, consumption level, frequency of drinking, behavioural impairment, marital and family functioning, and occupational status. The attrition rate from treatment and the degree of acceptance of treatment have also been used as measures of outcome. While abstinence does appear to be the most popular outcome criterion, two distinct reservations have been expressed. The first doubts the wisdom of employing it as the sole outcome measure (Pattison, 1966). Indeed, data have been published disputing the assumption that the achievement of abstinence necessarily results in the amelioration of problems, a large number of totally abstinent alcholics being rated at follow-up as overtly disturbed (Gerard *et al.*, 1962). The second reservation relates to the empirical fact that a proportion of treated alcoholics are apparently able to resume normal, non-alcoholic drinking while still maintaining stability in other adjustments (Davies, 1962; Kendell, 1968; Pattison, 1966).

A two-year follow-up of a sample of married male alcoholics, who had been the subjects of a controlled treatment trial, has helped cast some light on the processes involved in the return to normal drinking. As a consequence, the study raises important questions concerning the optimum planning of alcoholism treatment services (Orford *et al.*, 1976). In this study, outcome was considered 'good' if the patient's wife reported five or fewer weeks containing any episode of unacceptable drinking and if, in addition, the patient reported five or fewer weeks containing any drinking amount of 200 g; outcome was considered 'bad' if the wife reported 26 or more weeks containing an unacceptable drinking episode and if, in addition, the patient reported 26 or more weeks containing any 100 g per day drinking. All other cases were considered 'equivocal'. Of 26 men with a good outcome, 11 were agreed by husband and wife to be abstaining and 10 were agreed to be controlling their drinking. Most of the latter had not shown lengthy periods of abstinence before reducing drinking. Controlled drinkers, however, reported fewer symptoms of serious alcohol dependence at intake (morning drinking, shakes, secret drinking, hallucinations, etc.), were more likely to have been sub-diagnosed as so-called alpha alcoholics (psychologically dependent)

* See also Chapter 14.

rather than gamma-alcoholics (physiologically dependent) and were more likely to have been briefly counselled rather than intensively treated. Abstainers reported more symptoms at intake, were more likely to have been sub-diagnosed as gamma-alcoholics and were more likely to have been intensively treated. These findings suggested to the authors that different intensities of treatment might be required for different sub-types of alcohol-dependent individuals—the more physiologically-dependent requiring relatively intensive approaches involving psychotherapy, drug treatment, and in selected cases in-patient care, the more psychologically dependent requiring simple counselling, reassurance, guidance, and advice concerning the dangers of continuing to drink excessively.

In the field of alcoholism treatment, the reaction against reliance on abstinence as a sole criterion of a successful outcome has resulted in the endorsement of multidimensional measurement of outcome (Foster *et al.*, 1972). Such a position holds that although the major purpose of treatment is the modification of the target problem behaviour (in this example, excessive alcohol consumption), the effectiveness of a particular method of treatment can best be evaluated in terms of its total consequences. In chronic alcoholism, the multiple-outcome argument has considerable appeal (Armor *et al.*, 1978) since the disorder has profoundly disruptive effects on social, marital, occupational, and other areas of functioning. In the setting of a multidimensional approach, a successful treatment outcome would be evaluated by such measures, as job and social adjustment, emotional stability, interpersonal involvement, and marital and sexual adjustment in addition to abstinence.

Such a multidimensional approach, however, is clearly not limited to the field of alcoholism. In the evaluation of the treatment of schizophrenia, for example, very similar arguments are quite easily applied. Indeed, it is argued that pessimistic references to the lack of progress since Kraepelin's day are understandable only in terms of a somewhat narrow notion of cure (Bennett, 1980). Leaving aside symptomatic recovery, the social adjustment of schizophrenics, according to this argument, has much improved since Kraepelin reported that about 17 per cent of in-patients treated at his Heidelberg Clinic were socially readjusted many years later. Bennett quotes a study published in the mid-1950s showing that 56 per cent of 111 hospitalized schizophrenics had 'recovered socially' 5 years later while a further 34 per cent, while socially disabled, were out of hospital. There is clearly much more to the treatment of conditions such as schizophrenia than drugs—indeed, when drug treatments are compared with placebo, they only explain 36 per cent of the variance of improvement (Davis, 1976). Hirsch, whose somewhat uncompromising endorsement of the therapeutic role of drugs provoked Bennett's doubts, has responded by questioning whether the social functioning of patients and the improvements and gains measured in the social functioning of patients represent a true 'treatment' effect or whether it is simply due to the fact that 'we have begun to overcome the untoward effects of the social attitudes that society applies to our patients and the treatments that psychiatrists have been applying to patients over the last 75 years' (Hirsch, 1980).

Whatever the final merits and demerits of this particular exchange, the fact remains that an exclusive concern with symptomatic recovery can lead to a neglect of social and behavioural functioning which, for the patient's relatives and friends as much as for the patient himself, may have as important implications and consequences. However, there are hazards inherent in any multidimensional approach to evaluating outcome, hazards illustrated by returning to the field of alcoholism treatment once more. In emphasizing the value of multiple-outcome criteria some researchers have committed the error of discounting the relevance of the alcohol consumption criterion. According to Armor and his colleagues, who have published a systematic review of alcoholism treatment, success has been claimed for some therapies on the basis of inferred psychological changes even though the intended objective (i.e. reduced excessive drinking) has not been achieved (Armor *et al.*, 1978). An ordering of outcome criteria is clearly required. In the field of alcoholism treatment, the primary objective remains the elimination of excessive alcohol use and the gross signs of physical and behavioural impairment which result from it even though complete social and psychological recovery of the patient may remain as the ultimate goal.

A similar situation exists in relation to the treatment of a psychotic illness such as schizophrenia. Ideally, treatment aims to restore the afflicted individual to complete physical, psychological health and social functioning but in practice the relief of the major symptoms of the illness, the prevention of secondary handicap, and the promotion of social rehabilitation are, at the present state of knowledge, more realistic therapeutic goals. The fact that, as we have seen, individual patients will still manifest very different patterns of response makes it imperative that our methods of diagnosis and treatment evaluation are as refined as possible. Otherwise, there is always the risk that alterations in the outcome of a patient's illness will be attributed erroneously to some intervention or other. The contrary is, of course, also true.

The problem of selection

A further issue relating to psychiatric treatment and cure concerns patient selection. Making sense of claims concerning the efficacy of psychotherapy is confounded by doubts as to the nature and representativeness of the populations selected for treatment. The abortive Maudsley–Tavistock psychotherapy study illustrates this problem neatly. At the outset of this carefully disigned trial, it was agreed that the aim should be to include only those patients 'who appeared to be highly suitable for the particular form of psychotherapy to be used' (Candy *et al.*, 1972). Selection of patients accordingly took place in three stages. First, psychiatrists working within a reasonable distance of the two centres referred patients who appeared to them to fulfil particular criteria for psychotherapy.

These criteria included: (1) Absence of serious physical or psychotic illness, (2) Absence of serious drug dependence, sexual deviation, or sociopathic disorder, (3) Discernible or lasting problems in interpersonal relationships, (4) No evidence suggesting the need for hospital admission, (5) At least average intelligence, (6) No previous formal psychotherapy, (7) Active motivation for treatment, (8) Willingness to participate in research, (9) Age between 18 and 45 years, (10) No objection to a relative being seen. A total of 113 patients were referred. Of these, 23 failed to return the screening questionnaire (which asked for details of the individual's difficulties, family circumstances and history, sexual experience, and occupation). Ninety patients remained for the second stage assessment. However, on the basis of the Tavistock psychotherapists' evaluation of the questionnaire responses, only 27 of the 90 were accepted to pass on to the third stage of the selection procedure. Each of the 27 were given an interview with one of the four Tavistock participants, an interview which lasted at least $1\frac{1}{2}$ hours and which was tape-recorded. The Tavistock participants then met and discussed each case and decided to accept 8. These 8 represented approximately 9 per cent of those individuals who had completed the questionnaires and 7 per cent of those patients identified as suitable for psychotherapy by referring psychiatrists. It might be argued that such a research study employed a particularly stringent set of selection criteria but it is worth pointing out that the Menninger study in the 1950s opened the way for psychotherapists to choose and choose carefully good outcome cases by under-writing the importance of being highly selective at the outset.

Even if the Maudsley–Tavistock study had somehow accumulated sufficient patients, and even had it shown the effectiveness of psychotherapy, such a positive finding would have to be set aside. For how can the efficacy of psychotherapy for patients regarded by psychiatrists as suitable for the treatment be judged when the overwhelming majority of these had been excluded from participation by the researchers themselves? Nor is the study unusual in its findings. The literature on the suitability of patients for psychotherapy is replete with statements emphasizing the fact that in practice suitable candidates for such treatment are selected in ways similar to those employed in this abortive study. In a recent review, Bloch (1979) summarized the good prognostic factors for long-term psychotherapy (Table 1). In the light of such statements, the question arises as to whether it is acceptable to provide an expensive and time-consuming therapy for people who can function independently without it, who may well obtain such relief as they require from treatment and other approaches of much less complexity and who can only be categorized as 'ill' with some stretching of that already elastic term. What constitutes motivation and 'realistic expectations' appears difficult to establish with any degree of reliability and validity while Bloch's fifth and seventh criteria merely serve to re-emphasize the message that dynamic psychotherapy is not for people in serious mental difficulties. The fourth criterion has the virtue of testability while the sixth serves to remind us

Table 1   Good prognostic factors for long-term insight-orientated psychotherapy
(Bloch, 1979)

(1) Reasonable level of personality integration and
     general functioning.
(2) Motivation for change.
(3) Realistic expectations of therapeutic process—
     reflecting 'psychological-mindedness'.
(4) Average intelligence—at least.
(5) Non-psychotic conditions (i.e. neuroses and the
     'milder' personality disorders).
(6) Presence of strong affect (e.g. depression,
     anxiety etc.) at time of assessment.
(7) Life circumstances free of any unresolvable
     crises

that it is therapy we are considering and not the provision of a course in self-exploration or a professional friend.

Once again, however, the problem of selection is not a problem peculiar to psychotherapy. Another, even more pressing example concerns the widespread use and therapeutic efficacy of psychotropic drugs in the treatment of depression. Obviously the manner in which 'depression' is defined is crucial to any discussion of the efficacy of this or that treatment. General practitioners still receive almost all of their formal psychiatric training within a hospital setting, use diagnostic nomenclature based on hospital experience and prescribe drugs that are to a very great extent developed for and evaluated in hospital psychiatric practice (Barber, 1981). Yet, in the light of the extensive epidemiological research which has been carried out into the prevalence and nature of psychiatric disorders in the community in recent years (Hicks, 1976; Goldberg and Huxley, 1980; Shepherd *et al.*, 1981), it is clear that hospital populations represent a relatively small and highly selective group of depressively ill people. The proportion of depressed patients clinically treated in this setting is estimated between 11 per cent (Nielsen *et al.*, 1965) and 92 per cent (Odegaard, 1972). The first figure is based on the sum of all depressive illnesses, the later only on psychotic depressions. This type of depressive illness shows a markedly unequal distribution among the various sites of psychiatric care. (Paykel *et al.*, 1970; Wing *et al.*, 1981). In the hospital setting, patients with serious, psychotic, suicidal, chronic, and treatment-resistant depressions tend to accumulate. Such an unequal distribution almost certainly has increased in the past ten years, since antidepressant treatment has made out-patient treatment possible in certain cases of serious depression (Helmchen, 1979). Indeed, it is now becoming quite difficult for hospital-based psychiatrists to find untreated depressive patients for study in the hospital setting (Little *et al.*, 1978).

However, largely on the basis of results obtained from hospital-based trials of antidepressants (Burt *et al.*, 1962; Medical Research Council, 1965; Wechsler *et al.*, 1965), widespread use of antidepressants and anxiolytics in the management of the numerically common anxiety and depressive states in the setting of general practice was encouraged. Such studies of the efficacy of antidepressants in depressed patients as have been undertaking in general practice suggest that while these drugs may exert a therapeutic effect it is far from clear the extent to which it is as antidepressants *per se* or through a non-specific sedative effect (Hare *et al.*, 1964; Porter, 1970; Wheatley, 1972). In their study of 82 patients referred by 21 Melbourne GPs, Blashki and his colleagues did demonstrate therapeutic superiority for amitryptiline in doses of 150 mg/day over amylobarbitone, 150 mg/day amitryptiline, 75 mg/day, and inert placebo (Blashki *et al.* 1971). However, once again patient selection suggests that caution should be exercised in interpreting these figures. Each GP took approximately six months to recruit 4 patients who met the rigorous clinical criteria for inclusion in the trial. Such a figure represents a tiny and possibly unrepresentative sample of the pool of depressed patients encountered by each GP during that time. Nor is such a measure of selectivity limited to studies of depression in the setting of general practice. A Medical Research Council multi-centre trial comparing lithium with antidepressant maintenance thereapy in unipolar depressive illness took $4\frac{1}{2}$ years to recruit 136 patients from 95 investigators working in 9 centres (Glen *et al.* 1981). One centre, Sheffield, managed to recruit only 1 patient while another centre, Glasgow, recruited 2, provoking the *Lancet* to ask, a trifle caustically 'What out of the hundreds of depressives who must have been treated in those cities in $4\frac{1}{2}$ years, made those 3 patients so uniquely suitable for this trial?' (*Lancet*, 1981).

A number of observers, commenting on the drug treatment of depressive illness in general practice, have drawn attention to the tendency of GPs to use sub-therapeutic doses of antidepressants (Johnson, 1974, 1981) their apparently interchangeable use of antidepressants and anxiolytics (Clare and Williams, 1981), and the low levels of drug compliance on the part of their patients (Johnson, 1981). Concerning compliance, the tendency of patients to discontinue taking psychotropic drugs appears to be due mainly to intolerance of side-effects and, in a small but sturdy minority, to the view that their 'illness' is a response to stress or an environmental event and is more appropriately dealt with by some form of psychological treatment. To date, we do not know enough about the natural history of depressive illness in general practice to feel confident that such defaulting is always against the best interests of the patient.

The use of a significant proportion of the psychotropics prescribed in general practice is for the relief of physical symptoms (Williams, 1978). It is alleged that they are also often used for social reasons and to provide temporary relief (Cooperstock, 1971, Lader, 1978). It is certainly true that the general practitioner, confronted by an often inextricable mix of physical, psychological, and social problems which so often characterize the contours of the problems presenting in this setting, is often forced to rely on psychotropic medication in eu of any more appropriate response. A *Lancet* editorial, (*Lancet*, 1978), eviewing this subject, repeated the observation, made by Shepherd and his olleagues a decade earlier (Shepherd *et al.*, 1966), to the effect that a ombination of drug therapy and reassurance was the commonest form of eneral practitioner psychiatric treatment, and commented that 'in view of the igh prevalence of psychological distress it is doubtful whether we shall see fundamental change in medical management'. The editorial went on to ote that 'although most (sedatives and tranquillizers) are safe in the short erm . . . we know little about their long-term effects on social and personal unctioning, their impact on physical health, and the extent to which they ositively and negatively reinforce other forms of treatment. Until we know the nswers, we may give one or two cheers for psychotropic drugs in the treatment f stress and distress, but certainly not three'.

The withholding of the third cheer reflects the fact that we still do not know the nswers to these questions. We do not know how far, if at all the depressions and nxieties presenting in the general practice and the community settings resemble hose familiar to psychiatrists working in out-patient clinics and hospital wards. valuating, for example, the efficacy of antidepressants in general practice emands that general practitioners are able to identify amongst the many atients who present with depressed mood as a symptom the relatively few who manifest the psychotic or endogenous forms of depressive disorder which are nown to be responsive to such medication. Guidelines concerning how they ight do this abound but their reliability is affected by the fact that there is much ontroversy concerning the appropriate classification of depressive disorders in eneral (Kendell, 1976). Much of the confusion is due to failure to distinguish etween the classification of patients and the classification of symptoms Kendell, 1969). While there is fairly general agreement that there are at least two inds of depression there is no agreement as to whether there are two or more iagnostic groups of patients which are relatively distinct from one another. everal cluster analytic studies have shown that there is a distinct group of atients suffering from psychotic depression (Pilowsky *et al.*, 1969; Everitt *et al.*, 971; Paykel, 1971) but this does not seem to be true of so-called neurotic epression. This has led Everitt and his colleagues to suggest that the most useful rm of classification will prove to be a combination of a dimensional system in elation to the neuroses and a categorical or typological one in relation to the sychoses (Everitt *et al.*, 1971). In the light of this slowly emerging consensus, it as been suggested that the attempt to arrive at a differential diagnosis in relation depressed patients is inappropriate (Garside, 1981). Two separate questions hould be asked rather than one; first, is the patient suffering from psychotic ndogenous depression or is he not? and, second, to what extent is the person ffering from neurotic reactive depression?

Such arguments concerning classification directly bear on issues such as atient selection and outcome studies. They affect studies relating to the

effectiveness of antidepressants, electroconvulsive therapy, and psychotherap
in the management of depressions presenting in hospital, out-patient, an
general practice patients. However, establishing the efficacy of treatments i
depression is circumscribed by additional problems as recent efforts to clarify th
question of ECT illustrate. Since the introduction of ECT over 40 years ago, th
role of the treatment in depression has been a controversial one (APA, 1978)
Clinical opinion has held that the actual seizure induced by the electricity is th
therapeutic factor but attempts to establish this by comparing ECT witl
'placebo' treatment (i.e. anaesthesia plus muscle relaxation but no electric shock
have produced equivocal results. Cronholm and Ottosson (1960) found that 4
depressed patients treated with electrically induced convulsions improved mor
than did 23 patients in whom the convulsions were shortened by lignocaine, bu
the patients were not allocated at random. Freeman and his colleagues presente
data which suggested that a course of bilaterally applied ECT which began witl
two placebo treatments produced significantly slower improvement than
course which included real ECTs from the outset (Freeman *et al.*, 1978)
However, Lambourn and Gill (1978) reported that depressed patients improve
as quickly with six sessions of placebo ECT as with six real unilaterally applie
treatments. In perhaps the best trial to date, Johnstone and her colleague
(Johnstone *et al.*, 1980) allocated 70 patients with endogenous depression define
by strict criteria on a random basis to a course either of eight simulated ECTs o
to a course of eight real ECTs. The improvement in terms of psychiatrists' rating
in the group of patients given the real ECT was significantly greater than that i
those given the simulated treatments but the difference between the two group
was small in relation to the considerable improvement of both groups over fou
week treatment period. No differences were found between the two groups a
one-month and six-month follow-up. These workers concluded that th
therapeutic benefits of electrically induced convulsions in depression 'were o
lesser magnitude and were more transient than has sometimes been claimed
However, subsequent correspondence concerning this trial illustrates th
problems inherent in the best of attempts to establish effectiveness. Critic
pointed to the fact that patients in the trial may well have been less seriousl
depressed than those for whom ECT is classically recommended (Birley, 1981
that the scales of measurement used may not have been the most sensitiv
(Callender and Jones, 1981), that the frequency of ECT (twice a week) wa
improper (Russell, 1981), three times a week being preferred by most clinicians
and that the anaesthetic used (methohexitone) is known to shorten convulsion
and, in consequence, may well have impaired the effectiveness of the real EC
(Jones and Callender, 1981). Indeed, Jones and Callender, reanalysing th
results, claimed to show that the real ECT was indeed significantly superior to th
simulated variety both in the short-term and over the six months follow-u
(Jones and Callender, 1981).

Trials of ECT illustrate another problem of patient selection which is tha

:linicians can withhold seriously depressed patients from a trial involving the ossibility of a placebo treatment with the result that only moderately depressed atients are included. It is difficult to allow for this in a trial's design. In the Northwick Park trial (Johnstone *et al.*, 1980), the possibility that not all the atients were seriously depressed is raised by the fact that 90 out of 109 depressed patients of appropriate age' were considered to be candidates for the reatment, a surprisingly high proportion. Here the selection problem is the opposite of that encountered in the Tavistock–Maudsley psychotherapy trial, in hat more patients than would ordinarily have been deemed suitable for ECT appear to have been included in the ECT trial whereas, of course, the opposite appears to have been the position in the case of the psychotherapy study.

The problem of treatment

If the deficiencies in the information available concerning the natural history of psychiatric disorders deter us from making premature deductions concerning reatment outcome, and if the idiosyncrasies in patient selection serve to warn us against hasty conclusions concerning the superiority or inadequacies of this or hat therapy, the problem of what constitutes the active therapeutic ingredient in any effective therapeutic intervention should prevent us assuming that the reatment works in the way that it was constructed to work.

At least six aspects of the treatment process can be identified in a manner that permits quantification: (1) the technique employed; (2) the particular degree of kill possessed by the therapists; (3) the objectives or goals of the treatment; (4) he actual amount or extent of the treatment; (5) the setting or context of the reatment, and (6) the involvement of the therapist and the patient receiving the reatment. Insufficient attention paid to each of these aspects of treatment is a major contributory factor to the current difficulties encountered by anyone attempting to establish the efficacy of the major psychiatric treatments on the basis of published work. Achieving an acceptable degree of standardization of he technique involved might appear relatively straightforward, at least with the physical treatments, but a glance at the research experience with regard to electroconvulsive therapy quickly reveals that this is far from the case. Attempts o establish the efficacy of ECT are bedevilled by such problems as the positioning of the electrodes (Hesche, 1978), the strength of the current (Gordon, 1981), the timing of the treatment in relation to the expected duration of the illness (Kukopulos *et al.*, 1977), and the production of cognitive impairment Lambourn, 1981). Recent double-blind studies (Freeman *et al.*, 1978; Lambourn and Gill, 1978; West, 1981) have helped clarify the overall question of ECT's effectiveness but the best designed of these studies produced the sobering conclusion that 'the effects of repeated electrically induced convulsions are of relatively short duration' (Johnstone *et al.*, 1980). The importance of patient election is underlined by criticism to the effect that seriously depressed patients, the very category that might be expected to show ECT in the best possible therapeutic light, may well be kept out of double-blind studies on the ethical ground that leaving such potentially suicidal patients with little or no treatment cover cannot be justified. Such an objection is not easy to circumvent.

Standardizing techniques is even more difficult in psychosurgery where the variety of interventions is remarkable and the task of making meaningful comparisons between the various published accounts of therapeutic results a truly herculean one (Valenstein, 1977). Of course the same observation can be made about drug trials. It might be thought that a drug such as amitriptyline as a therapeutic intervention could be standardized quite efficiently. Yet, in the absence of documentation concerning dosage, compliance, and serum levels, the variation that is possible and which might well account for outcome differences between two apparently similar studies is substantial.

Substantial variation too occurs in relation to the treatment effects exercised by particular degrees of therapeutic skill. Yet in that area, namely psychotherapy, where technical knowledge, specialized training, and clinical expertise might well be expected to account for a significant proportion of the treatment variance, the findings suggest quite the reverse. There is remarkably little evidence, for example, that the different psychoanalytical orientations achieve very different results, for all their particular claims to possess explanatory truth and therapeutic power. Indeed, astute and sympathetic observers concede that the analytical schools will disappear as discrete entities as, in Storr's words, 'research discloses the common factors which lead to a successful outcome in psychotherapy' (Storr, 1979). The problem is compounded by the bewildering elasticity of the term 'psychotherapy'. A recently published handbook lists 64 different forms of 'innovative' psychotherapies (Corsini, 1981) so that in the circumstances it is perhaps not surprising that there are almost as many definitions of the process of psychotherapy itself (Wolberg, 1977; Frank 1978; Strupp, 1978; Storr, 1979). The most sophisticated does appear to be that of Meltzoff and Kornreich (1970) which terms it 'The informed and planned application of techniques derived from established psychological principles, by persons qualified through training and experience to understand these principles and to apply these techniques to modify such personal characteristics as feelings values, attitudes and behaviours which are judged by the therapist to be maladaptive or maladjustment'.

But at the heart of such a definition is the assumption that it is indeed training experience, and techniques which together effect change. Yet such research as has been undertaken provides little supportive evidence. The Philadelphia study comparing psychoanalytically-derived psychotherapy, behaviour therapy, and the impact of an introductory in-depth assessment suggested quite the opposite. The results of this study, as Marnor pointed out in the introduction (Sloane, *et al* 1975) 'offer little comfort to those adherents of either group (psychoanalytically derived psychotherapy or behaviour therapy) who are involved in passionately proclaiming the inherent superiority of this particular brand of therapy over all others'. Such differences as occurred appeared to be more a matter of degree than of substance and, more important, it emerged that the therapist's style and certain behaviours during the interview were of greater therapeutic significance than the elaborate nature of his theory and his technique. Behaviour therapists, for instance, tended to be more directive, more concerned with symptoms, less concerned with childhood memories and despite their reputation for coldness and clinical involvement, warmer and more active therapists. Tape-recorded interviews showed that they made as many interpretative statements as did the psychotherapists. Given the similarities between the two approaches in practice, it is not clear from the study whether the behaviourists and the psychoanalysts did use fundamentally different therapeutic approaches to reach the same therapeutic conclusions or whether the effectiveness of their treatments was due to factors common to both. But the patients themselves were in no doubt. Those who improved attributed their improvement less to the theoretical framework within which they had been treated and more to the personality, enthusiasm, and involvement of the therapists by whom they had been treated.

One of the most remarkable reviews of research on the efficacy of psychotherapy is the 'meta-analysis' conducted Mary Lee Smith and Gene Glass at the University of Colorado (Smith and Glass, 1977). Meta-analysis is described as 'the statistical analysis of a large collection of analysis results from individual studies for the purpose of integrating the findings' (Glass, 1976). Such an analysis is in contra-distinction to causal, narrative discussions of research studies which generally suffer from significant methodological difficulties. Smith and Glass inspected more than 1 000 published studies, retained 500 as appropriate and fully analysed the results of 375 controlled investigations. To be selected, a study had to have at least one treatment group compared to an untreated group or a different therapy group. The definition of psychotherapy employed was that of Meltzoff and Kornreich (1970) and studies in which the treatment was labelled 'counselling' but whose methods fitted this definition were included.

The most important feature of any outcome study is the magnitude of the effect of therapy. The definition of the magnitude of effect or 'effect size' was the mean difference between the treated and control subjects divided by the standard deviation of the control group. Thus an effect size of $+ 1$ indicates that a person at the mean of the control group would be expected to rise to the 84th percentile of the control group after treatment. The effect size was calculated on any outcome variable the researcher choose to measure. The effect sizes of the various 'independent variables' were 16 features of the study described or measured as follows:

(1) Type of therapy.
(2) Duration of therapy in hours.
(3) Whether it was group or individual.

(4) Experience, in years, of therapist.
(5) Whether clients were neurotic or psychotic.
(6) Age of clients.
(7) IQ of clients.
(8) Source of clients.
(9) Whether therapists were trained in education, psychology or psychiatry.
(10) Whether therapists and clients were similar, socially and ethnically.
(11) Type of outcome measure taken.
(12) Number of months after therapy outcome measured.
(13) The reactivity of the outcome measure.
(14) The date of publication of the study.
(15) The form of publication.
(16) The internal validity of the research design.

Two points deserve to be highlighted from this intriguing and imaginative approach. The first is that the symptoms which appeared to respond best were anxiety and depression whereas attempts to change attitudes tended to founder. (The most striking finding in this regard was that the average treated client is better off than 83 per cent of those untreated with respect to fear, anxiety, and self-esteem.) The second point is that there is not a great deal to choose between the various therapies. The average effect sizes for 10 different types of therapy are shown in Table 2. Psychodynamic therapy is described as 'Freudian-like', that is to say dynamically-based and achieves an average effect size of approximately 0.6 of a standard deviation. The average of over 200 effect size measures from approximately 100 studies of systematic desensitization was 0.9 sigma, the largest

Table 2   Effects of ten types of therapy on any outcome measure (Smith and Glass, 1977)

Therapy	Average effect size	No. of effect sizes	SE of mean effect size	Media treated person's percentile status in control group
Psychodynamic	0.59	96	0.05	72
Adlerian	0.71	16	0.19	76
Eclectic	0.48	70	0.07	68
TA	0.58	25	0.19	72
Rational	0.77	35	0.13	78
Gestalt	0.26	8	0.09	60
Client-centred	0.63	94	0.08	74
Systematic desensitization	0.91	223	0.05	82
Implosion	0.64	45	0.09	74
Behaviour Modification	0.76	132	0.06	78

average size of all the therapies. Correlations between duration of therapy, experience of therapists, group versus individual, and effect size were negligible whereas those between effect size and IQ of the clients and the similarity of the clients and therapists ethnically and socially were highly significant.

Of course, it has been objected that lumping together theories into broad classes obscures real differences between them (Presby, 1978) and that the inclusion by Smith and Glass of reports of undetermined reliability in their analysis invalidates their conclusions (Eysenck, 1978). It is probably too early to determine the true merit of such work (Costello, 1980) but some shortcomings, encountered in such an approach, could be avoided in the future.

Other studies of the efficacy of psychotherapy all point in the same direction—there is precious little evidence that the specific elements of this or that orientation are crucial to outcome (Luborsky *et al.*, 1975; Bergin and Lambert, 1978; Hogan, 1979; Luborsky *et al.*, 1980; Rounsaville *et al.*, 1981). In the light of such findings, it has been suggested that a more hopeful direction of research would be to explore 'therapeutically relevant' qualities of the patient, the therapist, and their interaction (Gelder, 1976; Frank, 1979). Frank (1978) has drawn attention to four features common to all forms of psychotherapies and which deserve much closer examination. The first concerns the special type of relationship, often described, between a therapist who offers help and a patient who seeks it. The second shared feature concerns the setting which is always sharply distinguished from the arena of daily living and can be identified as a sanctuary and place of healing. The third common ingredient is the cognitive structure or conceptual scheme employed while the fourth is a procedure which each therapy prescribes, which requires the active participation of both patient and therapist and which is believed by both to be the means of restoring the patient's health. Common effects of such therapies include the production of some degree of emotional arousal, the expansion of a patient's horizons and an increase in his options, the arousal and maintenance of the patient's hope for improvement, and the enhancement of the patient's sense of personal integration and security.

Summary

The meticulous review by Hogan (1979) of the status of psychotherapy indicates the extent to which psychiatric research in general has some way to go before the therapeutic effectiveness of the various treatments in psychiatry, and the precise elements in each treatment which contribute to efficacy, can be identified with any precision. Helmchen (1979) has identified a number of unsolved problems relating to the treatment of depression which, slightly modified, can be applied to psychiatric treatments in general. First, is the fact that the concepts of therapy and prophylaxis and particularly their relationship to each other are unclear. Secondly, the extent to which it is safe to generalize from the results of treating patients at the severe end of the illness spectrum is not known. Thirdly, psychiatric classifications are insufficiently oriented towards therapeutic considerations. Fourthly, the proportion of various psychiatric conditions which are resistant to the various therapies applied to them is unclear as are the explanations of such resistance.

Knowledge is also lacking concerning the role and the nature of suggestion and of the extent to which a therapist's effectiveness can be related to his/her role as a placebo exploiting the suggestibility of the patient. A well recognized admonition in medicine—'treat as many patients with the new remedies while they still have the power to heal'—relates to one aspect of such a suggestibility. Even supposedly well-proven techniques, such as behaviour modification, may lose their impact with the passage of time. The precise nature of so-called 'spontaneous remission' also deserves more scrutiny than it ordinarily receives and in this respect it is interesting to recall Bergin's suggestion that it may be the result of people in distress seeking help from friends and other help-giving sources (Bergin, 1963). Of course the whole issue of which came first, social networks and supports or psychological health, is currently amongst the thornier of problems facing psychiatric researchers (Vaillant, 1979; Henderson, 1981). However, evidence of the effectiveness of placebos, faith healing, spontaneous remission, leaderless groups, social support, and other variables apart from the practitioner and his theories and skills does not necessarily indicate that the professional has no influence. Rather it raises two significant issues. First, psychiatrists, and particularly psychotherapists, may play a far smaller role than hitherto recognized in determining whether the patient improves. Second, even if the practitioner is indeed important, the evidence of the influence of such factors as the placebo should generate inquiry into whether traditional measures of therapeutic competence are valid.

References

American Psychiatric Association (1978). Task Force Report 14. *Electroconvulsive Therapy*. American Psychiatric Association, Washington, D. C.
Armor, D. J., Polich, J. M., and Stambul, H. B. (1978). *Alcoholism and Treatment*. John Wiley Interscience: New York and Chichester.
Barber, J. H. (1981). Depressive illness in general practice. In Recent Advances in the Treatment of Depression. *Acta Psychiatrica Scandinavica Supplementum* 290, **63**, 441–446.
Bennett, D. H. (1980). Commentary on current trends in the medical treatment of schizophrenia. In *Current Trends in Treatment in Psychiatry* (Edited by Tennant, T. G.) Pitman Medical: Bath.
Bergin, A. E. (1963). The effects of psychotherapy: negative results revisited. *Journal of Counselling Psychology*, **10**, 244–250.
Bergin, A. E., and Lambert, M. J. (1978). The evaluation of therapeutic outcomes. In *Handbook of Psychotherapy and Behavior Change* (Edited by Garfield, S. L., and Bergin, A. E.), 2nd edition. John Wiley: New York.

Bielski, R. J. and Friedel, R. O. (1976). Prediction of tricyclic antidepressant response. *Archives of General Psychiatry*, **33**, 1479–1489.

Birley, J. L. T. (1981). The Northwick Park ECT Trial. Letter. *Lancet*, **i**, 222.

Blashki, T. G., Mowbray, R., and Davies, B. (1971). Controlled trial of amitriptyline in general practice. *British Medical Journal*, **1**, 133–138,

Bleuler, M. (1974). The long term course of the schizophrenic psychoses. *Psychological Medicine*, **4**, 244–254.

Bloch, S. (1979). Assessment of patients for psychotherapy. *British Journal of Psychiatry*, **135**, 193–208.

Burt, C. G., Gordon, W. F., Holt, N. F., and Hordern, A. (1962). Amitriptyline in depressive states: a controlled trial. *Journal of Mental Science*, **108**, 711–730.

Callender, K., and Jones, G. (1981). The Northwick Park ECT Trial. Letter *Lancet*, **1**, 283–284.

Candy, J. Balfour, F. H. G., Cawley, R. H., Hildebrand, H. P., Malan, D. H., Marks, I. M., and Wilson, J. (1972). A feasibility study for a controlled trial of formal psychotherapy. *Psychological Medicine*, **2**, 345–362.

Cheung, H. K. (1981). Schizophrenics fully remitted on neuroleptics for 3–5 years—to stop or continue drugs? *British journal of Psychiatry*, **138**, 490–494.

Clare, A. W. (1980). *Psychiatry in Dissent*. 2nd. edition. Tavistock, London.

Clare, A. W., and Williams, P. (1981). Factors leading to psychotropic drugs prescription. In *The Misuse of Psychotropic Drugs* (Edited by Murray, R., Ghodse, H., Harris, C., Williams, D., and Williams, P) Special Publication No. 1. Gaskell: The Royal College of Psychiatrists, London.

Cooper, D. (1967). *Psychiatry and anti-psychiatry*. Ballantine, New York.

Cooperstock, R. (1971). Sex differences in the use of mood modifying drugs: an explanatory model. *Journal of Health and Social Behavior*, **12**, 238–244.

Corsini, R. J. (1981). *Handbook of Innovative Psychotherapies*. Wiley, New York.

Costello, R. M. (1980). Alcoholism treatment effectiveness: slicing the outcome pie. In *Alcoholism Treatment in Transition* (Edited by Edwards, G., and Gravi, M.) Croom Helm, London.

Creese, I., Burt, D., and Snyder, S. (1978). Biochemical action of neuroleptic drugs: focus on the dopamine receptor. In *Handbook of Psychopharmacology*, Vol. 10, *Neuroleptics and Schizophrenia* (Edited by Iversen, L. L., Iversen, S. D., and Snyder, S. H.) Chapter 2. Plenum Press: New York and London.

Cronholm, B., and Ottosson, J-O (1960). Experimental studies of the therapeutic action of electroconvulsive therapy in endogeneous depression. *Acta Psychiatrica Scandinavica*, Supplementum, **145**, 35, 69–101.

Davies, D. L. (1962). Normal drinking in recovered alcohol addicts. *Quarterly Journal of Studies on Alcohol*, **23**, 94–104.

Davis, J. (1975). Overview: Maintenance therapy in psychiatry: 1. Schizophrenia. *American Journal of Psychiatry*, **132**, 1237–1245.

Davis, J. (1976). Recent developments in the drug treatment of schizophrenia. *American Journal of Psychiatry*, **133**, 208–214.

Everitt, B. S., Gourlay, A. J., and Kendell, R. E. (1971). An attempt at validation of traditional psychiatric syndromes by cluster analysis. *British Journal of Psychiatry*, **119**, 399–412.

Eysenck,, H. J. (1978). An exercise in mega-silliness. *American Psychologist*, **33**, 5, 517.

Falloon, I., Watt, D. C., and Shepherd, M. (1978). A comparative controlled trial of pimozide and fluphenazine decanoate in continuation therapy of schizophrenia. *Psychological Medicine*, **8**, 59–70.

Foster, F. M. J., Horn, J. L., and Wanberg, K. W. (1972). Dimensions of treatment outcome: a factor-analytic study of alcoholics' Responses to a Follow-Up Questionnaire. *Quarterly Journal of Studies on Alcohol*, **33**, 1079–1098.

Frank, J. D. (1978). General psychotherapy: the restoration of morale. In *American Handbook of Psychiatry*. (Edited by, Arieti, S.) 2nd edition. Chap. 17. 117–132. Basic Books, New York.

Frank, J. D. (1974). Psychotherapy: The restoration of morale. *American Journal of Psychiatry*, **131**, 271–274.

Frank, J. D. (1979). The present status of outcome studies. *Journal of Consulting and Clinical Psychology*, **47**, 2, 310–316.

Freeman, C. P. L., Basson, J. V., and Crighton, A. (1978). Double blind controlled trial of electroconvulsive therapy (ECT) and simulated ECT in depressive illness *Lancet*, **i**, 738–740.

Freud, S. (1932). Explanations, applications and orientations. Lecture 34 *New introductory lectures on psychoanalysis standard edition*, **22**, 1–182.

Garside, R. F. (1981). Bimodality and the nature of depression. Letter. *British Journal of Psychiatry*, **139**, 168–176.

Gelder, M. G. (1976) Research methodology in psychotherapy—Why bother? *Proceedings of the Royal Society of Medicine*, **69**, 505–508.

Gerard, D. L., Saenger, G., and Wile, R. (1962). The abstinent alcoholic. *Archives of General Psychiatry*, **6**, 83–95.

Gibson, A. C. (1978). Depot injections and tardive dyskinesia. *British Journal of Psychiatry*, **132**, 361–365.

Glass, G. V. (1976). Primary, Secondary and Meta-Analysis of Research. Paper presented as presidential address to the 1976 Annual Meeting of the American Educational Research Association, San Francisco, California, April 21.

Glen, A. I. M., Johnson, A. L., and Shepherd, M. (1981). Continuation therapy with lithium and amitriptyline in unipolar depressive illness: a controlled clinical trial. *Psychological Medicine*, **11**, 409–416.

Goldberg, D., and Huxley, P. (1980). *Mental Illness in the Community: The Pathway to Psychiatric Care*, Tavistock, London.

Gordon, D. (1981). The electrical and radiological aspects of ECT. In *Electroconvulsive therapy: an appraisal* (Edited by Palmer, R. L.) Chapter 10. Oxford University Press, Oxford.

Gostin, L. O. (1975). *The Mental Health Act from 1959 to 1975: Observations, Analysis and Proposals for Reform* Vol. 1 MIND Special Report, London. MIND (National Association for Mental Health.

Halleck, S. (1974). Legal and ethical aspects of behavior control. *American Journal of Psychiatry*, **131**, 381–387.

Hare, E. H., McCance, C., and McCormick, W. O. (1964). Imipramine and "Drinamyl" in depressive illness. A comparative trial. *British Medical Journal*, **i**, 818–820.

Helmchen, H. (1979). Current trends of research on antidepressive treatment and prophylaxis. *Comprehensive Psychiatry*, **20**, 3, 201–214.

Henderson, S. (1981). Social relationships, adversity and neurosis: an analysis of prospective observations. *British Journal of Psychiatry*, **138**, 391–398.

Hesche, J., Roder, E., and Thielgaard, A. (1978). Unilateral and Bilateral ECT. *Acta Psychiatrica Scandinavica*, Supplementum, **275**, 37–40.

Hicks, D. (1976). *Primary Health Care* HMSO, London.

Hirsch, S. R., Gaind, R., Rohde, P. D., Stevens, B. C., and Wing, J. K. (1973). Outpatient maintenance of chronic schizophrenic patients with long-acting fluphenazine: double-blind placebo trial. *British Medical Journal*, **i**, 633–637.

Hirsch, S. R. (1980). Current trends in the medical treatment of schizophrenia. In *Current Trends in Treatment in Psychiatry* (Edited by Tennent, T. G.) Pitman Medical, Bath.

Hogan, D. B. (1979). *The Regulation of Psychotherapists* Vol. 1. Ballinger, Cambridge, Mass.

Hogarty, G., and Ulrich, R. (1977). Temporal effect of drug and placebo in delaying relapse in schizophrenic outpatients. *Archives of General Psychiatry*, **34**, 297–301.

Hogarty, G., Goldberg, S., Schoder, N., and Ulrich, R. (1974). Drug and sociotherapy in the aftercare of schizophrenic patients. II. Two year relapse rates. *Archives of General Psychiatry*, **31**, 603–609.

Hutt, R., Parsons, D., and Pearson, R. (1979). *The Determinants of Doctors' Career Decisions*. Institute of Manpower Studies. University of Sussex, Brighton.

Jacobs, M., Thompson, L. A., and Truxaw, P. (1975). The use of sexual surrogates in counselling. *Counselling Psychologist*, **5**, 73–77.

Johnson, D. A. W. (1974). A study of the use of antidepressant medication in general practice. *British Journal of Psychiatry*, **125**, 186–192.

Johnson, D. A. W. (1978). The prevalence and treatment of drug-induced extrapyramidal symptoms. *British Journal of Psychiatry*, **132**, 27–30.

Johnson, D. A. W. (1981). Depression: Treatment compliance in general practice. In Recent Advances in the Treatment of Depression. *Acta Psychiatrica Scandinavica, Supplementum 290*, **63**, 447–453.

Johnson, D. A. W., and Breen, M. (1979). Weight changes with depot neuroleptic maintenance therapy. *Acta Psychiatrica Scandinavica*, **59**, 525–528.

Johnstone, E. C., Crow, T. J., Frith, C. D., Carney, M. W. P., and Price, J. S. (1978). Mechanism of the antipsychotic effect in the treatment of acute schizophrenia. *Lancet*, **i**, 848–851.

Johnstone, E. C., Deakin, J. F. W., Lawler, P., Frith, C. D., Stevens, M., McPherson, K., and Crow, T. J. (1980). The Northwick Park Electroconvulsive Therapy Trial. *Lancet*, **ii**, 1317–1320.

Jones, G., and Callender, K. (1981). The Northwick Park ECT Trial. Letter. *Lancet*, **i**, 500–501.

Karasu, T. (1981). Ethical aspects of psychotherapy. In *Psychiatric Ethics* (Edited by Bloch, S., and Chodoff, P.) Chapter 6, 89–116. Oxford University Press, Oxford.

Kendell, R. E. (1968). Normal drinking by former alcohol addicts. *Quart, Journal of Studies on Alcohol*, **24**, 44–60.

Kendell, R. E. (1969). *The Classification of Depressive Illnesses* Maudsley Monograph No. 18 Oxford University Press, London.

Kendell, R. E. (1976). The classification of depressions: a review of contemporary confusion. *British Journal of Psychiatry*, **129**, 15–28.

Kernberg, O. F., Burstein, E. D., Ciyne, L., Appelbaum, A., Horwitz, L., and Voth, H. (1972) Psychotherapy and psychoanalysis: final report of the Menninger foundation's psychotherapy research project. *Bulletin of the Menninger Clinic*, 1–2.

Kukopulos, A., Reginaldi, D., Tondo, L., Bernabei, A., and Galiari, B. (1977). Spontaneous length of depression and response to ECT. *Psychological Medicine*, **7**, 625–629.

Lader, M. (1978). Benzodiazepines—the opium of the masses? *Neuroscience*, **3**, 159–165.

Laing, R. D. (1967). *The Politics of Experience*. Penguine, Harmondsworth.

Lambourn, J. (1981). Is cognitive impairment one of the therapeutic ingredients of ECT? In *Electroconvulsive Therapy: An Appraisal* (Edited by Palmer, R. L.) Chapter 11, 97–105. Oxford University Press, London.

Lambourn, J., and Gill, D. (1978). A controlled comparison of simulated and real ECT. *British Journal of Psychiatry*, **133**, 514–519.

Lancet (1978). Editorial: Stress, distress and drug treatment **4**, 1347–1348.

Lancet (1981). Multicentre Depression. Editorial. ii, 563–564.

Leff, J., and Vaughn, C. (1981). The role of maintenance therapy and relatives' expressed emotion in relapse of schizophrenia. A two-year follow-up. *British Journal of Psychiatry*, **139**, 102–104.

Leff, J., and Wing, J. K. (1971). Trial of maintenance therapy in schizophrenia. *British Medical Journal*, **3**, 599–604.

Lewis, A., (1979). Psychiatric dicta. *The Late Papers of Sir Aubrey Lewis*. Oxford University Press, London.

Little, J. C., Kerr, T. A., and McClelland, H. A. (1978). Where are the untreated depressives? *British Medical Journal*, i, 1593–1594.

Luborsky, L., Singer, B., and Luborsky, L. (1975). Comparative studies of psychotherapies: is it true that 'everyone has won and all must have prizes'? *Archives of General Psychiatry*, **32**, 995–1008.

Luborsky, L., Mintz, J., Auerback, A., Christopher, P., Bachrach, H., Todd, T., Johnson, M., Cohen, M., and O'Brien, C. P. (1980). Predicting, the outcome of psychotherapy. *Archives of General Psychiatry*, **37**, 471–481.

McGarry, L., and Chodoff, P. (1981). The ethics of involuntary hospitalization. In *Psychiatric Ethics* (Edited by Bloch, S., and Chodoff, P.) Chapter 11, 203–219. Oxford University Press, London.

McKeown, T. (1976). *The Role of Medicine: Dream, Mirage of Nemesis?* Rock Carling Monograph. Nuffield Provincial Hospitals Trust, London.

Malan, D. H., Bacal, H. A., Heath, E. S., and Balfour, F. H. G. (1968). A study of psychodynamic changes in untreated neurotic patients. *British Journal of Psychiatry*, **114**, 525–551.

Medawar, P. B. (1972). *The Hope of Progress*. Methuen, London.

Medical Research Council (1965). Report by Clinical Psychiatry Committee. *British Medical Journal*, i, 881–886.

Meltzoff, J., and Kornreich, M. (1970). *Research in Psychotherapy*, Atherton, New York.

Nielsen, J., Juel-Nielsen, N., and Stromgren, E. (1965). A five-year survey of a psychiatric service in a geographically delimited rural population given easy access to the service. *Comprehensive Psychiatry*, **6**, 139–165.

Odegaard, O. (1972). Epidemiology of the Psychoses. In *Psychiatrie der Gegenwart*, II/I (Edited by Kisker, K. P., Meyer, J. E., and Muller, C.) 2, Aufl, Springer, New York.

Orford, J., Oppenheimer, E., and Edwards, G. (1976). Abstinence or control: the outcome for excessive drinkers two years after consultation. *Behaviour Research and Therapy*, **14**, 409–418.

Pattison, E. M. (1966). A critique of alcoholism treatment concepts with special reference to abstinence. *Quarterly Journal of Studies on Alcohol*, **27**, 49–71.

Paykel, E. S. (1971). Classification of depressed patients: a cluster analysis derived grouping. *British Journal of Psychiatry*, **118**, 275–288.

Paykel, E. S., Klerman, G. L., and Prusoff, B. A. (1970). Treatment setting and clinical depression. *Archives of General Psychiatry*, **22**, 11–21.

Petursson, H. (1979). Prediction of lithium response. *Comprehensive Psychiatry*, **20**, 3, 226–241.

Pilowsky, I., Levine, S., and Boulton, D. M. (1969). The classification of depression by numerical taxonomy. *British Journal of Psychiatry*, **115**, 937–945.

Porter, A. M. W. (1970). Depressive illness in a general practice. A demographic study and a controlled trial of imipramine. *British Medical Journal*, i, 773–778.

Presby, S. (1978). Overly broad categories obscure important differences between therapies. *American Psychologist*, **33**, 5, 514–515.

Redlich, F. (1977). The ethics of sex therapy. In *Ethical Issues in Sex Therapy and Research* (Edited by Masters, E. H., Johnson, V. E., and Kolodny, R.) Little Brown: Boston.

Richardson, H. L. (1966). Intramyocardial lesions in patients dying suddenly and unexpectedly. *Journal of the American Medical Association*, **195**, 254–260.

Roth, L. H. (1980). Mental health commitment: the state of the debate. *Hospital and Community Psychiatry*, **31**, 385–396.

Rounsaville, S. J., Weissman, M. M., and Prusoff, B. A. (1981). Psychotherapy will Depressed Outpatients: Patient and Process variables as predictors of outcome. *British Journal of Psychiatry*, **138**, 67–74.

Rubin, M., and Slonicki, A. (1967). A proposed mechanism for the skin-eye syndrome. In *Neuropsychopharmacology* (Edited by Brill, H.) International Congress Services, No. 129. Excerpta Medica Foundation, Amsterdam, 661–679.

Russell, R. J. (1981). The Northwick Park ECT Trial. Letter. *Lancet*, **1**, 98.

Shepherd, M. (1981). Psychiatric research in medical perspective. *British Medical Journal*, **282**, 961–963.

Shepherd, M., Cooper, B., Brown, A. C., and Kalton, G. W. (1966). *Psychiatric Illness in General Practice*. Oxford University Press, London.

Shepherd, M., Cooper, B., Brown, A. C., Kalton, G. W., and Clare, A. W. (1981). *Psychiatric Illness in General Practice*. 2nd. Edition. Oxford University Press, London.

Sloane, R. B., Staples, F. R., Cristol, A. H., Yorkston, J. J., and Whipple, K. (1975). *Psychotherapy Versus Behavior Therapy*. Harvard University Press, Boston.

Smith, M. L., and Glass, G. V. (1977). Meta-analysis of psychotherapy outocme studies. *American Psychologist*, **32**, 752–760.

Storr, A. (1979). *The Art of Psychotherapy*. Secker and Warburg/Heinemann, London.

Strupp, H. H. (1978). Psychotherapy research and practice: an overview. In *Handbook of Psychotherapy and Behavior Change* (Edited by Garfield, S. L., and Bergin, A. E.) 2nd. Edition. Wiley, New York. Chapter 1, 3–22.

Sudhoff, K. (1925). *The Earliest Printed Literature on Syphilis* (Adapted by Charles Singer). Florence. 172.

Szasz, T. (1971). *The Manufacture of Madness* Routledge and Kegan Paul, London.

Vaillant, G. E. (1979). Natural history of male psychologic health. *New England Journal of Medicine*, **301**, 23, 1249–1254.

Valenstein, E. S. (1977). The practice of psychosurgery: a survey of the literature. (1971–1976) In *Psychosurgery* Appendix 1–1–1–143 U.S. National Commission for the Protection of Human Subjects of Biomedical and Behavioral Research. US DHEW Publ. No. (OS) 77–0002.

Vedrine, J. (1967). Les hyperthermies liées à l'administration des neuroleptiques. In *Actualitie du Therapeutique Psychiatrique*. (Edited by Lamber). Masson, Paris. 332–350.

Wechsler, H., Grosser, G. H., and Greenblatt, M. (1965). Research evaluating antidepressant medications on hospitalised mental patients; a survey of published reports during a five year period. *Journal of Nervous and Mental Disease*, **141**, 231–239.

West, E. D. (1981). Randomized double blind controlled trial of ECT. In *Electroconvulsive Therapy: An Appraisal.* (Edited by Palmer, R. L.) Oxford University Press, London.

Wheatley, D. (1972). Drowsiness and antidepressant drugs in mild depressive illness. *British Journal of Psychiatry*, **120**, 517–519.

Williams, P. (1978). Physical ill-health and psychotropic drug prescription—a review. *Psychological Medicine*, **8**, 683–693.

Wing, J. K., Bebbington, P., Hurry, J., and Tennant, C. (1981). The prevalence in the general population of disorders familiar to psychiatrists in hospital practice. In *What Is A Case?* (Edited by Wing, J. K., Bebbington, P. and Robins, L. N.) Grant McIntyre, London. Chapter 6, 45–61.

Wolberg, L. R. (1977). *The Technique of Psychotherapy* Grune and Stratton, New York.

Mental Illness: Changes and Trends
Edited by Philip Bean
© 1983 John Wiley & Sons Ltd.

CHAPTER 8

Changing clinical practice, 1950–1980

ALFRED MINTO

*Formerly Consultant Psychiatrist, Mapperley Hospital,
Nottingham, now Medical Director, Rampton Hospital.*

The thirty years from 1950 span the most active phase or psychiatric history since the development of asylum practice in the mid-nineteenth century. In retrospect, one wonders whether the energy needed to develop extensive 'hotel' facilities for the insane sapped the drive to find out the causes of mental illness and limited the search for active treatment.

As the large mental hospitals developed—some like small townships with their own railway stations and goods yards—the enlightened attitudes of Tuke and Connolly were lost and 'treating the patient as much in the manner of a rational being as the state of his mind will possibly allow' was replaced by a return to locked wards, rigid discipline, and legal sanctions. Often mental hospitals were ill-funded, poorly staffed institutions, where poor nutrition, overcrowding, and poor standards of hygiene effectively reduced the flimsy benefits of available medical treatment. It is a sharp reminder of the quality of life in mental hospitals in the English speaking world that as late as 1927 Goldberger (Goldberger, 1927) was able to show that pellagra in the State Hospital, Jackson, Mississippi, occurred only in patients and never in staff; that the disease was caused by the diet given to the patient; could be cured by a proper diet; and was readily preventable by such a diet.

And even with such knowledge of the medical problems arising from the poor general care of the mentally ill, the belief was still strongly held even in the 1940s that schizophrenia predisposed patients to tuberculosis—with no reference to the very poor living standards in existence in nearly all mental hospitals of that era as a very likely contributory factor to mental patients developing TB. Despite these difficulties, psychiatrists were, in the main, committed to the idea of finding physical causes of mental disease. It was a common observation when a chronic psychotic developed a severe physical illness that there was often a remarkable improvement in his mental state. In epilepsy it was well known that pre-ictal severe behaviour disorder would often disappear after the patient had had an epileptic seizure. Such observations strengthened the hypothesis of mental illness having a genuine physical cause and led to the development of physical methods of treatment. Earlier crude devices—bloodletting, emetics, and purgatives in an earlier era—were replaced later by the concept of focal infection as a cause of disease. Treatment arising from this involved the pulling of teeth and the removal of many an innocent tonsil. Much effort was applied to finding ways to directly effect physical change in the brain by the use of organic therapies. These efforts reached a peak in the 1930s with Sakel's insulin coma therapy (Sakel, 1933), drug induced convulsions in the treatment of schizophrenia (Meduna, 1935), and electroconvulsive therapy (Cerletti and Bini, 1938). Surprisingly, as early as 1888 the Swiss psychiatrist Burckhardt had carried out the first psycho-surgery in an attempt to curb violent behaviour in a patient, but his work was not developed until 1935 by Moniz (Moniz, 1935). This pioneer work was much amplified and developed by Freeman and Watts in the United States (Freeman and Watts, 1942).

These developments in treatment were not fully explored because of the Second World War, but one important technique, drug induced abreaction, was developed in the combat situation for the management of war neurosis, e.g., severe anxiety state or hysterical dissociative symptoms released under severe stress (Sargant and Slater, 1941). This treatment showed probably for the first time, outside the mental hospital setting, that psychiatry as a discipline was not just theory and detention, but that patients could be treated effectively. One obvious effect was the prevention of the grossly crippling shell-shock cases found after the First World War. The effect of the Second World War on psychiatric practice was dramatic in two ways—technical and social. Some aspects of technical change will be examined later, but great benefit came to the mental hospitals as a result of general medical advances; penicillin for acute infections especially syphilis, isoniazide and streptomycin for tuberculosis, and better and more effective drugs for the treatment of infective disease of the bowel. With these new therapies much of the misery of physical disease in mental hospitals was eliminated leaving staff better able to pursue psychiatric care instead of the physical drudgery of nursing so many patients with severe physical illness, e.g. general paralysis of the insane, in addition to mental symptoms.

Western society was still in a state of turmoil after the war. A new egalitarianism had given rise, not only towards political change, but to an unwillingness to accept the pre-war social patterns of which the mental hospital was the archetypal authoritarian example. It is therefore not surprising that this change in social attitude combined with genuine possibilities of effective treatment should give sharp impetus to major changes in mental health practice. Although the stigma of mental illness was, and to some degree still is, a strong feature of public response, the war seemed to have softened some of the more retributive attitudes towards mentally ill people allowing the development of dramatic changes in the old asylums. Four factors influenced the sudden burst of psychiatric activity of the early 1950s.

1. Changes in the social structure and community attitudes with a greater concern for individual liberty and community acceptance of the responsibility for sick people, including the mentally sick.
2. A movement within the mental hospitals themselves to bring the social practices of hospital more into line with ordinary community.
3. The development of specific medical treatments which dramatically affected the way in which mentally ill patients coped with their disorders.
4. The development of out-patient, domiciliary, and day hospital facilities.

Changes in social attitudes

The immediate post-war period was marked by optimism and great social change e.g. the Welfare State in the United Kingdom—but at the same time there had been a loosening of the old family patterns with extensive movement of individuals to new homes far distant from their family. Perhaps the sharpest evidence of this was seen in England where there was a marked increase in certification of old people who were admitted to mental hospitals—from 31,000 in 1948 to 45,000 in 1954—nearly one-third of the total mental hospital population of 152,000 at that time. Despite this trend, it is interesting to note that in 1964 only 5 per cent of the elderly in the United Kingdom were in institutions.

People were more aware of their rights as citizens than in pre-war years. The aspirations of the community stemmed from the conviction that having overcome Naziism we must continue to expand and protect the liberty of the individual, especially if that individual was unable, by reason of infirmity to look after his own interests. The idea of all people being responsible for the provision of health care was an important stimulus to changes in the mental health field, since more resources became available, particularly in the United Kingdom with the development of the National Health Service.

Changes in professional attitudes

In addition to the very substantial improvements in mental hospitals arising from the elimination of much of the gross physical disease affecting many patients, the post-war era was marked by optimism about treatment and its beneficial effects which, in retrospect, were somewhat naive. But supported by this new hopefulness for recovery from mental illness, which was simply not there before the physical treatments were introduced, some workers were already reviewing the traditional professional attitudes towards psychiatric patients. In an era where no effective therapy existed, the agonizing miseries of chronic depression, the disintegration of the schizophrenic to a state of total withdrawal from his environment, and the physical decay of so many patients must have been daunting to all staff working in mental hospitals. With the new therapies there was the possibility of trying out some of the psychological approaches which would have had little hope of success previously. Despite the many problems besetting mental hospitals in the first half of the twentieth century, the beginning of an enlightened attitude to the management of mental illness had been apparent since the early 1900s when, for example, nearly half of the first 1,500 in-patients admitted to the Boston Psychopathic Hospital were in a voluntary category. By 1930 a similar category had been introduced in England by the Mental Treatment Act of 1930. In 1950 there was ready recognition of the fact that most psychiatric illness could be treated in a more free and relaxed setting than had been traditionally provided. This approach reached its first full expression when Bell at Dingleton, Rees at Warlingham Park, and MacMillan at Mapperley in Nottingham unlocked the doors of their 3 mental hospitals in the face of much scepticism, sadly led largely by other psychiatrists and nurses who could not face the clear responsibility inherent in such a mental hospital setting. If a hospital is open, psychiatrists and nurses have to enter into a dialogue with patients and it is no longer possible to avoid dealing with the patients' viewpoint. The traditional device of turning a key in a ward lock will no longer be sufficient. It is not therefore wholly surprising that the pioneers of the open door policy—last practised in the mid-nineteenth century—should have met derision and rejection of their proposals. The implementation of an open door policy forced professional staff to regard the patient as an equal with the right to demand respect of his personal dignity and to be offered treatment in a shared partnership arrangement with his professional advisers. Mental hospital staff who were working in a prison-like environment did not have to make great efforts to meet the patients' needs and aspirations—certainly there seemed little awareness of the need to explain to a patient what was involved in treatment, how it might work, what benefit might accrue to the patient and also, what harm it could do. I do not recall anybody telling patients when electroconvulsive therapy was given without anaesthetic or muscle relaxant that it was well known that cracked vertebrae, dislocated jaws, and even serious damage to the hip joints, could be side-effects of the treatment.

Opening up mental hospitals introduced a new and dramatic ingredient into the psychiatric process. If a patient did not like the proffered treatment programme he could simply walk out of hospital whereas patients in closed hospitals were not immediately able to do so. (Up to 1960, voluntary patients in England had to give 3 days notice of their intention to leave hospital, a condition much easier to apply in a closed setting.) The simple device of opening the doors was important but it could not have contributed much to treatment if that was all that happened. It soon became clear in those hospitals where the open door policy had been adopted that patient choice radically altered the traditional psychiatric ideas about prognosis, especially on the thorny topic of anti-social behaviour in the mentally ill. It was soon obvious that the previous lengthy periods of in-patient treatment were unnecessary in most cases. Not only was the old system a waste of scarce psychiatric resources but it was detrimental to the patients because they so easily became institutionalized and, more seriously, lost their place in society. It is from this viewpoint about loss of contact with society that the much abused concept of the 'revolving door' policy arose. This policy accepted that at the time of his discharge a patient might not be wholly recovered, but accepted further that he might be well enough to cope albeit at a limited level, in the community. If the strain was too great on him, he might well have to return for further treatment, but in the meantime he had again been back with his family, perhaps even started work, and generally be seen by his family and friends to be very much a living being and not a forgotten shadow in a remote locked up institution. This development in mental hospital practice was reinforced by the new therapies to be described later, together with the development of out-patient, domiciliary, and day care facilities. That the policy worked is beyond dispute. It we look, for example, at the effect of an open door/revolving door policy in Nottingham, we see a hospital where the in-patient population had been decreased from 1,300 in 1948 to under 500 in 1980. MacMillan in discussing his work said, 'Clinically, we were convinced of the good effects and advantages to the patients, but clinical impressions are not sufficient. Independent factual scientific data is required to assess the actual effects, and also to convince sceptics, critics and doubters' (MacMillan, 1970). The Nottingham psychiatric register which was set up in 1958 made an attempt to assess accurately whether the effects of the new policy were simply fads in the eyes of the practitioners operating the service, or whether there was real substance in the idea that such a service really did benefit the most important member of the programme—the patient. One thousand and twelve (1,012) of the new contact cases in 1962 were followed for a 6-year period. The results proved very interesting. Sixty per cent of men and 57 per cent of women did not receive any in-patient care. Twenty-nine per cent were admitted once and 6 per cent twice. One person was admitted 11 times and two persons 10 times during the 6-year period but, of the 167 men and 254 women who were admitted as in-patients, only 3 men and 10 women spent 2 years of more in hospital.

It has been said that achievements of this kind would not have been possible without the development of specific drug therapies. I have wondered over the years about the validity of this viewpoint and I cannot really accept it. Indeed, it is my view that one of the main advantages of drug therapy was that it enabled authoritarian psychiatric staff to maintain a hold over patients, without which they would have been reluctant to become involved in the very important implications of open-door short-stay mental hospital policy. I have a strong suspicion that the retention of the magic of drug therapy has enabled many psychiatric personnel to accept the reality of a genuine therapeutic contract with patients, only because at the back of their minds these workers give greater weight to the efficacy of the drugs than to the wider social values of a more respectful approach to the patient and his treatment. It was, in some ways, a surprising development in psychiatric practice in the past 30 years that, as psychiatrists pushed out into the community becoming involved as much in an educative role as in direct medical activity, so opinion on the role of the psychiatrists in dealing with severe mental illness became sharply divided. On the one hand, Szasz (1963) was saying that 'in a free society no-one should be cast into the role of mental patient against his will' since he believes there is no such thing as mental disease. His references to mental hospitals being prisons and alleged patients not really being sick undoubtedly touched raw nerve endings amongst those doctors whom he described as practising 'coercive psychiatry'. Most psychiatrists can well see the validity of his remarks if one thinks of neurotic patients who are uncomfortable with their life situations, exhibiting 'dis-ease' with their various problems of self-fulfilment, faulty interpersonal relationships and, in the most over-publicised area of all, sexual activity. In such areas there can be little doubt that any form of compulsory psychiatric treatment is pointless and would represent a serious infringement of individual liberty.

Treating the wildly overactive manic psychosis or a dangerously deluded paranoid is a very different problem. To ignore the social disturbance invariably associated with severe mental disease is an example of socially irresponsible behaviour, apart from denying the right to treatment to patients who, by the nature of their mental turmoil, are unable to make an informed decision to seek help for the problems affecting them and caused by them. Even Szasz (1963) suggests that action be taken against an 'aggressive paranoid person who threatens violence'. He says 'legally he should be treated like a person charged with an offence; psychiatrically it would be desirable of course if he were not incarcerated in an ordinary jail but in a prison hospital...' This must be an excellent example of the double-think that has marked this author's various propositions about mental illness in the past 20 years.

Much of this high-flung debate is sheer window-dressing with all parties adopting a pure stance which rapidly drops into actions seen by the one side as a deprivation of liberty and by the other as society protecting itself from the depredations (often more imagined than real) of the mentally ill, and at the same time providing humane treatment facilities. Both camps have said their disparate pieces and both have reached roughly the same position—that it is important to respect individual liberty, but society needs to make some provision for those whose state of mental disturbance prevents them from living amicably with other people without creating nuisance and with due respect for the liberty and rights of others.

The disappointing spin-off from all this debate was the opposite to what might have been expected. Having settled for provision of a caring process, one would have looked for substantial improvement in the ways in which care was provided for those with chronic mental disease but this has not been the case. The mental hospital scene has been one of steady and increasing resistance to the provision of psychiatric treatment and long-term support to a group of sick people who do not respond to current treatment. Sadly, the revolving door has turned more rapidly for the long-stay schizophrenic than for any other patient group. It is almost as though the patient's inability to be cured has become a personal insult to his treaters, who respond to his continuing disability as if it were a specific act of non-cooperation in the treatment process rather than a distressingly constant malady over which the patient has little control. There can be few states more pathetic than the withdrawn, hallucinated, neglected, and sometimes starving schizophrenic, barely capable of existence let alone a decent quality of life, who is left to 'enjoy' his miserable state in the wholly spurious name of individual liberty. That such an outcome to the disowning of the chronic schizophrenic by the psychiatric services was not more clearly foreseen appears at variance with the wide acceptance of the concept of institutionalization with the apathy, loss of interest, passivity, and deterioration of personal habits described by Barton (1959). If such a state readily developed in the hospital setting, it is a not surprising but very serious indictment of much current practice, that frequently few steps were taken to help stimulate and protect the chronic psychotic on his return to the community. As Hirsch (1976) has said, we changed the status of these patients from 'chronic institutionalised patients to a new equally undesirable status as lonely, single persons, homeless or inadequately housed, often residing in flop homes, prisons or the park benches with a high prevalence of unemployment and self-neglect'.

It is regrettable that more and more psychiatric resources have been applied to patient groups least needing medical care whilst the serious neglect of an overtly ill group of patients continues to exist. Not all psychiatric practice has developed in this way and in many hospitals interesting and effective steps have been taken to curtail disability and minimize handicap arising from chronic disease. Graded occupation with work routines involving industrial-type processes replaced the craft therapies of an earlier era, encouraging patients towards a return to ordinary life in the community. This enables patients to earn money for their efforts, producing a stimulus to efficient working habits which better equip patients for the often difficult return to life outside hospital. By such programmes, much can be achieved in reducing the handicaps caused by pre-morbid factors such as lack of education and working skills; primary handicaps such as slowness, social withdrawal, affective flatness, and poor initiative and motivation; and finally, the secondary handicaps of long-term institutionalization. By the early 1960s, it was apparent in mental hospitals where such activity had been pursued, that the final step of discharge could best be achieved if the patient could be supported initially by social workers and later, by community psychiatric nurses. The rapid development of the community psychiatric nurse may partly have been to give some gloss to the often criticized short stay treatment policies being developed, but there are other factors of some interest and importance. Nearly all community support in the 1950s had been given by social workers who were, by training, much involved in a Freudian style of thinking about mental illness. They were not very experienced in coping with the brisk and often threatening presentation of chronic psychosis. One found that great weight was given to the expressed thought of patients with dire predictions of imminent breakdown, often leading to requests for urgent re-admission to hospital. With the introduction of the psychiatric nurse, we had a new approach where the nurse trained in actually living with patients in the ward situation was much more matter of fact about the expressed illness and tended to look more for a reasonably settled behaviour pattern in the patient, allowing him to live without causing offence to the community—a tacit acceptance that a substantial degree of mental illness can exist with the patient still presenting to his fellow citizens as an acceptable, albeit odd, person.

It is only fair in this context to add that the maintenance of patients in the community is greatly enhanced by the effects of drug therapy, without which many patients would be unable to cope with the problems constantly affecting them in terms of the force of their diseased inner experience, together with the stress of ordinary living.

Specific medical treatment

By the early 1950s, physical treatment was well developed in most mental hospitals with insulin coma therapy, electroconvulsive therapy, and psychosurgery particularly prominent. There was some activity in the drug field such as continuous narcosis and the use of amphetamines and barbiturates in the neuroses.

Insulin coma therapy

Until the late 1950s and early 1960s nearly all mental hospitals had insulin coma units treating large numbers of schizophrenics with the classical technique outlined by Sakel, in units which needed substantial investment of medical and nursing manpower for their operation. The procedure was bedevilled by a fairly high level of serious complications (prolonged coma, epileptic seizures, and a variety of neurological disasters) but there is little doubt that these units had a very major impact on the attitude to illness in mental hospitals at that time. It may well have been that the technical skills needed for the treatment process lifted the standing of psychiatric staff from the position as minders of patients, to one of truly active therapists with genuine 'medical' skills. Whatever the reason for the impact on the staff, some aspects of the treatment were undoubtedly of great benefit to patients. Treatment was carried out in small groups in living conditions generally much better than on the ordinary wards with staff/patient ratios unheard of in routine mental hospital practice, so that the caring interaction between patients and staff was far superior to anything that the patient might have experienced previously. The way of life for 'insulin' patients was superior to that available in the rest of the hospital. It could be said that the very dangers of the therapy ensured a high staff involvement in patient care.

And some patients undoubtedly did show a real improvement whilst having this treatment, but the overall results were always very mixed, hedged about with a variety of reservations about the type of schizophrenia likely to respond well to the treatment. In some of the reported studies, results claiming remission gave figures of 59.4 per cent in New York, 59.1 per cent in Switzerland, and 66 per cent in Germany (quoted in Kalinowsky and Hippius, 1969), figures which give a favourable 2:1 ratio for insulin treatment compared with an untreated group. Relapse was, however, frequent occurring in up to 50 per cent of cases and long term prognosis was not satisfactory. When we take into consideration the criteria for successful outcome, acute onset, exogenous type of psychosis with high levels of reactive psychogenic material, and the schizophrenoid psychosis of Langfeldt (1937), most current psychiatrists would say that such cases have an excellent prognosis with rapid remission of symptoms without extensive treatment regimes. The more severe forms of schizophrenia, of paranoid hebephrenic and simple types did much less well with insulin therapy, suggesting to this writer that the psychosocial factors involved in the treatment were probably of greater importance than any direct chemical action of insulin on the brain itself. The real value of insulin coma therapy must lie in its importance in directing the minds of psychiatric personnel to the need for, and the great benefits of, good quality interpersonal relationship between patients and staff together with the encouragement of a more research-minded approach to psychiatric problems than had been seen previously in mental hospitals.

Electro-convulsive therapy

From the first description of ECT by Cerletti and Bini in 1938 until the early 1950s there was a steady increase in the use of this treatment with little attempt at scientific evaluation of the benefits. Looking back it seems incredible the amount of time and effort expended on arguments about the merits of different electrical wave-forms and current strengths, when so little was done to enquire into the effects and results of treatment. One gets a clear impression of doctors fascinated by the gadgetry being used, with little real interest in the patients. A typical example of this was the continuation of additional stimuli during the actual convulsion, despite the observation that no response was ever elicited during, and, for a minute or so, after convulsion (Kalinowsky, and Hippius, 1969). A refinement was introduced in this treatment in the early 1950s with the development of combined anaesthesia and muscle relaxation techniques which did a great deal to spare patients the tension and fear associated with ECT, as well as making the treatment much safer despite the added risk of anesthesia. Crushed vertebrae and joint dislocations became a thing of the past eliminating a serious disadvantage of this treatment. Unilateral ECT was first described by Thenon in 1956 in Argentina and the advantages confirmed by Lancaster *et al.* (1958) with less confusion and reduction of memory impairment as a result of unilateral application.

Despite an enormous literature on the subject there is still no single theory which begins to explain the action of ECT. Explanations range from the psychological (fulfilling a desire for punishment, unconscious hope of death) to the idea that the brain is physically damaged by ECT (Friedberg, 1977). Recent works suggest that the effect may be due to a potentiation of the action of 5HT, dopamine, and possibly noradrenaline, if depletion of these transmitters is a genuine cause of depressive symptoms (Grahame-Smith *et al.*, 1978). There has been a steady decline in the use of ECT in the past 10–15 years, the writer, for example, in recent years using ECT in mainly the depressive phase of manic-psychosis with a very rare use in schizophrenia where the patient appeared markedly depressed, in addition to other process symptoms. Antidepressant drugs have superseded ECT in the treatment of neurotic depression and, to a large extent, phenothiazines and other major tranquillizing agents have become the main treatment for schizophrenia. From a situation in the early 1950s where, in a 1000 bed hospital, the writer would be giving ECT to up to 40 patients twice weekly, by 1980 in Nottingham, this had dropped to a treatment of perhaps 7 to 10 patients weekly for a similar population catchment area.

Despite the disputes about how ECT works, and some claim that it does not really work at all, there is little doubt in my mind that there are some forms of life-endangering depressive illness where ECT is still the most valuable treatment available to psychiatrists. The agonizing states of chronic depression seen in an earlier era, simply have not developed to that stage since the use of ECT, and there is no doubt in my mind how much this therapeutic success has contributed to changing the miseries of the 1930s mental hospital into altogether more hopeful places to be treated in today. It would probably be fair to say that the full value of ECT applies to a small well-defined group: mainly depressive illnesses, and that whenever psychiatrists shifted their interests from the mechanical aspects of treatment to the effect of treatment on patients, it was a relatively straightforward exercise to assess the valid use of ECT. What is so incredible is that it took so long before ECT and its effect on patients, was properly evaluated and how, even now, scientifically acceptable trials of ECT are few in number.

Psycho-surgery

Since the original work of Moniz in 1936, psycho-surgery has passed through two distinct phases; an almost abandoned attack on patients—40,000 operations up to 1950 in the United States and 10,365 leucotomies in England between 1942 and 1954—which was followed by a period of sharp disillusionment with psycho-surgery until more recent attempts to introduce very accurate operative techniques, to destroy pin-point areas of brain tissue purported to control specific areas of human conduct. It is very doubtful if these modern day phrenologists of the innards of the brain have any greater claim to accuracy in their predictions than their nineteenth century predecessors who, more modestly and less dangerously, settled for prediction based on surface lumps and bumps. There is some agreement about brain targets that might be important, but it is clear from the literature that there are also large areas of disagreement about techniques to be used. There is better agreement about the type of patient most likely to respond to psycho-surgery, sadly derived mainly from accumulated knowledge of the often horrendous failures of leucotomy in the past 30 years. Many permanently damaged shells of post-leucotomized human beings still languish in our mental hospitals as living testimony to this speculative and frequently ill-advised approach to the treatment of mental illness.

In describing the three main physical treatments in vogue in the first 20 years or so of this study, one is struck again and again by the blind acceptance of them, despite their obvious immediate dangers, long term disabling effects in many cases, and finally, their clear lack of real value to the patients exposed to these treatments. It is to be hoped that the serious defects in responsibility for evaluation of these treatments will never be repeated in future, with psychiatrists organizing their discipline to ensure proper study and evaluation of any new treatment processes that may be introduced.

Drug therapy

The pharmacological aspects of drug therapy are dealt with elsewhere in this book.* From the original observations of Laborit, who produced artificial hibernation as an anaesthetic technique, to the work of Delay and Deniker also (1952) on chlorpromazine there has been a steady development of drugs which affect the ills of the mind for the better, and in safety. In essence, these drugs dampen down the intensity of the patient's reactions to his illness, producing greater benefits in the most severely disturbed patients and, to use Anton-Stephen's terms, often cause 'psychic indifference' to surroundings and symptoms without loss of awareness or contact with the environment (1954).

It is no exaggeration to say that the use of phenothiazines and, to a lesser extent, the butyrophenones, have revolutionized the treatment process in mental hospitals. Whereas previously patients might go for weeks, and sometimes months, exhibiting grossly disturbed behaviour after admission the use of these drug treatments would give to a patient a degree of relief from distress arising from his symptoms which was, at times, so near-miraculous that it was scarcely believable. Much of the physical, frankly combative aspects of patient care was simply no longer necessary, and calm reigned in wards which previously had strong resemblances to the worst kind of snake-pit.

*See also Chapter 10.

Whilst it would be correct to say that these drugs were less effective in more chronic states of illness, even in the long stay wards there were real benefits from their use. Restless, awkward patients were more amenable and less totally absorbed in their inner experience, after drug treatment so that genuine attempts at rehabilitation could be introduced. These more approachable patients could be persuaded to emerge from their psychotic cocoon with improvement in self-care, involvement in useful work, and a consequent diminution in all the oddness of appearance and behaviour, which hitherto had meant that the only place they were not conspicuous was in the company of other untreated patients. Combined with the new liberalism in mental hospitals described earlier, this was truly the watershed of the past three decades with a sense of purpose and achievement in psychiatry, where previously there had been an unhealthy preoccupation with either wholly psychological approaches or acute mechanical interventions with little commitment to long term care. In many cases the two approaches failed to alter the mental state and then the patient was relegated to a back ward to sink further and further into the miseries of this condition.

Two small points spring to mind which vividly illustrate the change. In my early days in psychiatry the textbooks described acrocyanosis of the ankles and feet—a common sign in schizophrenia. It was, of course, a sign of the non-treatment of the illness with patients sitting about for hours on end, totally unstimulated, and even encouraged to stay out of sight as much as possible because there were not enough staff to look after them, except at a very basic physical level. By 1960 the blue-footed schizophrenic was a defunct species in hospitals, where the initial impetus of drug therapy had enabled adequate rehabilitation to be carried out. The other appalling and depressing area of mental hospitals at that time was the airing court system, where patients marched around in circles without halt for the whole of the period of exercise. During this demoralizing spectacle the unfortunate nursing staff stood around watching the patients repeating a process which they had seen hundreds of times before. After the introduction of the phenothiazines, airing courts became a thing of the past since patients were usefully employed in departments like industrial therapy units.

These benefits were added to by the introduction of depot neuroleptics, which permit greater control of drug treatment especially in the out-patients community care setting. Renton *et al.* reported (1963) that 46 per cent of schizophrenic out-patients had failed to take medication and even in the in-patient setting. Hare and Wilcox (1967) reported that 20 per cent of patients failed to take medication given to them by nursing staff. The most definite confirmation of the importance of regular medication came from Hirsch *et al.* (1973) who carried out a double blind trial of Fluphenazine and Decanoate, in which 66 per cent of patients on placebo relapsed within 9 months, compared with only 8 per cent of those on active drug treatment. Unhappily, the depot preparations are more toxic (Rifkin *et al.*, 1977) and it is clearly most important to maintain high standards of care for patients on such treatment. The very ease of giving these drugs has, I suspect, led to poor supervision in many cases with little attempt to ensure that the drugs are not, in fact, simply keeping the patient in a chemical straight-jacket controlling his symptoms, but, with a very low quality of life because of the tiredness and muscle control problems so common as side effects. It is in this field that the community psychiatric nurse can be so important, not only as the person who maintains a regular treatment programme but also to monitor any disadvantages of such treatment to enable early adjustment of dosage.

Over the past few years, the problems of disturbance of gait and tardive dyskinesia appear to be more common than in the early days of phenothiazine therapy and it may be that long term use of these preparations is going to become more hazardous to patients than has been accepted to date. Allowing for these reservations, the benefits accruing from the neuroleptics over the past 25 years, have been of inestimable value. Mental hospitals have been transformed from huge institutions holding battalions of steadily deteriorating psychotics, into active therapeutic communities with good results, high turnover of new cases, and infinitely better services for long standing patients.

Drug treatment of depression has been useful and effective with many more patients being successfully treated by primary care physicians without recourse to psychiatric facilities. There remain patients with depressive illnesses which are resistant to drug therapy, but such cases are now few in number so that one whole area of psychiatric despair has been almost completely removed by these new therapies.

Before 1950 the most active group of patients in mental hospitals suffered from chronic epilepsy, but their activity was usually purposeless and often violent. With the development of adequate anti-convulsant treatment, the problem of the long standing epileptic has disappeared, and we no longer have large wards full of religiose irritable epileptics, passing through successive phases of behaviour disorder, major seizures, and confusion on an almost regular cycle. This is an example of what was formerly a mental illness which presented great difficulties in management, suddenly being reduced both in number and severity by an appropriate organic therapy.

Community services

Out-patient psychiatry has expanded greatly in the past 30 years despite increasing evidence that most psychiatric illness is dealt with in the primary care setting. In studies conducted by the General Practice Research Unit of the Institute of Psychiatry in London, 15,000 patients at risk, were studied over a 12-month period. 2,000 of them, i.e., 14 per cent of the patients, consulted a family doctor about a psychiatric condition but only 1 in 20 of these patients was referred for specialist care. Presumably this means that most of the illness was minor and the only serious cases were sent to psychiatrists. Strangely, this is not my own experience in 20 years consultant practice, mainly in an English industrial city, Nottingham (catchment population 400000) where referrals were generally for minor problems with only a small proportion of major illness—for example, in any one year, this population was throwing up only 50 new cases of schizophrenia a year, which worked out at about 3 or 4 cases per consultant per annum. The general impression was of out-patient psychiatry serving a useful function more at a counselling level than a formal medical model.

The growth of day hospitals in the Western world has been rapid and extensive, with two separate types of unit operating. The first, short term and treatment orientated, the second, long stay and supportive of patients who are unlikely to work again in open employment but can function in a protected environment. Even in such a unit there is always a throughput but this is affected much more by economic factors, recession and employment, than by purely psychiatric factors. In the era of full employment in England, most day hospital facilities which had some form of industrial therapy, could expect a high proportion of patients to return to work. In the present period of high unemployment, opportunities for the mentally ill have decreased (as indeed they have done for all disabled people). In highly competitive Western industrial societies those with chronic and disabling disease, both physical and mental, will always be seriously disadvantaged in the employment field. A great deal of public money could be saved by the development of day-care facilities with a suitable sheltered employment component. Such a service is undoubtedly better for patients who can continue to live in the community partly supporting themselves, albeit in subsidized workshops, instead of being total care problems in hospital. There seems little reason why we cannot provide services where all forms of disability can be helped in the same facility; the brain and skill of the paraplegic setting up the machine to be operated by the stabilized chronic psychotic, with the product being packed by a mentally handicapped person. There are still many barriers to such developments but is surely the next big step towards integration of mentally ill people in the community.

And what of the future?

After 30 years practice, I feel I should speculate a little about the future. The whole pattern of mental illness in the younger age groups has changed with a sharp reduction in long stay hospital care. Mental illness beds in England have been reduced in numbers to levels which seemed impossible when I started in the field. The worst of the treatment problems of past times can now be substantially modified by available therapy which will undoubtedly improve in efficacy and safety as biochemical research pinpoints organic causes of some of the more severe psychiatric illnesses, e.g. schizophrenia and severe affective disorder—perhaps even to a degree which will eliminate the need for psychiatrists as the only therapists of this type of illness. Just as the TB specialist disappeared with streptomycin, the smallpox experts with vaccination, psychiatrists may be faced with a situation where a doctor can, by drug therapy, cure those illnesses which currently absorb a large part of psychiatric resources.

If some other form of practitioner can give the 'phrenia pill', what will the psychiatrist be left with? Not much that will need mental hospital facilities but a lot of people who are just plain old-fashioned, miserable, and fed-up with their life situation and who need the ministrations of a social educationist more than those of an expensively trained psychiatrist. The tide of ageing people continues to rise steadily and with it, the likelihood of increasing numbers of mentally ill amongst the elderly. It may well be the final irony that psychogeriatrics, the neglected area of Western psychiatry in 1980, will be the only area in which future psychiatrists can continue to exercise their special skills.

References

Anton-Stephens, D. (1954). Preliminary observations on the psychiatric uses of chlorpromazine (Largactil). *J. Ment. Science*, **100**, 543.

Barton, R. (1976). *Institutional Neuroses*. Wright, Bristol.

Cerletti, U., and Bini, L. (1938). L'Elettroshock. *Arch Gen di Neurol. Psichiat e Psiloanal.* **19**, 226.

Delay, J., and Deniker, P. (1952). 38 Cas de Psychoses Traite Par La Cure Prolongée et Continué de 4568 RP. *Ann. Med-Psychol.*, 110, 366.

Freeman, W., and Watts, J. W. (1942). *Psycho Surgery*, Springfield, C C Thomas.

Friedberg, J. (1977). Shock treatment, brain damage and memory loss: a neurological perspective. *Am. J. Psychiat.*, **134**, 9, 1010–1016.

Goldberger, J. (1927) Pellagra, its nature and prevention. *Pub. Health Report*, **42**, 2193.

Grahame-Smith. D. G., Green, A. R., and Costain, D. W. (1978). Mechanism of the Antidepressant Action of ECT. *Lancet*, **1**, 254.

Hare, E. H., and Wilcox, D. R. C. (1967). Do psychiatric patients take their pills? *Br. J. Psychiat.*, 113, 1435–1439.

Hirsch, S. R. (1976). Interacting social and biological factors determining prognosis in the rehabilitation and management of persons with schizophrenia, in *Annual Review of the Schizophrenic Syndrome, 1974–75*. (Ed. R. Cancro) Brummer Mazel. New York.

Hirsch, S. R., et al. (1973). Out-patient maintenance of chronic schizophrenic patients with long acting pheno thyazines British Medical Journal. (1) 633.

Kalinowsky, L. B., and Hippius, H. (1969). *Pharmacological, convulsive and other somantic treatments in Psychiatry*. Grune and Stratton, New York.

Lancaster, N. P., Steinert, R. R., and Frost, I. (1958). Unilateral electro-convulsive therapy. *J. Mental Science*, **104**, 221.

Langfeldt, E. (1937). The prognosis in schizophrenia, and the factors influencing the course of the disease. *Acta Psychiat et Neurol.* Supp. 13.

MacMillan, D. (1970). The Function of the Nottingham Register in (Eds.) Wing, J. K. and Bramsby, E. R. *Psychiatric Case Registers, D.H.S.S. Statistical Report Series No. 8.* H.M.S.O. London.

Meduna, L. J. (1938). General Discussion of Cardiazol Therapy. *Am. J. Psychiat.* 94 (Supp) 40.

Moniz, E. (1936) *Tentatives opératoires dans le traitement de certaines psychoses* Paris: Masson et Cie.

Renton, C. A. Affleck, J. W. Carstairs, J. M., and Affleck, A. D. (1963). A follow up of schizophrenic patients in Edinburgh. *Acta Psychiat. Scand.* **39**, 584–600.

Rifkin, A., Quitkin, F., Rabiner, C., and Klein, D. F. (1977). Pluphenazine decandate, fluphenazine hydrochloride and placebo in remitted schizophrenics. *Arch. Gen. Psychiat.*, **34**, 43–47.

Sakel, M. (1938). The pharmacological shock treatment of schizophrenia, nervous and mental diseases. *Monograph Series. No. 62.* New York NMD Pub. Co.

Sargant, W., and Slater, E. (1940). Acute war neuroses. *Lancet*, **2**, 1–181.

Szasz, T. S. (1963). *Law, Liberty and Psychiatry.* Macmillan, New York.

Mental Illness: Changes and Trends
Edited by Philip Bean
© 1983 John Wiley & Sons Ltd.

CHAPTER 9

Clinical trials

PETER TYRER
Consultant Psychiatrist, Mapperley Hospital, Nottingham

Not so many years ago you could be sure that by introducing the subject of clinical trials to psychiatrists a lively, and not always amicable, debate would follow. You would doubtless hear at least three arguments whose differences are apparently irreconcilable. In their most pure form the arguments would run something like this.

1. Psychiatry is an art, and the art is unique. Psychiatry is not mental science but mental intuition. The training of psychiatrists does not involve teaching the scientific foundation of psychiatry, which does not exist, but should help the trainees to be more understanding and receptive to their patients' real problems. These problems are rarely what they appear to be and a psychiatrist has to travel on a long journey to get to the source of the mental conflict. This journey is unpredictable in direction and distance. Navigational aids are few, although some cartographers have pointed to the presence of 'royal roads' to take on the first part of the journey. When the journey is complete it will take an individual route that is highly unlikely to be retraced again, as patients and their problems are unique. Clinical trials are of no value in psychiatry because they only answer the superficial questions that are not important. Trials belong to science, not to psychiatry, and they have not place in the subject until the real measures—psychiatric ill-health—have been identified by the pioneers.

2. Experiments are for animals, not for man. If a man becomes ill it is our duty to give him the best treatment we have for the condition. Anything less than this is a travesty of medical care.

Clinical trials are experiments on man and should have no place in a democratic society. We all know that patients involved in clinical trials do not really give consent to take part because the experimenter only gives them a tiny part of the information they need to reach a decision. How else could you persuade so many patients to take part in experiments when they will only receive a placebo. If you said to each patient 'do you mind taking part in an experiment in which you may receive a new treatment that we don't know much about or a pill that contains nothing but chalk' how do you think they would reply? Of course, the doctors can't tell them that, so they resort to a form of deceit such as 'we are investigating some treatments for your condition that we know to be effective but we should like to see which is the best'.

Psychiatric patients are the ones most likely to be harmed by the deception practised in a clinical trial. They come for help because they are frightened and insecure and they want the doctor to be honest and open throughout his dealing with them. Psychiatric patients always fear a conspiracy and the cold experimenter in the clinical trial feeds these fears and may ultimately give credence to them.

3. No psychiatric treatment can be recommended until its effectiveness has been shown in a well-designed clinical trial. All treatment is experimental and each new therapy has to be compared with existing treatments under controlled conditions before it can be recommended. Each new procedure has to satisfy the test of comparison with no treatment before it can qualify as therapy. It is not sufficient for psychiatrists to hide behind the complexities of their subject and say that proper experimental comparisons cannot be made in their field. Everything from the application of leeches to free association on the psycho-analyst's couch can be subjected to controlled comparison provided that the basic principles of experimental design are followed.

One reasons why some psychiatrists are not prepared to submit their treatments to clinical trial is arrogance. They believe their treatments are adequate and need not be tested in conventional ways. No doctor likes to believe that the years he has spent training for a particular form of treatment have been wasted because the treatment is no good, but most are strong enough to expose themselves to this possibility by the independent judgment of a clinical trial. The surgeons did this in their assessment of the value of radical mastectomy for breast cancer. They were prepared to reassess their position when results showed that the radical operation, with its intricate and delicate techniques, had no better outcome than simple mastectomy followed by radiotherapy (Atkins *et al.*, 1972). Why should psychiatrists be different? Those whose only justification for the value of their treatments is blind faith often find it personally wounding to postulate that their cherished beliefs might be wrong. Rather than put them to the test they pretend that the form of improvement they are achieving is somehow immeasurable without personal assessment; or that the selection criteria for treatment are impeccable; or random allocation to two or more treatments is not ethically justifiable.

And so the debate could continue. I would like to think that some progress had been made in the last few years and views about the value of clinical trials would not be quite so extreme. Perhaps a small minority still argue that clinical trials are inappropriate for psychiatry, whilst those who take the opposite view and argue that clinical trials constitute the only key to progress in psychiatric treatment are also diminishing in number.

Despite a measure of greater understanding there is still prejudice about clinical trials. One curious prejudice is a xenophobic one. The concept of the controlled clinical trial is usually attributed to Anglo-Saxons, beginning with James Lind in 1747 and given its proper scientific weight by Austin Bradford Hill in 1945. The British have retained a somewhat proprietorial attitude to clinical trials which of course extends to those countries who have absorbed the Anglo-Saxon tradition. But apart from any inferences based on national stereotypes the political system of each country is also thought to affect the capacity to carry out clinical trials. In the stable democracies fair play is assured and a clinical trial will be expected to be carried out properly. But in totalitarian states freedom to express two opposing points of view is always constrained. So, it is assumed, that the clinical trial will always be subject to outside pressures both in its design and the interpretation of its results, and therefore cannot be accepted as a proper record of events.

This is a complex line of reasoning that can easily be turned on its head. The capitalist system of rewarding free enterprise shows itself in the vast number of drug trials carried out in the western hemisphere, in which there is constant pressure on the participants to produce favourable results and a consequent return on investment when the drug is marketed (Blackwell and Shepherd, 1967). Even so, capitalism, unlike other systems which exist elsewhere, is less affected by the political significance of the results of the trial. The Soviet biologist, Lysenko, was allowed to get away with grossly distorted and inaccurate claims that genetic changes could be induced by environmental control only because these views were politically acceptable. But a clinical trial does not allow a political option. When Molotov, in a candid moment, observed that 'the trouble with holding an election in a democracy is that you cannot be sure who is going to win', he described precisely the position of the participants in a clinical trial, who must maintain an agnostic position despite all pressures to commit themselves beforehand.

What is a clinical trial?

Those who come new to the argument over clinical trials will doubtless wonder what is the nature of the debate. It is really hard to understand why there is controversy when one reads the bare essentials of the reasoning behind clinical trials. Nothing could be more prosaic and unequivocal. In the words on one of its most staunch advocates, Bradford Hill,

a clinical trial is a carefully, and ethically, designed experiment with the aim of answering some precisely framed question. In its most rigorous form it demands equivalent groups of patients concurrently treated in different ways. These groups are constructed by the random allocation of patients to one or other treatment. In some instances patients may form their own controls, different treatments being applied to them in random order and the effect compared. In principle the method is applicable with any disease and any treatment (Hill, 1955).

In therapeutics the clinical trial is invariably concerned with benefit and harm. Under the 1968 Medicines Act of the United Kingdom a clinical trial involves administration of a drug about which there is sufficient evidence of 'effects which may be beneficial to the patient' and the trial 'is for the purpose of ascertaining whether, or to what extent, the product has those or any other effects beneficial or harmful' (Medicines Act, 1968).

But what exactly is the 'precisely framed question' mentioned by Bradford Hill. The nature of the question, and the experimental technique designed to answer it, often leads to the conflict of science and humanity. If the question is a straightforward one, such as 'is an accepted treatment X more effective when given for time Y than for time Z' then Science will usually be allowed to go ahead without argument, as, for example, in comparing short-term and long-term admission periods for alcoholic patients (Willems, *et al.*, 1973). If the question is the more common one that has to be asked early in the testing of all new therapies, 'is the treatment better than no treatment?' then ethical considerations intrude. The Hippocratic oath requires doctors to prescribe treatment 'for the good of my patients according to my ability and judgment and never do harm to anyone' and the comparison of new unknown treatment with no treatment (or the deceptive placebo) is not part of Hippocratic teaching. Other questions are controversial because of the status of the patients concerned. Thus, clinical trials in psychiatric practice involving the mentally handicapped or patients admitted on compulsory orders are under suspicion because the subjects constitute a captive population who may find it difficult to refuse a request to take part in the study.

But it would be wrong to infer that as each clinical trial presents a unique set of problems no useful purpose is served by discussing them as a whole. If we leave out some of the less informed parts of the debate already quoted, we are still left with six difficult issues where the arguments for and against clinical trials are evenly matched. These are (i) status of the participants, (ii) consent and how it should be obtained, (iii) answers to the questions asked by the trial and interpretation from them, (iv) random allocation to trial groups, (v) economy of the trial procedure compared with other methods, and (vi) developments that lead from clinical trials. Psychiatry adds its own special twist to these issues because of its unusual position among the medical disciplines. The two halves of controversy are shown in Table 1. They are interrelated so that those who argue against clinical trials tend to adopt all the contrary arguments shown in the table. Within psychiatry important differences in attitudes have been demonstrated between biological psychiatrists, who feel that psychiatry is wedded to medicine and should follow the same paths of investigation and evaluation, and psychothe-

Table 1   Controversial issues in clinical trials

	For	Against
Status	A scientific evaluation of treatment	Dehumanizes the patient and makes him a case
Consent	Informed consent seldom a problem if design of trial appropriate	Informed consent rare, deception common.
Answers	Answers precise questions	Answers are too restrictive to be clinically relevant
Random allocation	Comparison of randomly selected groups ensures absence of bias	Random selection and control groups are ethically unsound
Economies	Most economical way of evaluating efficacy	Efficacy only decided by years of successful use
Development	Leads to logical use of treatment and study progress	Leads to blinkered vision and funnelled progress

rapists, who stress the uniqueness of mental experience and are less enamoured of scientific method in psychiatry (Kreitman, 1962; Toone *et al.*, 1979). It is probably fair to say that biological psychiatrists and psychotherapists would align themselves on opposite sides when discussing clinical trials and their respective positions would be the same as in the table.

Status of the participants

Every clinical trial is an experiment. It is hoped to derive enough information from the experiment to make general predictions and thereby help other patients. But the promise of good in the future does not justify harm in the present, and in most clinical trials the shadow of harm is in the background. Unfortunately, animal experiments, particularly in psychiatry, only go some way towards predicting the response in man. The next step, i.e. testing the response on human beings, is a considerable one and is always accompanied by the doubt that untoward affects of the treatment may not have been detected and may not appear in the animal experiments anyway. In short, each patient is a 'guinea pig' and no amount of obfuscation can deny the fact. The patient or subject is being asked to make some sacrifice for the benefit of humanity, and although the sacrifice is usually very small, involving only a slight risk of unwanted effects, it is nonetheless important, not least because the patient rarely has full knowledge of the risk involved.

Psychiatry has endeavoured to accommodate to this difficulty in its support for clinical trials but has not really succeeded. In the Declaration of Hawaii, made at the 6th World Congress of Psychiatry in Honolulu in 1977, it was stated that 'every patient must be offered the best therapy available' even in clinical research. (This statement is a rephrasing of earlier declarations at Nuremberg (1947), Geneva (1948) and Helsinki (1964) and, ultimately, of Hippocrates.) However, at a later stage of the proceedings the original statement in the Declarations of Hawaii appears to have been qualified. Research with a patient can now be justified once voluntary participation is established and 'there is a reasonable relationship between calculated risks or inconveniences and the benefit of the study' (World Psychiatric Association, 1977). These statements are incompatible, as the second implies that risks can be taken with the individual if the potential benefit of the study to mankind is sufficiently great. The concept of sacrificing one for the good of the whole is an ancient one and there is no reason why it should not be present in clinical trials, but it is important to admit the fact because it alters the status of the patient. If the person making the sacrifice is fully aware of what he is doing, such as when Jonas Salk injected himself with his polio vaccine in 1954, this is acceptable, but if the person is an unwitting sufferer of a disorder, which may affect his judgment and comprehension how can he take the same risk with equal understanding?

The irony is that 'the best therapy available' is conventionally decided by comparison clinical trials in which at least one group will not receive the best treatment. There is greatest conflict when the treatment under test has been an established treatment for many years even though its efficacy has not been formally tested. In psychiatry the most topical example is electroconvulsive therapy (ECT). After Cerletti and Bini published their work on its use in 1938 it rapidly became accepted as the treatment of choice for severe depressive illness and has only been partially superseded by the antidepressant drugs. Because of its unfortunate aesthetic image ECT has been strongly criticized by the antipsychiatry lobby while being equally strongly defended by most psychiatrists. When past evidence for its efficacy was sought it was embarrassing to find that the treatment had not been satisfactorily tested (possibly because it was introduced before the clinical trial era). Recent controlled studies using simulated ECT have yielded conflicting results (Lambourn and Gill, 1978; Freeman *et al.*, 1979; Johnstone *et al.*, 1980), suggesting that the powerful therapeutic effects of ECT might not be due to the electric shock administered. Yet at the time these trials were mounted ECT enjoyed such unqualified supremacy as the best treatment and many considered it unethical for it to be withheld.

Consent and how it should be obtained

As the status of the patient in a clinical trial differs from that in ordinary practice it is all the more important to obtain an adequate level of consent from the patient before entry into a trial. The term 'informed consent' is usually employed in this regard and is often considered essential by an ethical committee before giving permission for a trial to go ahead. Unfortunately, fully informed consent is almost impossible to achieve as it carries with it a full understanding of the clinical issues and risks involved. It is better to state the circumstances in which consent is unlikely to be satisfactorily informed or voluntary. In the Declarations of Nuremberg (Mitscherlich and Mielke, 1947), brought out after the trial of German physicians accused of crimes involving experiments on human subjects these reservations are put as follows:

The voluntary consent of the subject is absolutely essential. This means that the person involved should have legal capacity to give consent; should be so situated as to be able to exercise free power of choice, without the intervention of any element of force, fraud, deceit, duress, overreaching, or other ulterior form of constraint or coercion; and should have sufficient knowledge and comprehension of the elements of the subject matter involved as to enable him to make an understanding and enlightened decision.

This knowledge includes 'all inconveniences and hazards reasonably to be expected' as well as an explanation of the 'nature, duration and purpose of the experiment'.

These requirements are a difficult enough for any group of investigators, but they are particularly difficult to achieve in psychiatry. The legal capacity to give consent is important and it follows therefore that patients admitted compulsorily to hospital should not be included in a clinical trial—even if they have the psychiatric disorder being investigated. So, recent studies of the efficacy of ECT have had to be restricted to patients receiving voluntary treatment. Free power of choice is a more diffuse concept and more difficult to define. Any patient being treated by a doctor is in a dependent position where he can be exploited. Although overt pressure to take part in a trial is rare, there are hidden pressures that are difficult to resist. These include exploiting the 'positive transference' that is often considered to be an essential part of the therapeutic relationship in psychiatry. The fear of being rejected following a refusal to take part in a clinical trial is a powerful reason to comply with the doctor's wishes. It is rarely expressed but must frequently affect the response to the doctor's invitation. Deceit of some form almost invariably comes into clinical trials. Formal deceit is a necessary part of the double-blind procedure that is central to the controlled trial. This requires that neither patient nor doctor knows exactly what treatment the patient is receiving, but the doctor at least knows what the alternatives are.

In several respects the pressures put on so-called volunteers to participate in clinical trials are greater than with patients. Once a new treatment has been satisfactorily tested in animals it is usual for it to be given to human subjects to determine factors such as dosage schedules and unwanted effects. In principle every volunteer knows the likely risks and gives informed consent; in practice it is quite a different matter. In the United States during the 1940s and 1950s the use of 'volunteers' from federal penitentiaries was widespread. The prisoners were given inducements to enter clinical trials, including improved living conditions.

more frequent visits from relatives and, in some cases, early parole, and so it was not surprising that many came forward. Some of the studies carried out would now be condemned out of hand by ethical committees. One shocking example was the administration of large quantities of alcohol to such volunteers for 7–12 weeks followed by sudden withdrawal to determine the nature of alcohol withdrawal phenomena in drinkers maintaining normal nutritional status. The outcome confirmed that epileptic fits, hallucinations, and paranoid psychotic features were all part of the alcohol abstinence syndrome (Isbell *et al.*, 1955) but one wonders at what cost to the 'volunteers' health.

It is current practice nowadays for most volunteers in studies involving new drugs to be employed by the drug firms concerned. These employees are placed under even greater pressure to take part in trials than a patient in a trusting therapeutic relationship with his doctor. Refusal to take part may carry many implications, such as a lack of promotion, or hints that the individual is not acting 'in the best interest of the company', or even allegations of cowardice from colleagues who have volunteered. Reassurances that these fears are completely unfounded, as indeed they are in most ethical pharmaceutical firms, do not alter the fact that the subject is dependent on the company for his livelihood and this alone may lead him to agree to take part in a clinical trial.

Several attempts have been made to overcome the vexed problem of consent. Some of them are obvious, i.e., always seeking consent from the parent or guardian before a child is subjected to any experimental procedure. The Medical Research Council (1963) in its guidelines on clinical investigations suggests that the clinician treating the patient should be part of a team of investigators who are all agreed on the procedures for recruiting patients so that there is no conflict between the scientific demands of the trial and the clinical needs of the subjects. However, those treating the patient often have an investment in the trial even if they are not organizing it. For example, it is now commonplace in multicentre trials, particularly in primary care, to pay participating physicians a standing fee for each patient enrolled. This practice, and the parallel one of paying patients to take part, cannot be justified on ethical grounds and must inevitably affect the quality of the consent obtained.

But because the inherent problems in obtaining informed consent are so difficult to resolve, I think it is more important to reinforce the power of bodies involved in approving and monitoring clinical trials than tightening up the consent procedure. The approval of the local ethical committee is now required in all parts of the United Kingdom before grants and facilities for clinical trials can be formalized, and the inclusion of lay as well as medical members has been all to the good. The ethical committee I served on until recently had a lay chairman who was a solicitor, and his contributions were invaluable in counter-balancing the sometimes blinkered perspectives of the medical members.

Another important function of an ethical committee is to comment on the scientific worth of a proposed clinical trial. In the strict sense of the term, a clinical trial which is above criticism in the way that patients have been recruited but which cannot achieve its objectives, is unethical. Patients (and clinicians) are being subjected to inconvenience and possible risk with no possibility of any long-term benefit from the results (except as a warning to others who might attempt to repeat the work in the same way).

An ethical committee can give advice before the study is mounted and prevent unnecessary labour. In the future it might also be helpful for ethical committees or National Research Centres to have details of all current and completed research in defined subjects, so that the potential research worker does not carry out a third-rate trial into a question that has already been answered by a first-rate study.

Answers to the questions

If the answers from a clinical trial lead to a major advance in treatment it is possible to overlook some of the controversial aspects associated with its execution. If, however, as in the example described above, the answer is of no value the trial has no justification. Bradford Hill's 'precisely framed question' is rarely the question that the average doctor asks about a treatment. More commonly, the doctor's question is simply 'does treatment X work?' This is not a precise question and it is pointless for the clinical trial to attempt to answer it.

Table 2   Factors affecting response to drug treatment and psychotherapy

Reserve factor	Drug	Psychotherapy
Dose	Strength of tablet	Intensity of treatment
Diagnosis	Homogeneous patients	Homogeneous patients
Duration of treatment	Response may be delayed for several weeks	Response may be delayed until after treatment is completed (the sleeper effect)
Vehicle of therapy	Form of capsule or tablet (excipient may affect absorption and distribution. Colour may also be important	Nature of therapist (gender and status) may affect response
Faith in therapist	Leads to 'placebo response' and better compliance	Positive transference an essential part of therapy.
Unwanted effects	If severe, course of treatment will not be completed	As for drug therapy
Individual variation in response	Pharmacokinetic differences	Specific nature of mental problem

The question that the trial ultimately answers is a restricted one but should none the less have wide application. The main reason for the restriction is the large number of factors that are independent of the main treatment but can greatly influence therapeutic response. If these were ignored very few clinical trials would yield positive results because the therapeutic effects of treatment would be swamped by other sources of variance, referred to as 'noise' by statisticians. Some of the noisiest factors are illustrated (Table 2) and apply equally to a 'hard' treatment such as a drug and a 'soft' treatment, such as psychotherapy.

A good clinical trial compensates for all these factors but, in doing so, may restrict the value of the results or, at worst, give misleading information. Therapeutics is full of examples of valuable treatments being prematurely abandoned because of inappropriate dosages being given or in the wrong way. The clinical trial answers a highly qualified question concerning efficacy and there is a danger that its findings may be irrelevant to clinical practice. If, for example, a new treatment accounts for, say 1 per cent of the improvement in a group of patients it is often possible to isolate this 1 per cent by using an experimental design that balances out the factors accounting for the remaining 99 per cent. A significantly positive effect of treatment may then be demonstrated but it is of no real clinical value despite the impressive rigour of the experiment. Psychiatric patients are more idiosyncratic than most in their response to treatment, as all readers who have been involved in clinical trials will be aware, and in statistical analyses the F ratios for 'between patient variation' are always higher than any other.

Random allocation is trial groups

An open clinical trial involves giving a new treatment to patients and recording the findings. But the real test of efficacy comes with the controlled trial, in which two or more treatments are compared, preferably under double-blind conditions. An essential feature of the experimental design is random allocation of patients to treatment, using various manoeuvres such as consulting tables of random numbers or even tossing a coin. This feature of clinical trials gets some people very angry, for it implies that a patient's fate is decided by a method akin to that of roulette. The criticism would be valid if the selection criteria for treatment were appropriate. In practice, and in no area of medicine is it more obvious than in psychiatry, the so-called appropriate selection criteria are usually indicators of good prognosis irrespective of treatment. This is why psychiatrists, no matter from what school they purport to belong, prefer to have young patients, who are presenting psychiatric symptoms for the first time, have stable premorbid personalities, and good psychological understanding of the possible nature of their symptoms. These patients do well with all therapists, who only differ amongst themselves in the degree of reluctance to discharge the patient once recovered.

At the other end of the continuum there are the difficult patients who tend to totter from one therapeutic failure to another, often with the psychiatrist making increasingly desperate attempts to transfer the patient to the arena of another specialist by arguing that an entirely different approach is needed. The outsider looking at this game of musical chairs, for that is what it is, would be pardoned a wry smile, (particularly when these creators of clinical acumen argue against random allocation on grounds of malpractice) for if treatments are to be adequately compared they must have an equal chance of getting both the potentially good and bad responders. Changing patients around in this way resembles the frequent changes of course that are characteristic of psychiatric treatment generally. As Bradford Hill (1963) observes 'ethically the doctor is in the same position (with random allocation of patients in controlled trials) in 'ringing the changes" within patients rather than between patients'.

A more bothering aspect of random allocation occurs when a placebo or similar non-active therapy is given at an early stage in the evaluation procedure. Comparisons are unavoidable yet the administration of a placebo to an ill patient when there are known effective alternatives is difficult to defend on ethical grounds. There are special designs that reduce the impact of placebo such as combining open and controlled trials (Amery and Dony, 1975) or alternatively there are cross-over designs which ensures that all patients receive active treatment at some stage. An example of this is illustrated in Figure 1 which also shows the importance of recording data after treatment has been withdrawn. In

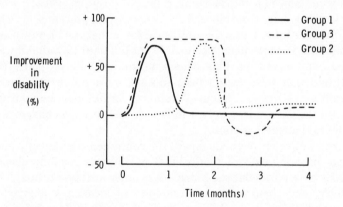

Figure 1   Hypothetical results from a clinical trial employing active and placebo treatment in each group
Group 1: Active treatment for one month followed by placebo
Group 2: Placebo for one month, active treatment for one month, then placebo
Group 3: Active treatment for two months, followed by placebo
In the example the active treatment is effective in relieving symptoms but produces a withdrawal reaction when given for two months

the hypothetical example active treatment is shown to be effective in reducing symptoms when given for one month with no ill-effects on withdrawal, but when given for two months regularly there is a temporary increase in symptoms on withdrawal suggesting that a degree of dependence has developed after a longer duration of therapy.

Economy of the trial procedure compared with other methods

One of the strong arguments in favour of the controlled clinical trial is that it settles disputes that may takes longer to resolve by other means. Another is that many fewer patients need to undergo experimentation compared with more traditionally forms of assessment—if what is called 'the weight of clinical experience' can be dignified as a form of assessment.

The arguments for and against controlled clinical trials are well illustrated by James Lind's trial on treatment for scurvy in 1747, described in detail by Hordern (1968). Lind chose a very small homogeneous group of patients, all with the clinical diagnosis of scurvy. He randomly divided them into six experimental groups of two patients each, and treated each group for six days with one of the alleged treatments for scurvy available at that time. The six treatments were cider, elixir of vitriol, vinegar, sea water, a purgative electuary, and citrus fruit (oranges and lemons). After six days the two patients receiving the citrus fruits dramatically improved; the others showed no response. The verdict was clear; citrus fruits contained an anti-scorbutic principle. Over the next 150 years citrus fruits, or later, the juice from citrus fruits, were used to prevent scurvy but were not always successful. Limes were substituted for oranges and lemons and, later, boiled and preserved lime juice was used. It was not until 1918 that it was found that boiled, or preserved juice had virtually no anti-scorbutic properties (Chick *et al.*, 1918) and that fresh lemon juice was the most powerful source of the subsequently anti-scorbutic principle, vitamin C. So although the controlled trial had revealed the answer to scurvy it took over 150 years to convert it into the correct clinical recommendation.

Some critics of other methods regard the controlled trial as only one of the many types of empirical observation that go towards deciding efficacy. But clinical trials have particular superiority over other methods although they are not infallible, and there are many examples of identically planned studies producing opposing results. Nonetheless, when the evidence derived from clinical trials is compared with other types of evidence it is generally more consistent and nowadays more likely to influence clinical practice. With the increasing number of new treatments introduced particularly in psychiatry, some efficient way of sifting the good from the indifferent is necessary, and clinical trials are the best means now available. With newer types of experimental design such as sequential analysis (Armitage, 1975) a trial can be stopped as soon as a statistical difference between treatments is achieved and this can be obtained with as little as 10 patients in such instances. Clinical trials are constantly being refined any economy in design is an important aspect of this. A good account of the many types of design intended for those thinking of carrying out a clinical trial (Johnson and Johnson, 1977) describes over 20 different varieties.

Developments that lead from clinical trials

If the critics of clinical trials were silent and it was universally accepted that no better way of assessing efficacy existed, would medical progress be inhibited or accelerated? I have no doubt that one of the first effects would be to include forms of therapy traditionally kept outside the empirical arena, and make them subject to more appropriate and stringent tests of efficacy. In psychiatry the dynamic psychotherapies are most in need of adequate evaluation. Although at least one valiant attempt has been made to assess them in a clinical trial (Candy *et al.*, 1972) in most instances obstacles have been put up which aborted the trial before it began. Several of the obstacles have already been defined. They could have been overcome had there been an open-minded spirit in the enterprise, but all too often clinical trials are viewed as the ugly tentacles of scientific method invading territory outside their domain. We in psychiatry are sometimes unduly humble, but now the subject is sufficiently sophisticated in research techniques to record or rate whatever the investigator feels it is important to measure, to record change in these ratings in response to treatment, and to compare different treatments whether they be pharmacological, behavioural, or psychological. All ethical objections can be overcome by using single case trials with repeated exposure to different treatments or by using one of the many alternative designs available. There is really no excuse for avoiding clinical trials for any form of therapy and the time is fast approaching when I believe that all new therapies will be considered experimental until they have been proved by clinical trials.

But it would be disastrous if clinical trials were regarded as the *sine qua non* of therapy. They are excellent at sorting treatment into 'efficacy league tables' but hopeless at creating new advances. They tend to channel investigators into conventional lines of enquiry and suppress what De Bono calls lateral thinking, the leap across logical thought to a completely new area of enquiry. Once the leap has been made, less imaginative scientists can carry out clinical trials, but the important steps have already been made. It would be most unfortunate if clinical research councils and other grant-giving bodies were to prefer supporting the 'safe' work of clinical trials rather than the risky ventures of new thinkers.

An analogy can be drawn from the progress of natural selection in evolutionary theory. Small, and at first indefinable, changes take place over several generations and the evolutionary line is developed. The major change to a new line occurs suddenly and dramatically; most such changes are of no value, only a few become more adapted and take over from the old. So it is with the evolution of clinical medicine and psychiatry; clinical trials only refine and develop the treatment 'species', the major shifts to new 'genera' and 'orders' of treatment come from unexpected and unpredictable advances in which clinical trials will rarely play a part.

The verdict

It is difficult to avoid accusations of bias in assessing the value of clinical trials in medicine, and to an even greater extent in psychiatry. Nevertheless, we can give two cheers for clinical trials, keeping the third cheer till our reservations have been overcome. There is no real rival to clinical trials in deciding the comparative value of one or more treatments and the scope of trials has continued to widen with improvements in design. If psychiatrists realize that clinical trials are not wedded to any psychiatric school and are equally fair to all therapies they would perhaps be more keen to use them. The reservations would then remain as ethical ones.

Randomization is defensible and, when used appropriately, cannot be faulted ethically, but the use of placebos and the difficult question of informed consent are rightly open to criticism. More effort is needed to design trials that avoid the need for placebos for disorders in which highly effective treatments already exist. These may involve the administration of placebos for short periods provided that all subjects also receive active treatment during the trial. 'Informed consent' now means very little and other safeguards are needed to ensure that patients are willing participants in clinical trials. It has to be admitted that the high-sounding declarations of world bodies have not clarified the issues in the way that was intended and the subject of consent needs re-examining in a less politicized atmosphere.

Etymology is another unfortunate aspect of controlled clinical trials that needs alteration. There is a pejorative double meaning to 'controlled' (which implies external pressure from an outside agency), 'clinical' (which also implies being detached, cold, and unsympathetic) and 'trials' (which also mean suffering). I suggest that a term such as 'systematic treatment evaluative procedure' (STEP), for all its polysyllables, is a better one that 'controlled clinical trial' because it is emotionally neutral. As language is determined by usage we could all make a start now towards making the change.

References

Amery, W., and Dony, J. (1975). A clinical trial design avoiding undue placebo treatment. *Journal of Clinical Pharmacology*, **15**, 674–679.
Armitage, P. (1975). *Sequential Medical Trials*, 2nd edn., Oxford: Blackwell.
Atkins, H., Hayward, J. L., Klugman, D. J., and Wayte, A. B. (1972). Treatment of early breast cancer: a report after ten years of a clinical trial. *British Medical Journal*, **2**, 423–429.

Blackwell, B., and Shepherd, M. (1967). Early evaluation of psychotropic drugs in man: a trial that failed. *Lancet*, **i**, 819–822.

Candy, J., Balfour, S. H., Cawley, R. H., Hildebrand, H. P., Malan, D. H., Marks, I. M., and Wilson, J. (1972). A feasibility study for a controlled trial of formal psychotherapy. *Psychological Medicine*, **2**, 345–362.

Chick, H., Hume, E. M., and Skelton, R. F. (1918). The relative content of antiscorbutic principle in limes and lemons: an experimental enquiry. *Lancet*, **(ii)**, 735–738.

Freeman, C. P., Basson, J. V., and Crighton, A. (1978). Double blind trial of E. C. T. and simulated E. C. T. in depressive illness. *Lancet*, **(i)**, 738–740.

Hill, A. B. (1963). Medical ethics and controlled trials. *British Medical Journal*, **1**, 1043–1049.

Hill, A. B. (1955). Introduction to medical statistics, 5th edition. *Lancet*, London.

Hordern, A. (1968). Psychopharmacology: some historical considerations. In *Psychopharmacology: Dimensions and Perspectives*. Ed. C. R. O. Joyce. pp. 95–148. Tavistock, London.

Isbell, H., Fraser, H. F. Wikler, A., Belleville, R. E., Eisenman, A. J. (1955). Experimental study of aetiology of 'rum-fits' and delirium tremens. *Quarterly Journal of Studies on Alcohol*, **16**, 1–25.

Johnson, F. N., and Johnson, S. (1977). *Clinical Trials*, Oxford Blackwell.

Johnstone, E. C., Deakin, J. F. W., Lawler, P., Frith, C. C., Stevens, M., McPherson, K., and Crow, T. J. (1980). The Northwick Park electroconvulsive therapy trial. *Lancet*, **ii**, 1317–1320.

Kreitman, N. (1962). Psychiatric orientation: a study of attitudes among psychiatrists. *Journal of Mental Science*, **108**, 317–328.

Lambourn, J., and Gill, D. (1978). A controlled comparison of simulated and real E. C. T. *British Journal of Psychiatry*, **133**, 514–519.

Medical Research Council (1963). Memorandum on Clinical Investigations. *Command 2382*. HMSO, London.

Medicines Act (1968). HMSO.

Mitscherlich, A., and Mielke, F., (1949). *Doctors of infamy: the story of the Nazi medical crimes*, Schuman.

Toone, B. K., Murray, R., Clare, A., Creed, F., and Smith, A. (1979). Psychiatrists' models of mental illness and their personal backgrounds. *Psychological Medicine*, **9**, 165–178.

Willems, P. J. A., Letemendia, F. J. J., and Arroyave, F. (1973). A two-year follow-up study comparing short with longstay in-patient treatment of alcoholics. *British Journal of Psychiatry*, **122**, 637–648.

World Psychiatric Association (1977). *Statement made at Sixth World Psychiatric Association Congress*, Honolulu.

Mental Illness: Changes and Trends
Edited by Philip Bean
© 1983 John Wiley & Sons Ltd.

CHAPTER 10

Pharmacological aspects of mental illness

RICHARD MINDHAM
Nuffield Professor of Psychiatry, University of Leeds

The use of drugs in the treatment of mental illness

Scarcely an issue in psychiatry has been so controversial as the use of drugs in the treatment of psychiatric disorders. Opinions vary from the enthusiastic to the antagonistic; some believe that recent developments in drug treatment represent the most important advances that psychiatry has ever seen: others believe that the use of drugs is both dangerous and based upon a false view of what psychiatric disorders represent. Whatever view one takes there is no doubt that drugs are widely used in the treatment of psychiatric disorders and are likely to continue to be so. It is now scarcely possible to deal with patients suffering from psychiatric disorders without some knowledge of the drugs used. The whole topic is more readily understood if it is viewed with some knowledge of the background to the development of the drugs concerned.

This chapter seeks to provide a very general account of the development of drug treatments in psychiatry.

Types of drugs used

In spite of the very large number of drugs marketed for use in psychiatry these fall into a relatively small number of major categories sharing their main characteristics. The action and use of the drugs is much more readily understood if they are grouped together in this way. Traditionally in pharmacology, drugs acting on the central nervous system have been classified according to their stimulant or depressant effects on it. These two major categories include a large proportion of drugs used in psychiatric practice. The drugs which have a stimulant effect on the nervous system include the antidepressant drugs from the earlier types, such as the amphetamines, to those in current use, the tricyclic drugs and the monoamine oxidase inhibiting drugs. Drugs which have a predominantly depressive effect on the activity of the central nervous system include the major tranquillizers and the sedatives; these will be dealt with in two separate groups as the ways in which they are employed in psychiatry are very different. It is convenient to add two

195

groups which include those drugs which will regularly induce psychosis when taken in small dosage, and those which cannot adequately be classified elsewhere. Inconsistencies in this approach will be evident but no truly satisfactory classification of the drugs used in psychiatry, or psychotropic drugs, has yet been prepared (Shepherd, 1972).

Medical concepts of mental illness

In general terms the use of drugs in psychiatric disorders is based on the notion that they resemble other medical conditions in certain respects, i.e. the individual is subject to a morbid process which is recognizable by the changes it produces and which continues until the morbid process is reversed either naturally or by treatment. The rational treatment of such disorders is by the use of a method which reverses the morbid process rather than by simply suppressing the symptoms it produces. Treatments as specific as this are only available for a restricted range of disorders, and many treatments are less specific and simply suppress symptoms and help the patient to endure the illness until a natural resolution of the disorder occurs.

Very few psychiatric disorders show all the characteristics of an illness; many more resemble medical disorders in some degree but not completely; others bear little resemblance to medical disorders at all. As knowledge increases a better understanding of psychiatric disorders may be achieved but at present the great majority are only incompletely understood. A lack of understanding of a disorder is not, however, a reason for not using the treatments available. Many well-established treatments in medicine were successfully used long before the mechanisms of their actions were known; this is particularly true in the case of the pharmacological treatment of psychiatric disorders. Furthermore, drug treatments used in psychiatry have been extensively evaluated, in contrast with most other methods of treatment in common use.

Antidepressant drugs

Until the 1950s there were no substances known which were capable of bringing about a persistent alteration in pathological states of elation and depression. Electroconvulsive therapy had come into use in the 1930s and had benefited a proportion of depressed patients, particularly those suffering from severe depressive illness. Sedatives had been used in controlling anxiety, agitation, and sleep disturbance but these had no more than the effect of relieving symptoms temporarily. Similarly, the amphetamines, although capable of temporarily lifting mood, did not show a lasting effect in depressive illness. The discovery of the first antidepressive drugs was to provide an important advance in treatment. Many psychiatrists who had worked in the years before the antidepressive drugs were discovered found it difficult to believe that mood could be changed by purely chemical means. Considerable scepticism still surrounds the use of drugs in disturbances of mood, and this makes the careful evaluation of the evidence of the effectiveness of these drugs particularly important, as well as a recognition of the relatively narrow range of disturbances for which they are appropriately employed.

There are two main types of antidepressive agents, and the antidepressive effects of both were discovered fortuitously. The tricyclic drugs will be described first as they have turned out to be more important in clinical practice. The monoamine oxidase inhibiting drugs and the amphetamines will then be described more briefly.

Tricyclic antidepressant drugs

The chemical substance iminodibenzyl has been known since the beginning of this century but it was only after the Second World War that the pharmacological effects of its derivatives began to be investigated. These studies were stimulated by the discovery of the important pharmacological effects of chlorpromazine which is chemically closely similar. When the full importance of chlorpromazine in psychiatric treatment was known the effects of related compounds were investigated. A Swiss psychiatrist, Kuhn, gave imipramine to several hundred chronically psychotic patients and discovered that it was helpful to the depressed patients rather than to those suffering from schizophrenia, who had shown the most benefit from chlorpromazine (Kuhn, 1958). Kuhn went on to describe many of the clinical characteristics of imipramine including the dosage required, the proportion of patients responding, the unwanted effects and the interval of two to three weeks between the initiation of treatment, and the early signs of response which are now recognized as being so typical of drugs of this group. Kuhn's work is a striking and historically important example of the value of carefully conducted but uncontrolled clinical evaluation of treatment. The main findings of these investigations have been fully confirmed by more extensive and scientifically rigorous studies.

Controlled studies of imipramine. Following Kuhn's work many more reports of the effects of imipramine followed, eventually leading to trials which included the use of control groups of subjects. The theoretical background to control trials of treatment in medicine and the way in which they are conducted is described elsewhere in this book (Chapter 9). Truly satisfactory controlled trials of imipramine are relatively few in number but are of great importance as many subsequent trials, in which the effects of drugs were compared with each other, refer back to them.

A typical controlled trial is that reported by Ball and Kiloh in 1959. Forty-eight depressed out-patients were given either imipramine 250 mg daily or placebo, and the results compared after four weeks' treatment. The patients were divided into those considered to be suffering from 'endogenous' or 'reactive' depressive illnesses. Amongst those suffering from endogenous depression 74 per cent of those who received imipramine responded as compared with 22 per cent of those receiving placebo; amongst those considered to be suffering from reactive depression, 59 per cent on the active drug responded as compared with 20 per cent on placebo. In this study unwanted effects were noted to be severe.

A number of similar studies were performed varying in detail and in the results they gave. In general, however, the trials suggested that imipramine was capable of suppressing symptoms in a proportion of patients and was more effective than pharmacologically inert control treatments.

A recurring criticism of trials then (and now) concerns the validity of comparing treatments where the difference between the treatments might be revealed to the observer and to the patient, through unwanted, and other effects. Attempts to overcome this involved the used of 'active' placebos which simulated the unwanted effects without showing the therapeutic effects. Such methods introduced different problems of interpretation.

At the time of the general introduction of imipramine into psychiatric practice the standard treatment for severe depressive illness was electroconvulsive therapy (ECT), and this naturally led to comparisons between the effects of ECT and imipramine. One of the best-known studies of this kind was that conducted under the auspices of the Medical Research Council of Great Britain in which the effects of ECT, imipramine, phenelzine (a monoamine oxidase inhibiting drug), and placebo were compared in a group of 250 moderately severely depressed in-patients of both sexes. ECT was the most effective treatment in the short-term (four weeks), but over a longer period (twelve weeks) both ECT and imipramine brought improvement to about two-thirds of the patients who received them. Phenelzine and placebo were associated with improvement in about a third of the patients who received them. This study shows fairly convincingly that, for the type of patients involved, ECT or imipramine give the greatest benefit. However, where a rapid response is needed, or depression is very severe, ECT still appears to be the preferred treatment.

Introduction of other tricyclic antidepressant drugs

Following the introduction of imipramine many new compounds of closely similar chemical formula were found to possess similar pharmacological properties. These were extensively investigated and their clinical effects compared one with another and with other treatments such as ECT and placebo. All of these compounds showed certain pharmacological effects in common: a delay in the onset of antidepressive effects; a tendency to produce drowsiness in varying degree; a range of unwanted effects arising from the anticholinergic actions of the drugs and a number of other undesirable effects. As new compounds of the group have been introduced advantages have been found to be less in the therapeutic effects observed, than in differences in unwanted effects. Naturally, attempts have been made to find substances which showed fewer, or less severe, unwanted effects of the more dangerous or unpleasant types. There are many accounts of the detailed investigation of imipramine and related drugs, e.g. Shepherd *et al.*, 1968; Silverstone and Turner, 1974; Mindham, 1979, 1982.

Tricyclic antidepressants are also useful in the treatment of nocturnal enuresis, particularly for short-term control of symptoms for holidays, etc. This effect is probably due to the anticholinergic action of the drugs.

Monoamine oxidase inhibiting drugs

Following the introduction of isoniazid and iproniazid for the treatment of pulmonary tuberculosis it was observed that the administration of either drug was occasionally associated with a euphoriant effect (Robitzek *et al.*, 1952). Subsequently it was reported that iproniazid had the effect of inhibiting the action of enzymes responsible for catalysing the oxidation of monoamines, simple nitrogenous substances which are widely distributed in the body including the brain. The euphoriant effect of iproniazid was attributed to a rise in brain monoamine concentrations consequent upon a slowing down in their destruction. There are two main groups of substances of this type; those that simply have the property of inhibiting the breakdown of monoamines and those which share this property and have in addition a stimulant effect resembling that of the amphetamines.

Evidence of the efficacy of monoamine oxidase inhibiting drugs in the treatment of depressive disorders has been less easily forthcoming than in the case of the tricyclic drugs. The results of trials have been variable and even conflicting. Evidence for efficacy is strongest for those with both monoamine oxidase inhibiting and stimulant effects. The Medical Research Council study described above showed phenelzine to be ineffective in severely depressed hospital in-patients. A number of studies has suggested that special groups of depressed patients may benefit from monoamine oxidase inhibiting drugs such as those with anxiety, phobic symptoms, and 'atypical' depressive states. Other studies have suggested that a restricted group of patients who metabolize the drugs more slowly, 'slow acetylators' may respond where others do not. Dosage may be particularly important and it would appear that some studies have used the drugs in inadequate dosage; this is particularly relevant to the suggestion that patients may vary widely in the speed with which they metabolize the drugs.

When monoamine oxidase inhibiting drugs had been in use for some years reports appeared of very severe headaches in a proportion of the patients receiving them. This was eventually recognized as an effect precipitated by the eating of cheese and a few other items of diet. The possible mechanisms were investigated in animals and it was shown that the monoamine oxidase inhibiting drugs had the effect of allowing amino acids from dietary substances to pass directly through the gut wall into the bloodstream, where they had the effect of dramatically raising the blood pressure; which was in turn the cause of the headaches (Samuel and Blackwell, 1968). These discoveries led to the general introduction of special diets free of pressor amino acids for patients taking the drugs. The proscribed foods included cheese of all kinds but especially ripe cheese, game and other matured foods, and a variety of beans, wines, and fruit which contained freely available amino acids in large quantities.

The monoamine oxidase inhibiting drugs also have other unwanted effects which include drowsiness or stimulation, nausea, dry mouth, postural hypotension, constipation, and impotence. Effects on the liver have also been described but these have never been firmly attributed to the effects of monoamine oxidase inhibiting drugs. Perhaps more important are the very large number of dangerous interactions between the monoamine oxidase inhibiting drugs and other drugs given in medical treatment.

The interaction with foodstuffs, the unwanted effects, and the uncertain or limited range of effectiveness has prevented the monoamine oxidase inhibiting drugs from occupying a central place in the treatment of depressive states. They have retained a place, however, and this is in the treatment of depressive states which include a good deal of anxiety, phobias, and somatic symptoms. Occasionally the drugs are combined with other drugs in the treatment of severely depressed patients who have failed to respond other forms of treatment. (For a fuller account of the monoamine oxidase inhibiting drugs see Tyrer, 1979 and 1982.)

The amphetamines

The amphetamines have been used for many years in combating fatigue in service personnel and in the treatment of various medical disorders. The drugs appear to have a direct stimulating effect on the ascending reticular activating system in the brain. They cause an increase in heart rate, a rise in blood pressure, they suppress appetite, and may elevate mood with restlessness, overactivity and increased physical performance and endurance. Although the amphetamines are undoubtedly capable of reversing depression of mood this effect only lasts while the drug is in the body in sufficient concentration. There appears to be no effect on any underlying disturbance which may be responsible for the appearance and persistence of depressive symptoms. Continued administration is impracticable because of the many side-effects produced, and the very serious risk of inducing dependency with a need for increased dosage to achieve a particular effect, and difficulty in discontinuing the drug for even a relatively short time.

Apart from the treatment of depressive states amphetamines have also been used to reduce appetite; to help in the disclosure of unpleasant material in abreactive or psychotherapeutic interviews; in the treatment of nocturnal enuresis; and for their paradoxical sedative effect in overactive children. Now the only generally accepted therapeutic use of amphetamines is in the treatment of narcolepsy.

Mode of action of antidepressant drugs

Strictly the mode of action of these drugs is not fully understood, nor can it be when the biological disturbances causing or accompanying depressive states are so incompletely known. Both the tricyclic drugs and the monoamine oxidase inhibiting drugs are known to alter the movement and metabolism of certain brain amines which are thought to act as neurotransmitters in the central nervous system; these pharmacological effects are thought to be in part responsible for the therapeutic effects observed.

In neurotransmission an impulse passes from one neuron to another by the release of a neurotransmitter substance from one cell which then stimulates the next. Normally the neurotransmitter substances, which are amines of various kinds, are removed from the inter-neuronal space by two processes: re-uptake by the cells which have released them, and breakdown to inert substances through the agency of enzymes, the amine oxidases. Tricyclic drugs have the effect of reducing the re-uptake of monoamine neurotransmitters and thereby prolonging their effects; monoamine oxidase inhibiting drugs inhibit the breakdown of the neurotransmitters and thereby extend the duration of their effects. Although the mechanism is initiated differently the final effect is thought to be similar; in each case the presence of the neurotransmitter substance being prolonged. Although these effects have been shown to occur the drugs may also have other important pharmacological effects, such as sedation, which may be important to their therapeutic effects. It is even possible that the pharmacological effects which have received such attention are of little clinical relevance.

A firmly established fact concerning both types of antidepressant drugs is that they must be administered for a period of some weeks before their therapeutic effects can be expected to appear. Conversely, effects of the drugs continue to be seen for a considerable time after administration of the drugs is discontinued. This has important implications particularly in the case of the monoamine oxidase inhibiting drugs where dangers of interaction of food and other drugs will continue after the drug itself has been stopped.

A large number of studies has been made of the relationship between the therapeutic effects of the tricyclic antidepressant drugs and the concentration of the drugs in the blood. No clear-cut relationship has been demonstrated but it does appear probable that very high plasma levels of some of the drugs do not produce such good results as more moderate levels. Although these studies are of great theoretical interest estimation of plasma levels of tricyclic drugs has not become a part of routine clinical practice.

Indications and clinical usage

Most psychiatrists use tricyclic drugs as first choice in the treatment of depressive states as evidence of efficacy and safety are firmer. A personal or family history of response to a particular tricyclic drug increases the chance of a good response in a further episode in the individual or in a relative. A history of neurotic premorbid traits has generally been held to suggest a poor response to tricyclic drugs. Depression of insidious onset suggests a good response to tricyclic drugs. The absence of a recognizable precipitant is not necessarily associated with a good response to treatment, just as the presence of an understandable cause does not mean that drug treatment will be of no value. In general psychotically depressed patients do well on tricyclic drugs especially where there are many 'vegetative' or 'vital' symptoms, which are evidence of bodily disturbance. The presence of delusions or hypochondriasis, possibly indications of severe disorder, are bad features of depressive illness as regards outcome of drug treatment. Biological predictors of antidepressant response include tests of urinary metabolites, cerebrospinal fluid amine concentrations, the response to amphetamines, erythrocyte catechol-o-methyl transferase concentrations, and the electroencephalographic characteristics of sleep, but none of these approaches is yet at the stage of clinical application, although they are all of great theoretical interest.

The choice of a particular tricyclic antidepressant drug is still largely a matter of clinical judgment and individual preference although the drugs do vary in the degree of sedation they may produce. Sedative properties might make the drugs particularly suitable for the treatment of agitated patients whereas stimulant properties might be expected to make the drugs more suitable for the treatment of retarded patients. Our knowledge of the properties of the tricyclic drugs indicate that they should be given in optimal dosage for a period of four to six weeks initially. During this time most of those patients who will eventually respond will have begun to do so. If clinical improvement occurs the drug should be continued for a total of eight to ten weeks during which time the improvement will progress and be consolidated. Where a patient fails to respond to a drug after an appropriate period the choice lies between giving electroconvulsive therapy, a quite different antidepressant drug, or changing to another tricyclic drug.

Should patients not respond to tricyclic drugs or, alternatively, it they show marked features of anxiety, phobias, or atypical depressive illness, then monoamine oxidase inhibiting drugs may be effective. Again these drugs must be given in adequate dosage for an adequate period of time if good therapeutic results are to be obtained. The patient should be warned of appropriate dietary restrictions.

In spite of the availability of many antidepressant drugs a proportion of patients do not respond; some of these will respond to electroconvulsive therapy, some will continue to be unwell until recovery occurs naturally, and a very small proportion will remain persistently depressed (Winokur, 1981).

Prophylaxis of depressive disorders using antidepressive drugs

A number of studies have attempted to discover whether the continued administration of tricyclic antidepressant drugs to patients, after they have recovered from a depressive illness which has responded to treatment, is associated with a lower rate of recurrence. Two studies of this kind will be described in more detail.

In a study conducted under the aegis of the Medical Research Council of Great Britain patients suffering from moderately severe depressive illness were initially treated with amitriptyline or imipramine and then, after full clinical recovery, were randomly allocated to six months further treatment with the drug to which they had recently responded, or to placebo. When continuation therapy was started all the patients were well but as the study progressed patients relapsed. The relative benefit to the patients was shown by the difference between the relapse rates among the patients who received the active drugs and those who received placebo. At the end of the six-month period of continuation therapy 22 per cent of those on the active drug had relapsed compared with 50 per cent of those on placebo (Figure 1). The only clinical factor which was associated with benefit from active treatment was the presence of minor symptoms at the time at which continuation therapy was commenced (Mindham *et al.*, 1973). A rather similar study was conducted about the same time in the United States of America. In this study all the patients received amitriptyline initially and were then divided into three groups to received amitriptyline, placebo, or no medication for six months. These groups were further subdivided into those groups who received supportive psychotherapy from a social worker in addition to other measures, and those who were followed routinely by psychiatrists. Thus

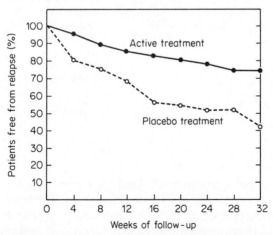

Figure 1   Proportion of patients remaining free from relapse in the two trial groups at 4-weekly intervals

Table 1　Antidepressant drugs

Official name	Common trade name	Daily dosage	Common unwanted effects	Closely related drugs
Tryclicic drugs and analogues:				
Imipramine	Tofranil	75–225 mg	Anticholinergic, i.e. dry mouth blurred vision difficulty with micturition	Desipramine Chlomipramine Trimipramine
Amitripytline	Tryptizol	75–225 mg	Anticholinergic Drowsiness	Nortriptyline Protriptyline
Doxepin	Sinequan		Anticholinergic Sedation	
Dothiepin	Prothiaden	75–225 mg	Anticholinergic	
Maprotiline	Ludiomil	75–300 mg	Anticholinergic Fewer effects on heart	
Mianserin	Bolvidon	40–200 mg	Anticholinergic as above	
Monoamine oxidase inhibitors:				
Phenelzine	Nardil	30–60 mg	Anticholinergic Postural hypotension Interaction with certain foods giving headaches	Iproniazid Isocarboxazid
Tranyl- cypromine	Parnate	10–30 mg	Insomnia Anticholinergic Interaction with foods Dependency	
Others:				
Dexam- phetamine	Dexedrine	5–60 mg	Insomnia, over- activity Dependency Psychosis	No longer in use as an antidepressant

there were six treatment groups in all. The trial showed an advantage, as far as relapse was concerned, to the patients who received amitriptyline irrespective of other measures (Paykel *et al.*, 1975). These studies appear to demonstrate conclusively that some patients benefit from continued medication for a six-month period after recovering from a depressive illness which had responded to the same drug. There are, however, many reservations which should be made as to the interpretation of the results and their application in clinical practice.

Major tranquillizers or neuroleptics

Before the Second World War no drugs were available for the control of violent behaviour which did not achieve this effect by producing sedation or even sleep. As a consequence mental hospitals either had to lock violent patients in padded rooms or to give them medication which prevented normal activities. Many of the sedative drugs used were themselves unsatisfactory; paraldehyde, for

Table 2 Major tranquillizers

Official name	Common trade name	Daily dosage	Common unwanted effects	Closely related drugs
Phenothiazines:				
Chlorpromazine	Largactil	75–1000 mg	Anticholinergic Drowsiness Extrapyramidal Cardiovascular effects Light sensitivity	Promazine
Thioridazine	Melleril	75–600 mg	Less likely to induce extrapyramidal effects Anticholinergic effects prominent Deposited in retina	Pericyazine
Trifluorperazine	Stelazine	10–60 mg	Many extrapyramidal effects Less anticholinergic	Fluphenazine Fluphenazine decanoate (depot)
Butyrophenones:				
Haloperidol	Serenace	1.5–200 mg	Extrapyramidal effects common Less anticholinergic action	Droperidol
Thioxanthenes:				
Flupenthixol	Depixol	3–18 mg	Extrapyramidal effects common	Flupenthixol decanoate (depot)

example, although rapidly effective, has a nauseating smell and when given by injection may lead to abscess-formation. Problems in the management of individual patients, when coupled with the overcrowding of mental hospitals, the availability of few therapeutic remedies for non-violent disorders, and the problems of institutionalization, meant that few therapeutic avenues were open to both patients and staff, leading to a very limited view of the future prospects for patients suffering from the major psychiatric disorders.

In the early 1950s the drug chlorpromazine was used clinically in France as an adjunct to anaesthesia, where it was found to calm patients without producing marked sedation. Prompted by these accounts Delay and Deniker (1952) used the drug in violent and excited patients and reported that control of symptoms was achieved without sedation. The same group of workers went on to use the drug in a more diverse group of psychiatric patients and reported good effects. The use of the drug rapidly spread, and enthusiastic reports came from all over the world. It was soon apparent that the drug was particularly valuable in the treatment of schizophrenia and was capable of controlling not only violence and overactivity, but many other symptoms including hallucinations, delusions, and passivity experiences as well.

Chlorpromazine itself has continued to be widely used but many more drugs of the same group have been developed, varying in their chemical composition, potency, and effects. There are three main groups of phenothiazines: the dimethylaminopropyl group of which chlorpromazine is one; the piperadine group of which thioridazine is the most important member; and the piperazine group which includes trifluorperazine and fluphenazine. Analogues of the phenothiazines have been developed; these share many of the pharmacological properties of the phenothiazine group but are different chemically; important groups are the butyrophenones of which haloperidol is the best known; the thiozanthenes of which flupenthixol is a well-known member; and a number of drugs which do not fit into these categories of which pimozide is an important example.

In the years after the original description of the action of chlorpromazine in psychiatric disorders, chlorpromazine itself, and other phenothiazines were more systematically assessed, particularly in the treatment of schizophrenia. An important study, among many, was that carried out by the United States Psychopharmacology Service Center Collaborative Study Group (1964) in which newly admitted acute schizophrenic patients were treated with chlorpromazine, thioridazine, fluphenazine, or placebo on a flexible dosage schedule and using a double-blind trial design. At the end of six months treatment global assessments of progress, which were carried out on the patients remaining in the trial indicated that all patients showed a tendency to improvement but of those on the drugs, 75 per cent were rated as 'much' or 'very much' improved whereas fewer than 40 per cent of those on the placebo were so rated. In addition, those patients who deteriorated proved to be on the placebo while none of the drug-treated group was worse. Global assessments were supported by evidence of improvement in individual symptoms. The study showed no particular advantage from any one of the drugs used, although other studies have suggested that individual drugs may be particularly effective in suppressing certain symptoms.

The advantages of continued treatment with major tranquillizers in schizophrenia have been less clear cut. A study performed under the aegis of the Medical Research Council of Great Britain showed an advantage to patients on active drugs, as compared with placebo, as regards the frequency of relapse in the year after recovery from the acute phase of the illness (Leff and Wing, 1971). The effect of drugs in established chronic schizophrenia is less clear. Some symptoms such as emotional disturbances and loss of drive, showing little response to drugs, and other symptoms, such as hallucinations and paranoid ideas, commonly responsive to drug treatment in the acute phase, tended to persist in spite of consistent and high dosage of appropriate medication. It appears that most of the acute symptoms of schizophrenia do respond to drug treatment but certain symptoms and some long-term effects, experienced by a minority of patients, are much less responsive.

Phenothiazines and their analogues are not only used in the treatment of schizophrenia; they have some effect on hallucinations and delusions occurring in other conditions including those arising from structural disease of the brain. This would suggest that whatever mechanisms are involved in the production of these symptoms they are not specific to schizophrenia. Phenothiazines are frequently used as sedatives in a variety of psychiatric conditions including agitated depressive states, restlessness in dementing patients, and in toxic confusional states arising from a wide variety of causes including that associated with alcohol withdrawal, or delirium tremens.

Phenothiazines are also used in conditions other than psychiatric disorders. Chlorpromazine is useful in the treatment of tetanus on account of its property of bringing about muscular relaxation. The phenothiazines generally have the property of reducing nausea and vomiting and some, such as prochlorperazine, have been especially developed for this purpose. A drug like prochlorperazine can be given by injection or by suppository, and this makes it particularly suitable for the control of vomiting. Chlorpromazine is useful in the control of hiccoughs due to pathological causes; this can be a most distressing symptom. Phenothiazines are also used as an adjunct to anaesthesia in a very similar way to that originally described. The phenothiazines potentiate the effects of a variety of drugs, and this is useful in combination with the analgesics especially where they are being given over a long period and in painful malignant disease.

Unwanted effects of phenothiazines and their analogues

A striking characteristic of chlorpromazine is that it has a very wide range of pharmacological effects. Some of these can be used therapeutically but invariably pharmacological effects are produced which are not a clinical advantage to an individual patient. These side-effects, or unwanted effects, are both interesting and important, and some of the major types will be briefly outlined.

All the drugs under consideration can produce other effects on the *central nervous system* if given in sufficiently large dosage. There are three common disturbances of motor function and these are: drug-induced Parkinsonism, akathisia, and acute and chronic dyskinesias. Drug-induced Parkinsonism was seen in some of the first patients to receive chlorpromazine, and for many years it was thought that changes in the motor system were essential if the effects on mental symptoms were to be brought about. Although varying in severity, drug induced Parkinsonism resembles naturally occurring Parkinson's disease, the subject showing tremor, rigidity, and difficulty in initiating movements, with a mask-like face, dribbling, and a characteristic small-stepping unsteady gait. Anticholinergic drugs of the type used in the treatment of Parkinson's disease are given to control drug-induced Parkinsonism where the symptoms are sufficiently severe to merit additional medication. Akathisia is a state of motor and subjective restlessness in which the patient cannot keep still and constantly has to shift his position, even during the night. This syndrome does not readily respond to treatment, and is particularly seen in patients receiving phenothiazines which are piperazine derivatives, such as trifluorperazine.

The dyskinesias are movement disorders in which there is grimacing, jerky, non-repetitive movements of the face, limbs, and tongue, with abnormal postures of the neck, head, and limbs. In the acute form the disturbances may be generalized, of very acute onset, and may produce bizarre and distressing postures, often of extreme extension of the body. These attacks are generally short-lived and benign. The more chronic forms of dyskinesia usually occur only after drugs have been given for months or years, and for this reason are called the 'tardive dyskinesias'. Most commonly only twitching movements of the mouth and tongue are seen, but the condition may be more generalized with twitching of the limbs, chest, and abdomen, and disturbance of gait, very much resembling the condition known as chorea. The tardive dyskinesias characteristically appear when the dosage of phenothiazines is reduced; then they may gradually disappear over a period of months, or alternatively may become a permanent neurological disorder. The full seriousness of this complication of treatment with major tranquillizers has taken some years to emerge, and a full knowledge of the disorder in terms of frequency and severity is not yet available. Treatment of tardive dyskinesia has been of very limited value (see Marsden *et al.*, 1983).

The major tranquillizers have many effects on the *autonomic nervous system*; these include blurring of vision, dryness of the mouth, retention of urine, hypotension, increased heart rate, and inhibition of ejaculation.

Jaundice occasionally occurs especially with chlorpromazine. This is a particularly interesting unwanted effect because it is a sensitivity reaction rather than a purely toxic effect on liver cells. The clinical picture is that of the obstructive type of jaundice appearing a few days after a single small dose of the drug. Recovery follows with withdrawal of the drug and takes roughly one month to become complete.

Major tranquillizers occasionally have effects on the bone marrow, suppressing its activity and very rarely leading to irreversible aplasia. The major tranquillizers have a number of effects on endocrine function: secretion of milk from the breasts may be seen, and is due to the effects of the drug on the secretion of the pituitary hormone concerned with lactation; menstruation may be interrupted; and, in men, impotence may be attributable to endocrine effects. Some of the drugs may be deposited in the lens and retina of the eye leading to deterioration of vision; this only occurs in patients who have received the drug over a very extended period of time. The drugs may make the skin more sensitive to the effects of light, leading to painful sunburn.

Mode of administration

The phenothiazines are given for a variety of psychiatric conditions but are particularly important in the treatment of the schizophrenias. As these drugs can obscure the clinical features of a mental illness they should be prescribed only after a definite diagnosis has been made, unless there are pressing reasons for doing otherwise. Caution is particularly important when a diagnosis of schizophrenia is being considered as it carries such serious implications for prognosis and for further management. The sedative action of the phenothiazines makes them of value in the management of psychiatric syndromes other than schizophrenia, such as agitation, delirium, and severe tension states; these compounds are best avoided in the milder psychiatric conditions for which effective alternatives are available.

Chlorpromazine and thioridazine are frequently given to patients who are restless, excited, or violent. They can be given by mouth or by injection according to the clinical requirements. The usual dosage is 25–100 mg three times a day but a much larger dosage can be used when necessary. In the excited patient 50–100 mg of either drug by intramuscular injection is quickly effective in controlling symptoms, and can be repeated. The less sedative drugs such as trifulorperazine and fluphenazine may be more suitable for the withdrawn or apathetic patient where excitement and restlessness are not leading problems.

Typically phenothiazine drugs have to be given to patients suffering from acute schizophrenia for several weeks before a marked improvement in symptoms is seen. After three or four weeks hallucinations and delusions become less prominent, and over a period of six to eight weeks in a proportion of patients symptoms disappear completely. It is a common practice to continue administration of phenothiazine drugs in patients in whom acute symptoms are well controlled for a period of six to twelve months, after which the drugs are then gradually withdrawn. If symptoms recur as the dosage is reduced it may be necessary to continue medication for a longer period. It should be remembered, however, that some patients suffer from recurrent episodes of schizophrenia with prolonged periods of remission in between so that continued medication is not necessary for all patients.

A minority of patient will either have persistent symptoms following the acute phase or will show a recurrence of symptoms if medication is reduced or withdrawn. When it appears necessary to continue treatment for an extended period of time it is worth considering the use of the more recently introduced long-acting phenothiazines. The main advantage of these preparations is to ensure the patient has received the drug, although they are less satisfactory in achieving good control of symptoms in the acute phase of the condition. The long-acting drugs now available are generally derivatives of very potent drugs which are themselves used in the management of acute schizophrenia. In the long-acting preparation slow release from an injection is achieved by giving the drug suspended in oil as an ester or salt of the original preparation. The drug is slowly released from an oil tissue depot and de-esterified, releasing the free drug into the bloodstream. Preparations of this kind extend the action of injections to between two and four weeks. A number of trials has demonstrated the effectiveness of this kind of preparation in the management of chronic schizophrenic patients; that by Hirsch and his colleagues (1973) dramatically showing the advantage of an active preparation of this kind as compared with placebo. Even patients for whom depot preparations are prescribed should not be kept on the drugs indefinitely; medication should be reviewed and, where appropriate, a trial of withdrawal of the drug made. It is important to recognize that relapse may take months to occur after the withdrawal of oral medication and in the case of depot treatment the period over which patients should be observed following the withdrawal of medication is correspondingly extended. In a high proportion of chronic schizophrenic patients withdrawal of medication will lead to the re-emergence of symptoms and a recognition of the need for continued medication. The risk of making a trial of withdrawal of medication has to be weighed against the advantages of stopping medication. The long-term risk of irreversible tardive dyskinesia is a major factor in favour of attempting to withdraw drugs.

Rauwolfia derivatives

For many years substances derived from the plant Rauwolfia serpentina have been used in the Indian subcontinent in the treatment of a variety of illnesses. In Western medicine a purified derivative, reserpine, has been used since the 1950s in the treatment of hypertension and as a tranquillizer in psychiatry. More recently synthetic reserpine-like compounds have been developed of which the best known is tetrabenazine. Rauwolfia derivatives are now little used but on account of their actions are of great theoretical importance.

The main effect of reserpine on the brain is to produce a depletion of amines over the course of a few weeks. Sedation is also produced and this has been attributed to a decline in the concentration of amines. The effect of the reserpine derivatives on the brain has led to their extensive use in pharmacological experiments particularly in testing the potency of drugs in stopping or reversing effects on the brain amines. The effect of reserpine lowering the blood pressure has been attributed to changes in amine concentrations in the autonomic nervous system.

Apart from its use in the treatment of hypertension reserpine has been used in the treatment of schizophrenia in controlling over-activity, restlessness, and violence. This group of drugs was introduced into psychiatry at about the same time as chlorpromazine and soon proved to be less effective and likely to produce more severe unwanted effects. The drugs are also useful in the treatment of some movement disorders, such as Huntington's chorea and dystonia musculorum deformans. The therapeutic effect seen in these disorders is probably attributable to a fall in the concentrations of some brain amines.

The principal unwanted effects of Rauwolfia derivatives are depression of mood and Parkinsonism, both thought to be due to a fall in amine concentrations in the brain. The depressive syndrome produced closely resembles naturally occurring retarded depression. There is evidence from the examination of the amine content of the brain of depressed subjects who have died by suicide, that there is a depletion of amines which is closely similar to that following the administration of Rauwolfia derivatives. Similarly in naturally occurring Parkinson's disease a specific depletion of dopamine has been found which may be reversed by the administration of large quantities of levodopa, the precursor of dopamine, by mouth. Thus the pharmacological effects of reserpine and its analogues in the brain, closely parallel two important diseases and to some degree have helped in their elucidation.

Hypnotics and sedatives

Drugs which have the effect of depressing the functions of the central nervous system have been known for many years; alcohol is probably the best known drug of this type. Such drugs induce a sense of relaxation, drowsiness, or even sleep, and this effect is accompanied by a reduction in tension and arousal, sometimes giving way to disinhibition. In large dosage intoxication may occur and be accompanied by unsteadiness, slurred speech, and slowness of movement. The pleasant effect of this group of drugs has made them particularly liable to abuse; the long-term effects of taking them have come to be very important.

Substances with these properties have been used in widely differing conditions and they are amongst the first drugs to be employed in psychiatric treatment. Drugs in this group include morphia and its analogues, paraldehyde, chloral, the bromides, barbiturates, and in more recent years the benzodiazepines. In psychiatry the sedative drugs were originally employed in the control of aggressive behaviour, with restlessness, agitation, and motor over-activity; or as hypnotics in inducing sleep; and in some cases for the control of epileptic fits. A major problem in using drugs of this type for the control of violent behaviour is that such improvement in behaviour as is obtained, occurs as a consequence of sedation, and this may make the subject sleepy and unfit for normal activities. As better drugs have become available for the treatment of psychotic disorders the use of sedatives has become restricted to a narrower range of conditions; these are the symptoms of anxiety and tension, and possibly, sleeplessness which are seen as a part of many neurotic disorders, and also in subjects who would not be regarded as suffering from psychiatric disorder. Although the indications for the use of the sedative drugs have narrowed the very large numbers of patients who

Table 3   Hypnotics and sedatives

Official name	Common trade name	Daily dosage	Common unwanted effects	Closely related drugs
Benzodiazepines:				
Diazepam	Valium	6–30 mg	Sedation Effects on driving Dizziness	Medazepam Clorazepate Clobazam
Chloridiaze-poxide	Librium		Depression of respiration	Oxazepam
Nitrazepam	Mogadon	5–10 mg	Prolonged drowsiness	Flurazepam Lormetazepam Triazolam Temazepam
Barbiturates:				
Amylobarbitone sodium	Sodium amytal	100–200 mg	Drowsiness, dizziness and ataxia Dependency Excitement and confusion Withdrawal fits	Butobarbitone Phenobarbitone Phentobarbitone
Others:				
Meprobamate	Equanil	1.2–2.4G mg	Drowsiness Dependency Withdrawal fits	
Chloral hydrate		0.5–2G mg	Gastro-intestinal irritation	

suffer from these disorders have led to their very wide use in the general population. The properties of some of the commonly used types will be briefly outlined.

The older preparations

The control of psychomotor over-activity has always figured prominently in the management of mentally disturbed patients. The use of opiates has been superseded by newer drugs which are more effective and less dangerous. The use of paraldehyde has also greatly declined, partly on account of its limited efficacy, its unpleasant smell and taste, but not least because of the risk of abscess-formation following its injection; it is still used by some workers in the treatment of status epilepticus because of its rapid onset of action. The bromides were not very satisfactory when used for the control of fits or insomnia, and their serious unwanted effects have led to their abandonment in therapeutics. Alcohol is unreliable as a hypnotic or sedative but chloral has retained a place as an effective and safe hypnotic, especially useful in the young and elderly in spite of its unpleasant taste.

Barbiturates

Among older drugs with a primarily depressive effect on the central nervous system the barbiturates have been used most widely in four different ways: to sedate and allay anxiety when given in small dosage; to induce sleep in larger dosage; to prevent or control convulsive behaviour in epilepsy; and to control the violent behaviour sometimes associated with the psychoses. Tolerance to the administration of the barbiturates occurs rapidly, largely due to an increase in the rate of metabolism in the liver brought about by the potentiation of the relevant enzyme systems. The barbiturates have a predominantly depressant effect on the brain, first reducing the activity of the neocortex and then affecting the brain stem and the spinal cord in larger dosage. Small doses of barbiturate release the cortex from inhibition. This effect can be recognized by an increase in electrical activity and by behavioural changes. Larger doses have a depressant effect on both the cortex and the reticular formation which is accompanied by drowsiness or even sleep. Behaviourally the administration of barbiturates results in a decline in the level of activity and in the precision with which more complex tasks are performed.

Barbiturates have been widely used as hypnotics and have been shown to be more effective than placebo in this respect. The concept of long and shortacting drugs has been questioned, and it seems that the duration of action is more likely to be related to dosage and potency than to differences in the rate of metabolism. Barbiturates are also used in the control of anxiety; controlled studies have confirmed their value in the treatment of chronic anxiety states.

In epilepsy phenobarbitone has retained a position as an important anti-convulsant in spite of the appearance of many newer drugs; it is more effective in grand mal and focal epilepsy and less effective in petit mal. Barbiturates can be used to control tension, agitation, and violence. However, when a patient is severely disturbed the degree of sedation produced by the high dose of drugs required to control the behaviour, is so great as to induce sleep or drowsiness which render normal activities impossible. There is another disadvantage in that the effects are short-lived, depending upon the continued administration of the drugs for the control of symptoms. Intravenous barbiturates can be used to facilitate interviews by allowing patients to disclose unpleasant information. The drugs are given by slow intravenous injection; and the effect appears to result from a drug-induced decline in the patient's reluctance to talk about his problems.

The main disadvantages of barbiturates are the drowsiness often associated with the therapeutic effects; the rapid rise in dosage required to achieve and maintain a particular effect; the serious risk of dependency developing if the drugs are prescribed over a long period of time; the associated risk of fits when the drug is withdrawn; and the common use of barbiturates for suicidal attempts which may be successful. Patients taking barbiturates may show a clinical picture of mild intoxication with impairment of mental functions, slurring of speech, ataxia, and nystagmus. These effects are particularly important when those taking them use dangerous machinery or drive motor vehicles. Quite a small dosage of drugs can impair judgment and motor functions and increases the risk of road accidents in very much the same way as alcohol does.

Non-barbiturate sedatives and hypnotics

Many attempts have been made to replace the barbiturates by drugs with the same general properties but without the most serious of their adverse effects. Many of these substances have been disappointing, and in spite of initial claims of certain advantages their general characteristics have closely resembled those of the barbiturates which they were intended to displace. Examples include meprobamate, glutethimide, Mandrax, a preparation containing methaqualone and diphenhydramine in combination; and more recently the benzodiazipines.

The benzodiazipines

In recent years the benzodiazipines have come into use as sedatives and hypnotics. Apart from their sedative effects the benzodiazepines are muscle-relaxants, anticonvulsants and appetite-suppressants. Although they vary in potency, diazepam being two to three times more potent than chlordiazepoxide, their pharmacodynamics are similar. Clinical trials have shown varying results but some evidence suggests that they are about as effective as barbiturates in the treatment of anxiety. Their main advantage lies in their relative safety; for example, ingestion of large doses has been followed by survival. Diazepam and chlordiazepoxide and other benzodiazepines can be used in most circumstances in which a mild sedative is required. Diazepam is also widely used as an anticonvulsant, and can be given by intravenous injection in status epilepticus. Nitrazepam is used mainly as an hypnotic.

Adverse effects include rashes, drowsiness, lapses of attention, confusional episodes, ataxia, slurred speech, excessive weight gain, and impairment of intellectual function. Physical dependence can be produced, and withdrawal is followed by an abstinence syndrome which may include fits (Petursson and Lader, 1981). In many respects the benzodiazepines resemble the barbiturates, and it is wise to warn patients of the likelihood of drowsiness, the dangers of driving, and the potentiating effect of alcohol.

A very large number of benzodiazepines have been developed and marketed; the choice is perplexing but the position is nothing like so complex as it might appear at first sight. Many of the drugs available are metabolized to common degradation products and may even share the same active principle.

The introduction of the benzodiazepines is a matter of some general interest, and it is illustrative of the problems of assessing the merits of new drugs when they are first brought into use. The drugs were seen as being less toxic than barbiturates; as producing their therapeutic effects with less sedation; and as presenting little risk of the induction of dependency. Furthermore claims for individual members of the group have been the shortness of duration of effect with no hangover period following their use, making the drug suitable for use as hypnotics; others are claimed to have prolonged effects making them especially suitable for the control of anxiety with the advantage of infrequent administration.

Experience has confirmed their general safety; but sedation and impairment of motor performance are clearly seen in a high proportion of those taking the drug in effective dosage. The risk of dependency is marked and follows the pattern of dependency described for other drugs which have a depressant effect on the central nervous system (Eddy *et al.*, 1965).

Evidence of strong tendency to induce dependency is now widely available. In the individual case doctors have difficulty in stopping administration of the benzodiazepines, and there are many reports of dependency, withdrawal effects, and other features of dependency. On the wider scale social ill-effects of the use of the drugs have been reported (World Health Organization, 1981). The sedative properties of the group of drugs is a matter of some controversy: they have come to be known as the 'minor tranquillizers' from the belief that their effect is not dependent upon a marked sedative effect. The term 'minor tranquillizers' appears to distinguish them from the distinct group of drugs used in psychotic disorders that are known as the 'major tranquillizers'. The reasons for regarding the benzodiazepines as different from other sedative drugs has never been universally accepted and is now widely questioned; the World Health Organization now regards all the drugs in this category as having broadly similar pharmacological and clinical effects.

Nitrazepam is a member of the group which has been promoted as a hypnotic. Experience has shown that this drug has a slow onset of action leading to a poor effect with patients having difficulty in getting off to sleep: this is coupled with prolonged pharmacological effects leading to drowsiness next day. These characteristics are clearly due to a relatively long half-life but may be due to the persistence of active metabolites in the blood. This preparation would probably have been better promoted as a sedative rather than as a hypnotic. Other examples exist, e.g. diazepam, of drugs which have been found to be excellent hypnotics but which have been promoted primarily as sedatives for round-the-day use for which they are less suited. The distinction between hypnotics and sedatives is in many ways an artificial one; the effect seen is partly dependent upon dosage and partly upon the duration of effect, this being largely a function of half-life.

Psychotomimetic drugs

Although many centrally acting drugs can occasionally precipitate psychotic reactions when administered in excessive dosage or to susceptible individuals, there is a group of drugs which, in relatively small dosage, regularly induces marked changes in perception, mood, and thought. Unlike the other psychotropic drugs the so-called psychotomimetic drgus are primarily of interest because of their capacity to provoke mental abnormalities rather than to suppress them. The readiness with which the drugs induce changes in perception, states of ecstasy, and mystical insight has led to their widespread use in religious ceremonies and by parareligious cults of many kinds. Many of the compounds occur naturally in various parts of the world, and in some cases their psychological effects have been known for centuries. The best-known psychotomimetic compounds are mescaline, lysergic acid diethylamide (lysergide or LSD), psilocybin, and phencyclidine. The pharmacological effects of an extract of the cactus peyotl was discovered by Lewin in 1888, and subsequently its active constituent, mescaline, was isolated. Lysergide was discovered in 1943.

The resemblance between the states produced by the psychotomimetic drugs and naturally occurring psychiatric conditions, especially schizophrenia, has led to their use in research into the possible causes and treatment of the psychoses. In pursuing possible chemical causes of the psychoses it was suggested that substances with actions similar to those of the psychotomimetic drugs might be produced in the brain in the course of various diseases and give rise to mental symptoms. Chemical similarities between some metabolites of the catecholamines and mescaline prompted the adrenochrome hypothesis for the causation of schizophrenia (Hoffer *et al.*, 1954). A number of naturally occurring ubstances which might be capable of producing hallucinations have been investigated but, so far, a satisfactory chemical basis of the symptoms of chizophrenia remains elusive. The states produced by the psychotomimetic rugs can also resemble a variety of other psychoses, including both the epressive and manic forms of the affective psychoses, epileptic psychoses, and sychoses associated with structural brain damage, as well as the psychoses iduced by other chemical agents.

On the supposition that substances which antagonize the effects of psychotoiimetic drugs in animals would be effective against the symptoms induced by the rugs in man, it was hoped that psychotomimetic drugs might be used to induce isychotic' behaviour in animals which would then be used to test the effects of arious drugs. This expectation is to some degree fulfilled in that phenothiazines ke chlorpromazine are usually effective in controlling the acute psychosis iduced by lysergide as well as the symptoms of acute schizophrenia, but the iethod has been of less general use than might have been expected when applied o animals.

The psychotomimetic drugs have several clinical types: the phenylethyimines, of which mescaline is the best known; the lysergic acid derivatives, of /hich lysergic acid diethylamide is the best known; and the indolamines epresented by psilocybin. There are, in addition, several other drugs of similar ction but of differing chemical composition.

The psychotomimetic drugs share many pharmacological properties in spite of ieir differing chemical formulae. The following account refers principally to the ctions of mescaline and lysergide as these are the most commonly encountered iembers of the group. Peripherally, the drugs have a stimulant effect on smooth iuscle and bring about a constriction of small blood vessels. Centrally, they timulate sympathetic centres, causing tachycardia, mydriasis, and elevation of lood pressure. Observations of the effects of the drug on the electroencephaloram are contradictory: experiments have variously suggested central and eripheral origins for the electrical discharges associated with visual halluciations. When given the drugs, many animals showed disturbance of behaviour 'hich has been regarded as a disintegration of both innate and learned patterns f behaviour. Experiments have included studies of the effects of the drugs, enerally mescaline or lysergide, on the web-building activities of spiders, the ostures of fish, the movement of snails, and waltzing in mice. Some animals emonstrate excitability after receiving the drugs; others exhibit a calming eaction.

Although the actions of all the psychotomimetic drugs are similar in many espects the clinical effects mentioned here are principally those of mescaline and 'sergide. Both mescaline and lysergide induce physiological changes which may e accompanied by changes in affect, perception, and cognition. However, the ffects produced are very variable, even in the individual patient, and are articularly dependent upon the social circumstance in which the drugs are

given. The following account is given of the sequence in which the effects ar
generally experienced.

The physical effects come on about thirty minutes after oral administratio
of the drug. There may be nausea, anorexia, vomiting, chest pains, dizziness
headache, sweating, tremor, incoordination, ataxia, and alternating feelings o
heat and cold. Autonomic effects include palpitations, blurring of vision, urinar
frequency, pupillary dilatation, tachycardia, and a rise in blood pressure. Th
somatic symptoms may be followed by a state of great anxiety and dread. As thi
dies away a state of euphoria or emotional lability may ensue. Thinking processe
may be slowed or accelerated and are irrational and loosely related. Perceptua
changes occur in about half the subjects taking the drugs: there may be change
in perspective and distortion of images; colours may appear to be more vivid
textures exaggerated, sounds distorted; the experience of body image and of tim
are often disturbed. Hallucinations can occur in any sensory modality and thes
are frequently abstract in form. The subject may feel detached from hi
environment and changed in himself, as with depersonalization experiences
Performance in tests of memory, attention, and dexterity declines. As the dosag
of drug is increased the changes in mental state come to resemble an acut
confusional state more closely.

The psychotomimetic drugs have been used in the treatment of a variety o
mental illnesses. Some workers have claimed LSD to have been of value i
neurotic states where they 'disturbed the barriers of repression' and allowe
patients to relive long-past events 'with frightening realism'. The use of LSD ha
been extended to group psychotherapy as well as individual therapy, and i
claimed to allow expression of unpleasant material and to enable a patient t
have insight into his emotional problems. Lysergide is claimed to be of value a
an adjunct to psychotherapy in the treatment of phobias, sexual neuroses, an
some psychopathic states (Sandison, 1964). At the same time attention is drawr
to the need for an experienced team to look after the patients receiving the dru
and to the dangers associated with its use. The published evidence suggests tha
psychotomimetic drugs have no established place in the treatment of menta
illness.

These drugs have become to be more important in psychiatry from the effect
of abuse rather than for their therapeutic effects. In the acute phase o
intoxication the subject may be a danger both to himself and to others; cases o
suicide and even homicide have been recorded. When the acute effects o
intoxication have died down abnormalities may persist which were not presen
before the drugs were taken; these include depersonalization, pseudo-hallucina
tions and other disorders of perception, anxiety, depression, mood swings, an
paranoid beliefs, and may last for a few days or be so prolonged as to b
indistinguishable from naturally occurring mental illness (DHSS, 1970). Th
acute effects can generally be terminated by giving chlorpromazine, by in

tramuscular injection. Concern that the illicit taking of lysergide might spread has led to the restriction of its manufacture in Great Britain.

Miscellaneous drugs

Lithium salts

The greater part of this section will concern the use of lithium salts in psychiatry. This substance, which occurs naturally in the body, was introduced initially as a sedative for the control of disturbed behaviour, and was subsequently advocated as a prophylactic treatment for both states of elation and of depression. Its evaluation occasioned a long and strongly contested controversy which has important implications for the evaluation of treatments of any kind whether they involve the use of drugs or not. For this reason the development of the use of lithium salts in psychiatric treatment will be described in some detail. Lithium salts have been employed in medicine for many years; initially in the treatment of rheumatoid arthritis and gout; and in this century as a salt substitute and, more recently, in psychiatry. In consequence a good deal was known about lithium salts before they were employed in psychiatry.

Lithium is a similar substance to sodium and shows many of its chemical, physiological, and pharmacological effects. It is widely distributed in the body and is capable of replacing sodium in nerve cells and in skeletal muscles. Lithium ions pass through the cells more slowly than sodium, and it has been suggested that changes induced by this effect have been responsible for some of the pharmacological effects observed.

Cade (1949) reported drowsiness in guinea-pigs following intraperitoneal injection of lithium salts and, subsequently, that lithium salts had a calming effect on manic patients. Schou *et al.* (1954) studied the effects of lithium salts in mania and reported a 'good' response in a proportion of patients. In 1963 Maggs reported a double-blind cross-over comparison between lithium salts and placebo in the treatment of manic patients and found lithium salts to be superior. The place of lithium slats in the treatment of mania is now widely accepted. They have a slower onset of action than some other treatments and are not effective in a high proportion of cases but may be of value for patients resistant to other forms of treatment. Hartogen (1963) and Schou (1963) independently suggested that lithium salts might exert a propylactic effect in patients who had suffered from mania. This claim has since been extended to include the prophylaxis of certain forms of depressive disorder although the evidence suggests that lithium salts are ineffective in the treatment of acute depression.

The introduction of lithium salts and the testing of their efficacy in preventing relapse in manic depressive psychoses has caused a controversy that is itself of considerable interest. Following the suggestion that lithium salts might be of value in preventing further episodes of affective illness their investigation went through a number of stages. After several open uncontrolled observations of their use reports of studies using retrospective controls, or a 'mirror image' design appeared. In this type of study the patient's progress before and after the introduction of the trial treatment are compared, and the effectiveness of the treatment is assessed.

Trials using retrospective controls carry some serious disadvantages. First, a 'mirror image' trial cannot be 'double-blind' so observer bias in favour of the new treatment can never be entirely excluded. Second, in this method the control period always precedes the period of trial treatment. This may lead to a number of biases that cannot be countered by the design of the study. For example, there may be changes in clinical practice or diagnostic conventions, or in the frequency of episodes of illness with the age of the patients; and these problems are particularly likely when the period of observation extends over many years. Third, it is well known that many factors influence the course of affective illnesses, even when there is considerable constitutional predisposition to the illness or even a regular phasic course. Extraneous influences are difficult to exclude in any event but more so when the period of observation is very long. Fourth, when patients who have just recovered from an affective illness are selected for a trial a bias in favour of the treatment subsequently given is introduced because, if the illness is recurrent, the patients are more likely to remain well just after an episode than if they had been studied from a randomly chosen point in the course of the illness. Finally, the criteria for assessment may have a bias in favour of the new treatment. This is particularly likely if the *number* of episodes of illness is chosen as a criterion of effectiveness of treatment. Electroconvulsive therapy tends to break up episodes of depressive illness, sometimes producing more but shorter periods of illness than are seen in the natural course of the disorder. It treatment with this effect has been employed in patients during 'control' period the subsequent withdrawal of the treatment could lead to fewer episodes of illness, and evidence in favour of the 'new' treatment.

Blackwell and Shepherd (1968) drew attention to the inadequacy of this type of study in a paper criticizing the method in detail, and illustrating many of these points by a retrospective study of the effects of continued medication in a variety of psychiatric patients, which demonstrated a spurious propylactic effect.

The appearance of Blackwell and Shepherd's paper was followed by a vigorous correspondence in the medical press. Possibly one of the most instructive letters came from two Swedish psychiatrists (Laurell and Ottosson, 1968) who stated that lithium salts had been so widely and rapidly employed in clinical practice in the Scandinavian countries that their use had become established clinical practice, making it virtually impossible to conduct a rigorous clinical trial of their efficacy without risking accusation of clinical malpractice and possibly legal proceedings. This letter emphasized the need for full and critical evaluation of new treatments *before* they are brought into general use *ontrolled trials of lithium salts*. In due course controlled studies of the use of thium salts in affective disorders were conducted.

Baastrup and his colleagues (1970) reported a well-controlled and rigorously onducted withdrawal study. The patients had all been taking lithium salts for a lapsing manic depressive illness, some with episodes of both mania and epression, others with episodes of mania or depression; and half of them had a lacebo substituted for lithium salts blindly and randomly. The investigators ho assessed the patients were also unaware of treatments the patients were eceiving, and their 'blindness' was maintained by the laboratory staff reporting ctitious plasma levels of lithium salts to the clinicians who then adjusted the osage of the placebo as though it were the active drug. This study showed that he patients withdrawn from lithium salts, whether they were suffering from ipolar or unipolar illness, had a higher relapse rate than those who continued on he drug.

To many this trial seemed to have answered former doubts but Blackwell 1970) made an important criticism of this type of study. He pointed out that to top the administration of a drug is not the same as initiating its use and that ffects might be produced that could be due to the withdrawal of the drug alone ather than to the re-emergence of an underlying condition. He illustrated this oint with the example of the barbiturates, in which the effects of administration nd withdrawal are quite different, the latter regularly producing fits and the ormer frequently producing sedation.

Subsequently a prospective study comparing the relapse rates in bipolar and nipolar manic depressive patients receiving lithium salts or placebo was eported (Coppen *et al.*, 1971). This trial was conducted in four centres. Patients vith a history of recurrent affective illness, some unipolar in type, others bipolar, vere allocated randomly to receive either lithium carbonate or placebo tablets of dentical appearance for periods of up to two years. The psychiatrist in charge ssessed the patients without knowing which treatment the patients were eceiving; a colleague took blood specimens and adjusted the dosage of lithium arbonate appropriately. Throughout the trial a record was kept of each atient's clinical ratings, the length of any hospitalization, and the nature of any dditional treatments given. Patients receiving lithium carbonate showed ignificantly less affective disturbance, judged by the length of both in-patient nd out-patient treatment for recurrences. The active treatment group also eceived significantly less additional medication and electroconvulsive therapy. ighty-six per cent of the patients on lithium salts were rated as showing 'little' or no' pathology compared with only 8 per cent so rated in the placebo group. ithium salts appeared to be equally effective in both unipolar and bipolar lisorders.

In a 'cross-over' study of patients who had been receiving lithium carbonate or periods of one to three years, Cundall and his colleagues (1972) found a very igh incidence of mania and hypomania amongst those who relapsed on placebo, uggesting that lithium salts were more effective in preventing relapse into mania or hypomania than into depressive states. Similarly, in a study by Hullin and his colleagues (1972) of 69 patients on lithium carbonate, 15 of 21 relapses were due to a manic or hypomanic state; and in 10 of these 15 there was a biochemical evidence of very low plasma levels of lithium.

The evidence suggests that lithium salts are effective in the treatment of manic states but not of depressive states. They are effective in the prevention of recurrence of both manic and depressive episodes in manic depressive illness, but are more effective in bipolar illness and in preventing relapse into mania than in the recurrent depressive type.

Now that the criteria of proof of the effectiveness of lithium salts in the prevention or relapse in manic depressive illness appear to have met Blackwell and Shepherd's stringent condition, it should not be forgotten that the methodological issues raised by them in 1968 are still valid and should be applied to any experiments on the effectiveness of supposedly prophylactic methods of treatment.

The use of lithium salts is now an established method of treatment for manic depressive illnesses. The technical aspects of the methods used in controlling lithium therapy and the many unwanted effects which have been reported are well documented.

Tricyclic drugs or lithium salts?

With the evidence of both the tricyclic antidepressants and lithium salts reducing the incidence of relapse in manic depressive illness there inevitably arises the question of how they compare in this respect and in what circumstances is one or the other to be preferred.

A study comparing the effects of imipramine, lithium carbonate, and placebo has been reported (Prien *et al.*, 1973). In this study patients who had suffered from recurrent affective illness, some of the unipolar depressive type and some of the bipolar type, in which there was a definite history of both manic and depressive phases, were given either lithium carbonate, imipramine, or placebo for a two-year period following discharge from the hospital after successful treatment for depressive illness. Among the patients classified as bipolar, lithium salts were associated with a lower rate of relapse than either imipramine or placebo; 69 per cent of the relapses were manic and 31 per cent depressive. Manic relapses occurred in 12 per cent of those on lithium carbonate, 67 per cent on imipramine and 33 per cent on placebo; depressive relapses occurred in 12 per cent of the lithium carbonate group, in none of the imipramine group, and in 55 per cent of the placebo group; i.e. the major difference between imipramine and lithium carbonate was in manic attacks; but the difference between lithium salts and the placebo was in both manic and depressive attacks. In the unipolar group 85 per cent of the relapses were depressive and 15 per cent were manic. Depressive relapses occurred in 36 per cent of the lithium carbonate group, in 29 per cent of the imipramine group, and in 85 per cent of the placebo group. Manic relapses occurred in a small percentage of each treatment.

The main conclusions drawn from this study were that in bipolar manic depressive illness lithium salts were superior to other methods in preventing relapse (as patients receiving them had a lower frequency of both types of relapse), and that in bipolar manic depressive illness, lithium carbonate and imipramine were equally effective in reducing depressive relapses and both were superior to placebo.

This study clarifies the relationship between the two methods of preventing relapse in manic depressive illness in a very helpful way and confirms the findings of earlier work on the effectiveness of the individual treatments.

Although we now have a considerable amount of information on the use of drugs in the prevention of relapse of manic depressive illness, there are still many questions to be answered. Are there other psychotropic drugs capable of preventing a recurrence of affective illness? Are there long-term effects of medication which might affect our choice of drug? How long should medication be continued? What dosage of drugs gives the best balance between clinical effects and unwanted effects? How can a choice be made among the drugs available? For example, lithium salts have a very narrow therapeutic ratio; their use must be controlled using estimations of plasma levels of the drug. On the other hand, tricyclic drugs do not require such fine control dosage, and would appear to have an advantage in this respect. The apparent advantages of tricyclic drugs could well be offset by long-term toxic effects that are as yet unknown. The information necessary to allow a rational choice of drugs to be made is not yet available; but it is likely to become available in due course, as our experience of their use grows.

In summary, the evidence now available suggests that both lithium salts and tricyclic antidepressants reduce the relapse rates in patients who have recovered from manic depressive illnesses. In preventing depressive relapses the two types of drugs are of similar potency, whereas in preventing manic relapses, lithium salts are more effective. When a patient has suffered from only depressive illness, a choice can be made on grounds of convenience; but when a patient has suffered from both manic and depressive episodes, lithium salts are to be preferred.

References

Baastrup, P. C., Poulsen, J. C., Schou, M., Thomsen, K., and Amdisen, A. (1970). Prophylactic lithium: double-blind discontinuation in manic-depressive and recurrent-depressive disorders. *Lancet* **ii**, 326–330.
Ball, J. R. B., and Kiloh, L. G. (1959). A controlled trial of imipramine in treatment of depressive states. *Brit. med. J.*, **2**, 1052–1055.
Blackwell, B., and Shepherd, M. (1968). Prophylactic lithium: another therapeutic myth? *Lancet* **i**, 968–971.
Blackwell, B. (1970). Lithium. *Lancet* **ii**, 875.

Cade, J. F. J. (1949). Lithium salts in the treatment of psychotic excitement. *Med. J. Aust.*, **2**, 349–352.

Coppen, A., Noguera, R., Bailey, J., Burns, B. H., Swani, M. S., Hare, E. H., Gardner, R., and Maggs, R. (1971). Prophylactic lithium in affective disorders. *Lancet* ii, 275–279.

Cundall, R. L., Brooks, P. W., and Murray, L. G. (1972). Controlled evaluation of lithium prophylaxis in affective disorders. *Psychological Medicine*, **2**, 308–311.

Delay, J., and Deniker, P. (1952). Le Congres de Psychiatrie et de Neurologie de Langue Française., p. 503 Masson et Cie, Luxembourg.

Department of Health and Social Security (1970). Amphetamines, Barbiturates, LSD and Cannabis; their use and misuse *Report on Public Health and Medical Subjects No. 124.* HMSO, London.

Eddy, N. B., Halbach, H., Isbell, H., and Seevers, M, H. (1965). Drug dependence: its significance and characteristics. *Bull. World Health Org.*, **32**, 721–733.

Hartigan, G. P. (1963). The use of lithium salts in affective disorders. *Brit. J. Psychiat.*, **109**, 810–814.

Hirsch, S. R., Gaind, R., Rohde, P., Stevens, B. C., and Wing, J. K. (1973). Out-patient maintenance of chronic schizophrenic patients with long-acting fluphenazine: double-blind placebo trial. *Brit. med. J.*, **1**, 633–637.

Hoffer, A., Osmond, H., and Smythies, J. (1954). Schizophrenia: a new approach. II Result of a year's research. *J. Ment. Sci.*, **100**, 29–45.

Hullin, R. P., McDonald, R., and Allsopp, M. N. E. (1972). Prophylactic lithium in recurrent affective disorders. *Lancet* i, 1044–1046.

Kuhn, R. (1958). The treatment of depressive states with G-22355 (imipramine hydrochloride). *Amer. J. Psychiat.*, **115**, 459–464.

Laurell, B., and Ottosson, J-O. (1968). Prophylactic lithium? *Lancet* ii, 1245–1246.

Leff, J. P., and Wing. J. K. (1971). Trial of maintenance therapy in schizophrenia. *Brit. med. J.*, **3**, 599–604.

Maggs, R. (1963). The treatment of manic illness with lithium carbonate. *Brit. J. Psychiat.*, **109**, 56–65.

Marsden, C. D., Mindham, R. H. S., and Mackay, A. V. P. (1983). Extrapyramidal movement disorders produced by antipsychotic drugs. In *The Psychopharmacology of Schizophrenia* Eds: Hirsch, S. R., Bradley, P. H. Oxford, Oxford University Press (In press).

Medical Research Council (1965). Clinical trial of the treatment of depressive illness. *Brit. med. J.*, **1**, 881–886.

Mindham, R. H. S., Shepherd, M., and Howland, C. (1973). An evaluation of continuation therapy with tricyclic antidepressants in depressive illness. *Psychological Medicine*, **3**, 5–17.

Mindham, R. H. S. (1979). Tricyclic antidepressants and amine precursors. In: *Psychopharmacology of Affective Disorders*, pp. 123–158 Eds: Paykel, E. S., Coppen, A. Oxford, Oxford University Press.

Mindham, R. H. S. (1982). The tricyclic antidepressants. In *Drugs in Psychiatric Practice* Eds: Tyrer, P., Mackay, A. V. P. (In Press).

National Institute of Mental Health. Psychopharmacology Service Center Collaborative Study Group (1964). Phenothiazine treatment in acute schizophrenia. *Arch. gen. Psychiat*, **10**, 246–261.

Paykel, E. S., Dimascio, A., Haskell, D., and Prusoff, B. A. (1975). Effects of maintenance amitriptyline and psychotherapy on symptoms of depression. *Psychological Medicine*, **5**, 67–77.

Petursson, H., and Lader, M. H. (1981). Withdrawal from long-term benzodiazepine treatment. *Brit. med. J.*, **283**, 643–645.

Prien, R. F., Klett, C. J., and Caffey, E. M., Jr. (1973). Lithium carbonate and imipramine in prevention of affective episodes. *Arch. Gen. Psychiat.*, **29**, 420–425.

Robitzek, E. H., Selikoff, I. J., and Ornstein, G. G. (1952). Chemotherapy of human tuberculosis with hydrazine derivatives of isonicotinic acid (preliminary report of representative cases). *Bull. Sea View Hospital*, **13**, 27–51.

Samuel, G., and Blackwell, B. (1968). Monoamine oxidase inhabitors and cheese: a process of discovery. *Hospital Medicine*, **1**, 942–943.

Sandison, R. A. (1964). Hallucinogens. *Practitioner*, **192**, 30–36.

Schou, M. (1963). Normothymics—'mood-normalizers'—are lithium and the imipramine drugs specific for affective disorders? *Brit. J. Psychiat.*, **109**, 803–809.

Schou, M. Juel-Nielsen, N., Strömgren, E., and Voldby, H. (1954). The treatment of manic psychoses by the administration of lithium salts. *J. Neurol. Neurosurg., Psychiat.*, **17**, 250–260.

Shepherd, M., Lader, M., and Rodnight, R. (1968). *Clinical Psychopharmacology*. English Universities Press, London.

Shepherd, M. (1972). The classification of psychotropic drugs. *Psychological Medicine*, **2**, 96–110.

Silverstone, T., and Turner, P. (1974). *Drug Treatment in Psychiatry*. London, Routledge & Kegan Paul.

Tyrer, P. (1979). Clinical use of monoamine oxidase inhibitors. In: *Psychopharmacology of Affective Disorders*, pp. 159–178 Eds: Paykel, E. S., and Coppen, A, Oxford, Oxford University Press.

Tyrer, P. (1982). Monoamine oxidase inhibitors. In: *Drugs in Psychiatric Practice* Eds: Tyrer, P., Mackay, A. V. P., Butterworth (In Press).

W.H.O. Expert Committee on Implementation of the Convention on Psychotropic Substances, 1971 (1981). Assessment of public health and social problems associated with the use of psychotropic drugs *Technical Report Series 656*. Geneva, World Health Organization.

Winokur, G. (1981). *Depression: The Facts*. Oxford, Oxford University Press.

Mental Illness: Changes and Trends
Edited by Philip Bean
© 1983 John Wiley & Sons Ltd.

CHAPTER 11

Contemporary behaviour therapy

DEREK JEHU
Professor, Psychological Services Centre,
University of Manitoba,
Winnipeg, Canada

According to a recent historian of the behavioural movement, it '... represents a revolution in the field of mental health: in less than 20 years, it has brought about a major reconceptualization of psychological problems and their treatment' (Kazdin, 1978, p. ix). Some corroboration of this admittedly committed view is available from several sources. Almost 10 years ago, a task force of the American Psychiatric Association concluded that '... behavior therapy and behavioral principles employed in the analysis of clinical phenomena have reached a stage of development where they now unquestionably have much to offer informed clinicians in the service of modern clinical and social psychiatry' (American Psychiatric Association, 1973, p. 64). A recent directory of graduate study in behaviour therapy in the United States lists 38 psychiatric residencies, 142 programmes in clinical or counselling psychology, and 21 schools of social work (Association for Advancement of Behavior Therapy, 1978). Among the countries in which professional organizations for behaviour therapy exist, are Australia, Brazil, England, France, Germany, Greece, Holland, Ireland, Israel, Japan, Mexico, Scotland, and the United States. It is estimated that there are now around two dozen journals devoted exclusively to behaviour therapy; and an *Annual Review of Behavior Therapy*, a yearly series of volumes entitled *Progress in Behavior Modification*, as well as innumerable books are available in the area.

A cross-sectional overview of such a widespread and rapidly evolving field is a hazardous enterprise, but in this chapter an attempt is made to identify some of the main features and issues in contemporary behaviour therapy; including its major characteristics and conceptual approaches, clinical and research practices, applicability and efficacy, and ethical principles.

Major characteristics

Among the major characteristics of behaviour therapy are the pursuit of a scientific approach, the utilization of a psychological model of abnormal behaviour, and the therapeutic application of knowledge from general psychology and its related disciplines.

Scientific approach

Perhaps the most commonly agreed characteristic is a commitment to empiricism and scientific method. Strong emphasis placed on the operationalization of concepts and the collection of data by valid and reliable techniques. Therapeutic procedures are described with precision so that they can be measured and replicated. Treatment interventions are experimentally evaluated using research designs that are as rigorous as the clinical conditions permit.

This scientific stance does not preclude the derivation or innovation of new therapeutic techniques from sources other than systematic research findings, such as uncontrolled case studies, always providing that these techniques are experimentally investigated and found to be of some therapeutic value before they become an accepted part of the behavioural repertoire. Nor should the emphasis on the scientific nature of behaviour therapy be taken to imply that all other forms of treatment are lacking in systematic investigation, clearly this would not be in accordance with the facts (e.g. see Garfield and Bergin, 1978; Meltzoff and Kornreich, 1970). Nevertheless, the experimental evaluation of therapeutic effectiveness is probably stressed more in behaviour therapy than in any other orientation. This self-corrective mechanism promises cumulative improvement in the help available to patients and perhaps constitutes the greatest hope for the long term viability and efficacy of the approach.

Psychological model of abnormal behaviour

For a variety of reasons (Erwin, 1978; Kazdin, 1978; Mischel, 1977) behaviour therapists generally reject the 'medical', 'disease', and 'intrapsychic' models of abnormal behaviour, in favour of a 'psychological' model. The disease model is accepted as appropriate when organic pathology can be shown to be a sufficient cause of the abnormal behaviour, but in other circumstances this is assumed, at least in part, to be acquired in the same manner as normal behaviour. Where there is no known organic basis abnormal behaviour is considered to be better conceptualized as a problem of living rather than a pathological disease state.

More specifically, abnormal behaviour is defined as a way of responding in certain situations that is unacceptable to the patient or other people. Thus, an agoraphobic housewife who responds with extreme panic in crowded shops may find this personally distressing, or the action of an exhibitionist who responds to a woman by exposing himself may be unacceptable to other people.

These and other forms of abnormal behaviour are assumed to be caused by certain organic factors, previous learning experiences, and contemporary conditions, operating singly or in combination in particular cases. When organic factors are present their adverse effects may arise either directly from some physical impairment or indirectly from the patient's psychological reactions to the organic factor concerned. Through his or her previous experiences a patient may have learned to respond in an abnormal manner, and in this psychological model it is assumed that the processes of such learning are essentially the same as those involved in the acquisition of normal behaviour. Finally, although some form of abnormal behaviour might have originated in an earlier organic condition or learning experience, it is precipitated by certain conditions in the patient's current environment or in his or her thoughts and feelings at the present time, and such contemporary conditions also determine the maintenance of the behaviour on future occasions. Thus, a sexual assault in the past may have led to the irrational belief that intercourse is likely to be a painful or unpleasant experience, consequently the current prospect of sex initiates anxiety and avoidance reactions. Likewise, a child's temper tantrums may be maintained if they are successful in producing parental surrender to his or her demands.

This aetiological approach is sometimes criticized for allegedly ignoring 'the causes' of problems, meaning those pathological internal processes that are assumed to be causal in an intrapsychic model. Exponents of a behavioural approach do deal with what they assume to be causal, that is those contemporary conditions that initiate and maintain the problems. These different assumptions are to be tested against the criterion of their relative usefulness as a basis for effective treatment.

Knowledge base in psychology and related disciplines

A third major characteristic of behaviour therapy is an attempt to apply principles and findings from many areas of psychology and related disciplines to the explanation, assessment, and treatment of psychological problems. These areas and disciplines include learning and cognition, developmental and social psychology, neurophysiology, and the sociology of deviance. Thus, a large body of empirical, systematic, and cumulative knowledge from such sources may be of continuing benefit to the understanding and treatment of psychological difficulties, just as anatomy, physiology, and biochemistry contribute to physical medicine.

Of course, while the contribution of psychology and related disciplines to therapeutic activities may be considerable, it is important to recognize the inevitable incompleteness and inadequacy of this knowledge, as well as the practical problems of converting it into feasible treatment interventions (Erwin, 1978; Kazdin, 1979). Moreover, such interventions can never be based entirely and exclusively upon derived psychological principles. Rather, these constitute a flexible guide to understanding and treatment, leaving much need and scope for the personal spontaneity, experience, judgment, and inventiveness of the individual therapist.

Conceptual approaches

The broad consensus on the major characteristics of behaviour therapy does not imply that it is a monolithic system, in fact it encompasses a variety of conceptual approaches. Among these are applied behavioural analysis, the neobehaviouristic stimulus – response approach, cognitive behaviour therapy, and social learning theory (Agras *et al.*, 1979; Kazdin and Wilson, 1978).

Applied behaviour analysis

This approach is most closely associated with the work of Skinner (1938, 1953) on operant conditioning. The focus is upon the modification of overt behaviour, rather than cognitive processes, and strong emphasis is placed on the importance of environmental factors in determining this behaviour. More particularly, it is regarded as a function of its environmental consequences. Thus, it is primarily these consequences that are manipulated therapeutically in order to modify behaviour in desired directions.

This aim is pursued by means of several operant techniques, including positive reinforcement, shaping, prompting, fading, chaining, extinction, time out, response cost, and stimulus control. Because these techniques require considerable therapeutic control over the patient's natural environment, they have been used most extensively with children, the mentally retarded, and hospitalized psychotic patients.

Neobehaviouristic stimulus – response approach

Leading contemporary exponents of this approach include Eysenck, Rachman, and Wolpe. They have attempted to apply the learning theories of Pavlov, Guthrie, Hull, Mowrer, and Miller, to the explanation and treatment of psychological problems. In particular the role of classical conditioning is stressed (Kazdin, 1978).

In contrast with the focus on overt behaviour in applied behaviour analysis, mediational variables are not eschewed in the neobehaviouristic stimulus – response approach. For instance, anxiety is assumed to underlie neurotic disorders although it is a hypothetical construct that cannot be observed. Thus, the treatment techniques of systematic desensitization and flooding which are most closely associated with this approach are directed towards the reduction of this underlying anxiety. It is, however, important to note that private events like anxiety are operationally defined and anchored in antecedent and consequent events, rather than being formulated in cognitive terms such as an expectation of harm.

Cognitive behaviour therapy

As the name implies this approach does emphasize the importance of cognitive concepts like expectations, perceptions, and interpretations as determinants of behaviour. It follows that the treatment techniques associated with the approach are directed towards the modification of maladaptive cognitions. For instance, the widely used interventive strategy of cognitive restructuring (Beck, 1976; Beck *et al.*, 1979; Ellis, 1970; Grieger and Boyd, 1979; Meichenbaum, 1977) is based on the proposition that many psychological problems are due to the patient's distorted perceptions, incorrect interpretations, or irrational beliefs, concerning himself and his life experiences. Thus, the various cognitive restructuring techniques are deployed to identify and modify these faulty thought patterns by means of rational argument, logical analysis, and assigned behavioural tasks. Other forms of intervention associated with cognitive behaviour therapy include covert conditioning, thought stopping, problem solving, and several self-control procedures (see review by Mahoney and Arnkoff, 1978).

The use of cognitive concepts that cannot be observed is criticized by some writers (e.g. Ledwige, 1978; Wolpe, 1978) as either irrelevant or detrimental to the development of behaviour therapy as an applied science. An opposing view (e.g. Beck and Mahoney, 1979; Franks and Wilson, 1979) is that cognitive processes are perfectly admissible as long as they are carefully defined, their role in treatment is well specified and replicable, and their therapeutic contribution is evaluated experimentally. The appropriate test of their utility is whether the inclusion of cognitive factors leads to novel and more effective interventive strategies with a broader range of psychological problems. It is too early to reach closure on this issue, but the development of the techniques mentioned above suggests that this criterion is likely to be surpassed.

Social learning theory

Bandura's (1977a) social learning theory is the most comprehensive conceptual approach in contemporary behaviour therapy. As we have seen, applied behaviour analysis is focused upon overt behaviour as a function of its environmental consequences, the neobehaviouristic stimulus – response approach is concentrated upon the classical conditioning of emotional reactions through the antecedent pairing of stimuli, while in cognitive behaviour therapy the emphasis is on faulty thought patterns. In social learning theory, the three regulatory systems of antecedent paired experiences, environmental consequences, and cognitive processes are integrated into a comprehensive theoretical framework, and each is regarded as especially influential on certain aspects of behaviour.

Particular importance is attached to cognitive processes. They are held to determine the influence of environmental events on behaviour. For instance, classical conditioning is not viewed as the automatic product of the temporal pairing of two stimuli, instead it requires that the individual recognize that the stimuli are correlated and that the occurrence of one predicts the occurrence of the other. Thus, it is a cognitive expectation that is learned in classical conditioning. Similarly, in operant conditioning, reinforcers are not regarded as automatic strengtheners of the behaviour they follow, but rather as sources of information and incentive, so that the individual learns to anticipate the consequences of his or her behaviour in particular situations and to regulate it accordingly. In general, cognitive processes determine which environmental events are attended to, how they are perceived, what is remembered, and the extent to which they might influence future behaviour.

Another feature of social learning theory is reciprocal determinism (Bandura, 1981). An individual's behaviour is not regarded as being determined by his environment in a unidirectional manner. Additionally, his behaviour influences the environment in which it occurs. Thus, the causal interaction between behaviour and environment is reciprocal, a person is both an agent and an object of environmental influence; an aggressive child creates a hostile environment, which serves to provoke his aggressive responses.

The therapeutic corollary of the social learning approach is self-efficacy theory (Bandura, 1977b). This is an integrative framework in which the alleviation of psychological problems is attributed to an increase in the patient's expectations of personal efficacy, brought about by various treatment techniques. Self-efficacy refers to the patient's belief that he or she has the ability to cope successfully with a threatening situation. This belief is based upon four sources of information; the patient's own behavioural performance in such situations, his or her vicarious experiences of the behaviour of other people in similar situations, his or her degree of physiological arousal, and verbal persuasion. There is evidence that the patient's own performance is the most potent influence on efficacy expectations.

These expectations are held to initiate, generalize, and maintain coping behaviour. Thus, if treatment procedures such as systematic desensitization, flooding, and modelling, can convince a phobic patient that he or she can cope with a threatening situation, then this expectation is likely to be accompanied by reductions in the anxiety and avoidance reactions evoked by that situation. Moreover, the expectation of coping with that situation may generalize to engender greater confidence in relation to other situations. Finally, the strength of the efficacy expectations may determine the maintenance of therapeutic change in the face of later adverse experiences, thus influencing the probability of relapse occurring.

There are criticisms of self-efficacy theory on both conceptual and empirical grounds (Rachman, 1978), but at the very least it is proving of considerable heuristic value, and the initial findings from the growing volume of experimental investigation are largely supportive of the theory.

Clinical practice

Assessment

Until quite recently the topic of assessment was relatively neglected in the behavioural literature despite its vital importance in clinical practice. Now there are several substantial books (e.g. Barlow, 1981; Ciminero *et al.*, 1977; Cone and Hawkins, 1977; Haynes and Wilson, 1979; Hersen and Bellack, 1976; Mash and Terdal, 1981) and two major journals (*Behavior Assessment; Journal of Behavioral Assessment*) devoted exclusively to this area.

In very broad outline, the content of a behavioural assessment includes a comprehensive and detailed specification of those aspects of the patient's functioning that are alleged to be problematic, a thorough exploration of the contemporary conditions that may initiate and maintain these problems, and an appraisal of the available resources that may assist or impede their treatment. This assessment forms the essential basis for the negotiation of therapeutic goals with the patient and the planning of an agreed treatment programme.

The emphasis on contemporary causes follows from the aetiological approach discussed above, and it is these causes that are the focus for behavioural treatment. It is impossible to alter events that have happened in the past, but it is feasible to try to modify any current conditions that are contributing to a patient's problem, and this is the strategy pursued in behaviour therapy. It should be noted that although the information collected in the assessment concerns these current conditions, it is very likely to be derived in part from an historical examination of the patient's previous experiences, for these can provide valuable clues to the factors that are initiating or maintaining the problem at the present time.

A wide range of methods is used to gather information in a behavioural assessment; interviews, paper and pencil instruments, direct observation, client records, and physiological techniques. Each of these has certain strengths and weaknesses in terms of coverage, reliability, and validity. Therefore, in order to achieve a balanced and comprehensive assessment, it is customary to implement a multimodal assessment scheme comprising a suitable combination of methods.

Some indication of the relative use of different methods by practising behaviour therapists is available in two recent surveys of samples drawn from the membership of the Association for the Advancement of Behavior Therapy in the United States. Swan and MacDonald (1978) obtained replies from 353 members, who gave the following estimates of the percentages of clients with whom certain methods were used:

Interview with identified client	89%
Client self-monitoring	51%
Interview with identified client's significant other	49%
Direct observation of target behaviours *in situ*	40%
Information from consulting professionals	37%
Role play	34%
Behavioural written self-report measures	27%
Demographic questionnaires	20%
Personality inventories	20%
Projective tests	10%

Table 1   Assessment procedures

Procedure	Therapists (%)	Clients (%)
Behavioural interviews	76.3	53.8
Behavioural observation	70.4	33.9
Behavioural surveys	49.4	20.3
Traditional interviews	46.3	24.7
Intelligence tests	34.6	8.2
Objective personality tests	31.5	10.2
Projective personality tests	19.8	4.8
Neuropsychological tests	19.8	2.3
Self-observation	3.5	1.8

Note. The first eight categories were supplied in the questionnaire. Self-observation was the only procedure written in an open category with any appreciable frequency. Client percentages are based on the number of therapists using the assessment technique. (Reprinted by permission from: Wade *et al.*, *The Behavior Therapist*, **2**, 3–6, 1979. Association for the Advancement of Behavior Therapy.)

In the second survey (Wade *et al.*, 1979), 257 therapists reported on the assessment methods they used and the percentages of clients assessed with each technique. The results are shown in Table 1, and the note to that table might account for the major discrepancy between the use of client self-monitoring in Swan and MacDonald's sample (51 per cent) and of self-observation among those who responded to Wade *et al.*, (1.8 per cent).

Despite the recent growth in interest and sophistication in behavioural assessment, there is still much to be accomplished. As Franks and Wilson put it '. . . by comparison with traditional psychometrics, behavioral assessment still has a long way to go . . .' Behavior therapists have developed many questionnaires, scales, and inventories, but the factor analytic studies, the item analyses, the various forms of reliability measurement, the normative studies, the large sample cross-validation investigations are still lacking. Standardized batteries with accompanying norms are the exception rather than the rule. It may well be that the general ill-repute of psychological testing in behavioral circles has resulted in the proverbial 'baby being thrown out with the bath water . . .' (1978, p. 167).

Treatment

Essentially behaviour therapy is an educational process in the broadest sense, in that it provides patients with opportunities for new learning experiences. These include certain non-specific factors, such as the therapeutic relationship, some understanding between therapist and patient concerning the causes of the problems, and the patient's expectation of receiving effective help. These factors are termed 'non-specific' in the sense that they operate not only in behaviour herapy, but also in most other forms of treatment. There is no implication that hey are intrinsically unspecifiable; indeed one of the aims of research in behaviour therapy is to describe them with greater precision, so that their contribution to the effectiveness of treatment may be enhanced. Thus, in contrast with earlier years, much more attention is paid to the conceptualization and investigation of the therapeutic relationship and other non-specific factors in contemporary behaviour therapy (De Voge and Beck, 1978; Ford, 1978; Wilson and Evans, 1977).

In addition to these non-specific factors, behaviour therapists utilize a range of procedures that are relatively specific to this approach. From these procedures an individualized treatment programme is constituted for each patient. The two surveys cited above contain some indication of the relative use of different procedures by behaviour therapists in the United States only. The percentages of clients with whom certain techniques were used are reported by Swan and MacDonald (1978) as follows:

Therapeutic relationship enhancement methods	58%
Operant methods	50%
Modelling methods	48%
Self-management methods	45%
Simulation and role play methods	44%
Attitude modification methods	43%
Fear reduction methods	34%
Self-instructional methods	30%
Aversion methods	18%
Expectation, hypnosis, and suggestion methods	16%

The findings of Wade *et al.* (1979) are shown in Table 2. Because of the different listings of procedures used in the two surveys it is difficult to compare the results directly, and in any case they cannot be regarded as more than indicative of recent practice.

Research practice

In view of the strong commitment to a scientific approach in behaviour therapy, it is not surprising that considerable attention is paid to the methodology of clinical research and to the experimental investigation of the efficacy, ingredients, and mechanisms of behavioural interventions (e.g. Kazdin, 1980; Kazdin and Wilson, 1978; Rachman and Wilson, 1980). It is probably true to say that no other form of psychological treatment has ever been subjected to such intensive evaluation, and the methodological advances that have been made are applicable to all testable treatment approaches rather than being restricted to behaviour therapy alone.

Table 2   Treatment procedures

Procedure	Therapists (%)	Clients (%)
Operant conditioning	60.7	31.9
Systematic desensitization	48.6	11.5
Modelling	33.5	11.4
Rational emotive therapy	14.4	6.6
Relaxation training	22.2	6.5
Assertion training	20.2	6.4
Cognitive restructuring	10.5	4.5
Covert conditioning	17.9	4.1
Behavioural rehearsal	9.3	3.8
Behavioural contracts	11.3	3.8
Self-management	7.4	3.7
Role-playing	6.6	2.5
Biofeedback	7.8	2.3

Note. Treatment procedures and percentages of clients were listed in response to an open-ended question. Only the more frequently listed treatments are included. Client percentages are based on the number of therapists using the treatment technique. (Reprinted by permission from: Wade et al.; The Behavior Therapist, 2, 3–6, 1979. Association for the Advancement of Behaviour Therapy.)

Treatment evaluation strategies

One of these advances is the delineation of several strategies for the evaluation of treatment, with guidelines for their use according to the stage of development of the intervention (Kazdin, 1980; Kazdin and Wilson, 1978). Initially, a treatment package strategy is likely to be appropriate, in order to ascertain whether a multi-component programme is effective in alleviating the problem being treated (Azrin, 1977). If so, then it is worthwhile investigating the contributions of specific components by means of the dismantling or constructive strategies. The dismantling strategy requires the experimental elimination or isolation of specific components in order to determine their role in treatment and to cast light on the therapeutic mechanisms producing therapeutic change. In the constructive strategy various components are added to a basic intervention to ascertain whether they enhance its effectiveness, so that a treatment package is established empirically rather than on the more usual ad hoc basis.

The parametric strategy consists of varying the presentation of treatment components, with the aim of maximizing therapeutic change. The variation may be quantitative or qualitative; for instance, the duration or mode of presentation might be investigated. In the comparative strategy the relative efficacy of different treatment packages is evaluated to determine which is the most effective for a particular problem. The influence of client and therapist characteristics on outcome is investigated by means of the client and therapist variation strategy, in which these individuals are either selected on the basis of the attributes being studied or these attributes are experimentally manipulated. Finally, the *internal structure or process strategy* is used to investigate what happens during therapy, rather than its longer term outcome. For instance, such questions as the nature of the interactions between the client and therapist might be addressed.

Early in the development of an intervention, the package, constructive, or parametric strategies are likely to be most appropriate. Once the intervention is demonstrated to be effective with a particular problem, then it can usefully be analysed by means of the dismantling, client–therapist variation, or internal structure strategies, as well as being compared to other interventions for the same problem.

Single case experimental designs

Another important methodological advance, contributed by operant conditioning and applied behaviour analysis, is the single case experimental design (Hersen and Barlow, 1976; Kazdin, 1980). Between group designs employ untreated or differently treated control groups to demonstrate the effects of particular interventions. In contrast, single case designs use each individual as his or her own control, and the effects of particular interventions are ascertained by examining the changes in his or her behaviour that accompany their implementation.

There are several advantages attaching to single case designs in evaluating therapy. The more traditional ways of approaching this task have been by means of anecdotal case studies or group control studies. Because of their uncontrolled nature the former do not demonstrate the efficacy of an intervention, although they may serve other useful purposes. Group control studies may demonstrate the efficacy of an intervention, but in terms of an average change across groups of patients, rather than in individual patients. It is the latter that is of primary interest in clinical practice, and single case designs do permit the controlled study of the effectiveness of treatment with individuals. Group control studies also require a relatively large and homogeneous pool of patients which may not be available, perhaps because of the rarity of the problem concerned, whereas single case designs are feasible in such circumstances. Furthermore, by the systematic implementation, addition, or withdrawal of specified components, these designs can be used to pursue the package, constructive, or dismantling strategies, and the effects of different interventions can be compared within the same individual. This capacity offers a cost-efficient bridge between the uncontrolled introduction of novel therapeutic interventions in clinical practice, and their evaluation in large-scale and resource expensive group studies. Finally, single case designs are not incompatible with group control studies. It is often quite feasible to examine both individual and average changes in the same investigation.

Single case designs are not without their limitations. Because of their focus upon only one or a small number of individuals, they are not the most appropriate means of investigating the influence of patient characteristics on the outcome of treatment. Similarly, the same consideration creates some problems in generalizing the findings from a single case design to a wider population of patients. There are problems also in interpreting the results of these designs. This is usually done by visual inspection of a graph, on the basis that any changes of sufficient clinical significance will be readily apparent. In practice, the data is not always so clearcut, and different judges do not always agree on the occurrence of therapeutic changes. Even when these do appear to be unambiguous by visual inspection, this may not be in accordance with the results of statistical tests of significance. In conclusion, there may be practical or ethical limitations on the implementation of single case designs. For instance, they require a delay of treatment until a baseline is established, and this may conflict with an urgent need for immediate intervention, such as when a problem constitutes a danger to the client or others. The limitations outlined in this paragraph do not negate the advantages of single case designs in the evaluation of therapy. There can be little doubt about their value when used to answer appropriate questions.

Evaluation of therapeutic outcome

This third area of methodological advance in behavioural research practice involves an expansion of the criteria used to evaluate the efficacy of treatment, and the development and application of more specific and varied measures of change (Kazdin, 1980; Kazdin and Wilson, 1978).

The most usual criterion of the effectiveness of an intervention is a *statistically* significant difference between the mean performances on some measure of a treated group compared to an untreated or differently treated control group. Other important patient-related criteria include the *clinical* significance of the therapeutic change, the proportion of patients who improve, and the breadth and durability of the improvements. Another set of criteria relate to the efficiency and costs of an intervention; including its duration, its method of administration, the degree of professional expertise required, the demands it places on patients, and its cost-effectiveness. There are also consumer-related criteria, such as the acceptability of the treatment to patients. Thus, therapy is evaluated against multiple and broad criteria, rather than the single test of mean change on a relatively narrow range of outcome measures.

Typically, these measures have comprised personality tests and global ratings of improvement. The behavioural methods of assessment discussed in a previous section can provide much more specific information. They are also more wide ranging and varied in their applicability. Many psychological problems are multifaceted, involving the patient's actions, cognitions, and affects. Often they are situation-specific, occurring in some circumstances, but not in others. Th various methods and instruments for assessment differ in their scope, validity, and reliability. In view of this variability along several dimensions, a wide range of measures in a multimodal assessment scheme is used to evaluate therapy, although this often entails some lack of correspondence among measures.

A major limitation in current research on behaviour therapy is the lack of attention to the longer term effects of treatment. For instance, Agras and Berkowitz (1980) examined two major journals in the field and found the median length of follow-up to be five weeks in the articles published in 1978. They contrast this with the median of 26 weeks in two major medical journals. Additionally, Flynn *et al.* (1977) found that of 289 studies reported in *Behavior Therapy* up to 1977, 67 per cent had no follow-up whatsoever. Fortunately, this serious deficiency is now being highlighted (Agras and Berkowitz, 1980; Agras *et al.*, 1979; Kazdin and Wilson, 1978; Mash and Terdal, 1979).

Applicability and efficacy

Compared to many other psychotherapeutic approaches behaviour therapy is applied to an exceptionally wide range of psychological problems. As shown in

Table 3   Problems treated

Problem	Therapists (%)
Anxiety	44.7
Child management	36.2
Marital relationships	30.4
Depression	24.9
Sexual dysfunction	12.1
Phobias	12.1
Interpersonal relationship	11.7
Vocational/educational/work	10.5
Psychosomatic/psychophysical	8.6
Family relationships	8.6
Assertion	8.6
Parent training	7.4
Obesity	7.4
Psychosis	7.4
Alcohol abuse	6.2
Retardation/handicaps	6.2

Note. Problems treated were listed in response to an open-ended question. Only the more frequently listed problems are included. the last three problems were treated primarily in inpatient settings, whereas all others were treated primarily in out-patient settings. (Reprinted by permission from: Wade *et al.*, The Behavior Therapist 2, 3–6, 1979. Association for the Advancement of Behavior Therapy.)

Table 3, there is some indication of this in one of the surveys of the United States membership of the Association for Advancement of Behaviour Therapy (Wade *et al.*, 1979).

This broad range of problems is treated by a diversity of behavioural interventions (e.g. see Table 2). Therefore, the question 'how effective is behaviour therapy?', is as meaningless as asking 'how effective is medical treatment?'. Instead, it is necessary to enquire about the effectiveness of specific behavioural interventions with particular problems.

This multiplicity of questions calls for an extensive review of the available evidence that cannot be undertaken within the confines of this chapter (see Kazdin and Wilson, 1978; Rachman and Wilson, 1980). The evidence is certainly uneven. For instance, it strongly supports the effectiveness of systematic desensitization and flooding in the treatment of many phobic disorders, and of the bell and pad method for the treatment of nocturnal enuresis. In contrast, the available evidence on the efficacy of various behavioural interventions with certain other problems, such as depression and antisocial behaviour, is much less extensive and conclusive. For example, the lack of adequate follow-up data on the longer-term effects of treatment is noted in the previous section. It is clear that there are limits to the usefulness and effectiveness of behavioural interventions. Like other forms of psychological treatment, they are of little value with problems such as florid schizophrenia or bipolar depression, which are much more likely to respond to appropriate drug regimes.

Professional ethics

Therapists of all persuasions are confronted by ethical issues arising from the selection of goals and interventions, the consent of a patient to a proposed programme, and the accountability of the therapist for its progress and outcome. Some principles for handling such issues are an important feature of contemporary behaviour therapy (Association for Advancement of Behavior Therapy, 1977; Martin 1975; Stolz *et al.*, 1978; Stuart, 1981).

The goals of treatment are chosen largely by the patient in accordance with his or her own wishes and values, although in consultation with the therapist. The major contribution of behavioural treatment *per se* is to provide effective ways of achieving these goals only after they have been selected by the patient on personal, social or ethical grounds. The role of the therapist in this task is to help the patient to explore alternatives and their consequences before deciding on the goals to be pursued. Inevitably, the therapist's own opinions and values will influence this process, and it is incumbent upon him or her to disclose these views to the patient so that he or she can take them into account when deciding between goals. Sometimes they will lead the patient to wish to seek treatment elsewhere, in which case the therapist will assist in making a suitable referral.

The therapist plays a larger part in the selection of intervention procedures, although certainly not to the exclusion of the patient. Among the factors considered by the therapist (Jehu, 1979) are the suitability of the procedures for the therapeutic task concerned, their feasibility in terms of available therapeutic resources, their probable efficacy in achieving the goals of treatment, and their efficiency in utilizing resources. They also have to be personally and ethically acceptable to both therapist and patient. One important factor influencing the acceptability of a procedure is its relative intrusiveness compared to possible alternatives (Wexler, 1973). By intrusiveness is meant the degree of external control involved in the procedure, especially if this control is of an aversive nature. Thus, a patient administered covert sensitization procedure would be less intrusive than therapist administered chemical aversion therapy. Similarly, the social reinforcement of desired behaviour by praise and approval is preferred to the suppression of undesired behaviour by punishment procedures such as time out or response cost. Generally speaking, more intrusive methods should be used only when less intrusive methods have failed, although the former should not be withheld when they are clearly necessary to achieve the therapeutic goals and the patient has given his or her informed consent to their use.

Such informed consent is an essential precondition for any treatment programme, and it is a key factor in the protection of patients' rights. It is usually held to require knowledge, voluntariness, and competency (Friedman, 1975). Patients have the right to adequate knowledge about what is involved in a proposed programme; including its goals and the procedures to be used, as well as its potential risks and benefits. Alternative programmes should be discussed and their relative merits and demerits fairly evaluated. It should be made clear to patients that they are free to refuse consent or to revoke it at any time. This consent should be given voluntarily and in the absence of any coercion or duress. It also requires competency, in that the patient can understand the information given and is able to make a reasoned judgment. Obviously, this implies that it will not be possible to obtain a valid informed consent from some psychiatric patients. In such circumstances, an equivalent consent should be sought from the patient's relatives or other authorized persons.

Finally, the therapist is accountable for the satisfactory progress of treatment. This requires that its effects are systematically monitored and evaluated, so that appropriate changes can be made in the programme when necessary. The data collected should certainly be made available to patient, and perhaps also to certain other persons or agencies, such as the patient's relatives or the institution employing the therapist.

Summary

Evidence from several sources attests to the growth and pervasiveness of behaviour therapy in the mental health field during the past 20 years. Among its major characteristics are a commitment to empiricism and scientific method, the adoption of a psychological model of abnormal behaviour, and the application of knowledge from general psychology and its related disciplines to the understanding and treatment of psychological problems. A variety of conceptual approaches is encompassed, including applied behaviour analysis, the neobehaviouristic stimulus–response approach, cognitive behaviour therapy, and social learning theory.

In behavioural assessment there is an emphasis on the contemporary causes of problems, although historical information is not neglected. Multimodal assessment schemes are drawn from a wide range of methods. Similarly, individualized treatment programmes are constituted from a broad range of interventions. These include non-specific components, such as a therapeutic relationship, as well as more specifically behavioural procedures.

Research practice in behaviour therapy has yielded significant methodological advances, including the delineation of treatment evaluation strategies, single case experimental designs, and extensions of the criteria and measures used to evaluate progress and outcome.

An unusually wide range of problems are treated by behaviour therapy, although the evidence currently available on the effectiveness of specific interventions with particular problems is uneven in its quality and notably deficient in longer term follow-up data.

The professional ethics of behaviour therapists require that the goals of treatment be selected largely by the patients, that any proposed programmes are acceptable to them, that their informed consents are obtained prior to treatment, and that the therapist be accountable for its satisfactory progress and outcome.

References

Agras, W. S., and Berkowitz, R. (1980). Clinical research in behavior therapy: halfway there? *Behavior Therapy*, **11**, 472–287.

Agras, W. S., Kazdin, A. E., and Wilson, G. T. (1979). *Behavior Therapy: Toward and Applied Clinical Science*, W. H. Freeman and Company, San Francisco.

American Psychiatric Association (1973). *Behavior Therapy in Psychiatry: A Report on the APA Task Force on Behavior Therapy*, American Psychiatric Association, Washington.

Association for Advancement of Behavior Therapy (1977). Ethical issues for human service. *Behavior Therapy*, **8**, 763–764.

Association for Advancement of Behavior Therapy (1978). *Directory of Graduate Study in Behavior Therapy*, Association for Advancement of Behavior Therapy, New York.

Azrin, N. H. (1977). A strategy for applied research: learning based but outcome oriented. *American Psychologist*, **32**, 140–149.

Bandura, A. (1977a). *Social Learning Theory*, Prentice-Hall, Englewood Cliffs, N.J.

Bandura, A. (1977b). Self-efficacy: toward a unifying theory of behavioral change. *Psychological Review*, **84**, 191–215.

Bandura, A. (1981). In search of pure unidirectional determinants. *Behavior Therapy*, **12**, 30–40.

Barlow, D. H. (Ed.). (1981). *Behavioral Assessment of Adult Disorders*, Guilford Press, New York.

Beck, A. T. (1976). *Cognitive Therapy and the Emotional Disorders*, International Universities Press, New York.

Beck, A. T., and Mahoney, M. J. (1979). Schools of "thought". *American Psychologist*, **34**, 93–98.

Beck, A. T., Rush, A. J., Shaw, B. F., and Emery, G. (1979). *Cognitive Therapy of Depression*, Guilford Press, New York.

Behavioral Assessment, Pergamon, New York.

Ciminero, A. R., Calhoun, K. S., and Adams, H. E. (1977). *Handbook of Behavioral Assessment*, Wiley, New York.

Cone, J. D., and Hawkins, R. P. (1977). *Behavioral Assessment: New Directions in Clinical Psychology*, Brunner/Mazel, New York.

De Voge, J. T., and Beck, S. (1978). The therapist – client relationship in behavior therapy. In M. Hersen, R. M. Eisler, and P. M. Miller (Eds.) *Progress in Behavior Modification*, Vol. 6, Academic Press, New York.

Ellis, A. (1970). *The Essence of Rational Psychotherapy: A Comprehensive Approach to Treatment*, Institute for Rational Living, New York.

Erwin, E. (1978). *Behavior Therapy: Scientific, Philosophical and Moral Foundations*, Cambridge University Press, Cambridge.

Flynn, J. M., Wood, R., Michelson, L., and Keen, J. (1977). *Publication trends in behavior therapy, 1970–1977*. Presented at the Annual Meeting of the Association for Advancement of Behavior Therapy, Atlanta, December, 1977.

Ford, J. D. (1978). Therapeutic relationship in behavior therapy: An empirical analysis. *Journal of Consulting and Clinical Psychology, 46*, 1302–1314.

Franks, C. M., and Wilson, G. T. (1978). Recent developments in behavioral assessment: commentary. In C. M. Franks, and G. T. Wilson (Eds.). *Review of Behavior Therapy*. Vol. 6., Brunner/Mazel, New York.

Franks, C, M., and Wilson, G. T., (1979). Cognitive process and procedures in behavior therapy: commentary. In C. M. Franks, and G. T. Wilson (Eds.). *Annual Review of Behavior Therapy*. Vol. 7, Brunner/Mazel, New York.

Friedman, P. R. (1975). Legal regulation of applied behavior analysis in mental institutions and prisons. *Arizona Law Review*, **17**, 39–104.

Garfield, S. L., and Bergin, A. E. (Eds.) (1978). *Handbook of Psychotherapy and Behavior Change: An Empirical Analysis* (2nd ed.), Wiley, New York.

Grieger, R., and Boyd, J. (Eds.) (1979). *Clinical Applications of Rational – Emotive Therapy*, Van Nostrand Reinhold, New York.

Haynes, S. N., and Wilson, C. C. (1979). *Behavioral Assessment*, Jossey-Bass, San Francisco.

Hersen, M., and Barlow, D. H. (1976). *Single Case Experimental Designs: Strategies for Studying Behavior Change*, Pergamon, New York.

Hersen, M., and Bellack, A. S. (1976). *Behavioral Assessment: A Practical Handbook*, Pergamon, Oxford.

Jehu, D. (1979). *Sexual Dysfunction: A Behavioural Approach to Causation, Assessment and Treatment*, Wiley, Chichester.

Journal of Behavioral Assessment, Plenum, New York.

Kazdin, A. E. (1978). *History of Behavior Modification: Experimental Foundations of Contemporary Research*, University Park Press, Baltimore.

Kazdin, A. E. (1979). Fictions, Factions, and functions of behavior therapy. *Behavior Therapy*, **10**, 629–654.

Kazdin, A. E. (1980). *Research Design in Clinical Psychology*, Harper and Row, New York.

Kazdin, A. E., and Wilson, G. T. (1978). *Evaluation of Behavior Therapy: Issues, Evidence, and Research Strategies*, Ballinger, Cambridge.

Ledwige, B. (1978). Cognitive behavior modification: a step in the wrong direction? *Psychological Bulletin*, **85**, 353–375.

Mahoney, M. J., and Arnkoff, D. (1978). Cognitive and self-control therapies. In S. L. Garfield, and A. E. Bergin (Eds.). *Handbook of Psychotherapy and Behavior Change* (2nd ed.), Wiley, New York.

Martin, R. (1975). *Legal Challenges to Behavior Modification*. Research Press, Champaign, Illinois.

Mash, E. J., and Terdal, L. G. (1979). Follow up assessments in behavior therapy. In P. Karoly, and J. Steffen (Eds.). *Towards a Psychology of Therapeutic Maintenance*, Gardner Press, New York.

Mash, E., and Terdal, L. (1981). *Behavioral Assessment of Childhood Disorders*, Guilford Press, New York.

Meichenbaum, D. (1977). *Cognitive Behavior Modification*, Plenum, New York.

Meltzoff, J., and Kornreich, M. (1970). *Research in Psychotherapy*, Atherton, New York.

Mischel, T. (1977). The concept of mental health and disease: an analysis of the controversy between behavioral and psychodynamic approaches. *The Journal of Medicine and Philosophy*, **2**, 197–219.

Rachman, J. (Ed.) (1978). Perceived self-efficacy: analyses of Bandura's theory of behavioral change. *Advances in Behavior Research and Therapy*, **1**, 137–269.

Rachman, S. J., and Wilson, G. T. (1980). *The Effects of Psychotherapy* (2nd ed.), Pergamon, Oxford.

Skinner, B. F. (1938). *The Behavior of Organisms: An Experimental Analysis*, Appleton-Century, New York.

Skinner, B. F. (1953). *Science and Human Behavior*, Macmillan, New York.

Stolz, S. B., and Associates, (1978). *Ethical Issues in Behavior Modification*. Jossey-Bass, San Francisco.

Stuart, R. B. (1981). Ethical guidelines for behavior therapy. In S. M. Turner, K. S. Calhoun; and H. E. Adams (Eds.). *Handbook of Clinical Behavior Therapy*, Wiley, New York.

Swan, G. E., and MacDonald, M. L. (1978). Behavior therapy in practice: a national survey of behavior therapists. *Behavior Therapy*, **9**, 799–807.

Wade, T. C., Baker, T. B., and Hartmann, D. P. (1979). Behavior therapists' self-reported views and practices. *The Behavior Therapist*, **2**, 3–6.

Wexler, D. (1973). Token and taboo: behavior modification, token economies, and the law. *California Law Review*, **61**, 81–109.

Wilson, G. T., and Evans, I. M. (1977). The therapist–client relationship in behavior therapy. In A. S. Gurman, and A. M. Razin (Eds.) *Effective Psychotherapy: A Handbook of Research*, Pergamon, Oxford.

Wolpe, J. (1978). Cognition and causation in human behavior and its therapy. *American Psychologist*, **33**, 437–446.

Mental Illness: Changes and Trends
Edited by Philip Bean
© 1983 John Wiley & Sons Ltd.

CHAPTER 12

Psychological treatment of psychopathology

MARTIN HERBERT
Reader in Clinical Psychology, University of Leicester

Introduction

The generic term 'psychopathology' refers, for the purposes of this chapter, to mental illness, the neuroses and psychoses of adulthood, and the emotional and conduct disorders of childhood and adolescence. The main focus of the discussion will be on the psychological treatments described (more often than not synonymously) as behaviour therapy, behaviour modification, or behavioural psychotherapy.* The crucial issues concern the value of this form of intervention, the scientific and theoretical status of behaviour therapy, and the ethical implications of its use with a vulnerable population.

Edward Erwin (1978), in an unsurpassed analysis of the scientific, philosophical and moral foundations of behaviour therapy, teases out the essentials of this form of treatment:

Behaviour therapy is a nonbiological form of therapy that developed largely out of learning theory research and that is normally applied directly, incrementally, and experimentally in the treatment of specific maladaptive behaviour patterns (p. 44).

The scientific status of behaviour therapy

Albino (1980) states that traditional psychotherapy is not a natural science, even though the value of its methods may often have been empirically evaluated. But it is the proud claim of many behaviour therapists that *behavioural* psychotherapy enjoys a scientific status which stands in sharp contrast to alternative psychological therapies, such as psychoanalysis. This *is* a critical issue, since explanations dealing with complex aspects of human functioning have tended, in the past, to be intuitive, literary or semantic, rather than scientific (see Farrell, 1970; Rycroft, 1970).

For the first time in history, it is claimed (see Beech, 1981; Kazdin, 1978) viable, testable and *successful* theories of human behaviour (adaptive and

*See also Chapter 11.

maladaptive) have been developed and applied to a large number and wide variety of psychopathological phenomena. If this can be demonstrated, it represents a dramatic breakthrough. It is platitudinous to assert that progress in the treatment of psychiatric disorders up to the 1950s was painfully slow and minimal; nevertheless not only is it a truism, but regrettably it makes the evaluation of recent therapeutic developments (methodologically difficult at the best of times) almost impossible to put in an objective and plausible perspective. For example, there is a temptation—to which the present author succumbs—to represent the advances of the last two decades in the application of psychotropic drugs to the psychoses (most notably) and behavioural/social learning principles to the neuroses (most particularly), as a quantum leap forward. However, it is only too easy to misinterpret modest gains in the alleviation of mental suffering and behaviour disturbance as highly significant, because they appear so when contrasted with a distinctly low base-rate (historically speaking) of success.

What is less in doubt (at least in the minds of those who have been around long enough to see the changes) is the transformation of attitudes within psychiatry from therapeutic nihilism—a pervasively static, custodial ethos—to a sense of optimism and forward movement. Certainly the research emphasis has shifted from a predominant concern with description and classification, to one which encompasses aetiological and therapeutic endeavours. There is much more of a feeling abroad today, that we have at least the beginnings of a pharmacological and psychological technology, such as to make a meaningful and reasonably 'normal' life in the community, a real posssibility for countless persons previously condemned to prolonged disability by their psychopathology.

Behavioural concepts of abnormal behaviour

Behaviour therapy is based upon a model in which abnormal behaviours are viewed not as 'behavioural neoplasms'—the outward and visible symptoms of some underlying quasi-disease process—but as the manner in which the client has learned to cope with the challenge and stress of living in a changing, complex and increasingly more impersonal social environment. O'Leary and Wilson (1975) state that since abnormal behaviour is learned and maintained in the same way as normal behaviour, as opposed to being a manifestation of inferred intrapsychic conflicts, it can be treated directly through the application of social learning principles rather than indirectly by 'working through' these underlying problems.

To be more explicit, in the learning theory canon, much (by no means all) of a person's 'normal' (i.e. prosocial, adaptive, functional) behavioural repertoire is acquired, maintained and regulated by its effects upon the natural environment, and the feedback it receives with regard to these consequences. This notion is extended to accommodate the 'abnormal' (i.e. antisocial, maladaptive, dysfunctional) behaviours, thoughts, and feelings which are subsumed under the rubric psychopathology; and so defined because they have unfavourable, disabling consequences in the short and longer term for the person himself/or those with whom he interacts.

The 'laws' of learning which are most appealed to as foundational in the narrower version of this model, are the law of classical conditioning and the law of effect. The scientific respectability of behaviour therapy rests heavily on the scientific status of behaviourism and learning theory, from which it is said to derive in such large part (e.g. Wolpe, 1976). The trouble here is that the evidence does not convince everyone (see Breger and McGaugh, 1965; Chomsky, 1971; Erwin, 1978). This is not the place to review the arguments, but the sceptics state that behavioural theories and laws are either unproven, tautologous, or too narrow in scope to accommodate the complex problems they are called upon to explain. Erwin (*op. cit.*) raises another issue when he poses the following embarrassing question:

Is it being claimed that there is some theory or principle of learning from which someone derived one or more statements describing a behaviour therapy technique? Who did this? Where in the entire behaviour therapy literature does anyone show how even *one* such statement can be derived?

Erwin is of the opinion that learning principles serve a heuristic rather than a logical function in generating therapeutic methods. And he acknowledges that this position is accepted by many practitioners and theoreticians. Kazdin (1978) observes, in his history of behaviour therapy, that the discipline has grown and diversified out of all recognition since its formal beginnings in the late 1950s and early 1960s. It is no longer the monolithic entity it once was, and certainly is not tied by an 'all-sustaining' behaviouristic umbilical cord. Nowadays, for example, it is difficult to find behaviour therapists who are fundamentalist or radical behaviourists. Most are cognitivists in some sense although their embrace of the cognitive realm ranges from the austerely constrained to the unashamedly wholehearted. Nevertheless, the controversy about the issue continues unabated (e.g. Ullmann, 1981; Grossberg, 1981). Indeed, as Kazdin (*op. cit.*) acknowledges, behaviour therapy has become so variegated in its conceptualizations of behaviour, research methods, and techniques, that no unifying schema or set of assumptions can incorporate all extant techniques. He states that although behaviour therapy emphasizes the principles of classical and operant condition- ing it is not restricted to them; it draws upon principles from other branches of experimental psychology such as social and developmental psychology. The importance of 'private events' or the cognitive mediation of behaviour is recognized; and a major role is attributed to vicarious and symbolic learning processes, for example modelling.

But what does it matter if the critics are correct in saying that behaviour therapy has no adequate unifying theory? Why not simply consider behavioural treatment as a technology? After all, the techniques can be utilized and researched *without* commitment to any distinctive foundational theory.

Erwin (*op. cit.*) is of the opinion that we cannot afford to ignore the study of the theoretical foundations. He addresses the issue as follows:

An adequate theory might also provide some important practical benefits. First, if better clinical techniques are to be developed, it will be helpful to know exactly which features of our successful techniques are therapeutically productive and why. The researcher consequently, needs some guidance concerning which are worth studying. Empirical data and sheer hunches will play some role here, but adequate theoretical principles might tell us that certain techniques have a greater antecedent likelihood of success than do others. Third, some behavior therapists are interested in explaining the origin and, more importantly, the maintenance of maladaptive behavior patterns. If we better understood the causes of alcoholism, sexual impotence, schizophrenia, and so forth, we might be able to treat these problems more effectively. The development of an adequate theoretical foundation might enhance our understanding of these matters. (p. xiii).

As it happens there are powerful arguments and evidence which make it inappropriate to view behaviour therapy simply as a technology. Its claim to scientific status arises from the fact that:

1. behaviour therapy practice and research is guided in part by specific experimental findings; the conceptualizing of assessment and the methodology of behaviour therapy are rigorous and sophisticated, building (as they do) on statistical-experimental foundations,
2. the empirical evidence that has been gathered in support of specific therapeutic claims is impressive; when behaviour therapists confirm the efficacy of particular techniques they may be confirming causal hypotheses and thereby offering explanations of behavioural change,
3. there are many behaviour therapists who add to their derivations from the learning theory literature by developing their own explanatory theories and testing them.

Behavioural assessment

Each of these points will be considered in the light of current practice with adult neuroses and childhood problems. A complete review of the evidence is impossible to encompass in one chapter; however, references are provided to the critical literature.

Behaviour therapists insist on carefully monitored (critics might say overly pedantic) pretreatment assessments—often along the lines of the conceptual framework provided in Figure 1, or some variation of it. They believe that the client is best described and understood by determining what he thinks, feels and does in particular life situations. The goal is eventually to help the client to

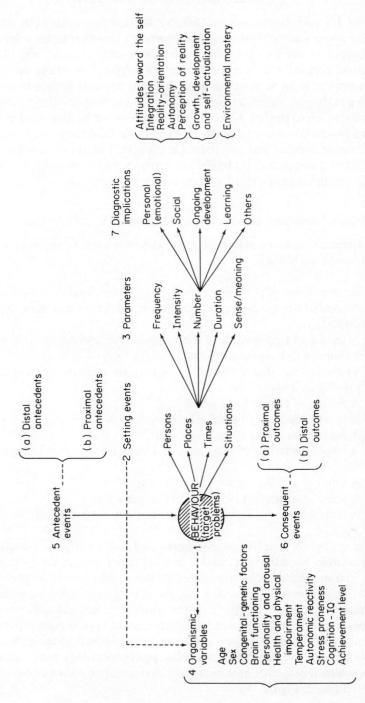

Figure 1   Reproduced with permission from M. Herbert: *Behavioural Treatment of Problem Children: A Practice Manual*, 1981. Copyright: Academic Press Inc. (London) Ltd

control his own behaviour and achieve self-selected goals. The assessment outline above can be illustrated with respect to the neurotic disorders.

Neurosis is not an easy term to specify in any definitive way. There are countless persons who survive the stresses of life, but whose survival is so restricted and in some cases marginal that they can only be said to be existing. Feeling as they do—alienated, unloved, unreal, and aimless—they cannot be said to be living life to the full. Some of these people would be diagnosed as suffering from a psychoneurosis (or neurosis). Neurosis is a shorthand term for something as pervasive as emotional disturbance or life problems; it can be applied to a set of attitudes; and it can also be defined narrowly and technically. Whatever the definition, the neurotic client is invariably a suffering person.

Behaviour: identifying target problems (1, Figure 1)

A behavioural assessment of neurotic disorders is likely to encompass a broad spectrum of problems:

(1) An avoidance of situations/people/objects one should not have to avoid;
(2) A sense of emotional turmoil (anger, fear, anxiety, dread, guilt, depression, disgust);
(3) A feeling of helplessness, of not being fully in control of one's life;
(4) feelings of unhappiness, distress, misery;
(5) Vague feelings that life is not being lived as meaningfully, effectively, or joyfully as it should be;
(6) A feeling of having lost control;
(7) A loss of the ability to make decisions;
(8) A loss of the ability to make choices;
(9) A loss of the feeling of being real, vital, committed to or enthusiastic about life;
(10) A sense of conflict, apathy, aimlessness;
(11) A sense of alienation (with self and/or society);
(12) A sense of being compelled to do things against one's will.

It is crucial in behavioural assessment and treatment to reformulate these complaints in operational terms, i.e. in overt terms of what the client says and does, and in a manner that lends itself to the quantifying of the problem.

For the purposes of this review it is useful to group symptoms according to traditional diagnostic labels. However, there is a general consensus in behavioural work that these classificatory labels are of limited value in formulating the nature of specific problems and planning treatment programmes. A very simple but effective way to conceptualize psychopathology behaviourally is to approach each case with the notion that behavioural excesses and deficits will be involved (see 3, Figure 1).

Behavioural excesses refer to behaviours which the client, with the help of the therapist, wishes to reduce or eliminate; in the case of deficit behaviours there is a need to increase them. Behavioural anomalies constitute a third target for modification. Neurotic anxiety, thus, constitutes (along with the obsessional thoughts and compulsive rituals such as incessant hand-washing it underpins) an *excess* problem. Extreme shyness; where it represents neurotic inhibition would be an example of a *deficit* problem. An instance of *anomalous* behaviour is the uncontrollable utterance of obscene words—a problem associated with Gilles de la Tourette's syndrome.

Situation specificity (2, Figure 1)

The situation specificity of normal behaviours has been well documented (Mischel, 1968). Maladaptive behaviours are no exception. The problems of a client suffering from phobic fears are not unidimensional (Lang, 1968; Rachman, 1978); each of the facets is complex, and they do not inter-correlate in any simple way. With regard to the particular components of an anxiety disorder, they are likely to consist of verbal reports of distress, cognitive, autonomic, and motor phenomena which display a degree of specificity with regard to persons, places, times and situations/circumstances, and indeed, with regard to each other. The specificity of, say, a phobic disorder must be carefully assessed in order to plan an effective programme of treatment. For example, Hodgson and Rachman (1974) consider what might occur if one or more of the three loosely coupled systems—subjective, physiological and behavioural—were discordant at any particular time, and more important from the therapeutic point of view, what might be expected if one of the systems was changing more rapidly or more slowly than the others (desynchrony). Evaluations of this kind, after a full analysis of a particular emotional disorder, might indicate which of the three systems is functioning most abnormally. In some circumstances, speedier therapeutic progress might be made if the therapy chosen for a particular client is based on this analysis. Thus, if the major component of the problem is behavioural then the treatment might focus on modifying the behaviour directly. Alternatively, if the predominant feature of the client's difficulties is the intensity of his physiological reaction then a direct concentration on the physiological overreaction might be indicated (see Rachman, 1978). Cognitive treatment would be given for problems with a prominent cognitive component (Bandura, 1978). The effectiveness of the matching of problem components and treatment modality has yet to be proven but it looks a promising research area (see Rachman, 1981; Zajonc, 1980).

Parameters (3. Figure 1)

What separates behaviours defined as 'neurotic' from the anxiety, avoidances, fears, indecisiveness and obsessions shown by all persons at one time or another, is the frequency (rate), intensity and persistence (duration) with which they are manifested, and the sheer number of problems with which they are associated.

These parameters are matters for careful individual assessment with any person with a suspected neurotic disorder. They are important not only for the understanding of the nature and ramifications of the problems, but for the highlighting of the ethical issues inherent in deciding whether to use a powerful change-orientated approach like behaviour therapy. The meaning of the problems for the client—the sense made of them, the 'pay-off' they provide—and, indeed, his family, also constitutes a vital element of the overall assessment.

The trouble with the terms 'psychiatric disorder' and 'psychoneurosis' is that it is not possible to draw clearcut lines of demarcation between those who fall into these categories and those who do not. We are referring, in most cases, to behavioural continua. A basic assumption of this chapter is that psychiatric disorders, by and large, are exaggerations, deficits or handicapping combinations of behaviours common to all persons. Here of course, lies the major 'booby trap' (tackled later) ticking away in that assumption, and the question it begs: 'Why and when and how do you intervene in someone's life (someone called a client)?'

Identifying controlling variables (4/5/6. Figure 1)

In identifying controlling variables two categories of controlling variables are generally considered: current environmental variables (antecedent and consequent events—5/6. Figure 1) and organismic variables (4. Figure 1) (see Herbert, 1981). The behavioural assessment is based on the concept of a functional relationship with the environment in which changes in individual behaviour produce changes in the environment and vice versa. The contemporary causes of problem behaviour may exist in the client's environment or in his own thoughts, feelings or bodily processes (organismic variables) and they may exert their influence in several ways: as eliciting or discriminative antecedent stimuli or as outcomes (consequences) of a reinforcing kind. The development of inappropriate strategies (or the failure to acquire appropriate strategies) for coping with life tasks, might be due to faulty training and or modelling or other environmental deficiencies. They might be a consequence of neurological defects or other inherited or acquired inpairments. Excellent accounts of the experimental derivations of these ideas are to be found in Bandura (1969) and Rimm and Masters (1979).

Organismic variables include individual differences produced by age, sex, genetic constitution, physiology, and by past learning. Behaviour therapists find it useful to distinguish the historical (distal antecedents) and the contemporary causes (proximal antecedents) of problem behaviour. Most people working in the behaviour therapy field adopt an interactional position—the view that behaviour results from an interaction between the current situation and individual differences (biological and psycho-social).

Proximal antecedents (5(b) Figure 1) *Contemporary influences*

A distinction is made between the direct and vicarious learning experiences that contribute to the acquisition of problematic behaviour and those contemporary influences which determine whether the client will perform the behaviour he has acquired. For example, in the conduct disorders—which are discussed later—some violent action which has been acquired by imitation or modelling, may not be performed, either because appropriate instigating conditions do not occur, or because the consequences of violence are likely to be unrewarding or unpleasant. Perhaps the most obvious instigating conditions for violent acts are various forms of aversive experience. In addition to aversive experiences, various incentives may also act as instigators of aggressive behaviour. Here, the instigation is the pull of expected reward rather than the push of aversive experience. Thus, violent and alternative responses are selected for performance on the bases of their anticipated consequences (see Herbert, 1978).

Proximal consequences (6(a) Figure 1)

Turning to the maintenance of problematic behaviour, this is postulated to be largely dependent on its consequences. Maladaptive actions that are rewarded tend to be repeated, whereas those that are unrewarded or punished are generally discarded. The reinforcement which strengthens an adolescent's disruptive behaviour—to take an increasingly typical example from the contemporary classroom—may be in terms of direct external reinforcement, vicarious or observed reinforcement or self-reinforcement.

Distal consequences and diagnostic implications (6(b)/7. Figure 1)

While it is true to say that clinicians delineate certain 'symptoms' as pathogno-monic of particular psychiatric disorders (see Hill *et al.*, 1979), the fact is that in our chosen area of neurosis and disorders of children, we are dealing with social rather than medical criteria of what is problematic. It is important to look not only at the immediate consequences of a client's behaviour, but also at the longer term implications (distal outcomes). What are the likely consequences of non-intervention in the problem for the person and his family? There are essentially two issues to be resolved at this stage of a behavioural assessment:

(a) Diagnostic: Is it a problem of sufficient seriousness to merit an intervention?
(b) Ethical: Is it ethically right to intervene so as to produce changes in the direction of goals X, Y, or Z?

One of the simplest ways to uncover a therapist's implicit or latent definition of mental health is to ask him how he decides that treatment is actually required. Problem behaviours are usually so-called, because they have a variety of unfavourable short-term and long-term outcomes. They are therefore referred to as maladaptive actions or dysfunctional thoughts and feelings; they are inappropriate in terms of several criteria which are assessed by the therapist. The diagnostic criteria are listed as distal outcomes (6(b) in Figure 1) and diagnostic implications (7 in Figure 1) with regard to (a) social, (b) personal, (c) developmental, and (d) work and learning implications. Ultimately, the professional judgment of a client's behavioural/psycho-social/mental status is made in individual terms, taking into account his particular circumstances. It involves an estimate of the consequences that flow from the client's specific thoughts, feelings and behaviours and general life-style, with particular reference to his personal and emotional well-being, his social relationships, his ongoing development and self-actualization, his ability to work effectively (and in the case of children) to learn academically, and his accessibility to socialization. All are subject to disruption in neurotic disorders, and are gravely affected in the conduct disorders of childhood and adolescence. Other factors to be considered are his self-esteem and competence.

There is no general agreement about the defining attributes of psychopathology or, on the opposite side of the coin, positive mental health. Jahoda (1958) provides an interesting discussion of these important issues. The criteria she lists as significant are included (see right-hand column in 7, Figure 1).

Evaluation

Behaviour therapy is characterized by the rigorous assessment and experimental evaluation of treatment—a tradition nurtured in experimental psychology. A variety of experimental research methods are used: between-group research designs and intra-subject-replication designs, the latter originating in operant conditioning research. Kazdin and Wilson (1978) provide a review of the issues and of research strategies. Most of the single subject ($N = 1$) designs involve a pretreatment period of measurement (base-line) of target problems (dependent variables), followed by the intervention or some systematic variation of the treatment (the independent variable). These variations include reversal designs, multiple base-line designs, changing criterion designs and multi-element base-line designs (Herbert, 1981).

Behavioural treatment

This section is organized by method and problem, a particular disorder being described in order to illustrate the application and success of a specific behavioural technique.

Treatment of phobic anxiety by systematic desensitization

Unadaptive (phobic) anxiety is formulated by behaviour therapists as a learned reaction, which is elicited in situations in which it is not objectively called for, in that no real danger exists. The dangers are often in the mind of the client, in the form of anticipated consequences of a dreadful kind, or other negative evaluations of the situation.

The assessment involves an investigation of the circumstances in which anxiety is *currently* experienced as well as conditions which may exacerbate or reduce it. Lang (1968) speaks of a process of discrimination training (by no means easy) for the client, such that he or she isolates the crucial events or other sources related to the experience of anxiety. External or internal events may elicit anxiety.

The procedure called systematic desensitization involves the presentation of the anxiety-provoking stimulus while preventing the anxiety response from occurring. This is achieved by training the client to engage in an activity that is incompatible with the anxiety reaction. The stimulus may be *imaginal* (conjured up by the client's fantasy in imagination) or presented *in vivo* (the client being exposed to the real life stimulus). Essentially the method involves the inhibition of anxiety aroused by minimally provocative stimuli (the lowest items of a hierarchy of anxiety-provoking stimuli) and the gradual and systematic progress—step by step—to more intensely disturbing (but now manageable) stimuli.

The model of systematic desensitization which stresses the role of respondent conditioning in the establishment of and maintenance of anxiety reactions (5b. Figure 1) has had its effects attributed to the principle of reciprocal inhibition, i.e. the application of an antagonistic response to anxiety, such as relaxation, in such a way that it weakens the bond between the phobic stimulus and the anxiety reaction.

Since the introduction of systematic desensitization for the treatment of phobies (and other affect-laden conditions) by Wolpe (1958), it has surely become one of the most painstakingly researched and 'dissected' procedures in behaviour therapy (see Mathews, 1978). It is a fine exemplar of the point made earlier, that by means of their preoccupation with the evaluation of outcomes and the unravelling of the active, necessary and sufficient ingredients in a therapeutic 'package', behaviour therapists are conducting a vital scientific exercise.

There can be little doubt that as a package, systematic desensitization works, both in the short and longer term (see *inter alia*, Gelder *et al.*, 1973; Paul, 1966, 1969; Rachman and Wilson, 1980) producing success rates of between 70 and 90 per cent, which represent substantially better than spontaneous remission rates.*

*The success of desensitization goes beyond fears and phobias related to social situations, death, injury, illness, animals, and sexual encounters. It has been successful in reducing existential anxiety, auditory hallucinations, anorexia nervosa, epileptic seizures, stuttering, depressions, and asthma attacks.

There *can* be a lot of doubt that we know how it works, despite the many explanations offered. This is scarcely surprising given the highly complex nature of clinical phobias (for which behavioural explanations provide an incomplete picture) plus the fact that systematic desensitization is made up of a multi-element package (Lipsedge, 1973).

A large number of investigations have demonstrated that the precise methods prescribed by the founder, Wolpe, are not vital to the success of the procedure; the only necessary condition for change seems to be exposure to the feared object or situation. The essential role of muscular relaxation and the presentation of heirarchies of anxiety-provoking stimuli, has been brought into question. In general, longer durations of exposure to phobic stimuli result in greater fear reduction, irrespective of type of fear (Mathews, *op. cit.*). We are left with the question 'What makes desensitization work? It has generated a plethora of theoretical speculation. Wilson and Davison (1971) have done a good deal to demolish Wolpe's original model of reciprocal inhibition—a situation in which one response (anxiety) is dampened or inhibited by simultaneously initiating an antagonistic response (for example, relaxation, assertion, or sexual arousal). In terms of learning theory, the procedures of systematic desensitization involve, at the very least, a combination of counter-conditioning (viz. conditioning a new relaxed state to the stimulus that previously provoked anxiety, thus eliminating the anxiety) and *extinction* (viz. the repeated presentation of the stimulus while preventing the anxiety response from occurring).

We are left with several interpretations: namely extinction, habituation, operant conditioning, and the attribution theory. With regard to attribution theory, the most recent contributions to the debate (see Bandura, 1977a, 1978) have centred around the postulation of various central cognitive processes to explain the success of systematic desensitization. Bandura proposes as the main therapeutic ingredient an increment in the phobic client's perception of self-efficacy. That is to say he comes to *believe* that he can cope with the dreaded situation and is thus able to do so. Bandura's research and theoretical elaborations on the concept of self-efficacy provides a nice illustration of the point made about the development of explanatory theories as a spin-off of systematically evaluated treatment programmes.

There have been several other attempts (see Davison and Wilson, 1972, 1973; Gaupp *et al.*, 1972; Murray and Jacobson, 1971; Rachman, 1978; Rosen *et al.*, 1972) to tease out the components of the method which make it effective and the reasons they do so.

In vivo work emphasizes the relationship between anxiety responses and consequences (6, Figure 1); the focus is on altering these responses by reinforcing a gradual approach to actual objects and/or situations, the concern being on changing what happens *after* approach behaviour occurs. This method, also called 'performance desensitization', 'shaping', or 'reinforced practice' is in contrast to symbolic desensitization, in which anxiety-provoking situations are

imagined, and has been shown to be more effective (e.g. Barlow *et al.*, 1969).
There is a spectrum of behavioural techniques involving exposure training, from the gently hierarchical (graded) approach of systematic desensitization to the eliciting of intense emotion, a feature of the method called *flooding* or *implosion*.

Treatment of phobic disorders by flooding

This is yet another model of change which stresses the importance of exposing the client to anxiety-provoking situations within a respondent extinction method.

These procedures involve exposing the patient to selected anxiety-arousing stimuli while being prevented from responding to them with his or her characteristic escape or avoidance behaviours. Where systematic desensitization takes the client gently and gradually through a series of anxiety-provoking stimuli—graded from least to most provocative—so as to minimize the fear experienced during treatment, flooding means just what its says: the client is exposed to the most anxiety-provoking stimulus for an extended period of time. Exposure may take place *in vitro*, by means of imagined imagery, or *in vivo*, by means of real-life experience. The client is encouraged to experience the stimulus cues fully and the anxiety evoked by these cues. The worst that could happen is imagined or experienced in this method. Exposure time is related to effectiveness—longer exposures producing greater reductions in avoidance behaviour; actual, real-life exposure is more effective than imaginal exposure (see Rimm and Masters, 1979).

Extinction of classically conditioned responses to anxiety-provoking cues is the rationale provided for the high level of success (Marks *et al.*, 1971; Marks, 1975; Watson *et al.*,1971) of these procedures in the case of fears and phobias. Extinction is assumed to occur each time the client is exposed to the conditioned stimuli at full strength. By repeating the procedure the stimuli eventually lose their capacity to elicit fright. The method is based upon experimental work on experimental neuroses and avoidance learning. As Walker *et al.*, (1981) explain the process:

Extinction is presumed to occur with each repeated presentation, since there is no traumatic event or physical harm experienced by the patient as the anxiety-related cues are introduced. Further, since the patient is not allowed to make the usual avoidance or escape response, there is no drive reduction or other reinforcing event that might strengthen the avoidance response pattern . . . essentially, implosion therapy and flooding represent a form of reality-testing under therapeutically controlled conditions. It is assumed that the process allows the patient to realise that the feared traumatic event actually will not occur and that avoidance is not necessary (p. 115).

An extensive review of the experimental literature (23 analog studies, 15 clinical population investigations) evaluating the flooding technique (Levis and

Hare, 1977) demonstrated its effectiveness with a wide variety of psychiatric and psychoneurotic problems, including anxiety and phobic conditions, and most notably those intractible problems of the past—the despair of the sufferer and the psychiatrist alike—obsessive-compulsive neuroses (see Rachman *et al.*, 1971; Hodgson *et al.*, 1972; Rachman *et al.*, 1973).

Treatment of obsessive-compulsive neuroses by flooding

Carr (1974) describes the obsessive-compulsive disorders as being characterized by a recurrent or persistent thought, image, impulse, or action that is accompanied by a sense of subjective compulsion and a desire to resist it. Foa and Tillmans (1980) repudiate the customary tendency to classify thoughts and images as 'obsessions' and repetitive actions as 'compulsions'. They prefer a functional classification (see ABC/parameters in Figure 1) where the distinction is based on the relationship between anxiety/discomfort and each class of symptoms. Thus behaviours (more rarely thoughts and images) that *reduce* anxiety are called 'compulsions' (for example, washing and checking); while thoughts, images, and actions that elicit anxiety or discomfort are termed 'obsessions'.

In general the literature on the use of systematic desensitization with obsessional and compulsive patients suggests that it is disappointing and costly in time. Its success appears to be limited to cases with recent onset of symptoms and to the application of *in vivo* rather than imaginal sensitization.

The treatment of choice for obsessive-compulsive disorders is flooding and response prevention—procedures that deal with anxiety as well as the compulsions associated with it (Foa and Goldstein, 1978; Foa and Tillmans, 1980; Meyer *et al.*, 1974). The evidence suggests that exposing the patient to distress-evoking situations *in vivo*, is more effective than fantasy or modelling alone. The method of exposure, be it rapid versus graduated, with or without participant modelling, does not alter its therapeutic potency.

The rationale for these procedures is Mowrer's (1960) two-factor theory of avoidance behaviour, which, although it does not accommodate *all* cases, is a widely accepted model of avoidance learning in psychopathology because it accounts rather well for the acquisition and maintenance of obsessional-compulsive behaviours of both categories (common in these neuroses) of washers and checkers.

Treatment of psychopathology by aversion therapy

In aversive therapy, a negative (aversive or noxious) stimulus is associated with a positive (pleasant) stimulus in order to change the response to the latter from one of approach to avoidance or escape. For example, an emetic drug may be administered in such a way that the client experiences nausea contingent upon drinking alcohol. Sometimes the negative stimulation is presented *simultaneously* with the behaviour (called 'classical' or 'respondent' counter-conditioning); sometimes the unpleasant stimulation is made *contingent upon* the occurrence of the behaviour (termed 'operant' counter-conditioning). Whether or not aversive therapy is a matter of conditioning is debatable.

Although therapeutic effectiveness of aversion therapy appears to be promising in the case of sexual deviations, self-injurious behaviour, and alcoholism (Rachman and Teasdale, 1969) there is controversy about its rationale and the ethics of its use.

Covert sensitization is similar to aversive therapy in that aversive stimulation is paired with an undesirable behaviour, but whereas in the latter the unpleasant stimulus is a nausea-inducing drug or electric shock, in the former it is an unpleasant scene or situation *imagined* by the client.

'Treatment' by non-specific influences

All the methods discussed so far raise problems when it comes to assessing their value; their effects are confounded by a variety of non-specific psychological factors common to all forms of therapeutic intervention.

Albino (1980) is of the opinion that there are three psychological principles commonly in use in all forms of psychotherapy: teaching, the provision of explanations (he refers to these agnostically as 'explanatory myths'), and persuasion (influence). Certainly the didactic role is embraced openly and wholeheartedly in behaviour therapy, (sometimes by self-discovery as in problem-solving methods). The provision of explanations is a conscious part of this process. Not surprisingly, behaviour therapists claim (Herbert, 1981) that the rationale of their methods has face validity for clients as all people, especially in their social interactions and in their role as parents are informal behaviour modifiers. They constantly make use of 'common sense' principles of learning and change (e.g. modelling, reward, and punishment).

Persuasion. Albino (op. cit.) is referring here to the powers of persuasion and influence which rest on practical knowledge or practice wisdom. The therapist offers reasons why the client should change his beliefs and/or behaviour. Lewis (1972) states that:

The central element of influence is that patients come, attend, and respond to the therapist, whether they come of their own will or are coerced. To influence is to sway another, whether for the moment or for life. Patients come for therapeutic influence because some of their Plans have gone awry ... Human Plans can suffer all (these) types of confusions and disconfirmations, and all (these) types of painful feelings result. But humans suffer many additional types of conflict given by their more complex symbolizing capacity. Influence in psychotherapy aims at correcting the confusion, disconfirmation, and errors of the patient's Plans. The desired end result for the patient is the possession of more reliable, more zestful, more loving and creative Plans (pp. 222/3).

For those who favour a social learning approach to the understanding of human problems and their remediation, there is no question of denying the importance of social influence in therapy. After all, social learning is concerned with explaining the development of behaviour in interpersonal, social settings. Influence is implicit in all social interaction because of the interdependence of human beings living in society. Helping, cooperative and therapeutic relationships are no exception, all being based upon mutual influence. Therapists influence clients and vice versa.

There have been many studies of the influence of the therapeutic relationship and such factors as the clients' expectations (expectancies) of receiving help. This matter of the client's beliefs about therapy leads us neatly into one of the crucial developments within behaviour therapy—the growth of cognitive features in both the theory and practice of the method. The therapist's influence upon the client may have its source in the provision of information or interpretations; changing behaviours, attitudes, values, and perceptions; teaching problem-solving and social skills; altering the client's attributions concerning past and present behaviours.

The client's positive expectations about the outcome of treatment and his attitude toward the therapist have been shown to be important (but not all-important) elements in determining the success or failure of programmes (see Lick and Bootzin, 1975; Meyer, 1975). There is a lack of consistency in the studies, which makes it difficult to give appropriate weight to the various components in treatment techniques. For example, some investigations provide evidence that therapeutic instructions alone increase the efficacy of experimental desensitization, while other studies fail to demonstrate the effect. And while the client's expectation that he will be helped by the therapy accounts for some of the improvement, it clearly does not account for all of the positive change. In the case of systematic desensitization there have been many controlled experiments in which the method has brought about greater change for the better than pseudo-therapy, applied to clients who have had expectations of help induced by the experimenter. The problem with placebo control groups to which behaviourally treated clients have been compared, is that they do not necessarily generate a client's expectancies of success to the degree that (say) desensitization does (Nau *et al.*, 1974).

If we assume that the expectation of help can facilitate therapeutic change, we have to evaluate several explanations of how it works. Erwin (*op. cit.*) puts forward the possibility that the client who believes he will be helped may have the incentive to test his belief by exposing himself to the phobic situation; also the client is 'under more demand' to show improvement than is the one who does not expect to be cured. For some practitioners it may be most convincing to accept that the therapy works, but is effective (at least in part) because of the client's *beliefs*. For others it is the belief and not the therapeutic trappings that bring about the improvement.

Cognitive explanations. The learning theorist Estes (1971) writes that for the lower animals, for very young children, and to some extent for human beings of all ages who are mentally retarded or subject to severe neurological or behaviour disorders, behaviour from moment to moment is largely describable and predictable in terms of responses to particular stimuli and the rewarding or punishing outcomes of previous stimulus-response sequences. In more mature beings, much instrumental behaviour and more especially a great part of verbal behaviour is organized into higher-order routines and is, in many instances, better understood in terms of the operation of rules, principles, strategies and the like. Bandura, (1977a) points to a therapeutic paradox, when he comments that'... explanations are becoming more cognitive. On the others hand, it is performance based treatments that are proving most powerful in effecting psychological changes. Regardless of the method involved, the treatments implemented through actual performance achieve results consistently superior to those in which fears are eliminated to cognitive representations of threats' (p. 78).

Interestingly, behavioural procedures may be among the most powerful methods of actually activating cognitive processes. Not surprisingly they are recruited for the remediation of a wide range of intra- and interpersonal problems. There is a delightful irony in the burgeoning literature on the cognitive aspects of behaviour therapy. Nowadays the approach encompasses a plethora of techniques that depend upon those mediating processes and private events which were once so passionately repudiated as 'ghosts in the machine'. Thus self-verbalizations, illogical thoughts, misperceptions and misinterpretations, attributions and self-appraisals (in other words what the client thinks, imagines, and says to himself) prior to, accompanying, and following his overt behaviour, become a primary focus for a therapeutic intervention.

Essentially, it is being claimed that people can be taught to eliminate some of their maladaptive behaviours by challenging their irrational beliefs and faulty logic or by getting them to instruct themselves in certain ways or to associate wanted behaviour with positive self-statements, and unwanted ones with negative self-statements or painful imagery. Depression, in particular, lends itself to the cognitive-behavioural approach. Most depressed clients manifest a high rate of intrusive negative thoughts, including ruminations about past negative events and thoughts about the hopelessness of the future and their helplessness in the face of their perceived dilemma. Beck's study of depression (Beck *et al.*, 1979) provides an excellent introduction to the intricacies of the cognitive approach (see also Lewinsohn *et al.*, 1976, and Seligman, 1975).

Seligman's formulation of clinical depression is in terms of learned helplessness. A sense of helplessness, it is posited, leads to cognitive and motivational deficits and emotional disturbance. These learned helplessness effects are determined in large part by the attribution which the client makes when he experiences a persistent 'disconnection' (independence) between his behavioural responses and their outcomes (see also Abramson *et al.*, 1978). What a person tells himself about his experience affects his behaviour. For example, one client may tend to attribute the causes of what happens to him to forces beyond his control, while another may see himself as having a major influence and say on the unfolding events of his life.

This notion generates practice methods which have proved very promising—methods (e.g. 'cognitive restructuring') that include the attempt to alter overt behaviour by modifying thoughts, assumptions, and interpretations; also strategies (e.g. in 'problem-solving' training) of analysing and responding to difficult or fraught situations. The client is trained to re-evaluate potentially distressing events so that when they are viewed from a more realistic perspective they lose their power to upset. This involves changing his characteristic ways of organizing his experiences, and then producing alternatives. Goldfried and Davison (1976) have developed a problem-solving approach which involves working through five stages in dealing with his problem: (a) general orientation; (b) problem definition and formulation; (c) generation of alternatives; (d) decision-making; (e) verification.

Treatment of stress disorders by problem-solving

The rationale for these methods is succinctly provided by D'Zurilla and Goldfried (1971):

Much of what we view clinically as 'abnormal behaviour' or 'emotional disturbance' may be viewed as ineffective behaviour and its consequences, in which the individual is unable to resolve certain situational problems in his life and his inadequate attempts to do so are having undesirable effects, such as anxiety, depression, and the creation of additional problems. (p. 107).

Although some of the therapeutic procedures commonly used in adult cognitively-orientated work can be understood by adolescents, many of them would not be suitable for children. Nevertheless, youngsters can be taught rational thinking, stress-inoculation techniques and problem-solving strategies (Herbert, 1981). Whereas the nature of the cognitive problems associated with adult anxiety and depression—to take two examples—can be conceptualized as *cognitive errors*, the cognitive problems and the focus of treatment in child cognitive-behavioural therapy are most often *cognitive absences*. Kendall (1981) explains that the child fails to engage in the cognitive, information-processing activities of an active problem-solver and refrains from initiating the reflective thoughts processes that can control behaviour. Indeed he may lack the cognitive skills needed to carry out crucial abstract, analytical mental activities.

The aim of training clients in problem-solving skills is to provide them with a general coping strategy for a variety of difficult situations. The method has been used to help adults deal with stress (see below), and children and adolescents to deal more effectively with a variety of conflict situations (e.g. arriving at mutually acceptable decisions with parents, developing cooperation with the peer group). Its prime advantage as a training method is the provision of principles so that the person can function as his own 'therapist'. It is a variant of self-control training, directed towards the objective of encouraging the client to think and work things out for himself.

Treating dysfunctional emotion by developing cognitive self-management skills

Stress-inoculation training has been used successfully by Meichenbaum (1972, 1977) in the self-management of phobic anxiety, anger, and pain. Clients are provided with a prospective set of skills and defences so as to deal with future crises. The training programme has three phases: (a) the first, educational in nature, provides the client with a conceptual framework for understanding the nature of his problem; (b) a number of behavioural and cognitive coping skills arising from the conceptual framework, are rehearsed by the client; and (c) the opportunity is provided for the client to practise his coping skills while being exposed to a variety of real stresses and/or practice by means of imagery and behavioural rehearsal. The evidence for the effectiveness of this and other forms of self-control training for the treatment of various disorders, has been supported by several controlled studies (Goldfried and Goldfried, 1975).

Cognitively-orientated theorists reinterpret *desensitization* in their own terms. Ellis (1971) assumes that the anxiety and avoidance behaviour associated with phobias result basically from irrational self-statements. These verbalizations are discouraged in desensitization thus reducing their potency. Beck (1976) believes that because the client is relaxed when presented with the phobic stimulus in desensitization, he is better able to deal with it objectively. The client may thus come to the conclusion that the fear is really irrational and therefore not dangerous after all.

Goldfried (1971) offers a coping interpretation of desensitization comparing it to a self-control technique whereby the client is taught how to relax himself in the feared situation. This is very much in the tradition of the stress inoculation/anxiety management programmes mentioned earlier. The interpretations proliferate, but perhaps this is no bad thing as they have generated productive research (see Rimm and Masters, 1979) and useful methods (see Mahoney and Arnkoff, 1978). For example, *covert modelling*, in which the client is requested to imagine himself coping adequately in a fear-arousing situation (*coping* with fear rather than mastering the situation so that no fear is experienced), has proved effective in decreasing anxiety (Cautela, 1971; Kazdin, 1973).

Sadly, it is only possible to speak of *promise* at this stage of the development of effective forms of cognitive-behaviour therapy (see Rachman and Wilson, 1980).

Rachman (1981, p. 287) traces the disappointments over the potency of cognitive – rational forms of therapy to two assumptions:

(i)   Most forms of this approach have assumed that affect is post-cognitive rather than pre-cognitive,
(ii) The approach is based on the implicit assumption that cognition and affect operate within the same system. If it is conceded that more than one system may be involved, then access between the systems (e.g. the accessibility of affective reactions by cognitive operations) is assumed to be possible and free.

Both these assumptions are open to doubt! This fragmentary account of an ongoing theoretical discussion and empirical exploration, is given here as an example of the heuristic potential of the behavioural approach. The point was made earlier that although a major part of the foundational theory for behaviour therapy has been drawn from the social learning theory literature, behaviour therapists are evolving and researching their own theories that are specially designed to explain clinical phenomena. Erwin (1978) sees Bandura's work on two types of expectancy—*outcome* and *self-efficacy* expectancies—as a particularly apt example of this kind of innovation.

Bandura (1977a and b) hypothesizes that the self (a central mediating system which is influenced by performance accomplishments, vicarious experiences, verbal persuasion and physiological states) distinguishes between *efficacy expectations* and *outcome expectations*. Efficacy expectations refer to whether the person believes he can or will perform certain behaviours, while outcome expectations refer to anticipated effects the behaviours are likely to have on the environment if performed. He adduces some evidence that efficacy expectations correlate better with actual performance in a behavioural approach test than scores derived from performance measures during treatment: such as the number of hierarchy steps completed. Bandura is of the opinion that the findings support his hypothesis concerning the self-system as a central mediating construct unifying all behaviour change data. This notion has not gone unchallenged (Tryon, 1981).

Bandura's theory suggests that psychological treatment methods work by altering the client's self-efficacy expectations. These expectancies derive primarily from the four sources of information: performance accomplishments, vicarious experience, verbal persuasion, and physiological states. The more reliable the sources, the greater are the changes in perceived self-efficacy. An increase in perceived self-efficacy will affect both initiation (the willingness to get involved in otherwise daunting situations) and persistence of coping behaviour (in the face of aversive experiences).

There are many behaviour therapists (e.g. Phillips, 1981) who are concerned to arrest the 'invasion' of cognitive behaviour therapists because of the dangers of the trend toward clouded concepts and methodology. She has this to say in her conclusion of a review of work carried out by behaviour therapists in which there was 'cognitive content':

Since the "cognitive" behaviour therapists reviewed above are really helping their clients their mixed techniques seem to be effective in most of the cases cited) one might ask what s the harm in confounding techniques anyway? The harm lies in the confusion created in the professional community. Behaviour therapy is still misunderstood and not accepted by the majority of the psychiatric establishment . . . Rather than cloud the issues, we need to sharpen the precision of our concepts and techniques. More careful behaviour analysis should be carried out on individuals, clients and in research populations (p. 15).

Phillip's position is summarized in the following hypotheses:

1. 'Cognition' is a category term which refers to a class of behaviours subject to external stimulus controls as are other behaviours.
2. Private events are not ignored by behaviourists: they have as much access to them as do 'cognitivists', through verbal report of clients and direct experience of their own. The former simply require more precise, operational definitions of their constructs.
3. Mediating responses categorized as images, perceptions, hypotheses, $r_g - s_g$ s, etc., are learned through interactions with the organism's external environment, as are more overt responses.
4. There is no disagreement that cognitive behaviours are, and always have been an important part of behaviour therapy. There is complete disagreement, however, with the implication that they must be treated differently or belong to a different world and are governed by laws different from other behaviours (p. 6).

Operant conditioning

We return to firmer ground when we look at the kind of technique which involves the systematic manipulation of the behaviour's consequences (6. Figure 1) so as to modify subsequent behaviours of the same type. This may involve the removal of rewards (positive reinforcers) that customarily follow a maladaptive response, or the provision of a reward following the display of a desirable response.

Although operant technology has been used successfully in cases of anorexia nervosa, and in modifying delusional statements in schizophrenics and also the secondary symptoms of psychotic patients, arising out of institutionalization (see Kazdin, 1978), to mention a small fraction of the wide spectrum of applications, this discussion will concentrate on their use with problematic children and adolescents. The issues raised by work with children illustrate the many variations of operant conditioning and other methods already mentioned in connection with adult patients, not to mention the complexities of work within families. It also throws into sharp relief the matter of ethics and behaviour therapy.

Childhood psychopathology

It is necessary to say something about the psychopathology of childhood. There is a surprisingly clear consensus in past and present studies, that children's behaviour problems can be classified into two main 'symptom clusters'. Despite great diversity in subjects, instruments, raters, and statistical analyses, empirical investigations consistently elicit syndromes of the *undercontrolled type* (conduct disorder, aggressive, externalizing, acting-out), and the *overcontrolled* type (emotional disturbance, personality disorder, inhibited, internalizing, anxious) (Herbert, 1978).

Treatment of conduct disorders by operant and other methods

There is a convergence between clinical and factor analytic studies with regard to the conduct disorders. The term refers to a syndrome (or constellation) of problems characterized by non-compliance, restlessness, irresponsibility, boisterousness, and aggression. It includes seriously antisocial acts as well as moderately troublesome behaviours. Not only is the prognosis with regard to the 'natural history' of the more severe conduct disorders a grave one (Herbert, *op. cit.*), but they tend to be resistant to traditional therapeutic interventions.

There is a vital need to identify those children who are at risk at the earliest possible moment so as to initiate therapeutic programmes before problem patterns become fixed. The evidence is unambiguous that there are significant links between childhood and adolescence and adult life. For example, it is those disorders involving disruptive, aggressive or antisocial behaviour which are most likely to persist into adolescence or (the evidence is reviewed in Herbert (1982)). General population surveys show that just under half of adolescent disorders have an onset before adolescence, while clinic-based studies suggest that the majority of adolescent psychiatric disorders have been manifesting themselves from early or middle childhood. There is a degree of continuity between early conduct disorder and juvenile delinquency. Most adult antisocial behaviour is antedated by similar behaviour in childhood. The behaviour of childhood, and in particular the *extremeness* and *variety* of psychopathology, provide better predictors of adult functioning—and in particular antisocial adult life-style—than the family background, social class of rearing, or particular type of childhood behaviour.

Training children (or retraining them) as part of a treatment programme, is potentially a long-term endeavour, and therefore the home becomes a crucial base for therapeutic work. The time span for change can be a long one—given some of the slowly evolving, complex psychological attributes under consideration (e.g. learning rules, developing resistance to temptation, empathy, and self-control). Some are internalized quickly (depending on self rather than external reinforcement). Some will remain for ever situationally determined. Time-scales vary, depending on the age and maturity of the child and the nature of the behavioural task.

The last 15 years or so have seen major advances in the behavioural treatment of children's problems. There is a wide range of empirically based therapeutic procedures from which to choose in planning an intervention. When it comes to the treatment of the conduct disorders, it is proposed by the present author that a history of maladaptive moral and social learning is central to many of the problems (Herbert, 1981, 1982). Such a notion gives urgency to the idea of treating them with the caregivers as the main mediators of change. Among the more optimistic developments in recent years has been the application of behavioural treatments to the alleviation of conduct disorders, an application linked fruitfully—given the psycho-social definition and evolution of these problems—to social learning theory (Herbert, 1978). Such a conceptualization has guided the present author in his work with hyperactive and conduct disordered children and adolescents at the Child Treatment Research Unit, University of Leicester. The methods elaborated, for the task of enhancing or making good the socialization process (described above) when it is going wrong, have been applied with encouraging effectiveness by parents (Herbert and Iwaniec, 1981). The systematic investigation of parents as formal and primary mediators of behavioural change began in the 1950s. Many studies of the feasibility and efficacy of using parents—particularly with conduct problems—have followed (Griffen and Hudson, 1978).

The common theme running through the rather heterogeneous collection of problems seen at the Child Treatment Research Unit is their quality of antisocial disruptiveness, and the social disapproval they earn because they flout society's sensibilities and rules, and because their consequences are so disturbing or explicitly harmful to others. Not surprisingly the behaviour therapy applied in the unit amounts to a multi-element package depending for its final shape upon the behavioural assessment. It might include several variations of the operant technology referred to above: *differential reinforcement* (positive reinforcement—social and sometimes material—of prosocial actions and removal of reinforcement or application of punishment contingent upon antisocial behaviours); also *time-out* from positive reinforcement (periods of 5 minutes for children below the age of 10), *response-cost*, and *over-correction* procedures. Incentive systems (*token economies*) are negotiated and contracted between parents and children, and some are linked to behaviour at school.

In the case of the older children, we tend to use more cognitively orientated methods (see Herbert, 1981) including *self-control training* (assertion and relaxation training, desensitization of anger, role-play, behaviour rehearsal); *problem-solving skill-training* (see Urbain and Kendall, 1980); *and social-skills training* (see Goldstein *et al.*, 1978). A technique which has proved to be invaluable (see Herbert, *op. cit.*) with hyperactive, impulsive children is *self-instruction training*—the development of children's skills in guiding their own performance by the use of self-suggestion, comments, praise, and other directives (Meichenbaum, 1977). Frequent use is made of *alternative response training*, a method that provides children with alternative modes of response to cope with provocative and disturbing situations, or activities that are incompatible with the undesired behaviours. *Contingency contracts* between parents and their children (particularly when adolescent) have also proved useful, in large part because of their functions in modelling skills of negotiating and finding solutions to conflict.

In a sample of 117 children (ages two to sixteen) with conduct disorders accepted for treatment at the Child Treatment Research Unit, a majority (83 per cent) were causing serious disruption within the family; they were often perceived by their parents to be 'out of control'. Using the framework for assessment in Figure 1 and behavioural methods (described above), 61 per cent were evaluated as successful (improved on several criteria); 21 per cent were moderately improved; and 18 per cent showed no improvement. A median figure of three months (and some 33 hours) of intervention to termination—but not including follow-up—was required. Similar results were obtained in a replication study of a sample of conduct disorders drawn from 36 consecutive mixed cases referred to the unit. Twelve of the 16 children who improved with treatment, maintained this improvement over a six-month follow-up period. Three of the four who deteriorated over this period responded to booster behavioural programmes.

Patterson and his colleagues at the Oregon Research Institute have been a prolific source of ideas and data on the subject (*inter alia*) of children's conduct disorders, notably aggression and stealing. They have evolved a treatment package which involves training parents in childmanagement skills (Patterson *et al.*, 1975). It is difficult to summarize such an extensive contribution but it is worth reporting the team's results with 27 conduct disordered boys referred to them in the period January 1968 to June 1972, and accepted for treatment. Training the families took an average of 31.5 hours of professional time. The treatment programme (parents read a semi-programmed text followed by a multiple-choice test; staff teach parents to pinpoint problem areas and collect appropriate data on them; the latter join a parent training group to learn appropriate change-techniques; home visits occur where necessary, lasting on average between 3 and 4 months. Most parents opted to work on reducing their offsprings' non-compliance to requests, but overall a further 13 behaviours in the conduct-disorder 'syndrome' were also pinpointed for treatment.

With regard to criterion measures such as the targeted deviant behaviours of the boys, an average 60 per cent reduction from base-line level to termination, was achieved. In 75 per cent of cases, reductions exceeded 30 per cent from base-line levels. In 6 cases the rate of problematic behaviour deteriorated. On another criterion—total deviant scores—the 27 boys showed a reduction from higher than normal overall rates (scores computed for normal boys over 14 'problem areas') to within normal limits. According to parental daily reports there was a significant drop in the level of reported problems during follow-up (data was obtained here on 14 families only). About two-thirds of the families reported marked reductions in the problems for which they were originally referred.

A successful replication of this work was conducted by Eyberg and Johnson

1974)—using the treatment package. Follow-up data were obtained monthly by the Oregon Research Institute for the first six months after termination of treatment, and every two months after that until a year after termination. Booster treatment programmes during follow-up took an average of 1.9 hours of professional time.

It has to be faced that there are many practical difficulties in working with populations on $N = 1$—i.e. with parents and teachers as the primary mediators of change—and in natural (which often means experimentally 'unnatural') settings. However, as Repucci and Saunders (1974) argue, the frontiers of behaviour modification are changing; and the central questions must be redefined to include the *social* application of behavioural techniques. As they put it:

In natural settings, the behaviour modifier faces a variety of problems that do not relate directly to theoretical issues in behavior modification and that are either nonextent or relatively inconspicuous in the laboratory or special research situation, where the investigator has almost complete control over the contingencies of reinforcement (p. 52).

Treating emotional disorders of children by systematic desensitization and modelling

Desensitization. We have seen that emotional behaviour can be controlled by different stimulus sources (e.g. the emotional arousal evoked directly by conditioned aversive stimuli). To eliminate maladaptive emotional responses in children, repeated non-reinforced exposure to threatening events (either directly or vicariously) has been used as the main thrust of treatment. However, clear evidence for the effectiveness of any variant of desensitization with children is still lacking (see Hatzenbuehler and Schroeder, 1978). Some case studies suggest the successful reduction of avoidance behaviour; others have failed. Evidence suggests that it may be preferable with the child who shows intense avoidance behaviour so that his voluntary participation is inhibited, to emphasize (initially) responses (e.g. relaxation) which are antagonistic to anxiety. With moderately avoident children—according to Hatzenbuehler and Schroeder (*op. cit.*)—active participation is preferable because of the assured advantage of behavioural rehearsal.

Modelling involves the systematic demonstration in actuality (or symbolically—on film) of a model displaying the required behaviour: a skill, an appropriate pro-social action, a coping strategy.

Modelling is the most frequently used and reliably effective strategy for reducing children's fears (see Herbert, 1981). However, it can be used in many situations including the teaching of new skills or alternative behaviours. It may have a promising preventive role in the area of stress-inoculation. Modelling can be combined with other procedures; thus modelling combined with desensitization may be very effective in the treatment of phobias, among the most common problems of children.

Ethical imperatives

A critical issue in psychiatry is the moral foundation of its therapeutic armamentarium. This issue is of concern throughout medicine, of course; but it is a particularly sensitive one in psychiatry because of the vulnerability of its clientele and the controversial nature of some of its methods. Psychiatric patients are not always a voluntary clientele, in the sense of seeing themselves as patients, of choosing to come into hospital, or of consenting to treatment. And even when consent is given, can it be said to be 'freely given' when the person is dependent on the goodwill of the staff of the institution in so many ways, or when fear or clouded consciousness limit his understanding of the treatment being offered, or its implications? Iatrogenic effects are a matter of controversy throughout the range of medical treatments, especially with regard to drugs, but the controversies somehow become much more emotive when (say) electroconvulsive therapy is the subject of debate. The risk of memory-loss, makes the method—the mechanics of which are perceived by some as a violation—a thoroughly questionable procedure.

Behaviour therapy seems to generate as much heated opposition among the critics as the physical treatments such as ECT and psychosurgery. The domain of behaviour therapy/modification is not infrequently broadened out of all recognition to include any method whose end-goal is behaviour change and modification. Thus behaviour modification, psychosurgery, ECT and brain-washing are merged to conjure up a scenario which combines images of a Clockwork Orange and Brave New World. It is a short series of steps from behaviour control to mind control to social control at this level of reportage. However, the sillier conjectures and extrapolations should not provide an excuse to dismiss the serious reservations of people who are aware of the defining attributes of the behavioural appraoch. It is also necessary to go beyond the 'you too!' defensive reflex. It is only too easy (and understandable, when the criticisms come gallingly from psychotherapists) to point out that all therapies, of whatever persuasion, are in the business of producing change; all involve social value judgements about undesirable and desirable behaviours. To the extent that they change people, they can all be accused of being presumptions, manipulative, and open to abuse. Indeed, the spiteful commentator might say that critics are particularly vocal in their criticisms of behaviour therapy because they suspect that it really works!

The concerns about behaviour therapy are related, *inter alia*, to the following issues:

(a) Behaviour control;
(b) The purposes to which behaviour therapy is put;

(c) The superficiality of the tratment;
(d) The dehumanizing quality of behaviour therapy.

Behaviour control

The criticism here is that the behaviour therapist controls, moulds, shapes or manipulates behaviour. Undoubtedly, 'behaviour modification' is a particularly unfortunate name for a therapy; it has sinister overtones, and the experimental/laboratory derived language which provides much of its terminology does little to encourage enough critics to explore the actual nature of current practice. Of course, *all* therapies involve influence!

The 'you too' rejoinder swiftly moves from the defensive to the offensive, and includes the claim that a particular feature of behaviour therapy is the respect paid to the integrity of the client by its democratic (as opposed to authoritarian) and participant (as opposed to unidirectional) therapeutic basis. Good practice is, or should be, like this—not simply on ethical grounds but for good theoretical reasons. Behaviour therapy is nothing if it is not about self-management. It respects the client:

(a) By focusing on observed behaviours (there is an absence of the 'hidden agendas' of some depth psychotherapies);
(b) By limiting treatment to helping diminish maladaptive functioning and increase adaptive functioning (rather than seeking to change 'deep structures' of personality);
(c) By carefully negotiating treatment goals with the client;
(d) By sharing (in most cases) the therapy, the thinking behind it, and decision-making, with the client.

It is claimed that by means of this sort of active client participation, the source of much of the influence in behaviour therapy is made explicit.

Behaviour therapists are accused of controlling behaviour as if clients exist in a vacuum of free will before entering treatment. Behavioural practitioners talk, on the one hand, of liberating clients from some of the unwanted controlling forces in their lives, but assume, on the other hand, a freedom of choice when it comes to accepting therapy. They tend to say, as do other therapists, that if a client requires help and requests it, then help should be provided. The difficulty with this comforting principle is that people can be *coerced*, in ways subtle and unsubtle, tangible and intangible, to 'seek' help. Some clients, for example in mental hospitals, are not in a position to ask for help or (to put it another way), clear enough about the issues to reject the offer of help.

Erwin (1978) points out the paradox that many behaviour therapists accept some form of determinism, but also try to distinguish between a free and coerced decision to change one's behaviour. For example, those behaviour therapists (a decreasing number) who accept the fundamentalist position of behaviourism, that all human behaviour is caused solely by a process of classical and operant conditioning, are stuck with a hard determinism which leaves no room for free choice. It would require much space and a linguistic philosopher to explore the implications of the free will and determinism debate for behaviour therapy. Erwin concludes that some decisions to seek therapy (for example by those who receive treatment as out-patients) which hitherto have been viewed as free and voluntary decisions may, in reality, be neither of these. It is of interest, given the growing use of the cognitive-behavioural method known as 'cognitive restructuring', to consider briefly Kelly's views on free will. He sees man as both free *and* determined (Kelly, 1955, p. 58). The construct system provides him with both freedom of decision and limitation of action—freedom, because it permits him to deal with the meaning of events rather than forces him to be helplessly pushed about by them, and limitation, because he can never make choices outside the world of alternatives he has erected for himself. Pervin (1970, p. 337) comments that man is free to construe events, but he is then bound by his constructions. Having constrained himself with these constructions, he is able to win his freedom over and over again by reconstruing (perhaps with the help of the therapist with his alternative 'explanatory stories') his life and his environment. According to Pervin 'man is not a victim of his past history or of his present circumstances—unless he chooses to construe himself in that way'. Even if this is a valid hypotheses it has no bearing on the person's decision at the pretreatment stage to accept behaviour therapy. The old and sharp dichotomies of free will and determinism, have become blurred. Many modern philosophers accept a 'soft determinism' in which free choice can exist even if every event does have a cause.

Purposes of behaviour therapy

The more strident (and this tends to mean ill-informed) commentaries drown out the reasoned critiques which voice genuine concern about the rights of children and institutionalized adults and, thus, more basically, the purposes of the treatment. There *have* been abuses of the method as court cases in the USA have revealed. We do have to examine closely the definition of purposes to which the best-intentioned and best trained practitioners are using the approach. A painstaking review of these crucial ethical issues by Stolz, *et al.* (1973, p. 1039), concludes as follows:

On the whole, the goal of behaviour modification, as generally practised is not to force people to conform or behave in some mindless, automation-like way. Rather, the goals generally include providing new skills and underdeveloped options and developing creativity and spontaneity.

This all sounds very well, but a *strictly enforced* code of practice which states and protects clients' rights, is still notable for its absence in the UK.

The apologias of 'gun lobbies', the world over, find echoes in the arguments of some behaviour therapists. Behavioural technology is as good as the person who applies it; the method is ethically neutral (see Erwin, 1978). Behaviour therapy has no inherent purpose other than therapeutic change—it contains no intrinsic message about how people ought to live. It is open to abuse like any other therapy. Here is a subject for debate which requires space far beyond the scope of this chapter.

For those who accept a consensus model of society, it is sufficient to say that behavioural treatments in homes, clinics and hospitals work to goals breadly endorsed by the community, e.g. relieving anxiety, increasing self-control, self-management and social skills, eliminating self-injurious, deviant or psychotic behaviours. It goes without saying that such a stance is far too complacent and simple minded with regard to the nature of society, deviance, mental illness and positive mental health (see Jahoda, 1958).

Behaviour therapists would probably claim that their working philosophy and particular concern is to relieve suffering – to provide the client with the ability for greater self-direction, by means of self-control and problem-solving training so as to embrace his personal freedom of choice. On balance, the evidence is that they achieve these purposes.

Superficiality

The charge that the method is superficial or trivial is best answered by examining, as does Gambrill (1977) the wide range of life problems, which have responded to this form of treatment.

The dehumanizing quality of behaviour therapy

Stolz *et al.* (*op. cit.*) reflect that some mental health professionals criticize behaviour therapy on the grounds that its underlying assumptions tend to dehumanize man. It has been said that a therapist is a humanist to an extent inversely proportional to his professing to know what is good for man *in general*, and actively attempting to help the client achieve this imposed aim. The relative modesty of the behaviour therapist's technology which depend upon cooperation for its highly specific treatment adjectives—most often the implicitly stated complaints by the client—scarcely fit him for the role of anti-humanist. Tharp and Wetzel (1969) note that, far from assuming an authoritative posture and considering the art of therapy as a secret cult, behaviour therapy is more willing to rally the support of non-professionals like parents, housewives and others, to participate in the treatment programmes—an essentially humanizing role.

The recent recognition of the client's essentially human qualities of thinking and reasoning by behaviour therapists—in their embrace of the cognitive—has undermined the once potent criticism that clients were perceived as anthropomorphized rats. The basic model expounded by Erwin (1978, p. 222) is that the practice of behaviour therapy does rest on moral foundations; it is right (permissible or obligatory) to help people who request help. The principle is fundamental to many therapists because they are aware of the suffering and despair of persons who receive no treatment or whose treatment has failed. What is wrong with the basic model according to Erwin is the idea that a more complex foundation for the practice of behaviour therapy is not required. He offers a list of principles (p. 222).

Conclusions

Behaviour therapy is not a system of ethics (Bandura, 1969, p. 87); whether or not its techniques are morally neutral, its application must give rise to acute moral questioning, especially when institutionalized delinquent and mentally ill persons or children constitute the clientele, or when problems like the so-called sexual deviations, are involved.

Principles are needed to cover the cases where clients do not comprehend the nature of a treatment and are not clear about what they want or need (if anything) in the way of help. Principles are required to cover cases where the therapy is painful (and pointing to the good that comes from dentistry does not absolve us from this concern). They are needed too, to cover the reversal experimental design where a deliberate effort is made, after an improvement, to return the client to 'square one', i.e. to reverse the effects (temporarily) of the treatment.

References

Abramson, L., Seligman, M., and Teasdale, J. (1978). Learned helplessness in humans. *Journal of Abnormal Psychology*, **87**, 49–74.
Albino, R. (1980). *Psychotherapy: is it more than persuasion and teaching?* Paper presented at the South African Society of Clinical Psychologists Conference—Durban, July 1980 (22 pages).
Bandura, A. (1969). *Principles of Behaviour Modification*. N. Y., Holt, Rinehart & Winston.
Bandura, A. (1977a). *Social Learning Theory*. Englewood Cliffs, N. J.: Prentice-Hall.
Bandura, A. (1977b). Self-efficacy: toward a unifying theory of behavioural change. *Psychological Review*, **84** (2), 191–215.
Bandura, A. (1978). Perceived self-efficacy. In S. Rachman (Ed.) *Perceived Self-Efficacy. Advances in Behaviour Research and Therapy*, **1** (4).
Barlow, D. H., Leitenberg, H., Agras, W. S., and Wincze, J. P. (1969). The transfer gap in systematic desensitization: an analogue study. *Behaviour Research and Therapy*, **7**, 191–196.
Beck, A. T. (1976). *Cognitive Therapy and the Emotional Disorders*. N. Y.: International Universities Press.
Beck, A. T., Rush, A. J., Shaw, B. F., and Emery, G. (1979). *Cognitive Therapy of Depression*, N. Y.: John Wiley.
Beech, H. R. (1981). Creating change. In M. Herbert (ed.) *Psychology for Social Workers*. London: MacMillan and British Psychological Society.

Breger, L., and McGaugh, J. L. (1965). A critique and reformulation of 'learning theory' approaches to psychotherapy and neuroses. *Psychological Bulletin*, **63**, 335–358.

Carr, A. T. (1974). Compulsive neuroses: A review of the literature. *Psychological Bulletin*, **81**, 311–318.

Cautela, J. R. (1971). *Covert modelling*. Paper presented at the fifth annual meeting of the Association of the Advancement of Behaviour Therapy, Washington D. C., September, 1971.

Chomsky, N. (1971). The case against B. F. Skinner. In *For Reasons of State*. N. Y.: Random House.

Davison, G., and Wilson, G. T. (1972). Critique of 'desensitization': social and cognitive factors underlying the effectiveness of Wolpe's procedure. *Psychological Bulletin*, **78**, 28–31.

Davison, G., and Wilson, G. T. (1973). Processes of fear-reduction in systematic desensitization: cognitive and social reinforcement factors in humans. *Behaviour Therapy*, **4**, 1–21.

D'Zurilla, T. J., and Goldfried, M. R. (1971). Problem solving and behaviour modification. *Journal of Abnormal Psychology*, **78**, 107–127.

Ellis, A. (Ed.) (1971). *Growth Through Reason*. Palo Alto, Calif: Science and Behaviour Books.

Erwin, E. (1978). *Behaviour Therapy: Scientific, Philosophical, and Moral Foundations*. Cambridge: Cambridge University Press.

Estes. W. K. (1971). Reward in human learning: theoretical issues and strategic choice points. In R. Glaser (Ed.) *The Nature of Reinforcement*. N. Y.: Academic Press.

Eyberg, S. M., and Johnson, S. M. (1974). Multiple assessment of behaviour modification with families: effects of contemporary contracting and order of treated problems. *Journal of Consulting and Clinical Psychology*, **42**, 594–606.

Farrell, B. A. (1970). Psychoanalysis: the method. In S. G. Lee and M. Herbert (Eds.) *Freud and Psychology*. Harmondsworth, Penguin, 53–62.

Foa, E. B., and Goldstein, A. (1978). Continuous exposure and complete response prevention in the treatment of obsessive-compulsive neuroses. *Behaviour Therapy*, **9**, 821–829.

Foa, E. B., and Tillmans, A. (1980). The treatment of obsessive-compulsive neuroses. In A Goldstein and E. B. Foa (Eds.) *Handbook of Behavioural Interventions: A Clinical Guide*. N. Y.: John Wiley, 416–500.

Gambrill, E. (1977). *Behaviour Modification: Handbook of Assessment, Intervention and Evaluation*. San Francisco: Jossey-Bass.

Gaupp, L. A., Stern, R. M., and Galbraith, G. C. (1972). False heartrate feedback and reciprocal inhibition by aversion relief in the treatment of snake avoidance behaviour. *Behaviour Therapy*, **3**, 7–20.

Gelder, M., Bancroft, J., Gath, D., Johnston, D., Mathews, A., and Shaw, P. (1973). Specific and non-specific factors in behaviour therapy. *British Journal of Psychiatry*, **123**, 445–462.

Goldfried, M. R. (1971). Systematic desensitization as training in self-control. *Journal of Consulting and Clinical Psychology*, **37**, 228–234.

Goldfried, M. R., and Goldfried, A. P. (1975). Cognitive change methods. In E. H. Kanfer and A. P. Goldstein (Eds.) *Helping People Change*. N. Y. Pergamon Press.

Goldfried, M. R., and Davison, G. C. (1976). *Clinical Behaviour Therapy*. London: Holt, Rinehart and Winston.

Goldstein, A. P., Sherman, M., Gershaw, N. J., Sprafkin, R. P., and Glock, B. (1978). Training Aggressive Adolescents in Pro-social Behaviour. *Journal of Youth and Adolescence*, **7**, 73–92.

Grossberg, J. M. (1981). Comments about cognitive therapy and behaviour therapy. *Journal of Behaviour Therapy and Experimental Psychiatry*, **12** (1) 25–33.

Griffen, M., and Hudson, A. (1978). *Parents as Therapists: The Behavioural Approach.* P. I. T. Press. Victoria, Australia.

Hatzenbuehler, L. C., and Schroeder, R (1978). Desensitization procedures in the treatment of childhood disorders. *Psychological Bulletin*, **85**, (No. 4) 831–844.

Herbert, M. (1978). *Conduct Disorders of Childhood and Adolescence: A Behavioural Approach to Assessment and Treatment.* Chichester, John Wiley.

Herbert, M. (1981). *Behavioural Treatment of Problem Children: A Practice Manual.* London: Academic Press; N. Y.: Grune and Stratton.

Herbert, M., and Iwaniec, D. (1981). Behavioural psychotherapy in natural homesettings: an empirical study applied to conduct disordered and incontinent children. *Behavioural Psychotherapy*, **9**, 55–76.

Herbert, M. (1982). Conduct Disorders. In B. Lahey and A. E. Kazdin (Ed.) *Advances in Child Clinical Psychology.* Vol. 5. N. Y.: Plenum Press.

Hill, P., Murray, R., and Thorley, A. (1979). *Essentials of Postgraduate Psychiatry.* London: Academic Press.

Hodgson, R., Rachman, S., and Marks, I. M. (1972). The treatment of chronic obsessive-compulsive neuroses: follow-up and further findings. *Behaviour Research and Therapy*, **10**, 181–189.

Hodgson, R., and Rachman, S. (1974). Desynchrony in measures of fear. *Behaviour Research and Therapy*, **12**, 319–326.

Jahoda, M. (1958). *Current Concepts of Positive Mental Health.* N. Y.: Basic Books.

Kazdin, A. E. (1973). Covert modelling and the reduction of avoidance behaviour. *Journal of Abnormal Psychology*, **81**, 87–95.

Kazdin, A. E. (1978). *History of Behaviour Modification: Experimental Foundations of Contemporary Research.* Baltimore: University Park Press.

Kazdin, A. E., and Wilson, G. T. (1978). *Evaluation of Behaviour Therapy: Issues, Evidence and Research Strategies.* Cambridge, Mass: Ballinger.

Kelly, G. A. (1955). *The Psychology of Personal Constructs.* Norton: New York.

Kendall, P. C. (1981). Cognitive-behavioural interventions with children. In B. Lahey and A. E. Kazdin (Eds.) *Advances in Child Clinical Psychology*, Vol. 4. N. Y.: Plenum Press.

Lang, P. J. (1968). Fear reduction and fear behaviour: Problems in treating a construct. In J. M. Shlien (Ed.) *Research in Psychotherapy*, Vol. 3. Washington D. C.: American Psychological Association.

Levis, D. J., and Hare, N. (1977). A review of the theoretical rationale and empirical support for the extinction approach of implosive (flooding) therapy. In M. Hersen, R. M. Eisler, and P. M. Miller (Eds.) *Progress in Behaviour Modification*, N. Y.: Academic Press.

Lewinsohn, P. M., Biglan, A., and Zeiss, A. M. (1976). Behavioural treatment of depression. In P. O. Davidson (Ed.) *The Behavioural Management of Anxiety, Depression and Pain.* N. Y.: Brunner/Mazel, 91–146.

Lewis, W. C. (1972). *Why People Change: The Psychology of Influence.* London; Rinehart and Winston.

Lick, J. R., and Bootzin, R. R. (1975). Expectancy factors in the treatment of fear: methodological and theoretical issues. *Psychological Bulletin*, **82**. 917–931.

Lipsedge, M. S. (1973). Systematic desensitization in phobic disorders. *British Journal of Hospital Medicine*, **9**, 657–664.

Mahoney, M. J., and Arnkoff, D. B. (1978). Cognitive and self-control therapies. In S. L. Garfield and A. E. Bergin (Eds.) *Handbook of Psychotherapy and Behaviour Change* (2nd Ed.) Chichester: John Wiley. 689–722.

Marks, I. M., Boulougouris, J., and Marset, P. (1971). Flooding versus desensitization in the treatment of phobic patients: a crossover study. *British Journal of Psychiatry*, 119, 353–375.

Marks, I. M. (1975). Behavioural treatment of phobic and obsessive-compulsive disorders: A critical appraisal. In M. Hersen, R. M. Eisler, and P. M. Miller (Eds.) *Progress in Behaviour Modification* (Vol. 1). N. Y.: Academic Press.

Mathews, A. (1978). Fear-reduction research and clinical phobias. *Psychological Bulletin*, 85 (2) 390–404.

Meichenbaum, D. H. (1972). Cognitive modification of test anxious college students. *Journal of Consulting Clinical Psychology*, 39, 370–380.

Meichenbaum, D. (1977). *Cognitive-Behaviour Modification: An Integrative Approach*. London: Plenum Press.

Meichenbaum, D. (1977). *Cognitive Behaviour Modification*. N. Y.: Plenum Press.

Meyer, V., Levy, R., and Schnurer, A. (1974). The behavioural treatment of obsessive-compulsive disorders. In H. R. Beech (Ed.) *Obsessional States*. London: Methuen.

Meyer, V. (1975). The impact of research on the clinical application of behaviour therapy. In T. Thompson and W. S. Dockens (Eds.) *Applications of Behaviour Modification*. N. Y.: Academic Press, 11–14.

Mischel, W. (1968). *Personality and Assessment*. N. Y.: John Wiley.

Mowrer, O. H. (1960). *Learning Theory and Behaviour*. N. Y.: John Wiley.

Murray, E., and Jacobson, L. (1971). The nature of learning in traditional and behavioural psychotherapy. In A. Bergin and S. Garfield (Eds.) *Handbook of Psychotherapy and Behaviour Change: An Empirical Analysis*. N. Y.: John Wiley.

Nau, S. D., Caputo, J. A., and Borkovec, T. D. (1974). The relationship between credibility of therapy and simulated therapeutic effects. *Journal of Behaviour Therapy and Experimental Psychiatry*, 5, 129–133.

O'Leary, K. D., and Wilson, G. T. (1975). *Behaviour Therapy: Application and Outcome*. Englewood Cliffs, N. J., Prentice-Hall.

Patterson, G. R., Reid, J. B., Jones, J. J., and Conger, R. E. (1975). *A Social Learning Approach to Family Intervention: Vol. 1. Families with Aggressive Children*. Eugene, Castalix Publishing Co.

Paul, G. L. (1966). *Insight Versus Desensitization in Psychotherapy*. Stanford, Calif., Stanford University Press.

Paul, G. L. (1969). Outcome of systematic desensitization II. In C. M. Franks (Ed.) *Behaviour Therapy: Appraisal and Status*. N. Y.: McGraw-Hill.

Pervin, L. A. (1970). *Personality Theory: Assessment Research*. N. Y.: John Wiley.

Phillips, L. W. (1981). Roots and branches of behavioural and cognitive practice. *Journal of Behaviour Therapy and Experimental Psychiatry*, 12 (1), 5–17.

Rachman, S. and Teasdale, J. (1969). *Aversion Therapy and Behaviour Disorders*. Coral Gables, Fl: University of Miami Press.

Rachman, S., Hodgson, R., and Marks, I. M. (1971). Treatment of chronic obsessive-compulsive neuroses. *Behaviour Research and Therapy*, 9, 231–247.

Rachman, S., Marks, I. M., and Hodgson, R. (1973). The treatment of obsessive-compulsive neurotics by modelling and flooding *in vivo*. *Behaviour Research and Therapy*, 11, 463–471.

Rachman, S., and Hodgson, R. (1974). Synchrony and desynchrony in fear and avoidance. *Behaviour Research and Therapy*, 12, 311–318.

Rachman, S. (1978). *Fear and Courage*. San Francisco, Freeman.

Rachman, S., and Wilson, G. (1980). *The Psychological Effects of Therapy*. Oxford: Pergamon Press.

Rachman, S. (1981). The primacy of affect: some theoretical implications. *Behaviour Research and Therapy*, 19, 279–290.

Repucci, N. D., and Saunders, J. T. (1974). Social psychology of behaviour modification: problems of implementation in natural settings. *American Psychologist*, **29**, 649–660.

Rimm, D. C., and Masters, J. C. (1979). *Behaviour Therapy: Techniques and Empirical Findings*. N. Y.: Academic Press.

Rosen, G. M., Rosen, E., and Reid, J. B. (1972). Cognitive desensitization and avoidance behaviour: a reevaluation. *Journal of Abnormal Psychology*, **80**, 176–182.

Rycroft, C. (1970). Causes and meaning. In S. G. Lee and M. Herbert (Eds.) *Freud and Psychology*. Harmondsworth, Penguin, 323–335.

Seligman, M. (1975). *Helplessness*. San Francisco; Freeman.

Stolz, S. B., Wienckowski, L. A., and Brown, B. S. (1975). Behaviour modification; a perspective on critical issues. *American Psychologist*, November 1975, 1027.

Tharp, R. G., and Wetzel, R. J. (1969). *Behaviour Modification in the Natural Environment*. N. Y.: Academic Press.

Tryon, W. W. (1981). A methodological critique of Bandura's self-efficacy theory of behaviour change. *Journal of Behaviour Therapy and Experimental Psychiatry*, **12**, 113–114.

Ullmann, L. P. (1981). Cognitions: help or hindrance? *Journal of Behaviour Therapy and Experimental Psychiatry*, **12** (1), 19–23.

Urbain, E. S., and Kendall, P. C. (1980). Review of social-cognitive problem-solving interventions with children. *Psychological Bulletin*, **88** (No. 1), 109–143.

Walker, C. E., Hedberg, A., Clement, P. W., and Wright, L. (1981). *Clinical Procedures for Behaviour Therapy*. N. J., Engewood Cliffs, Prentice-Hall.

Watson, J. P., Gaind, R., and Marks, I. M. (1971). Prolonged exposure: a rapid treatment for phobias. *British Medical Journal*, **1**, 13–15.

Wilson, G. T., and Davison, G. O. (1971). Processes of fear reduction in systematic desensitization: Animal studies. *Psychological Bulletin*, **76**, 1–14.

Wolpe, J. (1958). *Psychotherapy by Reciprocal Inhibition*. Stanford, Calif., Stanford University Press.

Wolpe, J. (1976). Behaviour therapy and its malcontents. 1. Denial of its bases and psychodynamics fusionism. *Journal of Behaviour Therapy and Experimental Psychiatry*, **7**, 1–5.

Zajonc, R. (1980). Feeling and thinking. *American Psychologist*, **35**, 151–175.

Mental Illness: Changes and Trends
Edited by Philip Bean
© 1983 John Wiley & Sons Ltd.

CHAPTER 13

Psychogeriatrics as a speciality

FELIX POST
Consultant Psychiatrist Bethlem Royal and
Maudsley Hospitals (retired)

Some demographic facts

One of the many unprecedented developments in the history of mankind during the present century has been the absolute and relative increase of the elderly. This has been most marked in the case of developed nations of the West, but a similar trend is beginning to show itself in the rest of the world.

In England and Wales out of a total population of 32.5 million only 1.5 million (4.7 per cent) were in 1901 aged 65 and over. By 1974, with a population of 49.2 million the proportion of the elderly had risen to 13.9 per cent (6.9 million). Furthermore, the proportion of very old people (aged 75 and over) had increased from 1.4 to 4.9 per cent (Arie and Isaacs, 1978). Until recently, the increase in the number of old people had been due to two factors: improved living standards as well as advances in medicine, and at the same time progressive reduction in family size. Large families had, however, still been the fashion in the early part of our century, but in contrast to all previous human experience more and more children survived into later adult life. Furthermore, the proportion of the elderly in Western populations rose on account of a concomitant relative decline of the younger age groups due to shrinking family size. Further expectation of life after the age of 65 until recently increased only slightly in the case of women, and hardly at all for men.

However, more recent figures from the United States have shown that by 1980 there had been an increase of people aged 65 and over to 22.5 million from 20 million in 1970 (then 10 per cent of the total United States population). This has been regarded as almost certainly related to a recent decline in mortality rates among the elderly: persons currently reaching their 65th birthday will, on an average, live 16 more years (Redick and Taube, 1980). It looks as if advances in medical care during later adult life are beginning to contribute to a further increase of the proportion of the old in Western populations.

Redick and Taube also estimate that the American population over the age of 64 will increase to 27 million by 1985, and to 32 million by 2000. Moreover, the

279

population aged 75–85 as well as 85 and over will increase far more steeply than the population below the age of 65. In fact, the proportion of persons aged 65–74 will be decreasing (presumably because of the relative decline of the younger population beginning to make itself felt). In addition, there will be even more old women by 2000, a fall of the male to female ratio from 64 in 100 to 48 males in 100 females. Similarly, in the United Kingdom the number of persons aged 65–74 will between 1977 and 1991 drop from 6.8 to 6.4 million while that for the age group 75 and over will continue to increase from 2.9 to 3.6 million (Central Statistics Office, 1979).

Increase of the aged population and mental illness

During the coming twenty or thirty years the absolute and relative increase of the elderly will make increasing demands on social and health services. Psychogeriatrics has indeed become one of the key issues of mental illness, and not only because there will be increasing numbers of people at risk of suffering from psychiatric disorders; in addition, it has come to be realized that older people are much more liable to suffer mental breakdowns than younger ones. This was one of the new facts on mental disorders enumerated in a book with this title by Dayton (1940), which was based on admission statistics to American mental hospitals. For instance, in New York by 1940 annual admission rates rose from 106 per 100 000 of persons aged 20–24 to 202 per 100 000 of those aged 60–64, and to 506 per 100 000 aged 70 and over. As Aubrey Lewis (1946) pointed out in quoting these figures, this tremendous increase of first admissions with rising age was partly due to the fact that in the United States mentally infirm old people tended to be admitted to psychiatric hospitals, when in this country they would more often have found shelter in local authority institutions. All the same, Lewis was probably the first psychiatrist in this country to place the new problem before the members of the Royal Medico-Psychological Association at their 1945 annual meeting: 'I think it is pretty clear where all this leads. We must regard the mental disorders of the elderly as likely to be responsible within the next thirty years for the bulk of the patients admitted to mental hospitals'.

Incidence figures based on admissions to mental hospitals are only a rough guide towards the more important prevalence rates in the community, but an early study of admission rates in London had pointed to the disorder which was mainly responsible for the increased psychiatric morbidity in old age. Norris (1959) calculated as follows: In the course of their lives, out of every 1000 males, only 8 will be admitted for schizophrenia; 8 for manic-depressive, including involutional psychoses, but 21 for the psychoses of old age. The figures for females were rather higher: out of 1000, 10 schizophrenics, 14 affective psychotics, and 28 senile psychotics. Almost all schizophrenic and most affective psychoses lead to first admission before the age of 60. Norris' figures showed that these functional psychoses made up less than half the mental illnesses suffered by

population in a lifetime; rather more than half of mental illness experience was
ccounted for by what she labelled as senile psychosis and by this she meant the
ementias of old age.

Their predominance over psychiatric disorders among the elderly has been
onfirmed by prevalence studies carried out in the community. Their results have
een summarized recently by Kay and Bergmann (1980). Prevalence rates
mong community subjects over the age of 60 or 65 for functional psychoses are
iven as between 1 per cent and 4 per cent, and those for the neuroses, mainly
eurotic depressions, as between 5 per cent and 27 per cent, with most
ivestigators reporting between 9 per cent and 12 per cent. These rates for
inctional psychoses and for neurotic and personality disorders are very similar
) those found in surveys covering all age groups. By contrast, organic psychoses
re very rare below the age of 60, but in elderly community subjects the
revalence rate for disabling dementia has been given as between 4 per cent and
4 per cent, with the majority of investigators reporting between 5 per cent and 6
er cent. Beyond the age of 90 it rises to around 20 per cent. In addition, mild and
ubious dementia has been reported in from 5–15 per cent of community subjects
ver the age of 65.

While the increased mental morbidity among older people is largely due to the
icreasingly frequent occurrence of organic mental illnesses, there is also much
iorbidity arising from so-called functional psychiatric disorders, and these differ
i some important respects in type and response to treatment from those
icountered in earlier life.

he clinical psychiatry of old age

sychological symptoms and defects may be the consequence of disease or
ructural changes in the brain, and the resultant psychiatric illnesses are called
ie organic mental disorders: where these conditions are severely disruptive, we
)eak of organic psychoses. Psychopathology of varying degree of severity may
so occur in the absence of brain disease or deterioration detectable by present
ethods of investigation. It has been suggested that not the structure of the brain
affected, but only its functioning, resulting in 'functional' psychiatric disorders,
id these have been further subdivided into the severely disabling functional
iychoses and the relatively milder neuroses and personality disorders. During
ie nineteenth century it came to be generally assumed that the cerebral causes of
iese 'functional' disorders would be ultimately discovered, and that all mental
sease was brain disease. The end of the century saw confirmation of this
'ediction in a number of instances, most strikingly perhaps in the discovery of
philitic brain disease as the cause of general paralysis of the insane. These
evelopments were, however, overshadowed by the revolutionary claims of
orkers like Janet and Freud to the effect that functional psychiatric conditions
ere neither due to brain disease nor were caused by degenerations as a sequel of

hereditary 'tainting', but that they were of emotional origin. Personality was weakened or warped by deleterious childhood experiences, and under the impact of various life stresses, personality disorders, neuroses, or much more rarely functional psychoses later made their appearance. Freud himself remained a child of the materialistic nineteenth century, and seems to have entertained a lingering belief in the ultimate discovery of biochemical foundations for the functional psychoses as well as for the workings of the unconscious in its shaping of personality and neurosis. He would not have been surprised by the recent discovery of biochemical abnormalities in some functional psychoses. However for practical purposes the distinction between 'organic' and 'functional psychiatric conditions remains useful.

Organic mental disorders

During earlier life, most mental disturbances caused by cerebral pathology are transitory and fully recoverable. These are, as most common examples the delirious states accompanying severe infectious diseases in childhood and later Younger adults, also, may suffer deliria in relation to severe physical illnesses but the commonest acute confusional states in them are nowadays those suffered by drug-dependant and particularly by alcoholic subjects. Full recoveries are usually possible, but, especially in relation to alcohol abuse, permanent brain damage may result. The supervening chronic organic mental disorder is characterized specifically by a severe defect in memory functioning. Far rarer but even more tragic, are the destructions of intelligence and personality which sometimes follows on the delirium of various types of encephalitis or epilepsy Other causes of chronic and irreversible mental impairment are cerebral trauma (in peace-time mainly accidents on the road or at work), and, often unavoidably the surgical removal of tumours. Of even greater rarity are the so-called presenile dementias, Huntington's chorea, Alzheimer's disease, and Pick's disease, to enumerate the least uncommon ones.

The situation is quite different in the case of elderly and aged persons. The ageing brain is particularly sensitive to reduction of oxygen supply and to circulating toxins, and older people even more than children are prone to become confused and delirious in relation to the many diseases which are their lot. *Acute confusional states* are often produced by myocardial infarction, by urinary retention from prostate enlargement, by severe pneumonia, etc. An even more common cause of acute confusion in the elderly is injudicious medication or faulty self-dosage with correctly prescribed medicines. Physical illness associated with delirium carries a very high death rate in old age, but surviving patient usually gain their previous mental level.

In contrast to what obtains in the case of younger people, the elderly, and especially the very old (some 20 per cent of them) suffer from gradual but sever mental deterioration due to progressive brain disease. There are basically two types of this devastation: In *multi-infarct dementia* areas of brain are destroyed by the sudden deprivation of their blood supply, the clinical manifestation of which is a stroke. It used to be thought that this event was caused by a local narrowing of small of medium-sized arteries, hence the old name of arteriosclerotic dementia. More recently it has been recognized that impaired blood supply more commonly has its source in the narrowing of large blood vessels at the base of the skull or in the neck, often combined with impeded cardiac action. Now, a stroke is not infrequently experienced by older people. The majority may suffer a temporary paralysis, speech disturbance, or confusion, and yet make good and long-lasting recoveries. However, massive cerebral damage or a succession of not necessarily very severe strokes will lead not only to pareses, disturbance of speech, writing, reading, or the recognition and handling of objects, but also to progressive decline of intellectual and other personality functions amounting to dementia. The rising prevalence of dementia during real old age is mainly due to the other type of progressive mental decline: *senile dementia*. This develops gradually, often in people who are otherwise quite healthy. Occasional disorientation in unaccustomed surroundings, repetitiveness of talk, minor forgetfulness, restriction of interests and increased egocentricity are apt to be regarded by relatives as due to normal ageing (which in fact they never are). However, sooner or later more obvious defects make their appearance. The patient looks increasingly vacant and bewildered. His talk becomes rambling, incoherent, and ultimately incomprehensible. Before this has happened it will have become obvious that the old person has become anecdotal, concerned only with the past, and given to the repetition of a few statements. Even without specific questioning it may become clear that he has little knowledge of more recent events, and that he does not remember what had occurred on the previous day. He fails to recognize even familiar persons, forgets instructions, but usually remains capable of correct immediate repetitions of sentences or numbers. At this or at an earlier stage, the patient may have become pathologically irritable or suspicious, believing that belongings he had hidden have been stolen, that he is being cheated, or that his spouse is unfaithful. Physical illness or excessive medication may produce a superadded confusional state with impaired consciousness, panicky restlessness and aggression, as well as dreamlike illusions and hallucinations. This senile delirium may prove fatal. More often the condition progresses to exhaustion from aimless restlessness, helplessness from loss of the ability to dress and to feed himself. Urinary incontinence is often an early sign of dementia, preceded by excretion in inappropriate places from disorientation. However, finally lack of control of both micturition and defaecation supervene, the patient becomes bedfast, and falls victim to bed sores and a terminal pneumonia.

There are probably two different types of senile dementia: one, starting somewhat earlier in old age with rapid dilapidation of speech and disabilities arising from more localized cerebral deterioration of areas governing motor functions, speech, and the recognition of objects. These patients tend to die within a few years of onset. With a later onset, senile dementia tends to be largely characterized by progressive memory failure alone. This leads to deterioration, and loss of self-care, but at the same time what has been called the social façade of the patient remains intact. He continues to be able to engage in superficial conversations, behaves like a lady or gentleman, and may be cheerful. In this way the casual visitor, and that unfortunately sometimes includes the family doctor, may doubt the family's complaint of unmanageable restlessness, decline of self-care, irascibility, and other unpleasant character changes. Patients of this kind tend to go on vegetating over long periods, for anything between 5 and 15 years after the first appearance of memory defects.

Regardless of type, senile dements and multi-infarct dements reach the same distressing terminal stage, though on account of the associated neurological defects, especially hemiplegia and other pareses, multi-infarct dements are more likely to be in geriatric, and senile dements in psychiatric care. It is estimated, however, that four out of five old age dements remain in the care of their families, and are admitted to hospital only shortly before death, if at all.

Functional mental disorders

Very little work has been done on the *neuroses* of elderly persons as they tend to remain untreated even more frequently than in the case of younger people. Almost half of the subjects of all ages in the populations surveyed have been found to exhibit mild and occasional morbid fears, states of anxiety or mild depression, as well as hysterical or obsessional episodes. The elderly are no exception, but neurotic disorders of a disabling kind were thought to be present in only 18 per cent of a community sample. In only 11 per cent the neurosis had started after the age of 65.

There were important differences between early-onset and old-age neuroses. Persons who had been chronically or episodically neurotic for most of their lives continued in old age to suffer from the same variety of phobic, anxiety, obsessive-compulsive, and hysterical conditions. By contrast, almost the only neurotic disabilities diagnosed for the first time in late life were anxiety states and, much more commonly, neurotic depressions. Late onset neurotics, unlike life-long neurotics had not exhibited neurotic symptoms as children and had not had disturbed relationships with their parents. Hypochondriacal fears (unreasonable health concerns) are the commonest symptom of all elderly neurotics, but, while life-long neurotics were often quite healthy during old age, many late onset neurotics had in reality poor health, with a higher death rate than normal old people. In fact, their neurotic symptoms might well have been precipitated by poor health, especially cardiovascular disease. Their social and financial status tended to be inferior to that of the life-long elderly neurotics, and ineffectual household over-activity with domestic neglect were more frequent in their case.

Finally, they more often gave an impression of mental senility, which was not confirmed to be progressive on follow-up (Bergmann 1971, 1978).

Very little is known about the fate of persons with *personality and psychopathic disorders* in later life. There is a strong impression that the extra-punitive types, often associated with delinquency, improve as the subjects age, while inadequate personalities become even more dependent. Some paranoid personalities may end up as senile recluses.

Turning to the more serious mental illnesses, *depressions* range from neurotic severity to psychoses, with dangerous and disabling mood disorders and associated delusional ideas. Descriptively, they hardly differ from the depressions of younger people; only hypochondriacal symptoms are once again more frequently encountered. In the past, when only the most severe mental illnesses were admitted to mental institutions, it was widely held that the senile melancholias were especially profound because they were characterized by bizarre delusions of guilt, of bowel stoppage, of emptiness of abdomen or head due to an imagined disappearance of organs from atrophy, rotting, etc. Patients thus affected only occasionally recovered with the only treatments then available: nursing care and prevention of death from starvation, physical illness, or suicide. It was recognized, however, that severe depressions in old age were not forms of senile dementia. Nowadays almost all more seriously ill elderly depressives sooner or later come under psychiatric care; in fact, they form the great majority of psychiatric patients seen below the age of 75, before the increasing incidence of dementing illnesses makes itself felt. It has become apparent that even in late life severe melancholia is relatively rare; most patients are only mildly deluded with self-reproach and self-belittlement. They have hypochondriacal fears rather than unshakeable false beliefs, and unpleasant physical sensations in the abdomen are their main symptoms. They are also anxious, restless, and importuning in their complaints. Many of them respond well to modern drug therapies under the care of their family doctors. However, some even of these moderately ill persons have to be referred to psychiatrists on account of poor response and of the strain they impose on their families.

In most younger patients, depressions occur only at widely spaced intervals, and there is some evidence that they become less disrupting as the patients grow older. However, most depressions requiring in-patient treatment first start only between the ages of 55 and 65. These tend to recur much more frequently, and this is even more strikingly the case in late life affective psychoses with elated moods and over-activity. *Manic illnesses* are not as rare in old age as used to be thought: they are moreover, in the elderly always associated sooner or later with depressive attacks (for details, see Post, 1978).

In the elderly, *suicide* is strongly related to depressive illness. In countries for which statistics are available only 10–15 per cent of inhabitants are over the age of 65, but 25–30 per cent of all suicides occur beyond that age. In fact, suicide rates increase steadily with rising age, and in the case of men do not even tail off at the highest ages. By contrast, attempted suicide is relatively rare in the elderly, only 5 per cent of parasuicides at all ages. Younger people commit self-injury (and much more rarely succeed in suicide) most often in settings of life stress of relatively trivial kinds rather than in the course of depressive illnesses. Most older people are driven to suicidal acts in depressions, of which in many cases their doctors had been or should have been aware (for details, see Shulman, 1978).

Paranoid psychoses are the only functional mental illnesses which are almost only encountered in later life. Persecutory ideas or systems of persecutory beliefs are hardly ever observed in children or younger adults, but the older we get the more suspicious we tend to become! The paranoid form of schizophrenia is of relatively late onset. Persecutory ideas are encountered in some manic-depressive illnesses of later adult life, and among the elderly the early stages of dementia may be accompanied by persecutory ideas. There is, however, a specifically old age form of paranoid psychosis which is not associated with depression or dementia, and which has been called *late paraphrenia*. It resembles the paraphrenic type of schizophrenia, which for a time had been singled out on account of persistent persecutory delusions and hallucinations in the absence of the disruption of other mental functions typical of paranoid schizophrenia. Most elderly paraphrenics suffer from very narrowly circumscribed symptoms: perhaps just the belief that people in the house create noises or smells to drive them out, or talk about them, or interfere with their belongings. On moving home symptoms may stop for long periods. These people are a trial to their neighbours, families, and often to the police. As a rule, admission to hospital only becomes ultimately necessary in the case of late paraphrenics, who suffer from more widespread delusions, and who are continually plagued by 'voices'. Unlike the first mentioned group of patients, they will sooner or later become unable to look after themselves, and are more likely to become abusive and aggressive. Most elderly paraphrenics have always been suspicious people, rarely ever happily married, and in many ways odd. An unduly high proportion suffer from longstanding deafness. The condition, therefore, is rare: only 10 per cent of admissions over 60 to mental hospitals have been reported as due to paraphrenia.

The special needs of elderly psychiatric patients

This brief descriptive sketch of the psychiatry of late life will have indicated the areas in which aged patients in comparison with younger ones are likely to have special needs. Most strikingly, the great majority of patients after the age of 75 require care and treatment for the severe disabilities caused by cerebral degenerative diseases, the organic mental illnesses. In addition, persons with ageing brains are unduly prone to develop in association with physical illnesses acute confusional episodes. However, these complications are largely dealt with by surgeons and by general as well as by geriatric physicians.

Dementias

Most multi-infarct and many senile dements also have serious physical defects and chronic physical illnesses as well as disabilities which require the skills and the facilities of geriatric physicians. Organic mental disorders were found to have been present, in addition to physical conditions under treatment, in 20.5 per cent of elderly patients in general medical wards and in 49.4 per cent of those in geriatric wards (Copeland and Gurland, 1978). Rather fewer dements (38.6 per cent) were in psychiatric in-patient facilities.

However, as mentioned earlier, only one in every five dements will be found in institutional rather than family care. It was also pointed out that after the age of 80 the proportion of dementing persons maintained in the community rises to 20 per cent of over 2 million, and of over 3 million in the near future. At the present time the vast majority of these severely handicapped persons and their caring relatives remain without benefit of psychiatry. Even without any advances in curative or ameliorating treatments, the hard lot of these patients and of their friends could be greatly improved. Given a sufficient number of psychogeriatricians, but more important of psychiatrically trained community nurses and social workers, every old person beginning to show signs of mental decline could and should be referred to the psychiatric services for assessment. Such a person would then become known to the psychogeriatric team at an early stage. In many cases no further action may be required at the time, but families would know where to turn as soon as difficulties arose. In most instances, it would not be difficult to find out that some help was needed. In cooperation with the family doctor, physical health might be improved. The burden of the family might be lightened by the provision of some domiciliary services or by arranging regular, not necessarily daily attendance of the old person at a day centre or hospital; short periods in hospital may afford relief. It is obvious that these are utopian proposals in the present, and, one fears in the near future, state of the economy. But without considerable expansion of psychogeriatrics, the present sequence of events will continue in the great majority of situations: months and years of increasing family suffering terminating in rejection of the patient by the family and demands for a so-called emergency admission. It has been shown that even under present circumstances well-led and marginally more adequately staffed psychogeriatric services can go quite a long way in responding to legitimate demands.

The expansion of psychogeriatric services will no longer be an utopian aim, if and when pharmacological means are discovered which probably may never cure established dementia, but which may well be able to arrest or retard its progress after early diagnosis. Increasing numbers will come under treatment, which will have to be continuous. Considerable research efforts will be needed to delimit various types of senile dementia, which are likely to respond differentially to the new therapies. Waste of resources will be avoided only by the careful monitoring of patients under treatment, and by other forms of operational research. Much of this research will be in the hands of clinicians rather than of pharmacological and other basic researchers.

Personality disorders and neuroses

As was demonstrated earlier, there are still considerable gaps in our knowledge of these conditions when they affect elderly persons in a disabling fashion. At the present time, family doctors rarely refer elderly people with these—relatively speaking—minor disorders to psychiatrists. No doubt this will change when it becomes increasingly realized that psychological treatments for these conditions can be just as effective as in the case of younger subjects.

However, first of all it should be pointed out that much effort expanded on trying to help unhappy old people is misdirected and wasteful of resources. For example, their loneliness is often a complaint which leads to referral to social workers. The meaning of loneliness needs, however, to be elucidated individually for each elderly person before instituting the appropriate measures. Family doctors, but perhaps more often geriatric physicians may be struck by the lonesome style of life of some of their patients; they may feel that this cannot be a good thing, and that something ought to be done, even though the patient does not complain of loneliness. Doctors and well meaning neighbours are not always aware of the fact that there are old people who have always been self-contained and often hostile towards and suspicious of other people, and that this attitude tends to increase in old age. So-called resocialization would be strongly resisted, and much more appropriate would be tactful supervision to ensure compliance with ongoing treatments and prevention of self-neglect, which may occur in some of these loners but not by any means the majority. Much more often, elderly patients voice the complaint of feeling lonely. This may be the realistic result of successive bereavements and the loss of all contemporaries from their circle. In this sad situation, befriending by social workers and by volunteers as well as persuasive direction towards clubs and other social amenities are certainly the correct measures. Rather more old people are lonely on account of physically caused immobility. In such a situation, more effective geriatrics should precede resocialization. Probably, many lonesome old people suffer from the milder kinds of neurotic depressions; these are often accompanied by domestic neglect. Doctors are apt to ask for domiciliary services when psychiatric treatment is indicated, and when social workers should be asked to concentrate their efforts not on the provision of services but on attempts at resocializing these clients. Bergmann (1971, 1978) (where more details on all this will be found) has pointed out that neurotically lonely old people tend to attract more domiciliary services than those with organic mental impairment who have far greater needs of them.

Quite apart from the useful results which can be achieved by pharmacological means in mild depressions, psychotherapists have begun to take an increasing interest in the neuroses of the elderly. Depending on the nature of the neurotic symptoms, treatments may be merely supportive, or rather more along psychodynamic (psychoanalytically oriented) lines, with the therapists being prepared to be actively directive, especially in crisis situations. (For a very useful discussion, see Kahana, 1979.) Finally, many old people suffer from morbid fears (phobias), especially of a kind that prevent them from leaving their homes or from their being left alone for a time by their caring friends. Behavioural therapies are in these circumstances just as effective as in younger subjects.

Functional psychoses

In older people severe depressions and paranoid illnesses respond even better to modern methods of treatment than do similar conditions of younger persons, but in the aged they may remain untreated for longer periods, even though the early recognition of serious depression is imperative for the prevention of suicidal acts. Every adequately trained psychiatrist is able to recognize and treat the functional psychoses of older people, but there are several reasons why psychogeriatric teams might be more effective:

Though usually hospital based, the psychogeriatrician and his co-workers are likely to have especially strong links with the community—with family doctors, social workers and voluntary auxiliaries, and he is thus in a especially good position to educate community workers in the early recognition of psychiatric breakdown in the elderly. That of dementing disorders is certainly desirable, but prompt ascertainment of depression may prove life-saving, and much general upset and suffering can be prevented by the early treatment of paranoid illnesses. On the basis of his experience, the psychogeriatrician tends to be more optimistic about old people than many general psychiatrists, and he will therefore often persevere longer when immediate results of therapy are disappointing. He should have more experience of the risks of drug treatments in the elderly, and less reluctance to use electroconvulsive treatments when indicated. Knowing that severely paranoid (late paraphrenic) patients will almost always remit with treatment, he will be less hesitant than colleagues without his specialized experience to advocate compulsory treatment which is often unavoidable with patients who from the very nature of their disorder lack realization of being ill and in need of treatment.

Additionally, but most importantly, while it is true that it is almost always possible to remove or greatly ameliorate the symptoms of affective and paraphrenic psychoses, in the case of the elderly there is a much greater and a much earlier tendency of severe recurrences. These conditions like almost all geriatric disorders are almost always continuity problems. The patients almost invariably need to be supervised for the rest of their lives by one or the other member of the psychogeriatric team. Only a quarter of hospital-treated depressives over 60 did not require further treatment (usually as out-patients) over a relatively short follow-up period of three years, and very few late paraphrenics fail to relapse within a few weeks or months after discontinuing maintenance drug therapy (Post, 1978). The long-term treatment with the currently used major tranquillizers is fraught with problems, and so is the use of lithium preparations, which are so effective in preventing serious and frequent recurrences, not only of mania but also of depression. The risks entailed in the use of these valuable therapeutic agents are obviously more likely to be avoided by psychiatrists with continuous experience with them in aged persons.

Some specific psychogeriatric skills

Hemsi (in press) has set out recently the numerous and highly important practical skills which successful psychogeriatric practice requires.

Almost everywhere in the Western world, old people and their families rely for medical care on publicly or insurance financed medical treatment. This tends to be hospital based, but with an even greater emphasis than in the case of adults, and even of child psychiatry, hospital services for elderly patients have to be community centred. Disability arising in them from mental disorders is mitigated by the network of support given by their families, neighbours, and to a far smaller extent by statutory and voluntary social services. It is almost always ill-advised to tear an elderly patient out of his social network for purposes of assessment and further investigations. Hospital admission may be unavoidable on account of the severity of the illness or of the absence or weakness of this network, but it should be arranged only after most careful thought. Attendance at an out-patient clinic or at a private consulting room, obviously does not entail any disruption of the patient's social support system, but it does require the use of transport. Insightful and only mildly ill elderly psychiatric subjects are in fact able to utilize private consulting and public out-patient services; but my own clinic for patients over 60 years of age was the only one in the whole hospital which did not have a waiting list, because mildly demented or neurotically depressed old people are rarely referred by their family doctors to psychiatrists. More seriously disordered patients could obviously be brought in for consultation by their relatives by public transport, by car, or ambulance. In fact, this is what happens in most countries where geriatric psychiatry has been developed. In the United Kingdom, the great majority of psychogeriatricians prefer to assess their patients personally in their own homes. They believe that the additional amount of time expended is more than balanced by the advantages gained from a domiciliary consultation. The patient is seen as he is functioning in his own customary environment, and his caring 'significant others' can either be interviewed at the same time, or at any rate preliminary contact with them can be established. This is not the place to argue for and against the merits or domiciliary consultations, but their popularity with many psychogeriatricians highlights what distinguishes them from other psychiatrists. While in the case of severely depressed, manic, paranoid, or demented old persons the verbal and non-verbal aspects of a therapeutic doctor–patient relationship are hardly ever lost, of far greater practical importance (even more so perhaps than in child psychiatry), are the assessment and therapeutic use of the patient's emotional and socially supportive relationships. The psychogeriatrician is the social psychiatrist *par excellence*, and even more than his generalist colleagues he has to learn how to utilize on his patients' behalf community resources. If he is wise, he will not attempt to work single-handed, but will seek assistance from his juniors, from family doctors, community nurses, social workers, and occupational therapists. All these members of his team should spend most of their time in patients' homes and not round the conference table, except for purposes of training and case discussions when there are especially difficult problems. One of the essential qualities of all the workers in a psychogeriatric service should be a flexible sharing of responsibilities and a willingness to step across interprofessional boundaries, even though the overall responsibility should almost certainly remain in the hands of the consultant psychogeriatrician, i.e. the senior doctor. He carries and additional burden which arises from the scarcity of resources: it is his painful task to allocate priorities, and see to it that the efforts of his colleagues are not directed towards achieving idealistic aims, which can so easily lead towards unintentional neglect of the needs of many equally disabled patients and their families.

The present status of psychogeriatrics as a specialism

In this chapter the special psychiatric needs of older people have been documented, and the specialized expertise embodied in psychogeriatrics has been demonstrated. In this final section, an attempt will be made to set out the present status of this speciality and with an eye to the future.

Birren and Renner (1980) have conservatively estimated that in the United States 10 per cent of the elderly will need help from psychiatric services at some stage. Assuming that each patient needed six hours of psychiatrist's time each year, this would by 1985 require 10 664 psychiatrists of the elderly. In fact, in 1975 there were thought to be only 20 psychiatrists in the entire United States regarded as experts in geriatric psychiatry! Considering the number of psychogeriatric associations and journals which have recently sprung up in North America, this figure would seem to be a serious under estimate for 1980.

For the situation in the United Kingdom during the year 1979/80 figures have been made available through a questionnaire survey by Wattis *et al.* (1981): At the beginning of the 1970s there were only some twelve psychogeriatricians running less than half a dozen special district services for mentally ill old people. By the time of their survey, Wattis *et al.* estimated that there were at least 120 consultant psychiatrists with a special commitment to the elderly, and they identified 87 health districts with specialized psychogeriatric services. Professor

Arie kindly informed me that the total number of health districts in the United Kingdom is 221, and there is thus still a considerable shortfall, most services being at the present time concentrated in Scotland and south-east England. Of the psychiatrists claiming to have special commitments towards elderly patients some 41 per cent worked as psychogeriatricians either full time or, when they also engaged in some private practice, during all of their health service sessions: 27 per cent worked with elderly cases at least half time, and the remaining 32 per cent gave only a few sessions to this specialized work. Most part-time psychogeriatricians also engaged in general adult psychiatry. They were in fact general psychiatrists with a special interest in the aged. Overall, some 68 per cent of these doctors professing psychogeriatric interest gave from half to all of their time to this specialized work. Wattis *et al.* report gives many more details, on junior medical staff, community nurses, social workers, physiotherapists, speech therapists, and occupational therapists. Training these professional people was one of the main tasks of psychogeriatricians, in which most were found to be fully engaged: 40 per cent had substantive or honorary academic appointments, and in the training programme of general psychiatrists in Britain psychogeriatrics had become a mandatory subject.

The present status of psychogeriatrics is clearly unsatisfactory: We recall that in the United Kingdom there were by 1974 some 2·5 million persons over the age of 75 (Arie and Isaacs, 1978), and that towards the end of the century this number may well rise to 3.6 million (Central Statistics Office, 1979). At a conservative estimate, 10–15 per cent of them will be suffering from mental disorders requiring medical attention, i.e. there are at the present time at least 250 000 potential patients over the age of 65 and only some 120 psychiatrists with special expertise in their illnesses. Some 360 000 patients may need psychogeriatric assessment, treatment and care in the future. Possibly, by now the situation in North America may be similar, but from personal knowledge in Northern, Central, and Western Europe, in South America and in the Soviet Union there are only very small groups of devoted psychiatrists struggling with the special needs of the elderly, and in research rather than in service settings.

One of the key issues of mental illness not treated in this volume, probably because it is shared by medicine and health care in general, is that demands are always likely to outgrow facilities. Obviously, these are unlikely to be increased in the present state of the economy. In the United Kingdom, at any rate, we shall be fortunate if during the next few years we can continue to mark time, and do not go into a prolonged, and disastrous decline, which will hit the aged population even more than the rest. Let us assume, however, that in due course energy shortages can be overcome and that with a more fruitful inclusion of the Third World there will once again be rising prosperity. In this setting, increased automation of industrial processes is likely to create greater wealth, and this will be available to employ increasing numbers of redundant workers in administration, service, and care. This shift from productive to unproductive occupations (using these terms in a false and materialistic sense) has been going on in the West since the Industrial Revolution, and is likely to be accelerated if 'progress' continues.

Even if more money and more manpower became available for the care of the sick in body and mind, as well as of the physically and psychological handicapped, the future of psychogeriatrics as a discipline comprising doctors, nurses, social workers, and other care personnel might still be a difficult one. It has to be faced that the care of the elderly may always appeal to fewer persons than will be needed. Moreover, psychiatry is an unpopular subject to medical students and even more to young doctors, and beyond that, the psychiatry of late life has to most psychiatrists far less appeal than child psychiatry, dynamic or behavioural psychotherapy, treating marital problems, etc. Most of the preconceptions on which this unpopularity is based are faulty. Psychiatric disorders of younger people occur almost always in persons with inborn or early acquired personality weaknesses, and their long-term course is often disappointing. By contrast, many late life disorders occur in people who have led healthy and successful lives, and whose remaining years can be made lastingly more tolerable by timely psychiatric intervention. It is hoped that general psychiatrists will gradually come to realize this and will become increasingly eager to become involved with older persons. Unless they have had interest and opportunity of special training in one of the psychotherapies or in work with psychopaths and delinquents, they may in any case find an extension of their interest from the decreasing number of younger people with affective, schizophrenic, or paranoid conditions towards older patients a natural development. We should then see a reunion of general and geriatric psychiatry, with psychogeriatrics becoming a research discipline rather than a sub-speciality. Demographic trends should further this development, if with a stabilized low birthrate the proportion of the aged in the adult population will again become more manageable after AD 2000!

Some concluding thoughts

Returning to the present reality, it may seem pointless to ask whether psycho geriatrics should become an officially designated speciality. This status has been denied to geriatric medicine by the Royal College of Physicians, but one of the leaders of British geriatricians, Bernard Isaacs (1981) has subsequently put an opposing point of view and encouraged 'a separate development, because general physicians and geriatricians are like bookends; they come out of the same mould; they perform the same task; neither can manage without the other; but they face in opposite directions; and when they cease to do so what they are supporting falls down'.

It could be said that the situation in psychiatry is somewhat different. There is not the same subdivision as that of medicine into highly specialized subdivisions, each requiring training in different, often highly complex technical skills. By contrast, child and adolescent psychiatrists remain much concerned with the assessment and treatment of adults (parents and care personnel); adult psychiatrists will continue to care for quite a number of elderly patients with functional disorders as well as with illnesses in younger persons caused by cerebral disease or deterioration; finally, the functional conditions coming to the attention of psychogeriatricians do not, as we have seen, differ all that much from those treated by psychiatrists dealing with younger adults. True, there are specialized psychotherapists and behaviour therapists, but their skills are also much used by general psychiatrists for patients of all ages. Psychiatry is a relatively new, and one hopes, rapidly developing branch of medical science, and premature crystallization into subspecialities might be regretted.

There is in the writer's opinion only one set of circumstances which may make the establishment of psychogeriatrics as an officially recognized speciality desirable: these are (1) the need for a pressure group to advocate adequate funding and staffing, (2) the greater power of a professional body in championing the cause of the aged, and (3) the desirability of monitoring developments in the psychogeriatric services separately from the psychiatric services for younger adults.

References

Arie, T., and Isaacs, A.D. (1978). The development of psychiatric services for the elderly in Britain, in *Studies in Geriatric Psychiatry* (Eds. A. D. Isaacs, and F. Post), pp. 241–261, John Wiley and Sons, Chichester, New York, Brisbane, Toronto.

Bergmann, K. (1971). The neuroses in old age, in *Recent Developments in Psychogeriatrics'* (Eds. D. W. K. Kay, and A. Walk), pp. 39–50, *British Journal of Psychiatry*, Spec. Pub. No. 6.

Bergmann, K. (1978). Neurosis and personality disorder in old age, in *Studies in Geriatric Psychiatry* (Eds. A. D. Isaacs and F. Post), pp. 41 – 76, John Wiley and Sons, Chichester, New York, Brisbane, Toronto.

Birren, J. E., and Renner, V. J. (1980). Concept and issues of mental health and aging, in *Handbook of Mental Health and Aging* (Eds. J. E. Birren and R. B. Sloane), pp. 3–33, Prentice-Hall Inc., Englewood Cliffs, N. J.

Central Statistics Office (1979). *Social Trends*, No. 9. Chart 1.3, HMSO London.

Copeland, J. R. M., and Gurland, B. J. (1978) Evaluation of diagnostic measures: An international comparison, in *Studies in Geriatric Psychiatry* (Eds. A. D. Isaacs, and F. Post), pp. 189–209, John Wiley and Sons, Chichester, New York, Brisbane, Toronto.

Dayton, N. A. (1940). '*New Facts on Mental Disorder*' C. C. Thomas, Springfield, Illinois.

Hemsi, L. (in press). Psychogeriatric care in the community, in *The Psychiatry of Late Life* (Eds. R. Levy, and F. Post), Blackwell, Oxford.

Isaacs, B. (1981). Is geriatrics a specialty? In *Health Care of the Elderly* (Ed. T. Arie), pp. 224–235, Croom Helm, London.

Kahana, J. R. (1979). Strategies of dynamic psychotherapy with the wider range of older individuals, *Journal of Geriatric Psychiatry*, **12**, 71–100.

Kay, D. W. K., and Bergmann, K. (1980). Epidemiology of mental disorders among the aged in the community, in *Handbook of Mental Health and Aging* (Eds. J. E. Birren, and R. B. Sloane), pp. 34–56, Prentice-Hall Inc., Englewood Cliffs, N. J.

Lewis, A. (1946). Ageing and senility. A major problem of psychiatry, *Journal of Mental Science*, **92**, 150–170.

Norris, V. (1959). *Mental Illness in London*, Maudsley Monograph No. 6, Institute of Psychiatry, London.

Post, F. (1978). The functional psychoses, in *Studies in Geriatric Psychiatry* (Eds. A. D. Isaacs, and F. Post) pp. 77–94, John Wiley and Sons, Chichester, New York, Brisbane, Toronto.

Redick, R. W., and Taube, C. A. (1980) Demography and mental health care of the aged, in *Handbook of Mental Health and Aging* (Eds. J. E. Birren, and R. B. Sloane) pp. 57–71, Prentice-Hall Inc., Englewood Cliffs, N. J.

Shulman, K. (1978) Suicide and parasuicide in old age: A review, *Age and Ageing*, **7**, 201–209.

Wattis, J., Wattis, L., and Arie T. (1981). Psychogeriatrics: a national survey of a new branch of psychiatry, *British Medical Journal*, **32**, 1529–1533.

Mental Illness: Changes and Trends
Edited by Philip Bean
© 1983 John Wiley & Sons Ltd.

CHAPTER 14

Alcoholism

PHILIP McLEAN
*Consultant Psychiatrist, Mapperley
Hospital, Nottingham*

Alcohol is the most frequently used psychoactive substance. Its use is common in most cultures even those which are primitive. The only exception to this is Muslim societies where alcohol is forbidden on religious grounds. Alcohol is available in a variety of forms which differ considerably in strength, colour, taste, smell, viscosity, and many other characteristics whose description requires the use of an elaborate jargon. Indeed no drug was ever better packaged. It is used frequently for pleasure, relaxation, or as part of social or religious ritual. Its consciousness altering properties are well known and appreciated by many. The effects and after effects of excess use are also well known and an experience of both drunkenness and a hangover is often considered to be part of growing up into manhood although not, at present anyway, into womanhood. Yet the alcoholic role is perceived as a self-destructive one surrounded by tragedy involving the lives of many others. This is a reality and is becoming more readily appreciated. There is growing awareness in government, in the media, in the courts, in some industrial corporations, in the medical profession, and in the community at large of the dangers and cost to society of the consequences of alcohol abuse and of alcoholism.

The word 'alcoholic' is an emotive one. To many it seems to imply social dereliction and degeneracy—the stereotyped homeless, vagrant, unemployed, unemployable, unlovable, meths drinking denizen of decayed inner cities—the 'skid-row bum'. Alcoholism implies a total lack of control over drinking and has to some extent fallen into disrepute in the eyes of patients and sometimes in the eyes of their helpers because of such pejorative connotations. I shall use the term 'alcoholic' to imply drinkers who show significant dependence on, or addiction to, alcohol and 'problem drinker' to imply someone whose drinking is repeatedly causing problems of itself or by its long or short term consequences, but who is not seriously addicted. This division is not hard and fast but has some usefulness. Clearly all alcoholics are problem drinkers but not all problem drinkers are alcoholics although many may become so.

Some sources refer to an epidemic of alcoholism and there is a current increase in the incidence and prevalence of alcohol problems. The numbers admitted to mental hospitals in England and Wales with a primary diagnosis of alcoholism or alcoholic psychosis shows a steady rise from 439 in 1949 to 12,751 in 1975 (Royal College of Psychiatrists, 1979). A very large number are admitted to general hospitals with one or more of the many physical conditions related to alcohol use. The cost is enormous—the annual cost of hospital care alone is £4,000,000 (Royal College of Psychiatrists, 1979). The total cost of alcohol problems to the community is much greater, probably immeasurably so for the data needed to make such calculations are notoriously difficult to obtain accurately. An estimate of the total UK cost of alcohol problems is between £248 million and £650 million annually at 1977 prices (Holtermann and Birchell, 1981) equivalent to £1,000 million at 1981 prices. The greater part of this cost comes from loss of output at work. Such figures cannot convey the cost in terms of misery and hardship to the alcoholic or problem drinker or to his family and friends. Evidence points to an increase in all indices of this since the end of the Second World War. Most indices, which are accepted as marking alcohol problems and alcoholism, are reaching the levels of 100 years ago when increasing concern led to the establishment of the 'Temperance' movement. Consumption of alcohol is also increasing particularly amongst the younger age groups and there are disproportionate increases in consumption by women (Camberwell Council on Alcoholism, 1980). Recent estimates by senior government ministers (Office of Health Economics, 1981) that there may be 750,000 'alcoholics' in England and Wales may be unreliable because of methodological problems, but they are consistent in magnitude with earlier figures (e.g. 500,000, DHSS, 1976) and do indicate a problem of some size.

The development of concepts of alcoholism

Although Thomas Trotter in 1804 urged the medical profession to view the 'inebriate' as sick it took almost 150 years for his advice to be heeded. For many years the inebriate was viewed as sinful, criminal, or as an atavistic degenerate but rarely as sick and hence not an appropriate receiver of the benison of medical care. Doctors who were interested in the alcoholic were few and far between, and even though many recognized the diseases brought on by alcoholism and knew that alcohol consumption was a probable aetiology, it was rare for them to mention it to patients. If it was mentioned it was as a bland exhortation to 'lay off the hard stuff', or to 'cut it down a bit'. These exhortations would be received with a submissive apparent acceptance. Honour was satisfied, the doctor had done what he could and the patient, duly discharged cured, inevitably celebrated that fact by drinking exactly as before.

There was no real conception of alcoholism by the doctors as anything other than an eminently understandable over-indulgence. Then came the disease concept. This arose out of the philosophy of Alcoholics Anonymous—a self-help group started in 1935 by a stockbroker and a surgeon (AA World Services 1955). AA rapidly evolved a total philosophy of alcoholism leading to a successful mode of coping with it. This involved acknowledgment of the powerlessness of the individual over alcohol and the realization that total abstinence was the only way for alcoholics to handle alcohol without disaster. This seems to have arisen from the influential views of Dr Silkworth who, in 1937, hypothesized an 'allergic response' to alcohol from the alcoholic. The notion of self-help seemed to be successful as a means of arresting the alcoholism of AA members. Because of this it was assumed that the philosophy underlying AA must therefore have been correct. This is to say that it became accepted that the alcoholic was in some way different from other drinkers in his response to alcohol; that this was innate and could only be avoided by the avoidance of alcohol. It followed that the alcoholic was born, not made and hence suffered from an 'illness'. The medical profession having previously been indifferent to alcoholism were now confronted by the alcoholic with a disease, and everybody knows that doctors treat disease. The 'disease concept' of alcoholism was elegantly formulated by E. M. Jellinek (1960) who produced a classification of 'alcoholism' according to drinking patterns. Partly as a result of Jellinek's discussions with the Ministry of Health in the 1950's, it became apparent that in Britain there was a far more extensive alcoholic problem than was previously accepted, and the 1950s saw the establishment of special treatment units based in psychiatric hospitals. These special units tended to be based on the use of group therapy over a long period of in-patient treatment with disulfiram (Antabuse) and sometimes other drugs as adjuvants. Referral to AA usually contributed the only after-care and the emphasis was on finding out why the patient drank so that he could then become totally abstinent. It was an obvious mixture of AA philosophy and the psychoanalytically orientated group therapy then favoured for the neuroses, together with some medical expertise during the withdrawal or 'drying out' phase, and to some extent this traditional form of treatment persists to this day. The disease concept reigned supreme—alcoholics were ill and needed medical treatment. It was anomalous. The need for medical treatment occurred because of an illness (alcoholism) which had been divined by a group of sufferers (AA) who felt that the best way of overcoming it was by self-help (the 'twelve steps' and the 'fellowship' of AA). In spite of this medical interest helped awaken the public and the government to the problems associated with alcohol. It provided evidence that there was a significant problem which could be helped by appropriate intervention as shown for example by a two-year followup study (Davies et al., 1956). This study contradicted the prevailing medical opinion that alcoholism was virtually untreatable.

Whether or not such interventions are labelled as medical treatment or whether or not the condition being intervened in is a disease was largely irrelevant in practice whilst the goal of intervention was abstinence in accord with AA philosophy.

The notion that persons who repeatedly drink so much that they become ill (cirrhosis), irresponsible (drunkenness, criminal acts, etc.), and socially derelict (divorce, unemployment, etc.), do so because of some as yet unknown disease process has especial benefits to those persons. Society should not stigmatize them for their acts when drunk as 'they couldn't help it' because of a disease. They should not be held fully responsible for their acts and should be accorded at least some of the privileges which are conferred upon the sick. Furthermore, they should be treated by the medical and nursing professions. If a treatment which provided a cure for the disease was not available, then medical research should set about finding one which could then be applied to more and more individuals in more and more specialist units. These are some of the logical implications of a disease concept of alcoholism. There have been others which are not so logical. If alcoholism were a disease with some sort of physical basis, why should it be treated in psychiatric hospitals? Presumably because its manifestations are behavioural and mental and because these manifestations require psychiatric skills for their control. If alcoholism is a *mental* illness leading to physical complications why is there a need for special units for it—what is wrong with the institutions for the care of mental illness, i.e. psychiatric hospitals? Again presumably because alcoholism is different from mental illness, mainly because the patients, with very few exceptions, turn out not to be mentally ill when detoxified and sober. And most alcoholics insist on a distinction between the alcoholic and the general psychiatric patient—which is tacitly acknowledged by the creation of special units separate from the psychiatric hospital.

Many diverse hypotheses have been formulated to explain the 'disease'. Each tended to lay emphasis on a single aspect of the alcohol problem, the cause of excess consumption being frequently confused with the effects. Many hypotheses stress psychological factors usually pointing to underlying personality abnormalities or to unconscious conflicts, frustrations, and anxieties which are relieved by repeated use of alcohol. Other theories stressed physical causes—allergy (Silkworth), 'Imbalance between front and back brains' (Dent). 'Brain damage leading to loss of control', 'a biochemical lesion in one of the steps in metabolism' (Mardones). 'An inherited pattern of individual metabolic peculiarities' (Williams), 'A symptom of a glandular disorder . . . with hypoadrenocorticism' (Tintera). More recently the tendency has been to stress the pharmacological properties of alcohol as a drug. This model views alcoholism as an addiction induced by the properties of the drug. Felix, in 1944 said, 'From the psychiatric point of view the alcoholic, and the drug addict differ chiefly in that they use different drugs' and Adnus in 1933 said, 'Alcohol is one of the addiction producing drugs. The characteristics of addiction are tolerance, craving and the withdrawal syndrome'. Lundquist (1951) distinguished alcoholism as physical dependence upon alcohol, from alcohol abuse with excess drinking leading to social problems. These examples of theories of alcoholism (all quoted from Moss and Beresford Davies, 1967) are included to illustrate their diversity and to suggest that most variables within an *individual* had been considered, each authority or school considering one aspect to be paramount and few individuals looking at multiple factors acting together.

Another feature of the period of the hey-day of the disease concept was the microscopic dissection of the alcoholic individual—the classical mode of pathological study. The essential question was considered to be: 'How does this alcoholic individual differ from a normal individual?' The net result of much endeavour was to discover that alcoholics differed from normals in no clear cut respects and most differences could be accounted for as the results not the cause of the alcoholic excess. However one at-risk group of individuals has been identified. This comprises young impulsive aggressive and unrestrained males especially those with deviant or alcoholic fathers (Robins, 1960; McCord *et al.*, 1960). It may be said with some truth that alcoholics do not differ markedly from others except in so far as they have harmed themselves by their drinking. There is very little to mark them as diseased. Jellinek himself acknowledged that his formulation of alcoholism as a disease lacked scientific validity, merely being presented as a working hypothesis with the aim of influencing medical and political attitudes to alcoholism—'for the time being this may suffice, but not indefinitely' (Jellinek, 1960, p. 159). Yet whilst Jellinek had doubts about the status of alcoholism as a disease the adherents of the disease concept have been reluctant to acknowledge them and have clung to a simplified dogma of disease as if their lives depended on it (since many of these are abstinent adherents of AA their lives may indeed depend on it!). This dogma has been maintained in the face of modern evidence which allows a much broader and variable interpretation of alcoholism' and also suggests alternatives to abstinence as a goal of treatment and, indeed, broadens the field of problems with alcohol which may be susceptible to treatment. Again, referring to Jellinek (1960, p. 35), 'By adhering strictly to our ... ideas about "alcoholism" and "alcoholics" created by Alcoholics Anonymous in their own image and restricting the term to those ideas, we have been continuing to overlook many other problems of alcohol which need urgent attention'. Before considering some aspects of the change from traditional to more modern concepts it is worth enumerating some of the problems associated with adherence to the traditional concepts.

The major difficulty caused by acceptance of the disease concept is that those agencies treating alcoholics will only cater for those with the disease, i.e. the obvious physically dependent, chronic alcoholic often showing or beginning to show social and physical deterioration. Thus there is no provision for the less severe forms or the forms of alcohol problems which do not conform to the picture of physical dependence, these being seen as manifestations of personality disorder, or illness other than alcoholism. Hence the less severe (and probably more easily reversed) or prodomal form of alcoholism is not recognized or treated until too much damage has been done for treatment to be effective.

Recently a preventive approach has been developed, which may bear fruit in the actual reduction in cost to nations and to individuals of alcohol problems. This approach would be feasible in terms of the disease concept only in terms of total prohibition of alcohol.

Secondly, a sick role for alcoholics may lead the patient to deny his own ability to change an established pattern or to prevent it evolving from a less severe to a more severe problem. The sick role may even precipitate an increase in severity which suggests that alcoholics behave in a manner determined by labels affixed to them by themselves or others. However, a case against labelling as applied to alcoholism has been convincingly argued by Lee Robins (1980).

Thirdly, the notion of loss of control inherent in the disease model of alcoholism is counter-productive. The idea that an abstinent alcoholic will lose all control over his consumption of alcohol when he has had any alcohol at all ('one drink, one drunk') has been proved false in many cases. It may often be a self-fulfilling prophecy in that the alcoholic will surrender what control he does have after only a small amount of alcohol because of his belief in the dogmatic statements of the disease concept. Similarly, the disease concept implies that total abstinence is the only cure. This ignores the reality of degrees of recovery and partial cures and often leads clinicians to fail to assess the functioning of their patients in terms other than those of drinking.

Finally, disease needs treatment. If doctors are treating the disease then they must have a satisfactory cure rate or they would not treat it. The notion of disease may through this type of thinking, lead to false hopes of cure by medical men. A passive recipient role for the patient is obviously prejudicial to his overcoming the problems of dependence or the consequences of his drinking.

The preceding paragraphs provide some reasons for doubting the validity and usefulness of the disease concept. Jellinek's formulation of alcoholism as a disease had some of its roots in his perception of the need to alert the medical profession and governments to the toll taken by alcoholism and to prod them into doing something about it. Discarding a rigid disease concept and replacing it with more flexible concepts of problems caused by drinking will continue to fulfil Jellinek's basically humane aim of enabling more individuals who are suffering because of their alcohol intake to receive help. The implications of much of the more recent thinking and evidence are that more individuals would benefit from a greater range of treatments, that such treatments may be given by a wider variety of agencies, and also that there are a range of strategies which may be undertaken by governments with the aim of preventing the onset of such problems.

There are some indications to suggest that, amongst those who are professionally involved in treatment of alcoholism and alcohol problems, the disease concept has already passed into history. 'Alcoholism is dead' is the war cry of those in the vanguard of the new orthodoxy. It is, however, difficult to understand the often aggressive attempts to undermine the faith in the disease

oncept of those in AA. Alcoholics Anonymous has done more for more
problem drinkers than any other group, including the medical profession, and
continues to fulfil a real need. Maybe its image as the leader in the field of
lcoholism treatment is a cause for envy. A recent article (Room, 1981) was
ntitled 'A Farewell to Alcoholism'. The Advisory Committee of the Department
f Health and Social Security has dropped the terms alcoholism and alcoholic in
avour of 'problem drinking' and 'problem drinker' deliberately in order to
xpand the remit of the services it suggests for treatment of these people (DHSS,
978a). In the White Paper, 'Better Services for the Mentally Ill', (DHSS, 1975)
he DHSS seemed to be undecided—'It is a disease which . . .' (p. 62, 8.1) and 'It
s not of itself a mental illness' (p. 62, 8.1). The DHSS has since moved firmly
way from considering alcoholism (and incidentally, drug addiction and sexual
eviancy) as a mental illness in its own right by recommending that alcoholism as
uch, rather than the mental conditions secondary to it (delirium tremens,
lcoholic dementia, etc.) should 'not be regarded as a mental disorder' (para
:13, 1978b).

The disease concept still lives on in some institutions and organizations. I
uspect that with the increasing media concern and interest in alcoholism as a
esult of increasing medical and research involvement over the past 10–20 years,
he population at large is only just beginning to move towards viewing
lcoholisms as a disease or condition rather than as a vice, a crime, or a weakness.
he disease model still continues to be a cornerstone of AA philosophy and many
reatment organizations still operate as if it were accepted that the problems
aced by their patients are a manifestation of disease to be diagnosed and treated
ccording to strictly medical practice.

Newer concepts of alcoholism

t is recognized that alcohol is a drug of addiction. It has the properties of
nducing tolerance, producing a withdrawal syndrome and causing craving—an
verpowering desire to continue the habit. Thus if taken in sufficient quantities
ver a long enough period alcohol will induce dependence with various
manifestations of behaviour and emotion. Most of these seem to be harmful and
estructive. There is a wide range of problems which may be caused by excessive
lcohol consumption ranging from occasional intoxication to severe brain
amage, with most excessive drinkers showing some degree of physical and
ental harm. The presence or absence of any given problem in any given drinker
s due to a wide variety of causes—personality, circumstances, attitudes of
thers, state of nutrition, body build etc., and the net result is a complex of
roblems along many dimensions for which the disease concept of alcoholism
ignificantly fails to provide a reasonable model. The degree of alcohol
ependence is one aspect of drinking to which much attention has been devoted
nd which is central to understanding alcoholics. This constellation of problems

has been summarized in the alcohol dependence syndrome (Edwards and Gross, 1977) and this term seems to be catching on as an alternative to alcoholism. The alcohol dependency syndrome is not a disease entity and implies no specific aetiology. It is merely a description of symptoms which commonly cluster together in certain individuals. Each of the elements of the syndrome may be present or absent and may be present in varying degrees and in differing degrees from time to time. The description of the syndrome allows it to change as alcoholics change through time and in varying environmental circumstances. It helps to abolish the 'all or none' problem of alcoholism as a disease. It can be seen as a psycho-physiological disorder (Edwards, 1977) and provides clinicians with some pointers to treatment goals and outcomes—the greater the degree of dependence the less likely the chances of a return to drinking under control. It also provides a reasonable basis for quantification of the severity of the disorder with a view to studies of the natural history and treatment outcome. Dependence is one aspect of alcohol problems, and relates to but must be differentiated from, 'alcohol related disabilities' in any assessment of patients. The disabilities are the harm, social, mental, and physical which ensues from excess alcohol consumption.

The alcohol dependence syndrome is composed of seven elements. It is obvious that some have a psychological slant and others a physical one, perhaps reflecting the movement of the drinker through predominantly psychological problems (craving, compulsion to drink, denial, etc.) towards mainly physical ones (shakes, sweats, fits, etc.) The syndrome is as follows:

(1) Narrowing of drinking repertoire. Drinking behaviour becomes habitual and loses some of its normal variability.
(2) Prominence of drink seeking behaviour.
(3) Awareness of a compulsion to drink. This is sometimes accompanied by loss of control.
(4) Increased tolerance to alcohol.
(5) Repeated withdrawal symptoms.
(6) Avoidance of withdrawal symptoms by relief drinking (especially in the morning).
(7) Reinstatement after abstinence.

There are other symptoms, notably alcoholic amnesias, which denote the onset of increasing harm from alcohol, and also denote increasing dependence, which might feasibly be included in the syndrome. The alcohol dependence syndrome is a useful concept and may be seen as forming part of a theory of alcoholism (Davies, 1980). Above a certain average level of consumption, habits develop as a result of an interaction of the individual's personality, cultural patterns, and circumstances with the chemical properties of alcohol. These habits constitute ependence, may take years to develop, and will be more strongly developed the reater the consumption which is, by and large, determined by availability to the ndividual. The dependent individual responds to increases in availability by ncreasing his consumption and is more likely to respond to stress by an increase f consumption than the non-dependent individual. As consumption increases) the physical symptoms of dependence predominate and harm in emotional,)cial, economic, and above a certain level, physical terms is more likely to evelop. Dependence of low degree does not necessarily mean harm, but the reater the degree of dependence the more likely harm is to have occurred. Davies)ecifically excepts from this theory those whose alcohol dependence is clearly :condary to major psychiatric illness such as manic depressive illness. These are :w in number.

The amount which it is safe to drink has been variously estimated. The Royal 'ollege of Psychiatrists (1979) estimated that an amount of alcohol equivalent to)ur pints of beer for men or three pints for women was an acceptable upper verage daily limit. Anstie's limit dating from the nineteenth century was roughly alf that. Davies (1980) states that the alcohol equivalent of two pints of beer aily is enough to produce dependence. Above 6 pints is likely to produce tissue amage.

lcoholism in relation to drinking in the community—a social dimension

Jntil recently studies of alcoholism concentrated on the alcoholic individual. As :ated earlier much effort was expended to explain how that individual was ifferent to others in a way which led to his excessive drinking. Usually there were o differences. The view taken was a microscopic one and the subject was the lcoholic. More recently research has taken a wider view aimed at the population t large, and placing the alcoholic in that population, in terms of his drinking, his narriage, family, criminal record, health, and work record amongst other spects of his life. Much data has emerged from follow-up studies and from tudies of populations in treatment to demonstrate a hitherto unsuspected lasticity in alcoholism which challenges the traditional view of the relationship f the alcoholic to drinking and drink, and which has led to new approaches to ·eatment on a much broader front, many of which seem to challenge the primacy f the doctor in the treatment of alcoholism. Numerous epidemiological studies ave concentrated upon the distribution of drinking behaviour within the opulation as a whole and the relationship between excessive drinking and ormal drinking (e.g. Cartwright *et al.*, 1975; O'Connor, 1978; Dight, 1976). tudies have also looked at the relationship of alcoholism, consumption of lcohol, and economic factors existing within a population under study and have erhaps pointed to ways in which alcoholism may be prevented. This is a Public lealth model of alcoholism.

The new orthodoxy has it that in any given population, consumption of

alcohol is determined by the availability of alcohol, itself determined by i
accessibility in both place and time, and price. This view also maintains tha
alcoholism can be said to occur in an individual at certain given levels o
consumption, and that approximate predictions of the number of alcoho
dependent individuals in a given population can be made if the distribution o
alcohol consumption is known for that population. The drinking habits o
population have become subject to mathematical analysis following the pro
position in 1956 by Ledermann (Ledermann 1956) that the frequency distr
bution of alcohol consumption follows a log-normal curve. If this is so, the
given the total consumption of alcohol by a population (data which is easil
obtained), the curve can be drawn and the numbers of persons drinking give
quantities can be predicted so that the numbers of heavy drinkers may b
predicted (data which are notoriously difficult to elicit accurately by direct mean
such as population surveys or sampling).

It has been argued that the frequency distribution curve is not an exact log
normal curve (Duffy, 1977, Skog, 1977) but that there is a positively skewe
unimodal, continuous distribution of alcohol consumption in most groups o
populations under study (De Lint and Schmidt 1971). This would seem generall

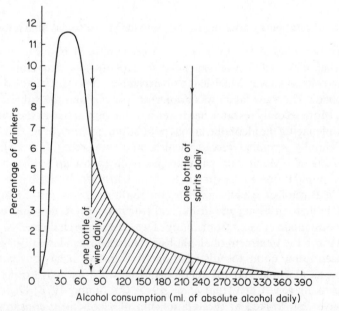

Figure 1   Typical log-normal frequency distribution curve of
alcohol consumption (Ledermann curve). The numbers of drinkers
at a given consumption level is related to the area under the curve to
the right of that level—hence the shaded area represents the
numbers drinking more than one bottle of wine per day

rue for it makes sense in a logical way to say that, leaving out total abstainers, ew people drink hardly at all, many people drink moderately, somewhat fewer ieavily, and very few very heavily. Furthermore, there is an upper limit of .lcohol consumption which is fatal and above which no one can drink. The Ledermann curve' is a graphical illustration of this sort of statement and the requency–distribution curve in reality approximates to a log-normal distri-)ution. Although it is now generally accepted that there is no fixed mathematical .elationship between the average per capita consumption of alcohol and the iumber of alcoholics (Office of Health Economics, 1981) the concept does allow .ertain conclusions.

The greater the per capita consumption of alcohol the greater the number of)roblem drinkers. Problem drinkers and alcoholics are likely to be consuming .bove about 15 cl of alcohol daily (about 2 bottles of wine or $\frac{1}{2}$ litre of spirits Iaily). The evidence suggests that all indices of problem drinking—drunkenness)ffences, cirrhosis mortality, and hospital admissions for alcoholism rise in line vith a rise in alcohol consumption by the population. One may argue about the iiceties of the interpretations of the figures and the data on which these figures .re based, but it seems as if the trend is clear—the more alcohol consumed, the ;reater the harm done by alcohol. As a general proposition it is probably more .ccurate when applied to large groups such as a whole country but it is also true vhen applied to individuals. Another important conclusion derived from this urve, is that a small change in average per capita consumption leads to a lisproportionately large change in the numbers of heavy drinkers and con- .equently in the extent of alcoholism. Since the converse is also true this .rgument has become the focal point of much that has been written with regard o the prevention of alcohol problems on a large scale.

The continuous unimodal characteristic of the frequency distribution curve eems to provide further evidence that there is no discrete population of .lcoholics and that there is no disease of alcoholism. Some critics have challenged his conclusion on the basis of the methodology of the studies on which requency–distribution curves are based. Furthermore, certain populations seem o be somewhat anomalous, e.g. Scotland where, according to Dight (1976), 3 per :ent of the population consume 30 per cent of the alcohol and Ireland where the .verage per capita consumption is relatively low, but where there are large iumbers of problem drinkers because of a large number of religiously motivated otal abstainers and a large number of very heavy drinkers. One is tempted to .peculate on the form of the frequency distribution curve of alcohol consumption n a society where alcohol is officially prohibited, as in Muslim countries, issuming that the researcher could get anyone to admit to any alcohol :onsumption whatsoever or find any data at all relative to this. In such a situation he curve might not be unimodal or continuous at all.

Relationships between gross national consumption and numbers of heavy lrinkers is fairly well established, but is there an established link between consumption and problems? It seems that there is. Shaw *et al.* (1978) considered this question in the light of evidence from two general population surveys of drinking in London, conducted nine years apart. (Cartwright *et al.*, 1975 Edwards *et al.*, 1972). Their conclusions support the view that there is a virtuall: linear relationship between perceived problems and consumption. If anythin, the trend is such that the number of problems increased disproportionately to th amount drunk. In individuals problems perceived were related to demographi data and to the drinking pattern for a given alcohol consumption. Thus for a given average weekly consumption problems would be present more for socia classes III, IV and V than for I and II, more for persons aged below 35 than fo persons over 35, and more for those who consumed erratically rather tha regularly. A man drinking 1 pint of beer each day of the week was less likely to report problems than a man who drank 7 pints of beer on one day in the week This latter relationship is interesting in that others have shown that cirrhosis i: more likely to be preceded by frequent moderate consumption than by les: frequent excess (Rankin *et al.*, 1975) and is likely to go some way toward: accounting for differences between, say, Scotland and France as examples o Northern European—binge drinking often of spirits with loss of control drunkenness and consequent problems and Southern European wine drinking with inability to abstain, and continuous use of the drink as a day-to-da' beverage. The Southerners have high indices of cirrhosis and physical harm bu low indices of social harm—drunkenness, marital disruption, etc. and the Northerners have high indices of social disruption (drunkenness, drunke violence, marital problems, etc.) but relatively low rates of cirrhosis.

Prevention of alcohol problems and the role of Government

A discussion of the epidemiological aspects of alcohol consumption leads to the question of what may be done to prevent the excesses of alcohol consumptior leading to alcoholism. Can the number of individuals requiring treatment be reduced? Those who adhere to the epidemiological approach suggest that it car and that the obvious way to do it is to reduce the total consumption of alcohol by the population at risk. There are precedents for this. During the period of Prohibition in the USA the indices of harm done by alcohol were all reduced. During both World Wars consumption of alcohol was markedly reduced and there was a concomitant reduction in indices of harm caused by alcohol. The converse is equally true. Between 1950 and 1975 per capita alcohol consumption in England and Wales increased by some 87 per cent and during that period there has been a rise in cirrhosis deaths by some 8 per cent, and the number of drunkenness offences have more than doubled (Royal College of Psychiatrists. 1979). Consumption of alcohol has also increased in the post-war period in 24 out of 25 developed countries studied by De Lint (1975)—the exception being France. French consumption was still highest of all but had dropped by some

12 per cent between 1960 and 1970 following the beginning of government interest in the harm done by alcohol to the nation's health in the 1950s—one Prime Minister, Pierre Mendes-France was held to some ridicule in the British press for urging the French to drink milk! France provides a model of an alcohol based culture. Jellinek (1960) estimated that 1 in 3 of the working population obtained their living wholly or partly from the production, distribution, or sale of alcoholic drinks.

The evidence that harm done by alcohol is related to total consumption was so convincing that Kendell (1979) was moved to propose that alcoholism is a political rather than a medical problem, in that it is to political and fiscal rather than medical measures that we should turn in our efforts to halt the rising tide of alcohol consumption and consequent problems. Political measures would have a preventive rather than curative influence. Kendell cites historical precedents for legislation altering the drinking habits of the nation. The tripling of duty on beer in 1690, increases in malt tax in 1791, restriction of public house openings by the Defence of the Realm Act of 1914 are British examples of legislation followed by a marked reduction of consumption. The Defence of the Realm Act, admittedly under exceptional conditions in the First World War, was also followed by immediate concomitant reductions in drunkenness offences and in alcohol induced mortality. On the other hand Kendell quotes Gladstone's 1880 reduction of the Alcohol Tax which was followed by an increase in alcohol consumption. Examples abound throughout the world to demonstrate links between changes in the laws governing availability of alcohol and consumption. In the USA Prohibition caused a considerable reduction in alcohol problems although few cases have been as dramatic as this. However a small change in the law produced a marked change in consumption in Finland in 1969 (Whitehead, 1975) when restrictions on the retail outlets of medium strength beer were lifted—the emphasis having previously been on promoting weak beers as a means of restricting alcohol consumption. In the year after this change alcohol consumption increased by 49 per cent, the increase being made up mainly by beer with consumption of strong spirits being little affected. It seems that new drinking practices were added unexpectedly to the old ones rather than being substituted for them, with a consequent increased in total consumption.

Two main aspects of the law may affect consumption. Licensing laws affect availability in terms of the age at which we can legally buy alcohol, the number of retail outlets where alcohol may be bought or consumed, those who may sell it, and the hours during which it may be bought or consumed. Secondly, the price of alcohol is largely a result of the tax levied on it and is thus amenable to control by government. The available evidence shows that restricted availability due to licensing laws tends to reduce consumption. The Clayson Committee (Scottish Home and Health Department, 1973) in Scotland and the Errol Committee (Home Office, 1972) in England and Wales made recommendations for changes in licensing laws, but these were largely rejected. Errol recommended relaxation

of licensing laws and a lowering of the minimum age for drinking. This wa
rejected by the government, fiercely attacked by the medical press, and
condemned as a 'boozer's charter' by the lay press. The Clayson Committee'
recommendations were also largely rejected but an important one was implemen
ted. Licensing hours in Scotland were extended and Sunday opening wa
allowed. Paradoxically this did not, as had been widely predicted, increas
drinking. It seems to have reduced it and moderated its intensity so that Scottish
drinking habits, especially the '10 o'clock rush' in which drinkers rate o
consumption would escalate in an attempt to achieve total satisfaction before
closingtime, became more like those in England (Wilson, 1980). Clayson wanted
to change the traditional Scottish pub, often seen as a male dominated place in
which to get drunk, into something more akin to a French café. One way of doing
this was to make the pub a place for the family, encouraging women and children
to accompany the men. This, it was hoped, would moderate the men's drinking
and also help to inculcate moderate drinking habits into the young, in the hope
that this is one way of enabling drinkers to habitually avoid excessive drink
ing. The work of Dight (1976) and of Davies and Stacey (1972) provided some
foundations for the views. They found that those children most likely to have
problems adjusting to drinking come from families with extreme attitudes to
drink being either strongly against drinking in any form or strongly involved with
drinking in excess. This view, that early experience of drinking within families is a
crucial variable in the constellation of factors which tend to make a given person
an alcoholic, is reflected in the extremely low rate of alcoholism amongst Jews
who introduce their children to sensible and modest drinking at an early age
(Clayson, 1977). The differences between rates of alcohol problems in France
and in Italy (both wine producing countries with high consumptions) have
been ascribed to differences in traditional attitudes towards childhood wine
drinking.

   These aspects of licensing law have been considered as beneficial in curbing the
epidemic of drinking problems from a preventive standpoint. They do not help
the established alcohol dependent although they may prevent others from
increasing their consumption to the point where chemical dependency intervene
and the drinker has less control over his consumption and begins to suffer
economically, physically, mentally, and materially and to cause suffering to hi
family and to others. It is obvious that preventing alcohol problems is better than
curing them since our ability to cure alcoholics is, at best, limited. In any case
curing established cases does nothing to reduce the prevalence of problems as fo
every cure, another case has its inception. The position is worse than this
Alcoholism is a condition in which relapse is frequent, so not only are there new
cases to be dealt with but also old cases which are in relapse. On the other hand
curing an alcoholic may have a bearing on the way the alcoholic influence
others—it may diminish Ledermann's 'boule de neige' effect in which excessive
drinkers tend to persuade others to match consumption, thereby creating heavy

drinkers, and consequently reduce the total number of cases. It makes sense to adopt an approach which makes it likely that the potential alcoholic drinks at a level below that which is likely to produce severe dependence. This is the crux of the preventionist argument.

The number of retail outlets may also be modified with a consequent change in total consumption. There are telling arguments (McGuinness, 1980) to suggest that reducing the number of licensed premises is one way of tackling the alcohol problem. McGuinness has calculated that a 1 per cent decrease in retail outlets would produce a 2 per cent decrease in total consumption of alcohol, and thus if the Ledermann hypothesis has any validity, a disproportionately large reduction in the numbers of excessive drinkers. The 1961 Licensing Act enabled the number of outlets to increase by allowing the sales of alcoholic beverages from supermarkets and grocers, although under some control, and this has been rightly criticized. It directly raises consumption by putting temptation in the way of the ordinary shopper, in the proportions calculated by McGuinness. It also raises the issue of increased availability to women, who still, one must assume, do most of the shopping, and lastly will tend to increase the incidence of theft of alcohol by shoplifting, a crime in which alcoholics figure all too largely. Others, e.g. Popham *et al.* (1975) in Canada dispute that there is any significant relationship generally between numbers of retail outlets and consumption arguing that changes relate to local customs.

Advertising is often indicted as luring people, especially the impressionable young into excess drinking; for example by suggesting that a few vodkas will endow the, drinker with wealth, sexual attractiveness, and sophistication. Advertisings defenders, the advertisers and their agents, all claim that the promotions on which they spend so much (around £100 million per year in Britain) merely serve to influence the preference between brands. That seems improbable but the opposite argument that advertising is a major factor in increasing consumption is equally invalid—the USSR with virtually no advertising has a tremendous alcohol problem. Some restriction of advertising seems desirable. McGuinness (1980) also made computations regarding the effectiveness of a cut in the advertising budget of the drinks industry. He calculated that in 1975 a reduction, in terms of pure alcohol consumed of 0.2 per cent would be achieved if the advertising budget was reduced by per cent.

A further preventive strategy is the traditional one of education. If the people are educated as to the risks inherent in drinking to excess then, the argument goes, their own intelligence and common sense will allow them to put that educational knowledge into practice and there will be a reduction in alcohol problems. Yet this type of education rarely seems to work out and the success of Health Education in virtually any field has been limited. People may become educated and often become quite knowledgeable but they fail to put that knowledge into practice in modifying their behaviour. In 1975 in the north-east of England an expensive campaign utilizing spot television commercials was launched. These concentrated on the harm done by excessive drinking and the possibility of treatment. They failed significantly to alter consumption of alcohol but did cause an increase in persons perceiving themselves as having a drinking problem and presenting themselves for treatment (Royal College of Psychiatrists). The overall value of education as a means of preventing alcohol related problems is debatable and probably not cost effective. More attention needs to be paid to refining such educational approaches.

Finally we come to what is regarded as the most potent force in controlling alcohol consumption, the price of drink. The evidence points to price being a most significant determinant of consumption and the assumption is again made (with good reason) that consumption determines the number of heavy drinkers. Thus, if alcohol becomes more expensive, less will be drunk and there will be fewer alcoholics and fewer problems caused by drink. Most of the price of alcoholic beverages is tax paid to the government so it follows that the government could directly change the extent of the alcohol problem by increasing the tax on alcohol. An increase in tax on drinks is often seen as one of the easiest and most profitable ways for the Chancellor of the Exchequer to raise more money at budget time, and he could justify changes by saying that he is doing it as a public health measure. The taxes on alcohol and tobacco have been labelled as 'selective health taxes' because of the links between those commodities and ill-health. There can be no doubt that the real price of alcohol has been dropping, at least since the Second World War. This becomes apparent by comparing the rise in price of alcohol relative to the rate of inflation, or relative to the increase in disposable income (what remains from gross income after taxes and necessary fixed expenditure such as rent), or even by estimating the time the average man has to work to buy himself a bottle of whisky. On all these indices in most industrialized countries the real price of alcohol is falling, and in the UK has fallen at a greater rate than in many other countries (Kendell, 1979). This has been coupled with a trend towards lowering the taxation on alcohol and a general increase in prosperity in the developed countries, at least until 1977. Changes in the real price of alcohol are mirrored by an inverse change in alcohol consumption. The relationship is almost linear in many countries studied (De Lindt and Schmidt, 1971; Royal College of Psychiatrists, 1979) as well as in Great Britain (Office of Health Economics, 1981) and it is probable that the more expensive the alcohol the less is likely to be drunk. Similar relationships between price and consumption are seen in many other marketed commodities but the trend is not all one way. In the First World War wages reached high levels and drink was not markedly increased in price but alcohol consumption was reduced by 50 per cent between 1913 and 1917 so that other factors—stricter licensing laws, loss of potential drinkers to the Army, diversion of raw materials away from alcohol production, etc., outweighed the natural market forces tending to increase alcohol consumption by relative lowering of price. A newspaper report

(Dean, 1981) claims that the Central Policy Review Staff (the 'think tank') has calculated that a 1 per cent rise in real income would raise beer intake by 0.7 per cent, spirits by 2.2 per cent, and wine by 2.5 per cent, another example perhaps of the tendency to add on drinking behaviours when the opportunities allow (beer is the staple drink, spirits and wine are luxuries to be afforded only at times of relative affluence).

This same report said by the Office of Health Economics (1981) to be unpublished but widely seen urged the government to increase the taxes on alcohol as a public health measure. Adjustments of the cost of alcohol can be attractive as a means of controlling alcohol consumption but disadvantages appear on closer consideration. A large amount of revenue comes to the government from this source and any government is unlikely to reduce its own income. The amount by which any alcohol tax is increased needs careful calculation to balance the greater revenue per unit sales against the net loss of revenue resulting from falling sales. Any net loss should take into account, however, the potential savings to be made by less hospital admissions, less time lost from work through alcohol problems, less accidents on the roads and at work, and from the other costly problems arising out of alcoholic excess. A second problem is that it is difficult for the population at large to see itself as at risk from alcohol problems and therefore to accept increased alcohol costs, however well meaning the rationale behind these increases. We are all aware of the disgruntlement felt by most of the public on Budget Day when the announcement is made of a few pence on the price of a pint of beer. The view of the public at large is that we should not have to pay extra for our pleasures because they (the alcoholics) need some kind of protection from themselves. A recent survey conducted by *The Sunday Times* (Lipsey, 1980) further illustrated public ambivalence over alcohol. Whilst most would favour much more severe penalties for drunken driving they would also oppose large increases in the price of their drinks. Governments could not survive too much of that kind of public censure so the price of alcohol is perhaps too sensitive a political issue to be able to be of much help in slowing the trend to higher consumption. It is in any case doubtful how much reduction could be achieved. Certainly it is naive to believe that, say doubling the price of alcohol would send consumption plummeting to the levels of 20 or 30 years ago. The Royal College of Psychiatrists (1979) recommended price increases such that the level of consumption would not continue to rise. This still leaves a very large number of problem drinkers who require treatment.

A third reason to be cautious on the price issue is that there is no selectivity about it. All drinkers are affected equally and there may be adverse consequences following significant rises in the cost of drinking. The very poor may continue to drink at the same, possibly minimal, level and deprive themselves or their families of necessities such as food or clothing, thereby increasing health problems as a result of measures designed to decrease them. Those who are severely dependent upon alcohol will find great difficulty in reducing consumption and may become forced to resort to theft to continue their habit. A further possibility is that illicit manufacture of drinks may increase with possible harm arising from impurities in such concoctions, e.g. methyl alcohol. The current level of home brewing and wine making is such as to cause some authors to express caution regarding the validity of estimates of alcohol consumption, especially at times of economic recession.

We have discussed some of the ways in which alcohol related harm may be reduced by direct government action aimed at simply reducing the total consumption of alcohol by the nation. It is likely that opposition to many of these measures will come from those in whose interest it is to have a high consumption of alcohol, and the attitude of the drinks trade has in the past been somewhat lukewarm towards recognizing that there is a serious alcohol problem in this country. They have tended to promote the view that alcoholics were different from non-alcoholics and that the cause of the problem lay in the person not the alcohol, denying the fact that alcohol is a psychoactive drug being seductively promoted in forms more diverse and more attractive than any other. Schmidt (1977) quotes the Association of Canadian Distillers in a submission to government in 1973: 'Alcohol and alcoholism are two entirely different subjects—while alcoholism is a major health problem, alcohol is not. Just as sugar is not the cause of diabetes, alcohol is not the cause of alcoholism'. In a way one can see what they mean but would they also say that cigarettes are not the cause of nicotine addiction or heroin a cause of drug dependency? Perhaps these attitudes are beginning to change and the brewers and distillers are realizing that excessive drinkers do their trade no good (it is a matter of speculation as to how the Scottish drinks trade would fare without Dight's 3 per cent drinking 30 per cent of the drink). Mr Patrick Jenkin, Secretary of State for Social Services addressing the National Council for Alcoholism in July 1981, stated that he believed the common ground between the drinks industry and those concerned about alcoholism was expanding and that there was an increasing air of cooperation and conciliation, as exemplified by the drinks industry funding certain posts in the council and in funding research projects.

At present it is uncertain how committed governments are to interventions in the drinking habits of the nation. There have certainly been great increases in concern and interest since the Ministry of Health in 1951 stated, in considering the request of an NHS consultant for permission to attend a WHO colloquium on alcoholism in Copenhagen that 'there was no alcoholism in England and Wales and that the subject hardly merited the time of a Consultant in the National Health Service' (Moss and Davies, 1967). This sort of attitude has changed enough for the government to establish treatment units and to institute an Advisory Committee on Alcoholism, amongst other things. But there is still caution in responding to newer epidemiological data which indicates ways in which concerted action might prevent rather than cure the problems of alcoholism. Control of consumption is the most significant aspect of prevention of alcohol problems. Edwards (1971) puts the case eloquently and succinctly.

'The reason why a person drinks abnormally is connected with both his personality and his environment; his drinking will in fact, result from an interaction of the two, so that, for example an anxious person living where alcohol is cheap and attitudes to drinking are permissive will be more likely to become an excessive drinker than an anxious person who finds alcohol more difficult to obtain and attitudes less approving. Since we are not able to manipulate personalities and produce a race with no neuroses the only realistic method of exerting a benign influence on the prevalence of chronic alcohol problems is by control of environmental conditions of drinking and it is the availability element that remains the prime candidate for control.'

Treatment

If successful preventive measures can diminish the numbers of problem drinkers treatment may become unnecessary. For the time being treatment needs are increasing however. The initial impact of preventive programmes is to reveal more problem drinkers thus increasing the needs for treatment. Obviously, the main interest of the medical profession lies in the treatment of alcoholic problems. A narrow perspective would suggest that because alcoholism is not a disease medical treatment is inappropriate, but because there are often medical problems, such as cirrhosis of the liver, peripheral neuropathy, etc. arising from the alcoholic problem medical agencies are inevitably involved. It is equally obvious that there are psychiatric problems arising from alcoholic excess; many of these problems have an undoubtedly physical origin (e.g. delirium tremens and rum fits), but their manifestations are so clearly in the realm of disturbance of mental functioning, and are so frequently accompanied by gross behavioural disturbances that the psychiatric services are inevitably involved for therein lies the expertise of psychiatrists, and psychiatric nurses. But what of the alcoholism itself? The features of alcoholism as outlined in the dependence syndrome are manifestations of mental events mediated by behaviour and as such are the stuff of current psychiatric practice. It is, in my view, quite appropriate that alcoholism, as distinct from its complications should be seen as a psychiatric problem. That is not to say that it is an exclusively psychiatric problem, as is say, schizophrenia, nor that psychiatrists are the only people capable of modifying alcoholics behaviour or drinking, patterns but persons with psychiatric experience and training are, among all the health care personnel, best fitted to deal with the manifold problems presented by alcoholism. Within that specialty there may well be a subdivision of labour so that the doctor deals with certain aspects of a problem or with certain patients, whilst the social worker, community nurse, or psychologist deal with others according to their individual area of expertise. Equally the severity of the presenting problems should decide what degree of psychiatric expertise is required, as in most cases of mental illness. The general practitioner may be able to deal with some, others may be able to be dealt with by voluntary counsellors in local councils on alcoholism, and others by fellow alcoholics in AA. The protean manifestations of alcoholism cover such a variety of areas that it is impossible for any one agency to claim total exclusive expertise.

The history of alcoholism treatment in the UK is of some interest. I have already noted the vast increase in the number of persons treated for alcoholism and alcoholic psychosis within the National health Service since its inception, and have also referred to the indifference of the Ministry of Health to Jellinek's overtures in 1951. However, interest at the Maudsley Hospital (Davies *et al.*, 1956) and at Warlingham Park Hospital (Glatt, 1955 and 1961) stimulated the involvement of the government. The models used in these two centres were different. Davies concentrated upon immediate problems and manipulation of social factors often combined with disulfiram (Antabuse) treatment and introduction to AA, whilst Glatt's unit at Warlingham Park concentrated more on group therapy often along AA lines with prolonged (12 weeks) in-patient stay in a specialized isolated unit. The latter approach was more influential originally and the publication of promising success rates by these units seem to have stimulated widespread interest in treatment. The British Medical Association and the Magistrates Association in 1961 (British Medical Journal Supplement, 1961) urged the setting-up of specialized in-patient units for treatment of alcoholics and this theme was taken up by the Ministry of Health which recommended that each Regional Board should set up a specialist unit of between 8 and 16 beds ('a convenient size for group therapy') and that 'treatment for alcoholism and *alcoholic psychosis* [my italics] should, as far as possible, be given in special units'. After-care was to be in cooperation with Alcoholics Anonymous (Ministry of Health, 1962). This was the first official commitment by the National Health Service to the treatment of alcoholism and was based on the received wisdom of what was needed rather than on objective scientific evidence. This advice was acted upon and two or three units in 1961 became thirteen by 1968 and twenty-one by 1975 with 434 beds (Orford and Edwards, 1977). Most of these units operated on the original Warlingham Park model and it is only within the past few years that emphasis has moved away from the notion that long-stay in-patient treatment, based on group therapy is the best treatment for alcoholism. The rationale behind this sort of treatment seemed to be psychotherapeutic (it is only by finding out the hidden reasons why we drink to excess that we can successfully become the total abstainers which we must become in order to live with our disease) but yet founded in the disease concept of alcoholism. If there were hidden reasons which could be uncovered and worked through then surely there would consequently be no disease and that individual would be able to enjoy a drink in a normal fashion without excess. This kind of treatment was a curious mixture of psychoanalytic theory, AA dogma and the disease concept, which, in spite of being largely irrational and unscientific, seemed to work, and indeed to work well enough for it to be believed to be the optimal form for all alcoholics. This belief was supported by a selection procedures whereby patients selected for admissions to the special units were those likely to have a successful outcome in psychotherapy. There was then considerable selection bias towards those patients who would probably do well anyway and a bias away from those with psychosis and severe social problems. Edwards *et al.* (1974) showed the predominance of social classes I and II in a special unit between 1953 and 1957 and a disproportionate representation of classes I and II even in an ordinary psychiatric hospital. This bias was still found in 1975 by Hore and Smith (1975), though it was then less marked.

There has long been a need for a move towards more comprehensive services for *all* alcoholics and problem drinkers with a consequent revision of the role of the special units. There was some acknowledgment of this in 'Better Services for the Mentally Ill' (DHSS 1975) which altered the 1962 view that treatment of alcoholism and alcoholic psychosis should as far as possible be given in special units (Ministry of Health, 1962). This White Paper said, 'These special units were not developed to replace the facilities offered by the existing psychiatric services', and 'The specialized units were seen more as central foci of expertise, knowledge and research which could coordinate and direct a more community based approach', with more use of day and out-patient facilities. It also recognized the need for continual evaluation of treatment and the need to be flexible in planning the policy of services. 'Most services are in some sense experimental.' The shift in official thinking away from selective, in-patient based, psychotherapeutically orientated special units towards a more comprehensive community based approach was continued in the 1978 Report of the Advisory Committee on Alcoholism ('The Pattern and Range of Services for Problem Drinkers', DHSS, 1978a)—'We intend that every person with a drinking problem should be able to find the help he needs' (p. 15). This report set a trend. It dropped the word 'alcoholic' and substituted 'problem drinkers'. It also suggested ways in which services might be organized to cope with the various presentations of problem drinking and also considered the range of agencies which might be involved. A preventive model was also advocated similiar to that put forward the previous year by the Advisory Committee (DHSS, 1977). This report placed great emphasis upon primary care—general practices, area team social workers, probation officers, and volunteers in shop front agencies who were to act as the major treatment resource and so avoid the need to increase the number of psychiatric inpatients. Specialized units were seen as of secondary importance in terms of supplying treatment to individuals although they were in the front line when it came to promoting ideas, research on treatment, and acting as centres of advice, expertise, and training for the far more numerous primary care personnel.

There is a trend in alcoholism treatment towards a variety of approaches.

Initially this arose out of dissatisfaction with a uniform treatment approach (Glaser, 1980) such as was seen in the early days of the Alcoholism Treatment Unit (ATUs). Glaser's view is that a match between individual patients and treatment modalities must be obtained if more success in treatment is to occur. An illustration of this is the use of lithium in alcoholism treatment (Merry *et al.*, 1976, Kline *et al.*, 1974). It is only a useful treatment for those alcoholics who are significantly depressed and in such patients it produces significant changes in drinking behaviour. In those not depressed the tendency is for them to increase their consumption of alcohol (Glaser, 1980). Obviously this is a mismatch. This kind of thing does emphasize the need for a variety of available treatments. Similarly, there is a corresponding need for a multidisciplinary approach within the ATUs utilizing teams comprising psychiatrists, physicians, social workers, psychologists, voluntary workers, and members of AA. However, to think in terms of a team working hand in glove is perhaps an exaggeration. More likely there should be liaison between all disciplines so that individual patients or their spouses relate to the discipline most likely to provide the techniques and style best suited to their particular problems. Initially doctors may be asked to make the diagnoses and assessments such as the degrees of harm or dependence, and the presence or absence of significant illness or psychotic disability which would require specific medical intervention. They may then refer patients on to appropriate treatment agencies.

Before embarking on treatment the goals should be defined. The traditional goal of alcoholism treatment is total abstinence. This idea, that the only way to overcome drinking problems is to avoid drink, stems from the disease concept and the Alcoholics Anonymous view of alcoholism. Anything less than total abstinence has been regarded as partial success or, more likely, imminent failure. That this is not always the case has been amply demonstrated since Davies (1962) first showed that persons diagnosed as alcoholics, with most of the hallmarks of serious dependency, can on follow-up be found to be drinking in normal fashion. More extensive studies, particularly that by Armor, Polich, and Stambul (Armor *et al.*, 1978) ('The Rand Report') have shown that up to 15 per cent of alcoholics have at follow-up returned to a normal pattern of drinking and have re-established a degree of control over their consumption. The controversy caused by the publication of the Rand Report was clear evidence of how much its objective data flew in the face of traditional thinking and assumptions. It was urged to be rejected as it was 'an alcoholics charter', as if there was a moral sense in which alcoholics who returned to drinking without harm had somehow got away with it, and escaped the just penalty of enforced abstinence. The question of whether alcoholics might be taught or enabled to drink in a normal or controlled way has now been raised. It has been addressed in the main by psychologists using behavioural change techniques derived from learning theory conceptualizing alcoholism as an aberrant pattern of learned behaviour with the drinker responding to and modified by internal cues (withdrawal syndrome), or external cues (e.g. opening time, sight of a bottle or of other drinkers). The whole process is complicated, however, by the presence of induced biological changes—tolerance and withdrawal (Edwards and Gross, 1976) for the degree of dependence seems to be crucial in determining the success of any strategy aimed at a return to controlled drinking (Hodgson, 1980). The presence of significant symptoms suggestive of biological change as opposed to those suggesting psychological processes mitigates against a return to safe controlled drinking. Biological symptoms of dependence never occur without psychological precedents. They are signs of an increasing degree of dependence and there is evidence that the degree of dependence can be validly estimated, and is a useful predictor of ability to return to drinking in moderation after the establishment of the dependence syndrome. We may view alcoholism as a continuum beginning with normal drinking and ending with continual drinking in the vicious circle of severe physical dependence, in which withdrawal symptoms necessitate relief drinking which leads to loss of control and excess which in turn leads to withdrawal symptoms (see Figure 2). It is clear that changes (reductions as well as increases) in consumption are possible up to some point on that continuum and that gradually biological variables increasingly intervene with a corresponding reduction in reversibility. As the drinker progresses, his chances of returning to 'normal' drinking are reduced, and the 'reinstatement of the syndrome after abstinence' (Edwards and Gross, 1976) becomes more and more rapid and inevitable. When discussing treatment goals this needs to be made clear to the patient. An estimate of the risks inherent in a return to drinking (preferably after a period of abstinence for detoxification)

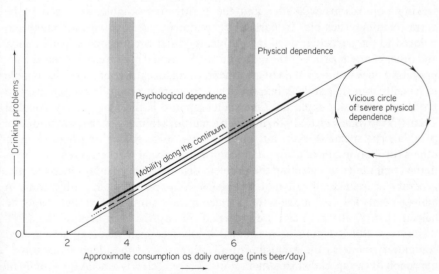

Figure 2   Diagrammatic representation of the continuum of drinking problems

should be made available to the patient. This can only be derived from a thorough assessment of the patient's degree of dependence.

Some patients receiving treatment aimed at total abstinence may eventually achieve a degree of control over their consumption of alcohol more or less by chance. Those chances can be increased by carefully planned treatment of a behavioural kind as reported by Sobell and Sobell (1978). They used a structured regime of discussion, drinking practice and training, social retraining to minimize drinking as a response to social cues, behavioural conditioning utilizing electric shock for control of excessively rapid consumption, and the use of videotapes for confronting the patient with his behaviour when drunk. Such extensive regimes are feasible but are time consuming and demanding a high degree of staff training. The commitment of such extensive resources is unlikely to occur in a widespread way at this time.

More severely dependent patients require to remain abstinent. They can be helped by the use of deterrent drugs such as disulfiram (Antabuse) or citrated calcium carbimide (Abstem) but a considerable amount of explanation of how these drugs may be incorporated into a one day at a time programme of abstinence as practised by AA may be needed. I believe that a description of the Antabuse/alcohol reaction is a more effective deterrent than is a test reaction in an artificially clinical setting. A considerable degree of support is needed for potentially abstinent patients and all should be referred to AA—it doesn't suit everybody but for some it is a complete answer. Work with spouses (if any) is essential to enable the patient's family to adjust to his newfound abstinence, to provide support and tolerance, and to adopt new roles.

With the recognition of a wider range of drinking problems the treatment seeking populations will alter and the treatment available will need to be correspondingly flexible. In particular, treatment needs to be individualized, tailored to the particular drinking problems, social circumstances, personality, and other characteristics of the individuals. The model of one centralized agency providing one system or style of treatment for all, usually rejecting those unable to benefit from that style is inappropriate to current needs. New responses to problems are being explored. One such response is the Community Alcohol Team (CAT) (Shaw *et al.*, 1978) in which a multidisciplinary team (psychologists, psychiatrists, social worker, nurse) of experts offers advice on counselling to others (probation officers, voluntary counselling, social workers, GPs, etc.) who in the community are meeting the problem drinkers. This method increases the general awareness of alcohol problems and provides an education in management. The advantage is that a much greater number of patients might be helped than if all treatment were carried out by the members of the CAT themselves. But it would be misguided if any treatment strategy emphasized community work to the exclusion of all others as did the older 'ivory tower' approach of the specialist treatment units. There is clearly a need for in-patient detoxification facilities for the more severely dependent and homeless alcoholics, whose requirements should never be neglected and whose needs for treatment must be met in any comprehensive service for alcohol problems.

Another approach is the 'core-shell model'. Here one centralized agency, usually a hospital unit fully assesses all patients needs and then refers patients to appropriate agencies such as social work, hostels, or probation. The special facilities of these agencies are closely matched to the needs of individual patients thereby providing a greater possibility of successful outcome. The 'core' itself contains specialists who in addition to assessment functions assist with the 'shell' agencies in an advisory and educational capacity, thereby building a large body of expertise which is spread over numerous agencies all directed towards helping the alcoholic in his recovery.

The detection of alcohol problems in the community

Treatment can be successful along a variety of dimensions but unless problem drinkers and alcoholics are detected or somehow encouraged to seek treatment early only a small proportion of those with problems will receive the help they need. It has been shown often that there are far more individuals with alcohol problems than receive treatment. Wilkins (1974) showed that in general practice as few as 5 per cent of alcoholics are recognized as such by their general practitioners. This is particularly so if the alcoholic is a woman. The failure to recognize alcoholism in patients may partially be accounted for by the GPs often reported pessimism about the outcome of treatment of alcoholics—they will treat anxiety, gastritis, neuritis, headaches, and the other ailments presented to them by alcoholics but if they connect these together into a diagnosis of alcoholism the patient is turned into a hopeless time consuming nuisance. This situation is not confined to GPs. The reluctance to diagnose alcoholism or serious drinking problems is shared by Probation Officers and Social Workers (Robinson, 1976). Robinson also observed that these groups of professionals are inclined to restrict themselves to the diagnoses offered by the patient or client. They tend to need additional evidence from a wife, parent or other involved party before they consider a diagnosis of alcoholism. There is a great deal of scope for education as a means of raising the awareness of various professionals to the existence of drink problems in their clients. Education of such professional groups should be conducted ideally in undergraduate, postgraduate, and in-service training. Within the medical profession undergraduate medical students need to be made aware of the possibility of alcoholic excess in the aetiology of conditions in most medical and surgical disciplines. Only by thus increasing the index of suspicion amongst doctors and at the same time making available ample treatment resources will problem drinkers be detected early before the onset of the worst of the morbidity, and at a stage in their careers when effective intervention is likely to be more successful. Availability of treatment services has to match an increased rate of detection unless the general practitioner or physician's knowledge of pointers to a diagnosis of alcoholism, and the level of his 'index of suspicion' of the condition is matched by his confidence in his own ability as a non-specialist to provide effective intervention. At this stage of the process the involvement of specialists as supporting, guiding and advising agents to the primary care doctor, or, for that matter, Social Worker or Probation Officer as envisaged by the DHSS, Advisory Committee Report (DHSS, 1978a) would be crucial. Once the primary care worker has had some success with a case of a type previously considered hopeless, he is likely to continue to improve his techniques with confidence. The process of encouragement of primary care workers to be able to treat most cases is seen by the Advisory Committee in 'The Pattern and Range of Services' as a long term one. They envisage it lasting up to 20 years.

Employers may also have a part to play in the detection of the excessive drinker, especially since the drinker is most likely to be a young male and in employment. Such detection might be considered part of a routine medical examination especially by the larger employers. Research in the USA and Scandinavia has indicated the possible use of such measures which are most appropriate when allied to an attitude by the employer compatible with recovery and rehabilitation of the worker (Murray, 1975). Similarly, since between 20 and 30 per cent of all general hospital admissions (including those serviced in casualty departments (Jarman and Kellett, 1979, Holt *et al.*, 1980)) may be excessive drinkers, there exists a need for rapid reliable detection methods. A questionnaire—The Michigan Alcoholism Screening Test—has been reported as being one of the few reasonable screening instruments for detecting alcoholism (Selzer, 1971; Murray, 1977). Blood tests to distinguish excessive drinkers or alcoholics have been assiduously sought by biochemists. The most reasonable one is to test for blood alcohol.

Any disparity between blood alcohol levels and apparent levels of intoxication indicating a degree of tolerance should arouse suspicion, especially if a high blood alcohol level occurs at an inappropriate time of the day. Blood alcohol levels can be accurately estimated from samples of breath using commercially available machines. Other blood tests have proved less successful although macrocytosis without anaemia is often found in the alcohol dependant (Wu *et al.*, 1974). Liver enzymes are often raised in excessive drinkers and return to normal on abstinence (Lamy *et al.*, 1975). None of these biochemical or haematological tests of itself has enough validity to be diagnostic but taken together may well provide clinicians as well as employers with some evidence to back up a suspicion that they may be faced by someone with a drinking problem. Confidence in the diagnosis is often crucial in breaking through the denial of problems frequently presented by the excessive drinker. Levels of liver enzymes are probably too sensitive to exclude all those who drink at safe levels, so false positives may occur. Virtually all those who regularly drink heavily will to have raised gamma glutamyl transpepdidase levels so false negatives are unlikely provided there are no other probable causes of liver damage (Whitehead, *et al.*, 1978).

The outcome of treatment

The outcome of treatment of alcoholism is not always what is expected as demonstrated by studies showing the return to normal or social drinking in those whose treatment was aimed at abstinence. Expectations of outcome have had to be modified, therefore, to allow a return to safe drinking to be seen as a good outcome. Many of those treating alcoholics find this adjustment difficult. Although the amount drunk tends to correlate quite well with the degree of problems experienced by both the drinker and by those around him, the drink itself is not the problem, it is the cause of problems in financial, physical, psychological, legal, or social aspects of life. The aim of most treatment is to reduce problems by reducing consumption or rearranging consumption temporally or spatially so that its consequences are diminished. Outcome should therefore logically be evaluated by some measurement of change in problems associated with drinking. Measurement of changes in individual consumption of alcohol is an easier way of evaluating outcome whilst making the assumption, often tacitly, that the less a person drinks the less problems he will have, and so by extension the happier he will be. Such moral undertones are echoes of the influence of the temperance movement. Account must be taken of these issues in any evaluation of outcome studies. Costello (1977, 1980) has used sophisticated statistical techniques to perform a meta analysis of all available outcome studies (initially over 300). He has found that the use of exclusion criteria by the treatment agency correlates with a high rate of good outcome and that some styles of treatment produced better outcomes than others—these were a therapeutic community orientation for in-patients, use of Antabuse, involvement of collaterals (spouses, family, friends, etc.) in the treatment, and an aggressive policy of after-care. Other features (AA, group therapy, counselling) were so common in his studies that they provided no discriminatory value. As for clients good outcome seemed mainly to depend on high social stability as evaluated by being married and being employed. Costello's approach may be open to criticism but it may also point the way towards designing programmes more likely to produce good outcomes, and tends to support the view that treatment works—a view which received something of a body blow when Edwards *et al.* (1977) published their report of a 1 year follow-up study which compared the difference in outcome between two groups of 50 married men. One group received extensive treatment of a conventional type including hospital in-patient treatment. The other group received no treatment but were given monthly follow-up visits by a social worker for evaluation only. Both groups had identical assessment interviews and were given advice about their drinking. There was no significant difference between the advice group and the treatment group at follow-up in measures of problems or in drinking behaviour. Both groups had significantly improved. The study was well controlled and any biases present would seem to have exaggerated the differences rather than produced the results found. Edwards *et al.*, (1977) were anxious that their study should not induce therapeutic nihilism recognizing the tyranny of the mean in statistical analyses and recognizing that if their assignment to treatment or advice groups had not been random, but based on well founded criteria of selection and matching, then the overall rates of improvement might have been even better. This fits in well with the reports of Armor *et al.* (1978), Sobell and Sobell (1978), and others that a good outcome to treatment can be expected, but that doubts exist over what elements of treatment contribute most to a good outcome with individual clients. Research is necessary to enable clinicians to obtain more precise and optimal matchings between patient characteristics and treatment modalities. It is not the existence of treatment that needs to be questioned but the style and content. It may eventually turn out that there is no such thing as specific treatment for alcohol dependence, and that the best that can be offered is general support to the patient and family whilst awaiting whatever it is that produces the spontaneous remissions which have been shown to occur. At least this sort of approach will emphasize the life saving aspects of medical treatment and may produce a better form of response to the inevitable crises which mark the lives of so many alcohol dependents.

Overall it seems that the rule of thirds applies to alcoholism treatment; one-third of patients do very well, one-third respond quite well, and one-third are not changed at all. This compares well with most psychiatric treatments and compares not unfavourably with treatment of many chronic physical complaints.

Conclusion

Alcoholism continues to be a major and increasing source of problems in society. Seeing alcoholism in its social context has opened up newer more rational modes of treatment with the realization that treatment must be matched to the individual and his particular drinking problems, and that problems with alcohol present in many ways—not all of them concerned with severe physical addiction. The way forward is clear. Treatment services need to broaden their scope to enable all problem drinkers to receive appropriate help. They must extend into the community and respond to those who are being increasingly detected as being in need of help. Much needs to be done to improve the awareness of these problems by the medical profession, social workers and other community agencies, whilst improvements in educating the professionals in this field is of paramount importance. The role of specialist units is changing from one which had the monopoly of treatment to one offering advice and education and assisting the primary care agencies in helping the individual but this is a gradual process and funds always need to be provided to enable these units to expand in this way.

This broader social view of alcoholism has opened up opportunities for prevention. Evidence has arisen that government has power to influence the health of nations by controlling alcohol consumption, and hence prevalence of alcohol problems, by various fiscal and legal measures. The benefits far outweigh the loss in revenue from alcohol. How far governments are prepared to grasp this nettle remains to be seen but it is to be hoped that treatment is not neglected totally in favour of prevention, merely because it is more expensive.

It has only been possible to make such clear recommendations through the application of the scientific research method to the alcohol problem. More research is required as well as a continuing evaluation of all measures of prevention and treatment.

References

Alcoholics Anonymous. A. A. World Services. New York, 1955.

Armor, D. J., Polich, J. M., and Stambul, M. B., (1978). *Alcoholism and Treatment.* Wiley – Interscience, New York.

British Medical Journal Supplement (1961). Vol. 1, p. 190.

Camberwell Council on Alcoholism (1980). *Women and Alcohol.* Tavistock, London.

Cartwright, A. K. J., Shaw, S. J., and Spratley, T. A. (1975). *Designing a Comprehensive Community Response to Problems of Alcohol Abuse. Report to the Department of Health and Social Security by the Maudsley Alcohol Pilot Project.* London.

Clayson, C. (1977). The role of licensing law in limiting the misuse of alcohol. In *Alcoholism: New Knowledge and New Responses.* Grant, M., and Edwards, G. (Eds.), Croom Helm, London.

Costello, R. M. (1977). Alcoholism treatment programming. Historical trends. In Madden, J. S., Walker, R., and Kenyon, W. H. (Eds.) *Alcoholism and Drug Dependence. A Multi-disciplinary Approach.* Plenum Press, New York.

Costello, R. M. (1980). Alcholism treatment effectiveness. Slicing the outcome variance pie. In *Alcoholism Treatment in Transition,* Edwards, G., and Grant, M. (Eds.), Croom Helm, London.

Davies, D. L., Shepherd, M., and Myers, E. (1956). The two year prognosis of 50 alcohol addicts after treatment in hospital. *Quarterly Journal of Studies in Alcohol,* **17**, 485–502.

Davies, D. L. (1962). Normal drinking in recovered alcohol addicts *Quarterly Journal of Studies in Alcohol,* **23**, 94–104.

Davies, D. L. (1980). Is there a leading theory? In *Alcoholism Treatment in Transition.* Edwards, G., and Grant, M. (Eds.) Croom Helm, London.

Davies, J., and Stacey, B. (1972). *Teenagers and Alcohol,* HMSO, London.

Dean, M. (1981). Can the Government put Britain on the waggon? *The Guardian,* 18th February 1981.

De Lint, J., and Schmidt, W. (1971). Consumption averages and alcoholism prevalence. A brief review of epidemiological investigations. *British Journal of Addiction,* **6**, 97–107.

De Lint, J. (1975). Current trends in the prevalence of excessive alcohol use and alcohol related health damage. *British Journal of Addiction,* **70**, 3–13.

Department of Health and Social Security (1975). *Better Services for the Mentally Ill.* HMSO London.

Department of Health and Social Security (1976). *Prevention and Health.* HMSO London.
Department of Health and Social Security (1977). *Report on Prevention by the Advisory Committee on Alcoholism.* HMSO London.
Department of Health and Social Security (1978a). 'The pattern and range of services for problem drinkers.' *Report by the Advisory Committee on Alcoholism.* HMSO London.
Department of Health and Social Security (1978b). *Review of the Mental Health Act 1959.* HMSO London.
Dight, S. E. (1976). *Scottish Drinking Habits. A Survey of Scottish Drinking Habits and Attitudes towards Alcohol.* Office of Population Censuses and Surveys. HMSO London.
Duffy, J. C. (1977). Estimating the proportion of heavy drinkers. In *The Ledermann Curve.* The Alcohol Education Centre, London.
Edwards, G., Chandler, J., and Hensman, C. (1972). Drinking in a London suburb. I. Correlates of normal drinking. *Quarterly Journal of Studies in Alcohol,* **6**, 69–93.
Edwards, G. (1971). Public Health Implications of Liquor Control. *Lancet* 1971 **2**, 424–425.
Edwards, G., Kyle, E., and Nichols, P. (1974). A study of alcoholics admitted to four hospitals. I. Social class and the interaction of the alcoholic with the treatment system. *Quarterly Journal of Studies on Alcohol,* **35**, 499–522.
Edwards, G., and Gross, M. M. (1976). Alcohol Dependence: Provisional Description of a Clinical Syndrome. *British Medical Journal,* **1**, 1058–1061.
Edwards, G., Orford, J., Egret, S., Guthrie, S., Hawker, A., Hensman, C., Mitcheson, M., Oppenheimer, E., and Taylor, C. (1977). Alcoholism: a controlled trial of "treatment" and "advice". *Journal of Studies on Alcohol,* **38**, 5. 1004–1031.
Edwards, G. (1977). The alcohol dependence syndrome. Usefulness of an idea. In *Alcoholism. New Knowledge and New Responses.* Edwards, G., and Grant, M. (Eds.) Croom Helm, London.
Glaser, F. B. (1980). Anybody got a match? Treatment research and the matching hypothesis. In *Alcoholism Treatment in Transition.* Edwards, G., and Grant M. (Eds.), Croom Helm, London.
Glatt, M. M. (1955). A treatment centre for alcoholics in a public mental hospital; its establishment and working. *British Journal of Addiction,* **52**, 55–92.
Glatt, M. M. (1961). Treatment results in an English mental hospital alcoholic unit. *Acta Psychiatrica Scandanavica,* **37**, 88–113.
Hodgson, R. J. (1980). Treatment strategies for the early problem drinker. In *Alcoholism Treatment in Transition.* Edwards, G., and Grant M. (Eds.), Croom Helm, London.
Holt, S., Stewart, I. C. Dixon, J. M. J., Elton, R. A., Taylor, T. V., and Little, K. (1980). Alcohol and the emergency service patient. *British Medical Journal,* **281** (2), 638–640.
Holtermann, S., and Birchell, A. (1980). The costs of alcohol misuse. *Government Economic Service Working Party Paper No. 37* HMSO, London.
Home Office (1972). *Report of the Departmental Committee on Liquor Licensing (Errol),* Cmnd. 5154, HMSO, London.
Hore, B. D., and Smith, E. (1975). Who goes to alcoholic units? *British Journal of Addiction,* **66**, 83–88.
Jarman, C. M. B. and Kellett, J. M. (1979). Alcoholism in the General Hospital. *British Medical Journal,* 1979, **2**, 469.
Jellinek, E. M. (1960). *The Disease Concept of Alcoholism.* Hillhouse Press. New Haven, Connecticut.
Kendell, R. E. (1979). Alcoholism: a medical or a political problem? *British Medical Journal,* 1979, **1**, 367–371.
Kline, N. S., Wren J. C., Cooper, T. B., Varga, E., and Canal, O. (1974). Evaluation of lithium therapy in chronic and periodic alcoholism. *American Journal of Mental Science,* **268**, 15–22.

Lamy, J., Beglin, M. C., Weill, J., Aron, E. (1975). Serum gamma-glutamyl transpeptidase and alcoholism. *Nouvelle Presse Medicale*, **4**, 487–90.

Ledermann, S. (1956). *Alcool, Alcoolisme, Alcoolisation*. Presses Universitaires de France. Paris.

Lipsey, D. (1980). Random B-tests backed. *The Sunday Times*. Dec. 28th 1980.

McCord, W., McCord, J., and Gudeman, J. (1960). Origins of alcoholism. *Stanford Studies in Sociology No. 1*. Stanford University Press.

McGuinness, L. (1980). An econometric analysis of total demand for alcoholic beverages in the United Kingdom 1956–1975. *Journal of Industrial Economics*, **39** (1), 85–109.

Merry, J., Reynolds, C. M., Bailey, J., and Coppen, A. (1976). Prophylactic treatment of alcoholism by lithium carbonate. A controlled study. *Lancet* (1976) **2**, 481–482.

Ministry of Health (1962). National Health Service. *Hospital Treatment for Alcoholics*. HM (62), 43.

Moss, M. C., and Davies, E. B. (1967). *A Survey of Alcoholism in an English County*. Geigy Scientific Publications, London.

Murray, R. M. (1977). Screening and early detection instruments for alcoholism. In *Alcohol related Disabilities* (Offset Publication No. 32). World Health Organization, Geneva.

Murray, R. M. (1975). Alcoholism and employment. *Journal of Alcoholism*, **10**, 23–26.

O'Connor, J. (1978). *The Young Drinkers*. Tavistock, London.

Office of Health Economics (1981). *Alcohol. Reducing the Harm*. OHE, London.

Orford, J., and Edwards, G. (1977). *Alcoholism. Maudsley Monograph No. 26*, Oxford University Press.

Popham, R. E., Schmidt, W., and De Lint, J. (1975). The Prevention of Alcoholism: Epidemiological Studies of the Effects of Government Control Measures. *British Journal of Addiction*, **70**, p. 125.

Rankin, J. G., Schmidt, W., Popham, R. E., and De Lint, J. (1975). Epidemiology of alcoholic liver disease: insights and problems. In Kharma, J. M. (Ed.): *Alcoholic Liver Pathology. International Symposium on Alcohol and Drug Addiction Series*. Alcohol and Drug Addition Research Foundation of Ontario, Toronto.

Robins, L. N. (1960). Deviant Children Grown up. A sociological and psychiatric study of psychopathic personality. Williams and Wilkins. Baltimore.

Robins, L. N. (1980). Alcoholism and labelling theory. In *The Labelling of Deviance* (2nd Edition), W. R. Gove (Ed.), Sage Publications, London.

Robinson, D. (1976). *From Drinking to Alcoholism. A Sociological Commentary*. John Wiley and Sons, London.

Room, R. (1981): A farewell to alcoholism? A commentary on the W.H.O. 1980 Expert Committee Report. *British Journal of Addiction*.

Royal College of Psychiatrists (1979). *Alcohol and Alcoholism. The Report of a Special Committee*. Tavistock Publications, London.

Schmidt, W. (1977). Cirrhosis and Alcohol Consumption. An epidemiological perspective. In *Alcoholism. New Knowledge and New Responses*. Edwards, G., and Grant, M. (Eds.), Croom Helm, London.

Scottish Home and Health Department (1973). Report of Departmental Committee on Scottish Licensing Law (Clayson) Cmnd. 5354. HMSO, London.

Selzer, M. L. (1971). The Michigan alcoholism screening test. *American Journal of Psychiatry*. **127**, 1653–1658.

Shaw, S. J., Cartwright, A., Spratley, T., and Harwin, J. (1978). *Responding to Drinking Problems*. Croom Helm, London.

Skog, O. J. (1977). On the distribution of alcohol consumption. In *The Ledermann Curve*. Alcohol Education Centre, London.

Sobell, M., and Sobell, L (1978). *Behavioural Treatment of Alcohol Problems*. Plenum Press, New York.

Whitehead, P. C. (1975). Effects of liberalising alcohol control measures. *Addictive Behaviour. An International Journal*, **1** (3),

Whitehead, T. P., Clarke, C. A., and Whitfield, A. G. W. (1978). Biochemical and haematological markers of alcohol intake. *Lancet*, May 6th, 1978. 978–981.

Wilkins, R. H., (1974). *The Hidden Alcoholic in General Practice*. Elek Science, London.

Wilson, R. (1980). *Population Trends*. Vol 22. 14–18.

Wu, A., Chanarin, I., and Levi, A. J. (1974). Macrocytosis of chronic alcoholism. *Lancet* 1974, **1**, 829–830.

Mental Illness: Changes and Trends
Edited by Philip Bean
© 1983 John Wiley & Sons Ltd.

CHAPTER 15

The asylum as community or the community as asylum: paradoxes and contradictions of mental health care

ANDREW SCULL
*Associate Professor of Sociology, University of
California, San Diego, USA*

Paradoxical as it may seem, any discussion of 'community care' for the mentally ill must begin by paying serious attention to the mental hospital. The current generation of mental health reformers has shown a remarkable tendency to seize upon statistics about reductions in the mental hospital census as a direct measure of the success of their endeavours. Moreover, their reiterated emphasis on the horrors endemic and inextricably part of the Victorian bins to which earlier generations consigned the mentally disturbed has helped to legitimize the notion that any change (though preferably a drastic change) must represent an improvement over what has gone before; and to deflect attention away from 'the demise of state responsibility for the seriously mentally ill and the current crisis of abandonment'. (Gruenberg and Archer, 1979, p. 498).

Though the prehistory of the asylum can be traced back to medieval religious foundations (the most widely known example in the English-speaking world being the monastic foundation of Bethlehem, or Bedlam, (O'Donoghue, 1913), its use as a major instrument of public policy has far less ancient roots. It is, instead, the private, profit-making madhouses of eighteenth-century England (Parry-Jones, 1972) and, to a far greater degree, the publicly funded county asylums and state hospitals of nineteenth-century England and the United States (Scull, 1979, 1981a; Grob, 1966, 1973; Rothman, 1971) which mark the advent of an approach to mental illness based upon the physical and symbolic segregation of 'lunatics'—their isolation in ever larger specialized and purpose-built institutions designed to contain and treat them. It is one of the ironies with which the history of psychiatry abounds that the emergence of the state sponsored asylum system was itself the outcome of a vigorous campaign for reform; and that, as with the current drive to return the mentally ill to the community, their segregation in these places was urged as being vital on both humanitarian and therapeutic grounds.

During the first half of the nineteenth century, the weight of informed opinion on both sides of the Atlantic embraced an extreme therapeutic optimism. Those who led the crusade to establish state-supported mental hospitals—people like Dorothea Dix in the United States and Lord Shaftesbury in England—saw themselves as rescuing the mad from maltreatment, neglect, and inhumanity, and ushering in a golden age of kindness, scientifically guided treatment, and cure. In this respect, their self-portrait is indistinguishable from their present day successors! But for Dix and Shaftesbury the certain recipe for neglect and abuse was to leave the mentally disturbed to the mercies of the community. More often than not, the troublesome qualities of the insane would ensure their confinement in some non-specialized environment—the gaol, the workhouse, or the private madhouse—whose structural deficiencies (to say nothing of the qualities of those in charge of those places) made harsh treatment all but inescapable. Even those not abandoned by their families were the unfortunate prey of ignorance, if not callous unconcern. The ministrations of the most devoted relatives, however well meaning, were all too likely to be misconceived, and thus to exacerbate rather than mitigate the underlying problem. Beyond this, 'relatives and dependents' were 'timid, unskilled, and frequently the objects of irritation'. (Hill, 1839, p. 6), and the home was precisely the environment that had nurtured the disturbance in the first place (Brislington House, 1806).

By contrast, the asylum was portrayed as a technical, objective response to the patient's condition, an environment that provided the best possible conditions for recovery. While relieving the community of the turmoil and disorder at least latently present in madness, it provided those suffering from the condition with a sanctuary, respite from a world with which they could no longer cope. Here they would find a home where they would be known and treated as individuals while their minds were constantly stimulated and encouraged to return to their natural state. Even the architecture and physical setting of the building could make a vital contribution to its success, by avoiding all impressions of confinement, emphasizing cheerfulness through aesthetically pleasing design, and allowing a maximum of organizational flexibility (Tomes, 1981; Scull, 1981a). Coupled with an expertly chosen and carefully supervised staff, this would secure kindly dedicated, and unremitting care, carefully adapted to the needs and progress of the individual case.

On the one hand, therefore, nineteenth-century reformists promoted a vision of the asylum as providing a forgiving environment in which humane care on a large scale was possible, in and through which a very substantial proportion of 'lunatics' could be restored to sanity. The converse of this, however, was an elaborate and prolonged campaign to impress others with the gross unsuitability of the family and community as arenas for the treatment of the insane, and with the need to insulate the insane from the pressures of the world. Repeatedly, the reformers used their speeches and memorials to contrast the horrors of these alternative dispositions with idealized portraits of the asylums' beneficence. Harnessing the combined forces of humanity and science, they had protected future generations of the insane from the trials endured by poor Mary Jones, a Welsh lunatic whose family had kept her

on a foul pallet of chaff or straw... in a dark and offensive room over a blacksmith's forge... here she had been confined for a period of fifteen years and upward. She was seated in a bent and crouching posture on her bed of nauseous and disgusting filth. Near to her person was a cup emptied from time to time into a chamber utensil. This last vessel contained a quantity of feculent matter, the accumulation of several days. By her side were the remnants of some food of which she had partaken... the stagnant and suffocating atmosphere, and the nauseous effluvia which infected it, were all but intolerable. (Hansard 81, 3rd. series, 1845 cols. 185–186)

Yet if the mentally disordered in the latter half of the nineteenth century were no longer subjected to confinement of this sort, the change in their situation was hardly the one the reformers had envisaged. The small intimate institution devoted to the cure and humane care of its inmates proved to be a chimera of its planners imaginations. By the last third of the nineteenth century, public asylums on both sides of the Atlantic had become mammoth institutions, huge custodial warehouses in which the conditions of the patients' existence departed further and further from those in the outside world, for their return to which their incarceration was still ostensibly preparing them. Even gross statistics serve as an accurate indicator of the basic character of these places. The average size of county asylums in England was little short of a thousand patients by the end of the century, and as in the United States, there were several 'hospitals of patients and employees of three thousand, four thousand, and even higher' (Hurd, 1916 vol. 1, p. 401; Scull, 1979). Necessarily in such vast lunatic colonies, 'all transactions, moral as well as economic, must be done wholesale', as their sheer 'number renders the inmates mere automatons, active on in this or that fashion according to the rules governing the great machine' (Browne, 1864, p. 18; Arlidge, 1859, p. 107).

Thus for active cruelty, the reformers had succeeded in substituting the 'monstrous evils' of 'idle monotony'. In what typically became 'a mere house of perpetual detention', there was an 'utter absence of any means of engaging the attention of the patients, interesting them in any occupations or amusements or affording them a sufficient variety of exercise outdoors'. (House of Commons, 1877 pp. 396–7, 388). Consequently, those who bothered to examine the inside of the asylum would find 'patients in the prime of life sitting or lying about, moping idly and listlessly in the debilitating atmosphere of the wards, and sinking gradually into a torpor, like that of living corpses'. Men and women 'who have lost even the memory of hope, sit in rows, too dull to know despair, watched by attendants; silent, grewsome machines which eat and sleep, sleep and eat' (Mitchell, 1894, p. 19; Massachusetts State Board Charities, vol. 4, 1867, p. xl; Maudsley, 1871, p. 427).

In the face of the growing crisis of institutional legitimacy to which these conditions ultimately gave rise, the early twentieth century witnessed a further round of reform, one designed to reinvigorate the asylum and restore it to its original curative function. David Rothman (1980) has recently dissected the American period of this second generation of reforms, those of the so-called progressive era, and shown, despite the ostensibly new emphasis on flexibility, discretion, and the carefully adapted treatment of the individual case, how vast the gap between rhetoric and reality remained; how little, in fact, was changed. Indeed, the failure of this episode to produce more than cosmetic 'improvements', such as the relabelling of asylums as mental hospitals, had already been documented indirectly by that explosion of sociological studies of the mental hospital as 'total institution' that marked the 1950s and 1960s. (Since that body of research plays an important yet controversial role in the community care movement, I shall discuss it at more length below.)

More vividly, and for a wider audience, the same basic message was periodically reiterated in journalistic exposes of the deficiencies of the mental hospitals. Perhaps best known of the latter genre, certainly in the United States, was Albert Deutsch's *The Shame of the States*. Although Deutsch was certainly no foe of institutional psychiatry, here the wheel seems once more to come full circle, with descriptions of the inmate circumstances bearing an almost eerie resemblance to the ones the original generation of reformers had proffered as irrefutable evidence of the need for an asylum system. At Byberry, for example, 'the male incontinent ward was like a scene out of Dante's Inferno. Three hundred nude men stood, squatted, and sprawled in this bare room, amid shrieks, groans, and unearthly laughter. Winter or summer, these creatures were never given any clothing at all. Some lay about on the bare floor in their own excreta. The filth covered walls were rotting away' (Deutsch, 1973, p. 49). Scenes he had witnessed elsewhere reminded him, as they did other observers, of nothing so much as the death camps they had recently viewed at Dachau, Belsen, and Buchenwald (cf. Orlans, 1948).

What is remarkable as one looks back on this 'two hundred year history of reform without change' (Rothman, 1980) is how consistently those in charge of the system, indeed society as a whole, sought to deflect attention away from the horrors of the present by resurrecting tales of the barbarities of the past. Indeed, it is perhaps not too much to claim that one of the main ideological tasks of the history of psychiatry has been to manufacture reassurance of this sort, supplying us with a seemingly inexhaustible store of exemplary tales to document the inhumanities of earlier generations and the heroic struggles through which we arrived at our present (relative) state of grace and enlightenment.

The first generation of reformers seized upon this splendid collective defence mechanism almost as soon as their visions began to turn sour. As early as 1845, surrounded by clear signs of the collapse of the very things they had previously urged as indispensable to the whole enterprise, they sought solace in the thought that 'the worse asylum that can at this day by possibility be conceived, will still afford great protection' to the poor lunatic, when compared to his fate a half century earlier (Thurnam 1845, p. 104). Later in the century, defenders of the asylum system subtly shifted their ground; the standard of comparison by which the 'success' of the asylums was to be judged was not the goals that the reformers had set for themselves, but rather the worst conditions madmen had been found in prior to the enactment of protective legislation. And given such a starting point it was naturally all but impossible *not* to find evidence of improvement, no matter how dismal the reality one confronted.

Ironically enough, in the most recent variant of this by now hallowed ploy the negative referent is not the squalor and viciousness of the period before the work of Pinel and Tuke liberated the mad from their chains and secured for them the blessings of treatment in the mental hospital. Nor is it some dark episode in the asylum's history when notwithstanding the existence of policy based on the best and most honourable of intentions, things went temporarily and inexplicably wrong. Rather, the new target of reformist energy, the evil crying out for abolition, is the mental hospital itself. Instead of basking in their role as 'the most blessed manifestation of true civilization the world can present' (Paget, 1866, pp. 34–35), even the most up to date institutions find themselves denounced as harmful and antitherapeutic, and their destruction is urged as 'one of the greatest humanitarian reforms and the greatest financial economy ever achieved' (Belknap, 1956, p. 212; see also Mendel, 1974; Szasz, 1970). Thus, over the past quarter of a century in what must surely rank as an extraordinary reversal of effort, the energy and resources once devoted to giving the illusion of reality to the chimera of the humane and curative asylum have instead been employed in the elaboration and documentation of its irredeemable flaws and deficiencies. From the late 1950s through the mid-1970s a veritable flood of social scientific research elucidated the baneful effect of confinement in an institution. The most famous and influential of these studies was undoubtedly Erving Goffman *Asylums*, though that work in many ways was simply the most rhetorically persuasive presentation of a widespread scholarly consensus.

Studies of institutions as diverse as research hospitals closely associated with major medical schools (Barabee, 1951), expensive, exclusive, and well-staffed private facilities (Stanton and Schwartz, 1954), and undermanned and under-financed state hospitals (Belknap, 1956; Dunham and Weinberg, 1960; Perrucci, 1974) all revealed a depressingly familiar picture. Apparently, 'life in a such community tended inexorably to attenuation of the spirit, a shrinking of capacity, and slowing of the rhythms of interaction, a kind of atrophy' (Miller, 1974, p. 54). In the light of this research, it now appeared that, so far from sheltering the disturbed and helping to restore them to sanity, the mental hospital performed 'a disabling, custodial function' (Hunt, 1957). Moreover, this conclusion appeared to be the more plausible in the light of the striking convergences among those working in such widely different settings, for as Belknap (1956, p. 232) put it, the very 'similarity of these problems strongly suggests that many of the serious problems of the state hospital are inherent in the nature of mental institutionalization rather than simply in the financial difficulties of the state hospitals'.

Echoing one of the central themes of this work, major American psychiatrists, particularly those in university settings, began to express fears that 'the patients are infantile... because we infantilize them' (Redlich, *preface* to Caudill, 1958, p. xi). Instead of being a positive influence, mental hospitals threatened to amplify and even produce disturbance. Such ideas also acquired widespread currency on the other side of the Atlantic, where the work of men like Duncan McMillan and T. P. Rees, British pioneers of the concept of the open hospital, was held to provide unambiguous support for the notion 'that much of the aggressive, disturbed, suicidal, and regressive behaviour of the mentally ill is not necessarily or inherently a part of the illness as such but is very largely an artificial by-product of the way of life imposed on them [by hospitalization]' (Hunt, 1957). Another British psychiatrist, Russell Barton (1965) even ventured to give this iatrogenic phenomenon the status of a new psychiatric label of its own—'institutional neurosis'.

Seen in the context of this general intellectual climate, many of the details of Goffman's arguments in *Asylums* are not in the least original. The importance of his essays lay rather in the skill with which he deployed and then extended conventional wisdom, and the adroitness with which he made use of limited evidence of often dubious validity to advance some extremely general claims. Though the reader is hard-put to recall the fact, Goffman's primary data source is a relatively brief period of field observation in a single hospital, St Elizabeth's in Washington, DC, a data base, which in other hands, would have produced still another ethnography of a particular institution. In this case, however, the outcome is a general delineation of an organizational type to which *all* mental hospitals belong—along with prisons, monasteries, military schools, old age homes, and concentration camps. Replete with vivid 'references to mortifications that disrupt, defile, assault, or contaminate the self' (McEwen, 1980, p. 147). Goffman's account of these 'total institutions' provides a powerful indictment of such places as engines of degradation and oppression, a finely rendered 'symbolic presentation of organizational tyranny, and a closed universe symbolizing the thwarting of human possibilities' (Perry, 1974, p. 353).

Oddly enough, given his interactionist sensibilities, the central feature of the portrait Goffman sketches is an inevitable and powerful structural determinism. By its very nature, the mental hospital (not unlike Dickens' Marshalsea) manufactures the human materials that justify its existence. The crucial factor informing a mental patient is his institution rather than his illness. And his reactions and adjustments, pathological as they might seem to an outsider are the product of the ill effects of his environment' (with all its peculiar routines and deprivations) rather than the natural outcome of an unfolding intra-individual pathology.

As I have suggested above, there are serious weaknesses in the evidentiary base on which these extraordinarily far-reaching claims rest. There is, for example, not even a token attempt in Goffman's work to confront the issue of what explains inmates' presence in the mental hospital in the first place. We are instead supposed to rest content with an unsubstantiated claim that they are the victims of 'contingencies', somehow 'betrayed' into the institution by their nearest and dearest (for reasons that remain entirely obscure). The 'blame' for their situation, then, lies not at all in their own conduct or mental state, but rather in a conspiracy of others to secure their exclusion from society. Likewise questions of the social location of madness, and of the kinds of existence to which hospitalization is an alternative are simply passed over in silence. And perhaps most notably of all, there is not even an attempt to generate valid and reliable evidence essential to any credible assessment of the respective contribution of intra-psychic and environmental influences to what he calls the 'moral career of the mental patient'. As Craig McEwen puts it, 'Goffman's analysis has persuaded readers as much by its literary power as by the weight of its evidence...' indeed it relies for its persuasiveness on our willingness to take 'literary metaphor as established fact' (McEwen, 1980, pp. 147–48).

Yet there is the no shortage of people (and policy makers) willing to make precisely that leap of faith. In the process, the chilling equation of the mental hospital and the concentration camp, originally the hyperbole of muckraking journalists, has now acquired the mantle of academic respectability. Ideologically this is a development of profound significance, for it has effectively legitimized 'community treatment', not by a careful demonstration of its merits (which would require systematic attention to its practical implementation); but by rendering the alternative simply unthinkable. Who, in the circumstances, would even attempt to dispute the claim that 'the worst home is better than the best mental hospital'? (Cumming and Cumming, 1957, p. 55).

It is this climate of opinion that over more than two decades allowed the portrayal of the simple decline in mental hospital censuses and in length of stay in the hospitals as an unambiguous reform and improvement. Measured in this crude yet easily quantifiable way, the 'success' of community care in both England and America is easily shown, though the speed and extent of the changes have varied between the two societies. From the earliest years of the state-funded mental hospital system in the nineteenth century a pattern was established in both societies of consistent and almost uninterrupted increase in-patient population. This remorseless increase was such that in the United States during the first half of the twentieth century, 'the public mental hospital population had quadrupled..., whereas the general population had only doubled' (Joint Commission, 1961, p. 7). In England, the timing of the rise was somewhat different, with the most spectacular increases coming in the last half of the nineteenth century, but even here the hospital census all but tripled between 1890 and 1950.

This pattern of uninterrupted growth was abruptly reversed in the mid-1950s.

Table 1   Resident population in state and county mental hospitals in the USA, 1950–1974

Year	Number resident	Year	Number resident
1950	512 500	1963	504 600
1951	520 300	1964	490 400
1952	532 000	1965	475 200
1953	545 000	1966	452 100
1954	554 000	1967	426 000
1955	558 000	1968	400 700
1956	551 400	1969	370 000
1957	548 000	1970	339 000
1958	545 200	1971	309 000
1959	541 900	1972	276 000
1960	535 000	1973	255 000
1961	527 500	1974	215 600
1962	515 600		

Sources: NIMH: *Trends in Resident Patients, State and County Mental Hospitals, 1950–1968*, Rockville, Maryland. *NIMH Statistical Note*, No. 114, Rockville, Maryland. (All figures rounded.)

First in England, then in the United States, the in-patient census began to fall. As Table 2 show, the population of English mental hospitals had decreased from little short of 150 000 in 1954 to some 83 000 in 1976. In the United States, the decline began a year later, and from a maximum of approximately 560 000 had fallen to a 193 000 some twenty years later. Allowing for population growth, of course the break with historical trends was even more dramatic than these data would indicate. In the United States, for example, had the size of the hospital population relative to the total population remained constant (and historically the tendency was for it to rise faster than the general population), by 1975 the mental hospitals would have contained some three quarters of a million people.

As comparison of Tables 1 and 2 reveals, once the in-patient census began to decline, it did so each and every year in both countries. This common experience is the more remarkable given that both societies were also experiencing a simultaneous and sharp increase in admissions to mental hospitals. Between 1955 and 1968, admissions to mental hospitals in England and Wales rose from 78 586 per year to 170 527; and although admissions dipped to 162 864 in 1970, this was still more than twice the number admitted in 1955. The rise in admissions has been equally steady and of similar magnitude in the United States. While approximately 185 000 were admitted to mental hospitals in 1956, by 1970 the figure was 393 000 (although, once more, there was a slight decline after this). Statistically speaking, therefore, the decline in mental hospital populations

Table 2   Resident population of mental
hospitals in England and Wales, 1951–1970

Year	Number resident	Year	Number resident
1951	143 200	1961	135 400
1952	144 600	1962	133 800
1953	146 600	1963	127 600
1954	148 100	1964	126 500
1955	146 900	1965	123 600
1956	145 600	1966	121 600
1957	143 200	1967	118 900
1958	142 800	1968	116 400
1959	139 100	1969	105 600
1960	136 200	1970	103 300

Sources: E. M. Brooke. 'Factors in the Demand
for Psychiatric Beds.' The Lancet (December 8,
1962): 1211, by permission (for 1951–1960).
Figures supplied by the Department of Health
and Social Security (for 1961–1970). All figures
rounded. London: HMSO.

reflects a policy of greatly accelerated discharge. In the United States, for
example, whereas, in 1950, the average stay in a state mental hospital was over
twenty years, by 1975 it was no more than seven months.

Still, if de-institutionalization has shared certain features in the two societies,
even the gross statistics in Tables 1 and 2 suggest that they have also been
important divergencies. For the first ten years, both England and the United
States experienced consistent but relatively small declines in their hospital
populations. But while the English in-patient census continued a mostly steady 2
or 3 per cent per annum decrease, the American hospital population began to
decline much more rapidly. The major source of the difference lies in the
treatment of the senile and the mentally ill elderly. In England, those over 65 do
not constitute a disproportionate fraction of those discharged from mental
hospitals. Beginning in the mid to late 1960s, however, the contrary is true in the
United States. Between 1969 and 1974 alone, the number of patients over 65 in
State and County mental hospitals nationwide fell by 56 per cent, from 135 322 to
59 685 (Senate Committee on Ageing 1976, p. 719). In individual States, the
decline, was steeper yet. In 1968, a memorandum from the New York State
Commissioner of Mental Hygiene ordered the implementation of more restrictive admissions of the elderly, leading to a fall in hospitals cases from 78 020
to 34 000 by 1973, a decrease of 64 per cent in 5 years. As Table 3 (p. 342) shows,
other states were even more 'successful' than this. As I shall discuss at greater
length below, this pattern of accelerated discharge below reflects and is dependent upon some broad differences in the practical implementation of the deinsti-

tutionalization in England and the United States. I have pointed out that one major ideological defence of the decanting of patients from mental hospitals has been the essentially negative one that life in a state-run 'total institution' was so irredeemably awful that the mere absence of its deforming, dehumanizing pressures must be an improvement. Some of the de-institutionalization's supporters have simply been content with this claim to be guided by a belated recognition of 'the limits of benevolence' (Gaylin, *et al.*, 1974), and have argued that this round of reform rests upon a prudent recognition of the need to concentrate on avoiding harm rather than doing good (Rothman, 1980). In most quarters, however, the movement back to the community has involved the invocation of millennial claims not very different from those that accompanied its predecessors in the history of psychiatric reform. In Paul Rock's apt phrase (personal communication) most of the advocates of community treatment have sought to picture the community as a kind of 'secular Lourdes providing inexpensive redemption'.

Gliding silently over the reality of the increasingly segmented, isolated and atomized existence characteristic of late capitalist societies, those active in promoting the community approach to serious forms of mental disorder argued that the very locus of treatment could prove therapeutic. By not segregating the mentally ill from the rest of us, the community approach would help to keep them integrated with their neighbours, and even where those linkages had already been strained or fractured, would more readily permit a re-establishment of social ties with 'normal' society. Instead of the passive and dependent behaviour nourished by institutional existence, community care would restore independence and initiative. Possibly with some assistance from an out-patient clinic located as a general hospital or, in the United States, from one of the new community mental health centres, patients would find their needs provided for with minimal disturbance to their existing living arrangements and in ways that preserved and protected their basic social capacities. To an extraordinary extent, however, expectations like these rested upon *a priori* reasoning rather than empirical demonstration; and, as Kirk and Thierren (1975, p. 217) have pointed out, the notion thay they even remotely correspond with actual outcomes is simply a myth, 'reflecting more the intentions and hopes of community mental health than the uncomfortable realities'.

In the midst of all the excitement about the replacement of the mental hospital and the breathless proclamations about the virtues of the community, few people noticed the degree to which the new programmes remained figments of their planners' imaginations. Nor did many appear to realize, for some considerable time, that despite all the rhetoric on both sides of the Atlantic about 'better services for the mentally handicapped', the reality was the much darker one of retrenchment or even elimination of state supported programmes for victims of severe and chronic forms of mental disorder. As Peter Sedwick put it, with pardonable sarcasm, 'the reduction in the register of patients...has been achieved through the creation of rhetoric of "community care facilities" whose influence over policy in hospital admission and discharge has been particularly remarkable when one considers that they do not, in the actual world, exist' (Sedgwick, 1981, p. 9).

After a quarter century, there is still a remarkable dearth of 'major research projects of academic respectability that can show either the extent of the need or the extent of the failure' of mental health policy (Jones, 1979, p. 557). Still, in recent years the implementation of community care has finally begun to attract more critical attention, much of it journalistic, but some of it (belatedly) from scholarly sources (Reich and Siegal, 1973; Arnoff, 1975; Kirk and Thierren, 1975; Scull, 1976, 1977, 1981b, 1981c; Senate Committee on Ageing, 1976; Wolpert and Wolpert, 1976; General Accounting Office, 1977; Bassuk and Gerson, 1978; Rose, 1979). In consequence, it is now generally conceded that on both sides of the Atlantic, a policy of de-institutionalization was implemented with little or no prior consideration of such basic issues as where the patients who were released would end up; who would provide the services they needed; and who would pay for those services (General Accounting Office, 1977, p. 39). What is perhaps more surprising, the massive reassignment of patients has continued in the face of continuing lack of attention to these matters, with the predictable consequences I shall discuss below.

Given the general emphasis on the therapeutic value of reintegration into the community (and leaving to one side the fact that 'the belief in the value of re-integration has been devoid of any systematic analysis of what constitutes a relevant community' (Kirk and Thierren, 1975, p. 213), one might have 'expected that, by now, a substantial body of research would have been built up to demonstrate the advantages that accrue when the educational, occupational, domestic, and protective functions of mental hospitals are taken over by alternative agencies. In fact, such studies [as exist] ... have been in the main, descriptive rather than experimental, and are rarely epidemiological in nature, so that it is difficult to know how far the results can be generalized' (Wing, 1978 p. 240). For example, the study of Pasamanick and his associates (1967) which is often cited as demonstrating the feasibility of maintaining schizophrenics in the community deals only with those who are members of intact families, who as we know, form only a very small percentage of long-term mental patients. Moreover, a subsequent follow-up study with even these patients produced much less favourable findings, possibly the result of the failure of the authorities to maintain adequate funding for the programme (Davis *et al.*, 1974). On the other side of the equation, we also lack thoughtful and careful analysis, based on a sufficiently representative sample of ex-patients, of the social and economic costs of maintaining such people in the community—defining cost in the broadest sense, and moving beyond a narrow concern with fiscal costs to the state to incorporate a consideration of human as well as monetary costs to the patients, their families, and the community at large.

Ex-patients, and those who would formerly have been sent to mental hospitals (for many jurisdictions have sharply cut back the criteria justifying commitment), are to be found, of course, in a wide variety of settings, and attempting to generalize about their situations is necessarily a hazardous business. The problem is intensified by 'the paucity of follow-up studies whose data can be generalized and compared, and that trace the movement of discharged patients through the labyrinth of psychiatric facilities and living conditions after their release' (Bassuk and Gerson, 1978, p. 50). And it is, of course, still more acute when one is discussing more than one country. Among state mental health bureaucrats, ignorance about the fate of their former charges is often so great that they may not even know where the discharged patients are to be found. A recent American study, for example, discovered with disconcerting regularity that 'information on what happened to former mental hospital patients and residents in institutions for the retarded was generally not available. Follow-up of released patients was generally haphazard, fragmented, or non-existent' (General Accounting Office, 1977, p. 95).

One thing is certain: the overwhelming majority of them are not being serviced by the new community mental health centres. The existence of several hundred federally sponsored community mental health centres in the United States has fostered the comforting notion (particularly among overseas observers (Jones, 1979)) that those discharged from state hospitals have simply been transferred to a setting that provides a more modern and effective way of delivering treatment. Such assumptions are quite natural. (After all, the patients are allegedly being discharged to receive 'community treatment' and the community mental health centres built as discharge units, are one of the few places where community treatment is conceivably being dispensed.) Nevertheless, they are also quite mistaken. Even if one disregards the centres uneven geographical distribution and their current fiscal problems, it remains the case that 'both their ideology and their most common services are not directed at the needs of those who have traditionally resided in state psychiatric institutions' (Kirk and Thierren, 1975, p. 210; see also Chu and Trotter, 1974). From the outset those running the new centres have displayed a pronounced preference for treating '"good patients" [rather] than chronic schizophrenics, alcoholics or senile psychotics' (Rieder, 1974, p. 11), in other words, precisely a desire not to treat the patients being discharged from state institutions. Unsurprisingly, therefore, studies show 'no large consistent relationship between the opening of centres and changes in state hospitals resident rates' (Windle and Scully, 1974, p. 11). Indeed, National Institute of Mental Health data demonstrate that 'public mental hospitals accounted for fewer referrals to community mental health centres [less than 4 per cent] than any other referral source reported, except for the clergy' (General Accounting Office, 1977, p. 69). Partly as a consequence community mental health centres 'have no direct bearing on the bulk of publicly funded mental health care in the public sector' (Rose, 1979, p. 44).

Nevertheless, some of those discharged from mental hospitals have benefited from the shift in social policy. Victims of an earlier tendency toward what the Wolperts (1976) have called 'overhospitalization', they have experienced few problems obtaining employment and housing, maintaining social ties, and so forth, blending all but imperceptively into the general population. Among those with more noticeable continuing impairment, rather as one might expect, ex-patients placed with their families seem on the whole to have fared best. Even here, they have been costs, sometimes serious costs. John Wing has recently expressed 'surprise' that, in view of the greatly increased likelihood of someone with schizophrenia living at home instead of in a hospital, so little research is being done on the problems experienced by their relatives (Wing, 1978, p. 245). His own work, and that of his associates, has provided us with much of what little data we do possess on this subject, and demonstrates that 'the burden on relatives and the community was rarely negligible, and in some cases it was intolerable' (Wing and Brown, 1970, p. 192). A good deal of the distress and misery has remained hidden because of families' reticence about complaining, a natural tendency but one which has helped to sustain a false optimism about the effects of the shifts to community treatment. As George Brown puts it, 'relatives are not in a strong position to complain—they are not experts, they may be ashamed to talk about their problems and they have come to the conclusion that no help can be offered which will substantially reduce their difficulties' (Brown *et al.*, 1966, p. 209). (Such conclusions may have a strong factual basis, in view of the widespread inadequacies or even absence of after-care facilities, and the reluctance, often refusal, of the authorities to countenance re-hospitalization.) The new policy has thus unquestionably seen 'a considerable burden being placed on the health, leisure, and finances of the families [involved]' (Wing, 1971, p. 189). The evidence may not be sufficient yet to warrant Arnoff's (1975, p. 1277) claim that 'the consequences of indiscriminate community treatment may often have profound iatrogenic effects... we may be producing more psychological and social disturbance that we correct'. But at the very least, we must recognize that 'if... state policy is to shift more responsibility on to the "family and community"... and if in practice this reads simply "the family" then the physical and psychological burdens on individuals will increase disproportionately' (Gough, 1979, p. 92).

Their public silence and lack of protest notwithstanding, more research into these families' situations is clearly essential. Yet even without that additional research, we know that one consequence of the new policies is all but certain: "community care", in this form at least, means tying down women in traditional servicing roles for their disabled kinfolk'. To put it another way, in the absence of 'genuine, socially funded resources of community care [attempts] to loosen the tyranny of the mental institution [proceed on at the price of] re-enforcing an archaic sexual division of labour' (Sedgwick, 1981, p. 80–82).

Yet whatever the difficulties encountered by these ex-patients and their

Table 3   In-patients over 65 in State Mental
Hospitals in selected States

	1969	1974	Reduction (%)
Alabama	2646	639	76
California	4129	573	86
Illinois	7263	1744	76
Massachusetts	8000	1050	87
Wisconsin	4616	96	98

Source: Senate Committee on Ageing 1976, p. 719.

families, they pale by comparison with the experiences of the greater number of ex-patients who have no families, or whose families simply refuse to accept responsibility for them. Particularly in the United States the precipitous decline in mental hospital populations from the mid-1960s onwards has been matched by an equally dramatic upsurge in the numbers of psychiatrically impaired residents of nursing homes. This trend is particularly marked among, but not confined to, the aged mentally ill. Table 3 suggests how rapid and complete the elimination of the elderly from American state hospitals has been. That the majority of these elderly people have simply been transferred from one institutional setting to another is suggested by the fact that between 1963 and 1969 the number of nursing home inmates with mental disorders virtually doubled (*NIMH Statistical Note No. 107*, p. 2), and evidence from the National Center for Health Statistics that shows a further 48 per cent increase through mid-1974, from 607 400 to 899 500 (General Accounting Office, 1977, p. 11).
· NIMH data show that by the mid-1970s, nursing homes had become the 'largest single place of care for the mentally ill', with 29.3 per cent of the direct care costs of mental illness or 4.2 billion dollars going to nursing homes operators while state hospitals accounted for only 22.8 per cent of direct costs (ibid.). More than 50 per cent of these nursing home residents were placed in facilities with more than a hundred beds, and more than 15 per cent in 'homes' with more than 200 beds (ibid., p. 16).

   These numbers alone might cause one to suspect that 'the return of patients to the community has, in many ways, extended the philosophy of custodialism to the community rather than ending it at the gates of the state hospital'. (Kirk and Thierren, 1975, p. 212). But there is a growing volume of more direct evidence which demonstrates this. The recent General Accounting Office study of the institutionalization reported 'a general tendency to place formerly institutionalized persons in those nursing homes where the quality of care was poorer and safety standards not complied with as rigidly as in other nursing homes... generally speaking, the more mental patients there were in a facility, the worse the conditions "(General Accounting Office, 1977, pp. 13–14). Despite their titles, these places frequently provided neither nursing nor a home. In the words of an Oregon Task Force, 'a typical day for a mentally ill person in a nursing home was sleeping, eating, watching television, smoking cigarettes, sitting in groups in the largest room, or looking out the window [*sic*]; there was no evidence of an organized plan to meet their needs' (cited in General Accounting Office, 1977, pp. 15–16). To make matters worse, state agencies typically provide few or no follow-up services, and little by way of effective supervision or inspection. In the absence of such controls and lacking the bureaucratic encrustations of state enterprises, nursing home operators have found ways to pare down on even the miserable subsistence existence characteristic of state institutions.

Of course, many discharged mental patients of all ages end up in other, perhaps still less salubrious settings—board and care homes and so-called welfare hotels. In Philadelphia, for example, a recent Temple University study revealed that some 15,000 ex-patients were living in approximately fifteen hundred boarding homes in the city. In New Jersey, a whole new industry has sprung up, utilizing the huge, cheap, run-down Victorian hotels in formerly fashionable beach resorts as accommodation for several thousand more discharged mental patients. In New York, there have been repeated media exposes of the massive concentrations of ex-inmates in the squalid single room occupancy welfare hotels of the upper west side of Manhattan, and in the Long Island communities surrounding Pilgrim and Central Islip State Hospitals. Many of the boarding homes in the latter area, in a pattern which is becoming all too familiar, were opened by those formerly employed by the state hospitals (see Meshnikoff, 1978). In Michigan, the pattern is depressingly similar: 'many of the foster care homes serving the mentally disabled were in inner-city areas with high crime rates, abandoned buildings, sub-standard housing, poor economic conditions, and little or no recreational opportunities. Of a total of 378 community placement residences in Detroit serving the mentally disabled 165 were located in the inner-city with 101 on one street. State officials attributed this to the availability of large homes at relatively low prices . . . and to restrictive zoning which limits after-care homes to the older, run-down sections of the city. Although the number of mentally disabled in these facilities was not known, it has been estimated to be several thousand. The only service being provided many released mentally ill patients was medication' (General Accounting Office, p. 18). In Nebraska, in an original variant on the ancient practice of treating the mad like cattle, the state placed licensing and inspection of the board and care homes in the hands of its State Department of Agriculture. Subsequent citizen complaints about the resultant conditions lead to the withdrawal of the licenses, but not the *patients*, 'from an estimated 320 of these homes, leaving them without state supervision or regulation' (General Accounting Office, 1977, p. 19).

Such systematic academic research as has been done on conditions in board and care facilities (and again the research is noticeable mainly by its absence) confirms this picture: Lamb and Goertzel (1971, pp. 29–31) concluded that: 'it is only an illusion that patients who were placed in board and care homes are "in the community"... These facilities are for the most part like small long-term state hospitals wards isolated from the community. One is overcome by the depressing atmosphere, not because of the physical appearance of the boarding home, but because of the passivity, isolation, and inactivity of the residents'. Kirk and Thierren (1975, p. 212) use remarkably similar language to describe their findings in Hawaii: 'many ex-patients are placed in "ward-like" environments where they are supervised by ex-state hospital staff, and they participate in a state hospital routine, albeit now "in the community". But many of these former patients do not even have the limited involvement provided by a day hospital. They spend the majority of their time in a boarding home which promotes dependency, passivity, isolation, and inactivity'.

In the United States over the past quarter century, with the wholesale assistance of federal funds—Supplemental Security Income (SSI), Medicaid, Medicare, and so forth—mental patients have been transformed into a commodity from which various professionals and entrepreneurs extract a profit. The consequence has been the emergence of a new 'trade in lunacy' (Parry-Jones, 1972) which in many ways bears a remarkable resemblance to the private mad-houses which were employed to deal with the mentally disordered and distracted in eighteenth century England. In that earlier period, any one could enter this business, and there was no regulation of its conduct, with the result that gross exploitation and maltreatment of patients were commonplace. Indeed, it was precisely the abuses to which this system was prone that led to a campaign for 'reform' and to the establishment of England's state mental hospitals (cf. Scull, 1979).

Again the cycle is repeating itself. We now live in a period, also hailed as a era of reform, when anyone can open a boarding home for mentally ill patients discharged from the state system—though the modern madhouse keeper relies on less blatant chemical restraints to subdue his charges, in place of the chains and strait-jackets of two centuries ago. Once more the mentally disturbed are at the mercy of speculators who have every incentive to warehouse their charges as cheaply as possible for the less they spend on the inmates, the greater their profits.

At the beginning of this paper, I alluded to the case of Mary Jones, one of a number of 'exemplary tales' (Goffman, 1961) the nineteenth-century reformers used to point out the horrors of the non-asylum treatment of the insane. Contrary to their expectations, horrors of a virtually identical sort continued to be generated by the new mental hospitals. Recent investigations suggest that they continue unabated in the new community settings. I must confess that beyond a certain point I have difficulty calibrating human misery, but certainly the condition of a Mrs Bond, an ex-patient found in an Illinois nursing home seems to differ little if at all from that of her Welsh counterpart of the mid-nineteenth century. As the Senate Committee on Ageing (1976, p. 756) reported:

Mrs. Bond was covered with decubiti (bed sores) from the waist down, that decubiti on the hips were the size of grapefruit and bones could be seen; that the meatus and the labia were so stuck together with mucous and filth that tincture of green soap had to be used before a Foley Catheter could be inserted; that her toes were a solid mass of dirt which stuck together and not until they had been soaked in TID for three (3) days did the toes come apart; that body odor was most offensive; edema of feet, legs, and left hand.'

On a less lurid level, we possess a handful of studies which systematically compare the social functioning and clinical condition of hospitalized chronic patients with those of their counterparts in quasi-institutional community settings. From both American and Canadian studies we have reports that fewer of the [hospitalized] patients were incontinent, fewer took no part in bathing, more were able to bathe without help, fewer took no responsibility for their own grooming, more dressed without assistance, fewer failed to dress and remain in hospital gowns, and more had money available and were capable of making occasional purchases' (Epstein and Simon, 1968; Swan, 1973). More dramatically, a number of studies appear to demonstrate a close correlation between the relocation of chronic patients and sharp increases in their mortality rate (cf. Marlowe, 1976; Aldrich and Mendkoff, 1963; Jasman, 1967; Markus *et al.*, 1971; but for contrary findings, see Markson and Cumming, 1976).

In view of the depths of misery and maltreatment associated with recent American mental health policy, Kathleen Jones' (1979, p. 567) claim that 'so far the United States has made a much better job of the business of deinstitutionalization' would, if accurate, constitute an even more damning indictment of British practice than she perhaps intended. Apparently, what led her to make this unfortunate assertion was the combination of a relatively intimate knowledge of the failures of British policies with a rather naive acceptance at face value of the claims made by American advocates of deinstitutionalization. And certainly at the level of rhetoric, Americans have by and large been the more active and shameless. Practically, however, the British experience has not (yet?) been quite as awful.

In part this is because de-institutionalization has simply not been as rapid or far-reaching in Britain. In general, the shift away from the mental hospital in both societies has been powerfully influenced by fiscal considerations, the savings realizable by substituting neglect for even minimal custodial care (Scull, 1977; Rose, 1979; Sheehan and Atkinson, 1974; Murphy and Datel, 1976; Rieder, 1974). In the United States, however; these pressures have been magnified by the fragmentation of the political structure. Care of the mentally ill has traditionally been a responsibility of the states, but de-institutionalization has allowed and has been promoted by the states' ability to transfer most of the costs of community support to the federal level. (The causal linkage is particularly plain in the case of the mass discharges of the elderly beginning in the late 1960s.) In the absense of this additional incentive, the rush to empty mental hospitals has been somewhat less headlong in Britain.

Ex-patients there have also for the most part been spared the excesses associated with the new trade in lunacy (Scull, 1981b). The chains of private board and care homes and the dilapidated welfare hotels, now so large a part of American mental health 'services', have few precise British equivalents. In part, this probably reflects the somewhat lower numbers of chronic patients discharged. Undoubtedly too it also mirrors the more entrepreneurial character of American capitalism, and the greater legitimacy accorded to the process of the privatization of state and welfare services (Spitzer and Scull, 1977) in a society still ideologically dominated by the myth of the benevolent 'invisible hand'.

All of these qualifications notwithstanding, the British experience with community care remains dismal enough in all conscience. As Peter Sedgwick points out, 'in Britain no less than in the United States, "community care" and "the replacement of the mental hospital" were slogans which marked the growing depletion of real services for mental patients; the accumulating numbers of impaired, retarded, and demented males in the prisons and common lodging houses; the scarcity not only of local authority residential provisions for the mentally disabled but of day care centres and skilled social work resources; the jettisoning of mental patients in their thousands into the isolated helpless environment of their families of origin, who appealed in vain for hospital admission (even for a temporary period of respite), for counselling or support, and even for basic information and advice...' (Sedgwick, 1981, p. 11).

Jones herself is not unaware of these catastrophic failures masquerading under the official guise of a 'revolution' in psychiatric care. It is her awareness of the failures that prompts her bitter comparison of British policy with an idealized, indeed mythological portrait of American practices. For her, much of the blame can be apportioned to administrative lapses. In particular, the reorganization of the British National Health Service in 1973, which eliminated any distinctive organization for the mental health services, left 'no administrative focus, no form for policy debate, and no impetus to personal development. The result is that the British services are now fragmented and to a large extent the personnel are demoralized' (Jones, 1979, pp. 565–566).

But while low morale and administrative chaos have certainly contributed to worsening the situation, they are scarcely the major sources of current difficulties. More centrally important is the absence of the necessary infrastructure of services and financial supports without which talk about community care is simply a sham. During 1973–74, for example, while three hundred million pounds was spent on the mentally ill still receiving institutional treatment, a mere 6.5 million pounds was spent on residential and day care services for those 'in the community'. Local authority spending on residential facilities for the mentally ill was a derisory 0.04 per cent of their total expenditure (Sedgwick, 1981, p. 95). Three years later, 116 out of 170 local authorities did not provide a single residential place for the elderly mentally infirm (*Guardian* January 13, 1976, cited in Sedgwick, 1981, p. 105). And more recently still, the intensifying fiscal crisis of the Thatcher–Reaganite years has simply reinforced the existing conservative hostility to social welfare services, and made the prospect of providing even minimal levels of supportive services still more remote.

Some fifteen years ago, George Brown and colleagues claimed that 'the acid test of a community service lies in whether it can meet the needs of the seriously handicapped persons who used, in the old days, to become long-stay mental hospital inmates' (Brown *et al.*, 1966, p. 10). On even the most generous interpretation of subsequent events, British and American policies have failed to meet that test. Nor should this occasion much surprise. Many of 'the most basic needs of the mentally disabled—above all the needs for housing, for occupation, and for community—are not satisfied by the market system of resource allocation which operate under capitalism' (Sedgwick, 1981, p. 77). Nor is it realistic to suppose they will be. In this most profound sense, then, Peter Sedgwick is surely correct when he concludes that 'the crisis of mental health provision . . . is simply the crisis of the normal social order in relation to any of its members who lack the waged based ticket of entry into its palace of commodities' (Sedgwick, 1981, p. 77).

References

Aldrich, C., and Mendkoff E. (1963). Relocation of the aged and disabled: a mortality study, *Journal of the American Geriatrics Society*, **11**, 105–194.
Arlidge, J. T. (1859). *On the state of lunacy and the legal provision for the insane* London: Churchill.
Arnoff, F. (1975). Social consequences of policy toward mental illness, *Science*, **188**, 1277–1281.
Barrabee, P. S. (1951). A study of the mental hospital: the effect of its social structure on its functions, Unpublished Ph.D. dissertation, Harvard University.
Barton, R. (1965). *Institutional Neurosis* 2nd edition, Bristol: Wright.
Bassuk, E., and Gerson, S. (1978). Deinstitutionalization and mental health services, *Scientific American*, **238**, 46–53.
Belknap, I. (1956). *Human Problems of a State Mental Hospital* New York: McGraw-Hill.
Brislingon House (1806). *Prospectus* (Bristol: privately printed).
Brown, G. W., Bone M., Dalison, B., and Wing J. (1966). *Schizophrenia and Social Care* London: Oxford University Press.
Browne, W. A. F. (1864). *The Moral Treatment of the Insane* London: Adlard.
Caudill, W. (1958). *The Psychiatric Hospital as a Small Society* Cambridge, Mass.: Harvard University Press.
Chu, F., and Trotter, S. (1974). *The Madness Establishment* New York: Grossman.
Cumming, E., and Cumming, J. (1957). *Closed Ranks* Cambridge, Mass: Harvard University Press.
Davis, A., Dinitz, S., and Pasamanick B. (1974). *Schizophrenics in the New Custodial Community* Columbus: Ohio University Press.
Deutsch, A. (1973). *The Shame of The States* New York: Arno.
Dunham. H., and Weinberg, K. (1960). *The Culture of the State Mental Hospital* Detroit: Wayne State University Press.

Epstein, L., and Simon, A. (1968). Alternatives to state hospitalization for the geriatric mentally ill, *American Journal of Psychiatry*, **124**, 955–961.

Gaylin, W. (1974). *Partial Justice* New York: Knopf.

· General Accounting Office (1977). *The Mentally Ill in the Community: Government Needs to Do More*. Washington D. C.: government Printing Office.

Goffman, E. (1961). *Asylums*. Garden City, New York: Doubleday.

Gough, I. (1979). *The Welfare State*. London: Macmillan.

Grob, G. (1966). *The State and the Mentally Ill* Chapel Hill: University of North Carolina Press.

Grob, G. (1973). *The Mentally Ill in America* New York: Free Press.

· Gruenberg, E., and Archer J. (1979). Abandonment of responsibility for the seriously mentally ill, *Milbank Memorial Fund Quarterly*, **57**, 485–506.

Hansard's *Parliamentary Debates*.

Hill, R. G. (1839). *A Lecture on the Management of Lunatic Asylums*. London:

House of Commons (1877). *Select Committee on the Operation of the Lunacy Law*. London.

Hunt, R. C. (1957). Ingredients of a rehabilitation program," *Milbank Memorial Fund Proceedings* 34.

Hurd, H. (1916). *The Institutional Care of the Insane in the United States and Canada*. Baltimore: Johns Hopkins University Press.

Jasman, K. (1969). Individualized versus mass transfer of nonpsychotic geriatric patients from the mental hospital to the nursing home, *Journal of the American Geriatrics Society*, **15**, 280–284.

· Joint Commission on Mental Illness and Health (1961). *Action for Mental Health* New York: Basic Books.

Jones, K. (1979). Deinstitutionalization in context, *Milbank Memorial Fund Quarterly*, **57** 552–569.

Kirk, S., and Thierren, M. (1975). Community mental health myths and the fate of formerly hospitalized mental patients, *Psychiatry*, **38,** 209–217.

Lamb, R., and Goertzel, V. (1971). Discharged mental patients: are they really in the community? *Archives of General Psychiatry*, **24,** 29–34.

Markson, E., and Cumming J. (1976). The post-transfer fate of relocated patients, in P. Ahmed, and S. Plog (eds.) *State Mental Hospitals: What Happens When They Close?* New York: Plenum.

Markus, E., Blenker, M., and Downs, T. (1971). The impact of relocation upon mortality rates of institutionalized aged persons, *Journal of Gerontology*, **26**, 537–541.

Marlowe, R. (1976). When they closed the doors at Modesto, in P. Ahmed, and S. Plog (eds.) *State Mental Hospitals: What Happens When They Close?* New York: Plenum.

Massachusetts State Board of Charities (1967). *Annual Report*.

Maudsley, H. (1871). *The Physiology and Pathology of the Mind* New York: Appleton.

McEwen, C. (1980). Continuities and discontinuities in the study of total institutions, *Annual Review of Sociology* Beverly Hills: Sage.

Mendel, W. (1974). Dismantling the mental hospital, in *Where Is My Home?* mimeo, Scottsdale, Arizona: National Technical Information Service.

Meshnikoff, A. (1978). Barriers to the delivery of mental health services: the New York City Experience, *Hospital and Community Psychiatry*, **29**, 373–378.

Miller, M. (1974). At hard labor: rediscovering the nineteenth century prison, *Issues in Criminology*, **9**, 91–114.

Mitchell, S. W. (1894). *Address before the American Medico-Psychological Association*. Philadelphia.

Murphy, J., and Datel, W. (1976). A cost-benefit analysis of community versus institutional living, *Health and Community Psychiatry*, **25** 165–170.

O'Donoghue, N. (1913). *The Story of Bethlem Hospital* London.

Orlans, H. (1948). An American Death Camp, *Politics*.

Paget, G. (1866). *The Harveian Oration*. Cambridge: Deighton, Bell.

Parry-Jones, W. (1972). *The Trade in Lunacy*. London: Routledge and Kegan Paul.

Pasamanick, B., Scarpitti, F., and Dinitz, S. (1967). *Schizophrenics in the Community* New York: Appleton-Century-Crofts.

Perrucci, R. (1974). *Circle of Madness* Englewood Cliffs, New Jersey: Prentice-Hall.

Perry, N. (1974). The two cultures and the total institution *British Journal of Sociology*, **25**, 345–355.

Reich, R., and Siegal, L. (1973). Psychiatry under seige: the mentally ill shuffle to oblivion, *Psychiatric Annals* **3**, 37–55.

Rieder, R. O. (1974). Hospital, patients and politics, *Schizophrenia Bulletin* **1974**, **11**, 9–15.

Rose, S. (1979). Deciphering deinstitutionalization, *Milbank Memorial Fund Quarterly*, **57**, 429–460.

Rothman, D. (1971). *The Discovery of the Asylum*. Boston: Little, Brown.

Rothman, D. (1980). *Conscience and Convenience*. Boston: Little, Brown.

Scull, A. (1976). The decarceration of the mentally ill: a critical view, *Politics and Society* **6**, 173–212.

Scull, A. (1977). *Decarceration: Community Treatment and the Deviant: A Radical View*. Englewood Cliffs, N. J. Prentice-Hall.

Scull, A. (1979). *Museums of Madness*. London: Allen Lane. New York: St Martin's Press.

Scull, A. (1981a). *Madhouses, Mad-doctors, and madmen: The Social History of Psychiatry in the Victorian Era*. London: Athlone; Philadelphia: University of Pennsylvania Press.

Scull, A. (1981b). Deinstitutionalization and the rights of the deviant, *Journal of Social Issues* (in press.)

Scull, A. (1981c). A new trade in lunacy: the recommodification of the mental patient, *American Behavioral Scientist*, **24**, 741–754.

Sedgwick, P. (1981). Psychiatry and liberation, unpublished paper, Leeds University.

Senate Committee on Ageing (1976). *The role of nursing homes in caring for discharged mental patients* Washington D. C.

Sheehan, D. N., and Atkinson, J. (1974). Comparative cost of state hospitals and community based in-patient care in Texas. *Hospital and Community Psychiatry*, **25**, 242–244.

Spitzer, S., and Scull, A. (1977). Privatization and state control: the case of the private police, *Social Problems*, **25**.

Stanton, A. H., and Schwartz, M. S. (1954). The Mental Hospital. New York: Basic Books.

Swan, R. (1973). A survey of a boarding home program for former mental patients. *Hospital and community Psychiatry*, **24**, 485–486.

Szasz, T. (1970). *The Manufacture of Madness* New York: Dell.

Thurnam, J. (1845). *Observations and Essays on the Statistics of Insanity* London.

Tomes, N. (1981). A generous confidence: Thomas Story Kirkbride's philosophy of asylum construction and management, in A. Scull (ed.) *Madhouses, Mad-Doctors, and Madmen* London: Athlone/Philadelphia: University of Pennylvania Press.

Windle, C., and Scully, D. (1976). Community mental health centers and the decreasing use of state mental hospitals. *Community Mental Health Journal*, **12**, 239–243.

Wing, J. K. (1971). How many psychiatric beds? *Psychological Medicine* **1**, 188–190.
Wing, J. K. (1978). Planning and evaluating services for chronically handicapped psychiatric patients in the United Kingdom, in L. I. Stein, and M. Test (eds.) *Alternatives to Mental Hospital Treatment* New York: Plenum.
Wing, J. K., and Brown, G. W. (1970). *Institutionalism and schizophrenia.* Cambridge: Cambridge University Press.
Wolpert, J., and Wolpert, E. (1976). The Relocation of released mental patients into residential communities, *Policy Sciences*, **7**, 31–51.

Mental Illness: Changes and Trends
Edited by Philip Bean
© 1983 John Wiley & Sons Ltd.

CHAPTER 16

District psychiatric services: psychiatry for defined populations

HUGH FREEMAN
Senior Consultant Psychiatrist, Salford Health Authority and Honorary Lecturer, Universities of Manchester and Salford

The history of medical care shows relatively few examples of services being planned and developed in relation to the needs of defined populations—at least until recently. In Britain and neighbouring European countries, both hospitals and primary medical care grew up piecemeal through the combined activities of religious foundations, private charities, individual entrepreneurs, and then increasingly of public bodies, both national and local. The result, naturally enough, was a hodgepodge of uncoordinated facilities, inadequate in most places and over-provided in a few; an inverse relationship developed, in fact, between the social and medical needs of different areas in England and the services available to them (Tudor-Hart, 1971). This is understandable in economic terms—there were more resources to provide them in places of greater wealth—but it certainly makes no sense in terms of human needs (which is presumably what these services are mainly for).

Over the course of time, the state became increasingly involved in responsibility for health and social care, culminating in Britain with the inception of the National Health Service in 1948. The special public provision for mental illness, which had been established on a national basis a century earlier, was then absorbed into the overall structure of the Welfare State, though the original plans for the NHS had in fact left out mental hospitals completely. The NHS took into public ownership all hospitals, except for an insignificant private sector, and since everyone now paid the same taxes to support them, it might have been expected that the new service would have seen a major priority in the need to equalize standards of provision throughout the country. But this would be to ignore all the realities of the political process. For over 20 years, the NHS actually followed the principle that 'Unto him that hath shall be given'; this was the case particularly for capital resources, and to some extent for manpower.

A rather similarly illogical situation may be found in the relationship of services for mental and physical disorder. Psychiatrc illness has always been one of the major afflictions of humanity, and any civilized society in the modern era has acknowledged the need to provide care and treatment to those who could not look after themselves because of it. If medicine had little to offer the mentally ill until recently, in terms of remedies with an established efficacy, the situation was not vastly better for somatic diseases; furthermore, it has never been in doubt that mental and physical health are closely related. Yet throughout the world, facilities for the mentally ill have been segregated into a separate category for almost as long as they have existed. This category has always been an inferior one in respect of status, resources, and the stigmatization of its patients, whatever may be the advantages of specialization of experience or of large hospital campuses. Psychiatric services have mostly been ill-coordinated with the overall pattern of medical and social care, and often fragmented in themselves so that, for instance, the staffs of mental hospitals have no responsibility for patients outside—a situation still to be found in many parts of Europe.

One further factor, though, that has usually distinguished psychiatric from general hospitals is some form of geographically defined responsibility; this resulted from mental hospitals nearly always being provided by a level of government, which had political boundaries and did not accept any financial responsibilities outside these. But since the geographical area was usually large—e.g. that of the London County Council, or a State of the USA—it was rarely possible for a meaningful working relationship to develop between any hospital and a particular community.

This paper is primarily concerned with the concept of District Psychiatry in Britain, though reference will also be made to experience in other countries. Among its origins was the need to overcome the two factors referred to above, i.e. the sporadic and geographically skewed development of health facilities on the one hand, and the segregated nature of mental hospitals on the other. For about a century, though, the mental hospital was the undisputed foundation of psychiatric care, until several alternative services started in the 1920s. These were—general hospital psychiatry (at first only for out-patients and at certain teaching hospitals); private psychotherapy, based on Freudian theory; child guidance clinics; and, after 1930, out-patient clinics operated by the staffs of mental hospitals. In terms of numbers, their impact was very small for some time, but they had a greater importance in demonstrating that the mental hospital was not the only possible focus of care, particularly in relation to such a wide spectrum as that of psychiatric disorder.

However, the Second World War then caused a delay of almost a decade before any major change could be seen in the delivery of psychiatric services. The only exception was a pioneering integrated service in Portsmouth, developed by Dr Thomas Beaton, which was little emulated and soon forgotten; it was too far ahead of its time (Freeman, 1962). But it should not be overlooked that mental hospitals then admitted only a very small proportion of those in the community with even serious psychiatric morbidity; usually, this was either because they caused unusual disruption or lacked supporting relatives (Mills, 1959).

By the early 1950s, there had been another very significant development—the discovery in France of the neuroleptics. Opinions may vary about the relative importance of the pharmacological action of these drugs, compared with social and psychological measures. Shepherd *et al.* (1961) maintained that the introduction of neuroleptics into more traditional hospitals acted as a catalyst, facilitating the shift towards a new pattern of care, rather than being the cause of that new approach. But what surely cannot be disputed is that they allowed the acute disturbances of psychosis to be controlled in most cases, without putting the patient to sleep. So that for the first time, it was possible to manage many seriously ill psychotic patients outside mental hospitals—in general hospitals, in their homes, and in the new types of facilities such as day hospitals that were being initiated. Certainly, it was remarkable that in both Britain and the USA, an apparently inexorable rise in the resident populations of mental hospitals suddenly reversed in 1954—shortly after the introduction of neuroleptics—and has continued downwards ever since. *Post hoc*, if not *propter hoc*. However, the same pattern was not seen in other countries and there seems no direct relationship between these falls in numbers and use of medication, economic or political circumstances or professional practices; any connections must be very complex.

Of course, large numbers of such people had always remained in the general community, but often at terrible cost to their relatives; (*Kilvert's Diary* and Leonard Woolf's autobiography give harrowing examples). What was new was that people with psychiatric illness were now staying out of mental hospitals, not because they feared them, but because a genuine alternative existed. At this same time, the more extensive use of ECT—particularly for out-patients—brought quick relief to many people with severe affective disorders who might previously have had to spend long periods in a mental hospital (Slater, 1981). However, Brill (1980) suggests that the radical developments of the 1950s in mental health services were part of a broader trend in public affairs. Although it had long been known that the social environment was an important influence on psychiatric disorders, the Second World War led to a greatly increased sensitivity to social issues, as well as a greater confidence in the ability of governments to overcome such problems by social engineering.

On the basis of such changes (sometimes called 'deinstitutionalization'), an Expert Committee of WHO (1953) contrasted the 'classical' system of care, dominated by the mental hospital, with a modern system, operating through a variety of services, which it regarded as 'tools' as the disposal of the medico-social team. Their new model also included the responsibility which any service should have for a defined population. Jones (1972) regards this overall change as resulting from 'Three Revolutions', i.e. pharmacological, legislative, and administrative, the latter including the open-door policy in mental hospitals, industrial therapy, part-time hospitalization, out-patient care, hostels, therapeutic social clubs, general hospital psychiatry, social work in the community, etc. This has also been described as the creation of a 'dispersed institution', in that the functions of the formerly all-purpose mental hospital (together with some new ones) are spread throughout the community served, but remain administratively intergrated.

Bennett (1978) considers that other influential forces in this process were the egalitarian philosophies of the Welfare State (with responsibility to ensure a minimum of civilized life for all citizens, including the mentally ill), general social changes (earlier marriage, smaller family size, longer life expectancy, etc.), and changes in psychiatry, including acceptance of the role of society in the genesis of illness and recognition that psychotic patients, for whom the mental hospital largely catered, are only a small proportion of those suffering from psychiatric morbidity. Wing (1979) sees a similar type of progression in the history of all socio-medical services, so that instead of being a means of segregation, their purpose becomes primarily that of protecting the affected person against stresses and preventing the development of secondary handicaps. In the USA, Backrach (1976) emphasized that changes of this kind were 'not just concerned with the location of care, but (were) also the expression of a philosophy... which strongly emphasizes people's self-determination and their right to control the forces that affect them'.

Community care

This topic will not be dealt with at length, since it is the subject of another chapter*, but at least some reference must be made because it was one of the fundamental tenets underlying District Psychiatry. Endless tedious argument has occurred over the precise meaning of this and related phrases, such as 'community mental health'. However, the best pragmatic view of the question was that of Rehin and Martin (1963) who said that a community mental health service was any scheme 'directed to providing extramural care and treatment... to facilitating the early detection of psychiatric illness or relapse and its treatment on an informal basis, and to providing some social work service in the community for support or follow-up'.

Community care was a phrase which became strongly associated in Britain with the 1959 Mental Health Act, though the Act itself in fact made no actual legislative requirement for such a policy to be followed, and in some senses was more an acknowledgment of changes that were already occurring. The trend towards community care combined the new practices of psychiatrists, who were pragmatically doing what they believed to be right, with some general anti-institutional feelings in public opinion. Parker (1971) states that community care 'attained a currency reached by few other slogans in the history of social policy in

*See Chapter 15.

this country... was easy to comprehend and offered clear-cut guidelines for policy and action'. While this may be true, whose responsibility it was to follow these guidelines was by no means clear.

Bennett (1978) considers that while 'community psychiatry' began in Britain as an attempt to provide treatment for psychiatric patients outside mental hospitals, its meaning later changed when it was used to describe a national plan for district-based services. Such a practice would have to be grounded in social psychiatry, i.e. the relationship of social factors to psychiatric illness and of that illness to society; it involved the aim of caring, not just for the identified patient, but for a whole population over a significant period of time. Wing (1979) regards this model as most suitable for people who would formerly have been at risk of becoming long-stay mental hospital patients, but not for individuals who were unlikely to have been in-patients for long, and still less for those who would never have seen a psychiatrist at all formerly; this is sometimes called 'secondary community care'. Intervention with the latter group would tend to follow the 'consultation' model of Caplan (1964), which was claimed to have a primary preventive value, and if it could be shown that much chronic disability could actually be prevented in that way, then there might be a case for thus shifting the main focus of psychiatrists' activities; but in fact, firm evidence for this is lacking. Wing, however, seems to discount the extra benefit which the moderately ill would gain from improving the availability of psychiatric treatment in the population, though both the present author (1963b) and Bennett (1978) saw service to a broadened clientele as one of the primary aims of community psychiatry. Freudenberg (1976), who was influential in the development of British mental health policy, states that community psychiatry 'assumes that people with psychiatric disorders can be most effectively helped when links with family, friends, workmates, and society generally are maintained, and aims to provide preventive, treatment, and rehabilitative services for a district. This means that therapeutic measures go beyond the individual patient.'

An American view by Serban (1977) describes community psychiatry as having three aspects—first, a social movement; secondly, a service delivery strategy, emphasizing the accessibility of services and acceptance of responsibility of the mental health needs of a total population; and thirdly, provision of best possible clinical care, with emphasis on the major psychiatric disorders and on treatment outside total institutions. Most British developments could be regarded as a combination of the second and third of these aspects. Granted the prevailing complex of values, beliefs and norms, such a reorientation of psychiatric care towards a more community-based structure was probably inevitable in the 1960s and 1970s, though this did not necessarily imply any change in the types of treatment or care employed. However, a 'community' includes institutions, which in turn include hospitals, and to some extent mental hospitals; it is the mode of use of these institutions which is of fundamental importance. They can either be closed systems in themselves, drawing in a selected group of clients and treating them by separation from their social contexts, or alternatively, they can be part of a service network, which has extensions into the population served.

Finally, it is worth mentioning a definition of community psychiatry by Sabshin (1966)—'the utilization of the techniques, methods and theories of social psychiatry and other behavioural sciences to investigate and meet the mental health needs of a functionally or geographically defined population over a significant period of time, and the feeding back of information to modify the central body of social psychiatric and other behavioural science knowledge'. This is contrasted with the public health model, particularly as advocated by Caplan (1964), which sees community psychiatry as being primarily concerned with applying techniques of prevention, at different levels, and with achieving such vague aims as 'positive mental health'. In the USA, the development of comprehensive community mental health centres was strongly influenced by Caplan's views, and started with the assumption that these facilities could prevent psychiatric illness, promote mental health, and improve the general quality of life. Such ambitious aims were not achieved, though; most in-patient care continued to be provided by the public mental hospitals and most out-patient care by private practitioners, while the centres made relatively little contribution to the major problems of chronic mental illness and dementia. This model, in fact, has little to say about making clinical care available to those who are currently ill, and its effectiveness remains entirely unproven.

Mechanic (1981) comments on Caplan's proposals that 'Some of the concepts implicit in preventive psychiatry are unfortunate not only because they are grandiose, naive, and an obvious projection of political values, but also because they continue to divert attention from making remedial efforts which are more consistent with existing knowledge and expertise.' Examples of these efforts, which are still inadequate in almost every country, include ante-natal and post-natal care, family planning services, and community facilities for those with chronic mental illness. Mechanic goes on to ask 'By what values do we divert attention from these needs to pursue illusory goals? The greatest weakness of preventive psychiatry in the 1960s was substitution of vague ideals for tangible action and a failure to specify clearly how psychiatric expertise could lead to the laudable goals that were advocated'. It is an unfortunate fact of life that so little is still known of the aetiology of most major psychiatric disorders that primary prevention of them is impossible to any significant extent. This has provided endless opportunity for the critics of psychiatry to lambast it for 'patching up', instead of preventing the illnesses from occurring. However, until scientific knowledge advances much further, psychiatrists have no alternative but to turn the other cheek to this, and develop as well as they can those measures of secondary and tertiary prevention which are now proved to be effective. Examples of these include the use of depot neuroleptics to prevent relapses of schizophrenia and the similar role of lithium in recurrent affective disorders.

Having pretensions to knowledge of primary prevention which simply does not exist serves no-one's best interests in the long run.

Proving effectiveness, however, is a problem with most changes in psychiatric care (or indeed, with medical care in general), evaluation being usually restricted to the level of monitoring processes, or of the utilization of resources. It consists of empirical studies, dependent on a shared ideology or common sense view of what is desirable, and would more accurately be described as 'enumeration'. Yet the actual objective of the service activities is improved outcome in individual clients or those around them, and without knowledge of this, one cannot be sure that the effectiveness of treatment programmes is really being increased, e.g. by more staff or facilities. Rehin and Martin (1963) emphasized that 'To demonstrate the efficiency of community care... it will not be enough to point to declining first admission rates... we shall need to know if the patient's illness has been more fully and more lastingly remitted, if his family are socially more capable of living a satisfactory life'. But in fact, objective evaluation of all professional activities is immensely difficult—'Clinicians... are convinced of the benefits accruing from clinical autonomy, improved channels of communication and the close liaison with community services... but such benefits... may be extremely difficult to measure and to demonstrate, partly because they concern intangibles' (Cooper and Morgan, 1973). These authors add that evaluation of community services is even more difficult than that of hospital services because of the problems of monitoring clinical change in that setting, and of identifying all the variables by which it may be influenced. Because of all these considerations, it cannot honestly be claimed that the superiority of the District or Community Psychiatry model over others has been scientifically established. It is easy enough to find drawbacks in it, but as Bennett (1978) points out, the mental hospital was never properly evaluated either, and always dealt only with a highly selected group of clients, leaving the rest to manage as well as they could outside.

Evolution of the district concept

Looking back, it is difficult to say at what point the District Psychiatry model fully emerged, or just how it came to be adopted in Britain as a national policy, though there are indications in the Annual Reports of the Chief Medical Officer, Ministry of Health in the mid-1950s, particularly 1958, where a definite change of attitude can be seen. In fact, there seems to have been a slow evolution over some time, which represented the final common path of a variety of processes that were then affecting the mental health scene. One of these processes was the influence on forward-looking psychiatrists of a number of pioneering ventures:

(i) The Amsterdam home treatment service: this was started by Querido in the 1930s as a means of dealing with the shortage of mental hospital beds in the city, caused by financial stringency. It became widely known in the early 1960s, and was then one of the most influential models in social psychiatry for some two decades. Starting with the practical necessity to minimize hospitalization, it went on to promote treatment of psychiatric disorder in the general community as a primary goal, and to work out theoretical formulations as a basis for this work Priority was given to the re-establishment of equilibrium in the patient's pattern of human relations—a process that was generally thought to take place better in the community itself. However, the service's administrative independence, in a separate category from both mental hospitals and private practitioners who undertook most of the out-patient care, was not a feature that was widely copied (Querido, 1968). An autonomous social psychiatry service was later developed nationally in Holland, mainly on the Amsterdam model.

(ii) Day hospitals: the first day hospitals (apart from some forerunners in Russia) were established in London and Montreal respectively in the late 1940s. They demonstrated that many psychiatric patients could benefit from a category of care intermediate between in-patient and out-patient status, thus introducing the principle of part-time hospitalization, which added a new element of flexibility to services. Later, it was demonstrated that a large proportion of those needing psychiatric care *could* be dealt with primarily as day-patients, though not necessarily that this was the best means of treating them. Arrangements for day care spread rapidly in Britain, and to a lesser extent in other developed countries; one of the reasons was a wish to save money, compared with in-patient treatment, though good quality day care proved to be expensive in staff time, and many of its clients might never actually have been admitted as in-patients (Farndale, 1963). In other words, there was a broadening of the psychiatric clientele to include a group with a lesser degree of morbidity than in people who would previously have been admitted to mental hospitals.

(iii) The Thirteenth Arrondissement service: during the 1950s, Dr Phillippe Paumelle started a unit where treatment and occupational therapy were available to psychiatric patients in a working class area of Paris. Developing from that, an association was established with both official and voluntary funds, which became responsible for all psychiatric care in that administrative area of about 200 000 people. The district was then divided into seven sectors, for each of which there was a multi-disciplinary team, which visited patients at home and remained responsible for them in all facilities, including the psychiatric hospital; hence the term *psychiatrie du secteur*. The orientation was strongly psycho-analytical, though in 1964, only 10 per cent of patients received individual psychotherapy. A small psychiatric hospital, day hospital workshop, social clubs, child psychiatry service, and various community organizations were developed for the area (Chick, 1967); however, this model was not greatly followed within France itself.

(iv) General hospital units in Lancashire: industrial Lancashire was noteworthy for a relatively large number of county boroughs, i.e. medium-sized towns which provided all their own services and were answerable only to the national level of Government. Each had a former municipal hospital with a large psychiatric observation unit, from which patients would usually be sent on to a mental hospital if they needed more than a brief stay. When the NHS began, the Manchester Hospital Region found itself with only one mental hospital per million people; these hospitals were all overcrowded, neglected and short-staffed. It was decided to use the very modest extra resources that became available to develop local psychiatric services in the observation units at general hospitals in several of the county boroughs. Although the evolution of this process is not well documented, a few influential doctors seem to have been responsible for it—as was the case at the national level. Originally, it was assumed that links would be preserved with the nearest mental hospital, particularly for long-stay beds. However, it soon became clear that the psychiatrists appointed to run these units preferred to 'consume their own smoke', i.e. to use only the beds within their own units, though of course, they did not take over the care of those chronic patients from their populations who remained in mental hospitals. Considering that they were largely setting off into uncharted territory, the enterprise and success of these psychiatrists in such places as Oldham, Bolton, Burnley, Blackburn, and Blackpool was remarkable, though they may have sometimes overstated their case, since the poverty of their resources probably restricted referrals to them. Nevertheless, their experience eventually came to the attention of those responsible for the development of the NHS, and the example of these units was a potent influence; Godber (1981), who played a key role in national policy at this time, states 'The Manchester Region experience did more to gain acceptance of the general hospital unit than anything else'. The claim, though, that these units dealt with *all* cases of psychiatric disorder in the catchment area requiring specialist attention raised questions about the boundaries of psychiatric responsibility that were never adequately faced.

Furthermore, the generalizability of this model could be questioned. In Kathleen Jones' view (1979) 'Each of the success stories in hospital/local authority coordination was based on a double accident: an administrative solution where hospital and local authorities were roughly coterminous... and an accident of personality which provided them with psychiatrists willing to reach out into the community and to experiment with a community-based service'. That individual personalities are often of critical importance is at present a rather unfashionable view, though an historical study of the service in Salford supported it strongly (Freeman, 1980). However, experimentation always has to start somewhere and, as Muir Gray (1979) has commented on the early Public Health movement, 'Essential for change to occur are *changeurs*, those individuals and groups who have the commitment and ability to realise the potential energy for change'. Without such examples, little new would happen.

It was also shown that a very similar model could be developed from a mental hospital, when this was situated actually within its catchment area—usually a county borough. The early experiment in Portsmouth has already been mentioned, but during the late 1950s, developments in York, Croydon (May and Wright, 1967), and Nottingham attracted much interest. In fact, the difference between a large general hospital unit such as Oldham (Freeman, 1960) and a medium-sized local mental hospital that had shed much of its chronic population was scarcely significant. Bennett (1978) criticized these arrangements on the grounds that they offered 'only specialized, segregated care for the mentally ill, who often retained their sick role', but this seems to underestimate the considerable achievement of breaking down mental hospitals' isolation.

British Mental Health Policy, 1948–60.

The early years of the NHS were preoccupied with setting up an administrative structure, repairing wartime neglect, and establishing uniform conditions for staff; even though most of these were miserably paid, the cost of the service soared far beyond the naive financial predictions on which it had been founded. The fact that very little new hospital building occurred for over 15 years at least had the positive effect of preventing any additional mental hospitals coming into being—something that was likely to happen at one time. In general, psychiatric services were little different from the 1930s, though Blacker (1946), in a far-seeing book, predicted that they would have to undergo enormous expansion and change if, as was necessary, they were to help wider categories of people suffering from psychiatric morbidity. Even for the NHS, the rate of increase was particularly small in psychiatry, which carried very little weight within the medical Establishment. In addition to this lack of resources, the tripartite administrative division of the NHS—into hospitals, family doctors and local health authority services—made effective development very difficult. Though the Macmillan Royal Commission had concluded in 1926 that mental disorder should be 'dealt with on modern public health lines', there was still very little sign of this happening. For instance, in some regions, a psychiatric patient requiring admission might be taken into any mental hospital which had a vacancy, however far this was from his home; if he had several readmissions, each might be to a different hospital, so that no continuity of care was possible.

Outside hospital, there was virtually nothing for the mentally ill except a more widely available service of family doctors—though hardly any of these had had teaching or experience in psychiatry. (The role of the GP in psychiatry, which is the subject of another chapter,* will not be discussed at any length here). In 1948, with the ending of the Poor Law, local health authorities were given the duty of providing officers (DAOs) who would undertake compulsory admissions to mental hospitals. Again, there was no requirement for them to have any knowledge of mental illness, and some very curious individuals undertook the job at times in the smaller authorities—a situation that remained unchanged with

* See chapter 17.

the 1959 Mental Health Act, except for the new title of Mental Welfare Officer. In a general sense, these were community social workers, but they were administratively subject to the Medical Officer of Health, though not normally able to expect any professional guidance from him or his medical colleagues. Very few doctors indeed in public health had any special training in psychiatry, and in fact, the rigid bureaucracy of local government had virtually no experience of employing professional staff with a caring function, who would expect to make their own decisions, on the basis of their professional skill. A few qualified PSWs did begin to be employed in more progressive local authorities—though there were only eight such PSWs in 1951. However, their position was usually a difficult one, and they tended to retreat into isolated corners of professionalism, viewed with suspicion or hostility by the rest of their colleagues, who were mostly untrained and of different social characteristics. This was the unpromising basis on which 'community care' had to be established.

As mentioned earlier, the total resident population of British mental hospitals began to fall in 1954, in spite of the fact that admissions were continuing to increase steadily—a trend encouraged by progressive psychiatrists, believing that more could be done therapeutically for patients who came in at an early stage of illness. In fact, substantial changes were brewing within the mental health services, even though little was yet to be seen on the surface; one reason for them was undoubtedly the recruitment of many doctors of high quality for psychiatry in the Armed Forces during the Second World War. Afterwards, most of these joined the NHS as psychiatrists, and they provided a marked contrast with the rather poor quality of medical staff that had usually been found in mental hospitals (and is still to be found in most other parts of the world). Amongst other things, these consultants were generally intolerant of the traditional system of hierarchical authority under a medical superintendent, which contributed much to the institutionalism of mental hospitals and which was completely incompatible with their status in the NHS. Their 'Oedipal' rebellion against this system, which eventually resulted in the abolition of superintendents (except in Scotland), was certainly a positive factor for change. Another was the therapeutic community concept, developed within wartime psychiatry by Maxwell Jones; although often honoured more in the breach than the observance, this was a potent ideological force, which caused many old habits to be questioned and added psychological and social dimensions to the more organically based regimes in psychiatry. The foundation of postgraduate psychiatric centres at the Maudsley Hospital, London and at Edinburgh did much to raise intellectual and research standards, though contributing little at this time to practical developments in psychiatric care.

Yet another influential concept was the Open Door, pioneered particularly in the late 1940s by George Bell of Dingleton Hospital in the Scottish Borders. Though the history of psychiatry contained many examples of institutions that had been operated without locked doors for certain lengths of time, the old norm had always re-established itself eventually, except for a favoured élite of patients. The rationale for this policy of locking up was never examined objectively—any more than the 'certified' status of most chronic mental hospital residents, who had no wish to leave in any case. Bell's example (achieved before neuroleptics were widely available) had a more permanent effect on this occasion, and ward doors were unlocked throughout the 1950s and 1960s, contributing to a more therapeutic atmosphere and to a greater acceptability of the hospitals to prospective patients. It was only some years later, when mental hospitals had taken on a new function of extensive psychogeriatric care, that the problem of the senile wanderer caused some doors to be re-locked—but this was for different reasons.

Mention has already been made of the first day hospitals, which brought a new kind of flexibility into psychiatric facilities, contrasting with the rigid administrative procedures of the mental hospital system. Out-patient care also grew rapidly, from the early years of the NHS, and became even more important with the Pharmacological Revolution that produced neuroleptics, antidepressants, and tranquillizers in the 1950s. Industrial therapy, with a rehabilitative aim, began to replace the unpaid labour of a minority of mental hospital patients in hospital ancillary departments; it found its most intensive development in the Industrial Therapy Organization at Bristol (Early, 1960). Therapeutic social clubs and hostels were set up in some areas, notably in Salford (Freeman and Mountney, 1967) and a few psychiatric beds became available in general hospitals, though only for highly selected patients. In its best Wakleyan tradition, *The Lancet* published a series with the title 'In the Mental Hospital', which focused on the changes that were stirring in that previously torpid scene, and in turn stimulated professional staff in psychiatry to attempt further new developments. One of these was the fostering of links between a psychiatric hospital and the population it served, particularly through the local authority health department; early examples of this kind of cooperation occurred in Nottingham (MacMillan, 1956), York, and Oldham.

Such changes resulted in a widespread feeling among psychiatrists and allied professions that progress was being seriously impeded by obsolete provisions of the law. Apart from the amendments of the 1930 Mental Treatment Act, these were still embodied in the 1890 Lunacy Act which, as Jones (1972) has pointed out, was preoccupied overwhelmingly with the need to set up safeguards against possible illegal detention, rather than with providing care to those who needed it. Its effect was to impose a rigidity on the whole system that made innovation, early treatment, and flexible use of resources extremely difficult. These legal operations were supervised by the Board of Control, a surprisingly progressive body, which in the 1930s had unsuccessfully tried to persuade local authorities to run their mental hospitals in a more enlightened manner. In the early 1950s, though, it found a way round some of the more irksome provisions of the law by allowing admission of patients to mental hospitals on a 'non-statutory' basis, to 'de-designated' wards. (Patients could only be admitted under the Lunacy Act to accommodation that was legally designated for that purpose.) By this means, psychiatric patients had the same legal status as medical patients in a general hospital; the arrangement clearly worked well, and provided the example for a fundamental reform of the law governing mental disorder.

As a result of these currents of opinion, a Royal Commission was set up in 1954; it reported three years later and recommended sweeping changes in the relevant law. The usual fate of such reports is to gather dust in some Whitehall pigeon-hole, but as luck would have it, the government of the day found itself short of new legislation, and embodied virtually all the Commission's recommendations in the Mental Health Act, 1959. Both the Report and the Act were founded on the beliefs that as a medical discipline, psychiatry did not need detailed legal control of its activities, and that the focus of its operations should shift, as far as possible, from institutions to the communities served by them. However, there has been a widely prevalent misunderstanding ever since that the Act legislated for a policy of 'community care', which in fact it did not. It certainly removed any possible legal barriers to the implementation of such a policy, and it gave permissive powers to local authorities to provide extramural services, specifically mentioning hostels among these. But the only positive duty for the authorities was the same as before—to provide officers who would undertake compulsory admissions under the Act. Furthermore, every successive government refused to 'earmark' for mental health purposes any of the money which local authorities received from them.

As MacMillan (1965) pointed out, the greatest weakness of national policy, in connection with implementation of the 1959 Act's objectives, was the dependence on local initiatives and on voluntary action by local authorities for the development of integrated services. Within the budget of each local authority, mental health had to compete with all other demands, and it was rare for it to get any significant share. Probably no more than lip-service was ever paid to the policy of setting up a network of community-based services as an alternative to mental hospitals, since the scale of money that would have been required for this task never existed in the local authority financial system. Most authorities did very little, and a significant number did nothing at all; even 20 years after the Act was passed, the differences between the best and worst authorities remained as wide as ever.

Further developments

In 1961, Tooth and Brook published an analysis of the fall in numbers of residents of mental hospitals whith had occurred during the past five years, and they unwisely (in statistical terms) continued this straight line down to zero for long-stay patients in 1975. This simplistic projection of a trend whose causes were largely unknown seems to have influenced Mr Enoch Powell, as Minister of

Health, to proclaim the forthcoming end of British mental hospitals, in a characteristically apocalyptic speech (1961). Instead, in-patient accommodation for psychiatric patients was to be provided in district general hositals (DGHs); the first national Hospital Plan for these hospitals was published in the following year, though the actual role of psychiatry in them remained ill-defined for some time. Unfortunately, what was omitted was a calculation of even the roughest cost of this exercise; had this been done, it would have been obvious that the price of replacing all mental hospitals in Britain was far beyond the resources that might conceivably be available. In fact, the 1962 Hospital Plan was simply the lumping together of uncoordinated ideas and hopes from different authorities, with no real thought as to where the capital was to come from for the new buildings, or the revenue to operate them. Considering the penny-pinching way in which the NHS had actually operated from the beginning, this profligate phantasizing was most extraordinary; yet it was to be repeated over and over again.

In 1963, the Ministry of Health published a 'National Plan' for community care; like the Hospital Plan (with which it was completely uncoordinated) it was merely an assembly of proposals by individual local authorities. It contained no obligation on them to provide these services, nor any guarantee that the proposals would actually be carried out. In the following year, the Ministry issued a circular to hospital authorities on 'Improving the Effectiveness of Psychiatric Hospitals'; it recommended changes of the kind that have been described above, and particularly urged hospital – local authority collaboration. However, as no extra funds were provided, its effect was limited. Apart from this circular, central Government issued practically no specific advice on mental health services in the 1950s and 1960s, though official approval was clearly given to such integrative arrangements as those in Nottingham (which all centred on one individual and largely collapsed on his retirement). The situation was an unusually fluid one, so that where a group of like-minded professional staff came together, they could strike out in a new direction, providing their ideas did not require spending much extra money. In this, the clinical autonomy of NHS consultants and their position outside administrative hierarchies was particularly important. There was a strong feeling of optimism abroad—communicated particularly at the Annual Conferences of the National Association for Mental Health—and those involved felt that the problems of mental disorder could be largely conquered on the basis of their professional skills, if the resources could be obtained to do it. This feeling was not shared, however, by Titmuss (1961), who emphasized the enormous scale of the needs to be met in community care, compared with the puny efforts so far directed at them; he proved to be at least partly right.

During the 1960s, several different models of services for defined communities were developed through local initiatives of this kind:

(a) In Salford, extramural services were begun by the local authority; a new consultant had access to all facilities serving the population, and obstacles to integration were removed. The social workers became active partners in policy-making and training (Freeman and Mountney, 1967). The fact that the Medical Officer of Health devolved his administrative control over the activities of the local authority mental health services down to specialist social workers and doctors (mainly NHS) was of crucial importance.

(b) In Nottingham, the local authority handed over direction of its social workers to the medical superintendent of the mental hospital, but did not contribute to the organization or facilities.

(c) In West Ham, a consultant without hospital attachments developed a community service centred on local authority child guidance clinics; hospital services for adult psychiatry were unchanged (Kahn, 1967).

(d) In Worthing, the mental hospital pursued an extramural policy of its own, uncoordinated with the local authority (Carse, *et al.*, 1958). Its success was claimed primarily on the basis of a substantial reduction in admissions, yet some years earlier, a high admission rate had been thought to indicate a successful mental hospital.

(e) In York, the mental hospital and local authority cooperated through a joint committee and personal relationships, but the nature of the service was unchanged (Freeman, 1963a).

(f) In Lancashire, consultants based in general hospital units developed integrated services, in which the local authorities cooperated, but provided few initiatives of their own.

In 1971, all these arrangements were thrown into a state of upheaval by the Seebohm reorganization of social services, which absorbed mental health social workers into unified departments for each local authority. Mental Health specialism came into disfavour because of the generic ideology of the new departments, which set up elaborate administrative hierarchies. Opinions remain divided as to the overall value of this exercise, but nearly all psychiatrists regarded it as a disaster (Society of Clinical Psychiatrists, 1977). Though most districts admittedly did not have a mental health social work service of high quality before Seebohm, those which had devoted resources to creating one found it disappearing before their eyes, as staff were shuffled and reassigned. Jones (1979) has pointed out that 'integration' of social work meant loss of the common understanding of professionals working in mental health, and thus a disintegration, which was particularly unfortunate since medical and social needs are often inseparable. An official view (Brothwood, 1973) was that 'many more social workers are now involved in helping the mentally ill' and that 'the area teams will provide the continuity of care', but reality has rarely corresponded to that.

The present era

The early 1970s was a period in which managerialism was thought to be the key to solving the major problems of society, and in addition to the implementation of Seebohm, it saw the reorganizations of the NHS and of local government. The NHS reorganization of 1974 has had a worse press than it deserves; its objectives were broadly right, but it made the fundamental mistake of introducing one tier of management too many. This may have been because the health district was a concept which only emerged at a fairly late stage of the planning; however, the 1982 reorganization has made the district the basic unit of management, which is important in the development of locally-based psychiatric services. Mental hospitals lost their separate management committees in 1974 and though this may have resulted in some drainage of resources to other specialities, the record of most HMCs was a dismal one, for which no obsequies are needed. As a result of local government reorganization, though, places like Bristol or Blackpool which formerly ran their own social services found themselves part of a large county. Though small is not always beautiful, the results of this situation were generally unfortunate.

Present mental health policy in Britain really dates from the publication of _Hospital Services for the Mentally Ill_ by the DHSS in 1971. It outlined 'the essential elements of a comprehensive integrated hospital and community service based on a department in a district general hospital', in this, '... the in-patient, day patient, out-patient, general practitioner and local authority services jointly form a comprehensive service for patients in an area, to be used as flexibly as possible, in which the emphasis is on rehabilitation, on the preservation of continuity of the patient's personal relationships and of his contacts with the local community'. It was said to be important that the DGH psychiatric department should be supported by psychogeriatric assessment facilities and by a well developed geriatric department. Even more important was 'the provision of adequate community services by local authorities... Without this, an effective comprehensive service cannot be provided'. Generally speaking, each area of 60,000 population was to be served by a multi-disciplinary therapeutic team, including a consultant psychiatrist, which had its facilities in a division of the hospital. Referral of long-stay patients from DGH units to mental hospitals was to be avoided and mental hospitals were expected to run down towards closure; this process might be accelerated by transferring the residue to other mental hospitals or to small 'community hospitals'. However, 'It should be the responsibility of the local authority social services department, where necessary, to find suitable residential accommodation for patients discharged from hospital'. Norms of provision were—0.65 day places per 1000 population; 10–20 beds per 250,000 for psychogeriatric assessment; at least six out-patient sessions per 100,000 per week; and small numbers of beds for children and adolescents. Sainsbury (1973) pointed out, however, that the precise objectives of the new pattern were not stated, and that the main proposals had not been the subject of research specifically to assess their effects.

This was a clearly formulated policy, which in its general objectives was non-controversial. However, its advice was over-rigid ('only in exceptional circumstances should a "division" admit a patient from outside its "district"'); it ignored the need for specialized services such as psychotherapy; it denied the possibility of new long-stay patients accumulating; its reliance on social service provision was completely at variance with reality; and it provided no reliable data on which its norms might have been based. Also, since the number of general hospital units was still quite small, it should have been made clear that the process of providing them throughout the country was bound to be a very long one indeed. In 1968, a pilot project had started in the Worcester area with the objective of providing a community-based service and closing the mental hospital (Hassall, 1976), but calculating the cost of this development on a nationwide basis might have resulted in a rethink of policy, particularly as the DHSS had to augment the local social work service in Worcestershire by paying for four additional salaries.

A symposium on this national policy (Cawley and McLachlan, 1973) contained a restatement of the official view by Brothwood, who emphasized that the hospital function was to provide medical and nursing care for those in whom this is the primary need, whereas there was no justification for making the chronically handicapped long-term hospital residents. However, long-term provision of beds and day places for the aged with severe dementia (ESMI) was added—though not necessarily in the DGH—as well as medium security beds, on a regional basis. Sectorization was commended since it improved communication between staff members, ensured continuity of treatment, and fostered cooperation with the area team of social workers; furthermore, somebody had to have the final responsibility for treating patients whom no-one else would willingly accept, such as chronic schizophrenics. It was also advised that the staff of a DGH unit should constitute a single entity with that of the related division of the local mental hospital. In 1970, 94 DGH psychiatric units were operational, though varying greatly in size, but they accounted for only 15.5 per cent of all hospital admissions of the mentally ill; by 1976, this proportion had risen to 23 per cent.

Wing (1973) pointed out that since the problems of chronically handicapped people are both medical and social, these two aspects of the service must be integrated to be effective—'An active supervisory service ... for chronic schizophrenic patients must form an essential part of any community care system' and continuity of contact must be maintained. It was likely that a locally based comprehensive service would attract an increased clientele, while research on emergency referrals (Gleisner *et al.*, 1972) showed that these were often handled by inexperienced staff, whereas an experienced multi-disciplinary team should be generally available, if unnecessary hospitalization was to be avoided.

Account had not really been taken of this need, nor of the build-up of new long-stay patients; Mann and Sproule (1972) calculated, on the basis of Camberwell data, that for a population of 170,000, these would require 20 long-term hospital places, 25 supervised hostel places, and 20 unsupervised places in sheltered accommodation. Excluding the latter, 0.26 places per thousand population would be needed, together with 0.65 beds for patients staying up to a year, giving a total of 0.91. However, this took no account of old long-stay patients, who also remained in substantial numbers.

As far as sectorization was concerned, psychiatrists expressed their concern that this should be interpreted flexibly, in view of the special interests of individual consultants, the legitimate preferences of GPs or patients, and varied local conditions, e.g. of population density. There was also the danger of professional isolation where consultants worked single-handedly, without sufficient contact with their peers. Birley (1973) pointed out that in 1970, there was an average of just over two psychiatric doctors in post, one of whom was a consultant, for each 60,000 of the population; this included child psychiatrists. In view of the huge number of people in the population suffering disabilities from neuroses, personality disorders, and interpersonal problems, it seemed unlikely that most of these could ever be dealt with by experienced specialist staff. There were also the many people with chronic disabilities from psychoses or organic brain syndromes, who had complex needs. In terms of staff numbers and quality, it seemed that only a rudimentary service could be provided for much of the country, which drew attention once more to the gross disparities of resources from place to place. Furthermore, much responsibility was now being shifted on to local authorities to replace functions of the mental hospitals; yet central Government could do little to influence local situations, whilst experience up to then could give no confidence that a reasonable level of community-based mental health services would be provided everywhere by the Social Services.

After lengthy consultations, Government policy was promulgated in the White Paper 'Better Services for the Mentally Ill' (DHSS 1975 (a)). This acknowledged that adequate supporting facilities in the community were not generally available, and laid down four main objectives: expansion of social services provision; relocation locally of specialist services; establishment of suitable organizational links within the service; and increase in staffing levels. The new pattern of staffing was to consist of (a) Primary Care Team—GPs, health visitors, home nurses, social workers, (b) Specialist Therapeutic Team—psychiatrists, nurses, social workers, occupational therapists, and psychologists (c) Social Services, and (d) Volunteers. The DGH psychiatric unit was to be seen 'not simply as an in-patient department but as a centre providing facilities for treatment on both a day and in-patient basis and as the base from which the Specialist Therapeutic Team provides advice and consultation...'.

It was acknowledged that there were many old long-stay patients who could not realistically be discharged, and that new long-stay patients were accumulating, some of whom would have to remain in hospital accommodation. The Government's aim was said to be 'not to close or run down the mental illness hospitals but to replace them with a local and better range of facilities'. Where a mental hospital served more than one Health District, it should be split into divisions, each serving a district and integrated with the staff and facilities there. There was to be a radical change in the balance of resources, decreasing those for in-patient care and increasing those for out-patient, day, and residential care within the community.

This contained a much more sophisticated approach than earlier statements, but although it drew attention to the financial aspects of the policy, it said very little as to how these were to be met. In fact, there was still no possibility of the necessary amounts of capital being available to build the required DGH units within any reasonable time-scale; in one Region alone, this would have required £100 million at 1980 prices (Brough, 1981). Nor was the likelihood any greater of all local authorities providing the scale of community services that were needed to make up for reduced hospital accommodation and to improve standards. Early and Nicholas (1981) reported that though the resident population of a Bristol mental hospital had fallen by 59 per cent over the period 1960–80, 23 per cent of the remaining patients needed sheltered accommodation outside; however, Avon Social Services had just closed the one hostel in the county, and were spending only 0.7 per cent of their budget on adult psychiatric services.

A year after the appearance of the White Paper, Freudenberg gave a semi-official restatement of the policy of District Psychiatry (1976). Acknowledging the view that psychiatric intervention 'should be intimately related to the processes which occur in social contexts in the community' (Grinker, 1975), he stated that one of the main determinants of a community-based policy had been recognition of the detrimental effects that large, often isolated institutions had on patients, particularly schizophrenics. The number of occupied psychiatric beds in Britain had fallen by 60,000 in the past 20 years, and it was hoped that hospitalization would be further reduced by screening of patients before every admission and by maximum use of out-patient and day care. The network of facilities in a district was seen as consisting of a number of small manageable components, all within easy reach of the community they serve. However, in view of national economic difficulties, a low-cost policy was advised, with less specialized facilities being established first. The same approach has been proposed by the present author (Freeman, 1979).

In Freudenberg's view, if responsibility is clearly related to a defined, manageable population area, the psychiatrist and multi-professional team will develop a thorough knowledge of psychiatric disorder there, and will be more closely linked to the primary care team. They become more aware of patients' social circumstances and networks and of the general characteristics of the community, including its agencies and representatives—'Without such reorientation the development of community psychiatry is not possible. In turn, the community eventually also demands a much greater say in the way service are run'. Freudenberg goes on to suggest that in these circumstances, preventio becomes more feasible, though it is acknowledged that much of this goes fa beyond the responsibility of psychiatry; of these preventive measures, crisi intervention seems to be the most directly relevant at present, though its effect are still unevaluated.

As far as the social service contribution to district services is concerned, da centres were being planned on the basis of 0.6 places per 1000 population, but a the projected rate of progress in 1976, it would take 25 years to provide this fo the whole country. Day centres provide shelter, occupation, and social activity they relieve the strain on caring families, give help with personal relationships, an encourage participation in work or community activities. Sheltered longer-sta accommodation was being recommended by the DHSS on the basis of 0.1 places per 1000 population, of which about half should be in staffed homes; th same prolonged time-scale as for day care was envisaged, but might be reduce by using cheaper forms of building. During this time, it was hoped that th number of DGH hospital beds would rise to 26000 and that the number o occupied psychiatric beds might have fallen to 65000—possibly a very over sanguine view.

As far as new long-stay patients were concerned (i.e. under age 65, and i hospital between one and three years), a DHSS study (1975), had projected need of 0.17 hospital places per thousand population, which might be provided i a 'hospital hostel', from which patients could attend a day hospital or centre However, the Camberwell register had indicated a larger need than this and i Salford, a figure of about 0.6 was forecast, consisting mainly of elderly patient with dementia (Fryers, 1979). The basic flaw in national policy which Macmilla had pointed out a decade earlier—that it depended on local authorities who wer often poor or unwilling—thus remained unchanged, though some improvemen had come with the system of joint financing. However, the progressive restrictio of public spending from 1976 onwards has meant that the time-scales forecast b Freudenberg no longer have much relevance; in fact, some local authorit services have actually been reduced. Bewley *et al.*, (1981) point out that 'new long-stay patients have is fact often had a long psychiatric career in othe hospitals previously; in their five-year follow-up of 1467 mental hospita patients, only 17 of the 81 'new chronic patients received had not earlier been i other psychiatric hospitals.

During the period 1970–75, psychiatric doctors and nurses in Britain increase in numbers by 31 per cent and clinical psychologists by 64 per cent; out-patien attendances increased by $11\frac{1}{2}$ per cent and day-patient attendances by 55 per cent but the total number of in-patient admissions did not change much overall (firs admissions actually decreased by 10 per cent). There seemed to have been som shift, therefore, from in-patient to day care, and an increase in the amount o professional time available per patient—though teaching, research, and administration would also make demands on this (Williams and Clare, 1981). To some extent, therefore, the objectives of national policy were being met, though little or nothing was yet known of their effect on patients.

Case registers monitor the actual use of psychiatric services, but their data cannot decide questions of 'need' or of value, which essentially depend on human judgment. A ten-year study by the Salford Register (Wooff *et al.*, 1982) showed that when 31 December 1968 was compared with 31 December 1978, there was virtually no change in the ratio of occupied psychiatric beds per thousand adult population. Hospital day patients increased from 0.28 to 0.69 per thousand, but day centre attenders were unchanged; the contribution of day care to the overall total of psychiatric care remained relatively small. Out-patients seen by doctors were also unchanged, but a substantial new category (3 per thousand) had emerged of psychotic patients attending for depot neuroleptic injections only and being usually dealt with by nurses. Psychiatric social work clients showed a minimal increase to 2.39 per thousand, but were almost matched by another new category—patients seen by psychiatric community nurses. The total one-day prevalence for all forms of care in adults had increased over the decade from 9.54 per thousand to 13.48, the difference being accounted for almost entirely by these two new categories. This supports the above view of Williams and Clare that increased staffing had permitted a genuine fall in case-loads; it also indicates an absolute expansion in 'community' care, but without any great effect on use of existing hospital facilities. In Salford, the specialist social work team had been retained after Seedbohm, but changed from being community-based to hospital-based; in some areas, though, such specialism has virtually disappeared, and social workers are no longer a regular part of the psychiatric professional team. In such circumstances, there is a tendency for most essential activities of social workers with the mentally ill to be taken over by community psychiatric nurses (CPNs).

Salford illustrates the dramatic growth during the 1970s of this form of care, which was unknown before 1954. Since psychiatric nurses have the greatest experience of the day-to-day care of the mentally ill, it would be illogical for those patients who live at home to be deprived wholly of nursing care, particularly now that long stay in hospital has become much less common. Furthermore, the development of depot neuroleptic treatment in schizophrenia made it particularly important that those patients who would not attend regularly at a hospital or clinic for their injections should receive them at home; only a nurse could realistically be expected to do this. A survey in 1980 showed that in England and Wales, there was an average of one CPN per 42,000 population (CPNA, 1981) but with enormous variations between districts. However, if these staff were to be universally available to psychiatrists and primary care teams, as well as to specialist services such as psychogeriatrics or child psychiatry, their numbers would have to go up four or five times. This would pre-empt all other possible growth in resources for years to come, which would be a central issue of national policy, yet the growth of the CPN service seems to have occurred almost entirely through decisions made at the local level. Difficult issues of accountability have also been thrown up, since it may be a matter of opinion whether the CPN is responsible to the psychiatrist, the general practitioner, or his nursing officer for the care of a particular patient. Many CPNs have a special link with a primary care centre, where they may hold a clinic to administer depot neuroleptics, or a regular supportive group, or assess patients referred to them by the GPs.

Alternative approaches

From what has been said, it will be clear that the District Psychiatry policy, as evolved in Britain, has remained fairly closely within the conventional models of medicine, nursing, and social work, but has extended outwards from institutions. Its theoretical basis is an eclectic, but fundamentally biological form of psychiatry. Furthermore, it has not generally required major contributions to be made to it by individuals or organizations within the population, but has been part of the structure of public services, financed by national and local taxation; as such, it has been to some extent paternalistic. Though experiments to provide treatment on a totally different foundation have been unconvincing (Berke, 1977), it has certainly been possible to develop local services within the NHS which depart substantially from the average.

These have mostly emphasized crisis intervention, making a multi-disciplinary team available to patients in their homes, sometimes on a 24-hour and seven-day week basis. The best known is that operated from Napsbury Hospital to the London Borough of Barnet (Scott, 1980); this aims to involve family and neighbours in the intervention process, and to identify psycho-social transitions which may have led to the situation. Since the service began operating, the hospital first admission rate has dropped by over 30 per cent—though it was previously well above the national average. The Napsbury service generates strong loyalties, but also antagonisms; it involves long hours of work for the staff, with possible stresses in their personal lives, and heavy travel costs. Hospitalization and financial data, though, tell nothing of the experiences or outcome of patients, nor of the feelings of relatives, GPs, or others in the community about the service they receive. These matters have still to be fully assessed.

Dingleton Hospital, which was referred to earlier, has an even longer experience of a community crisis intervention service, but for a very different, largely rural population. It undoubtedly benefits from a particularly high standard of general practice and from a close-knit society in the small Border communities. However, especially in city areas, there may be significant numbers of people suffering from psychiatric disorders who are not part of any meaningful social network; in these cases, crisis intervention may have much less to offer. Though the work of Langsley *et al.* (1969) has often been cited in support of the 'preventive' approach, Pullen (1981) has demolished the credibility of its data. There is also the problem that the personal and interpersonal crises which occur in any population are so many that it would be quite impossible to intervene professionally in most of them. Nor has it been proved that such intervention would have the positive results that have been claimed for it. Mechanic (1981) states that crisis intervention theory is based on a vague conceptualization that environmental trauma and lack of coping ability cause mental illness, but that the evidence for this is incomplete and far from secure. Nor is there much evidence that the advocated type of troubleshooting, although perhaps valuable in reducing distress, has any impact on the rate at which mental illness occurs, or that it would necessarily be directed at those who are likely to become ill if untreated.

As a partial alternative to the DGH-centred model, Gleisner (1982) has developed a mental health centre in a converted house in Tameside, where intervention follows non-clinical lines as far as possible. Professional role differences are minimized, patients have access to their case-notes, and no stock of medication is carried; however, conventional treatment and care are also available within the district service. A similar service operates in the London Borough of Lewisham (Brough, 1981). Since no reliable evaluative work has yet been done on any of these alternative strategies, though, their claims can only be described at present as 'not proven'. Preliminary evidence suggests that they are tending to reduce the rate of first admissions, much more than that of readmissions; if so, data would need to be collected over a good many years to show whether or not this change was helpful to patients in the long run.

Social networks

Psychiatry, which concerns itself with whole communities, rather than with individual patients alone, must clearly have an involvement with the social structures of these communities and with their environments (Freeman, 1978). Psychiatrists who have a district responsibility will have the opportunity to become very familiar with living conditions in their territory, and may well intervene when overcrowding or high-rise accommodation, for instance, seem to be affecting people adversely. Within each community, the pattern of social networks—a factor first clearly analysed by Bott (1957)—seems to be relevant to much psychiatric disorder, particularly non-psychotic conditions. Deficiencies in the social environment are a well established consequence of being mentally ill, while some of the increased prevalence of neurotic morbidity observed, e.g. in the lowest social class can be partly explained by deficiencies of social bonds (Henderson, 1980). However, finding which of these elements is primary, or whether a third leads to both, is a problem on which research continues. The relationship of psychiatric disorder to social factors is extremely complex and, as Goldberg and Huxley (1980) point out, not only may different social factors be important in different diseases, but the same social factors may operate differently in different conditions.

District Psychiatry in Britain, though, is a concept which has not developed on a theoretical basis such as that of social networks, but rather through pragmatic action, and it has been mainly studied from the viewpoint of social administration. It has required psychiatrists particularly, among the professional staff involved, to step out of their traditional clinical role, and to intervene actively in social situations, as well as in the process of developing services. Its character up to now has been strongly influenced by the relationship between primary medical care and specialist services within the NHS – a relationship which has been well analysed by Goldberg and Huxley (1981). Overall, the commonest reason for referral by a general practitioner to a psychiatrist is failure of the patient to respond to the GP's initial treatment—which is usually medication. One of the most important forms of activity developed recently by psychiatrists in district services is that of regular visits to primary health centres, where consultations can be held with the primary care team and patients seen nearer to their homes. In some cases, but by no means all, a useful dialogue develops between specialist and primary care staff as a result of this regular contact.

Wing (1979) has summarized the essential characteristics of a mental health service for a community as that it should be—responsible, comprehensive, and integrated. This is an appropriate goal to which the further evolution of District Psychiatry could aim, but it has to be acknowledged that the present situation of public spending in Britain makes the achievement of formulated plans for it a matter for the distant future. In a discussion document (DHSS, 1981) various possible methods were indicated by which resources might be transferred from the hospital to the community sector, but if total resources are too restricted, such measures cannot improve things much overall. Bewley *et al.* (1981), however, consider it illogical that the NHS, which is 'the authority responsible for those who are ill', should expect local authorities to provide continuing care for the chronically ill 'when they do not have the resources to provide adequately for those many other services for which they have a mandatory statutory duty'. Although the number of very old people in the population is continuing to increase rapidly places in local authority residential homes in England actually fell by 9000 from an already inadequate level between 1976 and 1981 (Grundy and Arie 1982). Since community support services are also failing to keep pace with these demographic changes the NHS—and particularly its psychiatric services—may well face psychogeriatric demands which jeopardize the whole system.

There are two other aspects of District Psychiatry which deserve mention—establishing priorities and maintaining continuity. If a service aims to deal with all the mentally disordered in a population, it is self-evident that this can only be done by focusing limited resources primarily on those groups who have the greatest need of them. To some extent, this will require a reversal of articulated demands, which are likely to come most strongly from those of higher social status, with less severe neurotic and personality disorders. Where psychiatry is mainly practised privately, clients of this kind are likely to take up most of the resources available. On the other hand, in terms of human needs, the three groups which most require these resources are those suffering from schizophrenia, dementia, and mental retardation. All are predominantly chronic conditions, difficult to treat by curative medicine, and needing prolonged care by relatives or public services; few demands come from the patients themselves, so that there must be positive discrimination in their favour. So far as psychotherapy for less severe conditions is concerned, it may be necessary for the specialist services in a district to follow a policy of 'benign neglect'. In other words, responsibility for it may have to be devolved back to the level of primary care, but with the offer of training and consultation for those professional staff involved.

Continuity is one of the most important aspects of psychiatric care, and at the same time one of the most difficult to achieve; in a condition like schizophrenia, where episodes of illness may occur over most of a lifetime, it may make all the difference between success and failure. In a district service, individuals may come and go, but the torch should always be carried on within the professional team. Over the course of years, their collective knowledge of their community and its people should be an asset of steadily increasing value. It does, however, demand an integrated structure of services within which it can be deployed.

Reference

Backrach, L. L. (1976). *Deinstitutionalisation*. (Department of Health, Education and Welfare). Washington: US Government Printing Office.

Bennett, D. H. (1978). Community psychiatry. *British Journal of Psychiatry*, **132**, 209–20.

Berke, J. (1977). *Butterfly Man*. London: Hutchinson.

Bewley, T. H., Bland, M., Mechan, D., and Walch, E. (1981). *British Medical Journal*, **283**, 1161–1164.

Birley, J. L. T. (1973). In Cawley, R., and McLachlan, G. (Eds.), *Policy for Action*. London: Oxford University Press.

Blacker, C. P. (1946). *Neurosis and the Mental Health Service*. London: Oxford University Press.

Bott, E. (1957). *Family and Social Network*. London: Tavistock.

Brill, H. (1980). Notes on the history of social psychiatry. *Comprehensive Psychiatry*, **21**, 492–9.

Brothwood, J. (1973). In Cawley, R., and McLachlan, G. (Eds.), *Policy for Action*, London: Oxford University Press.

Brough, D. (1981). Unpublished address to seminar of the Royal College of Psychiatrists.

Caplan, G. (1964). *Principles of Preventive Psychiatry*. London: Tavistock.

Carse, I., Panton, N. E., and Watt, A. (1958). A district mental health service. The Worthing experiment. *Lancet*, **i**, 39–41.

Cawley, R., and McLachlan, G. (1973). *Policy for Action.* London: Oxford University Press.

Chick, J. (1967). In Freeman, H. L., and Farndale, J. (Eds.), *New Aspects of the Mental Health Services.* Oxford: Pergamon.

Cooper, B., and Morgan, H. G. (1973). *Epidemiological Psychiatry.* Springfield: Charles C. Thomas.

C. P. N. A. (1981). Report of a Survey on Community Psychiatric Nursing. Birmingham: Royal College of Nursing.

Department of Health and Social Security (1975, a). *Better Services for the Mentally Ill.* Cmnd. 623. London: HMSO.

Department of Health and Social Security (1975, b). *Statistical Report Series, No. 12.* London: HMSO.

Department of Health and Social Security (1981). 'Care in the Community' (Discussion Document). London.

Early, D. F. (1960). The industrial therapy organisation (Bristol) *Lancet,* ii, 754–7.

Early, D. F., and Nicholas, M. (1981). Two decades of change: Glenside Hospital population surveys 1960–80. *British Medical Journal,* **282,** 1446–49.

Farndale, J. (1963). In Freeman, H. L., and Farndale, J. (Eds.) *Trends in the Mental Health Services.* Oxford: Pergamon.

Freeman, H. L. (1960). Oldham and district psychiatric service. *Lancet,* i, 218–21.

Freeman, H. L. (1962). The Portsmouth mental health service 1926–52. *The Medical Officer,* **107,** 149–51.

Freeman, H. L. (1963a). In Freeman, H. L., and Farndale, J. (Eds.), *Trends in the Mental Health Services.* Oxford: Pergamon.

Freeman, H. L. (1063b). 'Community mental health services: some general and practical considerations'. *Comprehensive Psychiatry,* **4,** 417–25.

Freeman, H. L. (1978). Mental health and the environment'. *British Journal of Psychiatry,* **132,** 113–24.

Freeman, H. L. (1979). In Meacher, M. (Ed.). *New Methods of Mental Health Care.* Oxford: Pergamon.

Freeman, H. L. (1980). 'Mental Health Services in Salford 1948–74'. Unpublished M.Sc. Thesis, University of Salford.

Freeman, H. L., and Mountney, G. H. (1967). In Freeman, H. L., and Farndale, J. (Eds.), *New Aspects of the Mental Health Services.* Oxford: Pergamon.

Freudenberg, R. K. (1976). Psychiatric care. *British Journal of Hospital Medicine,* **19,** 585–92.

Fryers, T. (1979). Accumulating long-stay in-patients in Salford: monitoring further progress. *Psychological Medicine,* **9,** 567–72.

Gleisner, J. (1982). A community mental health centre. *British Journal of Clinical and Social Psychiatry* (1), 71–73.

Gleisner, J., Hewett, S., and Mann, S. (1972). In Wing, J. K., and Hailey, A. M. (Eds.), *Evaluating a Community Psychiatric Service.* London: Oxford University Press.

Godber, G. E. (1981). Personal communication.

Goldberg, D., and Huxley, P. (1981). *Mental Illness in the Community.* London: Tavistock.

Grinker, R. R. (1975). In Hamburg, D. A., and Brodie, K. H. (Eds.), *American Handbook of Psychiatry,* Vol. 6. New York: Basic Books.

Grundy E. and Arie T. (1982). Falling rate of provision of residential case for the elderly *British Medical Journal,* **284,** 799–802.

Hassall, C. (1976). The Worcester development project. *International Journal of Mental Health,* **5,** 44–50.

Henderson, S. (1980). A development in social psychiatry. The systematic study of social bonds. *Journal of Nervous and Mental Disease*, **168**, 63–9.

Jones, K. (1972). *A History of the Mental Health Services*. London: Routledge and Kegan Paul.

Jones, K. (1979). In Meacher, M. (Ed.), *New Methods of Mental Health Care*. Oxford: Pergamon.

Kahn, J. H. (1967). In Freeman, H. L., and Farndale, J. (Eds.) *New Aspects of the Mental Health Services*. Oxford: Pergamon.

Langsley, D. G., Flowenhaft, K., and Machoptha, P. (1969). Follow-up evaluation of family crisis therapy. *American Journal of Orthopsychiatry*, **39**, 753–8.

MacMillan, D. (1956). 'An integrated mental health service'. *Lancet*, **ii**, 1094–5.

MacMillan, D. (1965). In Freeman, H. L. (Ed.), *Psychiatric Hospital Care*, London: Baillière.

Mann, S., and Sproule, J. (1972). In Wing, J. K., and Hailey, A. M. (Eds.), *Evaluating a Community Psychiatric Service*. London: Oxford University Press.

May, A. R., and Wright, S. L. (1967). In Freeman, H. L., and Farndale, J. (Eds.), *New Aspects of the Mental Health Services*. Oxford: Pergamon.

Mechanic, D. (1981). In Bloch, S., and Chodoff, P. (Eds.), *Psychiatric Ethics*. London: Oxford University Press.

Mills, E. (1959). *Living with Mental Illness*. London: Routledge and Kegan Paul.

Ministry of Health (1962). *A Hospital Plan for England and Wales* Cmnd. 1604. London: HMSO.

Ministry of Health (1963). *Health and Welfare: the Development of Community Care*. Cmnd. 1973. London: HMSO.

Muir Gray, J. (1979). *Men Against Disease*. Oxford: Oxford University Press.

Parker, R. (1971). In *Proceedings of the 1971 Annual Conference of the National Association for Mental Health*. London: NAMH.

Powell, J. E. (1961). In *Proceedings of the 1961 Annual Conference of the National Association for Mental Health*. London: NAMH.

Pullen, I. (1981). Unpublished address to seminar to the Royal College of Psychiatrists.

Querido, A. (1968). *The Development of Socio-Medical Care in the Netherlands*. London: Routledge and Kegan Paul.

Rehin, G. F. and Martin, F. M. (1963). In Freeman, H. L., and Farndale, J. (Eds.) *Trends in the Mental Health Services*. Oxford: Pergamon.

Sabshin, M. (1966). In Roberts, L. M., Halleck, S. L., and Loeb, M. B. (Eds.), *Community Psychiatry*. Madison: University of Wisconsin Press.

Sainsbury, P. (1973). In Cawley, R., and McLachlan, G. (Eds.), *Policy for Action*. London: Oxford University Press.

Scott, R. D. (1980). A family oriented psychiatric service to the London Borough of Barnet, *Health Trends*, **12**, 65–8.

Serban, G. (1977). In Serban, G. (Ed.), *New Trends of Psychiatry in the Community*. Cambridge, Mass.: Ballinger.

Shepherd, M., Goodman, and Watt, D. C. (1961). The application of hospital statistics in the evaluation of pharmacotherapy in a psychiatric population. *Comprehensive Psychiatry*, **2**, 1–9.

Slater, E. (1981). Interview. *Bulletin of the Royal College of Psychiatrists*, **5**, 178–81.

Society of Clinical Psychiatrists (1977). *Psychiatry and the Social Worker*.

Titmuss, R. (1961). In *Proceedings of the 1961 Annual Conference of the National Association for Mental Health*. London: NAMH.

Tooth, G. C., and Brooke, E. M. (1961). Trends in the mental hospital population and their effect on future planning. *Lancet*, **i**, 710–13.

Tudor-Hart, J. (1971). The inverse care law. *Lancet*, **i**, 405–12.

Williams, P., and Clare, A. (1981). Changing patterns of psychiatric care. *British Medical Journal*, **282**, 375–7.

WHO (1953). *Third Report of the Expert Committee on Mental Health*. London: HMSO.

Wing, J. K. (1973). In Cawley, R., and McLachlan, G. (Eds.), *Policy for Action*. London: Oxford University Press.

Wing, J. K. (1979). In Meacher, M. (Ed.), *New Methods of Mental Health Care*. Oxford: Pergamon.

Wooff, K., Freeman, H. L., and Fryers, T. (1982). Psychiatric service use in Salford: a comparison of point-prevalence ratios 1968–1978, *British Journal of Psychiatry*. (in press)

Mental Illness: Changes and Trends
Edited by Philip Bean
© 1983 John Wiley & Sons Ltd.

CHAPTER 17

Mental illness and general practice

RACHEL JENKINS
Clinical Lecturer,
General Practice Research Unit,
Institute of Psychiatry,
University of London

MICHAEL SHEPHERD
Professor of Epidemiological Psychiatry,
General Practice Research Unit,
Institute of Psychiatry,
University of London

Introduction

It has been established for well over a decade that primary care physicians come into contact with, and are responsible for treating, the bulk of psychiatric disorder (Shepherd *et al.*, 1966), and that a relatively small proportion of the mentally ill who consult general practitioners reach the attention of psychiatrists, and an even smaller number are admitted to psychiatric hospitals. This chapter aims to examine some of the major issues which confront general practitioners as they deal with the large numbers of psychiatrically ill patients who pass through their surgeries, and to discuss the implications of these issues for mental health planning in the future. These include problems of definition, of the distinction between psychiatric and social morbidity, the distinction between illness and illness behaviour and its effects on the treated population, the accuracy of our knowledge concerning aetiology, treatment, and prognosis, and the role of the GP in prevention.

Table 1 compares general practitioner consultation rates for diagnosed psychiatric disorders with rates of out-patient and day-patient attendances and with rates of admissions to psychiatric hospitals and units. Since the most recent national figures available for general practitioner consultation rates for psychiatric disorders are those obtained from the Second General Practice Morbidity Survey, November 1971 – November 1972, the other figures are also presented for 1972. It can be seen that general practice consultations for identified psychiatric disorder outnumber psychiatric out-patient attendances by roughly

Table 1   Comparative rates of attendances at different levels of psychiatric care in the NHS for all ages and both sexes combined in 1972. (Rates quoted per 100 000 general population)

	GP consultations†	OP attendances*	Day hospital† attendances	Psychiatric† admissions
ICD 290–315 Mental disorders	32 520	3 329	4 848	378

*Obtained from Morbidity Statistics from General Practice, 1971–72. Second National Study.
†Obtained from In-patient Statistics from the Mental Health Enquiry for England, 1977.

10 : 1 and psychiatric admissions by roughly 100 : 1. This demonstrates one of the overwhelming reasons why primary care is of crucial importance in the care of the mentally ill: the sheer numbers seen and treated by general practitioners are enormous, while only a small proportion are dealt with by hospital psychiatrists. It is at the level of primary care that detection of illness occurs, and it is here that resources devoted to preventive psychiatry need to be devolved.

In 1973, the World Health Organization listed some of the other major reasons why it considered that the GP is best placed to deal with the primary care of mental illness. First, very many of the mentally ill present with a physical complaint and do not consider themselves to be in need of psychiatric care. Secondly, physical and mental illness frequently coexist. Doctors used to be trained to diagnose only one illness in a patient rather than several, and there is evidence that psychiatrists frequently miss physical disorder (Koranyi, 1979) while GPs miss psychiatric disorder (Goldberg and Blackwell, 1970). Thus exclusive preoccupation with one speciality may be disastrous for the individual patient. Thirdly, many psychiatric disorders are connected with family problems and social difficulties, and are only understandable when viewed against this background. The good GP may carry much of this in his head while the psychiatrist has to spend valuable time obtaining the relevant information. And lastly, GPs are best placed to provide long-term follow-up, and are available to the patient at his next relapse when the psychiatrist has often moved on to another post.

Pathways to psychiatric care

In order to describe and understand the structural position of the general practitioner in our system of mental health care, and the practical implications of such a position, Goldberg and Huxley (1980) described a system of filters in psychiatric health care, based upon the earlier theoretical writings of Lewis, Mechanic, and others. The model presented (see Figure 1) consists of five levels, each level representing different populations or strata of individuals. Individuals pass from one level to another by passing through a filter. Level 1 represents the

	The community	Primary medical care		Specialist psychiatric services	
	Level 1	Level 2	Level 3	Level 4	Level 5
	Morbidity in random community samples	Total psychiatric morbidity, primary care	Conspicuous psychiatric morbidity	Total psychiatric patients	Psychiatric in-patients only
One-year period Prevalence median estimates	250	230	140	17	6 (per 1000 at risk per year)
	Fist filter	Second filter	Third filter	Fourth filter	
Characteristics of the four filters	Illness behaviour	Detection of disorder	Referral to psychiatrists	Admission to psychiatric beds	
Key individual	The patient	Primary care Physician	Primary care Physician	Psychiatrist	
Factors operating on key individual	Severity and type os symptoms; Psycho-social stress; Learned patterns of illness behaviour	Interview techniques; Personality factors; Training and attitudes	Confidence in own ability to manage; Availability and quality of psychiatric services; Attitudes towards psychiatrists	Availability of beds; Availability of adequate community psychiatric services	
Other factors	Attitudes of relatives; Availability of medical services; Ability to pay for treatment	Presenting symptom pattern; Socio-demographic characteristics of patient	Symptom pattern of patient; Attitudes of patient and family	Symptom pattern of patient, risk to self of others; Attitudes of patient and family; Delay in social Worker arriving	

Figure 1: The pathway to psychiatric care. Reproduced by permission of Tavistock Publications Ltd. from D. Goldberg and P. Huxley: mental illness in the community

community or the general population at large. Level 2 represents patients attending primary care physicians, irrespective of whether or not the physician has detected the illness. Thus, the first filter between Level 1 and Level 2 consists of those factors which determine whether or not an individual will go to see his doctor. Although Goldberg and Huxley assert that it is largely the characteristics of the individual which determine this illness behaviour, it is also affected by the patient's previous experience of his doctor and whether the doctor in the past has offered encouragement or discourages attendance. Level 3 consists of those patients attending primary care physicians who are identified as 'psychiatrically sick' by their doctor. This has been termed the 'conspicuous psychiatric morbidity' of general practice, as opposed to the 'hidden psychiatric morbidity'. The second filter, between Levels 2 and 3, is represented by the doctor's ability to detect psychiatric disorder among patients in the second level, and passage through this filter is affected by the characteristics of both doctor and patient. Level 4 is represented by patients attending psychiatric out-patient clinics. The primary care physician is largely responsible for such referrals, and is, therefore, the main component of the third filter, although again the characteristics of the patient play some part in his referral, as well as the known characteristics of the consulting psychiatrist.

Level 5 is represented by patients admitted to psychiatric units and hospitals. here the psychiatrist represents the fourth filter in deciding who is admitted to the in-patient beds, although many other factors also operate on this filter, such as the availability of beds and of nursing care. It is possible for an acutely ill psychiatric patient to short-circuit the system and to pass directly from Level 1 to Level 5, passing through Level 4.

Comparison of Level 3 with Level 2 shows how selective the second filter is. The GP only detects about a half to two-thirds of psychiatric illness presenting in his surgery. Should this level of detection be improved? Is the course of conspicuous psychiatric morbidity better than that of hidden morbidity? Goldberg and Blackwell (1970) showed that patients with 'hidden' illness have as many symptoms as those with 'conspicuous' illness, and that hidden illnesses do not have a better prognosis. Johnstone and Goldberg (1976) showed that if a family doctor was made aware of these hidden illnesses, then the patients were more likely to get better quickly and would have fewer symptoms when seen at follow-up a year after their initial consultation.

Marks *et al.* (1979) have studied some factors associated with general practitioners' ability to detect psychiatric morbidity. Close observation of general practitioners suggests that the most important factor determining their likelihood of detecting minor psychiatric morbidity is their ability to conduct a simple mental state examination in an empathic manner, coupled with an understanding of the association of psychiatric morbidity with social dysfunctioning. Many general practitioners have not been trained in postgraduate psychiatry, and in fact often conform to the attitude that it is better not to ask questions lest one 'opens the flood-gates' or 'makes it worse'.

The nature and extent of psychiatric disorder recorded in general practice

Table 2 compares episode rates for psychiatric conditions recorded in general practice with admission rates to psychiatric hospitals for each major diagnostic category of mental illness.

Table 2 General practice episode rates for psychiatric illness and admission rates to psychiatric hospitals for the year 1972, by diagnosis and and sex. (Rates quoted per 100 000 population)

ICD category	Episode rates recorded in general practice*		All psychiatric† admissions	
	M	F	M	F
290–313 All mental disorders	9 230	19 800	318	435
290 Senile and presenile dementia	50	100	12	27
291.4 Organic psychosis	30	40	5	2
295 and 297 Schizophrenia and schizoaffective and paranoid states	140	220	68	70
296 Affective psychosis	210	520	32	68
298.9 Others and unspecified psychoses	10	20	22	32
300 Psychoneuroses	4 740	6 670	30	68
301–302 Personality disorders and sexual deviation	100	70	38	36
303,4 Alcoholism and drug dependence	130	80	30	9
305–309 Other psychiatric conditions	2 750	6 020	11	14
310–315 Mental retardation	50	50	2	2

*Obtained from Morbidity Statistics from General Practice, 1971–72. Second National Study.
†Obtained from In-patient Statistics from the Mental Health Enquiry for England, 1977.

Reference to this table shows that for general practice, episode rates for psychoneuroses exceed half of all psychiatric consultations. These form the largest single category, followed by ICD categories 305–309 which includes somatic disorders of psychological origin, tension headache, insomnia, etc., which contribute a further third to the psychiatric consultation rates. All other categories, that is mental retardation, dementia, the psychoses, personality disorders, alcoholism, and drug addiction only form one-sixth of consultations for psychiatric disorders in general practice. The picture for psychiatric admissions is completely reversed. Here, admissions for psychoneuroses form roughly one-tenth of all admissions, with ICD categories 305–309 making a negligible additional contribution, and all other categories including mental retardation, dementia, the psychoses, personality disorders, alcoholism, and drug addiction contributing the bulk of psychiatric admissions. The preponderance of the psychoneuroses in general practice has considerable significance for the practice of psychiatry in the primary care setting, not only in its treatment, but also in its detection and diagnosis, and in the appropriate training of the general practitioner for this task. Since minor psychiatric morbidity, that is the psychoneuroses, somatic conditions of psychological origin and the personality disorders, may form well over 80 per cent of all psychiatric episodes seen in general practice, the remainder of this chapter is largely devoted to this category, although the issues dealt with frequently extend throughout psychiatry.

The natural history of minor psychiatric morbidity

Two early studies suggested that about half of these disorders are of brief duration (less than a year) and are probably related to environmental stresses, while the other half are relatively long-standing and are associated with personality disorders (Kedward and Cooper, 1966; Cooper *et al.*, 1969). This difference appeared to be unrelated to the treatment prescribed. This view received further support from Murphy (1977) who underlined the significance of personality factors in determining outcome.

Mann *et al.* (1981) reported a prospective study of a representative cohort of general practice attenders with identified minor psychiatric morbidity, providing evidence that at the end of twelve months, half of the patients in such a cohort will be better. Detailed examination of the pattern of illness over the course of the twelve months demonstrated that a third had improved within the first six months, a third pursued a variable intermittent course, and a third had chronic persistent symptoms.

The outcome of psychiatric disorder is poorly predicted by diagnosis and clinical phenomena alone (Bleuler, 1968; Sims, 1975; Wittenborn *et al.*, 1977; Mann *et al.*, 1981). For minor psychiatric morbidity, factors which have been found to predict the duration of the illness are the initial severity of symptomatology (Huxley *et al.*, 1979; Mann *et al.*, 1981), and the continued presence of social stresses. Huxley *et al.* (1979) suggest that poor material conditions are important predictors of a long duration of illness while Mann *et al.* (1981) found that stresses and lack of support within the domains of social life, marriage, and family life significantly affected outcome of minor psychological morbidity. These are all domains to do with social networks which have been shown to play a key role in the outcome of major psychiatric illness (Vaughn and Leff, 1976) and physical illness (Medalie and Gouldbourt, 1976). The study by Mann *et al.* (1981) also examined the hypothesis that personality abnormality is associated with a poor prognosis. In their study, personality abnormality was not associated with final outcome at the end of twelve months, but it made a marginal contribution to the prediction of which patients displayed a chronic pattern of illness over the twelve-month period. It seems that the precise role of personality in the outcome of these disorders is not yet fully understood.

Physical morbidity associated with psychiatric illness in general practice and in the community

Depressed patients frequently offer physical symptoms to their GP for diagnosis and treatment instead of their psychological complaints. It has been suggested that this phenomenon occurs because patients believe that doctors expect to hear about physical complaints. However, there are several alternative explanations which may also contribute. A patient may have had a physical symptom for some time, but in a period of emotional stress and perhaps depression, the physical symptom may seem to worsen and is, therefore, presented to the doctor as the main complaint instead of the emotional problems. Depressed patients are frequently more introspective than usual, and examine their internal body sensations more closely than normal. There is still stigma attached to psychiatric illness, and it is more socially respectable to have a physical illness than a psychiatric one. Friends, relatives, and doctors often share this view. Depression can be secondary to a painful or worrying physical illness or symptom and while it is of course then appropriate for the patient to offer the physical problem to the GP, the onus remains on the general practitioner to be aware of the likelihood of the secondary depression, to detect it and to offer appropriate therapy.

In addition to these clinical phenomena, there is also a real association of physical illness with psychiatric illness. Eastwood and Trevelyan (1972) demonstrated this primary association in a London group practice during a health screening programme on 1470 individuals who received psychiatric and physical examinations in a carefully designed study of a random sample of a general practice population, using independent assessments of the physical and psychiatric states using objective methods, and strict criteria for diagnosis and use of a control group. The authors found that individuals with psychiatric disorder had a significant excess of ischaemic heart disease over controls. The psychiatric disorder could not be secondary to worry over the heart disease, since most individuals had not experienced angina and had no idea that they had ischaemic heart disease. In addition, psychiatric cases had a significant excess of other physical disorders over the control group. Thus, 17 per cent of the psychiatric group had had two major plus several minor physical conditions, compared with only 2.4 per cent of the controls.

Eastwood and Trevelyan (1972) suggest that their findings support the notion that individuals have a generalized propensity to disease, whether physical or psychological. Certainly their data refute the hypothesis that the physical morbidity of the neurotic patient is equivalent to that of the non-psychiatric patient, but that the latter tend to complain more and consult more frequently. More recently Murphy and Brown (1980) attempted to test the hypothesis that stressful circumstances lead to organic disease by first inducing a psychiatric disturbance, i.e. psychiatric disorder is a mediating link between the experience of a life event and the onset of organic illness. However, their study has various methodological difficulties which will need to be overcome before confidence can be placed in the findings—they used a control group from a different geographical and social area than that of the study group; their data are retrospective; they failed to measure or control for social supports, known to be an important influence in the relationship between life events and onset of both physical and psychiatric illness; physical disorder was assessed largely by self-report from the patients and objective scoring methods such as ECGs, lung function tests and blood sample tests, and complete physical examinations were not performed; assessment of physical and psychiatric disorder were not carried out independently of each other by separate investigators blind to the other assessments. Further, the control women were not assessed physically so that their somatic status was undetermined, and the authors do not present data concerning individuals whose organic disorder preceded their psychiatric disorder.

Sims and Prior (1978) reported an increased mortality from organic illness in patients with severe neurosis in a ten-year follow-up period after psychiatric hospital treatment. It seems likely that long-standing physical illnesses such as rheumatoid arthritis may cause secondary psychiatric illness. However, the association persists when this mechanism is excluded. Therefore, whether psychiatric illness can cause physical illness remains an open question. At present the most valuable model remains that of Eastwood and Trevelyan (1972) who support the notion that individuals have a generalized vulnerability to disease whether physical or psychological.

Social factors associated with psychiatric illness in general practice and in the community

More information is available concerning the relationship between psychiatric morbidity and social factors. There is accumulating evidence that social factors may affect the onset, course, and outcome of both physical and psychiatric disorders (Cassel, 1974). The literature assessing the role of social factors in psychiatric disorder may be broadly classified into that concerned with acute life events, chronic social stresses, social supports, and social disability. Psychiatric illness has important social consequences, not only for the individual, but also for his family, and for society in general. It is of importance to the GP to understand how far research has progressed in this region, since his understanding of the role of social factors in the aetiology, course and outcome will affect his formulation and management of the individual case, as well as his role in preventive psychiatry.

Confusion arises in the literature because of the problems of what to measure as indicators of specific social factors and how far questions of validity and reliability must be resolved before accepting the data from any measuring instrument.

Chronic social difficulties

Chronic social difficulties such as financial hardship, social isolation, migration, and low social class have been shown to be associated with an increased prevalence of mental illness although interpretation is by no means clear (e.g. Liem and Liem, 1978). Some of the evidence for this association will be discussed in detail as its implications for the general practitioner's recognition and management of mental illness are considerable.

Faris and Dunham's classic ecological study in Chicago (1939) showed that first admissions for schizophrenia were more prevalent in poor, socially disorganized central areas of the city, while those for manic depressive psychosis were random. Hare (1956) confirmed Faris and Dunham's findings for schizophrenia, but found that admissions for manic depressive psychosis were more common in the wealthier parts of Bristol. Considerable debate has centred around the question of whether the high rates of schizophrenia in certain impoverished neighbourhoods are due to schizophrenics drifting into the poorer, more socially disorganized areas as a result of their handicapping illness, or whether their illness was in fact precipitated by the adverse conditions encountered in such a neighbourhood. Evidence to support the 'drift' hypothesis came from Goldberg and Morrison's findings (1963), that fathers of a random sample of male schizophrenics had a higher occupational status at the same stage of life and that the schizophrenic sons had fallen either in occupational level or below the level predicted by their school careers. Hare *et al.* (1972) compared the occupational histories of schizophrenics with those of patients with other diagnoses. No significant difference was found between schizophrenia and neurosis when the highest occupational status achieved by a patient before the onset of his illness was compared with that of his father at the time of the patient's birth. By the time of the patient's first hospital attendance, more schizophrenics than neurotics were in a lower social class than their fathers and the status of the schizophrenics continued to decline, thus showing that the patient's fall from a higher to a lower level of occupation was due to 'drift', occurring after the onset of illness rather than to 'selection', the failure of the patient ever to achieve his expected occupational level.

However, the relationship of chronic social difficulties to the onset of manic depressive psychosis and of minor psychiatric morbidity, remains much more confused. Srole *et al.* (1962) in the Midtown Manhattan Survey found that the proportion of people rated as 'impaired' and as 'incapacitated' was significantly higher in both those with lower status occupations and those whose fathers had low status occupations. Leighton *et al.* (1963) in the Stirling Community Study compared the prevalence of mental illness in 'integrated' and 'disintegrated' communities. They reported that mental disorder was associated with low socioeconomic status, but the level of integration of the community overrode this association and the rate of mental disorder was lower in low status persons in integrated communities than in high status persons in disintegrated communities. Both these studies have been criticized on the grounds of diagnostic over-inclusiveness.

Nielsen (1962) and Kay *et al.* (1964) examined social factors in relation to psychiatric disorders in old age and did not find any association between mental illness and social class. Hagnell (1966) in a careful 10-year follow-up of Essen-Möller's original survey (1956) found that low socioeconomic status was not related to mental illness, the tendency being in the opposite direction. People in the lowest income groups and the lowest occupational status had the least risk of developing mental disorder, both at the beginning and end of the 10-year follow-up period. Hagnell did find a particularly high risk of mental disorder in the wives of skilled artisans.

Comstock and Helsing (1976) in a large US community survey found that depressive symptomatology was least common among the upper socio-economic groups (identified by level of education, income, and employment status). This finding was repeated by Finlay-Jones and Burvill (1978) in a community survey in Perth, Australia, where the prevalence of minor psychiatric morbidity was higher in the lower social classes.

Brown *et al.* (1975) found a large social class difference in the prevalence of depression in a study of a random sample of women in Camberwell. This difference was particularly noteworthy among women living at home with young children. Brown and Harris (1978) argued that the data provide evidence for four specific factors which confer greater vulnerability to depression in the presence of major life events. These are the existence of an intimate, confiding relationship, the loss of a mother before the age of 11, and lack of employment in the mother. However, a re-analysis of Brown and Harris' data using log-linear models (Tennant and Bebbington, 1978) does not confirm this contention.

Thus, with some exceptions, notably Hagnell, community surveys suggest that minor psychiatric morbidity is commoner in those of low social class. Is this association caused by 'drift', as in schizophrenia, or by selection pressures, or does it reflect a causal relationship between social adversity and minor psychiatric morbidity? Hare *et al.* (1972) found that 35 per cent of neurotic patients at first attendance were of higher social class than their fathers at the time of the patient's birth, while 14 per cent were of lower social class than their fathers. Thus, overall downward drift had not occurred. When the authors compared parental social class at the patient's birth with the highest social class achieved by the patient before his first attendance, there was a rise in social class of 36 per cent and a fall in social class of 13 per cent of the neurotic patients. Thus, in addition the neurotics had not been selected into a lower social class than that of their parents. The observed relationship between social class and minor psychiatric morbidity may, therefore, reflect a causal relationship, the nature of which remains unspecified.

However, the picture changes when studies of primary care attenders are examined, as these studies are dealing with patients who have passed through the first filter to attend a primary care physician. The most comprehensive study of the first filter was that carried out by Tischler *et al.* (1975a and 1975b) in the United States. A one-year sample of Connecticut Mental Health Centre patients ($n = 808$) was compared with a random sample of 1095 responders from the catchment area using the Gurin scale to measure psychological impairment and recording various demographic and social features. The groups which over-used the services compared with what would have been predicted from their distribution in the impaired population were the unmarried, the unemployed, those who lived alone, and those with no religion. Three groups, under-utilizing health services compared with the expected rates were middle-aged women, adults over the age of 30, and those in low income brackets. In this country, Cooper (1972) reported on the social circumstances of 81 chronic neurotic patients identified by their general practitioners and 81 matched controls (surgery-attenders with no known psychiatric symptoms) from the same practice. The chronic patients were found to have poorer housing conditions and lower income.

Hesbacher, *et al.* (1975) collected data on 1130 mainly neurotic patients from 7 family practices in Philadelphia and related sex, race, and social class to symptomatology scores. Social class was significantly correlated with symptomatology in both sexes, with higher class patients being less symptomatic than lower class patients; this relationship was independent of sex and race.

Thus, the relationship between symptomatology and social class remains as patients attend their general practitioners, and are diagnosed by them, even though evidence exists that some of the psychologically-impaired in low income groups in the United States are under-utilizers of the health services there (Tischler *et al.*, 1975b).

(b) Life events

Acute social difficulties, or life events, have received much attention recently (Dohrenwend and Dohrenwend, 1974). Brown and his colleagues (1973) attempted to record life events systematically, to measure their severity, and to exclude events which could possibly have been influenced by the patient. A higher frequency of such events has been found in schizophrenics (Brown *et al.*, 1973a; Paykel, 1974), and in neurotics (Cooper and Sylph, 1973) than in the general population. Brown *et al.* (1973b) proposed the now generally accepted view for schizophrenic patients that 'a person predisposed for... genetic, constitutional or other reasons... will also have some chance of developing the disorder following life events' i.e. that life events serve to precipitate recurrence of symptoms in persons already predisposed to schizophrenia. However, they proceed to suggest that, for depressive conditions, the condition may be actually caused by the life event, rather than merely precipitated. While the concept of reactive depression is deeply embedded in clinical psychiatric practice, the research evidence for the causal associations between life events and depression is still conflicting and the requisite carefully controlled prospective studies have not been performed. Horowitz *et al.* (1977) did not find the expected relationship. A recent critical review of the field (Tennant *et al.*, 1981) points out that hospital-based studies have failed to distinguish clearly between depressive illness and illness behaviour, and community studies have failed to distinguish clearly between normal distress responses and depressive illness. These writers conclude that many of the studies from which a causal connection between life events and depressive illness is inferred are weak methodologically and that, at the present time, a causal connection between life events and depression is suspected but remains unspecified.

(c) Social supports

In community studies, the conceptualization of social isolation has advanced to a study of social networks. Nielsen (1962) and Kay *et al.* (1964) found that old people in the community who were mentally ill have more restricted social contacts than those who were well. Restricted social contacts are also character-istic of people who commit suicide (Barraclough *et al.*, 1970; Sainsbury, 1973). Henderson *et al.* (1978) compared psychiatric patients with matched controls for the size and nature of their reported social network. They found that patients have smaller networks and less effective interaction with the 'primary attachment figure' than controls. In another study (Henderson *et al.*, 1980) they found that the availability and adequacy of loving, intimate relationships was negatively related to the presence of neurosis. The associations between neurosis and lack of social ties was stronger for women than for men. Their findings lend support to those of Brown and Harris (1978) who suggest that lack of an intimate, confiding relationship with husband or boyfriend, is an important vulnerability factor augmenting the causal effect of severe life events.

It has been proposed that not only is lack of social networks harmful, but that social support (conceptualized as information leading the subject to believe that he belongs to a network of communication and mutual obligation) is positively beneficial. Evidence of the effects of social support on normal growth, mortality, degenerative and infectious disease, as well as mental illness has been extensively reviewed (Cobb, 1976; Gore, 1978).

The precise nature of the interaction between stress and support is under debate and remains unsolved. Two major alternatives have been identified. First, stressful life events may cause and precipitate illness while social support decreases the incidence of illness, and each acts independently of the other. Several studies find that good crisis support and coping behaviour do not have an interactive effect in reducing the impact of high life event stress, instead they are independently related to neurosis (Miller and Ingham, 1976; Andrews *et al.*, 1978; Liem and Liem, 1978; Tennant and Bebbington, 1978).

A second alternative is that social support may act by decreasing the likelihood of encountering stressful life events (e.g. Myers *et al.*, 1971) or by decreasing the impact of life events (Nuckolls *et al.*, 1972; Brown and Harris, 1978; Kessler, 1979). Such an interactive effect has been widely discussed (Cassel, 1974; Henderson, 1977) but significant methodological criticisms remain (Tennant and Bebbington, 1978).

An additional effect which may complicate matters is that stressful life events may elicit social support which then protects against illness in either an independent or an interactive fashion. Furthermore, the two major alternatives are by no means necessarily mutually exclusive. Research in this field has been bedevilled by methodological problems of measurement and research design. There are further confounding factors which need to be kept in mind. For example, the association between poor social support and psychiatric morbidity may be exaggerated by neurotics downrating their social milieu or it may be the consequence of long-term illness, with social support melting away in the face of prolonged neurotic behaviour. The few studies that relate to prognosis rather than aetiology demonstrate that social support plays a key role in outcome in schizophrenia (Vaughn and Leff, 1976), depression (Bullock *et al.*, 1972), and minor psychiatric morbidity (Huxley *et al.*, 1979; Jenkins *et al.*, 1981; Holahan and Moos, 1981).

Familiarity with the role of social stresses and supports is of considerable importance to the primary care physician not only for his understanding of individual patients but also for his intervention in treatment and in primary prevention.

High risk groups amongst general practice attenders

Sex is a much studied variable in relation to risk. Women have a higher risk than men of manic depressive psychosis (Slater and Cowie, 1971), of parasuicide (Kennedy *et al.*, 1974), and of minor psychiatric morbidity (Finlay-Jones and

Burvill, 1977), while men have a higher risk of suicide (Kennedy *et al.*, 1974) and of problem drinking (Edwards *et al.*, 1973). There is no sex difference in the prevalence of schizophrenia when all age groups are combined, or in the prevalence of senile dementia when allowance is made for the fact that women live longer than men.

The differences in vulnerability between the sexes for affective disorders may be due to constitutional or environmental reasons. It has been observed that women are more likely to recognize psychiatric health problems in themselves than are men (Horowitz, 1977), that women are more likely to consult doctors than do men (Shepherd *et al.*, 1966) and that doctors are more likely to detect psychiatric illness in women than in men (Marks *et al.*, 1979). Thus, some of the observed difference in prevalence rates may be artefactual, produced by better detection and reporting of illness amongst women. However, the existence of these artefactual mechanisms does not exclude the possibility that some of the observed sex difference is real, either due to inherited (e.g. Weissman and Klerman, 1977) or acquired risks (e.g. Gove and Tudor, 1972). Gershon *et al.* (1975) review the evidence for X linkage in affective disorders, and for autosomal linkage with sex-related liability thresholds, and conclude that neither hypothesis can account for the generally observed excess of female vulnerability to affective disorders. The authors conclude that being female appears to be an environmental rather than a familial determinant of liability to affective illness.

Are women more environmentally predisposed to depression than men? Do women experience more life events, more chronic social stress or less social support than do men? There has been much speculation that woman's traditional housewife role leads her to experience more chronic social stress and less social support than is experienced by men at work (e.g. Gove and Tudor, 1972; Nathanson, 1980). However, specific attempts to perform comparative studies between men and women have been few. Uhlenhuth and Paykel (1973) studied life events retrospectively in men and women for a period of twelve months, and found that women did not experience more life events than men. Brown and his colleagues have not replicated their work on life events and specific vulnerability factors on men. Measurement of the quality of social support is still in its infancy. Thus, evidence for women's greater environmental predisposition to depression remains incomplete.

Marital status is another characteristic with which high risk groups have been associated. Goldberg *et al.* (1976) report higher prevalence rates among the separated and the divorced. These findings were confirmed by Henderson *et al.* (1980). This may be due either to the hypothesis that individuals with recurrent minor psychiatric morbidity may be more prone to marital disharmony, or to the hypothesis that marital disharmony and lack of a supportive intricate relationship increases vulnerability to the pathogenic effects of life events. Marital status also influences illness behaviour. Goldberg *et al.* (1976) found that the single, separated, and divorced with psychological distress were more likely to consult their general practitioners than the married and the cohabiting with psychological distress. These data support the work described earlier on social networks and social support. However, Pearlin and Johnson (1977) provide further reasons why the unmarried state is associated with a higher prevalence of depression. This work provided evidence that economic hardship and social isolation are more heavily concentrated in the unmarried population and indeed, that the unmarried are more vulnerable to equivalent levels of these chronic states than are the married. The authors also implicated parenthood as a particular strain for the unmarried, and concluded that about 70 per cent of the association of the unmarried state with depression is attributable to the differential exposure and vulnerability of the unmarried to the stresses of economic hardship, social isolation, and parenthood. It may be that the differential vulnerability of the unmarried, found by Pearlin and Johnson, is due to their lack of social support from an intimate spouse.

Employment status is a further variable which may affect the risk of mental disorder. Community surveys in the United States (Tischler *et al.*, 1975a; Weissman and Myers, 1978) and in the United Kingdom (Williams *et al.*, 1981) find a higher proportion of unemployed amongst the depressed population than amongst the normals. These surveys are of course cross-sectional and do not permit causal interpretation. Brown and Harris (1978) also implicated unemployment as one of four specific vulnerability factors in women. In view of the dramatically rising numbers of unemployed in Britain at the current time, this issue of the effect of unemployment on mental health requires further investigation. Particular groups who may have special needs are the long-term unemployed and the never-employed school leavers. The demands they place on the primary care services have yet to be assessed.

Issues in the treatment of mental illness by general practitioners

Current issues in the treatment of psychiatric illness in the primary care setting include the high level of prescription of psychotropic drugs, the value of psychotherapy, and the use of other health care professionals besides doctors to take on responsibility for both short and long-term support for the psychiatrically ill.

(a) Psychotropic drug prescription

Much public and professional concern has been expressed about the increase in prescriptions of psychotropic drugs over the last 10 to 15 years (Parrish, 1971; Williams, 1980) now accounting for 15 per cent of all prescriptions dispensed at retail chemists. Which patients receive such drugs? How long is treatment continued and are psychotropics efficacious? Dunnell and Cartwright (1972), in a nationwide survey, found that 11 per cent of adults had taken psychotropics within the previous two weeks. Murray *et al.* (1981) have replicated this finding in a household survey of West London. The authors make the point that in a prevalence survey of psychotropic consumption, the chances of being identified vary directly with the duration of the period over which prevalence is measured and with the duration of the prescription. Therefore, if in the last decade the increase in psychotropic prescription has been to individuals consuming them on a short-term basis, such short-term consumers have a much smaller chance of being detected in such prevalence surveys than have medium and long-term users. Thus, the apparent lack of increase in psychotropic consumption in the decade between the study reported by Dunnell and Cartwright (1972) and that by Murray *et al.* (1981) is probably explained by the supposition that the surveys have mainly detected medium and long-term users, whose numbers have not changed over the intervening period. There have been no prevalence surveys of psychotropic consumption designed specifically to detect short-term users.

Women are higher users than men (e.g. Parrish, 1971) and this holds across all age groups (Murray *et al.*, 1981). Prescriptions of psychotropic drugs are commoner in the older age groups than the young (e.g. Skegg *et al.*, 1977), in particular hypnotics (Parrish, 1971). The relationship between social class and consumption of psychotropics is more conflicting. Some workers have found that prescription rates are higher among middle-class patients (Parry, 1968; Dunnell and Cartwright, 1972), while others have found no relationship between drug use and social class (Manheimer *et al.*, 1968; Cooperstock, 1971; Linn and Davis, 1971; Fejer and Smart, 1973).

Are psychotropic drugs prescribed appropriately? Here it is important to examine studies where diagnoses have been made using measures of psychological health, independently of the doctor who prescribes. A relationship has been found between prescription of a psychotropic drug and high scores on standardized questionnaires designed to detect psychiatric morbidity (e.g. Farmer and Harvey, 1975; Harris *et al.*, 1978; Uhlenhuth *et al.*, 1978). Murray *et al.* (1981) using the General Health Questionnaire (Goldberg, 1972) as a screening instrument to detect minor psychiatric morbidity, found that 17 per cent of the men and 27 per cent of the women with high GHQ scores were consuming psychotropic drugs, whereas by contrast only 5 per cent of the male and 10 per cent of the female low GHQ scorers consumed these drugs. However, since low GHQ scorers preponderate in the population, in fact less than half of the drug consumers had high GHQ scores (46 per cent of the male and 48 per cent of the female consumers). Thus, there are many people taking psychotropics who do not have detectable psychiatric morbidity. Murray and her colleagues argue that their data do not support the view that psychotropic drug consumption is indiscriminate and unnecessary because, apart from the errors inherent in using the GHQ as an indicator of psychiatric caseness, there is evidence that GPs prescribe psychotropics, especially hypnotics, for physical conditions, and in addition it is reasonable to suppose that some individuals who were GHQ positive have reverted to GHQ negative but are still on therapy. (Such continued prescription for a limited period might be reasonable medical practice in the case of antidepressants but detrimental to the patient in the case of minor tranquillizers.) However, Harris *et al.* (1978) found no difference in the psychoneurotic scores of those currently being prescribed drugs and those whose drug prescription had recently been discontinued, i.e. there was no demonstration of any curative effect. Thus, there still seems room for the argument that many individuals without specific indications for psychotropic treatment continue to receive psychotropic medication.

While few would argue that schizophrenia and manic depressive psychosis are not reasonable indications for drug treatment, not only for the acute illnesses, but also for the prevention of relapse, a considerable body of opinion holds that the presence of minor psychiatric morbidity is not an indication for psychotropic treatment. One view is that since symptoms of depression, anxiety, and fatigue may arise from the stress of poverty, unemployment, poor housing, fear of unwanted pregnancy, and so on, then the prescription of pills may prevent the sufferers from organizing themselves in an effective manner to change these social hardships (Lader, 1975). However, neurotic illnesses are unpleasant, disabling and have harmful consequences for the family and the wider community, and the doctors' traditional responsibility has always been to the individual rather than to society at large. This issue underlines the need both for research into the causation, treatment, and prevention of minor psychiatric morbidity and for accurate prescribing by GPs. Not only is there evidence that GPs miss much psychiatric illness (Goldberg and Blackwell, 1970), but also that they tend to over-diagnose anxiety states and under-diagnose depression (Mann *et al.*, 1981), and that as a consequence they over-prescribe anxiolytics and under-prescribe antidepressants. In addition, many antidepressants are prescribed in inadequate dosages, and may be discontinued too soon, precipitating early relapse (Mindham *et al.*, 1973) while anxiolytics are prescribed for too long, running the risk of dependency. Long-term prescription of anxiolytics may have to be considered if life-long anxiety exists.

(b) Psychotherapy

The place of psychotherapy in general practice has recently been reappraised by Madden (1979). While it is no longer possible to deny that the bulk of psychiatric illness in the community is dealt with in general practice, psychotherapy is extremely time-consuming. In the average practice where 1 in 10 consultations concern a mental disorder (Royal College of General Practitioners, 1979) it is debatable how much time the GP could reasonably be expected to give each of his patients with psychological problems. Madden takes the view that steady support, a sympathetic and understanding attitude, a sophisticated understanding of the complexities of human behaviour is needed in all patient care. Whether classical psychotherapy has a place in general practice is controversial. Psychotherapy is so costly that access to it within the hospital system is grossly limited, and it is hard to see how the GP can provide what the specialist cannot (Madden, 1979). In answer to this issue, some have suggested the attachment of social workers or health visitors to general practice, as less expensive personnel than doctors, to deal with psychiatric cases by psychotherapy. Others, including Madden, would argue that a better solution is for psychiatrists themselves to become much more involved in the community care of psychiatric patients, implying a greater cooperation of hospital and community doctors to see patients together and to discuss management. It is pertinent to inquire here how far each of these alternatives has been put into practice and assessed.

(c)   Social work attachment schemes*

Corney and Briscoe (1977) have shown that doctors refer differently to social workers if they have access to an attachment scheme, possibly because only then does the social worker's skill in dealing with complex social and emotional problems become manifest to the general practitioner (Forman and Fairbairn, 1968). However, does such referral have a preventive function, and does such an attachment scheme have a beneficial effect on the duration of minor psychiatric morbidity in that practice? Cooper *et al.* (1975) designed a study to assess the therapeutic value of attaching a social worker to a metropolitan group practice in the management of chronic neurotic illness. They compared the psychiatric and social status of a group of patients before treatment, and one year later, with the status of a control group treated only by conventional methods. Thus, the comparison was between the experimental service and existing services alone. Patients in both groups received medication from their own doctors as usual and could be referred to specialist agencies in the normal way. While the initial clinical and functioning scores of the two groups were similar, those of the experimental group improved significantly more during the follow-up year than those of the control group. The authors concluded that the experimental service conferred some benefit on the patient population. Corney (1981) assessed the effectiveness of social work interaction on a group of 'acute' and 'acute-on-chronic' depressed women. She found that the experimental group did not improve more than the control group in either psychiatric or social ratings. However, when the experimental group was divided into the 'acute' and 'acute-on-chronic' illnesses significant improvements were apparent for the 'acute on chronic' group but not for the 'acute' group when referred to a social worker. Further analysis showed that the difference was due to the positive effect on

*See also Chapter 18.

acute-on-chronic patients rather than to any negative effect of social work on 'acutely' depressed patients. Thus, both these studies lead to the conclusion that social work interaction is helpful for patients with longstanding conditions.

It has been proposed that, in view of social work's contribution to health care, social agencies should be based on general practice boundaries rather than on geographical areas.

(d) Psychiatric attachment schemes

Should psychiatrists be more involved in the community? Schemes of attaching psychiatrists to general practice have been carried out but not as yet evaluated in a controlled manner. A psychiatrist attachment is unlikely to decrease psychiatric referrals by an amount which justifies the psychiatrist's time in the surgery as referrals are low anyway. Does a psychiatrist attachment improve psychiatric care at the primary care stage? It seems likely that it would do if the session were structured so as to enable plenty of opportunity for joint assessments and for discussion on formulation and management between general practitioner and psychiatrist. Thus, it should probably be used primarily as a teaching method. Williams and Clare (1981) have examined the national statistics and interpret the data as showing that although the relative numbers of psychiatrists have increased, they actually each deal with fewer patients than in the past, and general practitioners are still coping with the bulk of psychiatric disorder. It may, therefore, be unrealistic to expect a shift of psychiatrists into the community and indeed undesirable to move psychiatrists into a multiplicity of service commitments at the danger of neglecting the most seriously ill patients (Cooper *et al.*, 1975). Williams and Clare, therefore, reiterate the call of the World Health Organization to strengthen the role of the general practitioner in the primary care of psychiatric illnesses.

(e) Referral to specialist services

Whom should the general practitioner refer to psychiatric out-patients? Mowbray *et al.* (1961), on studying doctors' referral letters to a psychiatric out-patient clinic found that most patients were referred, not on the basis of diagnosis, but for abnormalities of conduct, social problems, or inappropriate responses to medical treatment. Several workers have found that pressure from relatives for referral is an important factor (e.g. Richards, 1960; Rawnsley and Loudon, 1962), and selective referral of young people and of men occurs (Shepherd *et al.*, 1966). Kaeser and Cooper (1971) note that GPs are more satisfied than the patients, and suggest that the referral process may be working more effectively as a means of disposal for the GP than as a step in securing effective treatment for the patient.

(f)   More psychiatrists or better general practitioners?

Pardes (1979) in the United States calls for the training of more psychiatrists to meet the country's needs both because of the relatively high prevalence of mental disorder in the general population (at least 15 per cent in US community surveys) and because there has been a rise in the utilization of mental health community services due to better education about mental illness, loss of the stigma which previously was associated with it, the emptying of the large long-stay hospitals into the community, and the increased health insurance coverage of the general population. Making the point that the proportion of undetected morbidity is high and that GPs are not always sufficiently trained to detect or to manage psychiatric disorder appropriately, Pardes argues for the unique capabilities of the psychiatrist and supports the view that mental health care would be best improved by the provision of more psychiatrists.

In this country, Shepherd (1974) supports the alternative viewpoint, namely that examination of the epidemiology of mental illness and its association with physical morbidity and social problems, leads to the conclusion that the GP should be strengthened in his role of delivering primary mental health care, and that training programmes and additional resources should be devoted to this end. It is in this context that the importance of social work attachment schemes becomes more apparent. However, it is important to bear in mind that, at present, urban general practice is unfortunately still losing many of its best traditional features such as home visiting, consultations without prior appointments, and the completely personal medical care provided by the best single-handed practitioners. This undoubtedly impairs the value of general practice as the site for mental health care.

Issues in the prevention of mental illness in general practice

What are the possibilities for prevention of mental illness at the primary care level? The material discussed already in this chapter should make it clear that an appropriate preventive model should take into account the multifactorial origin or psychiatric illness and the concept of risk factors. However, only a few of the contributing factors may be modifiable. Should prevention be aimed at reducing the occurrence of risk factors in the community, such as unemployment or poverty, or at strengthening protective factors such as social networks, in particular marital relationships which may reduce the impact of the risk factors, or at early crisis treatment once psychiatric morbidity has begun? Evaluation of preventive measures is fraught with difficulties (Flanagan, 1971) of measurement and design. Some social changes have become widespread before their specific value in reducing psychiatric morbidity has been established.

In practice, preventive work so far has been aimed at parenting, at vulnerable children, at health education, and at crisis intervention. Raphael (1976) discussed the need for psychiatric involvement in family planning work, particularly in relation to adolescent unwanted pregnancy and its frequent consequence of abortion, adoption, poor child rearing, and marital breakdown from early inappropriate marriage, all of which increase the risk of psychiatric morbidity.

Changing practices during childbirth which promote bonding between mother, father, and infant have been widely introduced and shown to improve parent–child relationships. However, it is not established how far this has prevented psychiatric morbidity.

Emotional disorders in children are often related to discord between the parents, and early intervention using marital therapy for the parents, and possibly early referral for the child may lessen the incidence of more severe disorders later in life.

The principle underlying effective crisis intervention is that of mobilizing social support for the individual and his family, and demonstrable benefits for crisis intervention have been reported following car accidents (Bordow and Porritt, 1979), surgery (Auerbach and Kilmann, 1977), and bereavement (Rosenheim and Ichilov, 1979; Raphael, 1977).

Other more practical measures which can be said to have placed a preventive role have been the lessening of psychiatric complications of syphilis and vitamin deficiency, lowered rates of birth injury, and elimination of lead from house paints (Lamb and Zusman, 1979). Atmospheric lead, derived from the exhaust fumes of petrol driven engines, remains a cause of much clinical concern because of its association with lowered IQ in children in the large city centres of both the US and UK (Rutter, 1980). The evidence of genetic contributions to the psychoses as well as to some forms of mental handicap make it imperative that the GP should be fully informed of the likely risks to offspring of contracting such conditions, and should be in a position to advise parents accordingly if approached.

The rising incidence of alcohol-related psychological and social problems have led to a call for prevention in the form of health education (De Lint, 1974) and for increased social control over the sale and consumption of alcoholic beverages. This raises the issue of whether it is ethically justifiable to intervene with well individuals to prevent the incidence of possible problems to an uncertain minority. Such interventions require a sound epidemiological basis.

Special issues within the doctor-patient relationship in general practice

(a) Consumerism

Observers of primary care in Britain have frequently called attention to the special relationship that exists between doctor and patient in the general practitioner's surgery, and the particular benefits which this relationship confers (WHO, 1973). However, this relationship must undoubtedly be affected by social changes in British culture and Ian Kennedy (1980) has drawn attention to the issue of consumerism and its impact upon the doctor–patient relationship. Kennedy suggests that consumerism, in the interest of the patient, has a role to play in establishing standards which doctors must meet in their practice, in measuring the doctor's performance in the light of these standards, and in creating means of redress for the patient and sanctions against the doctors if these standards are breached.

How far a relationship with patients which rests on trust can withstand the tensions and demands of a consumerist approach from patients has yet to be seen. Private litigation, suing doctors or hospital administrators, or others involved in medical care, is becoming increasingly common in this country, although there has yet to be a case concerning mental health in primary care.

The BMA states 'The ideal personal doctor service can exist only when the limits to it set by the state are so wide that in day-to-day practice there are no practical constraints'. The Royal Commission of the NHS proposed the introduction of a professional audit, with doctors reviewing and evaluating their own and their colleagues' clinical methods with a view to improvement. So far the BMA have rejected this, together with the notion of extending the powers of the Ombudsman.

The evaluative studies reviewed earlier indicate that there is certainly a need for improvement in the training of general practitioners to diagnose and adequately treat the volume of psychiatric morbidity which confronts them daily. It would seem right that the impetus for this should come as a positive move from the medical profession, based upon proper consideration of the needs of the primary care services, rather than as hasty and ill-considered defensive action resulting from private litigation.

Certification

The role of general practitioners as dispensers of certificates of incapacity for work has long been contentious (e.g. Morris, 1965). Those who assert that medical certification as practised today is a misuse of general practitioner's time argue that the doctor's time should not be wasted on administrative duties, and that examination by the doctor is usually a meaningless formality, since it is the patient who decides when he is fit to work (e.g. Handfield-Jones, 1964). However, still more serious issues arise when considering certification for mental illness. The doctor is under a legal obligation to provide accurate information (National Health Service Act, 1946) but this may conflict with his obligation to act in the best interests of the patient. The best interests of the patient may not always be served by disclosure to an employer of a psychiatric diagnosis, and may lead to lack of promotion or even loss of job. Doctors, therefore, often apply rather vague terminology on the medical certificates of mentally ill patients, with the consequence that DHSS statistics on medical certificates given for mental illness cannot be regarded as an accurate estimate of certified absence from work occasioned by mental illness (Jenkins, 1980).

What is a case of mental illness in general practice?

This question is of crucial importance to primary care physicians as well as to epidemiologists. On this question, whether explicit or implicit, rest decisions concerning detection, prevalence, treatment, and prognosis. Aubrey Lewis (1953) emphasized our ignorance — 'If we are determining the needs that must be met in the NHS, we must first estimate the prevalence of disease; yet for mental disease in all its forms, this is at present impossible, largely because we are unsure what is to be included'. This question is of obvious significance when considering minor psychiatric morbidity, frequently associated as it is with social stress and often of brief duration.

Approaches to the problem of 'caseness' may be divided into the moral, the social, and the empirical. Depressive neurosis and anxiety neurosis precipitated by social stress are identical in symptom content with depressive and anxiety neuroses apparently not associated with social stress, and yet a body of medical opinion holds that because these conditions are so common, and because their causation is apparently obviously social, they constitute part of ordinary human living and are not to be regarded as illnesses, and it is wrong to treat them as such. This line of reasoning confuses several issues and is certainly not upheld elsewhere in medicine, nor indeed elsewhere in psychiatry. For example, tuberculosis occurring in overcrowded, damp housing conditions was always recognized as an illness and treated as such long before medical science was able to identify the tubercle bacillus. Acute schizophrenia precipitated in a vulnerable individual by a severe life event is still regarded as an illness requiring therapy. These examples serve to illustrate the separate questions which need to be examined independently of each other. Is it an illness? How is it caused? Does it need treatment? Those who argue that social causation precludes application of the term illness are making a value judgment which only serves to cloud our observations of the psychoneuroses.

The sociological view of 'caseness' is that a case is an individual who presents himself to a doctor, i.e. a person who has measured himself against his own and society's values of illness and health, and has decided that he needs to consult a doctor, (e.g. Parsons and Fox, 1952; Mechanic, 1966). This view is taken further by medical positivists who consider mere attendance at a doctor's surgery to be insufficient, and assert that the presence of a treatable condition must be confirmed before illness can be said to be present (e.g. Redlich, 1976). Thus, this pragmatic view of 'caseness' is that it depends not upon symptomatology but is rather defined by the process of attending a doctor and being diagnosed by him, so that the key decisions on what is an illness are not made by epidemiologists but rather by the patient and his family doctor. However, this standpoint inextricably confuses illness with illness behaviour, thus removing the opportunity to study illness behaviour independently.

The empirical view of 'caseness' is obtained from standardized techniques of assessment of symptoms, and defines individuals as cases if they display symptoms of comparable severity to those seen and treated by psychiatrists in their clinics, regardless of the individual's illness behaviour. Such case finding instruments, which operate on the severity and number of psychiatric symptoms, calibrated against hospital patients, always produce a distribution of patients without a clear division between cases and normals, and at present, the decision of 'caseness' is thus arbitrary. However, use of these instruments has resulted in far less variation between recent estimates for rates of illness in random samples of populations than were reported in studies carried out before such instruments were available (the early 1970s), which lends support to the reliability of this approach. Both the empirical approach and the sociological approach make positive statements about the necessary criteria for caseness: the empirical approach requiring the presence of symptoms of sufficient severity, the sociological approach requiring the presence of illness behaviour on the part of the individual and the medical view requiring additional diagnostic abilities on the part of the doctor. The moral view on the other hand imposes exclusive criteria only, i.e. it makes a statement about what is not illness rather than what is illness, and cannot be logically applied elsewhere in medicine or psychiatry.

A comparison of the empirical and the sociological approaches raise the question of whether it is possible for someone to be mentally ill who does not see himself as ill? This has been rephrased as 'Do psychiatrists have the right to go out into the community and impose "illness" on an unsuspecting individual?'. However, if caseness is to hinge upon an individual's decision to attend a doctor, this propensity to illness behaviour fluctuates between geographical areas and chronological periods, depending upon the attitude of the individual towards his doctor, so that prevalence estimates would fluctuate in a similar manner regardless of the attributes of the disease. It would also lead to the exclusion of many people whom, by any common sense standard, one would qualify as ill.

This point is cogently put by Lewis (1953) who takes the view that social adaptation cannot be a criterion of mental illness because criteria of social malfunctioning vary from population to population. We need to search for firmer criteria of mental illness which apply to all populations. Some authors assert that such firm criteria do not exist (Szasz, 1971), while Lewis took the view that mental illness may be defined as the qualitatively altered function of some part of the total; such as thinking, perception, or mood. Both views accept that social deviance is not mental illness. However, as Lewis argues, to deny a social content in the idea of health in no sense implies denying it a social context. He concludes that 'although the social effects of disease, like the social causes, are extremely important, it is impossible to decide from them whether a condition is healthy or morbid'.

Resolution of this question of 'caseness' is important not only for the question of ascertaining who is ill, but also for deciding whom to treat. Those who assert that minor psychiatric morbidity is not 'illness' because it is a social reaction to such widespread factors as poor housing or unemployment, go on to argue that doctors should not treat afflicted individuals, as this would have the political consequence of reducing the fervour with which people might otherwise seek to change their social conditions (e.g. Lader, 1975). The counter-argument here is that to leave an individual untreated has foreseeable consequences not only for that individual but also for others in terms of disturbed family relationships, increased sickness absence (Fraser, 1947), impaired productivity (Hamburger and Hess, 1970), accidents (Adler, 1941), social problems (Cooper and Sylph, 1973), and possibly physical illness (Murphy and Brown, 1980). Certainly it has never been argued in general medicine that doctors should refrain from treating cholera cases so as to exert political pressure upon the government to improve the water supply, even at a time when pathogen had not been identified. The issue of what is a psychiatric case has still to be resolved.

Conclusion

This chapter presents some discussion of current issues concerning mental health in general practice. Consideration of these issues inevitably overlaps with the wider issues in psychiatry. Promiment among these are the themes of aetiology, natural history, treatment, and prevention. A fundamental problem in this field is the question of what is a case of mental illness, which is discussed here with specific reference to minor psychiatric morbidity detected and treated in general practice.

References

Adler, A. (1941). The psychology of repeated accidents in industry. *American Journal of Psychiatry*, **98**, 99–101.
Andrews, G., Tennant, D., Hewson, D., and Vaillant, G. E. (1978). Life event stress, social support, coping style and risk of psychological impairment. *Journal of Nervous and Mental Disease*, **166**, No. 5, 307–316.
Auerbach, S., and Kilmann P. (1977). Crisis intervention: a review of outcome research. *Psychological Bulletin*, **84**, 1189–1217.
Barraclough, B. M., Bunch, J., Nelson, B., and Sainsbury, P. (1970). The diagnostic classification and psychiatric treatment of 100 suicides. In *Proceedings of the 5th International Conference for Suicide Prevention, London*. (Ed. R. H. Fox). International Association for Suicide Prevention: Vienna.
Bleuler, M. (1968). A 23 year longitudinal study of 208 schizophrenics and impressions in regard to the nature of schizophrenia. In *The Transmission of Schizophrenia* (Eds. D. Rosenthal and S. S. Kety), pp. 3–12. Pergamon Press.
British Medical Association (1980). *Handbook of Medical Ethics 1980*.
Bordow, S., and Porritt, D. (1979). An experimental evaluation of crisis intervention. *Social Science and Medicine*, **13A**, 251–256.

Brown, G. W., Bhrolchain, M., and Harris, T. P. (1975). Social class and psychiatric disturbance among women in an urban population. *Sociology*, **9**, 225–254.

Brown, G. W., and Harris, T. (1978). *Social Origins of Depression.* A study of psychiatric disorder in women. Tavistock: London.

Brown, G. W., Harris, T. O., and Peto, J. (1973b). Life events and psychiatric disorders. Part 2: Nature of causal link. *Psychological Medicine*, **3**, 159–176.

Brown, G. W., Sklair, F., Harris, T., and Birley, J. L. T. (1973a). Life events and psychiatric disorders. Part 1: Some methodological issues. *Psychological Medicine*, **3**, 74–87.

Bullock, R. C., Siegel, R., Weissman, M., and Paykel, E. S. (1972). The weeping wife: Marital relations of depressed women. *Journal of Marriage and Family*, **34**, 488.

Cassel, J. (1974). An epidemiological perspective of psychosocial factors in disease aetiology. *American Journal of Public Health*, **64**, No. 11, 1040–1043.

Cobb, S. (1976). Social support as a moderator of life stress. *Psychosomatic Medicine*, **38**, No. 5, 300–314.

Comstock, G. W., and Helsing, K. J. (1976). Symptoms of depression in two communities. *Psychological Medicine*, **6**, 551–563.

Cooper, B. (1972). Clinical and social aspects of chronic neurosis. *Proceedings of the Royal Society of Medicine*, **65**, 501–512.

Cooper, B., Fry J., and Kalton, G. W. (1969). A longitudinal study of psychiatric morbidity *British Journal of Preventive and Social Medicine*, **23**, 210–217.

Cooper, B., Harwin, B. G., Depla, C., and Shepherd, M. (1975). Mental health care in the community: an evaluative study. *Psychological Medicine*, **5**, 372–380.

Cooper, B., and Sylph, J. (1973). Life events and the onset of neurotic illness: an investigation in general practice. *Psychological Medicine*, **3**, 421–435.

Cooperstock, R. (1971). Sex differences in the use of mood-modifying drugs: an explanatory model. *Journal of Health and Social Behaviour*, **12**, 238–244.

Corney, R. H. (1981). Preliminary communication. Social work effectiveness in the management of depressed women: a clinical trial. *Psychological Medicine*, **11**, 417–423.

Corney, R. H., and Briscoe, M. E. (1977). Social workers and their clients: a comparison between primary health care and local authority settings. The Team – 2. *Journal of the Royal College of General Practitioners*, **27**, 295–301.

De Lint, J. (1974). The prevention of alcoholism. *Preventive Medicine*, **3**, 24–35.

Dohrenwend, B. S., and Dohrenwend, B. P. (1974). *Stressful Life Events: Their Nature and Effects.* John Wiley & Sons: New York.

Dunnell, K., and Cartwright, A. (1972). *Medicine Takers, Prescribers and Hoarders.* Routledge and Kegan Paul: London.

Eastwood, M. R., and Trevelyan, M. H. (1972). Relationships between physical and psychiatric disorder. *Psychological Medicine*, **2**, 363–372.

Edwards, G., Hawker, A., Hensman, C., Peto, J., and Williamson, V. (1973). Alcoholics known and unknown to agencies: epidemiological studies in a London suburb. *British Journal of Psychiatry*, **123**, 169–183.

Essen-Möller, E. (1956). Individual traits and morbidity in a Swedish rural population. *Acta Psychiatrica Scandinavica*, Suppl. 100.

Faris, R. E. L., and Dunham, H. W. (1939). *Mental Disorders In Urban Areas: An ecological study of schizophrenia and other psychoses.* University of Chicago Press: Chicago.

Farmer, R. D. J., and Harvey, P. G. (1975). Minor psychiatric disturbance in young adults. *Social Science and Medicine*, **9**, 467–474.

Fejer, D., and Smart, R. (1976). The use of psychoactive drugs by adults. *Canadian Psychiatric Association Journal*, **18**, 313–320.

Finlay-Jones, R. A., and Burvill, P. W. (1977). The prevalence of minor psychiatric morbidity in the community. *Psychological Medicine*, 7, 474–489.

Finlay-Jones, R. A., and Burvill, P. W. (1978). Contrasting demographic patterns of minor psychiatric morbidity in general practice and the community. *Psychological Medicine*, 8, 455–466.

Flanagan, J. C. (1971). Evaluation and validation of research data in primary prevention. *American Journal of Orthopsychiatry*, 41, 117–123.

Forman, J. A. S., and Fairbairn, E. M. (1968). *Social Casework In General Practice*. Oxford University Press: London.

Fraser, R. (1947). The incidence of neurosis among factory workers. *Medical Research Council*, Industrial Health Research Board No. 90, London.

Gershon, E. S., Baron, M., and Leckman, J. F. (1975). Genetic models of the transmission of affective disorders. *Journal of Psychiatric Research*, 12, 301–317.

Goldberg, D. P., and Blackwell, B. (1970). Psychiatric illness in general practice. A detailed study using a new method of case identification. *British Medical Journal*, 2, 439–443.

Goldberg D. P. (1972). Detecting psychiatric illness by questionnaire. *Maudsley Monograph 21*.Oxford University Press.

Goldberg, D., and Huxley, P. (1980). *Mental Illness In The Community. The Pathway to Psychiatric Care*. Tavistock Publications: London.

Goldberg, D., Kay, C., and Thompson, L. (1976). Psychiatric morbidity in general practice and the community. *Psychological Medicine*, 6, 565–569.

Goldberg, E. M., and Morrison, S. L. (1963). Schizophrenia and social class. *British Journal of Psychiatry*, 109, 785–802.

Gore, S. (1978). The effect of social support in moderating the health consequence of unemployment. *Journal of Health and Social Behaviour*, 19, 157–165.

Gove, W. R. and Tudor, J. F. (1972). Adult sex roles and mental illness. *American Journal of Sociology*, 78, No. 4, 812–835.

Hagnell, O. (1966). *A Prospective Study Of The Incidence Of Mental Disorder*. Svenska Bokforlaget Norstedts: Lund.

Hamburger, M., and Hess, H. (1970). Work performance and emotional disorders. In *Mental Health and Work Organisations* (Ed. McLean, A), pp. 170–195. Rand McNally.

Handfield-Jones, R. P. C. (1964). Who shall help the doctor? Ancillaries, prescriptions and certificates. *The Lancet*, 2, 1173–1174.

Hare, E. H. (1956). Mental Illness and social conditions in Bristol. *Journal of Mental Science*, 102, 349–357.

Hare, E. H., Price, J. S., and Slater, E. (1972). Parental social class in psychiatric patients. *British Journal of Psychiatry*, 121, 515–524.

Harris, G., Latham, J., McGuiness, B., and Crisp, A. H. (1978). The relationship between psychoneurotic status and psychoactive drug prescription in general practice. *Journal of the Royal College of General Practitioners*, 27, 173–177.

Henderson, A. S. (1977). The social network, support and neurosis. The function of attachment in adult life. *British Journal of Psychiatry*, 131, 185–191.

Henderson, S., Byrne, D. G., Duncan-Jones, P., Scott, R., and Adcock, S. (1980). Social relationships, adversity and neurosis: A study of associations in a general population sample. *British Journal of Psychiatry*, 136, 574–583.

Henderson, S., Duncan-Jones, P., McAuley, H., and Ritchie, K. (1978). The patient's primary group. *British Journal of Psychiatry*, 132, 74–86.

Hesbacher, P. T., Rickels, K., and Goldberg, D. (1975). Social factors and neurotic symptoms in family practice. *American Journal of Public Health*, 65, 148–155.

Holahan, C. J., and Moos, R. H. (1981). Social support and psychological distress: a longitudinal analysis. *J. Abnormal Psychology*, **90**, 365–370.

Horowitz, A. (1977). The pathways into psychiatric treatment: Some differences between men and women. *Journal of Health and Social Behaviour*, **18**, 169–178.

Horowitz, M., Schaffer, C., Hiroto, D., Wilner, N., and Levin, B. (1977). Life event questionnaires for measuring presumptive stress. *Psychosomatic Medicine*, **39**, 413–431.

Huxley, P. J., Goldberg, D. P., Maguire, G. P., and Kincey, V. A. (1979). Predictions of the course of minor psychiatric disorders. *British Journal of Psychiatry*, **135**, 535–543.

Jacobs, S. C., Prusoff, B. A., and Paykel, E. S. (1974). Recent life events in schizophrenia and depression. *Psychological Medicine*, **4**, 443–453.

Jenkins, R. (1980). Preliminary Communication: Minor psychiatric morbidity in employed men and women and its contribution to sickness absence. *Psychological Medicine*, **10**, 751–757.

Jenkins, R., Mann, A. H., and Belsey, E. (1981). The background, design and use of a short interview to assess social stress and support in clinical settings. *Social Science and Medicine*, **15E**, 3, 195–203.

Johnstone, A., and Goldberg, D. (1976). Psychiatric screening in general practice. *The Lancet*, **1**, 605–608.

Kaeser, A. C., and Cooper, B. (1971). The psychiatric patient, the general practitioner, and the outpatient clinic: an operational study and a review. *Psychological Medicine*, **1**, 312–315.

Kay, K. D. W., Beamish, P., and Roth, M. (1964). Old age mental disorders in Newcastle-upon-Tyne. Part II: A study of possible social and medical causes. *British Journal of Psychiatry*, **110**, 668–682.

Kedward, H. B., and Cooper, B. (1966). Neurotic disorders in urban practice: a 3 year follow up. *J. Royal College of General Practitioners*, **12**, 148–162.

Kendall, R. E. (1975). *Role Of Diagnosis In Psychiatry*. Blackwells: London.

Kennedy, I. (1980). Consumerism in medicine. *The Listener*, **104**, 777–780.

Kennedy, P., Kreitman, N., and Ovenstone, I. M. K. (1974). The prevalence of suicide and 'parasuicide' (attempted suicide) in Edinburgh. *British Journal of Psychiatry*, **124**, 36–41.

Kessler, R. C. (1979). Stress, social status and psychological distress. *Journal of Health and Social Behaviour*, **20**, 259–272.

Koranyi, E. K. (1979). Morbidity and rate of undiagnosed physical illnesses in a psychiatric clinic population. *Archives of General Psychiatry*, **36**, 414–419.

Lader, M. (1975). The social implications of psychotropic drugs. *Royal Society of Health Journal*, **95**(b), 304–305.

Lamb, H. R., and Zusman, J. (1979). Primary prevention in perspective. *American Journal of Psychiatry*, **136**, 12–17.

Leighton, D. C., Harding, J. C., Macklin, D. B., MacMillan, A. M., and Leighton, A. H. (1963). *The Character of Danger*. Psychiatric Symptoms in Selected Communities. The Stirling Community Study of Psychiatric Disorder and Sociocultural Environment, Vol. III. Basic Books: New York.

Lewis, A. (1953). Health as a social concept. *British Journal of Sociology*, **4**, 109–124.

Liem, R., and Liem, J. (1978). Social class and mental illness reconsidered: The role of economic stress and social support. *Journal of Health and Social Behaviour*, **19**, 139–156.

Linn, L. S., and Davis, M. S. (1971). The use of psychotherapeutic drugs by middle-aged women. *Journal of Health and Social Behaviour*, **12**, 331–340.

Madden, T. A. (1979). The doctors, their patients and their care: Balint reassessed. *Psychological Medicine*, **9**, 5–8.

Manheimer, D. I., Mellinger, G. D., and Balter, M. B. (1968). Psychotherapeutic drugs: Use among adults in California. *California Medicine*, **109**, 445–451.

Mann, A. H., Jenkins, R., and Belsey, E. (1981). The twelve month outcome of patients with neurotic illness in general practice. *Psychological Medicine*, **11**, 535–550.

Marks, J., Goldberg, D. P., and Hillier, V. F. (1979). Determinants of the ability of general practitioners to detect psychiatric illness. *Psychological Medicine*, **9**, 337–353.

Mechanic, D. (1966). Response factors in illness—the study of illness behaviour. *Social Psychiatry*, **1**, 11–20.

Medalie, J. H., and Goldbourt, U. (1976). Angina pectoris among 10 000 men. II. Psychosocial and other risk factors as evidenced by a multitude analysis of a five year incidence study. *American Journal of Medicine*, **60**, 910–921.

Miller, P. McC., and Ingham, J. G. (1976). Friends, confidantes and symptoms. *Social Psychiatry*, **11**, 51–58.

Mindham, R. H. S., Howland, C., and Shepherd, M. (1973). An evaluation of continuation therapy with tricyclic antidepressants in depressive illness. *Psychological Medicine*, **3**, 5–17.

Morris, J. N. (1965). Sickness absence: return to work? *Proceedings of the Royal Society of Medicine*, **58**, 821–825.

Mowbray, R. M., Blair, W., Jubb, L. G., and Clarke, A. (1961). The general practitioner's attitude to psychiatry. *Scottish Medical Journal*, **6**, 314–321.

Murphy, E., and Brown, G. W. (1980). Life events, psychiatric disturbance and physical illness. *British Journal of Psychiatry*, **136**, 326–338.

Murphy, H. B. (1977). Which neuroses need specialist care. *Canadian Medical Association Journal*, **115**, 540–543.

Murray, J., Dunn, G., Williams, P., and Tarnopolsky, A. (1981). Factors affecting the consumption of psychotropic drugs. *Psychological Medicine*, **11**, 557–560.

Myers, J. K., Lindenthal, J. J., and Pepper, M. P. (1971). Life events and psychiatric impairment. *Journal of Nervous and Mental Disease*, **152**, 149–157.

Nathanson, C. A. (1980). Social roles and health status among women: the significance of employment. *Soc. Sci. & Med.* **14A**, 463–471.

Nielsen, J. (1962). Geronto – Psychiatric period prevalence investigation in a geographically delineated population. *Acta Psychiatrica Scandinavica*, **38**, 307–310.

Nuckolls, K. B., Cassel, J., and Kaplan, B. H. (1972). Psychological assets, life crisis and the prognosis of pregnancy. *American Journal of Epidemiology*, **95**, No. 5, 431–441.

Pardes, H. (1979). Future needs for psychiatrists and other mental health personnel. *Archives of General Psychiatry*, **36**, 1401–1408.

Parrish, P. A. (1971). The prescribing of psychotropic drugs in general practice. *Journal of the Royal College of General Practitioners*, **21**, Supplement 4.

Parry, H. J. (1968). Use of psychotropic drugs by U. S. Adults. *Public Health Reports*, **63**, 799–810.

Parsons, T., and Fox, R. (1952). Illness, therapy and the modern urban American family. *Journal of Social Issues*, **8**, 31–44.

Paykel, E. S. (1974). Recent life events and clinical depression. In *Life Stress And Illness* (Eds. E. K. E. Gunderson and R. H. Rahe), pp. 134–163. Charles C. Thomas: Springfield, Illinois.

Pearlin, L. I. and Johnson, J. S. (1977). Marital status, life status and depression. *American Sociological Review*, **42**, 704–715.

Raphael, B. (1976). Primary care and the prevention of psychiatric disorder: Family planning, antenatal care and childbirth. *Australian Family Physician*, **5**, 1087–1109.

Raphael, B. (1977). Preventive intervention with the recently bereaved. *Archives of General Psychiatry*, **34**, 1450–1454.

Rawnsley, K., and Loudon, J. B. (1962). Factors influencing the referral of patients to psychiatrists by general practitioners. *British Journal of Preventive and Social Medicine*, **16**, 174–182.

Redlich, F. C. (1976). Editional reflection on the concepts of health and disease. *Journal of Medicine and Philosophy*, **I**, No. 3, 269–280.

Richards, H. (1960). *Psychiatric referrals from general practice.* (Unpublished dissertation), University of London.

Rosenheim, E., and Ichilov, Y. (1979). Short-term preventive therapy with children of fatally ill patients. *Israel Annals of Psychiatry*, **17**, 67–73.

Rutter, M. (1980). Raised lead levels and impaired cognitive and behavioural functioning. A review of the evidence. *Developmental Medicine and Child Neurology*, **22**, 1, Supplement 42.

Sainsbury, P. (1973). Suicide: Opinions and facts. *Proceedings of the Royal Society of Medicine*, **66**, 579–587.

Shepherd, M. (1974). General practice, mental illness and the British National Health Service. *American Journal of Public Health*, **64**, 3, 230–232.

Shepherd, M., Cooper, B., Brown, A. C., and Kalton, G. W. (1966). *Psychiatric Illness In General Practice.* Oxford University Press: London.

Sims, A. (1975). Factors predictive of outcome in neurosis. *British Journal of Psychiatry*, **127**, 54–62.

Sims, A., and Prior, P. (1978). The pattern of mortality in severe neuroses. *British Journal of Psychiatry*, **133**, 299–305.

Skegg, D. G., Doll, R., and Perry, J. (1977). Use of medicines in general practice. *British Medical Journal*, **1**, 1561–1563.

Slater, E., and Cowie, V. (1971). *The Genetics Of Mental Disorders.* Oxford University Press: London.

Srole, L., Langner, T. S., Michael, S. T., Oper, M. K., and Rennie, T. A. C. (1962). *Mental Health In The Metropolis: The Midtown Manhattan Study.* McGraw-Hill: New York.

Szasz, T. S. (1971). *The Manufacture of Madness.* Routledge and Kegan Paul: London.

Tennant, C., and Bebbington, P. (1978). The social causation of depression: A critique of the work of Brown and his colleagues. *Psychological Medicine*, **8**, 565–575.

Tennant, C., Bebbington, P., and Hurry, J. (1981). The role of life events in depressive illness: is there a substantial causal relation? *Psychological Medicine*, **11**, 379–389.

Tischler, G. L., Henisz, J. E., Myers, J. K., and Boswell, P. C. (1975a). Utilization of mental health services. Patieahood and the prevalence of symptomatology in the community. *Archives of General Psychiatry*, **32**, 411–415.

Tischler, G. L., Henisz, J. E., Myers, J. K., and Boswell, P. C. (1975b). Utilization of mental health services II: Mediators of service allocation. *Archives of General Psychiatry*, **32**, 416–418.

Uhlenhuth, E. H., Balter, M. B., and Lippman, R. S. (1978). Minor tranquillizers —clinical correlates of use in an urban population. *Archives of General Psychiatry*, **35**, 650–655.

Uhlenhuth, E. H., and Paykel, E. S. (1973). Symptom configuration and life events. *Archives of General Psychiatry*, **28**, 744–748.

Vaughn, C. E., and Leff, J. P. (1976). The influence of family and social factors on the course of psychiatric illness: A comparison of schizophrenic and depressed neurotic patients. *British Journal of Psychiatry*, **129**, 125–127.

Weissman, M. M., and Klerman, G. L. (1977). Sex differences and the epidemiology of depression. *Archives of General Psychiatry*, **34**, 98–111.

Weissman, M. M., and Myers, J. K. (1978). Rates and risks of depressive disorders in a U.S. suburban community. *Acta Psychiatrica Scandinavica*, **57**, 219–231.

Williams, P. (1980). Recent trends in the prescribing of psychotropic drugs. *Health Trends*, **12**, 6–7.

Williams, P., and Clare, A. (1981). Changing patterns of psychiatric care. *British Medical Journal*, **282**, 375–377.

Williams, P., Jenkins, R., and Tarnopolsky, A. (1981). Psychotropic drug consumption in unemployed males. (In preparation.)

Wittenborn, R., McDonald, D. C., and Maurer, H. S. (1977). Persisting symptoms in schizophrenia predicted by background factors. *Archives of General Psychiatry*, **34**, 1057–1061.

World Health Organization. (1973). *Psychiatry and Primary Medical Care*. Distributed by the Regional Office for Europe, WHO Copenhagen.

Mental Illness: Changes and Trends
Edited by Philip Bean
© 1983 John Wiley & Sons Ltd.

CHAPTER 18

Social work practice and mental disorder: current issues and some prescriptions

RON BAKER
Formerly Professor of Social Work, University of New South Wales, Australia

It is a particularly significant point in time to examine the contribution that social work can make in working with, and on behalf of, the mentally disordered. Social work is currently in a divided and demoralized state. Its social value and effectiveness is under intensive scrutiny by social workers and those in other professions and its credibility is being questioned by the general public. To many, the processes of social work practice are a mystery. Yet it is a professional occupation that has an extensive history and may be viewed as a 'living' system with its own goals, values, purposes, organizations, processes, and practice theories. Its ideology is said to contain both 'cause' and 'function' (Howe, 1980). As a cause its task is to bring to public attention the personal pains and disadvantages that people experience, which are not being appropriately catered for. As a function it operates within social welfare policies and programmes to ameliorate the disadvantages and social injustices experienced by citizens.

Social work is a professional occupation which is sanctioned by the community. It is also under the constant influence of economic, political, ideological, and other normative factors which underpin contemporary society. The relationship between sociostructural factors (e.g. class, age, sex, race, etc.) and social work is in itself a difficult one to examine. When the added task is to explore social work practice geared to a particular field or group, such as the mentally ill, the exercise becomes even more complicated.

One way to proceed is to identify and analyse 'internal' factors in social work, and 'external' factors in society which currently appear to be influencing the nature, quality, and direction of social work practice in general. As this exploration unfolds, the gaps, discrepancies, and issues relevant to social work with the mentally disordered will emerge. This will suggest prescriptions for social work practice and education in the future and be the focus of the last section of this chapter.

Internal forces and issues within professional social work. International contexts and historical perspectives

Viewed as a specific occupation social work, at least in Britain, can be traced back to the middle of the nineteenth century. Smith (1965) records how welfare workers were provided with in-service training in assisting the poor. As a helping discipline which could be studied in higher institutes of education its beginnings are evident at the turn of this century when several schools of social work opened in London, Amsterdam, Berlin, and New York (de Jongh, 1972). Only the New York and London schools had fraternal contact, both being sponsored locally by the Charity Organization Society. Today there are over 500 schools in more than 70 countries which are located in every region of the world (Kendall, 1978). These schools are affiliated through the International Association of Schools of Social Work (IASSW) which has its secretariate in Vienna. It is estimated that there are at least another 500 schools which are as yet unaffiliated to the IASSW. Four international organizations collectively provide an infrastructure for the development of different aspects of professional social work. They are the International Federation of Social Workers, (IFSW), the International Council on Social Welfare (ICSW), the United Nations (UN), and the IASSW (Skidmore and Thackery 1976).

Under the auspices of the UNs Social Commission five surveys directly related to social work have been undertaken from 1950–1971. These focused on patterns of training (1950), a directory of Schools of Social Work (1955), core content and methods used in teaching social work practice (1958), trends in educating for different levels of practice (1964), and new approaches in training social work and other welfare personnel (1971). The occupation of social work has rapidly developed throughout the world in the last 80 years. The reasons for this are complex and cannot be adequately discussed in this chapter, though in passing it is worth noting that they are frequently associated with the unintended consequences of industrialization, urbanization, technological change, weakening of nuclear and extended family systems, occupational mobility, the decrease of religious influence, and capitalism. On the latter it is of interest to note that social work is certainly not the prerogative of Western European capitalist societies having developed to a sophisticated degree in at least three European communist countries (WHO, 1974).

Psychiatric social work as a specialism has had a limited history both in terms of time and place (Timms, 1964). It developed as an exclusive form of social work practice in Britain and America from 1920. In the UK, special programmes for social workers in the mental health field were established in London, Manchester, and Edinburgh Universities with the first mental health course being offered in the London School of Economics in 1929. Holders of a certificate or diploma in psychiatric social work were eligible for membership to the Association of Psychiatric Social Work (APSW). In most countries such specialized training did not develop, even in those that had close cultural and language ties to Britain, such as Australia.

Following the recommendations of the Seebohm report (HMSO, 1970) and along with the amalgamation of eight 'specialist' independent social work organizations (e.g. child care, medical social work, psychiatric social work, etc.) into the British Association of Social Work (BASW) in 1970, the APSW disappeared. However, at least two universities (Leeds and Manchester) continue to offer educational programmes for social workers wishing to specialize in the mental health field.

In summary, it can be said that professional social work is an internationally recognized and sanctioned activity in developed and developing countries of the world. Despite this it is currently experiencing intense stress and divisions within its own ranks. Why is the discipline is such a parlous state? Some believe that it is due to confusion and disagreement about its purposes, functions, and practice theory (Butrym, 1976). Others link it to a lack of evidence concerning its effectiveness (Mullen and Dumpson, 1972; Fischer, 1979; Rees and Wallace 1982), whilst others still argue that it is unworkable in its present form and prescribe that it should be dismantled (Brewer and Lait, 1980). That a crisis exists is acknowledged by social workers in Britain, America, and Australia.

Hollis (1980), an internationally esteemed American practice teacher, writes,

we are faced today with tremendous obstacles, the general public is critical of the poor, critical of the social programmes we have helped to develop, and critical of us.

A British Association of Social Work (BASW) statement on social work education (BASW, 1979) recently observed that,

social work education is varied and complex in organization and often seems confused to social workers themselves, and even more to the general public, potential recruits, and members of other helping professions.

And in the most comprehensive survey ever undertaken of Australian social work and welfare education Learner (1979) comments,

educational courses, both Social Work and the wider range of other social welfare courses do not appear to produce workers with clear objectives and clearly differentiated skills and tasks.

This writer too (Baker, 1978), drawing on experience of practice and education in the UK and Australia expressed his concern in the following words:

Our discipline presents a fragmented profile; its credibility and relevance are questioned from all sides, and it often becomes an undefended scapegoat for not preventing or alleviating a myriad of social problems. It is my impression that this crisis is compounded by many social workers who are confused about their functions, unclear about their knowledge skill and value base, equivocal about their professional identity, and who agonize endlessly about the very existence of their discipline.

Huntington (1980) analyses the crisis as being due to a discrepancy between social work's stated occupational identity and what practitioners actually do, and, differentiation within an occupation in which its practitioners segment into different groups and base their practice on divergent ideologies, values, knowledge, and skills depending on work setting and clientele. These views are supported by Butrym (1976) who believes that social work must resolve two fundamental issues if it is to overcome its present crisis, namely, a specification of its central functions and the place of political action in its practices.

Any serious analysis of the special contribution that social work may be able to make in the field of mental illness must occur with an understanding of the 'internal factors' which contribute to social work's malaise. Therefore this discussion will proceed by examining the problem of defining social work and exploring what has come to be known as the generic-specialist controversy. Where possible, these basic social work issues will be related to social work practice in the mental health field.

Defining social work: problems and issues

"Definitions are a kind of scratching and generally leave a sore place more sore than it was before".

S. Butler

Throughout its history social work has struggled to formulate an acceptable definition of itself (BASW, 1977; Crouch, 1980). Kendall (UN, 1950) reports an international study in which 33 countries provided a definition. She categorized these in three ways, as individual charity which expressed itself in alms giving and voluntary service; as an organized activity under government or voluntary auspice dealing with economic dependency; and as a professional service available to all citizens under government or non-government auspice. Such diversity led her to conclude over 30 years ago that 'no definition of social work can be formulated that would be accepted in all countries and might be put forward as an international definition'. Nevertheless, she culled some 'strivings' and 'tendencies' from the 33 definitions which indicated that it was viewed as a helping activity, a social activity, and a liaison activity through which disadvantaged people could utilize community resources. One notes in this historic writing a lack of attention to the creation of new resources, of structural and organizational change, of involvement in policy development and planning, of changing public attitudes to stigma, and drawing attention to violation of human rights all of which are activities which many social workers would deem appropriate today.

In some respects contemporary definitions continue to be unsatisfactory, tending to be over-generalized and tautologous. The following is one such example:

Social work has been described as a social institutional method of helping people, individually or collectively with their social problems and their social functioning. Social workers provide helping services in terms of what is known as social work practice (Siporin, 1975).

Over the years social work practice has come to be recognized by the predominant 'method' used by practitioners, and definitions of 'casework', 'groupwork', 'community work', and 'administration' are available. However, these do not attempt to define the common elements and processes that may inhere in social work practice as a whole. Rather they refer to specific methods which a social worker might use in working with different sizes of client groups. The last decade, however, has seen a serious and sustained attempt to define the 'wholeness' of social work practice and identify its common elements and processes through what has come to be called the generic or unitary approach (Boehm, 1959; Bartlett, 1970; Pincus and Minahan, 1973; Goldstein, 1973; Siporin, 1975; Specht and Vickery, 1977; Olsen, 1978; Baker, 1975, 1976, 1978, 1980a, 1980b, Baker and Campbell 1976, Baker *et al.*).

An amalgam of these descriptive definitions provide a progile of what competent social work may consist of:

(1) Social work practice is a systematic, goal-directed, 'planned change' activity (Pincus and Minahan, 1973). As such it is concerned with, (a) activation of constructive change in welfare systems, (b) activation of constructive change between people and welfare systems, (c) activation of constructive change between people, (d) activation of constructive change within people, (e) the creation of new services, resources, and welfare systems to serve disadvantaged people (Minahan and Pincus 1977), and (f) the prevention of change if this is assessed as being detrimental to people, particularly those already disadvantaged.

(2) Social work practice is an activity bedded in human rights (UN, 1948) from which flow humanitarian and professional values (IASSW, 1976; BASW, 1977; AASW, 1980; NASW, 1980) and common practice principles (Lewis, 1972) based on social justice and trust.

(3) Social work practice entails assessment, planning, focused intervening, recording, and evaluation skilfully undertaken (Baker, 1978).

In addition, a number of common roles, tasks, and strategies are selectively applied to promote or prevent change in line with the values and principles listed in item (2) (Baker, 1976).

(4) Social work intervention is informed by social and behavioural science theory, by insights and experience gained from the occupation itself, from the organization under the auspices of which it comes, from legislation, and from the personal ideologies of the practitioner.

(5) Social work practice requires a developed capacity for clear thinking,

disciplined feeling and self-awareness, and an ability to engage constructively in conflicting and collaborative interaction with people (Towle, 1954).

The above definitive statements represent a cross-section which can be currently found in the literature. However, they arouse little agreement among the main body of social workers. The claim that has been made for psychiatry that experts from all over the world are now beginning to be able to agree upon standards of definition that are not dependent on local social values' (Wing, 1978), cannot be made for social work. (Some assert of course that such a claim cannot be made for psychiatry either (Szasz, 1961, 1971; Wootton, 1981).) The lack of clarity about the nature and functions of social work practice has a direct bearing on work with and on behalf of the mentally disordered. Utting (1978) finds social workers working with the mentally ill confused about their tasks and lacking confidence in carrying them out even when they think they know them. Olsen (1979a) reporting on a follow-up study of long stay patients 2–5 years after being discharged from a psychiatric hospital says:

In many instances the individual problems went unrecognized, the meeting between social worker and client represented no more than contact, the social work goals were not stated or understood by the client or those with whom he lived, the emphasis was on long term intervention, the strategies employed to meet needs were limited and mainly confined to work with individuals, there was little evaluation of the effectiveness of social work services in meeting stated needs and the majority of patients remained disadvantaged.

These findings are in line with other research which shows that much of practice in social service departments in the UK is unrecognizable in terms of the profile of competent social work sketched earlier (Stevenson and Parsloe 1978). It is evident, for example, that social workers either delay in recording their work or do not do it at all (Stevenson and Parsloe, 1978, p. 66). If a similar study were conducted in Australia it is this writer's impression that similar findings would emerge.

Of course it would be naive to suggest that the divisiveness and disillusionment which social workers experience is wholly due to a lack of agreed definitions of social work practice, but it does seem to play a significant part. It leaves practitioners unsure about their occupational identity and wondering whether they have anything in common with other social workers. In 1970 an esteemed practice scholar opined that for social work to overcome its identity and definitional crisis it must identify,

an area of central concern that is, (1), common to the profession as a whole, (2), meaningful in terms of the profession's values and goals, (3), practical in terms of available and attainable knowledge and techniques, and (4), sufficiently distinctive so that it does not duplicate what other professions are doing (Bartlett, 1970, p. 86).

I agree. Until this becomes the collective concern of all social workers, social work will remain a house divided against itself, struggling to gain internal cohesion and external credibility.

The generic–specialist controversy and the current state of social work practice theory

Social work practice theory is in an under-developed state. Within it there is much diversity and sloppy thinking, all of which combine to produce practitioner, educator, and public confusion.

Here 'practice theory' is distinguished from 'theory for practice' following a number of writers (Siporin, 1975; Evans, 1976; Baker, 1978; Curnock and Hardiker, 1979) and refers to those frames of reference formulated by social workers to describe and prescribe their own practice. Theory development may be seen on a continuum (Figure 1) on which there are a number of crucial stages. Much of social work practice theory remains untested and may be said to lie to the left of the dotted vertical line on the continuum.

There are many different conceptual frameworks which have been proposed. Some, as already mentioned, claim to contain common and basic elements of all social work intervention and collectively, these are referred to as generic models. (Sometimes they are also called 'unitary' or 'integrated' models.) Others link social work specifically to a 'field' (e.g. medical social work), 'setting' (school social work), 'social problem' (poverty, unemployment), particular 'client group' (the mentally disordered or physically handicapped), or to a specific 'method' of intervention (case-work, group-work, community work). Over the years the last mentioned has had a dominant influence over practice and education. Though this is now on the wane the 'method' approach still has a significant hold on the way social workers describe themselves and how they are seen by employers, other professionals, and the public.

The proliferation of approaches without an agreed common base has led to divisions and polarized positions being adopted by social workers themselves. Numerous textbooks have been written promoting this method or that, which has had the effect of reinforcing the unsubstantiated position that specific 'methods' or 'fields' actually exist. Within social work itself there is currently an intensive controversy as to whether what is unique by way of knowledge and skill to a method, field, or target group, can be distinguished from what is generic to

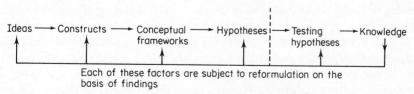

Each of these factors are subject to reformulation on the basis of findings

Figure 1 Theory development continuum

all social work. Social workers are ambivalent about which camp they put themselves in and readily become confused or defensive about the issues. Despite the lively and at times turbulent debate engendered by the generic–specialized controversy (see 'Social Work', 1981) in the USA, Britain, and Australia, one writer seems to sum up the position in all three countries when he observes;

specialization by client group has persisted. In addition specialization by social work method has continued largely unchanged with the predominance of social casework, and that this continues despite the fact that no substantial discussion about the nature and focus of specialist practice has taken place (Cypher, 1980, p. 81).

For as long as such a state of affairs persists social workers will remain confused about their own practice theory. Rigorous theoretical analysis and empirical research needs to be undertaken to determine what is generic and specialized in practice and what constitutes practitioner competence. Some evidence suggests that this is beginning to occur (Clarke and Arkava, 1979; Booth *et al.*, 1980; Hill, 1980).

Social work with and on behalf of the mentally disordered has long been regarded as a specialist area of practice, so the generic–specialist debate is particularly pertinent to it. Many books, journals, and educational programmes have been devoted to identifying the specialist knowledge and skill thought to be required to work in the field of mental disorder (Mind, 1976a, 1976b; Olsen, 1976). Genericists argue, however, that much of this knowledge and skill is relevant to all social work intervention and that the generic approach provides a more comprehensive service to the mentally disordered, their families, and the community. A number of 'case' studies are now available supporting this claim (Hartman, 1974; Webber, 1977; Vickery, 1976; Evans, 1978; Olsen, 1978; Coulshed, 1980; Scurfield, 1980). For some within social work the generic–specialist controversy is irrelevant. Barter (1979, 1980) whose particular commitment is to services for the mentally ill, cites evidence which indicates that neither 'generic' nor 'specialist' oriented workers are more effective in meeting the needs of the mentally disordered and their families. He argues that the present controversy merely draws attention and energy away from what is really required of the social worker, which is greater awareness of the organizational and political obstacles to the provision of adequate resources for the mentally ill. He prescribes that the social worker must 'develop new (and probably quite practical) helping techniques based on a more informed understanding of mental disorder' (Barter, 1980, p. 17). Barter would see the social worker acting more as an advocate, coordinator, and enabler. His position is appealing and would find support from reformist and radical social work theorists who frequently point to the environmental factors (political, economic, legal, ideological, organizational) which are claimed not only create social problems but also prevent social workers from being able to provide appropriate services (Corrigan and Leonard, 1978; Pritchard and Taylor, 1978, Simpkin, 1979; Galper, 1975, 1980).

But Barter's position obscures significant facts about our understanding of mental disorder. Mental illness is a complex concept, difficult to define. Its causes are even more difficult to establish with any degree of reliability. Hence it becomes difficult if not impossible to know what kind of new and practical intervention techniques need to be developed. Barter's plea for social workers (and others!) to understand the 'natural history' of mental disorder is a caution against superimposing theoretical interpretations whether psychoanalytic, Marxist, existentialist, or whatever on to people and situations. In the experience of this writer this is all too prevalent a tendency among psychiatrists and social workers.

But we must ask, what is actually known about the aetiology of most mental disorders? Thorough research reviews all point to the same fact. There are numerous theories of causation but only the organic psychoses are explainable by facts (Nurse and Gleisner-BASW (undated); Wing, 1978; Ineichen, 1979). As many as seven 'models of madness' have been identified (Siegler and Osmond, 1976; Bates, 1977) each having their own protagonists, disciples, and interventive techniques. In a world of many religions one becomes sceptical about all of them!

In such a working reality the social worker will be hard put to develop new or effective approaches to work with the mentally ill. Particularly when she/he is unclear or confused about social work's own practice theory. It remains to be seen whether the present generic–specialist battle being waged within social work itself will have positive or negative outcomes for social work practice in the field of mental illness. What it has done so far is to spawn some important seminal research into practice theory which hopefully will now be replicated by social workers in the mental health field (Curnock and Hardiker, 1979; Hardiker and Storz, 1979; Rees, 1980; Huntington, 1980). Such research would focus on the special knowledge and skill required of a competent social worker in working in this field. Once this has been identified educational programmes could be developed accordingly to prepare practitioners for such specialist practice. As will be evident, however, such a research focus requires that the kinds of questions already posed be resolved, i.e. what is the nature of social work practice, what are its basic processes, what is the relationship (if any) between its basic and common processes, and its specialist activities in the mental health field.

A third issue dividing social work internally concerns the different positions taken up by social workers on the place of ideology and social work practice, the relationship between them and whether social work does or should take on an explicit political role.

Ideology, politics, and social work practice

In recent years practitioners have become increasingly aware of how social welfare policies impact on their practice and the various constraints that prevent them doing an effective job. These constraints directly concern the power base of the social worker and what seems to determine the degree of practitioner power being experienced is related to a combination of the following factors:

(1) Control over tangible resources,
(2) Demonstrable competencies which the social worker is able to bring to bear on practice situations,
(3) The right to define the problem and practice reality,
(4) The range and levels of accountability to employer, agency, clients, legislation, the public, and the profession.

Social workers have become ultra-sensitive to the fact that they act as vehicles of social welfare policy and often function as social control agents (Green, 1975). Social workers are sanctioned to intervene in people's lives with a societal expectation to assist the disadvantaged, victimized, and disturbed, yet at the same time they are restricted in resources and power to do a competent job of work. This is particularly the case when one considers the place of the social worker in the field of mental disorder (at least in Britain and Australia). In what is essentially a secondary setting for social work few practitioners are involved in the formulation of policy for the mentally ill or their families. Important decisions in terms of assessment, intervention, and hospital or community care are made by psychiatrists, psychologists, 'counsellors' of one kind or another and nurses, and the social work role is essentially prescribed by the psychiatrist. A 'treatment'–'illness' ethos persists and dominates the field of mental disorder usually ignoring the lack of evidence for this approach and neglecting the different 'models of madness' which have been identified.

Social workers feel under 'psychiatric' domination and question the medical model which has traditionally been and remains the predominant way in which mental disorder is viewed. Thus they experience a classic double-bind situation, often feeling impotent or blamed for incompetence yet not given the power over resources or the autonomy to define their own practice reality. Anger, disillusionment, and cynicism are common outcomes. The dynamics of this situation have been exposed by radical social work writings which have increased dramatically in recent years. This literature has had a powerful and unnerving influence on many social workers. To briefly summarize the main thrust of the radical perspective: the central proposition is that traditional and reformist forms of social work only serve as a conservative force in capitalist society and therefore function to maintain the *status quo*. Thus social work reinforces social injustices in a myriad of ways by 'cooling out' victims of the system rather than working to create structural, organizational, and ideological change. People are 'helped' to adjust and adapt to dominant values rather than the values themselves becoming targets of change. Such social work becomes an instrument of the ruling class through which the poor and other disadvantaged groups are controlled by benevolent professional caretakers. The extent to which social work is aligned with a society in which self-help, individualism, competition, and achievement rule, guarantees that its social change mission is doomed to fail (George and Wilding, 1976). The result is a form of social work that is primarily concerned with *means* not *ends*, *individual* not *structural* change, methods of intervention rather than their *effectiveness* and with *social functioning* rather than social justice. Pritchard and Taylor (1978) put it succinctly:

We may have a welfare orientated capitalist system (although even this is open to major question) but the fundamental point about our society remains not its welfare but its capitalism. Given this sort of approach social work must be seen as an institution of the state which exists to perpetuate an unworkable and undesirable system. Moreover as its primary function is to 'rehabilitate' some of these elements in society which are not 'integrated' social work performs part of the invaluable task of legitimating the existing structure.

The point is well made by other radical writers (Galper, 1975, 1980; Corrigan and Leonard, 1978) that social workers as well as clients can be rendered powerless or feel strait-jacketed by the dominant ideologies that govern their working world. Radical writers appear agreed that social work will only become a real force for change if and when the discipline adopts a critical, preferably Marxist, ideology (Findlay, 1978; Galper, 1975, 1980; Corrigan and Leonard 1978).

The radical position has had a major impact on the hearts and minds of social workers. It has forced them to re-evaluate their practice and the nature, quality, and ideological bias of their professional education. For many it challenges the cherished and deeply held belief that change is possible in reformist, incremental, and democratic ways. It poses a full frontal attack on much of interpersonal therapeutic helping, indicting case-workers and group-workers for using special knowledge and skills for political ends, whether this is done consciously or not. Lastly, it affronts social work's self-image which is inherent in the rhetoric that it exists to assist people, to change inequitable social systems, and to create new resources (Robinson, 1972; Cooper, 1977; Cowger, 1977). The radical challenge is to the very basis and nature of social work and what is its real relationships to the 'external' world. It exposes contradictions between social work's ideological commitments and the way the practitioner may be functioning to control and manipulate disadvantaged people on behalf of élites in capitalistic systems. A heightening of awareness about such matters allows few social workers to rest easy and is likely to make them highly anxious and insecure.

Yet there are many unresolved questions and issues which cannot be appropriately dealt with here. For example, one might ask: what is the actual, not merely the theorized relationship between an ideological position and acts of practice? Is there a necessary or linear relationship between them? Can there be more than one ideology at any one moment in time which significantly influences the roles and tasks of practice and strategies of intervention? If so, which predominate at different times, for which problems and purposes and to what effects? There are no clear cut or simple answers. That a relationship would appear to exist between ideologies, practice acts, and outcomes seems self-evident, but the nature of this relationship is unclear. These and other crucial questions lend themselves to empirical research. That social workers are asking them at all is a significant step forward and reflects real strength in such a young discipline, particularly when compared with the lack of such questioning in the more established disciplines like medicine and law. The plea is made here that empirical research should occur before the premature foreclosure of these important questions. In the meantime social work must continue to operate in something of a vacuum with limited knowledge and inconclusiveness about its functions and effectiveness. In the process of working these out, established patterns of practice and education are unsettled, and turbulence is felt at every level (Righton and Richards, 1979; Huws Jones, 1980). This effects the relationships social workers have with other professional workers. This is particularly so in the field of mental disorder, where, as has already been suggested, social workers feel their role is prescribed by others, where their power of decision-making and policy development is very limited, where they command few resources, where a medical–illness–treatment model predominates, and where they are usually expected to accept a subservient role.

In summary, this section has identified some crucial issues within social work that seem to contribute to its crisis. These concern social work's struggle to find a clear occupational identity and comprehensive definition of itself, the generic–specialist controversy, the state of its practice theories, the effectiveness of social work intervention, and the relationship between ideologies, practice acts, and outcomes. All these issues have a direct bearing on social work practice in the mental health field. Until they have been systematically addressed and substantially resolved by social work itself, practitioners will remain unsure of themselves and their discipline, and be unclear whether their particular contribution to the field of mental disorder is as a generalist social worker or as a specialist operating in a unique arena of social intervention. It is obvious that future forms of personal social service delivery and programmes of social work education will depend on how the above questions and issues will be dealt with.

Contexts for social work practice with the mentally disordered: the 'external' factor

Germain (1980) points out that social work occurs in a dynamic environment in which there are long standing and new social problems. She claims and is supported by Millar (1979) that little progress has been made in America over the last 100 years in eliminating poverty, unemployment, racism, sexism, and urban blight. Others argue that the same is true for Britain and Australia (Townsend, 1979; Stretton, 1979).

Additionally, a host of new social problems of direct concern to all service professionals has been generated by dramatic technological, social, and cultural changes particularly in the last twenty years. For example, advancements in micro-chip technology have led to the development of computers, information storage and retrieval systems, and cheap audio-visual recording equipment which can invade privacy and threaten human rights. Such technology is changing the world of work, creating structural unemployment, increasing bureaucratization and depersonalization of personal welfare systems, and shifting male and female roles in society, and within the family. New life-saving technologies can now prolong life by mechanical means, create test-tube babies, and produce toxic waste in the production of nuclear energy that remains lethal to life for hundreds of years. These factors and many others place great strain on the adaptive capacities of individuals, groups, and communities to tolerate the form of change and the speed with which it occurs. Social work is expected by society to be in the forefront in handling the stress and anxiety that new technologies and ideas engender. To keep practice relevant the practitioner is forced to constantly review his/her knowledge, skill, value, and assumptive base. As Reynolds (who is quoted by Germain) has observed, 'practice is always shaped by the needs of the times, the problems, the fears they generate, the solutions that appeal, and the knowledge and skill available'. The task of connecting changing reality to appropriate practice responses makes very heavy demands on the social worker's energies and quite frequently leads to 'burnout' (Daley, 1979). Moving from the broader social context to the intimate link that exists between societal values and mental disorder Jones (1979, p. 3) writes, 'What we define as mental illness depends on the norms of society, what it is prepared to tolerate and what it finds intolerable. Modes of care and treatment evolve out of complex interactions between rival philosophies'. Social workers operate at the interface between what 'society' chooses to define as a social problem and the behaviour of people which expresses their needs, wishes, conflicts, stresses, and aspirations. Thus, the practitioner is constantly faced with vying and sometimes totally conflicting definitions of reality coming from the people being served, social expectations and norms, and professional values (IASSW, 1976; BASW, 1977; NASW, 1980). To make appropriate assessments and interventions within such a context is no mean feat. The whole thing is made more difficult (some would say impossible!) when one takes into account current structural and administrative arrangements for the provision of services of the mentally disordered, particularly in Britain. Jones's (1979) comprehensive and critical analysis makes for depressing reading. The vision for future development contained in the 1959 Mental Health Act has never become a reality. It was envisaged that an integrated system of hospital to community care would be developed. With naive optimism it was thought that large mental hospitals would become relics of the past as they gave way to a range of community resources. Help for the mentally disordered and their families was to be available in the community, the mentally ill would largely be treated over short periods in general hospitals, resources would be made available to the family, and, in the process, the stigma of mental illness would disappear. Optimism turned to a 'trough of unconcern' as mental health services continued to be starved of resources and the few research projects geared to prove the benefits of 'community care' did not bear out that this was necessarily the most appropriate approach (Wing, 1978, p. 204).

Professor Jones points out that the word 'integration' was little understood and hardly thought through. The experiment of 'integrating' mental with general hospitals, psychiatry with general medicine, administrative structures for mental with physical illness, and psychiatric with other kinds of social workers has had disastrous consequences. Distinctive knowledge and skills for working in the field of mental disorder have become seriously attenuated. Jones is scathing about the present services for the mentally ill,

they have no distinctive framework, no senior administrative staff appointments, no clear or integrated statistics on which to base monitoring or evaluation and no specialized administrative training. At the primary care level they rest on the concept of using a team trained in the care of physical illness, without mental health skills for the care of conditions they do not understand (Jones, 1979, p. 13).

This is by no means an isolated view. Another expert in the field, a professor of social work, writers,

Mental health in spite of the conscience money made available after each public inquiry and scandal is currently severely restricted by political neglect, resource limitations, an outdated legislative framework and unproven therapeutic strategies. In consequence we have a forsaken cause and staff confounded by contradictory feelings of hope and frustration (Olsen, 1979).

It has been estimated that in Britain 180 000 people are discharged from mental hospitals each year and one in seven of the population receives treatment for psychiatric disorder at some time in life. Spending forcasts for local authorities for 1979–1980 showed that only 1.2 per cent was allocated to the mentally ill compared to almost 23 per cent for children and 37 per cent to the elderly and young physically handicapped. Capital expenditure forecasts show similar negative discrimination with 4.2 per cent for the mentally ill, 19.1 per cent for the mentally handicapped compared to 27.5 per cent for children and 43.9 per cent for the elderly. Such expenditures have been devised despite the forward looking policies contained in the white paper entitled, 'Better Services for the Mentally Ill' (HMSO, 1975). Why it occurs is anyone's guess. But it seems related to the greater 'popularity' of children, the physically disabled, and the elderly in arousing sympathetic responses in the media and the public. These groups may therefore become more important than the mentally ill to politicians intent on catching votes.

There is little doubt that mental disorder, whether long past or only minimally present is still stigmatized in Britain and elsewhere. Many cases have been reported of ex-psychiatric patients being unable to get work or keep a job once it is known that they have had psychiatric treatment (Knight, 1977; Melville, 1977). Stigma is alive and well everywhere! (WHO, 1978). One wonders why it is so chronically persistent. Is it due to ignorance, fear, the need for a scapegoat group, or conscious or unconscious acting out of ambivalence from policy makers and resource holders toward the mentally ill? Research is urgently needed to find some answers.

Though the problems and gaps identified above have focused on the British scene they are by no means restricted to it. An international working party made up of 21 experts from 16 countries, working under the auspice of the World Health Organization (WHO, 1978) concluded that at least six factors led to constraints in mental health services development.

(1) Widespread lip service was paid to integrated and comprehensive community services but their actual development was patchy or non-existent.
(2) Though it was agreed that there was a chronic lack of tangible resources the persistence of stigma and ignorance about mental illness was the major obstacle. To quote a significant section of the report,

the greatest impediment to progress lay in the minds of men rather than in their pockets or purses. Bias, prejudice, fear and ignorance seemed to be the root cause of inertia and resistance which the public, mental health care professionals, national policy and programme planners and governments alike displayed and it was those attitudes which determined the relatively low levels of capital and revenue funding and of recruitment which superficially appeared to be the impediments to progress (WHO, 1978, p. 29).

(3) No country was keeping satisfactory statistics or information or doing enough to ensure that appropriate information was getting to the public, mental health professionals, policy and programme developers, and legislators.
(4) Existing resources were not being maximally used or adapted to changing community needs or the ideology of community care. Thus even available resources were not being redeveloped to create alternative community resources such as protected employment, controlled and subsidized 'sheltered' accommodation, day centres, as well as personal and family support services.
(5) There is ineffective coordination and administration of resources which prevents the delivery of comprehensive community mental health care.

(6) There is a lack of political will to give to the mentally disordered and to mental health programmes a greater share of national resources.

The report ends with nine recommendations which are:

(1) Greater professional intervention in the fields of public relations, press, radio, and television to overcome ignorance and stigma.
(2) More factual information about mental disorder and community mental health care philosophies should be made available to the public, to legislators, and administrators.
(3) Mental health service personnel in mental hospitals and community mental health care teams require continuing education programmes in which they can regularly update their knowledge about progressive changes of practice in community mental health.
(4) Education authorities should take greater responsibility for teaching principles of mental health in schools.
(5) Staff deficiencies should be overcome by channelling monies from capital funding to staff development.
(6) Radical reappraisals of training programmes and role definitions of mental health workers should be undertaken and then made public.
(7) Lack of resources can be partially overcome by the redeployment of existing resources.
(8) Poor coordination to be overcome by better administrative training and research, by greater participation of a wider range of field workers, and by establishing clear objectives and specific responsibility at the national, regional, and local levels so that an integrated service can develop.
(9) Mental health legislation to be regularly reviewed and liberalized so it remains consistent with generally accepted human rights.

These are over-generalized and conservative recommendations. Yet they do point the way to some of the changes that are needed. Social work has the potential to contribute to these by taking on roles of education, advocacy, consultancy, coordination, research, advising, policy development, and planning.

This section has focused on some 'external' factors which impinge upon the practice of social work in work with and for the mentally disordered. It is evident that stigma persists, and that there is a lack of political and social goodwill toward the mentally disordered which expresses itself through inadequate tangible resources and up-to-date progressive legislation. Further, the coordination of existing resources (personnel, buildings, knowledge, skills) leaves a great deal to be desired, and words that are frequently used such as 'teamwork', 'integration', 'community care' are concepts with little concrete meaning at present.

Future trends for social work practice in the mental health/illness field

As has been shown both social work and psychiatric services are in a fragmented and stressed state. It would be a foolish person indeed who forecast future trends with any real confidence. At its worst, special services and structures for the mentally disordered and their significant others, could become even more fragmented and lacking in coordination and direction. Social work as we know it today could disappear to be replaced by another named personnel undertaking similar tasks such as 'community psychologists', 'clinical sociologists', 'community mental health nurses', 'social psychiatrists', etc. It is assumed here that the disappearance of social work would be detrimental to both the psychiatric services and the people who use its facilities. The main reasons being that competent social workers provide a unique social dimension to understanding and intervening appropriately in the psychosocial problems of the mentally ill. The expertise in this beleaguered field is already in very short supply and to reduce this even further would be detrimental to all concerned. The main issues facing all mental health service professionals have been identified by Smyth (1979) as the future use and viability of psychiatric hospitals, the development of integrated community services, establishing workable links between hospitals and social service departments, providing accommodation and employment opportunities for people who have been or are mentally disordered, developing relevant retraining programmes, and creating humane facilities for the elderly mentally infirm (Gray and Isaacs, 1979). He pinpoints the major deficits in the present 'system', to be intolerable conditions in some mental hospitals, demoralized and negative attitudes among staff, vast gaps in community services, and a lack of family supports. To tackle these major problems requires the collaborative effort of politicians, economists, sociologists, social administrators, planners, the whole range of professional personnel within the service, and of course the consumers.

The limited question posed here is, in the light of possible future developments in social work theory and practice itself what might its particular contribution be to the future development of the mental health services? The rest of this discussion rests on three interconnected assumptions:

(a) That '*community care*' remains the strategy of choice over institutional care,
(b) That *integration* of resources and facilities is the goal to be aimed at and the means of achieving more effective services for the mentally disordered and their families,
(c) That the principle of '*normalization*' (O'Brien, 1980) and other principles derived from this which are discussed in the recent paper 'An Ordinary Life' (Kings Fund Centre, 1980) as applied to the mentally handicapped are also directly relevant for the mentally disordered.

These principles are briefly stated as follows (with the words 'mentally disordered' replacing those of 'mentally handicapped' in points (2) and (4)):

(1) The 'normalization principle' is defined (Wolfensberger, 1977) as 'the utilization of culturally valued means in order to establish and/or maintain personal behaviours, experiences, and characteristics that are culturally normative or valued'.

(2) Mentally disordered people have the same value as anyone else and so the same human rights.

(3) Living like others within the community is both a right and a need.

(4) Services must recognize the individuality of mentally disordered people.

The gaps, deficiencies, and needs are clear. How may social work help to deal with them? Some possible answers may be forthcoming in this exercise of crystal ball gazing if we examine some directions being taken within contemporary theory and practice and then suggest their likely implications for agencies and service delivery, interdisciplinary relationships, social work education, and work with people who carry the label 'mentally disordered'.

Contemporary intra-occupational developments

There is a growing commitment within social work to strengthen and reinforce its power base by demonstrating through empirical research that it is a discipline of social intervention firmly based on the skilful performance of selected practice tasks which are applied to achieve specific and explicit goals (Sainsbury, 1980). There will be much greater emphasis on competence and outcomes of social work intervention which will replace what some have seen as an excessive concern with clarification of its purposes, values, knowledge bases, 'methods', conceptual frameworks (NASW, 1981), theoretical/ideological underpinnings (whether by Freud, Parsons, or Marx, etc.), and professional status. Hopefully in this process social workers will become more skilled in practice, disciplined in approach, research-minded, and modest in their claims. I believe that these trends will accelerate in the next decade or two.

Social workers will also become very conscious of the way they are 'used' by society to facilitate individual, interpersonal, and community well-being as well as being pressed to be agents of social control. They will become hypersensitive to the relationship between ideology and practice and carefully examine the influence different ideologies (political, practice, employers', societal, professional, personal, etc.) may be having in the way they assess, intervene, and evaluate outcomes. They are likely to challenge with increasing vigour and competence those ideologies which devalue people and their human rights and expect social workers to act primarily as control agents. I would anticipate that social workers will increasingly become advocates and resource people to the powerless and disadvantaged, and engage in social action both with them and on their behalf. In consequence they will be viewed even more ambivalently by the public and other human service professionals than they are today. To be continuously at the centre of controversy by having a commitment to make public unpalatable facts about injustice and inadequate resources, will lead to a backlash effect which will push social workers to develop stronger supportive organizations, such as their professional body, a union, or both.

Let me now move from the general to the particular. Perhaps the most misused words within the mental health service for over twenty years have been 'community care'. The phrase has become a glib piece of terminology which has been used as a political expedient. Wing (1980, p. 215) speaks for many when he says:

It is not sufficient to discharge someone 'into the community' and to think that this act alone is a form of community care. The concept of community care is an artificial one when applied to people with no social roots, few social skills, and an inability to make useful social contacts for themselves.

Wing was referring particularly to community care, or lack of it, for long stay psychiatric patients who had been discharged into the community without adequate preparation or resources. A number of action research demonstration projects can be cited which have developed different forms of community care for particular problems (fourteen of these are described in a book edited by Meacher, 1980). Some local authorities in Britain (Westminster Social Service Dept., 1977; Dowrick, 1980) have sponsored important research and produced useful ideas. Similarly, new services have been developed in the USA (Marx, Test, and Stein, 1973; Stein, Test and Marx, 1975; Baldwin 1975; Grumet and Trachtman, 1976; Benedetto, 1977; Drake and Wallach, 1979) and Australia (Maller 1971, 1976a, 1976b). What most of these initiatives have in common is that they largely represent independent efforts undertaken by committed professionals with limited resources and power. Further, such projects have been very slow in getting off the ground and those which provide evidence of the validity of a new community service meet obstacles, by way of organizational and professional vested interests and dominantly medically oriented 'treatment' ideologies, that slow down or prevent the new service from becoming established. Olsen (1979a), a social worker and an authority on the services for the mentally disordered, draws on expert opinion and cites research findings which show how poorly the concept of community care has been thought through, and lacks the resources to make it a reality. He suggests a line of action for social work that is both clear and unequivocal,

if community care is to remain the strategy of choice over institutional care then much more thought needs to be given to the political, organizational and professional difficulties that confront it. For social workers this means the development of a practice which is firmly rooted in a unitary framework.

That social workers and others should direct their attention and interventive efforts towards the political, organizational, and professional obstacles to the creation of an integrated community care system is a view that would be shared by many in the field (Simpkin, 1979; Meacher, 1980; Olsen, 1979b). What is particularly worth noting is that Olsen (along with Leonard, 1975) believes that social workers are most likely to maintain an organizational and political focus if their practice is rooted in a unitary (generic) approach. There is a growing interest around the world among practitioners, educators, and students in applying and researching the use of conceptual frameworks for unitary practice. And there is every indication that this will continue into the foreseeable future. A drastically condensed resumé of the approach will only be possible here and only touch on segments of two frameworks. Pincus and Minahan (1973) who are possibly the most influential of unitary practice theorists have formulated a four 'systems' model. Within these 'systems' four categories of people are identified:

(1) The client system—the consumers or beneficiaries of the service.
(2) The change agent system—all those involved in providing the service.
(3) The target system—the people and/or situations to be changed.
(4) The action system—those people who are sympathetic to the need for particular changes to be brought about and who can be mobilized to assist the change agent system to bring these about.

In applying this framework the social worker (or team) considers these four systems in every problematic situation. Assessments about possible causes would be made and an action plan arrived at in which process and outcome goals are specified for work with each system. Pincus and Minahan have identified eight generic skills which the 'change agent system' would use selectively and differentially to achieve explicitly stated goals. What this model does is to commit the practitioner (or team) to the following:

(1) Assess, plan, and intervene in a more comprehensive way than was possible within the traditional 'methods' approach of case-work, group-work, and community work. Such an approach forces the practitioner/s to look beyond the person/group who are the problem carriers and are labelled clients or patients.
(2) It commits the change-agent system to consider carefully who and what might be additional or alternative targets of change to clients, e.g. the agency itself and its hours or service, or an employer who is antagonistic to employing anyone with a history of mental disorder.
(3) It points to intervention at the indirect as much as the direct service levels, that is: coordinating significant and sympathetic others to effect changes for example in the Mental Health Act, working to develop new resources such as a residential facility for disturbed adolescents, or demystifying mental illness and reducing stigma by educating public attitudes.

Figure 2   Multirole practitioner model

Another generic framework developed by this writer stands either independently of, or can be complementary to the Pincus and Minahan formulation (Baker, 1980). Five interlocking models comprise this framework and one of the models aims to specify what the general tasks and roles of practice are (Baker, 1976). Figure 2 clarifies this formulation.

What is suggested by the model on its outer perimeter is that there are eight general tasks of practice which when competently performed are referred to as generic skills. In addition at least thirteen common roles of practice can be identified each containing role specific tasks within them. In the reality of any practice situation the tasks and roles interweave or follow one another in rapid succession. Some tasks and roles seem better understood and described in the literature than others. The initial pilot research of this model showed that certain tasks and roles tended to cluster together. This was related to where the practice act occurrred, the problem/s being addressed, agency policies and procedures, and the ideologies of practice which were pre-eminent. Differing profiles of practice emerged in different agencies and when these were evaluated against job descriptions significant discrepancies became evident. Some positions having an explicit 'community work' bias in their job specification in fact involved the practitioner in doing essentially direct service work. Other social workers, particularly those who were located in clinical agencies, had the roles of advocate, researcher, educator, and coordinator excluded from their job descriptions. The study showed how employers and sometimes other helping professionals are in a position to determine the form and direction that social work intervention takes which can be irrelevant to people using the service and ignore a host of structural factors (economic, political, organizational, ideological) which can be significantly linked to human problems. The unitary approach clearly challenges established patterns of intervention in which human problems and needs are defined essentially in terms of individual and family pathology. It further challenges agency policies and processes in which prescriptions for intervention are geared only to problem carriers. The way problems are defined will to a large extent determine the direction intervention takes and the way scarce resources are used. The unitary approach offers alternative definitions of reality for social workers and other mental health service personnel. It tells the practitioner (and team) to assess more comprehensively, to take personal, interpersonal and structural factors into account, and to work out programmes of intervention which may be well beyond 'the person with the problem'. It expects the social worker at least to know the range of common roles of practice and as far as possible to develop minimal competence in all of them, for they are all needed.

By integrating the Pincus and Minahan and Baker models it can be seen how such a practice could develop (Figure 3).

The arrows from the multirole model which are directed to each of the four 'systems' are intended to show how the role clusters may be differentially applied to work for change in each system. The application of such a model by an intra- or interdisciplinary team would mean that, once overall outcome goals had been established, different members of the team, possibly working in pairs, would be responsible for selecting and executing a number of roles which were regarded as important to achieve change in a specific system. The team would report on developments within their own system regularly, they would monitor each other's work and ensure that overall goals were kept to the fore. Within the field of mental disorder one pair might work to assist clients by offering support, advice, and 'therapy', another pair might research needed changes in the Mental Health Act and advocate policy changes (target system), a third pair could work as brokers and coordinators to develop sheltered cheaper accommodation or new employment opportunities for recently discharged long-stay patients, or bring together families of the mentally disordered and assist them to become a self-help group (action system). A fourth pair working as researchers, advocates, and enablers might direct their energies to changing those aspects of the change-agent system itself that was making it difficult for people to use the service, e.g. by offering the service only 5 days a week from 9.00 am – 5.00 pm or long delays in making telephone contact with staff in the agency, etc. It has been suggested that the unique contribution that social work can make in work with and for the mentally disordered is in being located at the interface between people, and their welfare and community systems (Prins, 1977). Being so located means that the social worker should have a detailed understanding of the needs of people in their community context, to know the community resources that exist to meet these needs, and be aware of gaps in provision. To understand and appropriately respond to these different interfaces requires the kind of broadly based practice

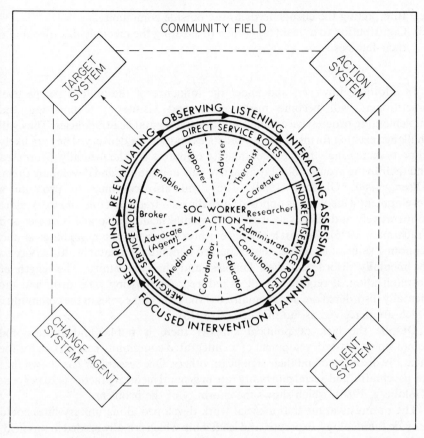

Figure 3

theory inherent in the unitary approach. Such a theory is also in line with the development of a truly integrated community care service for the mentally disordered, which has been the wish but not the reality for many years.

It is envisaged that the near future will see increasing attempts to develop an integrated community care programme for the mentally disordered, which social workers will attempt to link to a unitary approach to practice.

Despite the plea by Olsen (1980) that 'we urgently require a theory of the purposes and process of the social worker's intervention in mental health' there seems little doubt that social workers will continue to undertake the traditional tasks which Prins (1976) describes as:

(a) Historians and biographers of the social situation,
(b) Offering personalized support and resources to clients and their significant others,

(c) Interpreting the clients needs to the outside community,
(d) Contributing to a 'team' approach in assisting the mentally disordered and their families.

In addition, however, and under the influence of the unitary perspective, practitioners will become more active and visible in formulating and implementing progressive community care and mental health policies. They will challenge existing forms of agency practices and service delivery. They are likely to press increasingly for new community resources for the mentally disordered and their living groups and play an active part in initiating and developing them. (Olsen, 1980; Gleisner, 1980). They will also continue to promote a developmental ideology as opposed to an illness – treatment one and work more cooperatively and effectively with other mental health personnel (Grumet and Trachtman, 1976). Research evidence accrues showing the psychological and economic value of an adequately resourced community mental health service to the mentally disordered, their families, and the community. The length of hospitalization, if required at all, is reduced, readmission rates drop and the mentally disordered are less stigmatized if they can carry roles in the community which are perceived as 'normal' (Segal, 1978).

Despite the lack of political support there is public and professional commitment to the development of an integrated community care service for the mentally disordered and their significant others. One researcher has shown that the psychiatric and social morbidity rate in general medical practice is 20 per cent (Goldberg, 1980), which shows the enormity of the problem.

The optimists argue that a social work developed along unitary lines could provide the ideology, expertise, and leadership which is badly needed in this field, and make a substantial contribution to the integrated service that is required. However, such an approach would have significant implications for users of the service, other professional caretakers within it, interdisciplinary team-work, service delivery, and current assumptions underpinning mental health services. The issues are only beginning to be identified and grappled with. They represent a significant challenge to social work practitioners, educators, and researchers and will need to be resolved before it becomes possible to say whether the approach is practicable and is a step forward. It seems likely that much energy and time will be expended by practitioners, educators, and students in dealing with them in the next decade. Some of the most crucial ones will be briefly discussed next and will complete this chapter.

The unitary approach and intra-occupational issues

(1) Social workers who have been trained in the traditional 'methods' approach to practice may have real difficulty in considering other approaches. They may prefer to hold on to what they know for different reasons: a belief that it is more

relevant, safer, effective, or easier for themselves. How may practitioners and educators can be best assisted to consider and test new approaches? Through educational programmes, action research projects, etc.?

(2) To what extent is highly specialized knowledge and skill required to work effectively in the field of mental disorder? Those who argue that it is push for specialized post-basic and post-graduate educational programmes. Others provide research evidence which indicates that the knowledge and skills required are best learned 'on the job' (Stout, 1976; Berg, *et al.*, 1978). Those who take the latter position need to demonstrate through their practice and research that the unitary approach is more effective in working in the mental health field than the other available methods.

(3) There are at least eleven conceptual frameworks for unitary practice available (Baker, 1980a). Research needs to determine which, if any, are most relevant for work in the field of mental disorder.

(4) If a unitary approach is to become viable a technology for operationalizing it will need to be developed (Stein, 1969). This will have to specify what the generic skills of practice are (Sainsbury, 1980), which are most effectively employed in dealing with different categories of mental disorder, and how they are best taught. Other instruments will need to be developed which allow teams to record their work with different systems, as well as means whereby process and outcome goals for the total planned effort are constantly being evaluated (Baker, 1982).

(5) The ambivalence and/or organizational inertia that such an innovative approach might generate will need to be combated by social workers. How is this best done?

(6) What kind of research programmes will have to be established to evaluate the effectiveness of a unitary approach to established 'methods' intervention? Factors which will need to be evaluated include whether the unitary approach does contribute more to the development of a community mental health service in getting new resources, influencing legislative changes, and reducing the stigma of mental disorder.

(7) The unitary approach means that social workers may intervene across a broad range of systems and have several target groups. This would occur in a context in which the practitioner is accountable to different groups, namely, clients, employers, the profession, and the community. Stress increases for the practitioner if his/her approach suggests one line of action whilst lines of accountability indicate another. Will the unitary approach be felt to be impracticable by social workers because of this and be rejected? Germain (1980) claims that very few social workers have autonomy to any degree in the US and she suggests that this is the central issue facing the discipline.

(8) Working in a team creates strains and tensions. In unitary practice these are likely to be related to how different roles are allocated to members of the team, the outcome goals, and specific strategies of intervention to be employed in achieving them. Members of the team may have different understandings of

unitary practice and/or find that they prefer to work in a more limited way with a particular mental disorder or technique, e.g. behaviour modification, family therapy, etc. How are these conflicts to be resolved constructively for all concerned?

(9) Students who develop knowledge and skill in the unitary approach are likely to find when in placements, and later as a graduate social worker, that the established methods prevail. This is likely to lead to disenchantment and cynicism of this (or any other) innovation. How can this be combated?

The unitary approach and interdisciplinary issues

(10) Will other mental health service personnel commit themselves to such an approach to community care or will it be interpreted as a social work takeover bid and lead to increasing interdisciplinary strife? In the light of some evidence which indicates that the roles of psychiatrist, psychologist, and social worker are undifferentiated, and that they all spend most of their time doing 'psychotherapy' (House *et al.*, 1978), it seems likely that the unitary approach will be seen as a threat to social workers and others alike, and represent an unwanted politicization of services for the mentally disordered. How may this be tackled constructively? Katz (1976) offers a model of community mental health practice which he claims holds the potential for integrating a variety of strategies.

(11) Can social workers with a unitary orientation work cooperatively with psychiatrists, psychologists, and nurses or is such interdisciplinary team-work a myth? Some claim that what was referred to as 'team-work' in the past was really everyone being subservient to the doctor/psychiatrist who made diagnoses and prescribed treatments within an illness–medical model. Within this framework some blame the difficulties that were experienced within the team on poor communication (Julia, 1976; Prins, 1976) and the fact that psychiatrists and social workers (in the UK at least) are accountable in different ways and to different organizational structures (National Health Service and Social Service Departments). This represents an essentially conservative view. An insightful analysis provided by Huntington (1980) suggests other, perhaps more significant reasons, for inter-occupational conflict. She argues that doctors are relatively free agents and have a great deal of power over the way they work. They essentially provide a 'contract' or 'fee-for-service' and their professional culture is one of autonomy and independent professional judgments. They are also primarily middle and upper middle class and male. Social workers on the other hand are employees, they work predominantly in large welfare bureaucracies often under the direction of non-social workers, they are usually young females, and are upwardly mobile coming from upper working and lower middle classes. For groups like these to genuinely cooperate with such different backgrounds is to say the least likely to be problematic. Issues relating to status, power, and who controls what and whom are at stake. Radical changes in who gains entry into

training programmes for these occupations and restructuring of professional education to incorporate extensive multidisciplinary education seems called for. Add the challenge that the unitary approach poses and the working relationships within the team is rich in the possibility for tension and negation of each others positions.

Goldberg (1980) having examined the role of social workers in relation to general practice in the mental health field asks what will be the future role of social work with psychiatrists, community nurses, health visitors, etc. and concludes that, 'until there is a fairly radical redevelopment of these resources and a redefinition of social work tasks there is very little hope of more positive well informed collaboration between social work and medicine or psychiatry'. She argues for 'a certain amount of specialization (information, practical service delivery, neighborhood work, groupwork) within the framework of an integrated social services department'. For Goldberg two important shifts need to occur before 'teamwork' and 'integrated community mental health care' can become a reality; a redefinition of social work tasks and effective interdisciplinary collaboration. It has been suggested in this paper that the unitary approach has the potential to address both these needs.

Unitary approach and agency organizational and 'case' processing issues

(12) Currently welfare agencies are structured on hierarchical lines. A 'director,' 'administrator', 'medical superintendent' is first among equals, as the phrase goes. Unitary practice would challenge this kind of structure and shift it to a horizontal one along the lines suggested by Jacques (1976). Within such a team decisions are made, roles delegated, and action strategies worked out, not in terms of ascribed or irrelevent status but on the basis of what particular expertise the team member can offer in dealing with a specific problematic situation. To accommodate such a form of practice may require significant changes in the way agencies organize their welfare service, i.e. individual accountability may give way to group accountability, personnel may need to be available more readily, and assessments and chosen interventions may be dependent on different kinds of evidence rather than 'expert' opinion or the dominant ideology of the agency.

(13) The processing of 'cases', or perhaps more appropriately termed 'problematic situations' would need to shift dramatically from handling of individual cases by a particular worker to one in which the team took an active part. A whole ideology and the current technology supporting it would have to change. Problematic situations would be assessed by an intake team. Goals would be arrived at collectively. Intervention would also be undertaken in such a way that it became a coordinated planned effort (Evans, 1978). As Evans points out:

unitary models of social work not only constitute a shift from an individualistic perspective on practice to an interactionist one but they also require a shift from individual forms of teamwork to joint ones if they are to be successfully implemented and developed. This relationship between models of practice and forms of organization of service delivery has been insufficiently appreciated or explored.

Unitary practice and the consumer

(14) The mentally disordered and their significant others may find it overwhelming to have a team of people concerned with their problems rather than one individual worker whom clients have a contract with is a major question. Would it be with one member of the team, the whole team, or the agency? And can any one member of a team be accountable to clients for work being done by other members of the team elsewhere? Unless these issues are properly resolved the recent thrust to demystify psychiatry and social work helping processes may come to an abrupt halt.

(15) Associated with the above is the extent to which clients can retain control and be an active participant in what is done on their behalf. The team may initiate action systems or intervene in target systems which are not understood or sanctioned by clients. To what extent does the unitary approach push social workers and others to act in this way? Thus members of the team may select bargaining or conflicting strategies with a target system at one remove, yet on behalf of clients, but the backlash of this may be experienced by the consumers and not the professionals. It is all too easy for democratic rights to be overridden, for self-determination to be undermined, and for the processes called 'helping' and 'planned change' to become a total mystery to those who are supposed to be the prime beneficiaries of these acts.

Summary

This chapter will satisfy no-one, least of all the writer, but it was not intended to. The present state of affairs in social work, psychiatry, and the organization of mental health services, is one of confusion, stress, and demoralization. In many respects this essay simply reflects the current reality. Some key issues have been identified which are 'internal' to social work and contribute to its present crisis. These include concern about its identity, functions, purposes, effectiveness, the place of ideology in social work practice and the generic–specialist controversy. Some 'external' factors were also discussed which appear to have a major influence on the quality and direction social work intervention takes. It was suggested that an increasing number of social workers find the formulation of a new practice theory called the unitary approach one with exciting possibilities. It is believed to have greater potential for contributing to the development of a community mental health care system than traditional social work methods, because of its interactionist ideology and commitment to multi-system intervention. However, at present the approach remains at a primitive stage of development. It needs to be tested practically, developed conceptually, and empirically researched. Then its value needs to be compared to other social work methods and orientations (case-work, group-work, community work, 'radical' intervention) to see which of these practice modes are more effective in assisting people labelled mentally disordered and changing socio-structural factors that devalue them, i.e. the stigma of mental disorder, age, sex, race, etc. A number of selected issues were briefly discussed relating to unitary practice which are likely to be of central concern to social workers in the next decade. At the end of the day social work will be accepted or rejected not on the basis of this or that practice theory or ideology. Rather its worth will be judged on the resources or *'facts'* it creates which improves the life of the disadvantaged and disturbed, and the *acts* it performs with, and on behalf of powerless people. Today social work is on trial; few feel sure or confident about what the verdict will be tomorrow!

References

Australian Association of Social Worker's Guide Lines For Ethical Practice in Social Work (1980). AASW.

Baker, R. (1975). Toward generic social work: a review and some innovations, *Brit. Jnl. of Social Work*, **5**, 2.

Baker, R., and Campbell, M. D. (1976). A model for the planning and promotion of change in generic social work, *International Social Work*, **XIX**, 2.

Baker, R. (1978). 2nd Edn, *The Interpersonal Process in Generic Social Work: An Introduction*, Preston Institute of Technology Press, Bundoora, Vic., Australia.

Baker, R. (1976). The multirole practitioner in the generic orientation to social work practice, *Brit. Jnl. of Social Work*, **6**, 3.

Baker, R., Campbell, M. D., Picton, C. (1976). Curriculum planning for the education of the generic social worker, in *Social Work In Australia: Responses to a Changing Context*, Ed. P. J. Boas and J. Crawley, Australia International Press, pp. 204–213.

Baker, R. (1980a). Building and implementing unitary social work practice—a personal account, *Contemporary Social Work Education*, **3**, 1.

Baker, R. (1980). *Exploring the Use of the Bio-psychosocial model in one Unitary Framework for Social Work Practice*, Unpublished paper, available from the author.

Baker, R. (1980b). Notes on a conceptual framework for unitary social work practice, *International Social Work*, **XXIII**, 4.

Baker, R. (1978). In praise of social work practice, *Australian Social Work*, **31**, 2.

Baker, R. (1982). Is there a future for integrated practice? Obstacles to its development in practice and education Paper presented at the 21st International Congress of Schools of Social Work, University of Sussex, Aug. 1982 (Mimeo).

Baldwin, B. (1975). Alternative services, professional practice and community mental health, *American Journal of Orthopsychiatry*, **45**, 5.

Barter, J. (1979). Prevention, in *Seebohm Across Three Decades* edited by J. Cypher, p. 138, BASW Publication.

Barter, J. (1980). 'Specialization in social work with the mentally ill, mentally handicapped, and elderly mentally infirm people and their families, *Specialization*, Edited by T. Booth, D. Martin, C. Melotte, BASW. Publications.

Bartlett, H. (1970). *The Common Base of Social Work Practice*, NASW.

BASW (British Association of Social Work) (1977). *The Social Work Task*, BASW Publications.

BASW (British Association of Social Work) (1979). *Social Work Education: The Way Ahead*, BASW Publications.

Bates, E. (1977). *Models of Madness*, University of Queensland Press.

Benedetto, R. (1977). The 23-hour bed: an alternative to hospitalization, *Health & Social Work*, **2**, 2, 74–88.

Berg, L. K., Cohen, S. Z., and Reid, W. J. (1978). Knowledge for social work roles in community mental health: findings of empirical research, *Journal of Education for Social Work*, **14**, 2.

Boehm, W. (1959). *Objectives of the Social Work Curriculum of the Future*, CSWE.

Booth, T., Martin, D., and Melotte, C. (1980). *Specialization: Issues in the Organization of Social Work*, BASW Publications.

Brewer, C., and Lait, J. (1980). *Can Social Work Survive?* Temple Smith.

Butrym, Z. (1976). *The Nature of Social Work*, Macmillan.

Clarke, F., and Arkava, M. (1979). *The Pursuit of Competence in Social Work*, Jossey-Bass.

Cooper, S. (1977). Social work: a dissenting profession, *Social Work*, **22**, 5, 360–367.

Corrigan, P., and Leonard, P. (1978). *Social Work Practice Under Capitalism: A Marxist Approach*, Macmillan.

Coulshed, V. (1980). A unitary approach to the care of the hospitalized elderly mentally ill, *British Journal of Social Work*, **10**, 1.

Cowger, C. (1977). Alternative stands on the relationship of social work to society, *Journal of Education for Social Work*, **13**, 3, 25–29.

Crouch, R. C. (1980). Social work defined, *Social Work*, **24**, 1, 46–48.

Curnock, K., and Hardiker, P. (1979). *Towards Practice Theory*, RKP.

Cypher, J. (1980). Specialization by stealth and design, In *Specialization: Issues in the Organization of Social Work*, Edited by T. Booth, D. Martin, and C. Melotte, BASW Publications.

Daley, M. (1979). Burnout: smouldering problem in protective services, *Social Work*, **24**, 5, 375–380.

de Jongh, J. (1972). A retrospective view of social work education, in, *New Themes in Social Work Education*, proceedings of the XVI International Congress of Social Work, The Hague 1972, International Association of Schools of Social Work, 1973.

Dowrick, C. (1980). Piloting a course through unchartered waters, *Social Work Today*, **11**, 23.

Drake, R., and Wallach, M. (1979). Will mental patients stay in the community? A social psychological perspective, *Journal of Consulting and Clinical Psychology*, **47**, 2, 285–294.

Evans, R. (1976). Some implications of an integrated model of social work theory and practice, *British Journal of Social Work*, **6**, 2.

Evans, R. J. (1978). Unitary models of practice and the social work team, in *The Unitary Model*, Ed. R. Olsen, BASW.

Findlay, P. C. (1978). Critical theory and social work practice, *Catalyst*, 3, 53–68.

Fischer, J. (1979). *Effective Casework Practice*, McGraw-Hill.

Galper, J. (1975). *Politics of Social Services*, Prentice-Hall.

Galper, J. (1980). *Social Work Practice: A Radical Perspective*, Prentice-Hall.

George, V., and Wilding, P. (1976). *Ideology and Social Welfare*, RKP.

Germain, C. (1980). The social context of clinical social work, *Social Work*, **25**, 6.

Gleisner, J. (1980). An experimental crisis centre, in *New Methods of Mental Health Care*, Ed. M. Meacher, pp. 133–135, Pergamon.

Goldberg, T. (1980). The role of social work in relation to general practice in the mental health field, in, *New Methods of Mental health Care*, Ed. M. Meacher, Pergamon.

Goldstein, H. (1973). *Social Work Practice: A Unitary Approach*, S. Carolina, University Press.

Gray, B., and Isaacs, B. (1979). *Care of the Mentally Ill Infirm*, Tavistock Publications.

Green, D. (1975). Social control and public welfare practice, in *Social Work In Australia: Responses to a Changing Context*, Ed. P. Boas and J. Crawley, Aust. Int. Press.

Grumet, G., and Trachtman, D. (1976). Psychiatric social workers in the emergency department, *Health and Social Work*, **1**, 3, 113–31.

Hardiker, P., and Storz, M. (1979). *Occupational Ideologies: An Exploratory Study of Welfare Practitioners' Assessments of Words of State Cases*, Sociograph No. 9, Caulfield Institute of Technology.

Hartman, A. (1974). The generic stance and the family agency, *Social Casework*, **55**, 4, 199–208.

Her Majesty's Stationery Office (1970). *The Committee on Local Authority and Allied Personal Social Services*, HMSO, (Commonly referred to as the Seebohm report following the chairman of this committee.)

Her Majesty's Stationery Office (1975). *Better Services for the Mentally Ill*, Cmnd. 6233.

Hill, M. (1980). *Specialization in Field Social Work: A Research Perspective*, BASW.

Hollis, F. (1980). On revisiting social work, *Social Casework*, **61**, 1.

House, W. C., Miller, S. I., and Schlachter, R. H. (1978). Role definitions among mental health professionals, *Comprehensive Psychiatry*, **19**, 5, 469–476.

Howe, D. (1980). Inflated states and empty theories in social work, *British Journal of Social Work*, **10**, 3, 317–340.

Huntington, J. (1980). *Social Work and General Medical Practice: Toward a Sociology of Inter-Occupational Relationships*, Ph.D. Thesis, University of New South Wales. Published as, *Social Work and General Medical Practice, Collaboration or Conflict?* Allen & Unwin, 1981.

Huws Jones, R. (1980). *Social Work Education in the 80's*, Presidential Address XXth International Congress of Schools of Social Work, Hong Kong.

IASSW (International association of schools of social work) (1976). *International Code of Ethics For the Professional Social Worker*, Adopted by the International Federation of Social Workers, Puerto Rico, Published in *ASWU/AASW News*, Nov/Dec. 1976.

Ineichen, B. (1979). *Mental Illness, The Social Structure of Modern England*, Longman.

Jacques, E. (1976). *A General Theory of Bureaucracy*, Heinemann.

Jones, K. (1979). Integration or disintegration of the mental health service: some reflections and developments in Britain since the 1950s, in *New Methods of Mental Health Care*, Ed. M. Meacher, Pergamon.

Julia, A. (1976). The history of the political and professional development of the social workers role with the mentally disordered, in *Differential Approaches in Social Work with the Mentally Disordered*, Ed. R. Olsen, BASW.

Katz, A. J. (1976). The duality of focus for social work practice in community mental health, *Journal of Social Welfare*, **3**, 1, 23–33.

Kendall, K. (1950). Social work education in review, *Social Service Review*, **24**, 3, 296–309.

Kendall, K. (1978). The IASSW 1928–1978: a journey of remembrance, *Reflections on Social Work Education 1950–1978*, IASSW.

Kings Fund Centre, (1980). *An Ordinary Life*.

Knight, L. (1977). The devastating stigma, *Community Care*, No. 175, 17th August.

Learner, E. (1979). *Education and Training for Social Welfare in Australia*, Dept. of Social Security, Australian Government Publishing Service.

Leonard, P. (1975). Towards a paradigm for radical practice, in *Radical Social Work*, Ed. R. Bailey and M. Brake, Arnold.

Lewis, H. (1972). The morality and politics of practice, *Social Casework*, **53**, 7, 404–417.

Maller, S. (1971). *Sheltered Existence: A Study of 142 Psychiatric Patients in Two Sheltered Workshops in Sydney*, Psychiatric Rehab. Association.

Maller, S. (1976a). *Fountain House: An Approach to Psychiatric Rehabilitation*, Psychiatric Rehab. Association.

Maller, S. (1976b). Buckingham House—a pilot project sponsored by the P. R. A., Psychiatric Rehab. Association.

Marx, A., Test, M., and Stein, L. (1973). Extrahospital management of severe mental illness, *Archives of General Psychiatry*, **29**, Oct.

Meacher, M. (1980). *New Methods of Mental health Care*, Pergamon.

Melville, J. (1977). Mental Block, *New Society*, 8/12/77.

Millar, S. (1979). Social policy on the defensive in Carter's America, *New Society*, 8th November.

Minahan, A., and Pincus, A. (1977). Conceptual framework for social work, *Social Work*, **22**, 5, 347–352.

Mind (1976a). *In Service Training for Social Work with the Mentally Ill*, Mind Publications.

Mind (1976b). *Mental Illness and the Health Component of Basic Social Work Training*, Mind Publications.

Mullen, E. J., Dumpson, J., and ass. (1972). *Evaluation of Social Intervention*, Jossey-Bass.

Nurse, J., and Gleisner, J. (Undated). Social aspects of chronic mental illness: a review of the literature, in *Aspects of the Social Care of the Mentally Ill: A Discussion Paper*: Published by Section 11 (Mental Health), BASW.

O'Brien, J. (1980). *The Principle of Normalization: A Foundation for Effective Services*, Georgia Advocacy Office.

Olsen, R. (1976 Ed.). *Differential Approaches in Social Work with the Mentally Disordered*, BASW, Publications.

Olsen, R. (Ed. 1978). *The Unitary Model*: BASW Occasional Paper No. 1.

Olsen, R. (1979a). Comment-Social work with the mentally disordered, *Social Work Today*, **10**, 42.

Olsen, R. (1979b). Constraints on the mentally disordered, *Social Work Today*, **10**, 43, 25.

Olsen, R. (1980). A model of emergency management, in *New Methods of Mental Health Care*, Ed. M. Meacher, pp. 127–132, Pergamon.

Pincus, A., and Minahan, A. (1973). *Social Work Practice: Method and Model*, Peacock.

Prins, H. (1976). The contribution of social work to the treatment of the mentally disordered, *in Differential Approaches in Social Work With the Mentally Disordered*, Olsen, R. (Ed.), BASW. Occ. Papers, No. 2.

Pritchard, C., and Taylor, R. (1978). *Social Work: Reform or Revolution*, RKP.

Report on a Working Group (1974). *Psychiatric Services*: Regional Office, of Europe WHO, Copenhagen.

Rees, S. (1980). *Social Work Face to Face*, Arnold.

Rees, S., and Wallace, A. (1982). *Verdicts on Social Work*, London, Edward Arnold.

Righton, P., and Richards, M. (1979). *Social Work Education in Conflict*, National Institute for Social Work Papers, No. 10.

Robinson, J. (1972). The dual commitment of social work, *British Journal of Social Work*, **2**, 4, 471–480.

Sainsbury, E. (1980). A professional skills approach to specialization, in *Specialization: Issues in the organization of Social Work*, Ed. T. Booth, D. Martin, C. Melotte, BASW.

Scurfield, R. (1980). An integrated approach to case services and social reform, *Social Casework*, **61**, 10.

Segal, P. (1978). Attitudes towards the mentally ill: a review, *Social Work*, **23**, 3, 211–217.

Siegler, M., and Osmond, H. (1976). *Models of Madness: Models of Medicine*, Harper & Row.

Simpkin, M. (1979). *Trapped Within Welfare*, Macmillan.

Siporin, M. (1975). *Introduction to Social Work practice*, Collier-Macmillan.

Skidmore, R., and Thackery, M. (1976, 2nd Ed.). *Introduction to Social Work*, Prentice-Hall.

Smith, M. (1975). *Professional Education for Social Work in Britain*, Allen & Unwin.

Smyth, T. (1979). The outlook for the mentally ill, *Social Work Today*, 10, 42.

Social Work, (1981). Conceptual frameworks II: second special issue on conceptual frameworks, *Social Work*, 26, 1.

Specht, H., and Vickery, A. (1977). *Integrating Social Work Methods*, Allen & Unwin.

Stein, H. (1969). Reflections on competence and ideology in social work, *Journal of Education for Social Work*, 5, 1.

Stein, L., Test, M., and Marx, A. (1975). Alternative to the hospital: a controlled study, *American Journal of Psychiatry*, 132, 5, 517–522.

Stevenson, O., and Parsloe, P. (1978). *Social Service Teams: The Practitioner's View*, HMSO.

Stout, D. (1976). Current mental health treatment modalities: a theoreticians nightmare, *Journal of Social Welfare*, 3, 1, 35–45.

Stretton, H. (1979). The Australian War on the Poor, *New Society*, 15th November.

Szasz, T. (1961). *The Myth of Mental Illness*, Harper.

Szasz, T. (1971). *The Manufacture of Madness*, RKP.

The National Association of Social Work Code of Ethics (1980). *Social Work*, 25, 3, 184–188.

Timms, N. (1964). *Psychiatric Social Work in Great Britain*, Routledge.

Towle, C. (1954). *The Learner in Education for the Professions*, Chicago University Press.

Townsend, P. (1979). *Poverty in the United Kingdom*, Penguin.

United Nations (1948). *Declaration of Human Rights*, Office of Public Information.

United nations (1950). *Training for Social Work: An International Survey*, United Nations Publications.

United Nations (1955). *Training for Social Work: Second International Survey,* United Nations Publications.

United Nations (1958). *Training for Social Work: Third International Survey*, United Nations Publications.

United Nations (1964). *Training for Social Work: Fourth International Survey*, United Nations Publications.

United Nations (1971). *Training for Social Welfare: Fifth International Survey*, United Nations Publications.

Utting, B. (1978). News, *Social Work Today*, May 8th, 9, 35.

Vickery, A. (1976). A unitary approach to social work with the mentally disordered, in *Differential Approaches in Social Work with the Mentally Disordered*, Ed. R. Olsen, BASW.

Webber, R. (1977). Using a unitary approach in student placements, *British Journal of Social Work*, 7, 4, 455–468.

Westminster Social Service Research (1977). *Provision for Community Services for the Mentally Ill in Westminster*, Clearing House for L. A. Research No. 9, Dec. 30th, 1977.

Wing, J. (1978). *reasoning about Madness*, Oxford University Press.

Wing, J. (1980). Comments and conclusions, in *New Methods of Mental Health Care*, Ed. M. Meacher, Pergamon.

Wolfensberger, H. (1977). The normalization principle and some major implications to architectural–environmental design, in M. Bednar, Editor, *Barrier Free Environments*, Hutchinson & Rees.

Wootton, B. (1981). Mental illness—letter to the editor, *New Society*, 12/2/81.

World Health Organization (1974). *The Role of the Social Worker*.

World Health Organization (1978). *Constraints in Mental Health Service Development*, Regional Office of Europe, Copenhagen.

Mental Illness: Changes and Trends
Edited by Philip Bean
© 1983 John Wiley & Sons Ltd.

CHAPTER 19

Mental illness in the third world

STEWART MacPHERSON
*Lecturer, Department of Social Administration
and Social Work, University of Nottingham*

Any attempt to generalize across the vast range of conditions to be found in the Third World is necessarily unsatisfactory. In what follows only a few of the major contemporary issues are indicated and it must be stressed that circumstances, problems, and possible improvements will be different for different parts of the world. The term 'Third World' itself is to dubious validity; it is used here as a somewhat crude heuristic device in full knowledge of the problems (Goldthorpe, 1975). As used in this context, it refers to those countries of the world which contain the vast majority of the human population; primarily rural, primarily in the southern latitudes, predominantly poor and for the most part enmeshed in the continuing processes of 'underdevelopment' which determine both their external patterns of economic and social relations with the powerful industrial nations, and their internal economic and social formations. Until relatively recently, debates on the nature of social change in the Third World were dominated by 'modernization theories', derived from Western economists, which placed almost total emphasis on the need for rapid penetration by western oriented market forces and productive processes. This approach assumed that the disruption, dislocation, and destruction of pre-existing social formations was the inevitable price of progress (MacPherson, 1982). These fundamental assumptions regarding the nature and direction of 'development' were basic to patterns of social provision, which in themselves were seen most often as both supportive of economic transformation and necessary to cope with the human costs of that transformation. More recently, attention has been focused on the concepts of development which emphasize the needs of the mass of Third World populations and attempt to correct the inequalities characteristic of earlier development strategies. Contemporary analysis of underdevelopment as a process highlights the continuing role of relationships between the unequal sectors of the world economy and focuses attention, within Third World countries, on those mechanisms which perpetuate and extend the patterns of inequality which are the most pervasive feature of the underdeveloped countries. Studies of housing (Drakakis-Smith, 1981), health (Doyal and Pennell, 1979), and social welfare (Midgley, 1981; MacPherson, 1982) have analysed both the distribution of resources in these areas and the principles which determine dominant policies, on the basis of these newer approaches to the study of underdevelopment. It is against this background, of past and present underdevelopment, that mental illness, and responses to it, must be seen.

It is now generally accepted that health problems in general in the Third World are the problems of poverty and underdevelopment; they are not, in terms of overall patterns or morbidity and mortality, exotic, unusual and outside the experience of Western societies. Similarly, the peculiarity and special nature of mental illness and mental health services in developing countries result essentially from poverty and underdevelopment; of education, of health service systems, of trained medical staff, of resources, transportation, and communications. In addition, and in this perhaps the developing countries simply demonstrate in sharper focus issues which are still real in the West, there is the major issue of traditional methods of dealing with mental illness. Currently, as will be seen in more detail below, considerable debate centres on the possible retention of traditional methods and their incorporation in 'modern' systems of health care delivery. Thus, while Western observers may be overwhelmed by what appears to them to be dramatically different patterns of mental illness and mental health services these 'do not derive from any difference in the spectrum of psychiatric disorders found in developing countries' (Asuni, 1975, p. 12).

The extent and nature of mental illness

Although the range of mental illness in Third World countries had generally been established to be similar to that in the developed countries there are significant differences in patterns of illness. At a general level, the demographic characteristics of Third World countries are important; populations tend to be poor, rural, young, and to have a high incidence of organic disturbances which predispose to psychopathology. In addition, rapid social change produces situations in which a proportion of the population is still essentially located in highly integrated traditional social organizations while others are more isolated and displaced, often having left the rural areas and migrated to urban environments. Again at a general level, the massive scale of health problems in the Third World has frequently led to questioning the significance of mental illness as a social problem. Here of course we must note the crucial distinction between 'social problems' and 'social conditions'; put very crudely, if mental illness is not acknowledged to be a problem of major concern, then it is not. Given the overall patterns of morbidity and mortality in the Third World, it is clear that problems of infectious disease and malnutrition are so great that responses to these are the first priority. However, arguments which may place services for the mentally ill lower in the scale of priorities are often linked by implication with an assumption that mental illness is not itself significant in extent. Such an assumption is, however, no longer tenable and the magnitude of mental illness in the Third World has been widely recognized in recent years (Diop, 1974; Baasher *et al.*, 1975; Binitie, 1976; Fine *et al.*, 1981).

Psychopathology in developing countries has been found to be similar in both characteristics and epidemiology to that reported in developed countries, but some differences have been noted. Given that about half the population is under fifteen years old in most developing countries the increased role of problems of children and adolescents rather than the elderly is not surprising (Mbatia, 1979; Varma *et al.*, 1980). Michels (1980) noted, in addition, 'the prominence of acute transient psychoses, the prominence of hysterical and projective mechanisms, the prominence of organic psychopathology, and the decreased prevalence of depression, obsessional pathology, guilt, and in general self-directed aggression'. German (1972), a psychiatrist working in East Africa, confirmed the overall similarity of psychiatry in Africa to psychiatry in other parts of the world. The differences which he noted were, he argued, in part due to physiological deprivation and physical disease and in part to cultural differences and illiteracy. The latter may be seen as coming dangerously close to the suggestion that the people fail to fit the models that Western psychiatrists bring with them to their practice in the Third World. Echoes of the 'modernization' approach referred to earlier may perhaps be found in his suggestion that if the comparison were to be made between contemporary psychiatric disorder in Africa and psychiatric disorder in Europe a hundred years ago the differences in patterns of psychopathology would be even less marked. From his perspective as a practising psychiatrist German confirmed that the prevalence of psychiatric morbidity was similar to that found elsewhere:

Schizophrenia, manic depressive disorder and organic psychioses exist in their familiar forms, although in different proportions; neurotic illness is widespread, although little studied; psychogeriatric problems are beginning to appear. Differences are mainly of a pathoplastic sort, and such differences as exist are likely to become less as development accelerates (German, 1972, p. 477).

There are very many similar statements in the literature, regarding patterns of psychopathology in Third World countries and based on clinical practice (Neki, 1975; Giel and Harding, 1976). Although obviously interesting in themselves, and extremely useful as indication of the nature of psychiatric practice they are, despite the best efforts of their authors, of limited usefulness as guides to overall patterns of psychopathology and mental illness. First of all, as will be seen in more detail later, access to health services is grossly uneven in all Third World countries; this is even more true of psychiatric services. People with greater access to hospital referral sources, and higher utilization rates, are more likely to present for psychiatric treatment than people without such access. Access and utilization will be affected by the physical distribution of facilities, ease of transportation, and socio-cultural factors. Utilization of health facilities in general will be affected by length of exposure to and familiarity with those facilities.

Furthermore, in relation to mental illness, there are numerous reasons why generalization from referred cases to whole populations is fraught with difficulty; people who are referred to the psychiatrist do not necessarily represent that segment of the society from which they originate. Communities vary enormously in the range and level of abnormal behaviour they are willing, and able, to tolerate within themselves; referred cases may more often represent the more extreme cases. Finally, of course, given the extremely low number of psychiatrists in Third World countries, extensive 'filtering' mechanisms operate to ensure that 'appropriate' cases are referred through the system. Unless information is collected systematically, commentary on the nature of mental illness and psychopathology is liable to be reduced to unreliable generalization from individual case referrals. There is therefore a need for full-scale surveys utilizing standardized epidemiological design.

A large number of surveys have in fact been conducted, in many parts of the world, and prevalence rates of mental illness calculated. The World Health Organization, in a review of these, and other work, concluded that:

Well conducted epidemiological studies in several parts of the world have shown no fundamental differences either in the range of mental disorders that occur or in the prevalence of seriously incapacitating mental illness. These studies indicate that such seriously incapacitating mental disorders are likely to effect at least 1% of any population at any one time and at least 10% at some time in their life (World Health Organization, 1975a, p. 8).

In the developing countries, as indeed elsewhere, the major functional psychoses from a large proportion of serious disorders, and, in addition, there are mental disorders related to infectious illnesses and other organic pathology (Giel, 1975). The prevalence of the psychiatric disorders of old age, and especially dementia, which are presently reported as relatively low, is generally seen as likely to rise. Two major factors may be noted as important here; first, life expectancy is increasing with improvements in health services and second, 'tolerance levels' are falling in many areas and traditional systems of social support are increasingly unable to cope with the demands put upon them. The incidence of some organic brain conditions is likely to fall with enhanced public health measures and more complete understanding of disease aetiology. With regard to the latter, the identification of a virus-like body as significant in the causation of kuru, an organic disease of the central nervous system, was perhaps one of the most dramatic and impressive examples of such advances in recent years (Hornabrook, 1976). Improvements in health services are also likely, however, to increase the number of surviving children with brain damage (Ashem and Jones, 1978). Increases in the incidence of brain injury from accidents, particularly those involving motor vehicles are also noted in many parts of the world.

Prevalence rates for epilepsy are higher in developing countries than elsewhere, and in many areas the number of cases is known to be seriously understated due to specific socio-cultural responses (Kapur, 1975). Alcohol-related disorders are increasing in very many countries; in very many urban areas alcoholism is already a serious problem. But increasing prevalence is not restricted to urban areas; in many rural areas of the Third World alcoholism is beginning to constitute a serious problem (Kiev, 1972).

According to the World Health Organization, 'the extent of other forms of mental disorder (psychoneuroses, emotional disorders, personality problems) is more difficult to define, but there is no evidence to support the view that such disorders are significantly less common that elsewhere' (World Health Organization, 1975a, p. 9). A number of studies have been carried out of patients attending curative health facilities (health centres, out-patient clinics), and these have found up to 20 per cent of patients with significant mental disorders (Giel, 1975). The general population surveys have found prevalence rates of 10 per cent or more. It is important to note that many of the patients at health facilities present with somatic symptoms and are frequently dealt with inappropriately (World Health Organization, 1975a). This is of major importance, as such patients may become frequent attenders at health facilities which are called upon to carry an enormous burden of work in the conditions of scarcity which prevail in the Third World. Presentation with predominantly somatic symptoms has been noted particularly in relation to depressive illness and the psychoneuroses.

In many Third World countries, it is the more dramatic forms of mental illness which gain public attention, as will be seen later, rather than the whole range of mental disorders. This in itself may go some way to explaining the importance given to some extreme mental disorders in the Third World. For example, 'certain forms of acute functional psychosis with florid symptoms have been described as common in Africa and elsewhere in developing countries. Lack of treatment facilities leads to the development of particularly severe forms of psychotic illness' (World Health Organization, 1975a, p. 9). From a review of the major surveys of mental illness in the Third World, the World Health Organization concluded that:

...mental disorders constitute a very serious problem in the developing countries: the functional psychoses occur ubiquitously, as serious mental disorders with an organic basis occur more frequently than elsewhere. Nonpsychotic mental illness forms a significant part of the case load in all curative health services. In addition, mental illness may present itself under various guises such as: physical complaints, criminal offences, suicide, frequent or prolonged absenteeism from work, dropping-out from school, etc. (World Health Organization, 1975a, p. 10).

While it must be acknowledged that the World Health Organization conclusions are soundly based on the available survey results, those results themselves must be treated with substantial caution. Giel, in a discussion of the difficulties inherent in assessments of the need for mental health services in developing countries, concluded that 'epidemiological surveys are unlikely to provide important leads on how to solve the mental health problems of the developing countries' (Giel, 1975, p. 28). He identified a number of serious problems with attempts to establish the prevalence of mental disorder. Most were those familiar in any survey-based methodology; four points are important here. First, and of particular importance in situations where those providing services, and making judgments are almost certainly from outside the community in question is that 'except for some outright psychotic mental phenomena, most other behaviour cannot be judged according to uniformly applicable and objective criteria for presence of pathology' (Giel, 1975, p. 24). Second, and again of general applicability, but of particular force in situations of general deprivation, he points to the lack of any consistent relationship between symptoms, the degree of disability, and the perception of that disability as 'illness'. There is evidence that under conditions of poverty the same amount of suffering is less likely to cause illness behaviour than it would in people who can afford to be ill (Dormaar *et al.*, 1974). Third, community surveys based on standard sampling may fail to trace chronically psychotic people, who may either be 'hidden' from the investigators, or quite commonly, have become vagrants. The fourth point, which is important for later discussion of mental health services, is that although community surveys may be attractive to planners as helpful in establishing basic morbidity rates of mental illness in the general population, such surveys are both inefficient and, more important, unlikely to provide much information about the need of people to attend mental health services should these be available.

Despite the fundamental problems encountered in attempts to establish the prevalence of mental disorder in Third World countries, a consistent theme in the literature is the relationship between rapid social change and mental illness. For many years, considerable stress was placed on the problems of social disruption, dislocation, and disorganization produced by rapid social change. Clifford (1966) for example, concluded from a review of sociological literature on modernization in Third World countries that previously well-integrated communities were becoming less cohesive and less able to deal with social problems. Traditionally, the rural family was self-sufficient, functioning as an integrated social and economic unit; every individual had clearly defined duties and obligations towards the family, community, and cultural group. Conversely, these groups were responsible for the welfare of the individual. Clifford argued, as have many others, that as the pace of social change quickened, traditional systems of social support were eroded. In particular, this erosion was seen to be accelerated by urbanization and associated patterns of rural–urban migration. As the young were drawn away to the towns and cities, rural communities were less able to provide support for all their members, especially the most vulnerable. In the urban areas themselves migrants find their expectations thwarted when housing and employment are scarce; in very many Third World cities the poor are crowded into slums or illegal squatter settlements, with only temporary employment, or none at all. The problems of urban poverty have been made worse by psychological problems; an example often quoted being the loss of cultural identity brought about by inter-marriage and the disintegration of traditional customs. 'In the towns we are faced not only with amorphous populations, shapeless, normless and often suspended between two ways of life, but also with the psychological effects of this hiatus' (Clifford, 1966, p. 6).

A number of other authors have also stressed the disruptive effects of urbanization and social change (Leon, 1972; Carstairs, 1973; Giel and Harding, 1976; Chakraborty, 1978). Writing on the effects of modernization in Iran, Farman-Farmaian (1964) argued that the destruction of traditional systems had resulted in serious psychological tensions and an increase in the incidence of psychiatric illness. Bulsara (1965) made a very similar case for India; modernization made people more insecure and vulnerable. For urban areas in particular, the poor have consistently been characterized as outside the mainstream of society. Very many studies have continued, and extended, the work of Oscar Lewis (1966) in graphically recording the hopelessness and social disorganization of the urban poor; despite the weakness of Lewis's work, both theoretically and methodologically (Valentine, 1968). In a recent study of mental health in Honduras, the urban barrio in question was described as a place 'where anomie, despair and disorganization are endemic' (Eisenberg, 1980, p. 77).

In general, however, more recent work on Third World urbanization has corrected the extreme views noted above. Despite the disruption caused by urbanization, anthropological research in particular has demonstrated that urban migrants are enmeshed in social networks and systems of social support. Social and economic links are maintained or developed between migrants and their home communities and new urban dwellers and urban groups with whom the new arrival has kinship or cultural ties. Numerous studies have examined the nature and extent of these links (Mangin, 1969, 1970; Safa, 1974; Safa and du Toit, 1975). In general, two conclusions emerge; first, an enormous variation and second the relatively greater importance of links within the urban situation than with the rural areas. Nonetheless, rural–urban links are important, and in Africa the maintenance of kinship ties and rural land rights by urban Africans, their patterns of visiting, plans to retire to the village, and attempts to give primacy to ethnicity over class in certain situations are common themes. Similar features have been noted by Levine and Levine (1979) in Papua New Guinea, where urbanization is relatively recent; here towns are characterized as 'ambivalent' and it is suggested that as 'a generation comes of age in the towns, they may (despite continuing ideological ties to rural areas) come to identify more strongly with urban life-styles' (Levine and Levine, 1979, p. 138).

The second sort of link is of major significance to the present discussion and is closely related to the first. Throughout the towns and cities of the Third World, the incoming migrant is likely to be assisted by some social group with which he has ties. These groups, whether formal or informal, will be of crucial importance in providing both material and social support to the migrant, together with the contacts and the information which assist the new arrival in establishing a new life in the town. The great variation in such grouping would appear to be related to the size of the urban area, the strength of traditional systems with which such groups are associated and the homogeneity of the urban group as a whole. Where such groups are to be found, however, their role is of great importance; in many areas the dominant feature of the social structure of urban communities may be these networks of relationships based on community of origin (Lloyd, 1979). Thus the patterns of urbanization are complex and generalizations are not simply difficult but dangerous. In specific situations, patterns of social relationships and social support are clearly of major relevance to considerations of mental health. Lloyd provides a useful summary:

> The ties of the immigrant to his co-villagers and to his home community not only needs to be stressed but also needs to be examined closely so that these differences in the nature of the relationships their intensity and the differential involvement of persons of high and low socio-economic status, is fully explored. We must distinguish clearly between the personal links which bind the migrant to his family in the rural area, and those which unite co-villagers in the city; and between associational activities which serve to develop the home area and those which are for the benefit of the city immigrants themselves (Lloyd, 1979, p. 140).

Considerable attention has been given here to the question of urbanization; this may appear contradictory given earlier emphasis on the fact that the populations of the Third World are predominantly rural. However, as will become clear the contradiction is one which is firmly embedded in the responses to mental illness in the Third World. Mental health services are essentially urban in character; not only are they maldistributed very unevenly in favour of urban areas, but their character is largely determined by assumptions imported from urban societies. Furthermore, the presumptions regarding the effects of modernization, noted earlier, continue to dominate responses to problems of mental disorder, despite contrary evidence. As suggested, it has been common for observers to assume a high degree of mental instability among recent migrants as a result of the trauma of sudden movement to very unfamiliar surroundings and the lack of traditional systems of support. Surveys of urban populations did, and still do, describe the maladjusted and thus apparently validate the hypothesis. Many more studies have, however, shown a different picture. For example, an epidemiological survey in Nigeria showed that those who had moved into the town were relatively healthy but that the incidence of symptoms of maladjustment was higher in the village—though it was not clear whether this was the direct effect of village life or because those individuals least able to cope gravitated to the villages (Leighton *et al.*, 1963). Overall it must be concluded that the evidence that mental illness is greater among migrants to urban areas is ambiguous. Even when it does appear that there are higher rates of mental disorder it is far from certain that the social and cultural differences between rural and urban areas are the main cause.

In summary, although sociologists and anthropologists accept that rapid social change causes structural tensions and social disruption, many believe that the psychopathological consequences of modernization have been exaggerated. To the extent that they are present, they are most certainly to be found in both rural and urban areas.

Perhaps most important of all neither the sharp division between 'rural–traditional' and 'urban disorganized' social systems nor the notion that development inevitably demanded massive psychological change are any longer tenable. If response to mental illness in the Third World is to be relevant, and effective for the mass of people, the complexity of the situations in which that illness arises must be acknowledged, and simplistic assumptions, related more to the underlying philosophies of imported treatment systems than the real needs of the people, must be avoided.

Contemporary responses to mental illness

Although many of those responsible for mental health services in the Third World have proceeded as if the societies in which they were working were blank pages waiting to be filled this is quite clearly nonsense. All existing societies had mechanisms for dealing with mental disorder. In recent years, considerably more attention has been given both to traditional concepts of mental illness and the coexistence of modern and traditional forms of treatment.

Very few authorities would now underestimate the significance of traditional beliefs regarding the nature and causation of illness in general or mental illness in particular (Kiev, 1964). Hammond-Tooke (1975) draws a sharp distinction between ideas of causation held by Western man and the non-Western traditionalist. The Western medical model operates 'on a mechanical universe basis', and the non-Western with 'a picture of the world (which) operates with a personalized model'. In very many traditional systems, 'the world is governed by forces conceived to be in the form of human-type intelligence-gods, nature spirits, ancestors, witches who are the causal agencies in illness and misfortune' (Hammond-Tooke, 1975, p. 25). There are of course wide variations among different societies in concepts of illness and methods of treatment; in a review of primarily African sources Asuni (1975) indicates something of the complexity:

Some recognise physical causes of mental illness; others do not. Some use physical methods of treatment; others do not. Consequently, in some cases greater emphasis is placed on social order and integration than on the individual. Some help the patient to live with his dysfunction rather than attempt a cure. Some exorcise the offending spirits; others do not, but make use of the spirit to the benefit of the patient. Some confine themselves to the psychoneuroses, others treat all psychiatric disorders. In general, . . . each system is geared to the fulfillment of the sociocultural needs of the society (Asuni, 1975, p. 16).

Although this may be discouraging for those who are looking for simple explanations of traditional approaches which may be then used whenever and wherever mental health problems are considered in the Third World, the complexity is a reflection of variation in the nature of societies; it is the relationship between traditional approaches and the societies in which they function which is their greatest strength. They are part of those societies, not alien systems imposed upon them.

In Papua New Guinea, which has been subject to a considerable degree of anthropological investigation, the link between anthropology and mental health services has been emphasized (Pataki-Schweizer, 1976). However, although numerous statements in that country have acknowledged the degree to which both the form and frequency of mental disorders are culturally determined, there would appear to be a considerable gap between rhetoric and the response of formal mental health services (Robin, 1979). Burton-Bradley, whose work on mental illness in Papua New Guinea forms the major part of all literature on the subject relating to that country, recognized the role that metaphysical concepts play in shaping attitudes to illness and illness-behaviour. However, his re-cognition carries the clearly implied judgment that existing systems are inferior:

Until magic has largely disappeared at the hands of modern logico-experimental science—and it is doubtful if this can be effected on a wide scale in the immediate future—it is apparent that there must be some form of rational integration of the two systems for some time to come . . . The situational logic has to be taken into account, and the model for therapy should bear at least some resemblance to indigenous concepts if it is to enjoy a greater level of acceptability (Burton-Bradley, 1969, p. 3).

However, others in Papua New Guinea express a more direct bias in favour of Western psychiatry. Moi, head of the mental health services, suggested that traditional attitudes to mental disorder were not only common among the general population, but also among administrators, planners, and health personnel. Such attitudes, he argued, 'constitute a major obstacle to the development of mental health services' (Moi, 1976, p. 17). He goes on to suggest that mental disorder will only lose its stigma when the efficiency of modern methods are acknowledged and in particular their success at integrating the mentally ill into society. Such defences of imported Western psychiatric methods are not uncommon in Third World countries and traditional beliefs and practices are very often seen as barriers to progress. As Robin (1979) points out, arguments about 'the need for successful integration into society and the necessity to prevent stigma of mental illness fails to recognize psychiatry's poor track record on both these dimensions' (Robin, 1979, p. 40). As an essentially alien, imposed, system in Third World countries, it is perhaps even more the case that psychiatry works against successful integration by hospitalizing patients and posting the vast majority of its personnel within institutional structures, removed from the community. In terms of creating a stigma of mental illness among the population, psychiatry is recognized as contributing to, and actually creating this process of stigma through the use of labels and other psychiatric procedures (Szasz, 1970).

In the majority of cases, although the importance of traditional systems may be acknowledged, there is at best only a half-hearted attempt to incorporate these into contemporary treatment processes. Despite very rapid social change, traditional belief systems would appear to be surviving in many parts of the world. In many African countries, for example, metaphysical conceptions of the world remain extensive and these are at considerable odds with the supposed rationality of Western , 'scientific' approaches (Lambo, 1969; Orley, 1970). Lambo (1978) has pointed to the difficulty of imposing Western forms of treatment in situations where contrary systems prevail in the traditional culture; 'modern science fails to satisfy the basic metaphysical and social needs of many people, no matter how sophisticated they are' (Lambo, 1978, p. 38).

A number of authors have discussed attempts to incorporate traditional healers with Western psychiatric practice, and in particular the importance of placing the sick person within a social context and using the indigenous therapeutic practices which are available in the community (Argandona and Kiev, 1972; Torrey, 1972). Although there is considerable variation in the forms of traditional practice encountered in different parts of the world, and indeed some divergence in the opinions of that practice, nearly all studies illustrate the basic recognition that indigenous therapeutic practices need to be integrated within the institutional health structure to make treatments viable and effective. Lambo accurately described the typical reaction to legitimizing traditional methods as well as the importance of using them:

To the Western eye, such lingering beliefs in ritual and magic seem antiquated and possibly harmful—obstacles in the path of modern medicine. But the fact is that African cultures have developed indigenous forms of psychotherapy that are highly effective because they are woven into the social fabric. Although Western therapeutic methods are being adopted by many African therapists, few Africans are simply substituting new methods for traditional modes of treatment. Instead, they have attempted to combine the two for maximum effectiveness. The character and effectiveness of medicine for the mind always and everywhere depend on the culture in which the medicine is practiced. In the West, healing is often considered to be a private matter between patient and therapist. In Africa healing is an integral part of society of religion, a matter in which the whole community is involved (Lambo, 1978, p. 33).

Considerably more attention has been given recently to traditional methods of dealing with mental disorders and the possibilities of integrating traditional and modern practice. A recent conference on mental health services illustrated both this trend and the considerable degree of antipathy towards traditional treatment which is to be found in very many Third World countries (Kiev *et al.*, 1980). There is a considerable way to go before the implications of Torrey's statement, made a decade ago are incorporated into practice: 'we can learn to be less ethnocentric and arrogant about our own therapy and more tolerant of others' (Torrey, 1972, p. 74).

The World Health Organization, recognizing that the function of traditional healers in treating mental disorder was controversial, adopted a somewhat cautious approach to the problem (WHO, 1975a). The wide social functions of traditional healers were acknowledged, as was their effectiveness in dealing with particular kinds of mental disorder. On the other hand, some stress was put on the possibility that some healers are 'unscrupulous, in both the methods they employ and their mercenary motivations' (WHO, 1975a, p. 11). The conclusions on the relationship between traditional and modern systems are somewhat ambiguous but display a marked lack of enthusiasm for traditional practice. It is suggested that close collaboration between traditional healers and psychiatrists is 'probably appropriate in only a few selected situations . . . however, those responsible for mental health services may have to recognize the function performed by healers, both therapeutically and in influencing attitudes' (WHO, 1975a, p.12). Although cooperation with psychiatrists was seen as very limited it was felt that more could be achieved at the village health worker level, particularly where such workers were drawn from the community itself. This was significant in two, perhaps contradictory, ways; stress on the village health worker adumbrated later development of the primary health care approach but also underlined the gulf between the extremes of the health service hierarchy in Third World countries. A brief examination of the emergence of primary health care and the role of mental health services within that approach will enable a clearer understanding of this fundamental contradiction.

Health services in the developing countries, the majority of which are former colonial territories, must be seen as reflecting dominant societal relationships (Segall, 1972; Navarro, 1974; Turshen, 1977a; Doyal and Pennell, 1979; Gish, 1979; MacPherson, 1980). Contemporary patterns of underdevelopment have their roots in colonialism; underdeveloped health services have grown out of colonial medical care systems. The metropolitan powers introduced their own health systems into their overseas territories at an early stage of colonial penetration; in many cases, this period was dominated by the military and the missions. Colonial administration hospitals were built initially to meet the needs of 'Europeans' and their families; they might have some minor provision for 'non-European' in-patient care, but this was more likely to be provided by mission hospitals (Beck, 1970; Schram, 1971). Characteristically, hospital provision was in the major centres of European settlement and economic activity (Gish, 1973; Benyoussef, 1977). Rural facilities, where these existed, were more commonly run by missions and other voluntary organizations; they were essentially currative, dispensing drugs to out-patients, with very limited in-patient facilities. To the extent that colonial services were extended to the indigenous population their distribution was again generally determined by patterns of economic activity, notably in primary export production. As for their style, the dominant theme was most often the desire to spread the scientific and orderly methods of Western scientific methods to peoples considered to be 'backward' and lacking in awareness of 'proper medical practice'. As Gish remarks, 'it was generally assumed that the administered people would prosper to the degree they became like those who administered them' (Gish, 1979, p. 205). With many others, Turshen (1977b) argues that the spread of the clinical medical model was inextricably linked to the spread of the capitalist mode of production; the values and underlying paradigm of the clinical model are connected to the forms of economic organization that characterize capitalist social life:

... medicine's failure to develop a positive definition of health results from the individualistic and ideological bias that pervades medical research and medical practice, structures relations between practitioners and patients, shapes the approaches selected for treatment (e.g. chemical or surgical intervention) and the technology employed, and rejects the initiation of collective social action by communities' (Turshen, 1977b, p. 49).

the legacy of colonialism was grossly inadequate services, extremely maldistri-buted in favour of urban areas and particular areas of high economic activity, which were generally irrelevant to the basic health needs of the majority. Further, an approach to health itself was established which was to a very great extent inimical to the levels present of appropriate health systems.

Political independence made little difference to health policies; the change was most often little more than 'the replacement of direct colonial administration by "independent" governments representing local strata and classes with an interest in sustaining the colonial economic relationships' (Leys, 1975, p. 9). Numerous studies of neo-colonialism and health have documented both the continuing injustice of health care systems in the Third World and the crucial in-terrelationships between those systems and those of the former colonial powers (Gish, 1971; Lall and Bibile, 1977; Doyal and Pennell, 1979). Most newly independent states attempted expansion of their health provision, but essentially in the form developed under colonialism. Despite stated objectives to the contrary, in most countries post-independence health allocations were biased as much, or more, in the direction of emerging élite and urban groups than had been the case before political independence (Lipton, 1977; Mburu, 1979; MacPherson, 1980). Although the fundamental nature of health provision changed little there was considerable expansion; most notably in the rapid growth of hospital provision and the drive to produce medical graduates. This provision was almost always in urban areas and widened the gulf between rural and urban populations. Although profound changes were taking place in a few newly independent countries, for example Tanzania (Kilama *et al.*, 1974; Gish, 1975), most countries emphasized 'growth'; health policies matched the dominant economic ideology. It was not until the 1970s that emphasis on 'growth' and 'gross national product' as the measures of 'development' began to give way to alternative view informed by the realities of conditions for the mass of people. By the end of the 1970s, it was possible to say, albeit with some qualifications, that 'the emergence of a new majority view of development focussed upon the needs of the most impoverished, including perhaps especially their nutritional and health requirements, has more or less "swept the development boards"' (Gish, 1979, p. 208).

International concern with health in developing countries began to reflect this 'new' view of development; there was more attention paid to the problems and issues of basic health services in rural areas (World Health Organization, 1973a, 1973b, 1974). The principles of the primary health care approach were enunciated by the Director-General of the World Health Organization in 1975; these have been the focus of attention by the international agencies ever since (World Health Organization, 1975b, 1979). The fundamental justification for the new approach was expressed in the major background study conducted for the World Health Organization:

Despite great efforts by government and international organisations, the basic health needs of vast numbers of the world's people remain unsatisfied. In many countries less than 15 percent of the rural population have access to health services ... The strategy adopted ... by many developing countries has been modelled on that of the industrialised countries, but as a strategy it has been a failure ... In sum, history and experience show that conventional health services, organised along "Western" or other centralised lines, are unlikely to expand to meet the basic health needs of all people ... Clearly the time has come to take a fresh look at the world's priority health problems and at alternative approaches to their solution' (Djukanovic and Mach, 1975, p. 7).

The conclusions of this study, based on an analysis of the failure of 'conventional' health services and the example of countries with successful, or potentially successful, basic health programmes emphasized the need for clear national health policies, the relationship between health and development strategies, the need for massive redistribution of resources and, fundamentally, the reorientation of health systems around community-based primary health workers. Of the countries examined by Djukanovic and Mach, Cuba, China, and Tanzania were those which provided the most dramatic results from the application of the primary health care approach. The Djukanovic and Mach study very clearly established the primary health care worker as the foundation of health systems in developing countries. In doing so, major emphasis was put on involvement of the community which the health worker served. This was examined in a further World Health Organization publication which suggested that basic health should be 'health by the people' (Newell, 1975). In all the examples presented by Newell the new systems of primary health care were either linked with pre-existing indigenous health systems or attempted to function in ways which were qualitatively similar to such systems; 'In this sense the new did not win over or destroy the old but achieved an adjustment that had some new qualities and techniques and provided a link between the present and the past' (Newell, 1975, p. 193). The key similarity between the successful examples discussed lay in community organization and it was argued that some significant advances could be made by this approach, whatever the wider socio-political context.

Others have placed much greater emphasis on the relationship between developments in health and social, economic, and political forces. In particular it has been argued that if genuine progress towards justice and the strengthening of communities is to be made this can only occur where there is a fundamental shift of power (Navarro, 1972; Rifkin and Kaplinsky, 1973; Sidel and Sidel, 1974, 1977; Feuerstein, 1976). In general, however, a more pragmatic approach has been dominant; 'present medical care systems are clearly inadequate, so if the choice is between offering primary health care or no health care at all, then the choice is obvious' (Benyoussef and Christian, 1977, p. 407). In September 1978, the Alma-Ata International Conference on Primary Health Care established primary health care as the model of health development in the majority of Third World countries. The Declaration of Alma-Ata stressed the 'existing gross inequality' in health status, and argued that health should be a main focus of overall social and economic development. The extent to which the new approach has gained acceptance is indicated by, for example, recent changes in World Bank policies, which now stress that 'Technical, social, and economic factors demand that for most of the world, it will be necessary to adopt or extend simplified systems of health care' (World Bank, 1980, p. 44).

However, optimism is by no means universal; Gish, for example, has expressed serious doubts regarding the recent wave of enthusiasm for primary health care. Suspicious that there has been little hard analysis of the issues and 'wishful thinking at best and cynicism at worst', he argues that 'the discussion appears to have moved in remarkably short order from almost total rejection of the traditional practitioner, the village health worker or even other types of "medical practitioners' than those with university degrees to idyllic glorification of these types of cadres' (Gish, 1979, p. 209). As Gish points out, there has been a failure to examine sufficiently the context of health programmes in countries such as Cuba, China, and Tanzania. Even where the appropriate conditions for success appear to be present there have been serious problems in attempts to radically reform the health systems. In Tanzania for example, despite major advances, rural health workers have been found to be careerist, deferential to the established medical hierarchy, and unsympathetic to the people among whom they worked (Raikes, 1973; Van Etten, 1976). Similar findings emerged from a recent study of community-level health workers in Papua New Guinea (MacPherson, 1980).

Primary health care has rapidly emerged as the dominant model for health service development; the approach focuses on the basic health needs of the majority of people, attempts to integrate promotional, preventive, and curative health, stresses the use of low-level manpower and relies heavily on community organization for health. Doubts regarding the real long-term success of this approach stem essentially from explanations of existing patterns of inequality in health conditions, access to health resources and approaches to health care. To the extent that these are the product of the 'development of underdevelopment' significant changes in health will depend not simply on health policies but on changes in the pattern of social, economic and political forces in developing countries (Frankenberg and Leeson, 1973; Sidel and Sidel, 1974; Aziz, 1978). From this perspective, improved health is not simply, or even primarily, a matter of medical systems but a much more complex question of the relationship between health and underdevelopment. As Gish argues, 'all activities concerned with health must begin with the specifics of underdevelopment in particular circumstances. Only from this background will it be possible to come to grips with the issues of improved health status as well as more relevant health and medical services in the Third World' (Gish, 1979, p. 210).

Services for the mentally ill must be seen in the context of the growth of health services in general, as outlined above. In particular, recent proposals for change have flowed from emphasis on primary health care and the acknowledgment of the gross inequalities in existing health systems. In virtually all Third World countries, formal provision for mental health problems is extremely limited. Where any services at all are available, they are most often in the form of mental hospitals. In general, such hospitals are large, isolated, serve a very large area, and have little contact with the communities from which patients come.

The large centralized hospital is commonly a legacy of colonial administration and fits the general pattern of a centralized, urban-based development of services. From the outset, such hospitals have been extensively used as custodial institutions, heavily used by the police and the courts; conversely, where hospital facilities do not exist, prisons are very often used to house the mentally ill (Mulaka and Acuda, 1978). The hospitals are almost always poorly staffed and grossly overcrowded; active treatment is generally limited to drugs and electroconvulsive therapy; 'rehabilitation and social therapy can rarely be carried out' (World Health Organization, 1975a, p. 14). Overall health budgets are relatively small in every Third World country and as Gish states, 'psychiatric hospitals in Third World countries are usually most unpleasant places, as in just about every other part of the world, mental patients are given very low priority in the allocation of health care resources' (Gish, 1977, p. 54).

In all Third World countries there are very few staff trained to meet mental health needs. In Ethiopia for example, with a population of twenty-seven million, there were 600 physicians in 1979, of whom one was a psychiatrist; in Zambia there were six psychiatrists and two hundred mental health workers for a population of four million (Kiev *et al.*, 1980, pp. 29, 31). Lippman's description of his work in Ethiopia illustrates graphically the realities of care for the mentally ill in very many of the poorest countries of the world:

The Amanuel (mental) Hospital in Addis Ababa is one of two such institutions in the country. In terms of number of patients, it was the largest hospital in Ethiopia, with an average census of between 530 and 570 inpatients. Since the hospital had only 300 beds available, most patients had to double up or in some cases triple up. Of the six psychiatrists in Ethiopia, three worked in Amanuel Hospital (two Bulgarians and myself).

In addition to inpatients, the physicians also saw about 50 outpatients daily who would line up for appointments beginning at 5 a.m. Due to the magnitude of the patient/physician ratio, pharmacological treatment constituted the main stay of therapy, although ECT was also provided for both in and outpatients, together with brief psychotherapy with suitable patients if their English, French or Italian was good enough ... (Lippman, 1980, p. 34)

Lippman's account is quoted at length as an unemotional description of the level of service available in very many Third World countries. It is recognized that Ethiopia is worse off than many countries, but the best part of this account is typical. Furthermore, 85 per cent of the patients at the Amanuel Hospital were from Addis Ababa and its environs; the vast majority of the population had no access even to these 'services'. The extreme scarcity of mental health services has been extensively documented; what little exists is concentrated in urban areas and provides minimal care. The hierarchical, drug-oriented characteristics of health systems in general may be seen to a more extreme degree in provision for mental illness.

Given the appalling levels of care available in conventional systems, which replicate Western treatment systems in conditions of extreme scarcity, attention has been given to the development of alternative strategies. Essentially, these strategies are seen as part of the overall 'primary health care' approach outlined earlier. Concern is with more adequate access for the mass of people, the provision of basic mental health care by primary health workers, and a fundamental re-orientation away from hospitals to community organizations as the focus of treatment. 'The development of basic health services at village level, with a supportive structure of health centres, district hospitals, and more central specialist facilities, offers the opportunity to provide mental health services on a limited scale' (World Health Organization, 1975a, p. 23). As yet, there are few examples of significant shifts in practice despite considerable rhetoric in support of such changes. An early example was the Tanzanian attempt to develop ultimately self-supporting 'halfway villages' for psychiatric patients throughout the country (Swift, 1972). Another, rather different example, is the attempt to develop community-oriented psychiatric care in Nigeria (Ayonrinde and Erinosho, 1979). Some successful programmes employing basic level health workers have been reported (Climent *et al.*, 1980) but in general significant change is predictably slow.

The constraints upon the development of accessible, relevant, and effective services for the mentally ill in the Third World are the same as those on the health systems of the Third World in general; the essential issues are not lack of knowledge but poverty, the imposition of alien systems, and the processes of underdevelopment which ensure the continuance of unjust and inappropriate policies. In virtually all Third World countries, the main source of care for the mentally ill is, and will continue to be—the family and the community. The capacity of families and communities to provide such care is being rapidly diminished by continuing underdevelopment. It remains questionable whether belated attempts to maintain and extend traditional forms of support will succeed in the face of contemporary social change without profound social, economic, and political transformation in the majority of Third World countries.

References

Argandona, M., and Kiev, A. (1972). *Mental Health in the Developing World: A Case Study in Latin America*, New York: Free Press.
Ashem, B., and Jones, M. D. (1978). Deleterious effects of chronic undernutrition on cognition abilities , *Journal of Child Psychology and Psychiatry*, **19**(1), 23–31.
Asuni, T. (1975). Existing concepts of mental illness in different cultures and traditional forms of treatment, in *Mental Health Services in Developing Countries* (Eds. T. A. Baasher *et al.*) pp. 12–17, Geneva. World Health Organization.
Ayorninde, A., and Erinosho, D. A. (1979). The development of a community psychiatric program at Igbo-Ora, Nigeria, *Nigerian Medical Journal*, **3**(5–6), 625–29.
Aziz, S. (1978). *Rural Development: Learning from China*, London: Macmillan.
Baasher, T. E. *et al.* (Eds.) (1975). *Mental Health Services in Developing Countries*, Geneva: World Health Organisation.
Beck, A. (1970). *A History of the British Medical Administration of East Africa*, Cambridge: Harvard University Press.
Benyoussef, A. (1977). Health service delivery in developing countries, *International Social Science Journal*, **29**(3), 397–418.
Benyoussef, A., and Christian, B. (1977). Health care in developing countries, *Social Science and Medicine*, **11** (6/7), 399–408.
Binitie, A. (1976). Mental health implications of economic growth in developing countries, *Mental Health and Society*, **3** (5–6), 272–85.
Bulsara, J. F. (1965). Social welfare in Indian conditions, in *Social Work in India* (Ed. S. K. Khinduka), Allahabad: Kitab Mulal.
Burton–Bradley, B. G. (1969). A traditional practitioner in Papua New Guinea, *Australian and New Zealand Journal of Psychiatry*, **3** (1), 1–4.
Carstairs, G. M. (1973). Psychiatric problems of developing countries, *British Journal of Psychiatry*, **123**, 271–77.
Chakraborty, A. (1978). Migration and urbanisation problems in Calcutta, *Mental Health and Society*, **5** (1–2), 72–78.
Clifford, W. (1966). *A Primer of Social Casework in Africa*, Nairobi: Oxford University Press.
Climent, C. E. *et al.* (1980). Mental health in primary health care, *WHO Chronicle*, **34** (6), 231–36.
Diop, S. M. B. (1974). *The Place of Mental Health in the Development of Public Health Services*, Brazzaville: World Health Organization.

Dormaar, M. *et al.* (1974). Psychiatric illness in two contrasting Ethiopian outpatient populations, *Social Psychiatry*, **9**, 61–9.

Doyal, L., and Pennell, J. (1979). *The Political Economy of Health*, London: Pluto Press.

Djukanovic, V., and Mach, E. P. (1975). *Alternative Approaches to Meeting Basic Health Needs in Developing Countries*, Geneva: World Health Organization.

Drakakis–Smith, D. (1981). *Urbanization Housing and the Development Process*, London: Croom Helm.

Eisenberg, C. (1980). Honduras: mental health awareness changes a community, *World Health Forum*, **1**(1, 2), 72–77.

Farman-Farmaian, S. (1964). Social work education and training, in *Social Welfare in a Developing Economy*, pp. 51–68. Faridabad: India, Planning Commission.

Feuerstein, M. T. (1976). Rural health problems in developing countries—need for a comprehensive community approach, *Community Development Journal*, **11**(1), 38–52.

Fine, S. H., Krell, R., and Lin, T. (Eds.) 1981. *Today's Priorities in Mental Health*, Boston: Riedel.

Frankenberg, R., and Leeson, J. (1973). The sociology of health dilemmas in the post-colonial world: intermediate technology and medical care in Zambia, Zaire and China, in *Sociology and Development* (Eds. E. de Kadt, and G. Williams) pp. 255–78. London: Tavistock.

German, G. A. (1972). Aspects of clinical psychiatry in sub-Saharan Africa, *British Journal of Psychiatry*, **121**, 461–480.

Giel, R. (1975). Problems of assessing the needs of the population, in T. E. Baasher *et al.* (Eds.), pp. 23–29.

Giel, R., and Harding, T. W. (1976). Psychiatric priorities in developing countries, *British Journal of Psychiatry*, **128**, 513–22.

Gish, O. (1971). *Doctor Migration and World Health*, London: Bell.

Gish, O. (1973). Resource allocation, equality of access and health, *International Journal of Health Services*, **3** (3), 399–412.

Gish. O. (1975). *Planning the Health Sector: The Tanzanian Experience*, London: Croom Helm.

Gish, O. (1977). *Guidelines for Health Planners*, London: Tri-Med.

Gish, O. (1979). The political economy of primary care and "health by the people": an historical exploration, *Social Science and Medicine*, **13c**(4), 203–11.

Goldthorpe, J. E. (1975). *The Sociology of the Third World*, Cambridge: Cambridge University Press.

Hammond-Tooke, W. D. (1975). African world—view and its relevance for psychiatry, *Psychologica Africana*, **16** (1), 25–32.

Hornabrook, R. W. (Ed.) (1976). *Essays on Kuru*. Faringdon: Classey.

Kapur, R. L. (1975). Mental health care in rural India: a study of existing patterns and their implications for future policy, *British Journal of Psychiatry*, **127**, 286–93.

Kiev, A. (Ed.) (1964). *Magic, Faith and Healing*, New York: Free Press.

Kiev, A. (1972). *Transcultural Psychiatry*, Harmondsworth: Penguin.

Kiev, A., Muya, W. J., and Sartorius, N. (Eds.) (1980). *The Future of Mental Health Services*, Amsterdam: Excerpta Medica.

Kilama, W. L., Nhondi, A. M., and Makene, W. J. (1974). Health care delivery in Tanzania, in *Towards Ujamaa: Twenty Years of Tanu Leadership* (Ed. G. Ruhumbika) pp. 191–217, Dar-es-Salaam: East African Literature Bureau.

Lall, S., and Bibile, S. (1977). The political economy of controlling transnationals: the pharmaceutical industry in Sri Lanka, 1972–1976, *World Development*, **5**(8), 677–98.

Lambo, T. (1969). Traditional African cultures and Western medicine, in *Medicine and Culture* (Ed. F. L. N. Poynter). London: Wellcome Institute.

Lambo, T. (1978). Psychotherapy in Africa, *Human Nature*, **1**(3), 32–39.

Leighton, A. A. *et al.* (1963). *Psychiatric Disorder Among the Yoruba*, New York: Cornell University Press.

Leon, C. A. (1972). Psychiatry in Latin America, *British Journal of Psychiatry*, **121**, 121–36.

Levine, H. B., and Levine, M. W. (1979). *Urbanisation in Papua New Guinea*, Cambridge: Cambridge University Press.

Lewis, O. (1966). The culture of poverty, *Scientific American*, **215** (4), 19–25.

Leys, C. (1975). *Underdevelopment in Kenya*, London: Heinemann.

Lippman, D. (1980). Psychiatry in Ethiopia, in A. Kiev *et al.* (Eds.), pp. 34–42.

Lipton, M. (1977). *Why Poor People Stay Poor: Urban Bias in World Development.* Cambridge: Harvard University Press.

Lloyd, P. (1979). *Slums of Hope?* Harmondsworth: Penguin.

MacPherson, S. (1980). *The Development of Basic Health Services in Papua New Guinea*, unpublished Ph.D. thesis, University of Nottingham.

MacPherson, S. (1982). *Social Policy in the Third World*, Brighton: Harvester Press.

Mangin, W. (1969). Mental health and migration to cities: a Peruvian case, in *Urbanisation and change* (Eds. P. Meadows, and E. Mizruchi), pp. 313–19, Reading, Mass: Addison Wesley.

Mangin, W. (Ed.) (1970). *Peasants in Cities,* Boston: Houghton Mifflin.

Mbatia, K. J. (1979). The nature of psychiatric morbidity in patients under 18 years at Muhimbili Hospital, Dar es Salaam, *East African Medical Journal*, **56** (4), 170–77.

Mburu, F. M. (1979). Rhetoric-implementation gap in health policy and health services delivery for a rural population in a developing country, *Social Science and Medicine*, **13**(A), 577–83.

Michels, R. (1980). Academic programs for developing countries, in Kiev *et al.* (1980), pp. 101–114.

Midgley, J. (1981). *Professional Imperialism: Social Work in the Third World*, London: Heinemann.

Moi, W. (1976). Organisation of mental health services in Papua New Guinea, *Papua New Guinea Medical Journal*, **19**(1), 15–18.

Muluka, E. A., and Acuda, S. W. (1978). Crime and mental illness, *East African Medical Journal*, **55** (8), 360–5.

Navarro, V. (1972). Health services in Cuba: an initial appraisal', *New England Journal of Medicine*, **287** (19), 954–59.

Navarro, V. (1974). The underdevelopment of health or the health of underdevelopment, *International Journal of Health Services*, **4**(1), 5–27.

Neki, J. S. (1975). The spectrum of mental disorders and the responsibility of the mental health services, in T. E. Baasher *et al.* (Eds.), pp. 18–22.

Newell, K. W. (1975). *Health by the People*, Geneva: World Health Organization.

Orley, J. H. (1970). *Culture and Mental Illness: A study from Uganda*, Nairobi: East African Publishing House.

Pataki-Schweizer, K. J. (1976). Curing and learning: the role of the clinical anthropologist in psychiatric health service, *Papua New Guinea Medical Journal*, **19** (1), 36–42.

Raikes, A. (1973). *Rural Development and Health Manpower*, Dar-es-Salaam: University of Dar-es-Salaam.

Rifkin, S. B., and Kaplinsky, R. (1973). Health strategy and development planning: lessons from the People's Republic of China, *Journal of Development Studies*, **9** (2), 213–32.

Robin, R. (1979). *Psychopathology in Papua New Guinea*, Port Moresby: University of Papua New Guinea.

Safa, H. I. (1974). *The Urban Poor of Puerto Rico: A Study in Development and Inequality.* New York: Holt, Rinehart and Winston.

Safa, H. I., and du Toit, B. M. (Eds.) (1975). *Migration and Development: Implications for Ethnic Identity and Political Conflict*. The Hague: Mouton.

Schram, R. (1971). *A History of the Nigerian Health Services*. Ibadan: Ibadan University Press.

Segall, M, (1972). The politics of health in Tanzania, in *Towards Socialist Planning* (Eds. J. F. Rweyemamu, *et al.*), pp. 149–66, Dar-es-Salaam: Tanzania Publishing House.

Sidel, V., and Sidel, R. (1974). *Serve the people—Observations on medicine in the People's Republic of China*. Boston: Beacon Press.

Sidel, V., and Sidel, R. (1977). Primary health care in relation to socio-political structure, *Social Science and Medicine*, **11** (6/7), 415–20.

Swift, C. R. (1972). Mental health programming in a developing country: any relevance elsewhere?, *American Journal of Orthopsychiatry*, **42**(3), 517–26.

Szasz, T. (1970). *The Manufacture of Madness*. New York: Harper and Row.

Torrey, E. F. (1972). *The Mind Game: witch Doctors and Psychiatrists*. New York: Bantam.

Turshen, M. (1977a). *The Political Economy of Health in Tanzania*, unpublished D. Phil. thesis, University of Sussex.

Turshen, M. (1977b). The political ecology of disease, *The Review of Radical Political Economics*, **9** (1), 45–60.

Valentine, C. A. (1968). *Culture and Poverty: Critique and Counter-Proposals*. Chicago: University of Chicago Press.

Van Etten, G. (1976). *Rural Health Development in Tanzania: a Case Study of Medical Sociology in a Developing Country*, Assen: Van Gorcum.

Varma, V. K. *et al.* (1980). Socio-demographic correlates of schizophrenia, affective psychoses and neuroses in a clinic in India, *Acta Psychiatrica Scandinavia*, **61** (5), 404–12.

World Bank (1980). *Health: Sector Policy Paper*, Washington: World Bank.

World Health Organization (1973a). *Interrelationships Between Health Programmes and Socio-economic Development*, Geneva: WHO.

World Health Organization (1973b). *Organizational Study on Methods of Promoting the Development of Basic Health Services*, Geneva: WHO.

World Health Organization (1974). *Training and Utilisation of Village Health Workers*. Geneva: WHO.

World Health Organization (1975a). *Organisation of Mental Health Services in Developing Countries*, Geneva: WHO.

World Health Organization (1975b). *Promotion of National Health Services*, Geneva: WHO.

World Health Organization (1979). *The Work of the WHO 1978–79*, Geneva: WHO.

Name Index

467

Subject Index

Note: The major legal cases have been cited in the subject index. For a more extensive list of legal cases cited see particularly the references at the end of Chapters 1 and 2.

A v. United Kingdom (1980), 33
Aavold Committee, 72
actions, human, 85–90
admissions, to mental hospitals, legal
    requirements, 40–42
advertising, and alcohol consumption, 311
Advisory Committee for Alcoholism, 317
Advisory Committee for Education, 33
after care, see community care
Alcoholics Anonymous, 298, 301, 318
alcohol, as drug, 304–305
    consumption levels and harm, 307–309
    damage from, 304–305
    social cost of, 312–314
    trends in consumption, 308–310
alcoholism, Chapter 14 passim
    cost to society, 298
    disease concept of, 298–303
    epidemiological features, 298–299
    in France, 308, 309–310
    in Scotland, 307, 308, 310
    treatment of, 143–144, 318
American Bar Association, 4, 6, 8
American Law Institutes, Model Penal
    Case, 11–12, 20
American Medical Association, 115
American Psychiatric Association, 45,
    102, 115, 150, 227
Amsterdam Home Treatment Service,
    357–358
antabuse, 299
anti-depressant drugs, general, 196–197
    amphetamines, 200–201
    clinical usage, 202

mode of action, 201
monoamine oxidase inhibiting drugs,
    199–200
prophylaxis of depressive disorders
    using anti-depressant drugs,
    203–205
tricyclic anti-depressants, 197–199
assessment of treatment in mental illness,
    138–140
Association for the Advancement of
    Behaviour Therapy, 227, 240
asylum, see also mental hospital
asylum, history of, 329–330
    in the 19th century, 330–333
    in the 20th century, 333–335
attribution theory, 256
Australian Association of Social Workers,
    415
aversion therapy, 258–259

Baxstorn v. Herold, 19, 61
behaviour control, 271–272
behaviour therapy, Chapters 11 and 12
    passim
    assessment in, 238–239, 248–254
    concept of, 229, 246–248
    methods of, 82, 233–234, 248–254,
    272–274
    scientific status of, 228–229, 245–246
behavioural movement, general, 227–228
    applicability, 239, 240
    knowledge base of, 229
    treatment in, 234–235
Bethlem hospital, see asylum